Bottom Line's HEALTH BREAKTHROUGHS 2018

BottomLineBooks
BottomLineInc.com

10 9 8 7 6 5 4 3 2 1

ISBN 0-88723-776-2

Selected articles in this book were written by reporters for HealthDay, an award-winning international daily consumer health news service, headquartered in Norwalk, Connecticut.

3 Landmark Square, Suite 201, Stamford, Connecticut 06901

BottomLineInc.com

Bottom Line Books is an imprint of Bottom Line Inc., publisher of print periodicals, e-letters and books. We are dedicated to bringing you the best information from the most knowledgeable sources in the world. Our goal is to help you gain greater wealth, better health, more wisdom, extra time and increased happiness.

Printed in the United States of America

Contents

3 • BRAIN HEALTH AND MEMORY

4 • CANCER CARE AND BREAKTHROUGHS

5 • CONSUMER HEALTH ALERTS

6 • DENTAL CARE UPDATES

7 • DIABETES CARE

11 • INFECTIOUS DISEASES

16 • NUTRITION AND FITNESS

17 • PAIN REMEDIES

Preface

We are proud to bring you the all-new *Bottom Line's Health Breakthroughs 2018*. This collection represents a year's worth of the latest health news and scientific discoveries in a broad spectrum of fields.

When you choose a Bottom Line book, you are turning to a stellar group of experts in a wide range of specialties—medical doctors, alternative practitioners, renowned nutrition experts, research scientists and consumer-health advocates, to name a few.

We go to great lengths to interview the foremost health experts. Whether it's cancer prevention, breakthrough arthritis treatments or cutting-edge nutritional advice, our editors talk to the true innovators in health care.

How do we find all these top-notch professionals? Over the past 40 years, we have built a network of leading physicians in both alternative and conventional medicine. They are affiliated with the world's premier medical institutions. We follow the medical research, and with the help of our partner HealthDay, an award-winning service that reports on evidence-based health news, we bring the latest information to our readers. We also regularly talk with our advisers in teaching hospitals, private practices and government health agencies.

Bottom Line's Health Breakthroughs 2018 is a result of our ongoing research and contact with these experts, and is a distillation of their latest findings and advice. We hope that you will enjoy the presentation and glean helpful information about the health topics that concern you and your family.

As a reader of a Bottom Line book, please be assured that you are receiving reliable and well-researched information from a trusted source. But, please use prudence in health matters. Always speak to your physician before taking vitamins, supplements or over-the-counter medication…changing your diet…or beginning an exercise program. If you experience side effects from any regimen, contact your doctor immediately.

The Editors, Bottom Line Books, Stamford, Connecticut.

CHAPTER 1

Allergies, Asthma and Respiratory Conditions

Sneezing and Wheezing Could Mean a Dust Mite Allergy

More than half of all Americans test positive for at least one kind of allergen. But there's one culprit that often gets overlooked by allergy sufferers.

What you may not realize: Dust mites, which thrive in warm, humid weather, are one of the most common household triggers for allergies and asthma. Dust mites are tiny, eight-legged creatures that are too small to be seen by the naked eye, but they can wreak havoc if you are allergic to them.

Dust mites lurk in beds, carpets, draperies and upholstered furniture and surfaces. Their primary food source is human skin cells that we shed naturally. In fact, each of us sheds enough cells each day to feed one million dust mites. And depending on its age, a mattress can harbor up to 10 million dust mites! *What you need to know to protect yourself...*

ARE DUST MITES TO BLAME?

Allergies to dust mites are caused not by the mites themselves, but rather by their waste particles and dead body parts. Since we are constantly exposed to dust mites, those of us who have a dust mite allergy are likely to experience year-round symptoms. These can include sneezing...runny nose...red, itchy or watery eyes...stuffy nose...postnasal drip... and cough. (Eczema and asthma symptoms can be triggered or exacerbated by contact with dust mites.) Because dust mite allergy symptoms are so similar to those caused by other common allergens, such as pollen, some patients fail to recognize when the ubiquitous little creatures are the cause of their allergy

---

Michael L. Lewin, MD, an allergist who has been practicing for 30 years. He has offices in New York City and Wilton, Connecticut, and is a faculty member of Weill Cornell Medical College in New York City. Lewin Allergy.com

symptoms or worsening symptoms due to another allergy.

If you have a dust mite allergy: You may notice that your symptoms are worse when you're in bed or when you first wake up in the morning. That's because of the high concentration of dust mites in mattresses and bedding. Your symptoms may also flare up when you're dusting or vacuuming—droppings can easily become airborne...or when the temperature and humidity are higher than usual.

EASY TESTS

There are a few testing methods that can determine whether you are allergic to dust mites.

The easiest is a skin-prick test: A drop of dust mite antigen is placed on the skin...the doctor lightly scratches your skin through the drop... and then watches to see if you develop redness, swelling or itching within about 20 minutes.

If you cannot have a skin test (some skin conditions and medications make the test unreliable), your doctor might recommend a blood test that looks for antibodies that are produced in response to specific allergens.

AVOIDANCE FIRST

As a first step to treating a dust mite allergy, it's a good idea to follow the strategies below to reduce the load of dust mites in your home. You can't eliminate them entirely, but reducing their number may be enough to lessen or eliminate symptoms. *To start...*

• **Cover your bedding.** Your bed has more dust mites than any other area in the house.

What helps: Cover your mattress, box spring, pillows and comforters with dust mite encasings. These encasings work by creating a barrier between you and the dust mites. These products, which are available online, are made of microporous fabrics with a pore size that is too small to be permeated by dust mites.

• **Hot-water washes.** Once a week, be sure to wash your bedding (sheets, blankets, mattress covers, pillowcases, etc.) in water that's 130°F or hotter. It will kill mites as well as their eggs.

• **Vacuum frequently.** Avoid wall-to-wall carpeting since it provides a large area for dust mites to inhabit. Vacuum your rugs, carpeting, drapes and other upholstered or fabric-covered surfaces once a week. A vacuum fitted with a HEPA filter will help prevent allergy-causing particles from getting stirred up in the air you breathe.

• **Steam clean.** A steam cleaner that produces superheated steam will kill mites and deactivate the allergy-causing proteins in their droppings. Consider steam cleaning carpets, drapes, upholstery, etc., once or twice a year.

• **Keep humidity low.** Because dust mites thrive in warm, humid environments, keep your humidity levels below 50%. Use a dehumidifier if necessary during the more humid months of summer. You can place it in the room(s), including the bedroom, where you spend the most time. To keep an eye on the humidity levels in your home, you can purchase a hygrometer online for less than $10.

• **Use a HEPA filter air purifier.** House "dust" contains copious amounts of skin cells and mites and their droppings, but you can reduce allergy symptoms by using a filtering mechanism to remove airborne particles. Portable HEPA units filter all the air in a room, trapping particles as they pass through. You can also consider a full-house filter for your HVAC system.

FOR ADDITIONAL HELP

If the steps above don't alleviate your symptoms, you may want to consider either over-the-counter or prescription medications such as antihistamines, nasal sprays or eye drops. If medication—plus environmental control—still doesn't give you adequate relief from your symptoms, you should consider allergen immunotherapy.

Allergen immunotherapy is the process by which the body builds immunity to allergens such as dust mites. This is accomplished by administering small, incremental doses of dust mite (or other antigens), prompting the immune system to respond by decreasing the body's reactivity to these substances.

Allergen immunotherapy can be administered by subcutaneous injections (commonly called allergy shots)—given in a doctor's office (usually weekly in the beginning, then once every few weeks for maintenance) for three to five years.

Help for Peanut Allergies

Fiber Is Your Friend

If a recent study is correct, fiber could help protect you from your peanut allergy.

Theory: Fiber may improve the antiallergy activity of gut bacteria by breaking down into short-chain fatty acids that could reduce the allergic response. More research is needed.

Cell Reports.

Patch Remedy for Peanut Allergies

A skin patch may help fight a peanut allergy. Nearly half of the participants who wore a patch that delivered small amounts of peanut protein to their bodies for one year were able to consume at least 10 times more peanut protein at the end of the year than they were able to tolerate at the start of the study.

Study of 74 children and young adults led by researchers at US National Institute of Allergy and Infectious Diseases, Bethesda, Maryland, published in *Journal of Allergy and Clinical Immunology.*

A newer method is sublingual immunotherapy—allergy drops. Allergy drops are made of the same antigens as allergy shots but are formulated into drops that are placed under the tongue.

Once you have been tested and your allergies have been identified, your doctor can prepare your allergy drops based on your test results. Allergy drops are an effective, safe and convenient way to treat allergy symptoms. Once your drops have been formulated, you take the first dose at your doctor's office and then continue treatment at home daily for three to five years.

Allergy Medication Alert

William Ondo, MD, director, Movement Disorders Clinic, Houston Methodist Neurological Institute.

Sedating antihistamines, such as Benadryl and Vistaril, can worsen symptoms of restless legs syndrome, a neurological condition. Nonsedating antihistamines, such as Claritin, don't appear to worsen symptoms as much—perhaps because they don't cross the blood–brain barrier as easily.

You Might Have a Tattoo Allergy

Johanna S. Youner, DPM, a certified laser specialist in private practice in New York City.

Allergies to tattoos are common, reports Johanna S. Youner, DPM. Allergic reactions, such as swelling, redness and a rash or bumps, can be caused by substances in tattoo pigments such as dichromate (green), cobalt (blue), cadmium (yellow) and mercury salt (red). And pigments contaminated with nickel sulfate also can cause allergic reactions. Choose inks or colors that do not contain these substances—ask the tattoo artist.

Nosebleeds and Spicy Food

Murray Grossan, MD, otolaryngologist, Tower Ear, Nose & Throat, Los Angeles, and author of *The Whole Body Approach to Allergy and Sinus Health.*

Can hot, spicy food cause nosebleeds?

It could. Food that contains capsaicin (a compound that gives chili peppers their spice) or allyl isothiocyanate (found in horseradish and hot mustard) irritates and inflames the mucous membranes in the nose, mouth and eyes, causing the nose to run and eyes to water.

This irritation can be good for nasal congestion, since it can temporarily relieve stuffed-up sinuses. Some nasal sprays even contain capsaicin. But when nasal membranes are thin and dry, this irritation can cause them to crack and bleed. Consult your doctor if you have frequent nosebleeds (more than once a week)—this may signal the need for an adjustment in the dosage of a blood thinner or an underlying condition, such as kidney disease.

Lungs That Smell

Frontiers in Physiology.

Newly discovered olfactory receptors in lung tissue trigger smooth muscle contraction/relaxation.

Takeaway: Scent molecules could affect drug treatments for asthma or other lung conditions.

Your Trombone Can Cause Lung Infections

Thorax.

Bagpipes, trombones and other wind instruments can harbor organisms that trigger "bagpipe lung," a potentially fatal lung infection.

Recommended: Clean instruments frequently and let them drip-dry between uses.

What's Really Causing That Annoying Cough?

Jonathan P. Parsons, MD, MSc, FCCP, professor of internal medicine at The Ohio State University College of Medicine and director of the Multidisciplinary Cough Clinic and the OSU Asthma Center at The Ohio State University Wexner Medical Center, all in Columbus.

The occasional cough is nothing more than your body's normal lung maintenance—a quick spasm that expels mucus or other irritants from the airways.

On the other hand, a cough that sounds unusual or is unpredictable (for example, there's no identifiable trigger or the cough occurs at different times of day)...severe...or long-lasting suggests that something else is going on—but what?

Surprising finding: A recent study published in *Annals of Family Medicine* found that a cough from a cold or the flu sticks around longer—for about 18 days, on average—than the one-week threshold that most people consider normal.*

But a cough's duration is not the only clue to its cause. While it's not surprising that infections such as pneumonia or whooping cough would lead to coughing, there are other conditions that most people wouldn't expect. *For example...*

•**Asthma.** People with asthma assume that they'll have moments of wheezing or breathlessness. But for some patients, a persistent cough is the only symptom.

What to watch out for: A wheezy-sounding cough that is usually worse at night. Frequent wheezing and/or coughing means that inflamed airways have narrowed, and it's a hallmark of poorly controlled asthma. Your doctor might recommend spirometry (a simple test that measures your lung capacity) or other lung tests to assess how well—or how poorly—you're doing.

My advice: If you have a wheezy cough but have never been diagnosed with asthma, see your doctor. If you know that you have asthma and find that you're using a "rescue" inhaler—a fast-acting bronchodilator that quickly relieves coughing and other symptoms—more than twice a week, see your doctor. You probably need to work harder to reduce flare-ups. This

**Note*: Be sure to see your doctor if a cough lasts for more than three to four weeks.

Salt Spray for Nosebleeds

Salt spray may relieve chronic nosebleeds, says Kevin J. Whitehead, MD. People with hemorrhagic telangiectasia (HHT) have as many as two nosebleeds a day.

Recent finding: People with HHT who sprayed a saline solution into their noses twice daily for 12 weeks got as much relief from nosebleeds as those who used the medicines *bevacizumab*, *estriol* or *tranexamic acid*. Nosebleeds in HHT are not very different from common nosebleeds, so saline spray might help those as well.

Kevin J. Whitehead, MD, associate professor of internal medicine at University of Utah School of Medicine, Salt Lake City, and leader of a study of 121 people with HHT, published in *JAMA*.

may include adjusting medication, avoiding pollen and air pollution, reducing stress and other measures.

•**Gastroesophageal reflux disease (GERD).** Most GERD patients suffer from both heartburn and coughs, but about one-third experience only a cough or unexplained sore throats. A GERD-related cough occurs when a surge of stomach acid reaches the voice box (the larynx). The irritation and inflammation that result from the acid can lead to a persistent, raspy cough.

What to watch out for: The cough sounds "barky" rather than wheezy. It gets worse when you lie down...after heavy meals...and/or when you consume certain trigger foods or drinks, such as spicy dishes, alcohol, chocolate, onions or citrus. You might also notice that your voice is more hoarse than it used to be.

My advice: For relief, take an over-the-counter (OTC) acid-suppressing drug such as *omeprazole* (Prilosec) or *ranitidine* (Zantac). Such a drug is unlikely to cause side effects and often is effective—although it might require long-term use (eight to 12 weeks) before your symptoms improve, so you should be monitored by a doctor.

Also important: Medication usually doesn't work unless you also make lifestyle changes. For example, don't eat large meals late at night. In fact, you should avoid food altogether for at least three hours before going to bed. Propping up your upper body with pillows also can prevent stomach acid from going upstream while you sleep.

•**Postnasal drip.** When there's a persistent drip of mucus from the sinuses, you're going to periodically cough. Typically, allergies are to blame. People with hay fever often have congestion and postnasal drip. The mucus can irritate the throat as well as the larynx and cause a nagging cough.

What to watch out for: A seasonal cough. If you mainly cough during the spring, summer and/or fall, an allergy-related cough is likely. This cough could sound barky and will probably get worse at night due to mucous drainage. It might be accompanied by other allergy symptoms such as a tickling in the throat, itchy eyes, sneezing, etc.

My advice: Reduce drainage by taking a daily OTC nonsedating antihistamine such as *loratadine* (Claritin) or *cetirizine* (Zyrtec).

Nasal steroid sprays are another effective alternative. They start working within hours, although it may take several days—or even weeks—to get the full benefit. Some brands (such as Flonase) are available in OTC versions.

•**ACE inhibitor drugs.** Patients who take these blood pressure–lowering drugs—such as *lisinopril* (Zestril), *captopril* (Capoten) and *enalapril* (Vasotec)—are told that they may experience occasional dizziness. They aren't always warned, however, about the nasty cough that can result in up to 20% of patients taking them.

What to watch out for: A throat tickle followed by a nagging, dry cough that begins anywhere from a few weeks to a year after starting the medication.

My advice: You can keep taking the drug if the cough isn't bothering you (and you're successfully managing your blood pressure). Switching to a different ACE inhibitor may help if you have a mild cough. Patients with severe coughs from ACE inhibitors are often advised to switch to a different drug class altogether—usually an angiotensin-receptor blocker (ARB) such as *losartan* (Cozaar) or *valsartan* (Diovan). They work like ACE inhibitors but without the cough.

A Powerhouse Snack

A handful of nuts every day can do more than lower risk for heart disease and cancer.

New finding: Adults who ate 20 g (about one-quarter cup) of either plain or salted walnuts, almonds, cashews, peanuts or other nuts every day cut their risk of dying from respiratory disease by nearly half and from diabetes by about 40%.

Possible reason: The antioxidants and nutrients in nuts that promote cardiovascular health also help fight other conditions.

Dagfinn Aune, PhD, postdoctoral research fellow, Imperial College London, UK.

More from Dr. Parsons...

When a Cough Is COPD or Cancer...

A chronic cough (persistent or episodic) may be the first symptom of two of the most serious lung conditions—lung cancer and chronic obstructive pulmonary disease (COPD), a lung disease that includes emphysema and chronic bronchitis. Both diseases are more common in people who smoke, once smoked or have had significant secondhand smoke exposure than in nonsmokers.

Important: Even though people who have never smoked are less likely than smokers to get COPD or lung cancer, it can still happen. Don't take chances. Anyone who has a cough for more than three to four weeks should see a doctor. And call your doctor anytime you cough up blood.

Hidden Smoking Danger

Liz Williams, project manager for the Berkeley, California–based nonprofit Americans for Nonsmokers' Rights. No-Smoke.org

Far too many people still smoke—and often do so in their cars, subjecting others inside the vehicle to the dangers of secondhand smoke...even if the window is open.

Latest development: Virginia is the latest of eight states and several municipalities (plus Puerto Rico) to enact laws that prohibit car-smoking when children are present. Similar legislation has been proposed in 12 other states.

"Car occupants exposed to secondhand smoke breathe air at levels much higher than what the EPA considers hazardous," notes Liz Williams, project manager for the Berkeley, California–based nonprofit Americans for Nonsmokers' Rights (No-Smoke.org).

Why it matters: Nonsmokers who breathe secondhand smoke have a 25% to 30% increased risk for heart disease...20% to 30% increased risk for stroke...and 20% to 30% increased risk for lung cancer.

What you may not realize: Thirdhand smoke—the sticky, smoky residue that clings to walls and other surfaces—can persist for years, according to research. Children are especially at risk because they can ingest tobacco residue just by touching contaminated surfaces (such as flooring and walls) and putting their hands in their mouths.

If a smoker has ever lived in your home, you might need to replace furniture, carpets and drapes to remove the ashtray smell. Washing walls might help.

Better: "Encapsulating" tobacco residues with a fresh coat of paint.

Bottom Line: Always insist on smoke-free environments, whether it's a public place or someone's home or car.

Faster Cold Recovery

Are sneezing, congestion and other cold symptoms making you miserable?

New finding: Adults who used zinc lozenges reduced the cold's duration—to about four days instead of the average seven.

Optimal dose: 80 mg a day. Avoid lozenges that contain citric acid (it binds to zinc and keeps it from working properly). If you take blood pressure drugs, antibiotics or other medications, check with your doctor before trying zinc.

Harri Hemilä, MD, PhD, research fellow, University of Helsinki, Finland.

5 Mistakes to Avoid If You Have Asthma

Gailen D. Marshall, MD, PhD, the R. Faser Triplett Sr. MD Chair of Allergy and Immunology at The University of Mississippi Medical Center in Jackson. His major research interests include factors affecting asthma risk and the effectiveness of integrative approaches to clinical care for asthma and other immune-based diseases. Dr. Marshall is in his third term as editor in chief of the *Annals of Allergy, Asthma & Immunology.*

Whether it's the wintertime pleasure of sitting next to a crackling log in the fireplace...or the summertime thrill of cooling off in a swimming pool, many of our most treasured seasonal pastimes can mean big trouble for some people.

Hidden threat: If you or a family member is among the 24 million Americans coping with asthma, such seemingly harmless activities could be a mistake.

Asthma, which inflames and narrows the airways, is serious business. Half of all adults with asthma have poorly controlled or even uncontrolled asthma, meaning they are at increased risk for sudden worsening of symptoms, which can lead to complications—such as persistent breathing difficulties and even death.

That's why it is imperative for asthma sufferers to avoid common missteps that may prevent them from properly controlling their condition. *Among the biggest mistakes...*

***MISTAKE #1:* Not seeing the right doctor.** Too many asthma patients—and even some doctors—fail to recognize the crossover component between asthma and allergies. For about one-third of adult asthma patients, acute episodes and poor control can be triggered by allergies to common substances such as mold, dust, pollen and animal dander. When the immune system of an asthma patient mistakes these substances for a foreign intruder, allergy antibodies (known as IgE) are produced and make their way to the lungs, often leading to an asthma attack.

An internist or a family doctor can manage asthma cases that flare up only occasionally. But for people with severe and persistent asthma (marked by repeated episodes of coughing, wheezing and/or difficulty breathing that take multiple medications to control), the best doctor is often an allergist, who can perform testing to determine whether a patient's asthma triggers are allergy-based.

My advice: Consider seeing an allergist if you have persistent asthma symptoms (described above) that limit everyday activities or you've ever had a life-threatening asthma attack. If an allergist is not available in your area, ask your doctor for a referral to a pulmonologist (a lung function specialist).

***MISTAKE #2:* Not getting treated for allergies.** To pinpoint allergies that may be contributing to their asthma, patients should undergo allergy testing as soon as possible after an asthma diagnosis.

Unfortunately, some asthma patients who learn they indeed have allergies don't get allergy shots, a form of immunotherapy that can reduce sensitivity to these triggers. Until this step is taken, repeated bouts of severe asthma symptoms are likely.

A relatively new treatment, sublingual immunotherapy (in which an allergen in tablet form is taken under the tongue) may be an option for certain allergy sufferers. If you're interested, talk to your doctor.

***MISTAKE #3:* Missing less obvious triggers.** Asthma triggers include anything—whether a true allergen or other irritant—that can aggravate symptoms. While most people already know about many of their own asthma triggers, such as strenuous exercise, rapidly breathing in cold air, certain medications, including nonsteroidal anti-inflammatory drugs like aspirin, *ibuprofen* or *naproxen*, or even strong emotions, many other triggers fly under the radar. What are some of these less obvious irritants?

- **Household plants.** Asthma attacks can be precipitated by mold spores that are often found in the soil of many household plants.

My advice: Mold-sensitive patients should minimize indoor plants and keep them out of rooms in which they spend a lot of time, such as the bedroom. If you want to have some plants in your home, you may want to try English ivy, a peace lily or a rubber plant. These plants have been found in research to reduce airborne toxins, including mold spores. *Note:* Keep English ivy, peace lily and the Indian rubber plant out of the reach of pets and children—these plants can be toxic if consumed.

- **Wood smoke.** Most people realize that cigarette and cigar smoke are irritants, but wood smoke is often overlooked, even though it too can trigger an asthma flare-up.

My advice: If you have asthma, avoid exposure to wood smoke from fireplaces, grills and open fires to avoid worsening symptoms.

- **Chlorine.** A dip in the pool can be invigorating and even help build lung function, but it can also take your breath away if the water is highly chlorinated. While not a true allergy, chlorine sensitivities can trigger chest tightness, coughing and wheezing.

My advice: If you have asthma, limit your exposure to freshly chlorinated pools—especially hyper-chlorinated public pools—and shower thoroughly afterward. If possible, swim in a saltwater pool.

Also, if chlorinated pools make your symptoms worse, be careful about using household cleaning products that contain bleach—only use these products in areas that are well-ventilated.

• **Candles and air fresheners.** Pleasant aromas from scented candles and air fresheners can irritate nasal passages and contribute to an asthma attack.

My advice: To prevent a possible allergic reaction, it's best to avoid scented candles and air fresheners.

MISTAKE #4: **Not getting a flu shot.** Getting an annual flu shot is especially important for asthmatics, who are at increased risk for dangerous flu complications, such as pneumonia. It's best to get the flu shot in October, but it's still helpful to get it up until March. Pneumonia vaccines, which can be given anytime during the year, are also recommended for people with asthma.

MISTAKE #5: **Not recognizing flare-up symptoms.** It's crucial that people with asthma watch for subtle warning signs—such as increasing shortness of breath while exercising or restless sleep—that indicate their asthma may be veering out of control.

Rule of thumb: Asthma is considered poorly controlled if wheezing or other symptoms occur more than twice a week or if you awaken more than twice a month with asthma symptoms. Other red flags include needing to use "rescue" inhalers, such as *albuterol* more than twice a week...requiring oral corticosteroids to treat severe attacks...and/or changing activity patterns (such as avoiding stairs, etc.).

• **Spices.** Powdered spices such as cumin, mustard and paprika don't just make for yummier food—they can also exacerbate asthma if inhaled. This can also happen with flour, powdered sugar and other products that are finely ground.

My advice: Whenever possible, avoid using finely ground ingredients. Fresh herbs and spices are much less likely to be inhaled. If you do need to use powdered ingredients, try putting on a fiberglass painter's mask when doing your food preparations.

Thunderstorms Can Trigger Asthma Attacks

Norman H. Edelman, MD, senior scientific adviser for the American Lung Association. He is professor of preventive medicine, internal medicine, and physiology and biophysics at State University of New York at Stony Brook.

Eight people in greater Melbourne, Australia, died as a result of a freak thunderstorm November 2016, and thousands more were hospitalized. The victims were not struck by lightning—they suffered asthma attacks. The Melbourne incident, which occurred when pollen and humidity were high, was not an isolated event. There is strong evidence that thunderstorms can increase the risk for asthma attacks. One study published in *Thorax* found that asthma-related visits to emergency rooms in the Atlanta, Georgia, area increased following thunderstorms.

The most likely explanation for "thunderstorm asthma" is that these storms can cause pollen already in the air to burst into tiny particles that are very easy to inhale deeply into the lungs. These tiny particles can be especially dangerous for people prone to allergy-induced asthma. When you have allergy-induced asthma, the pollen that can trigger, say, hay fever also can trigger an asthma attack.

An alternate theory proposes that downdrafts of cold air associated with thunderstorms might increase pollen concentrations low in the atmosphere, where the pollen is then more likely to be inhaled. It also is worth noting that lightning can generate ozone gas, and ozone is known to trigger asthma attacks.

What to do: If you have allergy-induced asthma, ask your doctor whether you should take special precautions when thunderstorms begin. For example, he/she might recommend taking an extra dose of an asthma-control medicine such as an inhaled corticosteroid...and/or remaining indoors as much as possible during the day following a thunderstorm.

10 Common Mistakes People Make When Using an Inhaler

Richard Firshein, DO, director and founder of The Firshein Center for Integrative Medicine in New York City and author of *Reversing Asthma.*

Imagine that you were prescribed one pill a day, and on some days you swallowed only one quarter...on other days, only one half. It doesn't sound good, right?

If you use a "metered-dose" inhaler, the most commonly used medication dispenser for a wide variety of lung conditions, odds are that you're getting less than half a full dose with each puff. Research suggests that up to 80% of patients incorrectly use this type of inhaler, which delivers a premeasured aerosol dose of medication. If you inhale a partial dose often, you may assume that the medication isn't working...or you may wind up with some serious side effects, such as a racing heart, a chronic sore throat or stomachaches. Or you could develop a condition called tachyphylaxis—when more of the medication gets in your bloodstream and less in your lungs, you develop a resistance to the medication.

Here are 10 mistakes you may be making with your metered-dose inhaler...

PREPARATION MISTAKES

•**Not shaking the inhaler well enough before each spray.** Because the canister contains both your medication and a propellant, without thorough mixing you cannot be sure that the proportions will be the same from puff to puff.

Better: Just before taking your dose, shake the inhaler vigorously for about 10 seconds.

•**Positioning the mouthpiece incorrectly.** Tilt your inhaler five degrees too high, and you'll send most of the medicine to the roof of your mouth rather than into your lungs. Five degrees too low, it'll hit your tongue. Either way, you'll swallow more of it than you inhale.

Better: Think about how you're holding the inhaler before beginning. Is it perpendicular to your windpipe? If not, adjust the position. The nozzle should be pointing directly to the back of your throat.

•**Tilting the chin.** Just as the inhaler's angle matters, so does the angle of your head. Even a slight shift up or down can change that angle, which will cause a considerable amount of medication to miss the target.

Better: If you're sitting, stand up—it's much easier to align your head and neck properly that way. Then make sure you're facing straight ahead with the bottom of your chin parallel to the floor.

COORDINATION MISTAKES

•**Releasing the medicine at the wrong time.** Aerosol lung medications are supposed to enter your lungs while you breathe in. If you dispense your medication too early, you won't have inhaled deeply enough to adequately pull the medicine into your lungs. Too late, and the dose may be sprayed into your mouth after you've completed most of your inhalation.

Better: Start your breath (through your mouth, not your nose!) before depressing the canister. About a second after you begin breathing in, squeeze the canister while inhaling deeply.

•**Jerking when dispensing a dose.** You've taken care to angle both the mouthpiece and your chin correctly, but a sudden movement when you dispense the medicine—such as when you press down on a canister-type dispenser—can move everything out of alignment exactly when the medication is spraying.

Better: Each time you use your inhaler, pay attention to how much force it takes to activate the spray—it may be less force than you've been using. Do your best not to move your hand or head while squeezing the inhaler between your forefinger and thumb.

•**Taking a breath too quickly.** If you pay attention exclusively to the "deep" part of the breath, you may inhale so fast that the medicine reaches only partway into your lungs.

Better: Picture your lungs expanding as you draw in the medication for about five seconds. Once your lungs are filled, hold your breath for 10 seconds, then breathe out slowly through pursed lips—not through your nose—as if you are whistling.

POST-DOSE MISTAKES

•**Leaping into a panicky second puff.** When you're struggling to breathe and the first dose from a quick-acting inhaler doesn't help, you probably want to put it right back up to your mouth and try again. But if you've misdirected the medication the first time—which could explain why you didn't feel relief—moving fast on the next round probably won't help, either. And if you've accidentally swallowed your medication, it could leave you feeling shaky. Trembling hands make it even less likely that you'll use the inhaler correctly, and things can snowball from there.

Better: For your second puff, pay close attention to your form. Shake the inhaler again. Stand up, look straight ahead and hold the device perpendicular to your windpipe. Begin to breathe in, and after one second, squeeze the canister. Keep breathing in slowly, as deeply as you can, then hold your breath for 10 seconds before exhaling.

•**Forgetting to rinse your mouth.** Even if you use your inhaler perfectly, odds are that some medication still will land in your mouth and on your tongue. Swallowing it can lead to sore throats and other side effects.

Better: After completing your exhalation, fill your mouth with water, swish it around and gargle briefly, then spit it out. Do not swallow.

•**Not cleaning the inhaler.** Although you can't see it, with each use your inhaler leaves a trace of propellant and medication in the mouthpiece. In time, that can build up and partially block the spray.

Better: At least once a week, remove the canister and rinse the plastic mouthpiece and cap under warm running water. If you see any residue, use soap as well. Do not rinse any other parts. Allow it to air-dry completely before replacing the canister and cap.

BIGGEST MISTAKE OF ALL

•**Ignoring the signs that you're doing it wrong.** If you regularly taste bitterness after a puff of an inhaled medication or if you use the inhaler and don't see improvement, don't just continue on. Continued misuse can lead to long-term side effects such as feeling jittery or developing stomachaches from swallowing more than you inhale. It also encourages the development of oral thrush, a yeast infection that can be stimulated by certain asthma medications. Thrush produces spotty white blotches on your mouth and can leave you with a chronic sore throat and difficulty swallowing. Even if you're using your inhaler correctly, you still may develop thrush—but the likelihood increases dramatically when medication winds up on the surface of your mouth, tongue and throat.

Better: When you notice any of the signs mentioned above, go back to the drawing board and review the advice in this article. If you still are concerned that you are not using your inhaler correctly, ask your doctor about using a spacer attachment. It's a tube that connects to the mouthpiece so that you can dispense a complete, single dose into it. Once all the medication is in the spacer tube, you breathe it in when you're ready—so there's no need to worry about clicking at exactly the right moment.

Beware of Adult-Onset Asthma Risks

Matthew Tattersall, DO, assistant professor of medicine, University of Wisconsin School of Medicine and Public Health, Madison.

Adults who develop asthma are 57% more likely to have a heart attack, stroke, heart failure, angina or other cardiovascular condition than adults without asthma, according to a recent study. It's unknown how asthma is linked to cardiovascular disease, but inflammation may be a factor. Symptoms of adult-onset asthma include persistent dry cough, shortness of breath and wheezing.

New Biologic Drug Tackles Hard-to-Control Asthma

J. Mark FitzGerald, MD, professor, respiratory health, University of British Columbia, Vancouver, Canada.

Len Horovitz, MD, pulmonary specialist, Lenox Hill Hospital, New York City.

Mario Castro, MD, professor, medicine and pediatrics, Washington University School of Medicine, St. Louis.

Alan Mensch, MD, chief, pulmonary medicine, Northwell Health's Plainview Hospital, Plainview, New York.

The Lancet, online.

A new injectable drug reduces flare-ups in patients with severe asthma that is not controlled by steroid inhalers alone, two recent trials show.

The drug, *benralizumab*, is a biologic that works by killing white blood cells called eosinophils. These are present in large numbers in such patients, and they have been linked to severe asthma.

If approved by the U.S. Food and Drug Administration, benralizumab would join two similar drugs—*mepolizumab* (Nucala) and *reslizumab* (Cinqair)—in fighting hard-to-control asthma, the researchers said.

"We can offer patients who frequently require courses of oral corticosteroids and have a certain level of eosinophils [an allergy-related cell easily measured in the blood] a very effective treatment," said study author J. Mark FitzGerald, MD. He is a professor of respiratory health at the University of British Columbia in Vancouver.

"With the right patient with the right characteristics, we can significantly modify the level of asthma severity," added Dr. FitzGerald, who had a hand in both trials.

The studies were funded by AstraZeneca, the maker of benralizumab, and published online in *The Lancet,* to coincide with the presentation of the findings at the European Respiratory Society meeting in London.

Dr. FitzGerald reports serving as a consultant to AstraZeneca.

One potential advantage of benralizumab is that it can be given less often, said Mario Castro, MD, a professor of medicine and pediatrics at Washington University School of Medicine in St. Louis.

"The treatments that we have now are done every two weeks or once a month, but benralizumab can be given every two months, which may lower the cost," he said.

The available drugs cost about $25,000 to $30,000 a year and are covered by insurance, including Medicare, said Dr. Castro, who coauthored an editorial accompanying the trial reports.

The current drugs have been approved for patients aged 12 and older, "but we are very interested in them moving to the next lower age range of six and above," he said.

"If you have severe asthma and you're not getting the control that you need, ask your doctor about these medications," Dr. Castro suggested.

In the first trial, more than 1,300 patients aged 12 to 75 were randomly assigned to one of three groups—benralizumab given every four weeks…benralizumab given every eight weeks…or a placebo. In addition, the patients continued to use high-dose inhaled corticosteroids and long-acting beta agonists inhalers to control their asthma.

Over 52 weeks, the researchers found that patients taking benralizumab had a 28% to 36% reduction in flare-ups, compared with a placebo. Patients on benralizumab also showed improved lung function.

The most common side effects were cold-like symptoms in 20% of those receiving benralizumab, versus 21% of those on a placebo, and worsening asthma, 12% versus 15%, respectively.

Four patients suffered from serious side effects, including one case of hives and two cases of herpes. One patient who was taking a placebo suffered chest pains. Because of side effects, seven patients receiving benralizumab and three receiving a placebo dropped out of the trial.

"About 10% of patients with asthma have severe disease, which flares in spite of current maximal therapies," said Len Horovitz, MD, a pulmonary specialist at Lenox Hill Hospital in New York City.

Compared with Nucala and Cinqair, benralizumab appears to work in a different way by reducing the number of eosinophils, cells that cause asthma, he said.

"Immune modulation has been on the forefront in treating many diseases, including cancer, but this drug represents a step forward in treating asthma," Dr. Horovitz said.

In the second trial, more than 1,200 patients were assigned to similar groups as in the first trial. The researchers found that benralizumab cut asthma flare-ups by 45% to 51%, compared with a placebo.

The most common side effects were worsening asthma in 13% of those receiving benralizumab, compared with 12% of those receiving a placebo, and cold-like symptoms experienced by 12% of patients in both groups.

Among patients taking benralizumab, four suffered serious side effects. One patient had allergic granulomatous (inflammation of blood vessels), one patient had a panic attack and one had paresthesia (pins and needles). Among those receiving the placebo, one had a skin reaction at the site of the injection. In all, 18 patients receiving benralizumab and three receiving a placebo dropped out of the study due to side effects, the researchers said.

One respiratory disease expert sees this new drug as another breakthrough in treating hard-to-control asthma.

"These biologicals treat patients that were previously untreatable, and these treatments are getting better and better," said Alan Mensch, MD, chief of pulmonary medicine at Northwell Health's Plainview Hospital in New York.

This Vitamin Can Reduce Asthma Attacks

Christopher Griffiths, PhD, deputy director for research at Centre for Primary Care and Public Health, Blizard Institute, Barts, and The London School of Medicine and Dentistry.

Vitamin D supplements can reduce asthma attacks, reports Christopher Griffiths, PhD.

Recent study: Patients who took vitamin D supplements every day had an average of 37% fewer asthma attacks that required oral corticosteroids. Vitamin D also cut the likelihood of emergency department visits/hospitalizations by 50%.

Important: Vitamin D should not be used as a substitute for regular asthma medications. *Editor's note*: The RDA for vitamin D is 600 IU. If you are age 70 or older, 800 IU.

What Is Third-Hand Smoke?

PLOS ONE.

Smoking deposits toxins on carpets, clothing and other surfaces. This third-hand smoke has been linked to liver and lung damage and could increase the risk for type 2 diabetes.

"You've Got a Spot on Your Lung"

Andrew J. Kaufman, MD, an expert in advanced minimally invasive thoracic surgery and thoracic surgical oncology. He is chief of the department of thoracic surgery at Mount Sinai Beth Israel and director of the Thoracic Surgery Airway Program and the Asian Thoracic Surgery Program at Mount Sinai Hospital, both in New York City. He is also assistant professor at the Icahn School of Medicine, part of the Mount Sinai Health System.

Imagine for a moment that your doctor has told you to get a routine chest X-ray or CT scan because you are having chest pain... are about to have shoulder surgery...or may have cracked a rib.

Then your doctor calls to say that the test unexpectedly detected a "spot" on your lung. Your first thought is, *It might be lung cancer!*...but take a deep breath.

Here are the steps you need to take to preserve your health and your sanity...

STEP 1: **Don't panic.** Most lung spots (dense areas within the lung that appear as white, shadowy areas on imaging tests) are not cancer. In fact, when doctors screen high-risk patients (people over age 55 who have smoked roughly 30 "pack years"—a pack year is defined as smoking one pack of cigarettes a day for a year) specifically for lung cancer, only about 1% to 2% of nodules that are detected on CT scans are cancerous.

When the spot is found incidentally—that is, during an imaging test that wasn't given because cancer was suspected—the risk is even lower.

Many conditions that don't have anything to do with cancer can cause a spot on the lung. *These include...*

• **Infection from tuberculosis,** pneumonia, bronchitis or other illness involving the lungs.

• **Inflammation from an autoimmune disease**—rheumatoid arthritis, for example, is a common cause of inflammatory lung nodules.

• **Scarring from pulmonary fibrosis or other lung disease.**

• **Environmental irritants,** such as asbestos, coal dust or silicone.

• **Environmental infection,** such as histoplasmosis, caused by fungus spores in bird or bat droppings. People can be exposed while demolishing old buildings, for example, or by spending time in bat-filled caves.

STEP 2: **Talk about your history.** If you've been told that you have a spot on your lung, make an appointment with the doctor who knows you best to review your medical history...take stock of your lung cancer risk...and decide your next steps.

First, your doctor, often in consultation with a radiologist, will want to compare the latest chest X-ray or CT scan with any previous imaging tests of your chest. It is possible that the spot has been there for years but wasn't previously identified. If the spot was present and hasn't grown for many years, the chance that it is malignant is low.

Next, discuss your recent health and personal risk factors for lung cancer with your doctor. Have you had a cough, the flu or a severe cold? Do you have an autoimmune disease? Have you had any risky environmental exposures? These all have the potential to cause lung spots.

If you have a history of another malignancy somewhere in your body, your doctor will want to rule out a metastasis to the lungs.

Of course, smoking history is very significant. Smokers have a higher risk for lung cancer... former smokers have a lower risk than active smokers...and nonsmokers have the lowest risk. For everyone, however, the risk for lung cancer increases with age.

Important: For reasons no one understands, the incidence of lung cancer is rising among never-smokers, especially women. Therefore, people who have never smoked should not assume that they can't have lung cancer. Any lung spot should be evaluated by an expert even if you don't have serious risk factors for lung cancer.

STEP 3: **Get follow-up testing.** If your nodule was found incidentally, you'll need focused follow-up imaging. For most people, the best option is a low-dose CT (LDCT) scan without IV contrast. This test gives a clear view of the nodule with minimal radiation.

The dose of radiation used in an LDCT is about the same as that used in a standard mammogram. The LDCT will let doctors see the size and qualities of the nodule.

For example...*

• **Small nodules**—spots that are less than one-fifth of an inch (5 mm) are very low risk but should be followed with surveillance in most cases. For example, such nodules should usually be monitored for two years at set time intervals to reveal if there is any growth in the nodule. A stable nodule without growth for two years is safely considered benign.

• **Larger nodules**—spots that are about one-third of an inch (8 mm) or greater demand a thorough workup. This may include a positron emission tomography (PET) scan, which involves an injection of radioactive tracers that light up to indicate areas that may be cancerous and would require a biopsy for confirmation, or a needle or surgical biopsy if the person's risk factors are high and the radiographic appearance warrants a tissue diagnosis.

• **Spiky nodules**—or those with an irregular surface—are generally more concerning than smooth nodules.

*The sizes and characteristics of nodules that require follow-up (as well as the schedule for such testing) may vary depending on the medical facility where you are receiving care. Many medical centers use the Fleischner Guidelines for Pulmonary Nodules, FleischnerSociety.org.

• **Solid and part-solid nodules**—meaning they have a solid density measurement throughout the entire spot or some solid component—are typically more concerning than nonsolid nodules.

• **More is usually better.** If your doctor says that you have multiple nodules (that is, more than one), the nodules are less likely to be cancer.

Because surveillance is the most practical way to determine whether a spot is dangerous, it's important to get expert recommendations. That's why decisions regarding surveillance are usually made by a multidisciplinary team that includes pulmonary doctors, thoracic surgeons and radiologists.

Even if a nodule is deemed benign, depending on your personal medical history, your doctor may recommend a yearly follow-up scan.

For example, if a person has a close relative with cancer (a first-degree relative such as a parent or sibling) or a history of heavy smoking, he/she will likely need an annual screening to check for new nodules that may develop and possibly become cancerous.

Important: You should not settle for an X-ray as a follow-up. An LDCT provides greater detail.

Among current or former heavy smokers, LDCT has been shown to reduce the risk for lung cancer deaths due to early detection. In the National Lung Screening Trial, more than 53,000 men and women (ages 55 to 74) who were current or former heavy smokers were randomly assigned to receive annual screenings with either LDCT or standard chest X-ray for three consecutive years. The LDCT group had 20% fewer lung cancer deaths than the X-ray group.

STEP 4: **Get a closer look.** If follow-up scans show that a nodule is getting larger and/or changing in appearance, your physician will need to take a biopsy to determine whether it's malignant.

If the nodule is easy to reach—for example, in the airway—a biopsy may be done with a very thin lighted instrument that is threaded through the mouth or nose and down the throat to snip off a piece of the nodule.

A needle biopsy may be preferred if the nodule is in the peripheral lung or near the chest wall.

A surgical biopsy that involves making an incision to remove a tissue sample may be needed if the approaches described above fail to make an adequate diagnosis or if the likelihood of cancer is considered high.

If lung cancer is diagnosed, then it is crucial to make a prompt appointment with a thoracic surgeon and/or oncologist to begin treatment.

Foods to Stop Lung Cancer

DrWeil.com

Apples, tomatoes and oranges provide antioxidants that help nourish the lungs. Carrots, yellow squash and dark, leafy greens provide antioxidants called carotenoids that protect lung tissue. Water helps flush out toxins. Whole-soy foods contain phytoestrogens that may have a protective effect.

Still the number-one recommendation: Do not smoke.

Secrets to Managing COPD

Dawn Fielding, RCP, AE-C, a licensed respiratory therapist and certified COPD and Asthma Educator based in West Haven, Utah. She is executive director of the Chronic Lung Alliance, a nonprofit organization involved in education and research related to chronic lung disease. She is also author of *The COPD Solution*.

If you are living with chronic obstructive pulmonary disease (COPD), the simple act of breathing can feel like you're pushing a boulder uphill.

What you may not know: Because your ability to breathe is affected by everything in your life—including your thoughts and emotions—few disorders have as strong a *mind-body connection* as COPD.

While most doctors talk to their patients with COPD about inhalers, oxygen therapy and sometimes even surgery, the additional approaches described here will help ensure the best possible results for those who have this disorder.

THE COPD SPIRAL

With COPD (which includes chronic bronchitis and/or emphysema), air can't flow easily into and out of the lungs because of a blockage in the airways, typically caused by excess mucus, inflammation or dysfunctional lung tissue.

Being unable to breathe is a primal terror. The constant worry and anxiety that accompany this fear push the body into a stress reaction that makes breathing even more difficult, triggering more fear and stress. The key is to break the spiral and create a steadier breathing environment.

In addition to proper breathing techniques that should be practiced regularly—such as pursed breathing (as though you're whistling) and belly breathing, which strengthens muscles that assist with breathing—try these simple steps...

***SECRET #1:* Change your thoughts.** When you have a negative thought—such as *I can't do this anymore because of my COPD*—your brain registers the emotion behind it and reacts by signaling the body to produce stress hormones and to speed up your respiration rate and blood pressure.

This is helpful in an emergency...say, if you fear an oncoming car and your body reacts to avoid a collision. But in the absence of an actual threat, the response can be physically harmful by lowering your body's natural defenses and sapping your energy levels.

What helps: Positive statements reduce anxiety, help you cope and tell your brain that it's OK to relax.

What to do: When you find yourself becoming stressed, stop! Break that cycle of anxiety by repeating a phrase, such as the following, to set your brain on a positive track...

- **"No more negativity...**I'll just focus on what I can do."
- **"One day at a time.** I got through yesterday. I'll get through today."

Positive thinking and deep breathing lower blood pressure, slow heart rate and make more oxygen available for breathing.

***SECRET #2:* Watch what you eat.** Food choices are a surprisingly important factor in controlling COPD symptoms.

Here's why: Breathing is a process that involves the exchange of carbon dioxide (CO2) and oxygen in the blood.

A person with COPD has a less efficient oxygen-CO2 exchange process. Anything that increases the amount of CO2 in blood (whether it's stress or a certain type of food, such as soda or sugary food products) revs up your breathing rate—which worsens COPD.

What to do...

- **Cut back on foods that increase levels of CO2 in the blood.** The worst offenders are carbonated beverages (even fizzy water)...and anything made with refined sugar or white flour (everything from cakes and cookies to certain breads and pastas).
- **Avoid caffeinated beverages, including coffee, tea and colas.** Caffeine "wakes up" your nervous system, causing your body to work faster, accelerating your breathing rate. Whenever possible, replace soda and other caffeinated beverages with water. Why water? It helps thin mucous secretions and transports nutrients throughout our bodies. For variety, choose flavored waters (such as those infused with lemon or mint).

***SECRET #3:* Do the right exercises.** For people with COPD, breathing alone is so physically taxing that it's crucial to also improve physical stamina.

In a recent study of people with COPD in *Respiratory Medicine*, researchers compared the benefits of specific types of exercise. All the study participants did cardiovascular exercise (such as walking and biking) twice a week for three months, but one group added more strength training (including weight training for the upper and lower body) than the other group.

Result: People who did the most *strength training* had much stronger muscles throughout the body, which resulted in more efficient breathing.

In addition to doing upper-body exercises, such as bicep curls, try the following three times a week...

•**Leg lifts.** This exercise targets large muscle groups that allow us to move about freely.

What to do: While sitting in a chair, straighten one leg and lift, foot flexed, as high as you can while keeping your back straight. Hold that position for a count of five, then lower your leg. Repeat five times with each leg. Don't worry if you cannot hold your leg up for very long—your strength will improve over time.

Also: Aerobic exercise is crucial—try to get *at least* 2,000 steps a day (use a pedometer or fitness tracker) while going about your daily activities, including getting the mail, going shopping, etc. Try to exercise when your energy levels are high...and check with your doctor about the best time to take your medications when exercising.

MAKE PEACE WITH COPD...

People with COPD can experience a wide range of troubling emotions, including denial, guilt, anger and depression. If you believe that you need help coping, consider joining a support group.

The American Lung Association (ALA) sponsors Better Breathers Clubs across the US. These groups are led by a trained facilitator and offer educational presentations as well as emotional support.

info To find a local group, call the ALA at 800-LUNGUSA...or look online at Lung.org (under "Support & Community," click on "Better Breathers Club").

When Indoor Temps Rise, So Do COPD Symptoms

Annals of the American Thoracic Society, news release.

High indoor temperatures can worsen symptoms of the lung disorder chronic obstructive pulmonary disease (COPD), particularly in homes with high levels of air pollution, researchers report.

The research included 69 people with moderate to severe COPD. The disorder includes emphysema and chronic bronchitis. Symptoms include shortness of breath, coughing and wheezing.

The study volunteers were assessed on the hottest days of the year. The mean outdoor temperature was 85 degrees Fahrenheit. The mean indoor temperature was 80 F, according to the study.

Even though 86% of the participants lived in homes with air conditioning, it wasn't turned on during 37% of the study days.

The patients spent most of their time indoors. On days they did go outside, they did so for an average of two hours.

As indoor temperatures rose, COPD symptoms increased in severity, and people had to use their "rescue" inhalers more often. These effects were even greater if there were higher levels of indoor air pollution, the study authors said.

The effects of higher indoor temperatures were felt immediately and lasted for one to two days, the authors said.

The findings were published in the *Annals of the American Thoracic Society.*

"Previous studies have found that the elderly are particularly vulnerable to the effect of heat and more likely to die or be hospitalized during heat waves," lead author Meredith McCormack, MD, said in a journal news release. She's an associate professor of medicine at Johns Hopkins University School of Medicine in Baltimore.

Dr. McCormack said the researchers believe this is the first study to find a link between indoor temperatures, indoor air pollution and COPD symptoms.

"Given that participants spent an overwhelming majority of their time indoors, which we believe is representative of patients with COPD generally, optimizing indoor climate and reducing indoor pollution represents a potential avenue for improving health outcomes," Dr. McCormack said.

info The American Academy of Family Physicians has more on COPD at FamilyDoctor.org.

COPD Linked to Falls

Cristian Oancea, MD, PhD, lecturer in pulmonary rehabilitation, Victor Babes University of Medicine and Pharmacy, Timisoara, Romania.

Having chronic obstructive pulmonary disease (COPD) could significantly increase the risk of falling, according to a recent study of 73 adults.

Why: People with COPD often don't get enough exercise, which can lead to loss of balance, and they're more likely to have other risk factors linked to falling, such as low blood oxygen levels.

If you have COPD: Talk to your doctor about ways to reduce your risk of falling, such as exercises to improve balance and using a cane.

COPD Warning

Study of 2,723 current or former smokers led by researchers at University of Michigan Women's Health Program, Ann Arbor, published in *The New England Journal of Medicine.*

Many smokers and former smokers have COPD symptoms well before they are diagnosed with the disease. The symptoms of chronic obstructive pulmonary disease (COPD) include shortness of breath, coughing and difficulty exercising. If you have these symptoms and are a smoker or a former smoker, see your doctor without delay. COPD is the third-leading cause of death in the US.

Sleep Apnea Treatment Falsely Maligned

Michael Breus, PhD, is a psychologist and sleep specialist in Manhattan Beach, California.

CPAP is still the gold standard for treating obstructive sleep apnea, reports Michael Breus, PhD. Recent research at the Adelaide Institute for Sleep Health in Australia had cast doubt on the cardiovascular effectiveness of Continuous Positive Airway Pressure (CPAP). But most people in the study were fairly sick, overweight and continued to engage in behaviors inconsistent with cardiac health, and their average use of CPAP was only three hours a night.

What's That Mean? Snoring vs. Sleep Apnea

National Institutes of Health/National Heart, Lung and Blood Institute, National Sleep Foundation, American Sleep Apnea Association, Merck Manual, University of Maryland Medical Center.

It's the middle of the night and once again you've been awakened by your partner's snoring. Is it simple snoring—or sleep apnea?

Snoring is a bummer—especially to your bed partner. But sleep apnea can be life-threatening. Here's how to tell these tricky terms apart.

SNORING 101

When the airways of your mouth, nose and throat relax during sleep, they get narrower. The tissues then vibrate as you breathe. Result: Snoring.

Just about everyone snores, at least sometimes. Temporary snoring can happen when your airways are narrowed by any upper-respiratory infection, including a cold or sinusitis, as well as by allergies. Drinking alcohol can relax the muscles of the throat and soft palate and lead to occasional snoring as well. So can some medications, such as tranquilizers, sleeping pills, antihistamines and beta-blockers. Pregnancy's hormonal changes, which relax muscles, can bring it on, too.

If you snore more than occasionally, however, you might have an enlarged uvula (the dangling tissue at the back of your mouth), which partially blocks the airflow. If you're overweight, you may have some extra tissue at the back of your throat that narrows the airway. And some people just naturally have a thicker soft palate or a deviated septum in the nose, which leads to snoring. Sleep position also can contribute—when you sleep on your back, gravity pulls your relaxed throat muscles down and partially blocks your airway.

SLEEP APNEA SIGNS

Snoring, even on a regular basis, doesn't mean you have sleep apnea. But it does mean that you should be on the lookout for these apnea signs...

- Constant, extremely loud snoring
- Gasping or choking
- Pauses in breathing
- Sudden awakenings with a snort
- Excessive daytime sleepiness
- Morning headaches

If you have sleep apnea, your breathing repeatedly stops while you sleep, sometimes for one minute or even longer. Each time you stop breathing, your sleep is disrupted but not enough to consciously wake you up. The poor quality of your sleep can increase the risk for high blood pressure, stroke, heart disease and type 2 diabetes. Extreme sleepiness during the day time, another symptom, can lead to falling asleep while driving—and thus, car crashes. There are two main types of sleep apnea:

Obstructive sleep apnea (OSA), the most common type, usually is caused by soft tissue at the back of your throat collapsing and blocking the airway. Your blood oxygen level drops, and your brain wakes you just enough to get you breathing again—even if you're not consciously aware that you've actually woken up momentarily. If you have OSA, you have five or more of these mini-awakenings every hour during sleep.

Central sleep apnea, where your breathing repeatedly stops and starts while you're asleep, is much rarer. It happens because your brain isn't sending the right signals to the muscles that control your breathing. Sometimes central sleep apnea is caused by a condition such as heart failure, but often the reason is unknown. (Some people have mixed sleep apnea—a combination of the obstructive and central sleep apnea.)

Bottom line: Losing even a small amount of weight, not smoking, skipping alcohol within four hours of bedtime, sleeping on your side and even doing anti-snoring throat exercises can help with a snoring problem, including sleep apnea. But if you think you or your bed partner might have sleep apnea, see your primary care doctor, who can evaluate you and, if needed, refer you to a sleep specialist. If you are diagnosed with this condition and the approaches above don't fix it, you may want to try an oral device that keeps your airways open or go with the medical gold standard, a continuous positive airway pressure (CPAP) machine.

Toxic Metals Found in E-Cigarette Liquid

Johns Hopkins Bloomberg School of Public Health, news release.

Electronic cigarette liquids can contain high levels of toxic and potentially cancer-causing metals, a recent study suggests.

"We do not know if these levels are dangerous, but their presence is troubling and could mean that the metals end up in the aerosol that e-cigarette users inhale," said study leader Ana Maria Rule, PhD, of Johns Hopkins Bloomberg School of Public Health in Baltimore. Dr. Rule is an assistant scientist in the department of environmental health and engineering.

Dr. Rule and her colleagues analyzed the liquid of five brands of so-called first-generation e-cigarettes, which resemble traditional cigarettes. (Newer e-cigarettes look like small cassette recorders with mouthpieces.)

The researchers found liquids in those brands contained the heavy metals cadmium, chromium, lead, manganese and nickel. These metals are toxic when inhaled, the researchers said.

In first-generation e-cigarettes, the cartridge of liquid is stored in close contact with the heating coil. When heated, the liquid creates the aerosol, or vapor, that users inhale. The researchers believe this heating coil is the main source of the dangerous metals.

"Perhaps regulators might want to look into an alternative material for e-cigarette heating coils," Dr. Rule said in a Hopkins news release.

The researchers did not examine the possible presence of the five metals in the aerosol.

Currently, the U.S. Food and Drug Administration requires e-cigarette makers to submit ingredient lists and information about potentially harmful ingredients, including four of the five metals detected in this study—nickel, lead, chromium and cadmium.

The agency has studied but not yet issued proposed rules on e-cigarette labeling.

"It was striking, the varying degrees to which the metals were present in the liquid," Dr. Rule said. "This suggests that the FDA should consider regulating the quality control of e-cigarette devices along with the ingredients found in e-cigarette liquids."

The findings were published recently in the journal *Environmental Research.*

info The U.S. National Institute on Drug Abuse has more about e-cigarettes at DrugAbuse.gov.

Will Worsening "Smoke Waves" Threaten Western US?

Jia Coco Liu, PhD, former graduate student Yale School of Forestry & Environmental Studies, New Haven, Connecticut.

Janice Nolen, assistant vice president, National Policy, American Lung Association.

Climatic Change, online.

Climate change, and the warmer summers it will bring, could blanket much of the western United States with persistent "smoke waves"—consecutive days of air pollution from wildfires, a recent study warns.

"More people in the western US are likely to experience high-pollution episodes from wildfires, and the pollution episodes are likely to be more frequent, last longer and be more intense," said study author Jia Coco Liu, PhD. She was a graduate student at the Yale School of Forestry & Environmental Studies when the study was conducted.

Northern California, western Oregon and the Great Plains will bear the brunt of the pollution, the researchers said.

Wildfires occur frequently in the vast, dry West. The smoke they produce can spread far beyond the burning landscape, and the full impact on human health is still unclear.

"The smoke has been long recognized as being harmful, and we're trying to understand how harmful," said Janice Nolen, assistant vice president of national policy with the American Lung Association.

According to Dr. Liu, wildfires are a major contributor to one component of pollution in the West—ambient fine particulates, or tiny bits of debris that can be practically invisible. Many studies have shown that these particles boost the risk of lung disease, Dr. Liu said, and some link it to heart disease.

STUDY DETAILS

For this study, Dr. Liu and her colleagues examined the levels of fine particulate matter in 561 counties in 16 western states from 2004 to 2009. Then they predicted what those levels will be from 2046 to 2051. They focused only on levels directly linked to wildfires.

Using what they called a mid-level prediction of climate change, the researchers estimated that incidents of two or more days of high pollution from wildfires will grow by 57% in frequency and 31% in intensity between the two time periods.

According to Dr. Liu, more than 82 million people will be affected. That number accounts for population growth, she said, and is equivalent to 57 million people today.

Moreover, the smoke-wave season will likely lengthen by 15 days, on average, in nearly two-thirds of the counties assessed. And more than half of the counties already suffering smoke waves will experience more intense smoke waves, the study predicted.

But about 19% of the areas could see less pollution from wildfires.

"It is hard to say exactly why some counties have fewer smoke waves," Dr. Liu said. However, she did say their prevalence depends on many factors such as weather, the number of trees in the area and their density.

WHAT THIS ALL MEANS

How might the extra pollution from wildfires affect health in the future?

Looking at Medicare recipients, the researchers predicted that more severe wildfires would boost the likelihood that the elderly will be hospitalized for respiratory diseases.

It's also possible that people could die earlier even if they're only exposed to the pollution for a brief time, said Nolen.

Recent research is revealing even greater impacts from pollution than previously reported. "The more we look into the body, the more we see that pollution affects systems like development in the womb," she said.

What should happen now?

Dr. Liu's team cited a need for better wildfire management and evacuation programs in high-risk regions. Nolen said the American Lung Association supports measures to reduce climate change and raise awareness about the long-lasting harms of wildfires.

The study was published online recently in the journal *Climatic Change.*

info For more about air pollution and health, see BottomLineInc.com/surprising-dangers-of-air-pollution.

How Yoga Helps a Cold

Tara Stiles, founder, Strala Yoga, based in New York City. StralaYoga.com

You hate taking decongestants when you have a cold, but what else can you do to breathe easier?

A calming yoga technique known as alternate nostril breathing can ease congestion and may help kick-start the immune system.

What to do: Sit up tall. Take your right hand and curl down your index and middle fingers into your palm. Press your ring finger over your left nostril and inhale for a count of four through your right nostril. Then close off your right nostril with your thumb so that both nostrils are closed. Hold your breath for a count of four. Release your ring finger and let all of your air out through your left nostril during a count of four. Reverse sides, and keep repeating for three to five minutes. Stop if you become uncomfortable at any time. If you have a chronic condition such as asthma or high blood pressure, check with your doctor before trying any special breathing techniques.

Lung and Liver Inflammation Reduced by Essential Oils

Environmental Chemistry Letters.

Compounds in essential oils made from cloves, anise, fennel and ylang-ylang may reduce lung and liver inflammation caused by air pollution, according to a new lab study. The oils reduced one cytokine (an inflammation marker) by 96%.

CHAPTER 2

Blood Pressure and Cholesterol

Don't Fall for These Blood Pressure Traps

When it comes to treating serious medical conditions, you would think that high blood pressure (hypertension) would be one of the nation's great success stories. Doctors test for it. Patients know the risks. And there are dozens of medications that treat it.

Yet the results are still disappointing. About one in every three American adults has hypertension...but only about half of them keep it under control.

Why are we still losing the battle against hypertension? Scientists now are discovering some of the traps that prevent people from adequately controlling their blood pressure. *What you need to know...*

TRAP #1: **Not treating soon enough.** Even though normal blood pressure is defined as below 120/80 mmHg, researchers continue to debate optimal blood pressure targets. In reality, most doctors don't consider treatment until readings reach 140/90 mmHg or above—the official definition of hypertension.

But recent research has shown us that is too late. The risks associated with hypertension—stroke, heart attack, kidney disease and vision loss, among others—start to rise at lower levels.

Important new finding: When researchers compared target blood pressure readings in more than 9,350 adults with hypertension and other cardiovascular risk factors, the results were striking. Those who got intensive treatment to lower their systolic (top number) pressure to below 120 mmHg were 27% less likely to die from any cause over a three-year period than those whose target was below 140 mmHg. In the study, diastolic (bottom number) pressure

Holly Kramer, MD, MPH, an associate professor in the department of public health sciences and the department of medicine, Division of Nephrology and Hypertension, at Loyola University Medical Center in Maywood, Illinois. She received the 2016 Garabed Eknoyan Award from the National Kidney Foundation.

was not measured because it tends to decline as people get older.

Starting treatment earlier than 140 mmHg to achieve a normal reading could save more than 100,000 American lives a year, the researchers estimated.

My advice: If your systolic blood pressure is 120 mmHg or above (or your diastolic pressure is 90 mmHg or above), tell your doctor that you want to be treated.

Note: If your systolic blood pressure is less than 150 mmHg, you may be able to avoid medication if you adopt healthier habits—not smoking...losing weight, if necessary...getting regular exercise...eating a well-balanced diet, etc. If these steps haven't lowered your blood pressure after six months, you may need medication. If systolic pressure is above 150 mmHg, medications may be needed in addition to lifestyle changes.

Caution: Intensive blood pressure treatment usually involves taking multiple blood pressure–lowering drugs, which increases risk for side effects, such as dizziness and lightheadedness. Therefore, blood pressure should be checked frequently (see below) and regular tests should be given for potassium and electrolyte levels. Electrolytes and kidney function should be checked within one month of starting a diuretic or when a dose is increased. After that, levels should be checked every six to 12 months.

***TRAP #2:* Not testing at home.** Don't rely only on the blood pressure tests that you get at your doctor's office. They can be too intermittent—and too rushed—to give accurate readings. Your pressure is likely to be artificially high...or artificially low, since people who are seeing a doctor often abstain from some of the things (such as drinking coffee) that raise it.

My advice: Buy a digital blood pressure monitor, and use it at home. Omron upper-arm blood pressure monitors (available at pharmacies and online for about $40 and up) are about as accurate as office monitors. A *JAMA* study found that 72% of people who tested at home had good blood pressure control versus 57% of volunteers who were tested only by their doctors.

What to do: Every day, check your blood pressure in the morning before eating, exercising or taking medication...and again in the evening. (If your blood pressure is normal, test every few months.)

Before testing, empty your bladder (a full bladder will cause higher readings). Then sit with both feet on the floor, and relax for five minutes. Rest your arm, raised to the level of your heart, on a table, and place the cuff on bare skin.

Do each reading twice: Measure your blood pressure once...wait a few minutes...then repeat—the second reading will be more accurate. Write down the readings, and share them with your doctor during your office visits.

***TRAP #3:* Taking the wrong drug.** About 70% of patients with hypertension require two or more drugs to achieve good control. Many will be given prescriptions for one of the newer drugs, such as an angiotensin-converting enzyme (ACE) inhibitor or an angiotensin receptor blocker (ARB). Some patients (such as those with heart failure) will need one of these drugs. Most people do not—at least not right away.

If you've recently been diagnosed with hypertension, consider a thiazide diuretic, such as chlorthalidone. It's an older drug that is available as a generic. It costs pennies a day, and studies have shown that thiazide diuretics lower blood pressure as effectively as other drugs, with less risk for heart failure and stroke. Thiazide diuretics may be paired with an ARB or ACE inhibitor, since these drugs are synergistic (each drug increases the other's effectiveness).

The caveats: Even though diuretics generally are safe, you'll urinate more often (they're known as "water pills" for a reason). Thiazide diuretics might also lower potassium levels in some patients—if so, your doctor may advise you to take potassium supplements. And diuretics can raise urate levels, triggering gout in some people.

***TRAP #4:* Not timing your medication.** Most people take medications when it's convenient—or at a set time, such as with their morning coffee. But blood pressure medication should be scheduled.

It's natural for blood pressure to vary by about 30 points at different times of the day. It almost always rises in the morning, which is why strokes and heart attacks are more common in the early hours. One study found that patients who took at least one of their blood pressure medications at night were about one-third less likely to have a heart attack or stroke than those who took all of their pills in the morning.

My advice: With your doctor's OK, take at least one of your blood pressure medications (not a diuretic) at bedtime to help protect you from blood pressure increases in the morning. Diuretics should be taken in the morning so that frequent urination won't interrupt sleep.

The Best Ways to Cut Back on Salt

Michelle Hauser, MD, MPA, a primary care physician, certified Le Cordon Bleu chef and nutrition educator. Dr. Hauser is also a postdoctoral research fellow in cardiovascular disease prevention at Stanford University School of Medicine, California. ChefInResidency.com

Has your doctor told you that you need to cut back on salty foods? You may already know that having too much sodium can increase blood pressure. Now a recent 20-year study published in the *Journal of the American College of Cardiology* says that individuals with the lowest sodium intake seem to have the lowest risk of dying early.

The salt threat: People who have high blood pressure, diabetes or kidney disease or who are African-American or age 51 and older are often salt-sensitive. That means they have a sharp increase in blood pressure when they eat salty foods and are at greater risk for stroke, heart attack and other dangerous health problems. However, many people don't realize that even those who are not salt-sensitive could have an increase in blood pressure if they eat too much sodium.

Here's the good news: There are many simple ways to reduce your sodium intake without sacrificing flavor!

A DOCTOR/CHEF'S TIPS FOR REDUCING SODIUM

The average sodium intake per day in the US is a whopping 3,400 mg (that's about one-and-one-half teaspoons of table salt). However, the American Heart Association advises just 1,500 mg per day (two-thirds of a teaspoon) or less for optimal health. It may be no surprise that fast-food items and deli meats have a lot of salt. But restaurant meals and store-bought sauces, salad dressings, soups and even bread tend to be loaded with sodium as well.

Michelle Hauser, MD, MPA, a primary care doctor and certified Le Cordon Bleu chef, says the absolute best way to cut back on salt is to prepare more meals at home using fresh, unprocessed ingredients. This not only enables you to control the amount of salt added to meals but also maximizes the flavor of food so that a little salt goes a long way.

Some people prefer to wean themselves off salt slowly, while others find it easier to go "cold turkey."

Either way, here are Dr. Hauser's flavor-packed suggestions...

- **Add some acid.** A few drops of a sour ingredient, like citrus juice or vinegar, wakes up the flavor in foods and enhances any salt you do use, allowing you to get by with less.

What to do: Add a squeeze of lime to low-sodium black bean soup (it will make the soup taste saltier and give it a Latin flavor)...include a teaspoon of balsamic vinegar in your homemade tomato sauce...add a few drops of Tabasco sauce (made from red peppers and vinegar) to chili...and use an orange juice–based marinade to tenderize and flavor chicken. Other tasty sources of acid include the juice of Meyer lemons or grapefruits.

Another option: Flavored vinegars—some are infused with herbs such as thyme or rosemary...others contain fruits like raspberries or figs.

- **Salt smart.** Do you have trouble knowing how much salt to add to your dishes? *Here's how to get maximum flavor without going overboard...*

What to do: To get the hang of this technique, try it with an unsalted sauce. Taste the sauce, taking note of the flavors. Sip some water, then add a few drops of an acidic ingredient to the sauce (see above) and stir. Taste again, noticing how much brighter and flavorful the dish is. Next, add a pinch or two of salt, stir and taste. If you taste the salt only on the tip of your tongue, the sauce is undersalted. Take a sip of water, and add another pinch or two of salt. The dish is perfectly salted when you taste the salt on the middle to the back of your tongue. The food is oversalted if the flavor hits the back of your throat.

•**Try these tasty all-natural salt substitutes.** Forget the potassium chloride salt-substitute sold in shakers at the grocery store—they can have a chemical or metallic taste. Fresh and dried herbs and spices add delicious flavors to your dishes and boost the impact of a small amount of salt.

What to do: You can buy fresh or dried rosemary, thyme and basil in grocery stores, but it's very easy to grow these herbs at home. Also, stock up on store-bought garlic and onion powders (not salts), cumin, coriander, Mexican oregano, smoked paprika and cayenne pepper.

Premade seasoning mixes—like Mrs. Dash Salt-Free Seasoning Blends, combinations of herbs, spices and dried vegetables—are available in grocery stores. But you may want to add some international flavor by using spice mixes from India, Asia, the Middle East or Africa. For example, Ras-El-Hanout is a Moroccan spice mix made of cumin, turmeric, allspice, coriander and pepper. You can buy this mix in gourmet cooking stores or online...or make it yourself (see the recipe at ChefInResidency.com).

•**Try roasting or grilling vegetables.** These high-temperature cooking methods cause a chemical reaction that releases hundreds of rich, savory flavor compounds (think of roasted or grilled mushrooms). With all this natural flavor, you'll never even miss the salt! The key is making sure that the surface of the food is as dry as possible before cooking (oils and seasonings are fine, but no added water).

Caution: Grilling and frying meats and fish can produce carcinogenic compounds, so avoid charring or overcooking these foods.

OTHER HELPFUL TIPS

•**Consider flaked kosher salt**—it has about half the sodium per teaspoon of granulated salt.

Note: Some people think sea salt is healthier than table salt.

The facts: There are small amounts of minerals and micronutrients in sea salt, but if you are getting the appropriate amount of sodium, these nutrients are not likely to affect your health. And sea salt contains just as much sodium as table salt by weight.

•**Get more potassium.** A high-potassium diet can blunt the effect of salt on blood pressure by increasing sodium excretion from the body. Eating a variety of fruits and vegetables is the best way to get the 4,700 mg per day of potassium suggested by the Institute of Medicine.

Good sources of potassium: Leafy greens, beans, potatoes, bananas, avocados, papaya, dried fruit, nuts and seeds, fish, chili peppers and powder, and even dark chocolate.

Caution: Check with your doctor before increasing your potassium intake if you have a chronic health condition (such as kidney disease) or take medication.

•**Add some interest to your plate by eating foods with a variety of colors, textures and flavors.** When you eat with all your senses, you will be less likely to need salt.

The Government's Sodium Advice? Don't Trust It

Steven Nissen, MD, chairman, department of cardiovascular medicine, Cleveland Clinic. He has more than 35 years of experience as a physician and is world-renowned for his work as a cardiologist, patient advocate and researcher.

When it comes to salt and your health, science seems to point left, right, up and down at the same time...

•**The American Heart Association wants every healthy adult to restrict sodium.**

•The FDA wants food companies to cut sodium in their products.

The goal—to cut the average adult's intake of sodium from 3,400 mg to 2,300 mg per day.

And yet...research has found that people who consume less than 2,500 mg of sodium per day are at higher risk for heart disease—and now a study reports that in healthy people without high blood pressure, there's no heart risk until they consume twice as much sodium as the average—7,000 mg per day!

Who's right? Should healthy people restrict sodium to prevent high blood pressure and heart disease? Can you believe the studies that point to a different conclusion? What if your blood pressure is high or edging up—should you watch your sodium?

For common sense grounded in science, we turned to one of the top heart specialists in the world, Steven Nissen, MD, chairman of the department of cardiovascular medicine at the Cleveland Clinic.

THE SCIENCE PROBLEM: WE'RE ACTING OUT OF IGNORANCE

Don't put much faith in either the government's public health campaign to get us to consume less sodium—or in the conflicting studies that suggest that a low-sodium lifestyle won't help and might harm.

Here's why: Bad studies. Or rather, the lack of good studies. The science is extraordinarily murky. The estimates used to come up with recommendations come not from clinical trials but from dietary recall studies, which are terribly unreliable, and from computer estimates that simulate what the effects might be.

In contrast, he pointed to Mediterranean diet studies. These are based on randomized double-blind clinical trials in which one group ate the diet for years and another group ate a different diet. These well-designed trials have proved that the Mediterranean diet can prevent heart disease.

There's no such research that shows that cutting sodium consumption in healthy people without high blood pressure will lead to any health benefit. We're not all the same—biology doesn't work that way. We have unique genetics and environments. If you're a construction worker in Houston in the summer, for example, salt restriction is probably not a good idea for you.

COMMON SENSE ABOUT SODIUM, SALT AND A HEALTHY HEART

Recommendations based on what is known scientifically...

•If you have high blood pressure, defined as a reading of 140/90 or higher, go on the sodium-restricted DASH diet, which includes dairy and plenty of fruits and vegetables—along with any medication you are prescribed. The combo of plenty of potassium and calcium and reduced sodium (a daily maximum of 2,300 mg) has been proven to reduce high blood pressure.

•If your blood pressure is borderline— with a systolic (upper) number between 120 and 139, for example—same advice. If you want to avoid needing meds, it's prudent to restrict salt and go on a DASH diet.

•If your blood pressure is normal—stop worrying about sodium and salt! Instead, pay attention to eating a healthy Mediterranean-style diet, with lots of vegetables, fruits, beans, nuts and whole grains, olive oil as the primary fat, regular consumption of seafood, moderate amounts of dairy and eggs, with less frequent, smaller servings of red meat—and, if you drink, a glass of wine with dinner.

Ironically, by eating in this style, you might actually take in less sodium than you do now—without resorting to low-sodium and salt-free products. That's because about three-quarters of the sodium in our diet comes from processed foods, not whole foods that we cook at home—even if we salt them.

Don't eat your dinner out of cans. Try an omelet—in spite of earlier concerns about cholesterol, eggs are very healthy foods. Eat apples and pears if you're hungry in between meals. If you eat like that, you won't overload on salt.

Tart Cherry Juice Lowers Blood Pressure

Study "Effects of Montmorency tart cherry (*Prunus Cerasus L.*) consumption on vascular function in men with early hypertension" by researchers at Northumbria University, United Kingdom, Northwest University, South Africa, published in *American Journal of Clinical Nutrition.*

Tart Montmorency cherries and their juice, already a popular natural remedy for gout, sore muscles and insomnia, may be good for your blood pressure, finds a recent study.

The cherries are rich in phytochemicals and had been shown to improve the function of blood vessels, stimulate the release of nitric oxide (which helps blood vessels expand) and reduce inflammation—in lab and animal studies.

So British researchers set out to see how cherries affect people.

In a randomized, crossover, blinded study, they gave 15 men with prehypertension—blood pressure levels of 130 systolic or higher, 80 diastolic or higher, or both—either a drink containing about four tablespoons (60 ml) of a tart cherry concentrate diluted in water or a similarly flavored drink that had no cherries. Two weeks later, they switched groups and redid the experiment.

Results: On cherry-drinking days, the men's systolic blood pressure dropped by an average of 7 mmHg. That's a significant effect, as strong as that provided by many hypertension drugs—and if sustained over five years or more, that kind of drop is linked to a 38% reduced risk for stroke and 23% reduced risk for heart disease. Diastolic blood pressure also dropped but not as dramatically. (The study, it should be acknowledged, was partly funded by England's Cherry Marketing Institute.)

Want to try it yourself? The researchers used a product called CherryActive Concentrate (made in England but available online in the US), from 100% Montmorency cherries. But be aware that fruit juice, and especially concentrate, is high in sugar—even without any added sugar.

If you want to take a more whole-foods approach, you can include tart cherries and tart cherry juice in your diet—along with other foods known to lower blood pressure, including celery, cocoa, red wine (as well as grapes and raisins), beet juice and soy foods, plus plenty of foods rich in potassium and calcium.

BP Med Decreases Risk for Fractures

Joshua I. Barzilay, MD, endocrinologist, Kaiser Permanente, Duluth, Georgia.

Blood pressure drug has a surprising benefit, we hear from Joshua I. Barzilay, MD. Thiazide diuretics, commonly prescribed to lower blood pressure, decreased risk for hip and pelvic fractures by 21%, compared with ACE inhibitors and calcium channel blockers, a new study of 22,000 older adults found.

Possible reason: Thiazide diuretics, such as chlorthalidone and indapamide, lower calcium excretion in urine, which may slow bone loss.

If you have thinning bones and/or an increased risk for fracture: Ask your doctor about taking a thiazide diuretic if you need blood pressure medication.

Aggressive Care Saves Lives

Analysis of a 2015 National Institutes of Health study led by researchers at Loyola University Medical Center, Maywood, Illinois, presented at a recent meeting of the American Heart Association.

Aggressive blood pressure treatment could save 100,000 lives a year. Current guidelines call for systolic pressure (top number) to be below 140 mmHg. But a recent study says that more lives would be saved with a goal of 120 mmHg or lower in people who are at high risk for heart disease.

Caution: Too-low pressure can cause dizziness that can lead to falls and broken bones.

Fluctuating Blood Pressure Linked to Cognitive Decline

Bo Qin, PhD, postdoctoral associate, Rutgers Cancer Institute of New Jersey, New Brunswick.

According to recent research, adults age 55 and older whose systolic (top number) blood pressure fluctuated by 15 points or more when measured regularly over seven years had a faster decline in cognitive function, including the ability to remember words, than those whose levels did not fluctuate as much.

Theory: Fluctuations may be a sign of inflammation and impaired blood vessels.

Obesity Is Not Always Bad for Your Heart: 1 in 7 Obese People Has Normal Blood Pressure, Cholesterol

Gregory Nichols, PhD, senior investigator, Center for Health Research, Kaiser Permanente, Portland, Oregon.

Carlos Lorenzo, MD, assistant professor, medicine, University of Texas Health Science Center, San Antonio.

Tracey McLaughlin, MD, associate professor, medicine, Stanford University School of Medicine, Stanford, California.

Preventing Chronic Disease, online.

Can people really be healthy and obese? In one of the largest studies to date, researchers quantified the number of US adults who are overweight or obese but don't have typical risk factors for heart disease and diabetes.

Of 1.3 million overweight and obese people studied, 14% had normal blood sugar, cholesterol and blood pressure readings, the study found.

Doctors use these "cardiometabolic" measures to help identify people at greater risk of having a heart attack or stroke or developing type 2 diabetes.

But calling these people "healthy obese" is a misnomer, said lead author Gregory Nichols, PhD, a senior investigator at the Kaiser Permanente Center for Health Research in Portland, Oregon.

LOW RISK FACTORS DOES NOT MEAN HEALTHY

"Just because they don't currently have risk factors doesn't mean they're not going to," said Dr. Nichols.

The study suggests that might be true: Less than 2.8% of overweight and obese people age 80 and older had zero risk factors, versus more than 29% of those ages 20 to 34.

The absence of risk factors doesn't mean they're healthy, either, Dr. Nichols added.

"They still have more joint problems; they're more likely to get certain cancers; they're at risk for kidney disease, and so on," he explained.

Plus, prior research has shown that obese people are more likely to die prematurely than people of the same age who are not obese.

Scientists don't know exactly why these fat-but-seemingly-fit people have normal blood pressure, blood sugar and cholesterol.

Dr. Nichols said diet and exercise or genetics may play a role. Or, he added, it may be a matter of timing.

The study provided a snapshot of overweight and obese adults at a point in time. Dr. Nichols said if he and his team had followed the study population over an extended period, they may have found that some people develop risk factors very quickly, while others take much longer to do so.

STUDY DETAILS

The new study involved 1.3 million overweight and obese adults served by four health systems in 11 states and the District of Columbia. Using each person's weight and height, researchers calculated body mass index (BMI), an estimate of body fat.

The large sample size allowed researchers to categorize obese adults by the severity of their obesity.

Using electronic medical record data, researchers looked for four risk factors—elevated blood pressure; elevated triglycerides (a type of fat found in blood); low HDL, or "good" cholesterol; and elevated blood sugar.

The study excluded people who already had diabetes. Dr. Nichols said that may explain why black adults, who are known to be at greater risk for diabetes than whites, were 28% less likely than whites in the study to have risk factors.

Across all overweight and obese adults in the study, the presence of risk factors varied widely. But with increasing levels of obesity, the likelihood of having at least one risk factor also increased.

Among participants who were overweight, 18.6% had no risk factors, but among obese participants, almost 10% had no risk factors. Among those considered morbidly obese, less than 6% had no risk factors, according to the study.

EXPERT COMMENT

Carlos Lorenzo, MD, an assistant professor of medicine at the University of Texas Health Science Center in San Antonio, suggested there may be significant variation in this population.

"Obese individuals who are metabolically healthy might represent one end of the spectrum of obesity," said Dr. Lorenzo, who was not involved in the study. Identifying people at greater risk for heart disease and diabetes based on their risk factors "may be important for prevention and treatment," he noted.

Endocrinologist Tracey McLaughlin, MD, said there is an "increasing movement" to identify subgroups of overweight and obese people at greater risk of metabolic disease who may benefit from weight loss.

"The jury is still out as to whether healthy overweight individuals benefit from weight loss," added Dr. McLaughlin, an associate professor of medicine at Stanford University School of Medicine.

WHAT TO DO IF YOU'RE OBESE...

Dr. Nichols said additional research is needed to understand who's most at risk and whether the measures used to assess risk factors are appropriate across different ages, races and ethnicities.

"If you're struggling with obesity and you don't have any of these risk factors, keep doing what you're doing," he said. "But don't assume that your health is really any better. You still need to think about diet and exercise."

The study appears in *Preventing Chronic Disease*, an online journal of the U.S. Centers for Disease Control and Prevention.

info The U.S. National Heart, Lung, and Blood Institute can tell you more about metabolic risk factors at NHLBI.nih.gov/health/health-topics/topics/ms/.

When Statins Don't Mix with Other Heart Drugs

Barbara S. Wiggins, PharmD, a clinical pharmacy specialist in cardiology at the Medical University of South Carolina and adjunct professor at South Carolina College of Pharmacy, both in Charleston. She is lead author of *Pharmacist's Guide to Lipid Management, 2nd Edition*. She also chaired the committee that created the American Heart Association's 2016 Scientific Statement on statin-related drug-drug interactions.

If you're taking a statin drug to help reduce your risk for heart attack or stroke, you wouldn't expect it to interact with another heart medication that your doctor may have prescribed...but it can.

What most people don't realize: The statin drugs that are taken by about one-quarter of American adults age 40 and older can interact with many medications that are needed to treat related cardiovascular conditions.

Even though combining a statin with other heart medicines usually offers more benefit than harm, it's important that these medications be closely monitored by one's doctor. Keep a list of your current medications and doses so that your doctor (and pharmacist) can evaluate them for potential drug-drug interactions (DDIs).

Latest development: The American Heart Association recently released a statement about these possible drug interactions, along with guidelines on how to avoid them. *What you need to know...*

WHAT ARE THE RISKS?

Millions of Americans take two or more drugs to reduce the risk for heart attack, stroke and other cardiovascular conditions. Multiple medications often are necessary to optimize treatment in patients who have more than one medical condition and are at risk for cardiovascular disease. Along with statins (used for lowering cholesterol), these drugs include fibrates (for lowering triglycerides)... blood thinners (for reducing clots)...calcium channel blockers (for high blood pressure and other conditions)...and many others.

When statins are combined with one or more of these other heart medications, a DDI can occur.

Important: If you're taking a statin, be sure to tell your doctor (and pharmacist) whenever any medication is added or taken away from your regimen or a drug dose changes.

POSSIBLE INTERACTIONS

Statin-related DDIs can range from mild muscle aches or weakness to a severe form of muscle damage known as rhabdomyolysis, which is rare but can be life-threatening. If you notice muscle pain and/or weakness, known as myopathy, tell your doctor right away.

Discuss with your doctor how to minimize side effects if you take the following combinations—even if you aren't currently experiencing side effects. You may not always tolerate these combinations.

• **Statin plus a fibrate.** Patients with high triglycerides or complex lipid disorders—such as metabolic syndrome, obesity and/or diabetes—sometimes are treated with both a statin and a fibrate drug. The fibrates include *gemfibrozil* (Lopid) and *fenofibrate* (Tricor). Gemfibrozil is particularly risky when combined with some statins.

The risk: Blood levels of *lovastatin* (Mevacor) and *simvastatin* (Zocor) can double or triple when combined with gemfibrozil. Gemfibrozil plus *pravastatin* (Pravachol) can increase blood-statin concentrations by more than 200%. When blood levels of a statin you're taking reach such high levels, it can increase risk for rhabdomyolysis.

Option: Choose the fibrate fenofibrate. According to the FDA's Adverse Event Reporting System, reports of rhabdomyolysis are 15 times lower with this drug than with gemfibrozil. However, fenofibrate is much more expensive, and not all patients will tolerate this drug.

Another option: Switch to the statin *fluvastatin* (Lescol). Unlike the three statins mentioned above, fluvastatin doesn't interact with gemfibrozil. For patients who must take one of the higher-intensity statins, such as *atorvastatin* (Lipitor), *rosuvastatin* (Crestor) or *pitavastatin* (Livalo), along with gemfibrozil, a lower statin dose can minimize the risk for side effects.

Note: Because the degree of risk versus benefit is different for all drugs, just lowering the dose is not always an option.

• **Statin plus warfarin.** Patients who are candidates for statins may also require a blood thinner. *Warfarin* (Coumadin) is often prescribed for patients with a high risk for stroke, heart attack or blood clots (including those leading to a pulmonary embolism). It's also used in people who have had a previous stroke or damage to a heart valve.

The risk: Statins may increase the effects of warfarin. When doses of warfarin are too high, it can lead to bleeding.

Warning signs: Bleeding gums when brushing your teeth...bloody urine or dark stools due to internal bleeding...or sudden, unexplained fatigue (possibly due to anemia). Some reports have found that warfarin plus simvastatin can cause up to a 30% change in a patient's International Normalized Ratio (INR), a standard measure of how quickly blood clots.

Option: Patients who show a marked change in INR might be advised to take pitavastatin or atorvastatin. They appear less likely to affect the INR than other statin drugs.

Note: When you first combine warfarin with a statin, or when you change a statin dose, you should have frequent blood tests to check your INR so the warfarin dose can be adjusted if needed—for example, two or three tests in the first week of treatment. Once the drug effects have stabilized and you have good clotting control, testing can be scaled back to once or twice a month.

Or in some cases, patients may be able to switch to *rivaroxaban* (Xarelto) or another one of the newer blood thinners instead of warfarin.

•**Statin plus a calcium channel blocker.** Many patients with high cholesterol also have high blood pressure, stable angina or some heart irregularities (arrhythmias)—all of which may be treated with a calcium channel blocker.

The risk: One drug in this class, *amlodipine* (Norvasc), may increase risk for muscle damage when combined with *simvastatin* or *lovastatin*. Other calcium channel blockers, such as *diltiazem* (Cardizem) and *verapamil* (Verelan), increase blood levels of simvastatin, atorvastatin and lovastatin.

Options: The degree of interaction is lower when amlodipine is combined with atorvastatin or pravastatin. Some patients may report occasional fatigue or muscle pain, but the dose of one drug could be lowered to avoid side effects.

The combinations of *diltiazem* with lovastatin or simvastatin, or verapamil with the same statins, can cause "moderate" increases in statin levels. However, lowering the statin dose might be all that's needed to prevent side effects, such as muscle pain and fatigue.

•**Statin plus antiarrhythmic drugs.** Patients with heartbeat irregularities (arrhythmias) often need to combine a statin with an antiarrhythmic drug.

The risks: Blood levels of digoxin (Lanoxin), a common drug in this class, may increase when it's combined with atorvastatin, leading to digoxin toxicity (nausea, vomiting, diarrhea, blurred vision, headaches and other symptoms). Patients who require this combination will need frequent tests (including blood tests) to detect toxicity before any troublesome symptoms kick in.

Dronedarone (Multaq), another antiarrhythmic agent, may increase blood levels of simvastatin, possibly leading to statin side effects.

Patients taking the antiarrhythmic drug *amiodarone* (Cordarone) may experience statin side effects when also using lovastatin or simvastatin.

Options: It's generally safe to use a heart-rhythm drug with one of the following statins—rosuvastatin, atorvastatin, pitavastatin, fluvastatin or pravastatin.

In patients taking lovastatin or simvastatin with an antiarrhythmic that increases the statin's blood level, a lower statin dose may be used and/or blood tests may be given to check for muscle damage.

What You Don't Know About Statins Could Hurt You

"Disentagling the Association between Statins, Cholesterol, and Colorectal Cancer: A Nested Case-Control Study," University of Pennsylvania School of Medicine, *PLOS Medicine*.

"Efficacy and Tolerability of Evolocumab vs Ezetimibe in Patients With Muscle-Related Statin Intolernance," American College of Cardiology, *JAMA*.

"Impact of incident diabetes on atherosclerotic cardiovascular disease according to statin use history among postmenopausal women," University of Massachusetts Medical School, *European Journal of Epidemiology*.

"How statistical deception created the appearance that statins are safe and effective in primary and secondary prevention of cardiovascular disease," University of South Florida, *Expert Review of Clinical Pharmacology*.

Cholesterol-lowering statins, touted as "wonder" drugs, are in the news—again. And the news is not all good. *Here's the latest on statins...*

•**It's cholesterol, not the drug, that protects against colon cancer.** Taking statins is statistically linked to lower colon cancer risk. But it's not the drugs that protect—it's having high cholesterol in the first place! University of Pennsylvania School of Medicine researchers reported in the journal *PLOS ONE* that colorectal cancer occurred at the same rate in participants with high cholesterol—whether they were taking a statin or not. In fact, a drop in cholesterol often preceded colon cancer diagnosis. But don't raise your cholesterol to avoid colon cancer!

•**Muscle pain side effects are real—but not as common as claimed.** Muscle pains are a common complaint in people who take statins—between 5% and 20% of people on the drugs complain of myalgia (muscle pain). Now, in the first major placebo-controlled, blind clinical trial, the American College of Cardiology confirms that statin-related myalgia is real—but only for 43% of people who complain of that side effect. The rest may have muscle pain, but it's not caused by their statin drug.

•**For women with diabetes, no heart benefit.** Statins aren't heart-protective for postmenopausal women newly diagnosed with type 2 diabetes. A 14-year study from the University of Massachusetts Medical School, published in *European Journal of Epidemiology*, found that newly diabetic women over age 50 had the same incidence of heart attack, stroke and cardiovascular-related death whether they were taking statins or not. (Ironically, one of the side effects of these drugs is an increased risk in women of developing diabetes in the first place.)

•**Overblown lifesaving claims.** In people at high risk for a first heart attack, claims that statins are protective are wildly exaggerated and based on a "statistical deception," concludes a University of South Florida analysis reported in *Expert Review of Clinical Pharmacology*. Let's say you read that taking a statin reduced the risk for a heart attack by 36%. But here's what really happened—3% of people taking a placebo had a heart attack, while 1.9% taking a statin had a heart attack. The absolute risk reduction is a mere 1.1 percentage points. That is, you'd need to give statins to more than 100 people to prevent one heart attack. The researchers concluded that for people at high risk for a first heart attack, statin drugs "fail to substantially improve cardiovascular outcomes" and their "modest benefits are more than offset by their adverse effects."

---

4 out of 5 People Prescribed Statins May Not Need Them

Study titled "Accuracy of the Atherosclerotic Cardiovascular Risk Equation in a Large Contemporary, Multiethnic Population" by researchers at Kaiser Permanente Northern California, University of California, San Francisco, et al. published in *Journal of the American College of Cardiology*.

Ever since new guidelines to identify who needs a statin were introduced in 2013, there have been skeptics. One major suspicion was that the cardiovascular risk calculator used to determine statin eligibility widely overestimated heart disease risk.

That could result in many people—potentially millions—taking these drugs when they shouldn't. But those concerns were theoretical, based on competing estimates of risk.

Now we have evidence from the first major study that actually looked at what happens with real patients.

The skeptics were right.

REAL PEOPLE'S HEARTS ARE SO MUCH HEALTHIER THAN WE THOUGHT

In this study, researchers put the risk calculator to the test by applying it to the population it was designed for—that is, men and women, ages 40 to 75, who did not already have diagnosed diabetes or cardiovascular disease, with an LDL cholesterol under 190 mg/dL. (If your LDL is above 190, current guidelines recommend a statin even if your risk is low.) Using a large database from Kaiser Permanente Northern California, they identified more than 300,000 men and women who in 2008 fit the profile of the ideal user of the calculator.

According to the cardiovascular risk calculator, the number of these patients who, over the next five years, would have a heart attack or an ischemic stroke (the most common kind) or die from heart disease should have been 10,150 people.

In reality, it was 2,061.

That's good news of course. But it means that cardiovascular disease was overestimated across the board—at every level of risk. It was found among both men and women and also among major ethnic groups including non-Hispanic white, non-Hispanic black, Asian-Pacific Islander and Hispanic people.

Not everyone in the study would have been a candidate for a statin—but about 30% were. And, based on this study, it appears that four out of five of them who would be candidates for statins based on the standard risk calculator don't need them.

How could the tests be so wrong? One possibility—the data from which the testing tool was created is based on studies from the 1990s, when more people smoked and developed cardiovascular disease at younger ages.

High-Fat Cheese OK for Your Heart?

High-fat cheese may be as good for you as the low-fat type, when eaten in moderation. In a 12-week study, people who ate three ounces a day of cheese with 25% to 32% fat content had the same blood-chemistry picture—including cholesterol and triglyceride levels—as people who ate three ounces a day of cheese with 13% to 16% fat. And there were no significant differences in body weight change between the groups.

Study of 139 people by researchers at University of Copenhagen, Denmark, published in *The American Journal of Clinical Nutrition.*

BETTER WAYS TO FIND OUT IF YOU NEED A STATIN

Here are a few approaches that may be more reliable...

- **Use a better risk calculator.** According to the Centers for Disease Control and Prevention, the Framingham score is an accurate predictor of cardiovascular risk when measured against actual patient outcomes.
- **If your doctor suggests a statin,** you may want to discuss getting a coronary artery calcium scan. It detects actual calcium deposits in your coronary arteries, which can predict heart disease before symptoms develop. There is some exposure to radiation involved.

For women only: Have you had a digital mammogram? You can skip the calcium scan. Instead, ask your radiologist about calcium that may have been seen in the arteries of your breasts, which correlates well with the coronary artery calcium score.

Chemo Boost

OncoTargets and Therapy.

Could statins work in combo with chemo? Cholesterol is a key component of cancer-cell membranes.

New approach: A cholesterol-fighting drug that kills tumors and reduces cell growth could be used in combination with standard chemotherapy.

New Cholesterol Drugs May Beat Statins, But Price Tag Is High

Marc Sabatine, MD, chair, cardiovascular medicine, Brigham and Women's Hospital, and professor, Harvard Medical School, Boston.

Gregg Stone, MD, director, cardiovascular research and education, NewYork-Presbyterian/Columbia University Medical Center, New York City.

Kausik Ray, MD, cardiologist and chair, public health, Imperial College London, UK.

James Underberg, MD, internist, NYU Langone Medical Center, New York City.

Donald Lloyd-Jones, MD, chief, preventive medicine, North Western University, and spokesman, American Heart Association.

New England Journal of Medicine.

American College of Cardiology annual meeting, Washington, DC.

Two different injectable drugs can lower cholesterol levels even further than statins do, potentially warding off future heart attacks or strokes, new research suggests.

However, some heart experts question whether the pricey medications, one of which costs roughly $14,000 a year to take, perform well enough to make them worth the extra money.

In fact, some cardiologists said the drugs should be reserved only for patients with the highest heart risks.

HOW THE DRUGS WORK

The drugs, *evolocumab* (Repatha) and *inclisiran,* both work by targeting PCSK9, an enzyme that regulates the liver's ability to remove "bad" LDL cholesterol from the bloodstream. By blocking the enzyme, the medications spur the body to screen out more cholesterol.

Clinical trial results showed that evolocumab was linked to a 15% reduction in the risk of major heart events in patients who are already taking statins due to heart disease. These events include sudden heart death, heart attack, stroke, hospitalization for angina, or surgery to reopen a blocked artery.

Evolocumab was also associated with a 20% reduced risk of heart attack, stroke or sudden heart death, said lead researcher Marc Sabatine, MD, chair of cardiovascular medicine at Brigham and Women's Hospital, in Boston.

"In patients with heart and blood vessel disease who are already on a statin, we know now that adding evolocumab reduces the risk of future heart attack or stroke, and it does it safely," Dr. Sabatine said.

Unfortunately, evolocumab did not reduce a person's overall risk of death, or their risk of dying from heart disease, noted Gregg Stone, MD, director of cardiovascular research and education at NewYork-Presbyterian/Columbia University Medical Center.

"The disappointing thing to me was there was absolutely no difference in mortality," Dr. Stone said.

Dr. Sabatine said that evolocumab, which costs about $14,000 a year, has been on the market for about two years now. It works by using artificial antibodies to block the receptors for PCSK9 in the liver.

By comparison, inclisiran is a next-generation PCSK9 inhibitor that works by reducing the ability of the liver to produce the enzyme, explained lead researcher Kausik Ray, MD, a cardiologist at Imperial College London, in the United Kingdom.

Inclisiran can reduce cholesterol by an additional 30% to 50% on top of statins, Dr. Ray's team found.

DOSAGES VARY FOR EACH DRUG

In addition, inclisiran appears to maintain its effectiveness longer, meaning that patients wouldn't have to visit the doctor as often for cholesterol-blocking shots, said James Underberg, MD, an internist with NYU Langone Medical Center in New York City.

The inclisiran dosage that produced the best results would require a person to get an initial shot followed by a booster three months later, Dr. Ray said. They then could wait up to six months before needing another shot.

By comparison, Dr. Underberg said, people must receive an injection of evolocumab either monthly or every other week.

"It's three or four injections a year versus what we're currently doing now, which is 24 or 12 injections a year," Dr. Underberg said. "It's a little more convenient for patients, potentially."

The safety data showed no serious ill effects from either drug, which may have even fewer side effects than statins, researchers reported.

EXPERT COMMENT

But heart experts aren't convinced the benefits of these drugs justify the cost, at least in most patients.

Leading cardiologist Donald Lloyd-Jones, MD, told the Associated Press that the results are modest and "not quite what we hoped or expected." He is chief of preventive medicine at Northwestern University and an American Heart Association spokesman.

"We should still probably reserve these for the highest-risk patients where statins are not doing a good enough job, at least at the price they are currently offered," said Dr. Lloyd-Jones.

Drs. Underberg and Stone noted that evolocumab decreases the absolute risk of a heart attack or stroke by about 1.3% at two years, and 2% at three years.

That means about 74 high-risk patients would have to be treated for two years to prevent one heart attack or stroke or death from heart disease, and that at three years 50 would have to be treated.

At that rate, after five years, just 17 high-risk patients would have to be treated, the authors said.

"In general, the drugs will probably be reserved for patients at high risk who will have a bigger treatment effect," Dr. Stone said.

The two clinical trials were funded by the drugs' respective makers—Amgen for evolocumab and the Medicines Company/Alnylam Pharmaceuticals for inclisiran.

Both trials were reported in the *New England Journal of Medicine*, to coincide with planned presentations at the American College of Cardiology annual meeting, in Washington, DC.

info For more about high cholesterol, visit the U.S. Centers for Disease Control and Prevention at CDC.gov

Americans' Cholesterol Levels Keep Falling

David Friedman, MD, chief, heart failure services, Long Island Jewish Valley Stream Hospital, Valley Stream, New York.
Satjit Bhusri, MD, cardiologist, Lenox Hill Hospital, New York City.
JAMA Cardiology, news release.

Healthier diets may be a factor in the ongoing decline in levels of unhealthy blood fats for Americans, recent research suggests.

According to the report from the U.S. Centers for Disease Control and Prevention, blood levels of total cholesterol, LDL ("bad") cholesterol, and the blood fats known as triglycerides have continued to fall among adults through 2014.

All of that may be adding up to improved heart health nationwide, with death rates from heart disease also on the decline, the CDC noted.

"Removal of trans-fatty acids in foods has been suggested as an explanation for the observed trends of triglycerides, LDL-cholesterol levels, and [total cholesterol] levels," wrote a team led by CDC researcher Asher Rosinger.

These trends "may be contributing to declining death rates owing to coronary heart disease since 1999," the study authors suggested.

One cardiovascular specialist was heartened by the news.

"Although heart disease remains the number one cause of death, we have made tremendous strides in lowering the number of people at risk," said Satjit Bhusri, MD, a cardiologist at Lenox Hill Hospital in New York City.

"As this study shows, through prevention and education we have helped lower cholesterol; a key risk factor in heart disease," he said.

The CDC team noted that between 1999 and 2010, blood cholesterol levels had edged downward among US adults aged 20 or over. The new report sought to determine if that improvement had continued through 2013-2014.

STUDY DETAILS

The study included data from more than 39,000 adults who had their total cholesterol levels checked, about 17,000 who had undergone LDL cholesterol level testing and nearly 17,500 who had their triglyceride levels tracked as part of the ongoing U.S. National Health and Nutrition Examination Survey.

Average total cholesterol fell from 204 milligrams per deciliter (mg/dL) of blood in 1999-2000 to 189 mg/dL in 2013-2014.

Between the relatively short span of 2011-2012 to 2013-2014, average total cholesterol levels plummeted by 6 mg/dL, the authors noted.

Average triglyceride levels also decreased—from 123 mg/dL in 1999-2000 to 97 mg/dL in 2013-2014, with a 13 mg/dL drop since 2011-2012.

Average LDL "bad" cholesterol levels fell from 126 mg/dL to 111 mg/dL during the study period, with a 4 mg/dL drop between 2011-2012 and 2013-2014, the CDC reported.

EXPERT COMMENT

David Friedman, MD, is chief of heart failure services at Long Island Jewish Valley Stream Hospital in Valley Stream, New York. He believes the findings "highlight that over the last number of years, American adults are paying heed and perhaps are being more mindful of cutting out fatty foods to a good degree."

In addition, "public health messages on cholesterol lowering, as well as patient adherence to medication for cholesterol treatment, all seem to be working," Dr. Friedman said.

The study was published online in the journal *JAMA Cardiology*.

Cholesterol's Impact on Heart Attack Risk May Change With Age

American College of Cardiology, news release.

Cholesterol's impact on heart attack may differ by age, recent research suggests.

The study found that younger heart attack patients are much more likely to have significantly low levels of HDL ("good") cholesterol, rather than high levels of LDL ("bad") cholesterol.

The findings might help doctors pinpoint which of their younger patients are in need of cholesterol-lowering therapies, the researchers said.

"We...want to look at prescribing patterns for statins in younger patients who are at increased risk for heart disease," said study lead author Bradley Collins, a fourth-year student at Harvard Medical School.

"Ultimately, we would like to develop new tools for calculating heart attack risk that are more applicable to younger people," Collins said in a news release from the American College of Cardiology (ACC).

Most people who get their cholesterol checked regularly know there is the bad LDL form, which clogs arteries, and the good HDL form, which can help keep arteries clear.

In the recent study, Collins' team tracked the medical records of more than 800 relatively young people—men younger than 45 and women younger than 50. All had been treated for heart attack at two large medical centers over the past 16 years.

The analysis revealed that these younger people who'd had a heart attack were more likely to have low levels of good cholesterol than high levels of bad cholesterol.

Specifically, low HDL cholesterol was seen in about 90% of the men and 75% of the women, the study authors said.

That suggests that different measures may be required to accurately spot heart attack risk in this age group, Collins said, and traditional tools for calculating heart attack risk may underestimate risk in these patients by putting too much emphasis on a patient's age.

"For many people, heart attacks can be prevented by following a healthy lifestyle," Collins stressed. People can increase their HDL cholesterol levels by quitting smoking, maintaining a healthy weight, increasing physical activity, eating more fruits and vegetables, and avoiding trans fats and other unhealthy fats, he said.

"When we identify individuals who have a higher risk, however, we can achieve the greatest risk reduction by combining a healthy lifestyle with medications," Collins added.

The researchers plan follow-up studies. "We are examining whether low HDL cholesterol also predicts risk for repeat heart attacks in younger patients, and whether there are genetic risk factors in this population," Collins said.

Statins May Boost Survival Odds After Cardiac Arrest

Ping-Hsun Yu, MD, National Taiwan University Hospital and College of Medicine, New Taipei City.

Suzanne Steinbaum, DO, director, Women's Heart Health, Lenox Hill Hospital, New York City.

Puneet Gandotra, MD, director, cardiac catheterization laboratories, Northwell Health Southside Hospital, Bay Shore, New York.

American Heart Association meeting, New Orleans, presentation.

The odds of surviving cardiac arrest seem higher for patients who've been taking cholesterol-lowering statins, a recent study shows.

Researchers in Taiwan studied the medical records of nearly 138,000 cardiac arrest patients. Those already using statins such as Lipitor (*atorvastatin*) or Crestor (*rosuvastatin*) were about 19% more likely to survive to hospital admission and 47% more likely to be discharged. Also, they were 50% more likely to be alive a year later, the study found.

"When considering statin use for patients with high cholesterol, the benefit of surviving sudden cardiac arrest should also be considered, as statin use before cardiac arrest might improve outcomes of those patients," said study author Ping-Hsun Yu, MD.

Dr. Yu is a researcher from the National Taiwan University Hospital and College of Medicine in New Taipei City.

The greatest survival benefit from statins was seen in patients with type 2 diabetes, Dr. Yu's team said.

Cardiac arrest is the abrupt loss of heart function. Death often occurs instantly or shortly after symptoms appear, according to the American Heart Association.

"We know that a large proportion of cardiac arrests occur due to coronary plaque rupture," said Puneet Gandotra, MD, director of the cardiac catheterization laboratories at Northwell Health Southside Hospital in Bay Shore, New York.

"This rupture leads to a snowball effect in arteries and can cause arteries to get blocked, resulting in a heart attack or cardiac arrest," he explained.

SO HOW MIGHT STATINS HELP?

"I feel that due to statin therapy, there is significant plaque stability and the effects of rupture are not as significant. Thus, an improvement in survival is noticed with patients on statin therapy who have cardiac arrests," Dr. Gandotra said.

Statins are often prescribed for patients after a heart attack or stroke as a way to prevent a second cardiovascular event. However, "this does not mean that everyone should be on statin therapy," Dr. Gandotra said.

These drugs can have side effects, such as muscle pain and weakness and higher blood sugar levels. In addition, the value of statins for preventing a first cardiac arrest or stroke is not conclusive, the researchers added.

Suzanne Steinbaum, MD, director of Women's Heart Health at Lenox Hill Hospital in New York City, said, "What we learn from studies like this is that [statins] have other benefits.

"A study like this gives me a reason to say, 'There are more reasons for you to take a statin than just to lower your cholesterol,'" Dr. Steinbaum said.

For the study, the researchers divided the medical records of almost 138,000 patients according to whether they had used statins for 90 days within the year before their cardiac arrest. The researchers also accounted for gender, age, other medical problems, number of hospitalizations, post-resuscitation and other variables.

Because more than 95% of the patients in the study were Asian, these results might not apply to other ethnic populations, Dr. Yu said.

For more about statins, visit the American Heart Association at Heart.org

Are There Alternatives to Statins?

Marc Sabatine, MD, MPH, chairman, TIMI Study Group and cardiologist, Brigham and Women's Hospital, Boston.

Nieca Goldberg, MD, medical director, NYU Langone Medical Center's Joan H. Tisch Center for Women's Health, New York City.

Journal of the American Medical Association.

Statins are the go-to therapy for lowering "bad" LDL cholesterol, but other treatments also can effectively reduce risk of future heart problems, a new evidence review reports.

These alternative therapies—including a heart-healthy diet, other cholesterol-lowering medications, and even intestinal bypass surgery—seem to confer the same level of heart health protection as statins when cholesterol levels decrease, according to the findings.

Nonstatin therapies reduced the risk of heart problems by 25% for each 1 millimole per liter (mmol/L) decrease in LDL cholesterol levels. That's very similar to the 23% reduction per 1 mmol/L decrease seen with statins like *atorvastatin* (Lipitor) and *simvastatin* (Zocor), the researchers said.

What's more, the benefits of these therapies stack up if more than one proves effective at lowering a person's cholesterol levels, said senior researcher Marc Sabatine, MD, a cardiologist at Brigham and Women's Hospital in Boston.

"The focus really should be not on a particular drug, but on reducing LDL cholesterol," Dr. Sabatine said. "These data show there are multiple interventions that can do that."

Dr. Sabatine and his colleagues undertook this evidence review in response to the increased role of statins in lowering cholesterol. Elevated cholesterol is a major risk factor for heart disease.

Statins, which work by reducing the liver's production of cholesterol, were taken by more than one-quarter of US adults aged 40 and over during 2011-2012, according to a national survey.

"The most recent guidelines in 2013 focused almost exclusively on statins and were silent on LDL cholesterol targets," Dr. Sabatine said. This caused some worry that doctors would prescribe a high-powered statin to patients, then wash their hands of the matter if the drug failed to lower cholesterol.

STUDY DETAILS

To see whether other cholesterol-lowering tactics would be as effective in protecting heart health, the researchers analyzed the results of 49 clinical trials. *These included 25 clinical trials for statins, as well as trials for...*

- **A heart-healthy diet,** which reduces the amount of LDL cholesterol you eat while increasing dietary components like fiber, which has been shown to help clear cholesterol from the bloodstream.
- **Zetia** (*ezetimibe*), a drug that blocks absorption of cholesterol in the digestive tract.
- **Bile acid sequestrants,** a class of medication that encourages the liver to draw more cholesterol from the bloodstream and convert it into bile acids.
- **Ileal bypass surgery,** which shortens the length of the small intestine by bypassing its final section. Again, this promotes conversion of cholesterol into bile acids by the liver.

The evidence review also included two trials with PCSK9 inhibitors, powerful cholesterol-lowering agents that also encourage the liver to clear cholesterol from the bloodstream. PCSK9 inhibitors were included even though trials are ongoing to assess their effectiveness in protecting heart health, Dr. Sabatine said.

These treatments have different levels of effectiveness in lowering LDL cholesterol, the study found. Zetia reduces cholesterol by about 20%, statins by 30% to 50% depending on dose, and PCSK9 inhibitors by as much as 60%, Dr. Sabatine said.

But the different trials showed that each unit of LDL cholesterol removed from the bloodstream protects heart health, regardless of how doctors are able to drive those cholesterol levels down.

"There is a linear relationship between what your LDL cholesterol level is and what your risk is of cardiovascular events," Dr. Sabatine said. "The relationship suggests that lower is better."

Statins remain the best option for cholesterol reduction, Dr. Sabatine said.

"They have the best established data set and are highly effective at lowering LDL cholesterol," he said. "But I think these data underscore that beyond that, if you don't have good control of your LDL cholesterol, it's not as simple as saying the person is on a high-intensity statin and I'm done."

EXPERT COMMENT

Nieca Goldberg, MD, is medical director of NYU Langone Medical Center's Tisch Center for Women's Health in New York City. She said the evidence review "supports that there are several options to lower LDL cholesterol and they all lower risk for cardiovascular disease."

Diet and exercise should be part of any cholesterol-lowering plan, regardless of what medications are prescribed, Dr. Goldberg added.

"Diet and exercise have other benefits, such as weight loss and lowering blood pressure," she said.

The study findings were published in the *Journal of the American Medical Association.*

Does "Good" Cholesterol Matter in Heart Disease Risk?

Dennis Ko, MD, MSc, senior scientist, Institute for Clinical Evaluative Sciences, Toronto, Canada.

Michael Shapiro, DO, member, American College of Cardiology Prevention of Cardiovascular Disease Section.

Robert Eckel, MD, professor, medicine, University of Colorado Denver, Anschutz Medical Campus.

Journal of the American College of Cardiology, online.

A large new study adds to questions about whether your "good" HDL cholesterol levels really affect your risk of heart disease.

The study, of nearly 632,000 Canadian adults, found that those with the lowest HDL levels had higher death rates from heart disease and stroke over five years. But they also had higher death rates from cancer and other causes.

What's more, there was no evidence that very high HDL levels—above 90 mg/dL—were desirable.

People with HDL that high were more likely to die of noncardiovascular causes, compared with those with HDL levels in the middle, the study found.

STUDY GOES AGAINST CONVENTIONAL WISDOM

The fact that low HDL was linked to higher death rates from all causes is key, said lead researcher Dennis Ko, MD.

That suggests it's just a "marker" of other things, such as a less healthy lifestyle or generally poorer health, he said.

That also means it's unlikely that low HDL directly contributes to heart disease, added Dr. Ko, a senior scientist at the Institute for Clinical Evaluative Sciences in Toronto.

"This study is going against the conventional wisdom," he said.

But the reality is, doctors are already shifting away from the conventional wisdom, said cardiologist Michael Shapiro, MD.

"Many people know that HDL is the 'good' cholesterol," Dr. Shapiro said. "But they may not know that the medical community is moving away from the idea that we've got to raise low HDL."

That's in part because of the results of several clinical trials that tested the vitamin niacin and certain medications that boost HDL levels.

The studies found that while the treatments do raise HDL, they make no difference in people's risk of heart trouble.

On top of that, Dr. Shapiro said, research has shown that gene variants associated with HDL levels have no connection to the risk of cardiovascular disease.

No one is saying that doctors and patients should ignore low HDL levels. Levels below 40 mg/dL are linked to a heightened risk of heart disease.

"That is a consistent finding," Dr. Shapiro said. "So we can reliably use it as a marker to identify patients at higher risk and see what else is going on with them."

Causes of low HDL include a sedentary lifestyle, smoking, poor diet and being overweight. And it's probably those factors—not the HDL level itself—that really matter, Dr. Shapiro said.

STUDY DETAILS

The current findings are based on medical records and other data from nearly 631,800 Ontario adults ages 40 and up. Over five years, almost 18,000 of them died.

Dr. Ko's team found that men and women with low HDL levels were more likely to die during the study period, versus those with levels between 40 and 60 mg/dL.

But they had increased risks of not only heart disease death, but also death from cancer or other causes.

People with low HDL tended to have lower incomes, and higher rates of smoking, diabetes and high blood pressure. After the researchers accounted for those factors, low HDL was still linked to higher death rates.

"But we couldn't account for everything," Dr. Ko said. And he believes that factors other than HDL number—such as exercise and other lifestyle habits—are what count.

"When you see that something [low HDL] is associated with deaths from many different causes, it's probably a 'generic' marker of risk, rather than a cause," Dr. Ko said.

At the other end of the spectrum, people with very high HDL—topping 90 mg/dL—faced increased risks of dying from noncardiovascular causes.

Dr. Shapiro called the finding "very interesting," but the reasons for it are unclear.

EXPERT COMMENT

Alcohol can raise HDL. So that raises the question of whether heavy drinking helps explain the link, said Robert Eckel, MD.

Regardless, there is no reason for people to try to send their HDL skyward using niacin or other medications. "Raising HDL with drugs is not indicated," Dr. Eckel said.

Dr. Shapiro stressed the importance of lifestyle: "Don't smoke, get regular aerobic exercise, lose weight if you need to."

Those things may, in fact, boost your HDL, Dr. Shapiro noted. But it's not the number that matters, he said, it's the healthy lifestyle.

The findings were published in the *Journal of the American College of Cardiology.*

CHAPTER 3

Brain Health and Memory

The Groundbreaking Alzheimer's Prevention Diet

As head of the renowned Alzheimer's Prevention Clinic at Weill Cornell Medicine and NewYork-Presbyterian, Richard S. Isaacson, MD, is on top of the latest research on Alzheimer's disease. Groundbreaking studies show that proper diet can make a real difference not only in slowing the progression of the disease but also in preventing it.

Here, Dr. Isaacson explains how we can change our eating habits to fight Alzheimer's. His recommendations are not specifically designed for weight loss, but most overweight people who follow this eating plan will lose weight—important because obesity more than triples the risk for Alzheimer's.

FEWER CALORIES

The Okinawa Centenarian Study (an ongoing study of centenarians in the Japanese prefecture of Okinawa) found that these long-lived people typically consume fewer calories (up to 1,900 calories a day) than the average American (up to 2,600 calories).

Lowering calorie intake appears to reduce beta-amyloid, particles of protein that form brain plaques—the hallmark of Alzheimer's disease. A 2012 study at the Mayo Clinic found that people who overate had twice the risk for memory loss...and those who consumed more than 2,142 calories a day were more likely to have cognitive impairment.

I generally advise my patients to try to have fewer than 2,100 calories a day. I can't give an exact number because calorie requirements de-

Richard S. Isaacson, MD, director of the Alzheimer's Prevention Clinic, Weill Cornell Memory Disorders Program at Weill Cornell Medicine and NewYork-Presbyterian, where he is an associate professor of neurology and director of the neurology residency training program, New York City. He is coauthor of *The Alzheimer's Prevention & Treatment Diet: Using Nutrition to Combat the Effects of Alzheimer's Disease.*

pend on body type, activity level, etc. Many of my patients tend to consume less than 1,800 calories a day, which may be even more protective.

Bonus: Calorie restriction also lowers insulin, body fat, inflammation and blood pressure, all of which can reduce the risk for cognitive impairment. It even improves neurogenesis, the formation of new brain cells.

LESS CARBS, MORE KETONES

Glucose from the breakdown of carbohydrates is the fuel that keeps the body running. But you don't need a lot of carbs. Ketones, another source of fuel, are healthier for the brain.

When you restrict carbohydrates, the body manufactures ketones from stored fat. On occasion, a "ketogenic diet" is recommended for some patients with Alzheimer's disease because ketones produce fewer wastes and put less stress on damaged brain cells. There's some evidence that this diet improves mild cognitive impairment symptoms (and theoretically may slow further damage).

We previously found in our clinic that patients consumed an average of 278 grams of carbohydrates daily before their first visits. We recommend reducing that slowly over the nine weeks of the diet plan to 100 to 120 grams of carbohydrates daily. (One sweet potato has about 23 grams.) The USDA SuperTracker website (SuperTracker.USDA.gov) gives carbohydrate amounts and other nutritional information for specific foods. Eat healthful carbohydrates such as beans and whole grains in moderation. Unlike refined carbs, they are high in fiber and can help to reduce insulin resistance and improve blood sugar control—which reduces risk for Alzheimer's.

FASTING

Some trendy diets recommend extreme fasts. With the Alzheimer's prevention diet, you'll fast—but mainly when you wouldn't be eating anyway, during sleep!

Several times a week, you'll go without food (particularly carbohydrates) for more than 12 hours. After 12 hours, the body starts making ketones. This type of fast, known as time-restricted eating, reduces inflammation, improves metabolic efficiency and improves insulin levels, insulin sensitivity and brain health.

How to do it: Eat an early supper—say, at about 5 pm. You won't eat again until after 5 am the next day. Your eventual goal will be to fast for 12 to 14 hours five nights a week.

MORE PROTEIN

The Institute of Medicine recommends getting 10% to 35% of calories from protein—go for the higher end. On a 2,000-calorie diet, that's about 175 grams. (Five ounces of cooked salmon has about 36 grams of protein.)

The amino acids in protein are important for memory and other brain functions. Protein-rich foods often are high in B vitamins, including folic acid and vitamins B-6 and B-12. The Bs are critical because they reduce homocysteine, an amino acid linked to poor brain performance and an increased Alzheimer's risk.

Which protein: Chicken, fish, nuts, legumes and eggs all are good choices. I recommend limiting red meat to one weekly serving because of potential associated health risks, including an increased risk for certain cancers...and because too much saturated fat (see below) can be a problem.

Helpful: Aim for four to eight eggs a week. They're high in selenium, lutein, zeaxanthin and other brain-healthy antioxidants.

LIMIT SATURATED FAT

A large study found that people who eat a lot of foods high in saturated fat—rich desserts, red meat, fast food, etc.—may be up to 2.4 times more likely to develop Alzheimer's disease.

Saturated fat limits the body's ability to "clear" beta-amyloid deposits from the brain. It also raises cholesterol and increases the risk for cardiovascular diseases—and what's bad for the heart also is bad for the brain.

Consuming some saturated fat is healthful—it's only in excess that it causes problems. The American Heart Association advises limiting it to about 5% to 6% of total calories. I recommend a little more—up to 10% of your daily calories. On a 2,000-calorie diet, the upper limit would be about 20 grams. (One ounce of cheese can have as much as eight grams.)

FISH, TURMERIC AND COCOA

Studies have shown that a few specific foods can fight Alzheimer's...

•**Fish.** A UCLA study found that adults who regularly ate foods high in omega-3 fatty acids (the healthful fats in fish) had a lower risk for mental decline. Other research has shown that low blood levels of DHA (a type of omega-3) are linked to smaller brain volume and lower scores on cognitive tests.

My advice: Eat one serving of fatty fish (such as wild salmon, mackerel and sardines) at least twice a week.

•**Turmeric.** In India, where people use the spice turmeric frequently, the risk for Alzheimer's is lower than in the US. This doesn't prove that turmeric is responsible (genetic factors, for example, also could be involved), but other evidence suggests that it's protective. Turmeric contains the compound curcumin, which has potent antioxidant and anti-inflammatory effects.

My advice: Use the spice in recipes—don't depend on supplements—because curcumin is fat-soluble and absorption is enhanced by the fat in foods.

•**Cocoa.** The flavanols in cocoa improve memory and other cognitive functions. They also have been linked to reduced blood pressure and improved insulin resistance.

My advice: Buy chocolate bars or cocoa powder that lists purified cocoa flavanols on the label.

It May Not Be Alzheimer's After All

Marc E. Agronin, MD, vice president for behavioral health and clinical research at Miami Jewish Health and an adult and geriatric psychiatrist and affiliate associate professor of psychiatry and neurology at the University of Miami Miller School of Medicine. Dr. Agronin is also author of *How We Age.* MarcAgronin.com

People joke about having the occasional "senior moment," but the humor partly deflects an unsettling concern: What if this memory lapse—forgetting an appointment, calling someone by the wrong name, losing your car in the parking lot, etc.—marks the beginning of an incurable mental decline? Not so fast.

Some middle-aged adults (defined roughly as ages 40 to 65) do develop early-onset Alzheimer's or other forms of dementia, but it's rare. Their flagging memories are much more likely to have simpler—and very treatable—explanations. If you have memory or other cognitive changes, it's critically important to seek early diagnosis and treatment before more serious problems ensue...or the changes become irreversible.

FORGETFULNESS HAPPENS

The fear of mental decline makes sense for older adults. While the prevalence of Alzheimer's disease and other types of dementia is nearly 10% at age 65, it jumps to up to half of those age 85 and older.

However, many patients in their 50s and 60s are convinced that the mildest mental slips mean that the worst is just around the corner. This is usually not the case.

Once you reach your mid-40s, your brain processes information more slowly. Memories are more transient than they used to be. Forgetting facts or incorrectly recalling details becomes more common. These are normal changes.

If you've noticed that you're more distracted or forgetful than usual, ask your doctor to perform a general checkup to rule out any obvious medical issues, such as a vitamin B-12 deficiency or a thyroid problem. If nothing is uncovered, it's still possible that something other than dementia is causing your cognitive symptoms. *Possible suspects...*

•**Medications.** If you're taking codeine or another opioid medication for pain, you expect to be a little fuzzy. But some of the drugs that affect memory aren't the ones that most people are aware of—or think to discuss with their doctors.

Examples: Cholesterol-lowering statins. A small percentage of people who take these drugs describe mental fuzziness as a side effect. The benzodiazepine class of sedatives/anti-anxiety drugs (such as Valium, Xanax, Halcion, etc.) can also cause cognitive problems and frequently affect memory. The mental effects are amplified when you take multiple drugs—say, one of these medications for sleep and another for daytime anxiety.

Don't overlook the possibility that some over-the-counter drugs—decongestants and antihistamines are common offenders—can also cause mental fuzziness.

Dr. Agronin's advice: Pay attention (and tell your doctor) if your cognitive symptoms seem to get worse after starting a new medication. You might need to change drugs or take a lower dose.

•**Mental health.** When you meet people at a party, do you remember their names? Or are you so nervous about making a good impression that their names don't register?

Anxiety and stress cause distraction, and it's impossible to form memories when you're not paying attention. Some people become so worried about memory problems that every slip causes them to freeze up and quit paying attention to what's happening around them. It becomes a self-fulfilling prophecy.

Depression is also linked to cognitive lapses, especially since it interferes with concentration...interest in activities...and sleep—all essential factors for good memory.

Dr. Agronin's advice: If you notice that your memory has good days and bad ones—and some days when it's horrible—it's reasonable to suspect that the problem is benign and you might just be going through an emotionally difficult time.

Talk to your doctor about what may be bothering you emotionally. If there's a problem with stress, anxiety or depression, get a referral to a mental health provider for a more thorough evaluation to assess your mood, thinking and behavior.

Important: Your doctor or a mental health professional should also talk to you about potential alcohol or recreational drug abuse, which can have a significant impact on cognition.

All of these conditions can be treated with medication, therapy and/or a variety of lifestyle changes, such as getting more exercise and practicing relaxation techniques.

•**Obstructive sleep apnea.** It's a common sleep disorder, particularly among those who

Early Signs of Alzheimer's

Lost Sense of Smell...

Difficulty identifying certain smells, such as lemon or smoke, could signal Alzheimer's disease 10 years before the onset of memory loss, according to a recent study of older adults.

Why: Alzheimer's can cause brain circuits to lose memory of certain smells.

Self-defense: If you or a loved one has difficulty identifying familiar smells, talk to your doctor about screening for Alzheimer's disease.

Mark Albers, MD, PhD, assistant professor of neurology, Harvard Medical School, Boston.

Apathy...

Families should watch older loved ones for emotional apathy and other behavioral changes such as suspicion or paranoia... greater-than-usual agitation or aggression... and loss of socially appropriate behavior. If new and sustained, these behaviors may be signs of mild behavioral impairment, an early indicator of Alzheimer's disease and other dementias.

Zahinoor Ismail, MD, FRCPC, a neuropsychiatrist and assistant professor of psychiatry and neurology at Hotchkiss Brain Institute, University of Calgary, Canada.

Difficulty with Navigating...

Difficulty navigating new surroundings may be an extremely early sign of Alzheimer's.

Recent finding: Study participants were tested on their ability to remember how to navigate a maze on a computer. People with preclinical Alzheimer's—based on analysis of fluid from around their brains and spinal cords—had significantly more trouble creating a map of the maze than people without the cerebrospinal markers.

Study of 71 people by researchers at Washington University School of Medicine, St. Louis, published in *Journal of Alzheimer's Disease.*

are overweight. A blocked airway during sleep impedes the flow of oxygen to the brain. This can occur dozens or even hundreds of times a night. Diminished nighttime oxygen can impair memory and concentration. Patients with sleep apnea also have a higher risk for stroke and heart disease.

Warning signs: Gasping, snorting or loud snoring during sleep...a dry mouth in the morning...morning headaches...and/or difficulty staying alert during the day.

The good news is that obstructive sleep apnea can be overcome almost completely with the use of a continuous positive airway pressure (CPAP) machine, a small bedside device that delivers mild air pressure through a hose to help keep the airways open. These machines can be noisy, and the mask or nose piece that connects to the air hose can be somewhat uncomfortable—but CPAP does work. And it's definitely preferable to a lifetime of brain fog.

•**Adult ADD.** People associate attention deficit disorder (ADD) with children, but it also affects 2% to 4% of adults—and most are never diagnosed. It's a lifelong neurobiological disease that makes it difficult to focus or pay attention.

People with ADD are easily distracted...may have a history of work problems...and often don't follow through on tasks at home. It's easy to confuse these symptoms with cognitive impairments.

ADD is usually diagnosed by taking a history from the patient and family members. If the patient then responds to medication such as *methylphenidate* (Ritalin), he/she is considered to have ADD.

Low Blood Pressure Alert

Risk for dementia is 15% higher among those with orthostatic hypotension (a condition in which blood pressure falls suddenly upon standing, resulting in dizziness and/or lightheadedness), according to a 24-year study of more than 6,000 older adults.

Theory: These brief periods of hypoxia, or lack of oxygen, may cause long-term damage to brain tissue.

If you have orthostatic hypotension: Talk to your doctor about drinking more water, wearing compression stockings and/or taking medication to raise blood pressure.

M. Arfan Ikram, MD, PhD, professor of neuroepidemiology, Erasmus University Medical Center, Rotterdam, the Netherlands.

Rosacea and Alzheimer's Risk

Alexander Egeberg, MD, PhD, associate professor of dermato-allergology, Herlev and Gentofte Hospital, University of Copenhagen, Denmark, and leader of a 15-year study of 82,439 rosacea patients, published in *Annals of Neurology.*

People with the common skin disorder rosacea are at higher risk for Alzheimer's disease, warns Alexander Egeberg, MD, PhD. Rosacea patients are 25% more likely, on average, to develop Alzheimer's disease than those without rosacea. The increased risk is greatest among women, who had a 28% greater risk. It is not known whether rosacea actually causes Alzheimer's, but the presence of rosacea in elderly people may aid in early detection and treatment.

Common Medications Increase Dementia Risk

Shannon Risacher, PhD, assistant professor of radiology and imaging sciences at Indiana Alzheimer Disease Center, Indiana University School of Medicine, Indianapolis, and leader of a study of 451 older adults, average age 73, published in *JAMA Neurology.*

Some frequently used medications increase dementia risk in older people. These drugs, which are used to treat common disorders such as asthma, depression and incontinence, have anticholinergic (AC) activity—that is, they block an important neurotransmitter called acetylcholine. They include *brompheniramine* (Dimetapp), *chlorpheniramine* (Chlor-Trimeton), *diphenhydramine* (Benadryl), *doxylamine* (Unisom), *oxybutynin* (Ditropan) and *paroxetine* (Paxil).

Recent finding: Older people who regularly took an AC drug had brain cavities up to 32% larger than other seniors. Increased cavity size reflects brain atrophy. AC-medication users also did worse on tests of brain function including short-term memory, verbal reasoning, planning and problem solving.

Self-defense: Older people who use an AC drug for a chronic condition should ask their physicians whether non-AC alternatives are available. A list of medications that have possible or definitive AC properties can be found by putting "Anticholinergic Burden (ACB) Scale" into any search engine. Drugs with an ACB score of 3 (found in the right-most column) are the most problematic.

The New Alzheimer's "Prescription"

Dean Sherzai, MD, a neurologist and director of the Alzheimer's Disease Prevention Program at Cedars-Sinai Medical Center in Los Angeles. A member of the American Academy of Neurology and the American Society on Aging, Dr. Sherzai is a former director of the Memory and Aging Center at Loma Linda University Medical Center. For more on brain health, follow him on Facebook at Team Sherzai.

Every now and then, researchers announce yet another "breakthrough" drug to halt mental declines or clear away the sticky brain plaque (beta-amyloid) that's the hallmark of Alzheimer's disease.

Unfortunately, the enthusiasm tends to fade as limitations of these drugs become apparent. The handful of medications that help ease the cognitive symptoms of Alzheimer's (such as memory loss and confusion) do not stop the disease's progression (see box on next page to learn what drugs are available).

What most people don't realize: Even though medication plays a role in treating Alzheimer's symptoms, certain lifestyle changes actually can slow the progression of Alzheimer's disease by 30% or more—something that is impossible with even the newest drugs.

Dean Sherzai, MD, one of the country's leading authorities on Alzheimer's disease explains more...

THE NEURO APPROACH

When I treat a person at risk for dementia or newly diagnosed with this disease or mild cognitive impairment (a condition that often precedes Alzheimer's), I recommend a set of lifestyle changes I call NEURO. This stands for Nutrition...Exercise...Unwind...Restful sleep... and Optimize mental/social activities.

People who practice each of these steps—and who also address health conditions, especially high blood pressure and diabetes, that increase the risk for and symptoms of Alzheimer's—can significantly slow the disease from progressing. Regardless of whether the person is also taking an Alzheimer's medication, these lifestyle steps are crucial.

What you need to know about the five-step NEURO approach...

STEP 1: **Nutrition.** With few exceptions (see next page), I don't often recommend individual vitamins, antioxidants or other supplements—the totality of your diet is more important because healthy foods contain a complex mix of nutrients that work together to give maximum benefit.

Best choice: A Mediterranean-style diet. This diet includes lots of fruits, vegetables, whole grains, beans, fatty fish and monounsaturated fats (such as olive oil). Research has shown that a version of this diet that emphasizes certain brain-healthy foods (such as berries and leafy-green vegetables) is especially effective.

Important findings: In a study that was published in *Archives of Neurology,* researchers tracked nearly 1,400 people—482 of whom had already been diagnosed with mild cognitive impairment—for an average of more than four years. They found that those with this condition who were most careful about following a Mediterranean diet were 48% less likely to develop full-fledged Alzheimer's disease than those who were more lax in their eating habits. And those who were still healthy at the start of the study were 28% less likely to develop symptoms in the first place.

Will supplements help when you are already eating well? Maybe—but the evidence isn't conclusive. *Supplements to consider...*

•**Vitamin B-12.** I've found that Alzheimer's patients with B-12 blood levels even at the lower end of the normal range (typically around 180 ng/L) sometimes have fewer cognitive symptoms when they take B-12 supplements.

•**Omega-3s.** Increasing blood levels of omega-3 fatty acids might help as well.

•**Vitamin D.** If vitamin D levels are low, a supplement may improve symptoms and help slow Alzheimer's progression.

STEP 2: **Exercise.** Exercise can slow progression by about 30% or more. Exercise works on multiple levels—it stimulates growth factors that maintain neurons (brain cells)...and increases circulation of blood in the brain, which promotes healthy cognitive function.

My advice: Get 30 minutes of exercise five or more times weekly.

What works well for some people: Riding a recumbent bike while watching TV.

STEP 3: **Unwind.** People who experience a lot of stress are up to two-and-a-half times more likely to develop Alzheimer's disease than those who have less or who deal with it more effectively.

Why? No one's sure, although it seems likely that the stress-related surge in cortisol and other hormones is harmful to the brain.

Exercise and volunteering are great stress reducers. Some people manage stress by keeping busy with hobbies...practicing yoga...and/or enlisting help from friends/relatives to deal with daily responsibilities. Do what works best for you—and make stress reduction a priority.

STEP 4: **Restful sleep.** Many Alzheimer's patients don't sleep well. Experts once assumed that poor sleep was merely an Alzheimer's symptom. But recent research suggests that a lack of restful sleep may play a role in the development and progression of the disease.

Important finding: A study in *JAMA Neurology* that looked at 70 older adults found that those who got less than five hours of sleep a night had higher brain levels of beta-amyloid than those who slept more than seven hours. Researchers speculate that poor sleep impairs the body's ability to clear beta-amyloid or other toxic molecules from the brain.

Also: Sleep apnea, a very common (and underdiagnosed) condition in which breathing intermittently stops and starts during sleep, reduces brain oxygen and is strongly linked to Alzheimer's.

If you frequently snore or snort during sleep, or you're tired in the morning despite having what you thought was a good night's sleep, your doctor might suggest a sleep study that measures brain waves and blood oxygen levels to detect apnea and other sleep disorders.

STEP 5: **Optimize mental/social activities.** People who stay mentally busy with hobbies, for example, and do other stimulating activities (such as playing challenging video games that require memory, problem-solving, hand-eye coordination, etc.) have smaller declines in memory and other cognitive functions...less Alzheimer's-related brain damage...and slower disease progression. They have a deeper "cognitive reserve," the neural connections (and brain size) that can forestall future impairments.

Once people start doing these new activities, it's both motivating and rewarding because the positive changes—including improved cognitive functioning—can occur within a matter of weeks.

MEDICATION CHOICES FOR ALZHEIMER'S

The drugs that are FDA-approved for treating Alzheimer's disease affect brain chemicals and can improve memory, alertness and concentration. *The two classes of these medications...*

•**Cholinesterase inhibitors** (Aricept, Exelon and Razadyne). These drugs block an enzyme that breaks down acetylcholine, a neurotransmitter that's vital for memory, language, learning and other cognitive functions. There are no serious side effects, but some patients may experience nausea, vomiting, diarrhea or other problems. If this occurs, an Exelon patch can be used.

•**N-Methyl-D-Aspartate (NMDA) receptor blocker** (Namenda). This drug affects glutamate, another brain chemical. It's approved

Surprising Traffic Danger

Dementia is more common in those who live within about 165 feet of a major road.

Reasons: Noise, pollution and disturbed sleep may damage the brain.

The Lancet.

for treating moderate-to-severe Alzheimer's, but it can also help patients with milder forms of the disease. In some patients, Namenda, which may cause side effects such as dizziness and/or headache, works best when combined with Aricept or another cholinesterase inhibitor.

Probiotics for Brainpower

Mahmoud Salami, PhD, professor of neurophysiology, Kashan University of Medical Sciences and Health Services, Iran.

When 52 patients with Alzheimer's disease took a probiotic supplement containing four billion units of *Lactobacillus* and *Bifidobacterium*, they showed improvement in memory and other cognitive test scores after 12 weeks.

Possible explanation: These probiotics may decrease inflammation in the brain.

If a loved one has Alzheimer's disease: Talk to his/her doctor about a probiotic supplement.

Safer Coma Recovery

Brain Stimulation.

In a first-time procedure, brief bursts of low-intensity focused ultrasound "jump-started" neurons and restored brain function in a coma patient. It could be an alternative to surgically implanted electrodes, a much riskier procedure.

Drawing a Blank...

Majid Fotuhi, MD, PhD, a neurologist and medical director, NeuroGrow Brain Fitness Center, McLean, Virginia. He is also author of *Boost Your Brain.*

Starting in their 40s, many people begin to have lapses in remembering names, occasional difficulty in finding a word and/or slowness in thinking speed (such as mentally adding numbers). Such occasional forgetfulness commonly occurs as we get older and is not necessarily a sign of dementia, as many people fear.

However, memory lapses that occur several times every day could be a sign of an underlying health problem and should be evaluated.

Many health conditions, including depression, thyroid problems and dehydration, can affect memory. Too much stress, too little sleep or a deficiency of vitamin B-12 can make someone forgetful, too.

Many medications, including tricyclic antidepressants, antihistamines and drugs that treat high blood pressure and cholesterol, can also cause memory loss. Your doctor may be able to prescribe other drugs that don't have this side effect.

Signs that memory lapses may be more serious include becoming lost in familiar places, asking the same question repeatedly and getting confused about time, people and places. If any of these signs occur, consult a neurologist.

You can quickly check your brain health with the free risk calculator developed by neurological researchers. Go to TheNeurocore.com/brain-fitness-risk-calculator. The good news is that many people can boost their brain health and performance within weeks.

This Memory Booster Smells Great

Mark Moss, PhD, head of psychology, Northumbria University, Newcastle upon Tyne, UK.

Need to remember to make a phone call or take your medication? A whiff of rosemary oil could help.

Recent study: 150 people over age 65 performed memory tasks either in a rosemary-scented room or in a room without scent. The aroma of rosemary significantly improved both mood and prospective memory (the ability to remember planned events and tasks).

Why: The herb contains compounds that boost the area of the brain involved in memory.

Best Nondrug Approaches for Parkinson's

Michael S. Okun, MD, professor and chair of the department of neurology and codirector of the Center for Movement Disorders and Neurorestoration at the University of Florida College of Medicine in Gainesville. He is author of *10 Breakthrough Therapies for Parkinson's Disease.*

The telltale tremors, muscle stiffness and other movement problems that plague people with Parkinson's disease make even the mundane activities of daily living—such as brushing teeth, cooking and dressing—more difficult.

What's new: Even though medications—such as *levodopa* (L-dopa) and newer drugs including *pramipexole* and *selegiline*—have long been the main treatment to control Parkinson's symptoms, researchers are discovering more and more nondrug therapies that can help.

Among the best nondrug approaches (each can be used with Parkinson's medication)...

Leukemia Drug for Parkinson's

There's new hope for Parkinson's patients.

New finding: Low-dose *nilotinib* (Tasigna), a drug currently approved for treating leukemia, increases dopamine and reduces toxic proteins in Parkinson's patients. The drug also caused improvements in cognition/motor function.

Journal of Parkinson's Disease.

EXERCISE

For people with Parkinson's, exercise is like a drug. It raises neurotrophic factors, proteins that promote the growth and health of neurons. Research consistently shows that exercise can improve motor symptoms (such as walking speed and stability) and quality of life.

For the best results: Exercise 30 to 60 minutes every single day. Aim to work hard enough to break a sweat, but back off if you get too fatigued—especially the following day (this indicates the body is not recovering properly). Parkinson's symptoms can worsen with overexercise. *Smart exercise habits...*

- **For better gait speed.** Choose a lower-intensity exercise, such as walking on a treadmill (but hold on to the balance bars), rather than high-intensity exercise (such as running), which has a higher risk for falls and other injuries.

A recent study showed that a walking group of Parkinson's patients performed better than a group of patients who ran.

Important safety tip: Parkinson's patients should exercise with a partner and take precautions to prevent falls—for example, minimizing distractions, such as ringing cell phones.

- **For aerobic exercise.** Use a recumbent bicycle or rowing machine and other exercises that don't rely on balance.
- **For strength and flexibility.** Do stretching and progressive resistance training.

Excellent resource: For a wide variety of exercises, including aerobic workouts, standing and sitting stretches, strengthening moves, balance exercises and fall-prevention tips, the National Parkinson Foundation's Fitness Counts book is available as a free download at Parkinson.org/pd-library/books/fitness-counts.

- **For balance.** Researchers are now discovering that yoga postures, tai chi (with its slow, controlled movements) and certain types of dancing (such as the tango, which involves rhythmic forward-and-backward steps) are excellent ways to improve balance.

COFFEE AND TEA

Could drinking coffee or tea help with Parkinson's? According to research, it can—when consumed in the correct amounts.

Here's why: Caffeine blocks certain receptors in the brain that regulate the neurotransmitter dopamine, which becomes depleted and leads to the impaired motor coordination that characterizes Parkinson's. In carefully controlled studies, Parkinson's patients who ingested low doses of caffeine—about 100 mg twice daily—had improved motor symptoms, such as tremors and stiffness, compared with people who had no caffeine or higher doses of caffeine.

My advice: Have 100 mg of caffeine (about the amount in one six-ounce cup of home-brewed coffee or two cups of black or green tea) twice a day—once in the morning and once in the mid-afternoon. *Note:* Even decaffeinated coffee has about 10 mg to 25 mg of caffeine per cup.

SUPPLEMENTS

Researchers have studied various supplements for years to identify ones that could help manage Parkinson's symptoms and/or boost the effects of levodopa, but large studies have failed to prove that these supplements provide such benefits.

However, because Parkinson's is a complex disease that can cause about 20 different motor and nonmotor symptoms that evolve over time, the existing research may not apply to everyone. *Some people with Parkinson's may benefit from...*

- **Coenzyme Q10 (CoQ10).** This supplement promotes the health of the body's mitochondria ("energy generators" in the cells), which are believed to play a role in Parkinson's. In a large study, people with Parkinson's who took 1,200 mg per day showed some improvement in symptoms over a 16-month study period. However, follow-up studies found no beneficial effects.
- **Riboflavin and alpha-lipoic acid** are among the other supplements that are continuing to be studied.

Important: If you wish to try these or other supplements, be sure to consult your doctor to ensure that there are no possible interactions with your other medications.

MARIJUANA

A few small studies have concluded that marijuana can improve some neurological symptoms, but larger studies are needed to show benefits for Parkinson's patients, especially for symptoms such as depression and anxiety.

However: Marijuana is challenging for several reasons—first, it is illegal in most states. If you do live in a state that allows medical marijuana use, it has possible side effects—for example, it can impair balance and driving...it is difficult to know the exact dosage, even if it's purchased from a dispensary...and with marijuana edibles (such as cookies and candies), the effects may take longer to appear, and you may accidentally ingest too much.

If you want to try marijuana: Work closely with your doctor to help you avoid such pitfalls.

SEEING THE RIGHT DOCTOR

For anyone with Parkinson's, it's crucial to see a neurologist and, if possible, one who has advanced training in Parkinson's disease and movement disorders.

Important finding: A large study showed that patients treated by a neurologist had a lower risk for hip fracture and were less likely to be placed in a nursing facility. They were also 22% less likely to die during the four-year study.

Neurologists are best equipped to treat the ever-changing symptoms of Parkinson's. For optimal care, see the neurologist every four to six months. The National Parkinson Foundation's Helpline, 800-4PD-INFO (473-4636) can assist you in finding expert care.

New Treatment for Essential Tremor

Travis Tierney, MD, PhD, a pediatric neurosurgeon at Nicklaus Children's Hospital, Miami, Florida.

Focused sound waves guided by MRI can be sent into the brain area called the thalamus to kill cells causing the tremor. The treatment is approved only for patients who are 22 or older and for whom standard medication therapy has not worked. Side effects, including numbness and tingling of the hands and face and difficulty walking, usually are transient.

"Epilepsy Gene Network" Identified in Brain

Imperial College London, news release.

Scientists say they have identified a gene network in the brain that's associated with epilepsy.

Although the research is in the early stages, the investigators hope their discovery can revive interest in finding new epilepsy treatments.

"Identifying groups of genes that work together, and then targeting these networks of genes, may lead to more effective treatments," said study senior author Michael Johnson. He's a professor of medicine at Imperial College London in England.

"Our proof-of-concept study suggests this network biology approach could help us identify new medications for epilepsy, and the methods can also be applied to other diseases," Johnson said in a college news release.

The newly discovered "epilepsy network" includes 320 genes believed to be involved in how brain cells communicate with one another. When the network malfunctions, it triggers epilepsy, the scientists said.

Epilepsy is one of the most common serious neurological disorders worldwide, affecting more than 50 million people, Johnson and his colleagues noted. People with the condition suffer seizures of varying severity.

"Despite almost 30 different drugs licensed for the condition, a third of people with epilepsy continue to suffer from uncontrolled epileptic seizures—despite taking medication," Johnson said.

In the past 100 years, not much progress has been made in finding improved therapies, and many drug companies no longer try to develop new medicines for epilepsy, he added.

Medications that restore normal function in this gene network could provide a new type of treatment, according to Johnson.

"The discovery of this network of genes linked to epilepsy opens avenues for finding new treatments. This uses an approach that is entirely different to the past 100 years of antiepilepsy drug development," Johnson said.

"Until recently, we have been looking for individual genes associated with diseases, which drug companies then target with treatments," he explained. "However, we are increasingly aware that genes don't work in isolation."

The study was published in the journal *Genome Biology*.

info The U.S. National Institute of Neurological Disorders and Stroke has more on epilepsy at NINDS.NIH.gov/.

Digital Media Danger

Dartmouth College.

Comprehension varies, depending on whether reading material appears in print or in a digital format (on a laptop or tablet).

Details: Digital users focused more on concrete details and less on the big picture...and were less likely to engage in abstract thought.

Time for Your Cognitive Checkup

Malaz A. Boustani, MD, the Richard M. Fairbanks professor in aging research at the Indiana University Center for Aging Research and founding director and chief innovation and implementation officer at the Sandra Eskenazi Center for Brain Care Innovation, both in Indianapolis. He is the recipient of the 2012 American Geriatrics Society Outstanding Scientific Achievement for Clinical Investigation Award. AgingBrainCare.org

One of your favorite actors appears on the screen, but you can't put a name to the face. Or you walk into the kitchen for—well, you walked in there for something, but you can't remember what.

Sound familiar? If so, you are probably at least middle-aged. These and other memory hiccups usually reflect nothing more than normal brain changes, but how can you be sure? It's a legitimate concern because up to 76% of cases of cognitive impairment aren't spotted by primary care physicians during the mild-to-moderate phases.

Recent development: You may have heard about the "annual wellness visit" that is now available as a Medicare/Medicaid benefit. As you might imagine, this free checkup includes standard tests (such as blood pressure), a review of screening tests, etc. But this exam also includes a thorough assessment to detect memory problems or other cognitive impairments. Some private insurance policies may also cover this type of exam.

Why it's important: People with Alzheimer's or other forms of dementia are typically diagnosed three to five years after they've developed impairments. The cognitive checkup offers the chance for earlier detection of a problem and the opportunity to develop an effective plan for coping with symptoms of cognitive impairment.

WHAT THE EXAM INCLUDES

During the annual wellness visit, your doctor will start with a general health assessment. If you're like most adults, you probably have one or more health issues—such as high blood pressure or diabetes—that increase the risk for cognitive impairments. Certain medications can also cause cognitive problems.

The exam (combined with subsequent tests) can also help identify reversible causes of cognitive declines, such as thyroid problems, low vitamin B-12 and depression.

After that, the exam will include...

- **Personal stories.** Your doctor will ask how your life is going. This is your chance to discuss any changes you might have noticed—maybe it's getting harder to balance your checkbook... perhaps you're forgetting to take medications (or you're taking them at the wrong times). Buttoning clothing might be harder...possibly you've slipped and fallen in the bathroom...or maybe you've felt depressed lately. Such self-reported observations can raise important red flags.

- **A conversation with a family member/close friend.** It's common for patients with cognitive changes to be unaware (or only partly aware) of how much they're affected. You may think that you're on top of daily details, but someone else in your life might notice that you keep missing appointments or taking wrong turns on your drive home. A different perspective is helpful.

My advice: I strongly encourage patients to bring someone with them to their wellness visits whether they suspect cognitive problems or not. The doctor or a member of the medical team may interview the person separately so that he/she can speak freely. If you and your companion say that your memory is good, there's a strong likelihood that everything's fine...and that you won't need further testing for another year.

POSSIBLE PROBLEM AREAS

If you have noticed changes in your memory or daily routines, your doctor will ask focused questions.

Examples: "During the last 12 months, have you noticed that confusion/memory loss is happening more often or getting worse?" "Did you need help from others during the last week in performing daily activities, such as grooming, walking or getting dressed?"

Problems in any of these areas could mean that you need...

- **Cognitive testing.** If your doctor suspects (based on the above discussions) that you might have some degree of cognitive impairment, commonly used tests include the Memory Impairment Screen (MIS)...the General Practitioner assessment of Cognition (GPCOG)...or the Mini-Cog. Each can be administered by a medical staff member in less than five minutes.

Example: The MIS is a verbally administered word-recall test. You might be asked to read four words—for example, checkers, saucer, telegram and bus—out loud. Then you'll be told to think of categories (such as "games") and come up with words that fit in each category. After a few minutes, you'll be asked to remember the four words you read earlier. You may also be asked to spell a word (such as "world") backward...or count back from 100 by sevens.

Patients who "fail" a test may have cognitive impairments—or they could simply be having an off day. Further evaluation by a neurologist, geriatrician or other specialist will be recommended.

WHAT'S NEXT?

If the wellness visit and subsequent testing point to a cognitive decline, you'll need appropriate follow-up.

Recent research: The collaborative care model (a team approach to care) has been shown to be more effective than the standard one-doctor/one-patient approach. With the collaborative approach, a team of clinicians (which may include a primary care doctor and memory care doctor) led by a care coordinator (a registered nurse or a social worker) works with the patient and family to improve quality of care.

In a study of 153 patients with mild-to-moderate Alzheimer's, patients who received collaborative care had fewer behavioral/psychological problems and were more likely to be given effective drug treatments than patients receiving "standard" care with one doctor.

Many patients can live a relatively normal life with cognitive decline, but they'll need a lot of help along the way. A collaborative program is the best way to provide it.

Note: All aspects of this care may not be covered by insurance.

Is It a Concussion?

Diane Stoler, EdD, a neuropsychologist in private practice in Boxford, Massachusetts, and author of *Coping with Concussion and Mild Traumatic Brain Injury.*

A concussion is typically diagnosed based on symptoms such as headache, blurred vision or confusion—sometimes hours or days after a head injury. If someone has taken a hard fall, can't recall events before or after a fall, loses consciousness (even briefly) or shows behavioral changes, take him/her to the emergency department, where neurological tests will be administered, along with a CT scan or MRI to see if there is any injury to the brain. If symptoms continue, neuropsychological testing by a neuropsychologist who specializes in brain injury can accurately diagnose a concussion.

Aha Moments Are More Accurate

Drexel University.

"Aha moments" tend to be more accurate than carefully reasoned conclusions.

Reason: Deadline-driven analytic thinking can lead to rushed ideas, while creative insights come suddenly after subconscious processing.

Want to Boost Learning and Memory? Time Your Exercise

Study titled "Physical Exercise Performed Four Hours After Learning Improves Memory Retention and Increases Hippocampal Pattern Similarity During Retrieval," by researchers at the Radboud University Medical Center in the Netherlands, published in *Current Biology.*

Cynthia Green, PhD, president and CEO of Total Brain Health and TBH Brands, LLC, Montclair, New Jersey, and founding director of the Memory Enhancement Program at the Icahn School of Medicine at Mount Sinai, New York City.

You already know that exercise is great for your mind as well as your body. Now brain researchers are uncovering exactly how exercise helps our brains learn and, more importantly, how best to retain what we've learned.

Exercise is key. But it's all in the timing.

To evaluate the recent research, we spoke with cognitive health expert Cynthia Green, PhD, president and CEO of Total Brain Health and TBH Brands.

LEARNING + TIME + EXERCISE = KNOWLEDGE

Researchers in the Netherlands asked 72 volunteers to learn 90 picture-location associations in a 40-minute exercise. The researchers did noninvasive brain scans to see how the different parts of the brains lit up.

Then the researchers asked about one-third of the volunteers to exercise immediately afterward...another third to exercise four hours later...and a third group to not exercise at all. The exercise was a garden-variety aerobic workout—35 minutes of interval training on an exercise bike, at an intensity of up to 80% of maximum recommended heart rate for each individual.

Then, two days later, all the volunteers were asked to repeat the task to see how well they retained what they had learned. They repeated the brain scans, too.

Results: Exercising immediately after didn't help—those folks didn't retain knowledge any better than those who didn't exercise at all. But the ones who exercised four hours later did significantly better than everyone else at retaining what they'd learned.

What happened inside their brains was even more interesting. For those who delayed exercise for four hours, the hippocampus—a part of the brain crucial to long-term memory—looked remarkably similar during the initial learning task and the one repeated two days later when they got correct answers. It lit up in the same pattern. For the other volunteers, not so much—when confronted with the same task again, they had to, in essence, relearn much of what they had learned earlier.

While this experiment didn't examine physiology directly, the researchers note that other studies have found that exercise boosts brain chemicals known as catecholamines, including dopamine and norepinephrine, which are key to memory and learning. Still, they're not sure why waiting four hours made a big difference. That's where future research will go. The study also didn't look at what happens if you exercise, say, two or three hours after learning something—or five. For now, all they know is that getting some aerobic exercise about four hours later helps you remember.

EXERCISE AND YOUR BRAIN

Dr. Green is all for using the recent research to help you consolidate learning. The next time you need to make sure new information sticks—when you've just immersed yourself in a big new work project—try heading to the gym or lace on your running shoes and go out for a jog four hours later, she suggests.

But Dr. Green also wants us to see the big picture when it comes to exercise and our brains. "We know exercise overall is one of the best things we can do for our brains, and studies have repeatedly demonstrated that aerobic activity benefits cognition," she said. Regular aerobic exercise—a rough total target of 150 minutes a week—is also key to maintaining cognitive health as you age, and it helps prevent dementia. But there's also growing evidence that strength training is also important for maintaining cognitive performance.

In other words, even if you don't care how buff you look, if you value your brain, when it comes to exercise—just do it.

BP Meds Cut Alzheimer's Risk

Analysis of the medical records of 784 patients with high blood pressure and mild cognitive impairment by researchers at Emory University, Atlanta, presented at the recent Alzheimer's International Conference 2015, Washington, DC.

People with mild thinking and memory difficulties who took an angiotensin-converting-enzyme (ACE) inhibitor, such as *captopril* or *lisinopril*...or an angiotensin-receptor blocker (ARB), such as *losartan* or *valsartan*...were less likely to develop Alzheimer's disease than similar patients taking other hypertension drugs. More research is needed, but if you are taking a medication for high blood pressure, ask your doctor if switching to an ACE or ARB drug is appropriate.

Alzheimer's Misdiagnosed

Melissa Murray, PhD, is assistant professor of neuroscience at Mayo Clinic, Jacksonville, Florida, and leader of a study of the brains of more than 1,600 people, presented at a recent Alzheimer's Association International Conference.

Two in 10 cases of Alzheimer's may be misdiagnosed, says Melissa Murray, PhD. *Reason:* There is no medical test that can definitively diagnose Alzheimer's. Instead, diagnosis is based on symptoms. Men seem to develop Alzheimer's at an earlier age than women, who typically develop it in their 70s or later...and men's symptoms may be behavioral or involve motor problems, while women's are more likely to involve memory issues.

Being Busy Is Good for Your Brain!

Study titled "The Busier the Better: Greater Busyness Is Associated with Better Cognition," by Sara B. Festini, PhD, Denise C. Park, PhD, and Ian M. McDonough, PhD, The University of Texas at Dallas, The University of Alabama, Tuscaloosa, published in *Frontiers in Aging Neuroscience.*

When you have too much to do, you might dream of spending time up a lazy river. But if you want to keep your brain sharp and your memory strong, you're better off staying busy.

Really busy—so busy that you feel like you have so many things to do that you can't possibly get them all done. So busy that you wish the day were longer. So busy that you sometimes stay up later than you want to in order to get everything done.

That's the surprising conclusion of a recent study of men and women ages 50 to 89. Researchers at the University of Texas at Dallas studied 330 participants who filled out a "busyness" questionnaire and then measured that against memory and brain function scores. *Results...*

- **The busiest ones processed information faster,** reasoned better, could remember more at one time and had a better recall of important moments in their own lives.
- **The strongest association was for "episodic" memory**—remembering specific times and places.
- **While participants in their 50s and 60s tended to be busier than those in their 70s and 80s,** the cognitive benefits of busyness remained a strong association at any age. "Our findings," the authors conclude, "offer encouragement to maintain active, busy lifestyles throughout middle and late adulthood."

It's an observational study, to be sure, so it doesn't prove cause and effect. Plus, the researchers note, it's well-established that chronic high stress levels can impair cognitive function, including memory—so there's no point to being so busy that you want to tear your hair out.

But it may be time to stop envying the lucky old sun, who keeps rolling around heaven all day. It's good to stay busy—at any age.

Animal Study Hints at Gene Therapy for Alzheimer's

Imperial College London, news release.

Gene therapy might one day offer a way to prevent and treat Alzheimer's disease, recent research in mice suggests.

Scientists at Imperial College London used a modified virus to deliver a gene called PGC1-alpha into the brain cells of mice. Previous research suggests this gene may prevent the formation of a protein called amyloid-beta peptide.

It's the main component of amyloid plaques, the sticky clumps of protein in the brains of Alzheimer's disease patients. These plaques are thought to cause brain cell death.

These very early findings could lead to a way of preventing Alzheimer's or stopping it in the early stages, according to study senior author Magdalena Sastre, PhD.

Alzheimer's is the most common type of dementia. It causes memory loss, confusion and changes in mood and personality. There is no cure.

"There are many hurdles to overcome, and at the moment the only way to deliver the gene is via an injection directly into the brain," Sastre said in a college news release.

It's also important to note that therapies that look promising in mice often don't work in humans.

"However, this proof-of-concept study shows this approach warrants further investigation," she added. Dr. Sastre is a senior lecturer in the department of medicine.

David Reynolds, PhD, chief scientific officer for Alzheimer's Research UK, said studies like this one are important because current treatments do not stop progression of Alzheimer's damage.

"This research sets a foundation for exploring gene therapy as a treatment strategy for Alzheimer's disease, but further studies are needed to establish whether gene therapy would be safe, effective and practical to use in people with the disease," Dr. Reynolds said in the news release.

The study was published in the journal *Proceedings of the National Academy of Sciences.*

info The U.S. National Institute on Aging has more about Alzheimer's disease at NIA.NIH.gov/alzheimers/publication/alzheimers-disease-fact-sheet.

Sound Waves to Heal the Brain

Science Translational Medicine.

Sound waves boost drug delivery. An implantable ultrasound device opens the blood-brain barrier and could improve the outcomes for patients with aggressive brain tumors. Currently, 99% of drugs for brain diseases and disorders are blocked by this barrier.

CHAPTER 4

Cancer Care and Breakthroughs

6 Ways to Beat Back Cancer

From time to time, we all hear about cancer patients who defy the odds and live longer than anyone predicted—or even, in some cases, have a complete remission. Why does this happen? No one knows for sure. Researchers are trying to understand this puzzle. *Here's what we've learned so far...*

SPONTANEOUS REMISSIONS

Some cancers simply disappear. We know, for example, that about 5% of patients with advanced kidney cancer will have spontaneous remissions. This doesn't mean that they're cured—the cancer could return at some point. But for some reason, these patients do much better than others.

Genetic factors surely play a role. Researchers have identified a number of "response mutations" in various types of tumors that somehow make them more likely to respond positively to treatments such as chemotherapy or radiation.

IMPROVE YOUR ODDS

Research is ongoing, but there's evidence suggesting that the six steps below are important in getting the best possible outcome—and can help prevent cancer from developing in the first place...

• **Take control and manage stress.** "Negative" emotions, such as anxiety and depression, are a normal response to a life-changing illness. Yet there's good evidence (both from human and animal studies) that chronic stress can make your body more susceptible to cancer growth—and that reducing stress may make a difference.

Lorenzo Cohen, PhD, the Richard E. Haynes Distinguished Professor in Clinical Cancer Prevention and director of the Integrative Medicine Program at The University of Texas MD Anderson Cancer Center in Houston. He is also a distinguished clinical professor at Fudan University Shanghai Cancer Center in Shanghai, China, vice-chair of the Academic Consortium for Integrative Medicine & Health, and a founding member of the International Society for Integrative Oncology.

Important research: A study published in the journal *Biological Psychiatry* found that breast cancer patients who participated in a 10-week stress-management program had an increase in cancer-controlling gene expression (such as type 1 interferon response genes) for improved immune function and a decrease in genes that control inflammatory molecules that promote cancer growth. An analysis of the 11-year survival data found that the women in the stress-management group lived significantly longer than those in the control group.

My advice: Engage in a stress-management activity every day (for example, meditation, yoga, relaxation techniques, etc.)...strive to bring that state of calm with you throughout the day...and get counseling if you need it.

- **Get a good night's sleep.** Poor sleep and disruptions in the body's biological clock (as occurs with shift work, for example) have been linked to the development of certain malignancies, including breast and prostate cancer. Now research is suggesting that sleep may play a role in cancer survival.

My advice: The sweet spot seems to be about seven hours of sleep a night. Some people need a bit more, but you don't want to get much less. Research has shown that the risk of dying from all causes—not just cancer—is higher in those who get less than six hours of sleep a night.

- **Watch your weight.** People with a higher body mass index (BMI) have greater concentrations of inflammatory molecules...more insulin resistance...and more estrogen and cancer-related growth factors.

And the effects can be significant. Obese patients are not only more likely to be diagnosed with cancer but also to have a cancer recurrence. They tend to have more complications from surgery, chemotherapy or other treatments as well.

My advice: People with a BMI of 27 or higher should make a serious effort to lose weight. They'll get a double benefit because the two main weight-loss strategies—a healthier diet and more exercise—will also improve cancer recovery and survival.

Important: Consult your doctor about the ideal time to lose weight during your treatment—it may not be appropriate at all stages of cancer care.

- **Get more exercise.** It is well known that regular exercise can help prevent many types of cancer. But can it also help cancer patients live longer? The jury is still out.

Thus far, observational studies—those that look at large populations of people—do suggest that it might make a difference. Exercise is believed to decrease circulating levels of cancer-promoting inflammatory markers and increase aspects of immune function that can help to control cancer growth.

My advice: Exercise at least 30 minutes a day at least five or six days a week. Any amount of activity helps—even 10-minute bouts every few hours count. Also avoid sitting for hours at a time.

- **Reduce exposure to toxins.** Cancer-causing chemicals are all around us. Hormone disrupters, such as bisphenol A (BPA) and parabens, are in some plastic bottles and cosmetics and can alter hormonal functioning and increase cancer risk. Carcinogens, such as formaldehyde and benzene, can be in wallpaper, paint, wood floor finishes and other household products.

My advice: Avoid personal-care products that contain parabens, phthalates, triclosan and synthetic fragrance. Use glass and stainless steel containers instead of plastic. Ventilate your home when painting or refinishing floors.

THE HEALTHY PLATE FORMULA...

To help fight cancer, it's important to make wise food choices throughout the day.

Here's how: Fill half your plate with vegetables (organic, if possible) at every meal, including breakfast. The other half should contain protein, fruits (preferably organic) and whole grains. Try replacing meat with sardines, salmon and other cold-water fish (loaded with omega-3 fatty acids) and beans at least four times a week for a healthy source of animal and plant proteins. Add spices and herbs, which are filled with healthy phytochemicals. It's also smart to eat fewer "white" foods, including white bread, white rice, etc. These and other high-glycemic foods are quickly converted to glucose, which increases levels of insulin and insulin-like growth factor (a cancer promoter).

Helpful: Meet with a dietitian to help guide you in healthy eating. To find a registered dietitian near you, consult the Academy of Nutrition and Dietetics, EatRight.org.

The Cancer-Carb Connection

Barry Boyd, MD, MS, a medical oncologist and founder and former director of the Integrative Medicine Program at Greenwich Hospital-Yale Health Systems, where he is currently the director of Cancer Nutrition. He is an assistant clinical professor and former director of Curriculum in Nutrition and Integrative Medicine at Yale School of Medicine in New Haven, Connecticut, and author of *The Cancer Recovery Plan.* DrBarryBoyd.com

---

More bad news for carb lovers: The same refined, low-fiber foods that contribute to obesity, diabetes and other serious conditions are now believed to increase one's risk for cancer—and to worsen outcomes in those who already have it.

Alarming new finding: In a study recently published in *Cancer Epidemiology, Biomarkers & Prevention*, people who ate the most high-glycemic (blood sugar–spiking) carbohydrates—foods such as white bread, white rice and russet potatoes—were 49% more likely to be diagnosed with lung cancer than those who ate the least.

Even though this isn't the first study to link "junk" carbohydrates to cancer, the evidence has now gotten strong enough that more and more medical experts are advising us to take a very close look at the quality of the carbs that we eat.

WHAT'S THE LINK TO CARBS?

Dietary carbohydrates are a critical driver of blood sugar (glucose) levels and must be tracked by people with diabetes to keep their blood glucose levels steady.

One of the most effective tools to do this is the glycemic index (GI), a ranking system of carbohydrates, which shows how quickly different foods increase levels of blood glucose. High-GI carbs raise blood sugar almost instantly...lower-GI foods (the "good" carbs, such as chickpeas, prunes and pearled barley) raise it more gradually.

We have known for a long time that people with diabetes are more likely to get cancer than those who do not have diabetes. More recently, we've learned that even in the absence of diabetes, many people are "prediabetic," with elevated blood glucose and insulin (the blood sugar–regulating hormone)—due to poor diet, a lack of exercise and other causes. Prediabetes makes people more likely to develop cancer...and puts them at greater risk for poor outcomes when they do.

Recent finding: A variety of cancers, such as breast, colorectal, endometrial and pancreatic, seem to be affected by high glucose and high insulin. It is clear that a "Western-style" diet—typically loaded with high-GI foods—creates some of the conditions that make it easier for cancers to thrive. *What happens...*

- **High-GI foods trigger an increase in insulin,** which results in a rise in insulin-growth factor (IGF-1). Both insulin and IGF-1 will promote the growth of cancer cells and inhibit their natural death.
- **Obesity,** particularly when there is excess fat in the belly area, is strongly associated with prediabetes, along with higher blood glucose and insulin. People with obesity have more inflammation, oxidative stress and estrogen—all of which increase cancer risks.

SELF-DEFENSE

Unless you already have diabetes or are at a high risk of developing it (for example, you are overweight or obese with belly fat* and/or have a sedentary lifestyle), I don't advise too much emphasis strictly on total carbohydrate intake or GI food ratings. I focus more on the quality of carbohydrates and, in practice, find that people who try to track the GI of all the foods they eat tend to give up healthy eating altogether because it becomes too much work.

Also, high-GI foods are just one part of the equation. Vegetarians (who generally eat low-

*Abdominal obesity is defined as a waist measurement of 40 inches or more in men and 35 inches or more in women.

GI foods) tend to have a lower risk for cancer. But is it because of their carbohydrate choices or because they're also more likely to be physically active and have lower body weights? The evidence isn't clear.

My advice: Follow an overall strategy that both controls blood glucose and may help you prevent/manage cancer. *Key steps…*

- **Limit weight gain through a prudent diet and physical activity.** You don't have to avoid all high-GI foods, but you should limit them. Consider eating plans (such as the Mediterranean diet) that emphasize whole grains, legumes, vegetables and other low-GI foods. Such diets have been linked to reduced risk for cancer-promoting obesity, diabetes and elevated blood glucose levels. Regular exercise has also been linked to a reduced risk and improved survival in many cancers—in part, by reducing insulin.

- **Avoid processed foods as much as possible.** They tend to be high in added sugar, which raises blood glucose very quickly.

One of the worst: Sugared soft drinks, which typically have the equivalent of 10 teaspoons of sugar per serving!

Important: Don't wait. Cancer usually develops after decades of exposure to high blood glucose, insulin, etc. The sooner you start eating a healthy diet, the better.

- **Cut back on red meat.** It is among the main sources of saturated fat in the American diet. Even if you mainly eat healthy carbohydrates, too much saturated fat increases the risk for insulin resistance (when the body becomes less sensitive to the hormone's effect, triggering the release of more insulin to compensate) and cancer.

- **Improve your gut health.** A healthy intestinal "flora" can help prevent obesity, along with preventing both insulin resistance and inflammation. It's another argument for eating low-GI carbs—they tend to be high in fiber and act as prebiotics, foods that promote the growth of healthy intestinal bacteria.

- **Ask about *metformin* (Glucophage).** It's a diabetes drug that reduces insulin resistance, decreases the production of glucose by the liver and lowers insulin levels. It's also less likely to cause weight gain than other diabetes medications. One large study found that it can reduce overall cancer risk by 31% in people with diabetes.

But it is not a miracle drug. Research has shown that lifestyle changes are more effective than metformin at preventing diabetes. Even so, more people should be taking it, particularly those who have trouble controlling high blood glucose/high insulin with diet and exercise alone.

FOR THOSE WITH CANCER

If you have cancer, try your best to stay active and eat well—during and after treatments. It's common for cancer survivors to deal with stress by overindulging in comfort foods. But research shows that those who maintain a healthy weight, are physically active and eat nutritious, low-GI carbs will be less likely to have a cancer recurrence.

Can Your Cell Phone Cause Cancer?

Devra Davis, PhD, MPH, president of Environmental Health Trust, a nonprofit scientific and policy think tank focusing on cell-phone radiation. She is a former senior advisor to the assistant secretary for health in the Department of Health and Human Services and a former member of the National Toxicology Program's Board of Scientific Counselors. She is author of *Disconnect: The Truth About Cell Phone Radiation*. EHTrust.org

You may have heard that cell phones have been linked to cancer but wondered if that could really be true. A recent study offers strong evidence that this is the case—cell phones and other wireless devices emit a type of microwave radiation termed radiofrequency radiation (RFR) that can cause brain cancer and other cancers.

Here are the findings and what to do to minimize this risk to your health…

THE NEWEST EVIDENCE

The government's National Toxicology Program (NTP) conducts scientific studies on toxins to see how they might affect the health of Americans. More than 90 studies show that the radiation emitted by cell phones and other wireless devices can damage DNA, the first step on the road to cancer.

In May 2016, the NTP published preliminary results from a two-year animal study on the health effects of cell-phone radiation—this was the largest study on animals and cell-phone radiation ever published.

One out of every 12 of the animals studied were affected by the radiation. Some of those that were exposed to daily, frequent doses of cell-phone radiation from birth developed glioma, a rare, aggressive type of brain cancer already linked to cell-phone use in people. (Glial cells surround and support neurons.) Other animals had precancerous changes in glial cells. And some developed rare tumors of the nerves around and within the heart called schwannomas. In contrast, a control group of animals not exposed to wireless radiation had no gliomas, no precancerous changes in glial cells and no schwannomas.

There are two crucial takeaways from this recent study...

1. For decades, many scientists and governments have embraced the following scientific dogma—the only unsafe radiation is "thermal" radiation that heats tissue, such as an X-ray. "Nonthermal" RFR doesn't heat tissue and therefore is safe. The latest study—during which animals exposed to RFR were monitored to ensure that there was no heating of tissue—contradicts this dogma.

2. Epidemiological studies that analyze health data from hundreds or thousands of people have linked gliomas and schwannomas to long-term cell-phone use—and this latest study found the same type of cancers in animals exposed to wireless radiation, strengthening the link.

EVEN MORE DANGERS

Gliomas and schwannomas aren't the only dangers. *Research links wireless-device use to a range of other cancers, diseases and conditions...*

•**Meningioma.** A recent study published in *Oncology Reports* showed that heavy users of mobile and cordless phones had up to twice the risk for meningioma, cancer in the protective coverings that surround the brain.

•**Salivary gland (parotid) tumors.** Salivary glands are below the ear and in the jaw—exactly where many people hold cell phones during conversation. A study published in *American Journal of Epidemiology* showed a 58% higher risk for these (usually) noncancerous tumors among cell-phone users.

•**Acoustic neuroma.** Studies show that heavy or longtime users of cell phones have nearly triple the risk of developing acoustic neuromas (also called vestibular schwannomas), noncancerous tumors on the nerve that connects the inner ear to the brain. Symptoms can include gradual hearing loss and tinnitus in the affected ear, along with balance problems, headaches and facial numbness and tingling.

•**Breast cancer.** A study published in *Case Reports in Medicine* describes four young American women, ages 21 to 39, who had tucked their smartphones into their bras for up to 10 hours a day for several years. Each of them developed breast tumors directly under the antennas of their phones. None of the women had the cancer-causing BRAC1 or BRAC2 gene, a family history of cancer or any other known risk factors.

•**Male infertility and potency.** Several studies link close contact with wireless devices—wearing a cell phone on the hip or using a laptop computer on the lap—with fewer sperm, sluggish sperm, abnormally shaped sperm, sperm with damaged DNA and erectile dysfunction.

•**Sleeping problems.** Research shows that people who use cell phones and other wireless devices in the hours before bedtime have more trouble falling asleep and staying asleep. Both wireless radiation and the "blue light" from screens suppress melatonin, a sleep-inducing hormone.

HOW TO PROTECT YOURSELF

Every step you take to reduce radiation is protective because exposure to radiation is cumulative—the higher the exposure, the higher your risk for cancer and other health problems.

The devices you should be concerned about include cell phones, cordless phone handsets and bases, Wi-Fi routers, wireless computers, laptops, iPads and other tablets, smartwatches, wireless fitness bands, iPods that connect to the Internet, wireless speakers, cordless baby monitors, wireless game consoles and any other type of wireless device or equipment such as thermostats, security networks, sound systems and smart meters.

•**Keep it at a distance.** To decrease your exposure to wireless radiation, keep wireless devices as far away from you as possible. *Just a few inches can make a big difference...*

•Never put the phone next to your head. Instead, use the speakerphone function or a wired headset or an earpiece.

•Never place a turned-on device in a pocket or jacket or tucked into clothing. Keep it in a carrier bag, such as a briefcase or purse. Never rest a wireless device on your body. This includes laptops and tablets—keep them off your lap.

•Never fall asleep with your cell phone or wireless tablet in the bed or under your pillow. Many people fall asleep streaming radiation into their bodies.

•Prefer texting to calling. And avoid using your cell phone when the signal is weak—radiation is higher.

•**Turn it off.** Putting your cell phone in "airplane" mode stops radiation. Also, look for the function key on your wireless device that turns off the Wi-Fi. Turn it off when the device isn't in use. There's also a function key to turn off Bluetooth transmissions. If you must use a Wi-Fi router at home, locate it as far away from your body as possible. And turn it off at night.

To stop a gaming console from emitting radiation, you need to turn it off and unplug it.

•**Don't use your cell phone in metal surroundings such as a bus, train, airplane or elevator.** Using the phone creates radiation "hot spots" that increase exposure.

Exception: It is OK to use a cell phone in a car if your phone is hooked into the car's Bluetooth system—this reduces radiation to the user.

•**Trade in the cordless phone.** Cordless phones and wireless routers that use a technology called DECT emit as much radiation as cell phones whether you are using them or not. At home, install telephones that get their signal by being plugged into a jack. Forward your cell phone to your landline whenever you're home.

Just Diagnosed with Cancer?

Mark J. Fesler, MD, an assistant professor of hematology and medical oncology at Saint Louis University Cancer Center and director of the Blood and Marrow Transplant Program at SSM Health Saint Louis University Hospital.

Getting a diagnosis of cancer is one of the scariest, most stressful situations a person can experience. Reeling from the distressing news and overcome with emotion, virtually all new cancer patients find it hard to know exactly what actions should be taken next.

What works best: Following certain steps the first week after a cancer diagnosis greatly reduces stress and sets the course for a treatment plan that involves good decision-making, stronger support systems and perhaps even an improved chance of recovery. *The steps below can be adapted to each patient's personal situation, but they will help bring order to what can otherwise be a chaotic and tremendously challenging time...*

•**Don't keep your cancer a secret.** Many patients keep their diagnosis to themselves at first. They may be in denial, don't have all the facts yet and/or don't want to worry loved ones. But it's much better to reach out to key family members and close friends right away.

Meet with close family members and friends individually or in a group to share your diagnosis and let them know that you would appreciate their support. You can give them more information at a later time. You could also call your friends and family members to give them the news, but don't communicate this information via text or social media.

The love and moral support as well as practical help with meals and rides that they can give will lessen your burden and anxiety much more than you realize.

•**See an oncologist within the first week after diagnosis.** There's a tremendous amount of anxiety during the time between the cancer diagnosis and the initial visit with an oncologist. I have observed that patients who see their oncologists right away tend to be less anxious.

Oncologists should make it a point to see newly diagnosed patients quickly, certainly within a week of diagnosis and sometimes even sooner. You should try to see at least one oncologist who specializes in your specific cancer subtype, for example, a gynecologic oncologist—if not on the first appointment, then during a second opinion (see below).

At the appointment, you'll get detailed information about the stage of your cancer...where it's located in your body...what kind of prognosis to expect...what treatment is most appropriate...and how it will affect your life. Having this knowledge often helps to ease anxiety.

To prepare for your appointment...

Write down a list of questions. You no doubt will have questions for the oncologist based on the initial conversation with your doctor. Be sure to write them down so that you don't forget them during the stress of your appointment.

In preparation for your appointment, you may also want to research your condition online, but restrict your browsing to well-respected sites, such as Cancer.gov (National Cancer Institute)...Cancer.org (American Cancer Society)...and Cancer.net (American Society of Clinical Oncology).

Important: Be cautious about drawing conclusions from information on the web. Data on cancer can be complicated, and treatments can change over a short period of time. And prognoses and other stats are usually based on medians or averages. Use the information you glean from the web to add to your list of questions for the oncologist.

Bring one to three people with you to the first oncologist visit. Patients are often so emotionally overwhelmed by the diagnosis that their brains do not process all the important information that's given to them during the appointment. Loved ones and/or friends can help listen, take notes and ask questions. They may also be able to tell the doctor about symptoms they've noticed that the patient isn't even aware of. I advise bringing as many as three loved ones or close friends because they can help the patient in different ways and will ask different questions. With your doctor's permission, you could also record the appointment (a recorder app on your smartphone is easy to use).

•**Consider a second opinion.** Ideally, you should get a second opinion before treatment begins, and it should be from a doctor not affiliated with the first. You should not feel uncomfortable telling your doctor about your plans for a second opinion—in the case of cancer, it's a very common practice and is even required by some insurance providers. Your doctor may facilitate the process of getting a second opinion with an unaffiliated doctor.

Having information you already received corroborated by a second opinion can be reassuring. And if the second opinion conflicts with the first, it's better to know that sooner than later. Insurance will usually cover the cost of a second opinion, but check with your insurance company or your insurance case manager, if you have one.

•**Address your stress.** After a cancer diagnosis, you may suffer from anxiety and/or lack of sleep. To take care of yourself, cut back on nonessential tasks so that you can focus on activities that will help relieve stress, such as getting more exercise and eating well. Talk to your doctor about the best exercise and diet for your specific situation.

Be sure to tell your doctor about any anxiety or depression you're feeling. He/she may refer you to a mental health provider, such as a therapist, psychologist or psychiatrist, and/or may prescribe a short-term medication, such as *alprazolam* (Xanax), to relieve anxiety and help you get some rest.

Also: Support groups can be beneficial. A good resource is Cancer.net (click on "Coping with Cancer," then on "Finding Support and Information" and finally on "Support Groups"). But some patients feel that support groups make them overly consumed by their diagnosis and choose not to join one. That's OK—the patient should decide the form of support that is best for him.

• **Learn about clinical trials.** Even though most people assume that clinical trials enroll only patients who are in very advanced stages of their illnesses, that's not true. There are clinical trials designed for different types and stages of cancer, but they may have very specific requirements. That's why you should ask your doctor early on about clinical trials that may be right for your case.

• **Ask about support services.** Keeping up with all the details of your illness can be overwhelming. A social worker can help with health insurance, financial aid, etc., free of charge. The medical center where your doctor practices may have social workers on staff or be able to refer you to one.

Weighty Cancer Risk

Marie-Béatrice Lauby-Secretan, PhD, scientist, International Agency for Research on Cancer, Lyon, France.

Overweight people are known to be at increased risk for cancer of the colon, esophagus, kidney, breast and uterus.

Now: A review of more than 1,000 studies found that eight more cancers are linked to excess weight and obesity—stomach, liver, gallbladder, pancreas, thyroid, ovary, meningioma (brain) and multiple myeloma (blood). The higher a person's body-mass index (BMI), the greater the risk.

Why: Excess fat produces hormones and inflammation linked to cancer growth.

Organ Transplants May Raise Skin Cancer Risk

A small study of organ-transplant recipients found an increased number of skin cancers. The study did not prove cause and effect—but it is possible that the medicines that suppress the immune system to prevent organ rejection also raise skin cancer risk.

Recommendation: Total-body skin exams should be a routine part of care after transplant surgery.

Analysis of the medical records of 413 organ-transplant recipients led by researchers at Drexel University, Philadelphia, published in *JAMA Dermatology*.

Very Hot Drinks Linked to Cancer

Robert H. Schiestl, PhD, professor of pathology, environmental health and radiation oncology at UCLA Schools of Medicine and Public Health in Los Angeles. UCLA.edu

The International Agency for Research on Cancer recently warned that consuming very hot beverages could increase esophageal cancer risk. It reached this conclusion after a review of 59 studies.

Beverages with temperatures above 149° Fahrenheit (65° Celsius) can scald the esophagus, the section of the digestive system that connects the throat to the stomach. This scalding appears to increase cancer risk. Less research has been done on the dangers of eating very hot foods, but it is reasonable to speculate that this probably carries similar scalding potential and esophageal cancer risk.

Smart response: There is no need to give up hot foods and drinks. Evidence suggests that this cancer risk exists only when beverages (and potentially foods) are regularly consumed at temperatures above 149°F. It is uncommon in North America and Europe to consume foods and beverages that hot—coffee and tea generally are consumed at temperatures no higher than 140°F, for example. At 150°F, your mouth and tongue would feel as if it were being burned. Consuming extremely hot beverages is more common in China, Iran, Turkey and much of South America.

Coffee, tea and foods are occasionally served at temperatures above 149°F in North America and Europe, however. If your initial sip or bite burns your mouth, be sure to wait a bit before consuming the rest. There's no need to worry that this initial sip or bite could cause cancer—the danger seems to develop only when very hot drinks or foods are consumed chronically, not occasionally.

NSAID Fights Cancer

Pan Pantziarka, PhD, coordinator, Repurposing Drugs in Oncology, London.

A new cancer fighter may be on its way. *Recent study:* Use of the prescription nonsteroidal anti-inflammatory drug (NSAID) *diclofenac* (Voltaren) was associated with less growth and spread of esophageal, breast, ovarian, lung and other cancers after surgery. Diclofenac was also reported to improve response to chemotherapy and radiation.

If you have cancer: Ask your doctor about this drug.

Saliva Test for Cancer

University of California, Los Angeles.

Traces of cancer can be detected in saliva in as little as 10 minutes. This genetic test, now in development, could detect multiple types of cancer from a single swab.

Expected cost: About $22.

Alcohol Linked to Cancer

Drinking alcohol can cause seven types of cancer. An analysis of studies conducted over the last 10 years determined that drinking increases the risk for cancer of the mouth and throat, esophagus, larynx (voice box), liver, colon, rectum and breast. Heavy drinkers were found to be at the highest risk, but even low-to-moderate drinkers were more likely to get these cancers than nondrinkers.

Analysis conducted by researchers at University of Otago, Dunedin, New Zealand, published in *Addictions*.

Joint Supplement Lowers Cancer Risk

Elizabeth D. Kantor, PhD, MPH, an assistant attending epidemiologist at Memorial Sloan Kettering Cancer Center, New York City, and coleader of a study of colorectal cancer at Harvard T.H. Chan School of Public Health, Boston, published in *International Journal of Cancer.*

Twenty-three percent reduction in colorectal cancer risk is linked to regular use of glucosamine and chondroitin supplements, reports Elizabeth D. Kantor, PhD, MPH. Glucosamine and chondroitin are thought to have anti-inflammatory properties, and this could explain why users of the supplements may have a lower risk for colorectal cancer.

Colon Cancer on the Rise in Younger Adults

George J. Chang, MD, professor in the department of surgical oncology, chief of the Section of Colon and Rectal Surgery and director of the Clinical Operations, Minimally Invasive and New Technologies in Oncologic Surgery Program at The University of Texas MD Anderson Cancer Center in Houston.

Most people do not get a colonoscopy until they are 50 years old. That's the age at which the American Cancer Society and other groups advise patients with average risk to have their first screening for colorectal cancer.

The unloved procedure is the best way to detect and prevent these often lethal cancers, which are second only to lung cancer as the leading cause of cancer deaths in the US. But people who wait until their 50th birthday to get this test might be making a big mistake. *Here's why...*

THE RISKS START EARLY

For reasons that aren't entirely clear, the incidence of colorectal cancers has risen in patients younger than the traditional screening age. Based on the current trend, the number is expected to grow—sharply in some cases—in the coming years.

Should young adults get a first colonoscopy in their 20s, 30s or 40s? For now, doctors will make this decision case-by-case. But the projected increase in cancer cases has led some experts to suggest that earlier screening—along with a more watchful eye for cancer symptoms—could be the most effective way to protect a group of patients that was previously thought to be low risk.

WHAT WE KNOW SO FAR

Overall, about 90% of colon cancers will be diagnosed in people who are age 50 or older—but the age of these patients is trending downward.

When researchers from MD Anderson Cancer Center looked at data from more than 393,000 patients who had been diagnosed with colorectal cancers, they found that the increasing risk for younger adults is expected to continue—specifically, within the next 14 years, about one in four rectal cancers and one in 10 colon cancers will be diagnosed in adults under age 50. In people over age 50, incidence of these cancers is declining.

WHY THE DIFFERENCE?

Even though it's still unclear why colon cancer is increasing in younger adults, possible causes include…

- **Obesity.** It's become more common for people to be overweight or obese at younger ages. People who are obese or overweight have higher risk for colorectal cancer than those of normal weight.
- **Poor diets.** A Western-style diet—high in processed foods, fast food and saturated fat, and low in fiber-rich plant foods—has been linked to higher cancer rates. People born prior to the 1970s tend to have a lower lifetime exposure to processed foods.
- **Lack of physical activity.** People who engage in routine exercise are less likely to get colorectal cancer. Exercise also increases survival in those who have already been diagnosed and treated for these cancers. Younger people seem to be less active than previous generations.

WHAT SHOULD YOU DO?

The standard guidelines (first colonoscopy at age 50…repeat every 10 years) apply only to people with an "average" risk of developing colorectal cancer. Others (such as those with a parent, sibling or child with colorectal cancer or symptoms including blood in the stool) might be advised by their doctors to have earlier/more frequent tests. *My advice…*

- **Understand your risks.** I don't recommend an across-the-board increase in routine colonoscopies. It's an expensive test with potential complications such as bleeding, perforation of the bowel or a reaction to the sedative used. We have to balance risks and benefits.

Who might need an earlier test: Patients with a strong family history of colorectal cancer (or a family history of precancerous polyps) should ask their doctors if they should be tested before age 50. If a family member was diagnosed at age 50, for example, then screening should begin 10 years earlier—at age 40. Other possible risk factors, such as obesity and/or a lack of exercise, could also warrant earlier testing in some cases.

Note: Highly sensitive fecal DNA tests may be able to identify patients who need colonoscopy before age 50, and virtual colonoscopy (which is noninvasive) is used sometimes for this purpose.

Important: If an older adult has had polyps removed, he/she should tell his children so that they can discuss earlier and/or more frequent colonoscopies with their doctors.

- **Don't ignore early symptoms.** Young people tend to disregard "minor" bowel problems, such as rectal bleeding (they often blame it on hemorrhoids)…an increase/decrease in bowel movements…or unexplained changes in the consistency of stool. Don't assume that your age means you cannot get colorectal cancer—take any bowel symptom seriously.

Example: If you've noticed rectal bleeding, ask your doctor if you should have an anal exam to rule out hemorrhoids or other causes.

Anemia is another common finding that can indicate colorectal cancer. It is most often identified during routine blood work or testing for symptoms such as fatigue.

If your doctor isn't convinced that your symptoms aren't caused by cancer, you should consider colonoscopy.

Better Colonoscopy Prep

It could be time to drop the "no eating" rule the day before having a colonoscopy, according to a recent study.

Details: Participants who were allowed to eat a small amount of low-fiber food (such as mac and cheese, yogurt and ice cream) were less hungry and their bowels were better prepared for the procedure than those restricted to the traditional clear-liquid diet.

Why: Low-fiber foods liquefy and don't stay in the bowel...and eating stimulates bowel movements, which help to clear the colon before colonoscopy.

Jason Samarasena, MD, assistant clinical professor of medicine, University of California, Irvine.

- **Eat the right foods.** The foods that make up a healthy diet—fruits, vegetables, whole grains, fatty fish, etc.—can also protect against colorectal cancers. Avoid (or limit) processed meats...charred meats (the "char" contains carcinogenic compounds)...sugary soft drinks... and fast food.

It's particularly important to get more fiber. According to the American Institute for Cancer Research, every 10 g of fiber that you consume daily can reduce the risk for colorectal cancer by 10%. Women age 51 and older need at least 21 g of fiber each day, and men in this age group require at least 30 g daily. There are lots of great sources of fiber—leafy greens, fruits, vegetables, beans, popcorn and wheat germ.

- **Be smart about exercise.** People who exercise are about 40% less likely to get colon cancer than those who are sedentary. Exercise affects insulin regulation, immune activity, inflammation and other factors that influence your risk for colorectal cancer. It also increases motility, the movement of food through the intestine. Increased motility reduces the time that potential carcinogens can affect the intestinal wall.

How much exercise? Any is better than none, although 30 to 60 minutes of moderate-intensity daily exercise—swimming, biking, fast walking, etc.—is ideal.

Lymphoma: New Treatments, New Hope

Elizabeth M. Adler, PhD. Trained in neurobiology, Dr. Adler conducted research and taught at Williams College and served as an editor at the journal *Science Signaling* and executive editor at *The Journal of General Physiology.* Following her own diagnoses with lymphoma and breast cancer, she shifted her focus from science research to science communication and cancer advocacy. She is author of *Living with Lymphoma: A Patient's Guide, 2nd Edition.*

Enormous scientific advances are radically transforming lymphoma treatment. If you're diagnosed with this cancer, your outlook is dramatically better than it would have been 20 years ago.

What you need to know about the many new weapons in the fight against lymphoma...

TREATMENT EVOLUTION

Lymphoma is a blood cancer that involves cells in the immune system called lymphocytes. There are many different kinds of lymphoma—the main types are Hodgkin's lymphoma and non-Hodgkin's lymphoma. Some grow so slowly—they are called "indolent"—that doctors may recommend a wait-and-see approach. Others are more aggressive.

Chemotherapy is the primary treatment. If a tumor is localized in one or a few lymph nodes, radiation may be used, but the cancer frequently affects more of the body.

In some cases, more advanced disease may require a combination of drugs and radiation. Surgery is rarely used for lymphoma treatment, although surgical biopsies are used in lymphoma diagnosis.

Unfortunately, the standard chemotherapy drugs—including *doxorubicin* (Adriamycin), *vincristine* (Vincasar PFS) and *cyclophosphamide* (Cytoxan)—kill not just cancer cells but also damage other rapidly dividing cells, such as those in the mouth, intestines, hair follicles and elsewhere. Side effects can include hair loss, painful sores in the mouth, increased risk for serious infection (due to a decrease in white blood cells), nausea, fatigue and "chemo brain."

The new drugs don't yet entirely replace these standard agents. But they reflect significant progress in our understanding of the biology behind lymphoma cells' growth and survival.

THE IMMUNOTHERAPY REVOLUTION

One major advance is a new era in immunotherapy, which uses the immune system's power to quell cancer. It's shown progress against different kinds of cancers and is now an important part of many lymphoma treatment plans.

Some approaches to immunotherapy rely on antibodies, compounds made by white blood cells that are one of the principal weapons of the immune system. Their function is to home in on a specific bacterium, virus or other enemy (such as a tumor cell) and tag it for destruction. In some forms of cancer immunotherapy, patients are given monoclonal antibodies synthetically cloned so that they can seek out a specific protein on the surface of malignant lymphocytes. That is, they turn your immune system against the cancer. Immunotherapy may also use other agents, including drugs, to unleash the immune system against the cancer.

The major immunotherapy drugs approved by the FDA against lymphomas and what they do...

•**Harnessing the immune system.** *Rituximab* (Rituxan), approved in 1997 against non-Hodgkin's lymphoma, is a monoclonal antibody that marks lymphoma cells for the immune system to destroy. This drug has been a major contributor to improved outcomes over the past two decades. It also inhibits tumor growth and promotes a process that signals lymphoma cells to die off.

•**Magnifying the effect.** *Obinutuzumab* (Gazyva) and *ofatumumab* (Arzerra) are two more recently approved monoclonal antibodies. Both work like rituximab but have been tweaked to modify their interactions with the immune system.

•**Opening the immune gates.** *Nivolumab* (Opdivo), another monoclonal antibody, approved in the treatment of Hodgkin's lymphoma in 2016, works to block "immune checkpoints." These are molecules that keep T-cells from attacking normal cells. Lymphoma cells can take over checkpoints for their own nefarious purposes. Monoclonal antibodies and other compounds can be used to neutralize those hijacked checkpoints, unleashing the body's immune system against the cancer.

•**Acting like a Trojan horse.** Monoclonal antibodies can also be engineered to deliver cancer-killing chemicals or radioisotopes. *Brentuximab vedotin* (Adcetris), first approved against lymphoma in 2011, recognizes a protein on the surface of certain cancerous lymphocytes and binds to it. Then it introduces a compound that only becomes toxic inside the lymphoma, causing less toxicity to other cells.

Is It Lymphoma?

The most common symptom is swollen lymph nodes—lumps, usually painless, that typically appear in the groin, in the armpit, on the neck or along the chin or collarbone. Other symptoms may include persistent fatigue, unexplained weight loss, fever, soaking night sweats, itching, coughing or trouble breathing and pain or swelling in the abdomen. A diagnosis is usually suggested by a physical exam and a profile of symptoms, followed by a biopsy. If confirmed, blood tests and radiology can hone the diagnosis.

OTHER PROMISING NEW DRUGS

Immunotherapy isn't the only new thing in lymphoma therapy...

•**Honing the attack.** Unlike conventional chemotherapy, which targets rapidly dividing cells, new "targeted chemotherapy" drugs disrupt the molecular pathways that cancer cells must maintain to survive. Two drugs—*ibrutinib* (Imbruvica) and *idelalisib* (Zydelig)—work this way.

•**Helping cancer cells die.** *Venetoclax* (Venclexta), approved in 2016 for a specific type of lymphoma (chronic lymphocytic leukemia), blocks a protein that supports tumor cell survival. Several other drugs that work similarly are now in development.

The search for new ways to treat lymphoma continues. Other innovations include antibiotics to quell infections that promote survival of certain kinds of malignant lymphocytes, and a technique that takes immune cells from the body, genetically alters them to fight cancer and returns them to circulation.

LIFE AFTER LYMPHOMA

Even when lymphoma is successfully treated, fatigue may persist. Medications such as tricyclic antidepressants, low doses of steroid and even stimulants may help in some cases. Acupuncture and, when needed, treatment for an underactive thyroid, may also help. Many people find that regular exercise is a most effective antidote.

The new drugs are approved only for specific lymphomas, often when they haven't responded to standard treatments, so which newer ones are right for you depends on your specific kind of lymphoma. Even with all these advances, survival carries no guarantee—even after five or 10 years, the disease can sometimes return. Treatment can increase the risk of other cancers, and can harm the heart and other organs. Discuss with your doctor what follow-up cancer screenings you should have, and reduce your risk for heart disease by not smoking, maintaining a health weight, eating healthfully and being active. Plus, the new immunotherapy can in some cases cause the immune system to attack other organs, leading to serious side effects, some life-threatening.

But none of that changes the fact that the prognosis for many people diagnosed with lymphoma is still better than it's ever been. It's a new day.

Music Eases Cancer Symptoms

Joke Bradt, PhD, associate professor of creative arts therapies, Drexel University, Philadelphia.

Music eases cancer symptoms, we hear from Joke Bradt, PhD. Music therapy (a personalized program of listening to or creating music designed by a music therapist) was effective in reducing pain, anxiety and fatigue in cancer patients, as well as improving their quality of life, a review of nearly 3,800 cancer patients found.

Benefits: Music may also reduce the need for anesthetics, decrease recovery time and shorten hospital stays.

To find a music therapist: Go to MusicTherapy.org.

Better Brain Cancer Treatment

Paul Brown, MD, radiation oncologist, Mayo Clinic, Rochester, Minnesota.

Stereotactic radiosurgery, which precisely targets radiation to a few small tumors, results in less damage to the patient's short-term memory and thinking skills than whole-brain radiation, a recent study of about 200 brain cancer patients concluded. The current method of radiation to the entire brain may be more appropriate for patients with large or more widespread tumors.

Hidden Cancer Risk

Nicholas Donin, MD, urologic oncology fellow, David Geffen School of Medicine at UCLA.

One in 12 cancer patients will develop a second unrelated cancer (not a metastasis of the original malignancy), a recent study of two million adults found.

Details: Those with bladder cancer were at greatest risk for an unrelated cancer—most often lung cancer.

Possible reason: People with bladder cancer often have risk factors for other types of cancer, such as smoking and exposure to workplace chemicals.

If you have any type of cancer: Be sure your doctors monitor for other cancers.

Melanoma Spreads Quickly

Molecular Cancer Therapeutics.–

Melanoma, the most dangerous form of skin cancer, quickly spreads to other parts of the body.

In development: A drug that reduces cancer-cell migration by 85% to 90%.

Bladder Cancer Alerts

Better Surgery for Bladder Cancer

A surgical technique called narrow band imaging (NBI) has been found to reduce recurrence for patients with early-stage bladder cancer. NBI's vision-enhancement technology allows surgeons to see and remove more tumors than in the traditional "white light" procedure.

Details: In a study of 965 patients, only 5.6% of those low-risk patients who underwent NBI surgery had tumors recur within 12 months, compared with 27.3% in the traditional surgery group.

Richard Bryan, MBChB, PhD, senior research fellow, University of Birmingham, UK.

Stubborn UTIs May Signal Bladder Cancer

In a recent study of more than 13,000 adults with a bladder malignancy, the cancer diagnosis took longer for those with UTIs—possibly because UTI symptoms, such as blood in the urine and frequent urination, also occur with bladder cancer. People with UTIs that don't improve after a single course of antibiotics should consult a urologist, who may recommend cystoscopy to examine the bladder.

Kyle Richards, MD, assistant professor of urology, University of Wisconsin School of Medicine and Public Health, Madison.

New Drug for Advanced Bladder Cancer

The FDA approved the immunotherapy drug *atezolizumab* (Tecentriq) for patients with metastatic urothelial carcinoma—the most common form of the disease. The drug is approved only for urothelial cancer that arises in the urinary tract. It is the first new treatment for this type of bladder cancer in more than 20 years. For that reason, the FDA approved it after only a Phase II clinical trial. Pricing, availability and insurance coverage are not yet known.

Jonathan Rosenberg, MD, a medical oncologist at Memorial Sloan Kettering Cancer Center, New York City, and leader of a study published in *The Lancet*.

Car Window Caution

Study of ultraviolet protection provided by glass in 29 cars by researchers at Boxer Wachler Vision Institute, Beverly Hills, California, published in *JAMA Ophthalmology*.

Car windows don't protect against UV rays. Windshields generally block 96% of cancer-causing UVA rays. But side windows block only 71%, on average. This could increase drivers' risk for left-eye cataracts and cancer on the left side of the face.

Self-defense: Wear sunscreen whenever you drive...consider buying special window-tint products that block 99% of UVA rays.

Melanoma Warning: Check Your Feet

Ryuhei Okuyama, MD, professor of dermatology, Shinshu University School of Medicine, Matsumoto, Japan.

When checking your skin for changes (in the size, color and/or shape of moles or for any that bleed), don't forget to examine the bottoms of your feet.

Recent finding: In a study of more than 100 melanoma patients, the deadly skin cancer was found to often be more advanced when it developed on the soles of the feet, possibly because this area is not examined as often as skin exposed to the sun.

Also: Repeated skin damage due to walking was identified as a possible trigger for melanoma on the soles of the feet.

New Drug for Advanced Melanoma

Caroline Robert, MD, PhD, is chair of dermatology, Institut de Cancérologie Gustave Roussy, Villejuif, France, and lead author of a study of 655 patients, presented at the 2016 meeting of the American Society of Clinical Oncology.

Pembrolizumab (Keytruda)—one of the medications used to treat former president

Jimmy Carter—helps the immune system fight cancer cells.

Recent finding: 40% of the patients given Keytruda were alive after three years, and 15% showed no sign of cancer. The drug is given intravenously every three weeks.

Among the more common side effects: Fatigue, itchiness, rash.

Self-Tanner Safety

Neal Schultz, MD, a dermatologist in private practice in New York City.

The only safe tan comes from a topical self-tanner. A real tan raises risk for skin cancer—especially if you use indoor ultraviolet tanning beds. And so-called tanning pills should never be used. They are not FDA-approved and can cause liver and retinal damage.

Most self-tanning products contain dihydroxyacetone (DHA), a nontoxic chemical that darkens the top layer of skin. Self-tanners are available as creams, lotions, sprays or wipes. For best results, exfoliate with lotion or pads containing 10% glycolic acid for three days before applying the self-tanner. This will help even out the top layer of skin and provide better absorption of DHA. If you're using a spray, cover your nose and mouth to avoid ingesting it.

Your tan should last for a week or so before it naturally fades. You will still need to use broad-spectrum sunscreen when outdoors, since faux tans will not protect your skin.

The Truth About Sunshine

Michael F. Holick, PhD, MD, a professor of medicine, physiology and biophysics at Boston University School of Medicine, where he directs the Bone Health Care Clinic and the Heliotherapy, Light and Skin Research Center. He is a leading expert on vitamin D and its link to osteoporosis, cancer and other diseases. Dr. Holick is author of *The Vitamin D Solution: A 3-Step Strategy to Cure Our Most Common Health Problems.*

It's a gorgeous summer morning, so you step outside to enjoy a touch of sun while sipping your morning coffee. But wait...what about sunscreen?

According to some medical organizations, any sun exposure is a serious risk factor for melanoma and other skin cancers. For this reason, Americans often are advised to get vitamin D only from foods and/or supplements. But not all medical experts agree with that advice.

To get a different perspective, we spoke with Michael F. Holick, PhD, MD, a leading expert on vitamin D and a firm believer that avoiding all sunshine can pose health risks that may be worse than those from sensible sun exposure.

His advice on finding the sweet spot for just the right amount of sun exposure...

A COMMON DEFICIENCY

Vitamin D is one of the most common nutrition deficiencies in the US. More than half of older adults are deficient—in part because the body's ability to synthesize vitamin D from sunlight declines with age.

Those with dark skin fare worst: Research has found that 40% of Hispanics and a staggering 84% of African-Americans over age 50 were vitamin D deficient.

Only a few foods (such as salmon, sun-dried mushrooms, cod-liver oil and, to a much lesser extent, egg yolks) contain vitamin D, so most Americans rely on fortified foods (such as milk and some breakfast cereals). Taking a vitamin D supplement helps, but it isn't the same as sunshine. The vitamin D produced by sunshine enters the bloodstream slowly and maintains its health-promoting biological activity for at least twice as long as supplemental D.

DANGERS OF LOW VITAMIN D

Humans have evolved to depend on sunshine. So what happens when you never go outside without wearing sunscreen—or rarely go outside at all? When used properly, a sunscreen with an SPF of 30 reduces vitamin D production by 97%. *Important health risks now being linked to low vitamin D levels...*

- **Multiple sclerosis.** You're five times more likely to get this disease if you live in North America or Europe than in the tropics. In the US, prevalence of this disease in northern states such as Maine, Minnesota and Washington is nearly double that found in sunnier areas.

• **Cancer.** There isn't conclusive proof that people with low vitamin D have an increased risk for cancer. But there's persuasive evidence from population and observational studies that people with sufficient vitamin D are 30% to 50% less likely to develop breast, colorectal or other cancers than those with vitamin D deficiencies.

• **Heart disease.** Vitamin D deficiency is associated with increased heart attack risk. People who live in sunny climates are also less likely to have high blood pressure.

Other health problems linked to vitamin D deficiency include osteoporosis, diabetes and depression.

THE REAL CANCER RISK

Dermatologists have long used the "C" word to warn people about the sun. It's true that chronic sun exposure increases one's risk for basal and squamous cell carcinomas.

While these "nonmelanoma" skin cancers are a significant health problem, they're fortunately among the easiest to cure and are rarely fatal. Meanwhile, the noncancer health risks from low vitamin D, such as those described earlier, generally outweigh the risks from these cancers.

Melanoma is another story. A frequently fatal cancer that results in some 10,000 deaths in the US each year, melanoma is strongly linked to sunburns. People who get only short-term and occasional sun exposure don't face the same risk. In addition, melanoma often develops on parts of the body with little (or no) sun exposure, such as the buttocks.

A SENSIBLE COMPROMISE

Let me be clear: I do not recommend sunbathing or tanning. I advise most adults to get just enough sun (without sunscreen) to help produce a vitamin D blood level of at least 30 ng/mL, as measured by a 25-hydroxy vitamin D blood test. The rest of the time, you should use sunscreen and wear a hat and other protective clothing. *My approach...*

• **Follow the "no sunburn" rule.** The amount of vitamin D produced by your body depends on such factors as the season, time of day, your geographic location and your pigmentation. I advise my patients to spend about one-half the time in the sun that it would ordinarily take them to get a mild sunburn. This should be done between 10 am and 3 pm (when the angle of the sun's rays maximizes vitamin D production).

During this time, expose your arms and legs to the sun (without sunscreen). Together, your limbs account for about half of your body's surface area. Exposing them to sun (with the rest of your body covered) should gradually increase your vitamin D level over four to eight weeks and then stabilize it.

• **Keep close track of the time.** While one's sun "dose" is highly individual, people with dark skin will usually be able to expose their skin to sunshine for up to 30 minutes, three times a week. If you're fair, five to 10 minutes is likely enough.

• **Use sunscreen the rest of the time.** I recommend using sunscreen with an SPF 30 rating whenever you're not getting your controlled sun dose.

Important: Be sure to use sunscreen on your face anytime you're outdoors. Very little vitamin D is produced via sun exposure to your face... and too much sun on your face, which gets sun whenever you're outdoors, will cause wrinkles and increase your risk for skin cancer.

• **Take a supplement.** Even if you enjoy regular "sun sessions," there will be times (particularly in the winter) when your body won't produce enough vitamin D. To ensure consistent adequate levels of vitamin D, a supplement (typically 2,000 IU daily for adults) will make up the difference. To determine your optimal dose of a vitamin D supplement, ask your doctor for advice. He/she may recommend a 25-hydroxy vitamin D blood test to check your body's vitamin D level.

Important: If you have had skin cancer or are at increased risk (due, for example, to family history)...or have a medical condition or take medication that increases your sun sensitivity, ask your doctor about appropriate sun exposure and the best ways to maintain adequate vitamin D levels.

Get the Very Best Cancer Care

Barrie R. Cassileth, PhD, the former Laurance S. Rockefeller Chair and chief of the integrative medicine department at Memorial Sloan Kettering Cancer Center in New York City. She is a founding member of the Advisory Council to the National Institutes of Health Office of Alternative Medicine and the founding president of the Society of Integrative Oncology. She is also the author of *Survivorship: Living Well During and After Cancer.*

A cancer diagnosis is always fraught with fear and anxiety—not to mention nagging questions about the best possible treatments.

Bridging the gap: While surgery, chemotherapy and radiation have long been the mainstay treatments for cancer, major cancer centers throughout the US now offer a variety of additional "complementary" therapies that help patients cope with a wide range of cancer-related problems.

Latest development: Recent studies continue to be added to the growing body of evidence supporting the use of such nondrug and nonsurgical therapies, which are used along with conventional cancer treatment.

LOOK FOR PROVEN BENEFITS

Only a small number of complementary therapies have been thoroughly tested with randomized, placebo-controlled clinical trials—the gold standard of scientific research. Some of these approaches have now been proven to work.

Common cancer symptoms that can be relieved with complementary approaches—some services may be covered by insurance, so check with your health insurer...

- **Less nausea.** Nausea and/or vomiting are among the most common symptoms cancer patients have—and among the most feared. Antinausea medications help, but they're not a perfect solution. That's why they're sometimes used in tandem with acupuncture, a complementary therapy that has been shown to be particularly effective.

Scientific evidence: When acupuncture was tested in a group of breast cancer patients being treated with a form of chemotherapy that's notorious for causing nausea, those who were given acupuncture for five days had one-third fewer episodes of nausea than those who were treated only with medications that were used for nausea, such as *lorazepam* and *diphenhydramine.* Self-acupressure, in which patients merely press on certain points, such as the PC6 point on the wrist (without using needles), can also help.

To find the PC6 point: Turn your hand so your palm is facing up and locate the area, which is between the tendons three finger widths from the base of the wrist. Massage the area for four to five seconds...or longer, as needed.

- **Pain relief.** Both gentle massage and acupuncture can reduce the pain that's caused by cancer (such as bone cancer) and cancer treatments (such as radiation)—and sometimes allow patients to take lower doses of medication, which can help reduce troubling side effects, including constipation.

Scientific evidence: A study that looked at nearly 1,300 cancer patients found that massage improved their pain scores by 40%...and the improvements lasted for hours and sometimes days after the massage.

Imaging studies show that acupuncture also helps by deactivating brain areas that are involved in pain perception. In one study, patients with chronic cancer pain were treated with either auricular acupuncture (needles placed in the ear) or with sham treatments. After two months, patients in the acupuncture group reported reductions in pain intensity of 36% versus 2% in the placebo group.

- **Less fatigue.** Only about 10% of cancer patients are physically active during treatment. But the vast majority can safely exercise before, during and after treatments...and exercise is among the best ways to reduce treatment-related fatigue.

Scientific evidence: When researchers at the University of Connecticut analyzed 44 studies focusing on patients with cancer-related fatigue, they found that those who exercised had more energy than those who were sedentary.

Any form of exercise seems to help. Yoga that focuses on gentle postures and breathing is good because it's easy on the body and has been shown to reduce anxiety and other stress-related symptoms.

Bonus: Cancer patients who exercise tend to live longer than those who don't stay active. A study of more than 900 breast cancer patients found that those who engaged in brisk walking for two and a half hours a week—the same level of exercise that's recommended for the general population—were 67% less likely to die during the nine-year study period than those who were sedentary.

- **Fewer hot flashes.** Both men and women who have hormone-dependent cancers (such as breast and prostate cancers) often experience hot flashes when they're given hormone-based treatments. Once again, acupuncture seems to help.

Scientific evidence: One study found that nearly 90% of patients with breast or prostate cancers who were given acupuncture had a reduction in hot flashes of nearly 50% that lasted at least three months.

HOW TO STAY SAFE

Virtually all oncologists and respected cancer centers in the US now support the use of complementary therapies, such as acupuncture and massage, to help cancer patients cope with nausea, pain, anxiety and other symptoms. These and other complementary therapies are used in addition to conventional treatments.

To find an evidence-based complementary oncology program: Look for a comprehensive cancer center at the National Cancer Institute's website, Cancer.gov/research/nci-role/cancer-centers/find.

Very important: When seeking complementary care, it's vital that the practitioner (including massage therapists, acupuncturists, etc.) be properly trained to work with cancer patients. Getting therapy at a comprehensive cancer center helps ensure that.

Also crucial: Cancer patients should always talk to their doctors before taking any supplements (herbs, vitamins, etc.). They can sometimes interfere with chemotherapy and other cancer treatments. For more on specific supplements, go to Memorial Sloan Kettering's website, MSKCC.org/aboutherbs.

New Drug Combo Fights Advanced Multiple Myeloma

S. Vincent Rajkumar, MD, chair of the Eastern Cooperative Oncology Group Myeloma Committee at the Mayo Clinic, Rochester, Minnesota.

When patients already receiving a standard two-drug treatment were also given the drug *daratumumab*, 43% had a complete response—there was no cancer left. That compared with 19% who had only the standard two-drug treatment. The success of the drug trio is significant because the disease can be controlled for a sustained period with this new regimen.

Talk Therapy Fights "Chemo Brain"

Study of 47 breast cancer survivors by researchers at Eastern Maine Medical Center, Bangor, and Lafayette Family Center, Brewer, Maine, published in *Cancer.*

About half of patients who get chemotherapy develop chemo brain, which causes them to have trouble following conversations or remembering steps needed to complete a project. Although medically considered mild, this can have a significant impact on personal and professional activities. In a small study, a specially developed form of cognitive-behavioral therapy called memory and attention adaptation training (MAAT) led to reduced memory problems and better processing speed. Patients who received MAAT also reported less anxiety about mental issues two months after the sessions ended.

CHAPTER 5

Consumer Health Alerts

13 Secrets Restaurants Don't Want You to Know

Eating out means trusting strangers to prepare and handle your food. Usually that trust is well-placed—but at times, the hectic pace and financial pressures facing restaurants result in corners being cut in ways that could jeopardize your enjoyment of the meal...or even jeopardize your health. *We asked a veteran waiter to share what restaurants don't want you to know...*

FOOD QUALITY AND SAFETY

•**Seafood stew, soup and pasta "specials" often feature fish that's too old to serve any other way.** Restaurants do not like to throw away expensive ingredients. When seafood is no longer fresh enough to serve on its own, it might be chopped up and served in a stew, soup or pasta dish, where sauces and other bold flavors can be used to hide its age. This can happen with meat and poultry, too, but it's most common with seafood, which has an especially short shelf life.

Tip from the waiter: It's generally OK to order a seafood stew, soup or pasta dish if it is on the regular menu. But when these are listed as specials, the odds are high that the restaurant is trying to sell past-its-prime seafood.

•**Restaurant menus rarely are cleaned.** Responsible restaurants take cleanliness very seriously. Almost everything in the kitchen and dining room is cleaned regularly—except the menus. At most restaurants, menus are rarely, if ever, wiped down, even though they are handled by many people and occasionally dropped on the floor.

Tip from the waiter: Wash your hands after you've ordered and handed your menu back to the waiter.

Darron Cardosa, who has more than 25 years of experience waiting tables in the New York City area. He is author of *The Bitchy Waiter: Tales, Tips & Trials from a Life in Food Service.* TheBitchyWaiter.com

•Complimentary bread or chips might have been served to other tables before yours. A Mexican restaurant in Michigan recently received negative press when it was caught taking chips and salsa that were not consumed at one table and serving them to a second table. That restaurant is far from alone—it is not uncommon for uneaten slices of complimentary bread to find their way onto multiple tables rather than get thrown away. And even restaurants that hold themselves to a very high standard usually send out the butter packages that accompany bread to table after table until they are used.

Tip from the waiter: It might be worth skipping complimentary premeal items such as bread and chips unless the restaurant has an open area where you can watch these items being prepared specifically for you.

•The week following an extended power failure might be the wrong time to eat out. Cash-strapped restaurants often cannot afford to throw away everything that was in their fridges and freezers after power outages, so ingredients may no longer be as fresh as they should be.

Tip from the waiter: If you want to eat out following a long power failure, choose a restaurant in a neighboring area that did not lose its power.

•You might not want to eat your leftovers if you saw how they were put into to-go containers. This task might be delegated to a busboy who has little training in hygienic food handling...or it might be done by a harried server who uses the same spoon to transfer multiple customers' partially eaten meals.

Tip from the waiter: Ask your server to bring to-go containers to your table, and then transfer your leftovers yourself.

•Your dessert might not be fresh even if the menu says desserts are "made fresh in house every day." Typically this means that one or two of the dessert options are made fresh each day, while others remain from earlier days.

Tip from the waiter: Before choosing a dessert, ask your server which desserts were made that day. Be leery of any dessert that features "chocolate crumble" or "chocolate crunchies" sprinkled on top. That chocolate topping might have been made by breaking apart stale chocolate cake, cookies or brownies that didn't sell in their original form.

BILLING AND SERVICE

•Billing mistakes are common—and rarely spotted. Servers are responsible for multiple tables at the same time—and billing mistakes are inevitable. But patrons rarely catch the mistakes, in part because roughly half of all restaurant customers do not bother to check their bills at all.

Tip from the waiter: If you do not want to take the time to check your bill closely, at least do a quick count to confirm that there are not more drinks, appetizers or entrées listed than you ordered. If at lunch, also make sure that you were charged lunch prices and not dinner prices for entrées, a particularly common billing error.

•The last tables seated often receive less-than-stellar service—but you can be treated better. If you walk into a restaurant shortly before its closing time, there's a good chance that both your server and the kitchen staff will be more focused on getting you out the door than on providing an enjoyable meal.

Tip from the waiter: Say something that sends a message to your server that you understand time is an issue, such as, "Don't worry, we won't order dessert"...and/or, "What can the kitchen prepare quickly?" This shows respect for the restaurant employees' priorities, greatly increasing the odds that they will show you respect in the form of a quality dining experience.

•Chefs are sick of the gluten-free trend. Restaurant employees usually are sympathetic when customers must make special requests because of allergies or other serious health concerns—but they hate it when they have to adjust dishes for customers who seem to be jumping on dietary fads. Gluten-free is the most prominent dietary fad at the moment, so servers and chefs might label you an annoyance if you ask to have a dish modified for a gluten-free diet—which could lead to a subpar dining experience.

Tip from the waiter: If you truly cannot consume gluten for health reasons—for example, you have celiac disease—preface your order with words to the effect of, "I know you have to deal with a lot of gluten-free requests these days, but I really am gluten-intolerant."

BEVERAGES

•**Wine sold by the glass could come from a bottle that has been open for days.** It even could come from a bottle that was originally ordered by another patron but rejected because that customer didn't like it.

Tip from the waiter: Order wine by the bottle, not by the glass, when possible. If you want only a single glass, boost the odds that it was opened recently by choosing something that's likely to be ordered often, such as the "house wine."

•**Your regular coffee actually might be decaf if closing time is near.** The regular coffeepot often is one of the first things emptied and cleaned by the restaurant staff at the end of the day. If you order a regular coffee after this has occurred, there's a good chance that you'll be given decaf with no mention of the substitution. (The reverse—receiving regular after ordering decaf—is much less common in well-run restaurants because the staff would not want to risk giving caffeine to a customer who, for example, has a heart condition.)

Tip from the waiter: If you really need a cup of regular coffee after a restaurant meal that concludes late in the evening—for example, if you're feeling drowsy and need to drive home—explain that to your waiter. He may be able to have a cup of regular coffee made for you. Or order cappuccino, which is typically made in an espresso machine one cup at a time.

•**Your water might not be as pure as you are told.** Some restaurants serve only filtered water...and some patrons pay extra for bottled water. But if there is ice in the water, that ice is almost certainly made from unfiltered tap water. Restaurant ice makers rarely have filters.

Tip from the waiter: If water purity is important to you, skip the ice.

•**Drink garnishes sometimes are germy or old.** That lemon or lime slice in your drink might have been cut hours earlier and then left to sit in an open, unrefrigerated container where numerous restaurant employees pick out pieces with their bare hands. Restaurants may have policies requiring the use of tongs for grabbing these garnishes, but rushed servers and bartenders frequently skip that.

Tip from the waiter: Tell your server to "hold the lemon" when you order a drink.

Rice Has Arsenic: How to Cook It Clean

Andy Meharg, PhD, professor and chair of plant and soil sciences, The Institute for Global Food Security, Queen's University Belfast, Northern Ireland. He tested methods of cooking rice for the BBC program *Trust Me, I'm a Doctor.*

Most of us eat rice, but most of us don't know that rice is the leading food source of arsenic, an element that occurs naturally in air, soil and water—and from contamination from industrial waste, pesticides and fertilizers.

The arsenic content of rice varies by where it is grown. For example, rice grown in California tends to have less arsenic than rice grown in Arkansas, Louisiana, Missouri and Texas. White rice tends to have less arsenic than brown rice.

Regular exposure to inorganic arsenic, the primary form of arsenic in rice grain, is linked to an increased risk for bladder, lung and skin cancers, heart disease and type 2 diabetes.

Good news: Cooking rice a certain way can eliminate most of the arsenic.

Recent study: Scientists from Queen's University Belfast tested three different methods of cooking rice to determine how they affected levels of arsenic.

***METHOD #1:* Researchers used a ratio of two parts water to one part rice, cooking the rice until all the water was either absorbed or steamed out.**

Result: Most of the arsenic still was present in the rice after cooking.

***METHOD #2:* Rice was cooked with five parts water to one part rice.** After cooking, excess water was drained off, and then the rice was rinsed under a running tap until the water ran clear.

Result: Arsenic was reduced by 50% compared with method #1.

***METHOD #3:* The rice was soaked in water overnight at room temperature.** It then was rinsed under a running tap until the water ran clear, drained and transferred to a saucepan with a ratio of five parts water to one part rice. The rice was then cooked and drained.

Result: Arsenic was reduced by up to 82% compared with method #1.

Bottom line: Use method #3.

Cooking instructions: Bring rice and water to a rapid boil over high heat, uncovered—this takes seven to eight minutes. Turn the heat down to medium-high. Boil white rice 10 minutes more. Boil brown rice 20 minutes more. Drain.

What to Do for Waxy Apples

Laura Cipullo, RD, CDN, a nutritionist in New York City. LauraCipullo.com

Is the wax on apples harmful? Sometimes it seems to remain even after apples are washed.

Apples have a natural waxy layer made of fatty substances and pectin. This natural protective layer helps maintain the apple's firmness and water content. Concerns about this layer arise when food companies apply an additional wax known as carnauba wax or shellac after apples have been washed and are set to transport. The additional wax is deemed safe by the FDA and helps to extend the shelf life of the fruit by cutting down on mold growth and moisture loss, but some apple skins may still contain harmful pesticides.

So what should you do? Clean your apples with a brush and a solution of one-quarter cup vinegar and three-quarters cup water. This practice is also good for organic apples, which have the least amount of added wax and pesticides but may be exposed to pollutants in the air.

OK to Refreeze Thawed Food?

You can refreeze food that has been thawed as long as the food was thawed safely in a refrigerator. If you put it in cold water or the microwave to thaw, you must cook the food before refreezing. As perishable foods begin to thaw at temperatures above 40°F, bacteria begin to multiply. Ground meat, poultry and seafood should remain safe in the refrigerator for one to three days after removing it from the freezer. Pork or beef roasts, chops and steaks are OK generally for three to five days.

Julie Garden-Robinson, PhD, RD, professor of nutrition and food safety, North Dakota State University, Fargo.

Unexpected Choking Danger: Soft Foods

Becky Turpin, director of home and community safety at the National Safety Council, a nonprofit organization based in Itasca, Illinois. She previously served as the adult injury prevention coordinator at University of Wisconsin Hospital and Clinics. NSC.org

A Connecticut woman choked on pancakes during a pancake-eating contest in April 2017 and died three days later. Around the same time, a Colorado man choked to death during a doughnut-eating challenge. It probably comes as no surprise that speed-eating contests are dangerous—but few people realize that soft foods such as pancakes and doughnuts pose any choking risk at all.

In fact, studies have found that soft baked goods are the second-most common cause of choking deaths, trailing only meat. Because soft foods seem so harmless, people sometimes take dangerously large bites and/or fail to chew sufficiently before swallowing. And if people drink beverages while they still have soft baked foods in their mouths or throats, these items can absorb the fluid and expand, potentially blocking airways. White bread and other baked goods made with white flour are particularly prone to this.

Peanut butter is another soft food that poses a major choking hazard. It's so thick and sticky that it can become lodged in the throat.

Be very careful with soft foods if…

•**You are in your 70s or older.** People produce less saliva as they age, greatly increasing their risk of choking. That's a major reason why most people who choke to death are age 75 or older.

•**You are taking a medication that lists dry mouth among its side effects.** This is a side effect of many medications.

•**You are drinking alcohol and/or talking while eating.** Intoxication and conversation increase choking risks—especially when combined.

info If someone starts choking, perform the Heimlich maneuver on him/her. For instructions, go to NSC.org and search "Choking Prevention and Rescue Tips."

Toxins in Your Fast-Food Packaging?

Laurel Schaider, PhD, environmental chemist, Silent Spring Institute, Newton, Massachussets.

Kenneth Spaeth, MD, MPH., chief, occupational and environmental medicine, Northwell Health, Great Neck, New York.

Foodservice Packaging Institute, statement.

Environmental Science & Technology.

Many grease-resistant fast-food wrappers and boxes contain potentially harmful chemicals that can leach into food, a recent study contends.

Testing on more than 400 samples from restaurants nationwide revealed that nearly half of fast-food wrappers and one out of five paperboard food boxes contained detectable levels of fluorine, said lead researcher Laurel Schaider, PhD. She's an environmental chemist at the Silent Spring Institute in Newton, Massachusetts.

Previous studies have linked some fluorinated chemicals such as perfluorooctanoic acid (PFOA) and perfluorooctanesulfonic acid (PFOS) to kidney and testicular cancer, low birth weight, thyroid disease, decreased sperm quality, pregnancy-induced high blood pressure, and immune system problems in children, the study authors said in background notes.

As a class, fluorinated chemicals are referred to as per- and polyfluoroalkyl substances (PFASs). They are used in a wide range of products, including carpeting, upholstery, floor waxes and outdoor apparel, the study authors said.

Major US manufacturers voluntarily phased out PFOA and PFOS for most uses starting in 2011, but other countries still produce them. These study results show that fluorinated chemicals are still widely present in food packaging, the authors said.

DIFFICULT TO IDENTIFY

"One of the challenges in avoiding exposure is you can't tell by looking at a wrapper whether it contains fluorine," Dr. Schaider said. "We can choose not to purchase a stain-resistant carpet or a stain-resistant coating on our furniture. But it's difficult for a consumer to choose food packaging that doesn't have fluorinated chemicals."

Some fast-food packaging is treated with PFASs to make the wrappers and boxes grease-resistant, Dr. Schaider said.

It has been found that PFASs can leach into food from packaging, Dr. Schaider said. Heat and grease appear to help the chemicals migrate into food, she added.

INDUSTRY RESPONSE

According to the Foodservice Packaging Institute, only "short-chain" fluorinated chemicals are still used in fast-food packaging. The "short-chain" chemicals "have been rigorously reviewed by the U.S. Food and Drug Administration and found to be safe for their intended use," the industry group said in a statement.

PFOA and PFOS are "long-chain" chemicals, and have been phased out, the institute said. "Today's food service packaging is no longer treated with 'long-chain' fluorochemicals, and instead use FDA-approved 'short-chain' fluorochemicals or even newer barrier coatings, which are free of any fluorochemicals," the group added.

STUDY DETAILS

For the recent study, the researchers said they gathered hundreds of samples from 27 fast-food chains in five metropolitan areas across the United States. They used particle-induced gamma-ray emission (PIGE) spectroscopy to analyze the samples for fluorine, Dr. Schaider said.

"Paper normally doesn't contain much fluorine, so we reasoned this would be a method of detecting the presence of PFASs," Dr. Schaider said.

The research team said it found that 46% of paper wrappers and 20% of paperboard box samples for foods like pizza and fries contained fluorine. The team also tested paper cups used for hot and cold beverages, but found no significant levels of fluorine.

Paper wrapper samples containing fluorinated chemicals ranged from about 38% of sandwich/burger wrappers up to about 57% of wrappers used for desserts, breads and Tex-Mex foods, the study authors said.

To validate their analysis, the researchers conducted a more detailed study on a subset of 20 samples, Dr. Schaider said.

In general, samples that were high in fluorine also contained PFASs. Six of the samples also contained a long-chain PFOA, even though the chemical is no longer widely used because of health hazards.

WHY ARE BANNED SUBSTANCES APPEARING?

PFOA could be present in these wrappers because recycled paper was used in their manufacture, Dr. Schaider said—an indication of how difficult it is to remove these chemicals from the environment.

Studies have shown that PFASs from consumer products accumulate in landfills and can migrate into groundwater, Dr. Schaider said. Fluorinated chemicals also are allowed in compostable food packaging.

"It seems incompatible to have these chemicals that never break down in paper that we want to compost," Dr. Schaider said.

LONG-TERM DAMAGE FROM FAST-FOOD WRAPPERS

There is particular concern regarding the long-term effects of these chemicals on children, said a chemical exposure specialist who wasn't involved in the study.

Fluorinated chemicals have been found in umbilical cord blood, suggesting that fetuses are exposed to PFASs, said Kenneth Spaeth, MD, chief of occupational and environmental medicine for Northwell Health in Great Neck, New York.

Approximately one-third of US children consume fast food every day, the study authors noted.

"With chemicals like this, exposure begins in utero and continues once we're born through childhood and into adulthood," said Dr. Spaeth. "That has real potential ramifications in terms of our health."

WHAT CONSUMERS CAN DO

It's unlikely that new regulations will be adopted to remove PFASs from products, Dr. Spaeth added. Instead, he recommended public pressure as a means for future change.

"A lot of products have become BPA-free, not because they were forced to but because of public concern and public outcry," he said, referring to Bisphenol A, an estrogen-imitating chemical used in plastics. "If consumers are waiting for public oversight, I don't think it's going to happen."

The study was published in the journal *Environmental Science & Technology.*

info For more about PFASs, visit the U.S. Agency for Toxic Substances and Disease Registry at https://www.atsdr.cdc.gov/pfc/health_effects_pfcs.html.

The Extra-Virgin Olive Oil Hoax

Larry Olmsted, author of *Real Food, Fake Food: Why You Don't Know What You're Eating & What You Can Do About It.* Based in Hartland, Vermont, he also writes the "Great American Bites" column for *USA Today.* RealFoodFakeFood.com

The "extra-virgin olive oil" in your kitchen is probably not extra-virgin at all. To qualify as extra-virgin, olive oil is supposed to be subjected to minimal processing and be made exclusively from fresh, high-quality olives. But a

Discount Coupons for Fresh Produce

SavingStar.com/coupons is free to join and gives cash back for items bought at major grocery chains. Earthbound Farm (EBFarm.com) offers recipes and coupons when you sign up for the Organic Bound guide. FreshExpress.com offers coupons if you sign up for the company's newsletter. Target occasionally offers produce coupons, especially through its mobile Cartwheel app, Cartwheel.Target.com (*recent example*: 25% off all produce). Organic Girl (ILoveOrganicGirl.com) offers coupons and promotions when you join its e-mail list.

MoneyTalksNews.com

highly publicized research report from the Olive Center at University of California, Davis, found that 69% of the olive oil sold as "extra-virgin" in the US does not meet those standards. The flavor of these fakes typically falls well short of the real thing. Also, a diluted or heavily processed olive oil might not provide the same cancer- and heart disease–fighting benefits of a true extra-virgin olive oil.

Producers get away with selling fake extra-virgin olive oil because the US government does little to enforce olive oil standards...and because most Americans have never tasted a true high-quality, extra-virgin olive oil, which makes it difficult to spot fakes.

What to do: Buy from trustworthy brands, such as California Olive Ranch (from $12.59 for a 500-ml bottle, CaliforniaOliveRanch.com)...Cobram Estate (from $12.99 for a 375-ml bottle, CobramEstate.com)...Whole Foods' 365 Everyday Value brand (from $6.99 for a 500-ml bottle)...and Oro Bailén (often $20 or more for a 500-ml bottle, OroBailen.com).

Or buy from an importer or a distributor of high-quality olive oils, such as Oliviers & Co. (OliviersAndCo.com) and Zingerman's (Zingermans.com). Alternately, you could join the Fresh-Pressed Olive Oil Club and receive three bottles of stellar olive oil four times a year ($99 per quarter for three 250-ml bottles, FreshPressedOliveOil.com).

Other good bets include any US-produced olive oil that has the "COOC" seal of the California Olive Oil Council on its label...or any Italian olive oil that says "100% Qualità Italiana." Extra-virgin olive oil produced in Australia is a reasonable choice, too—Australia enforces the world's strictest extra-virgin olive oil standards.

Note: To read research results from the University of California, Davis, go to OliveCenter.UCDavis.edu and click on "Research" and then "Reports."

New Dangers for Supplement Users

Mark A. Moyad, MD, MPH, the Jenkins/Pokempner director of complementary and alternative medicine at the University of Michigan Medical Center, department of urology, in Ann Arbor. He is the primary author of more than 150 medical journal articles and author, with Janet Lee, of *The Supplement Handbook*.

By now, you know that the supplements you pop to stay healthy may turn harmful if you also take certain prescription and/or over-the-counter medications.

What you may not realize: Scientists are still uncovering what the interactions are—and just how dangerous they can be. *What you need to know to stay safe...*

THE LATEST FINDINGS

When researchers at the University of Minnesota recently looked at data from more than 23 million scientific studies, they identified thousands of potential drug–supplement interactions—including some that have only recently been recognized.*

The danger zone: Some supplements increase drug levels by slowing their breakdown in the body. Some accelerate drug metabolism/breakdown and reduce the desired effects.

*To search for drug–supplement interactions, go to the National Library of Medicine's website NLM.nih.gov/medlineplus/druginfo...or the fee-based Natural Medicines Comprehensive Database, NaturalDatabase.com.

Other interactions are additive: Drugs and supplements can act on similar pathways in the body and increase the overall effects—and the risk for side effects.

PARTICULARLY RISKY

In the meta-analysis mentioned above, researchers discovered that echinacea, a popular herbal remedy for colds and other infections, reduced the activity of *exemestane* (Aromasin), a drug used for breast cancer. In fact, echinacea interferes with a number of chemotherapy drugs, including cyclophosphamide and fluorouracil. *Other drug–supplement interactions*...

•**Iodine.** Most Americans get enough iodine from salt, seafood, whole grains and other foods. But some people take supplements because they believe that extra iodine will improve thyroid health. The truth is, the supplement only helps if there's a true iodine deficiency.

Serious interaction: *Levothyroxine* (Synthroid and Levoxyl), a synthetic form of thyroid hormone that treats low thyroid (hypothyroidism). High doses of supplemental iodine—300 micrograms (mcg) or more—can interfere with thyroid function. When this happens, a dose of levothyroxine that was previously effective can suddenly stop working.

My advice: Do not take supplemental iodine unless you have been shown (via urine or blood tests) to be deficient, and your doctor OKs it. Supplements often contain 500 mcg to 1,000 mcg of iodine—far more than the recommended daily allowance of 150 mcg.

Helpful: Be cautious when taking any supplement that's dosed in micrograms. Anything that's measured in millionths of a gram requires careful minimal dosing.

•**Fish oil.** It has a number of proven benefits—lowering very high triglycerides (500 mg/dL and above)...improving pain from rheumatoid arthritis...slowing the progression of lupus...and even easing mild-to-moderate depression.

Serious interactions: All blood thinners—including not only the popular prescription blood thinner *warfarin* and newer blood thinners, such as Eliquis and Xarelto, but also over-the-counter drugs with blood-thinning effects, including nonsteroidal anti-inflammatory drugs (NSAIDs) such as aspirin and *ibuprofen* (Motrin).

Fish oil has a blood-thinning effect because it inhibits the ability of platelets to stick together and form clots. This can be beneficial since blood clots in the arteries are the main cause of heart attacks. But combining fish oil with other blood thinners can cause excess bleeding during surgery or dental procedures...or from wounds or internal injuries (such as ulcers).

My advice: Ask your doctor if you can take fish oil along with your usual blood thinner. The blood-thinning effects of fish oil are dose-dependent—you're less likely to have problems at typical doses of, say, 2,000 mg or less daily.

Don't make this mistake: If you're taking fish oil for high cholesterol, stop. A lot of my patients have been told that it lowers LDL "bad" cholesterol. Not true. At doses of 1,000 mg or more, it can actually raise LDL five to 10 points or more.

•**GABA (gamma-aminobutyric acid).** It's a neurotransmitter that's present in the brain and other parts of the body. In supplement form, it has a calming effect and is thought to lower cortisol, the body's main stress hormone.

Serious interactions: Sedative drugs, including opioids (such as codeine) and antianxiety medications, such as *lorazepam* (Ativan) or *alprazolam* (Xanax). Taking these drugs with GABA can cause excessive sedation.

My advice: Never combine sedatives—whether they're "natural" or pharmaceutical—without checking with your doctor.

•**St. John's wort.** This herbal supplement has been shown to be as effective as prescription antidepressants in treating mild-to-moderate depression—and with fewer side effects.

However, when combined with SSRI (selective serotonin reuptake inhibitor) antidepressants, such as *escitalopram* (Lexapro) or *paroxetine* (Paxil), or other types of antidepressants, the supplement can cause medication-induced serotonin syndrome. This dangerous "overdose" of serotonin, a neurotransmitter that affects mood, can cause swings in blood pressure and heart rate, along with such symptoms as heavy sweating, diarrhea and extreme agitation. But that's not all.

Serious interactions: An increasing body of evidence shows that St. John's wort can interact with many other prescription drugs, including warfarin, *digoxin* and other heart medications, antiseizure drugs, certain cancer drugs and birth control pills. You must let your doctor know if you're taking St. John's wort.

•**L-arginine.** L-arginine increases blood levels of nitric oxide, a naturally occurring molecule that dilates blood vessels and can reduce blood pressure by 20 points or more. Some men take it for erectile dysfunction (ED).

Serious interactions: L-arginine can interact with all prescription blood pressure medications, causing blood pressure to drop to dangerously low levels, resulting in dizziness, blurred vision or even a loss of consciousness. The supplement can also cause dangerous drops in blood pressure in men taking ED medication.

My advice: Always check with your doctor before taking a blood pressure drug or ED medication with L-arginine.

Lawn Mower Warning

Wilko Grolman, MD, PhD, professor of otolaryngology, University Medical Center Utrecht, the Netherlands.

Lawn mowers, leaf blowers and loud music can cause temporary hearing loss that lasts up to several hours and may even lead to permanent hearing loss.

Research research: When volunteers wore earplugs during a four-hour 100-decibel concert, only 8% had temporary hearing loss, compared with 42% who didn't wear earplugs. And 12% of those who wore earplugs reported developing chronic tinnitus (ringing in the ears) compared with 40% of those who didn't wear them.

Your Smoke Alarm Might Not Be Working

Susan McKelvey, communications manager for the National Fire Protection Association (NFPA), a nonprofit organization based in Quincy, Massachusetts, that has been working to eliminate fire deaths since 1896. NFPA.org

Your smoke alarms and carbon monoxide detectors might not be working properly—even if you never let their batteries run out or they are hardwired into your home's electrical system. That's because sensors in these alarms can fail over time.

To stay safe, replace a smoke alarm 10 years after its date of manufacture—an anniversary that can come sooner than 10 years after you installed the device depending on how old the smoke alarm was when you installed it.

For carbon monoxide detectors, check the manufacturer's website for replacement details if this is not spelled out on the device and you no longer have its instructions.

Dates of manufacture typically are printed on the backs of smoke alarms and carbon monoxide detectors, so you might have to remove them from walls or ceilings to check them.

More than 20% of residential fire deaths occur in homes where there were smoke alarms but those alarms were not working properly, either because of expired batteries or nonfunctional alarms.

Replace an alarm before the 10-year mark if it continuously "chirps" or displays a flashing red light or if its alarm does not sound when you press the "test" button (when battery replacement is not the issue).

Smoke alarms can cost less than $10 apiece, and carbon monoxide detectors can cost less than $25, so there is little financial reason to continue using an older unit. Make sure that the new alarms you install have been approved by a recognized independent testing lab such as Underwriters Laboratories (look for the "UL" logo on the packaging).

Stay Healthy When Traveling

Ask your hotel for wellness perks—some offer yoga and other exercise classes. Request a jogging map or guidance from the concierge. Research dining options featuring healthful foods. Request a room with a standing shower—bathtubs and hot tubs are harder for the cleaning staff to keep clean—and also request a smoke-free, pet-restricted room. Never go barefoot in your room—wear socks to protect against germs. Use antibacterial wipes on in-room phones, remotes, light switches, faucets and alarm clocks. Ask for an upgrade to a preferred-guest floor—they get the best housekeeping and are the least noisy.

Fortune.com

Certain Neighborhoods May Harm Sleep

Study by researchers at Stanford Sleep Epidemiology Research Center, Stanford, California, presented at a recent meeting of the American Academy of Neurology in Vancouver, Canada.

People living in neighborhoods that are lit up with signs and streetlights are more likely to report sleep problems than people living in areas with little nighttime lighting. Those exposed to higher light levels were more likely to report fatigue, wake up confused during the night and have excessive sleepiness and impaired functioning.

What to do: Invest in black-out curtains.

Update: Airport Scanner Radiation

David Brenner, PhD, DSc, director, Center for Radiological Research, Columbia University Medical Center, New York City.

Airport full-body scanners that use X-ray radiation were removed from US airports in 2013. Passengers now stand in a booth with their arms raised for screening with full-body millimeter-wave radiation scanners that use low-level radio frequency technology. This is virtually the same type of radiation used in microwave ovens but at a much lower intensity. There is no evidence that low-intensity millimeter wave exposure poses any health hazard. The backscatter scanners that used low-intensity X-ray radiation were removed from airports after concerns were raised that the X-ray exposure could damage DNA and raise the long-term risk for cancer—and that the body images they produced were too revealing.

Antibacterial Soap OK?

Philip M. Tierno, PhD, professor of microbiology and pathology, New York University School of Medicine, New York City.

A recent FDA ruling bans 19 chemicals in antibacterial soaps, including triclosan, hexachlorophene and phenol. Manufacturers have not shown that these ingredients are safe for long-term use and more effective in preventing illness than plain soap and water, the FDA stated. These antibacterial soaps must be off the market by September 6, 2017. (But the ruling does not ban these chemicals in cleaning products.) The agency is now considering a ban on other antibacterial ingredients, including benzalkonium chloride and chloroxylenol.

Washing your hands with plain soap and water is the best way to remove germs—scrub for at least 20 seconds. If soap and water are not available, use an alcohol-based hand sanitizer.

Are Hypoallergenic Cosmetics Worth the Extra Expense?

Melissa Kanchanapoomi Levin, MD, a dermatologist in private practice in New York City. MarmurMedical.com

There are no federal standards that determine what can be labeled hypoallergenic, but in general, these products omit certain ingredients, such as fragrance and preservatives, that have been shown to cause skin reactions. But that does not mean that a hypoallergenic product won't cause any irritation or reaction. These products are often simple formulations of regular cosmetics that contain fewer ingredients to minimize the risk of allergic reactions.

In my practice, I am seeing a growing number of patients with sensitive skin. If a patient has a history of eczema, acne, rosacea or psoriasis...a pigmentation disorder...a skin infection or sensitivity...and/or other inflammatory skin conditions, hypoallergenic products—along with consistent and gentle skin care—are needed to minimize irritation. Hypoallergenic skin-care products and cosmetics may also help prescription or nonprescription skin treatments work better.

Hair Products Linked to Hair Loss

Tina Sigurdson, assistant general counsel for the Environmental Working Group (EWG), a nonprofit environmental health research and advocacy organization. EWG maintains a database called Skin Deep, which offers health and safety ratings for thousands of personal-care products. Ewg.org/skindeep

More than 21,000 consumers have lodged complaints about WEN Cleansing Conditioners, a line of hair-care products heavily advertised on television. Many of the complaints cite significant problems such as hair loss and serious skin irritation. But despite this flood of complaints...an alert issued by the Food and Drug Administration (FDA)...and at least one class-action lawsuit, the products remain on the market. It's not clear which ingredients in the WEN conditioners may be causing the problems—which contributes to the FDA's inability to address the issue more strongly.

Hair-care and other personal-care products including cosmetics, toothpaste, mouthwash, baby wipes, baby powder, shaving cream and body wash are virtually unregulated by the government. The FDA has no authority to recall these items, and manufacturers are not required to confirm that the products are safe to use. Legislation that would increase FDA oversight of personal-care products is being considered by the Senate. But any changes are unlikely to take effect for many months.

What to do: Never assume that a product is safe because its packaging or advertising features words such as "Natural," "Healthy" or "Gentle." The use of these words is unregulated when it comes to personal-care products, so they often mean little or nothing.

Example: The makers of WEN Cleansing Conditioners have used the word "Natural" in their marketing materials even though these products contain synthetic chemicals—including at least one known to cause allergic reactions.

Fitness Trackers Might Not Help You Lose Weight

Mitesh Patel, MD, assistant professor of medicine and health-care management at Perelman School of Medicine and The Wharton School at University of Pennsylvania, Philadelphia. He is director of the Penn Medicine Nudge Unit, which steers providers and patients toward better health decisions. HealthcareInnovation.upenn.edu

A study published in *JAMA* found that dieters who wore fitness trackers for 24 months lost significantly less weight than dieters who did not—7.7 pounds versus 13 pounds, on average. Fitness trackers are wearable digital devices that measure fitness data such as the number of steps taken each day and calories burned. Their makers often boast that these devices promote weight loss, something this study calls into question.

But other research suggests that while these devices alone often are not effective, they can be paired with "engagement strategies" to promote weight loss and fitness, such as using them in a social way.

Example: The tracker's data could be shared with friends or family members for peer support...or a group of friends could wear fitness trackers and compete to see who can walk the farthest each week.

It also is worth noting that the recent study gave fitness trackers to people who already were participating in diet and exercise programs. In doing so, it might have accidentally undermined the healthy habits these people previously had established by asking them to change something that was already working.

What to do: Before purchasing a fitness tracker, use a smartphone fitness tracker app—a popular one is Health Mate by Withings. These apps are not quite as accurate as full-fledged fitness trackers, but they are a good way for smartphone owners to confirm that they will use a tracker before investing money in one. One of the reasons that trackers sometimes are ineffective is that many people discontinue use within a few months.

As noted above, if you buy a tracker, share your tracker results with friends or, better yet, enlist those friends into a fitness-tracker competition.

Also, set reasonable fitness goals for yourself. Use your smartphone app or fitness tracker to determine your current daily activity level, and then set a personal daily target that is perhaps 1,000 to 2,000 steps above this. Increase this target slowly over time.

Wow! Insurance Pays for This...

Charles B. Inlander, a consumer advocate and health-care consultant based in Fogelsville, Pennsylvania, was the founding president of the nonprofit People's Medical Society, a consumer advocacy organization credited with key improvements in the quality of US health care. He is author or coauthor of more than 20 consumer-health books.

My friend just received a 40% discount on a fitness watch. And after a dental procedure, he paid nothing for acupuncture to help ease the pain. His wife recently saved more than $800 on hearing aids. The surprising thing is that all these savings were benefits of their health insurance plan. Such benefits vary from state-to-state and plan-to-plan, but there are some widely used services and programs that your health plan may cover.

Important: The onus is on you to find out about these programs (see below) and enroll in them. *What you should check out...*

- **Weight-loss programs, grief counseling and more.** Are you having a hard time shedding those extra pounds? Chances are your health plan will pay all or most of the cost of a weight-loss and/or nutritional counseling program (often affiliated with a hospital and led by certified nutritionists). Your plan may also cover 10 or more sessions of grief counseling or even life coaching (which helps individuals cope with stressful work or life situations) as long as you see a licensed therapist (such as a psychiatrist, psychologist or social worker). Most health plans also offer disease/condition-management programs ranging from diabetes control to pain management. These plans often assign nurses, counselors and others to work directly with you to effectively deal with your condition. You may need a doctor's prescription or order to enroll in some of these programs—check with your insurer for details.

Here's how: If you are enrolled in traditional Medicare, check with your Medicare supplemental carrier for services. If you are in a Medicare Advantage Plan, check your plan website or call for details. If your insurance plan is through your employer or a health exchange, contact the insurer.

- **Healthy living.** Don't want to pay hefty gym membership fees? You could be in luck! Most larger health insurance carriers have healthy-living programs available through their plans.

Examples: Blue Cross Blue Shield 365... Cigna Healthy Rewards...and Humana Vitality offer a wide range of incentives to keep you active and healthy. Most pay all or part of gym membership fees for you and your family through programs such as Silver Sneakers. You may also be eligible for 10% to 50% off personal-training sessions. Other programs offer you reward points for participating in fitness activities, such as Zumba classes, swimming programs, etc. You can then "cash in" the points for rewards ranging from cameras to walking shoes. Other programs pay for smoking-cessation classes.

•Save hundreds on these special services... Chances are your health insurer has partnered with companies offering health-related products and services at steep discounts. For example, recent offerings by some plans include a more than $800 discount on Lasik eye-correction surgery...up to 70% off teeth whitening...partial payment for massage therapy for pain management...and much more.

Beware: Discount programs change regularly, adding new or discontinuing little-used services. So check regularly with your carrier to find out what's being offered.

Health Insurance Alert If You Work Past Age 65

Aaron Tidball, manager of Medicare operations at Allsup Inc., a nationwide service based in Belleville, Illinois, that helps guide people with Social Security disability and Medicare. AllsupInc.com

Two-thirds of baby boomers plan to work past age 65—the age at which they become eligible for Medicare—according to a study by the Transamerica Center for Retirement Studies. One of the challenges they might face is determining whether they can and should remain on an employer's health insurance plan or make the switch to Medicare. And it often is a very tricky choice that even human resources departments may not fully understand. *What you need to know if you plan to work (or already are working) past age 65...*

•The number of workers that your employer employs dramatically affects your health-care options. If there are 20 or more employees, the employer is required to offer you the same coverage after you turn 65 that it offers its younger employees. This means you generally can remain on this group plan—and it is considered "primary coverage"—unless the employer's prescription drug coverage is not considered "creditable." For more information, put "CMS: creditable coverage" into a search engine and go to the CMS.gov site listed.

If your employer has fewer than 20 employees, you almost certainly should sign up for Medicare. That's because Medicare generally is considered to be your primary health coverage...and your employer-based insurance, should you choose to continue to be covered, becomes "secondary" coverage (unless your employer opts to provide primary coverage to employees age 65 and over, though this is rare). That means the employer-based coverage will pay only the portion of your eligible health-care bills that Medicare does not cover. In this case, if you failed to sign up for Medicare, you would have to pay the lion's share of your medical bills out of pocket.

For details and exceptions to these rules, including how they apply to disabled employees, go to Medicare.gov/Pubs/pdf/02179.pdf.

Caution: It sometimes is difficult to know whether a company has 20 or more employees under Medicare rules. A seemingly small company might legally be part of a larger organization...while a seemingly large company might actually have many part-time or contract workers who do not count toward the 20-employee threshold. Ask your company's human resources department.

•Medicare could be the better option even if you can choose your employer's plan as primary coverage. In decades past, employer health insurance plans almost always were more attractive than Medicare. But many employer plans have become less appealing in recent years—deductibles, co-pays and premiums have grown larger, while in-network medical-provider options have shrunk. So an increasing percentage of employees age 65 or older now would be better off switching to Medicare.

To figure out if Medicare is the better choice for you, start by going to Medicare.gov and putting "Which insurance pays first?" in the search box.

If your employer's coverage has a four-figure deductible and a 20%-or-higher copay after that, for example, there's a good chance that Medicare would be better.

Helpful: Although ordinarily you must enroll with Medicare within a few months before or after you turn 65 to avoid late-enrollment penalties, if you stick with your large employer's plan as primary coverage, you don't have to sign up for Medicare at that point. The penalties do not apply as long as you sign up within eight months after the date your employer coverage ends or your employment ends, whichever comes earlier.

•**If you are at a small company and do sign up for Medicare, it sometimes makes sense to also keep your employer plan despite the extra cost.** This isn't common because the combined premiums of Medicare Part B (which covers medical services and supplies), Medicare Part D (which covers prescription drugs) and employer health coverage get pricey. But dual coverage could be best if you have a serious medical condition whose costs would be well-covered by the employer plan but not by Medicare. Ask your health-care providers if they can help determine whether you would face significantly different out-of-pocket costs or coverage gaps for your current needs if you don't keep your employer coverage in addition to Medicare.

•**Your spouse and dependents cannot stay on your employer's health plan if you leave it for Medicare.** It might be worth continuing your employer coverage even if Medicare makes more sense for you as an individual, especially if your employer's plan is the best way for your family members to obtain affordable high-quality health insurance.

However, there might be a way you could keep family members on your large-company employer plan even when you switch to Medicare for your own coverage. This involves COBRA coverage, which might be available to extend your family coverage, typically for up to 18 months, after you switch to Medicare. Ask your employer's human resources department for details.

THE HSA MEDICARE MISTAKE

Medicare often is discussed as if it is a single service, but it actually includes several components that eligible Americans could opt to sign up for at different times. Among these components is Medicare Part A, which covers hospital costs. There generally are no premiums for Medicare Part A, so people often are advised that they might as well go ahead and sign up for this "free" part of Medicare as soon as they become eligible even if they intend to remain on an employer's coverage.

For many employees, that can be a costly mistake. That's because more and more employer plans now include high deductibles and a Health Savings Account (HSA), a type of tax-advantaged savings account that can be used to pay medical bills. If you sign up for Part A and continue to make HSA contributions, you will face tax penalties. So if you opt to remain in an employer plan that includes an HSA, do not sign up for Part A until you leave this plan. (Rules differ for a spouse covered under your plan. For details, type into a search engine, "AARP: Can I have a health savings account as well as Medicare?" and go to the AARP website.)

Caution: Do not file for Social Security retirement benefits if you wish to continue contributing to an HSA. Starting Social Security anytime after age 65 automatically begins your Part A coverage up to six months retroactive to your Social Security sign-up date. If you made HSA contributions during that six-month period, you likely will face tax penalties.

Medicare Advantage Limits Doctor and Hospital Choices

Study by Henry J. Kaiser Family Foundation, reported in *The Wall Street Journal.*

Medicare Advantage plans often don't let members go to their preferred hospitals. The plans typically limit hospital and doctor choice—and in return, offer lower out-of-pocket costs than traditional Medicare, plus bonuses such as prescription-drug coverage and gym memberships. But plan directories may contain incorrect, confusing or outdated information and can be difficult to navigate. The plans are most likely to exclude hospitals that specialize in treating rare or complicated conditions. Among 409 plans studied, only 23% offered broad networks including 70% or more of the hospitals in a county...61% had medium-sized networks, including 30% to 69% of county hospitals...16% had narrow networks, including fewer than 30% of county hospitals.

How to Choose the Right Hospital for You

Steven Z. Kussin, MD, gastroenterologist and founder of the Shared Decision Center of Central New York. He has taught at Albert Einstein College of Medicine and Columbia College of Physicians and Surgeons, both in New York City. He is author of *Doctor, Your Patient Will See You Now: Gaining the Upper Hand in Your Medical Care*. He appears on WKTV in Utica, New York, as *The Medical Advocate*.

Sooner or later, nearly everyone winds up in a hospital. It might be for testing...an ER visit...or treatment for serious illness.

If you get hit by a bus, the best hospital is the closest one. Fortunately, most health problems aren't that pressing. It makes sense to choose a hospital with the best record for treating patients with your particular condition.

How can you tell which hospital? It may not be easy. You can't trust the billboards that appear in metropolitan areas. (Hospitals and other health-care facilities spend billions on advertising every year.) Recommendations from friends and family members generally are based on limited anecdotes and are not authoritative. Even your doctor might not have the best advice. *Here's how to find the right hospital for you...*

DIFFERENCES MATTER

People spend more time shopping for flat-screen TVs than choosing hospitals. They just assume that all hospitals provide more-or-less equal care.

They don't. One study found that heart attack patients who went to higher-quality hospitals had a 1% increase in survival. That is significant in itself, and for patients who need procedures for certain conditions such as some cancers or abdominal aortic aneurysms, the differences are starker. There might be a three- or four-fold difference in survival and complication rates between great and so-so hospitals.

CHOOSE THE BEST

Everyone wants to use a hospital that's close to home. Your local hospital may be superb, but you can't count on it.

To find the best, investigate the following...

• **Web-based lookups.** *There are many resources to choose from including...*

• Medicare's Hospital Compare (Medicare.gov/hospitalcompare)

• Why Not the Best (WNTB.org)

• The Leapfrog Group (Leapfrog Group.org).

These and other websites use publically available data to rate hospitals on various measures of performance—death rates from serious conditions (such as heart failure and pneumonia)...frequency of hospital-acquired infections...patient satisfaction...etc.

On these websites, you plug in your zip code to find hospitals in your area. You then can check to see how well (or poorly) each hospital manages patients with various conditions.

These web-based services are useful even when they don't discuss your particular condition. Some hospitals cultivate a culture of excellence. If they rate highly in one area, they're more likely to do well in others.

• **Hospitals farther away.** When patients are given a choice, they almost always choose the hospital that's closest to home. It might be the best hospital in your area—but a better one might be just a little farther away.

Surgical death rates tend to be higher at small, local hospitals than at regional medical centers. Hospitals that treat large numbers of select patients do better than those that treat fewer. If you're seriously ill and need a risky procedure, you should be willing to drive the extra miles to get the best possible care.

In one interesting study, patients were given a hypothetical scenario. They were asked to imagine that they had pancreatic cancer and needed surgery...and they could choose among different hospitals. All of the patients preferred having surgery locally if the risk of dying was the same as at a regional hospital. But when they were told that the risk of dying was twice as high at a local hospital, 45% still chose to stay close to home!

Don't use a second-rate hospital just because you're reluctant to travel. For routine procedures, it probably doesn't matter—the risks will be negligible wherever you go. But for serious illnesses or higher-risk procedures, a large, regional medical center probably will be the safer choice.

• **Number of patients.** Suppose that you need a back operation or a bypass procedure. Do you want to go to a hospital that does a handful of procedures a year? Or should you choose one that packs them in by the hundreds?

An analysis by *US News & World Report* found that the risk for death for patients with congestive heart failure and chronic obstructive pulmonary disease was 20% higher at facilities that saw the fewest patients.

My advice: Choose a hospital that treats a lot of patients with your particular condition—ask a hospital administrator or patient-care supervisor how many of your procedures are done each year. If you can't get this information, ask the surgeon how many he/she does. One study found that endocrine surgeons who did 100 or more operations a year accounted for 5% of total complications, while those who did three or fewer a year accounted for 32%.

• **Doctor qualifications.** Your doctor's experience is just as important as your hospital's. As mentioned above, doctors who see a lot of patients with similar conditions tend to have better track records. Those who work at top medical centers usually are better than those at smaller facilities—but not always.

ProPublica (a nonprofit investigative news service) looked at data from more than 2.3 million Medicare patients. The analysis revealed that a small number of surgeons accounted for about 25% of all surgical complications. Some had complication rates that were two or three times the national average, and some of them worked at the nation's most prestigious medical centers.

It's difficult to assess a doctor's competence. One thing you can do is ask other doctors, including your own, about a particular doctor's expertise. In addition, you can check out his/her education on the Web. It might sound snobbish, but other things being equal, I'd prefer to see a doctor who went to a great college, medical school and training program rather than lower-tier institutions.

You also can ask a prospective surgeon about his/her success and failure rate and rates of complications. Some surgeons won't discuss these matters. The good ones probably will be proud to do so.

Helpful resource: Healthgrades.com allows you to enter medical conditions and procedures into a search window and then provides the doctors who treat them and their Healthgrades ratings.

• **Patient satisfaction.** Patient satisfaction isn't a perfect proxy for quality, but you might glean some useful information. Check the patient-satisfaction measures on hospital-comparison websites.

How long did it take for nurses to answer calls? Were the doctors warm or brusque? Was the food delicious or dreadful? These might seem like minor considerations, but research has shown that patient satisfaction and good health care often go together.

Best Hospital in the US: Mayo Clinic

US News and World Report study, "Best Hospitals 2016–17."

The Rochester, Minnesota, clinic earned an overall top ranking plus first place for eight of 16 specialty areas. Second was the Cleveland Clinic, followed by Massachusetts General Hospital in Boston...Johns Hopkins Hospital in Baltimore...and UCLA Medical Center, Los Angeles. Nearly 5,000 US medical centers were compared in 16 specialties and nine conditions and procedures. Evaluators looked at patient survival rates and infection rates...quality of nursing staff...and patient satisfaction.

To see the full list: Go to Health.USNews.com/best-hospitals.

Your Post-Heart Attack Survival May Depend on Choice of Hospital

Emily Bucholz, MD, PhD, resident physician, Boston Children's Hospital.
Donald Lloyd-Jones, MD, chair, preventive medicine, Northwestern University Feinberg School of Medicine, Chicago.
New England Journal of Medicine.

Older heart attack victims who receive immediate high-quality care from their hospital often wind up with a long-term survival advantage, a recent study reports.

Medicare recipients can gain as much as a year of additional life if they are treated at a hospital that has a better track record of keeping all heart attack patients alive for the first 30 days after their emergency, the researchers found.

"It really does make a difference where you go for care," said study author Emily Bucholz, MD, PhD, a resident physician at Boston Children's Hospital. "It's not just about surviving that acute period. The benefits you accrue by being treated at a hospital that does really well will persist over your entire remaining life span."

STUDY DETAILS

In the study, researchers reviewed nearly 120,000 Medicare-covered heart attack patients treated at 1,824 hospitals across the United States between 1994 and 1996. The review included an average 17-year follow-up to track how long the patients lived.

Hospitals were ranked as "high-performing" or "low-performing" based solely on the 30-day survival rates of the heart attack patients, who were an average of 76 years old.

The research team discovered that victims treated at so-called "high-performing" hospitals had an overall increased life expectancy, compared with others treated at hospitals where more patients die during the first month of care. But the study did not prove a cause-and-effect relationship between level of hospital care and longer life.

The average survival advantage amounts to between nine months and a year, the investigators found.

"One year is actually a fairly substantial amount of time for these patients," Dr. Bucholz said. "From a policy level, investing in initiatives that improve short-term performance actually have long-term implications for patient outcomes."

The study did not examine what helped some hospitals provide better care for heart attack patients, but Dr. Bucholz said the "general consensus is it's a lot of factors."

The study was published in the *New England Journal of Medicine.*

WHAT MAKES A BETTER HOSPITAL

One important factor indicating high-quality care could be whether hospitals are closely following the guidelines for treating a heart attack, said Donald Lloyd-Jones, MD, chair of preventive medicine for the Northwestern University Feinberg School of Medicine in Chicago.

For example, hospitals should promptly get patients on a multiple-drug regimen that reduces their risk of a second heart attack, and should follow-up regularly with patients to make sure they're taking their medicine, said Dr. Lloyd-Jones, a spokesman for the American Heart Association.

Dr. Bucholz suggested that these hospitals also might be communicating better. Studies have shown patients do well if there's strong communication between paramedics, emergency room doctors, cardiologists and nursing staff.

In addition, Dr. Lloyd-Jones said, social, economic and ethnic differences in the communities served by hospitals can influence 30-day survival rates. But he also said that the researchers controlled for that in this study. It's something that must be done when comparing hospitals in different parts of the United States.

Dr. Lloyd-Jones said the study presents an "interesting and compelling" case that heart attack patients gain a permanent leg up if they receive high-quality immediate care.

"That gap never closes," he said. "If you get off to a better start in those first 30 days by being treated at a high-performing hospital, these data suggest there's a persistent benefit."

HOW TO FIND THE BEST HOSPITAL NEAR YOU

People can find high-performing hospitals near them by going to Medicare's Hospital Compare website, Dr. Bucholz said.

The website uses your address to locate nearby hospitals, and then compares them using a variety of quality measures including patients' experiences, timely and effective care, complications, readmissions and deaths.

info To review local hospital performance using Hospital Compare, visit the U.S. Centers for Medicare and Medicaid Services at https://www.medicare.gov/hospitalcompare.

Medical Coding Mistakes Can Cost You Big

Pat Palmer, who has more than 20 years of experience contesting medical bills as founder of Medical Billing Advocates of America, a patient-advocacy company, Roanoke, Virginia. She is author of *MBAA's Guide to Surviving Your Medical Bills: What You Need to Know Before You Pay a Dime.* BillAdvocates.com

There is a five-digit "CPT" code for every medical procedure that health-care providers perform. If one of these Current Procedural Terminology (CPT) codes is entered incorrectly by your provider on a claim submitted to your insurance company or Medicare, the result could be big out-of-pocket costs for you—and errors such as these are extremely common. One recent study by the US Department of Health & Human Services found that a staggering 42% of Medicare claims for "evaluation and management" were incorrectly coded.

Insurance companies and the Medicare system shoulder much of the cost of miscodings, but patients can face inflated bills, too, in the form of higher co-pays...overcharges that must be paid out of pocket before deductibles are met...or outright denials of coverage because misentered codes refer to procedures deemed not medically necessary.

What to do: When you receive an Explanation of Benefits (EOB) statement from your insurance company or Medicare following medical treatment, read the description listed for each service provided. (If an EOB does not provide descriptions, just a series of five-digit alpha-numeric codes, enter these codes into a website such as HealthcareBlueBook.com to find descriptions. If your EOB provides neither codes nor descriptions, contact your insurer and request the CPT codes—these must be supplied upon request.)

Be especially wary if...

- **The same code appears more than once.** It's possible that you received the same treatment multiple times...but it also is possible that you have been double-billed.
- **A straightforward office visit is coded as something more extreme.** A "level 5" office visit—with the CPT code 99215—should be listed only if you had a life-threatening condition, for example.

What to do: Enter any code you think is questionable into Medicare's National Correct Coding Initiative Edit (CMS.gov/NationalCorrectCodInitEd). If a description does not sound like the procedure or treatment you received, call the provider's office and ask whether the code is accurate. Sometimes office personnel acknowledge miscoding when prompted this way and will make corrections.

If you are told that the original coding is correct but you remain skeptical, send a letter to the provider's billing department officially disputing the bill. Or you can hire a medical billing advocate to contest the bill for you.

What to Do with an "Incidentaloma"

Stella K. Kang, MD, MS, an assistant professor of radiology and population health at NYU Langone Medical Center in New York City. She is author or coauthor of more than two dozen scientific papers that have been published in the *Journal of the American College of Radiology, Clinical Oncology* and other leading medical journals.

You're having abdominal pain and visit your primary care physician. As part of the workup, your doctor orders a CT scan of your abdomen and pelvis to rule out possible causes, such as an infection. The results arrive two days later, and there's nothing obviously wrong with your bowels. *But...*

In the report accompanying the scan, the radiologist noted an incidental finding (IF)—a spot on your kidney that was "too small to characterize."

Is it a harmless cyst...or a tumor that might grow and spread if left untreated? Should your doctor ignore it for now...or order more tests, possibly opening a medical Pandora's box that could perhaps entail a biopsy and raise radiation exposure? More and more patients and doctors are facing such questions.

Incidental findings—when a physician investigating a specific problem finds another possible problem (known in doctor-speak as an "incidentaloma")—are on the rise, in part because scanning technology is more precise than ever before.

Eye-opening statistics: On average, about 40% of all scans reveal an incidental finding. For two common imaging tests—CT of the abdomen and pelvis...and CT of the thorax (below the neck and above the abdomen)—IFs are now detected 61% and 55% of the time, respectively. *Basic types of IFs...*

- **High risk.** This type could cause real harm, even death, if it's not discovered and dealt with. *Example:* A large cancerous kidney tumor.
- **Intermediate risk.** This type has some potential to cause future harm, with a need for medication or other treatment. *Example:* A kidney stone that is asymptomatic.
- **Low risk.** This type has a greater than 99% chance of never causing harm. *Example:* A benign kidney cyst, which does not interfere with kidney function.

Why it gets tricky: Even though the discovery of an abnormality can sometimes be lifesaving (when an asymptomatic malignancy is found, for example), there are few medical standards for reporting and managing IFs—often leading to unnecessary testing and treatment of low- and intermediate-risk IFs.

BEST STRATEGIES

Here are ways to increase the likelihood that IFs are responded to safely and effectively—but unnecessary follow-up is avoided...

- **If your doctor orders any type of imaging test (X-ray, CT, PET or MRI scan, for example), ask about the likelihood of an IF.** You should know before the test whether or not it's likely to uncover an IF—so you're less apt to be surprised and frightened if an IF is found.

Helpful: Before the test, ask your doctor to give you a quick overview of high-, intermediate- and low-risk IFs commonly produced by the test.

To ensure that you are made aware of any IFs from an imaging test, ask to receive a copy of the radiologist's report so that you can discuss it with your doctor.

- **Partner with your primary care doctor.** With its array of specialists and subspecialists, medical care is increasingly fractured—making it more likely that specialist-ordered testing will follow the discovery of any IF, including those that are intermediate- and low-risk.

Best: Even if a specialist ordered the test, talk over the results with your primary care physician. He/she is likely to have a sense of your overall health and preferences regarding medical interventions such as testing.

- **If there's an IF, get an accurate description of the risk.** Sometimes a doctor will talk in vague terms about the risk from an IF—for example, "It's probably not going to hurt you." But that's not enough information to effectively partner with your doctor in deciding if more testing is appropriate.

Best: Ask for a statistical estimation of risk. Is the likelihood of harm (such as cancer that could metastasize or an enlarged blood vessel that could rupture) from the IF one out of 10? One out of 1,000? If the numerical level of risk is hard to understand, ask the doctor to explain it another way.

- **Ask if the American College of Radiology (ACR) recommends further imaging for this type of IF.** The ACR, the professional organization for radiologists, has guidelines for further investigation of some of the most common IFs, such as thyroid nodules, ovarian nodules and IFs discovered during abdominal CTs.

Best: Ask your physician if there are ACR guidelines for your IF and if he is following them.*

•**Ask your doctor to consult with the radiologist.** When certain IFs don't fall under ACR guidelines, radiologists don't always agree about their significance or management. One radiologist might recommend further testing. Another might say no additional testing is necessary. A third might not make a recommendation, letting the primary care physician decide what to do next.

Best: If your test has an IF with unclear implications for management, your doctor might schedule a joint consultation with the radiologist so the three of you can talk through your options—a strategy that is effective but underutilized.

•**Get a second opinion.** When a lesion is indeterminate (unclear in importance), consider asking your doctor to have another radiologist take a look at the result.

Best: Ask your doctor to recommend a consultation with a subspecialist—for instance, if the IF is on the kidney, talk to a radiologist who is expert in examining the kidney.

WHEN FOLLOW-UP IS NEEDED

Some IFs require follow-up testing and medical care. *Discuss follow-up options with your doctor for...*

•**Lung nodules**—a risk factor for lung cancer—found during a CT of the thorax.

•**Coronary artery calcification**—a risk factor for a heart attack—detected during a CT of the chest or a CT of the abdomen and pelvis.

•**A solid lesion on an ovary,** which could be a tumor, revealed by an abdominal and pelvic CT.

•**Enlarged lymph nodes,** which may be related to infection or malignancy, found during a pelvic MRI.

•**Enlarged aorta (aneurysm) found by an abdominal CT.** If this major blood vessel is enlarged, you could be at increased risk for it to break open and cause severe bleeding that could be fatal.

*To read the American College of Radiology's guidelines on incidental findings, go to Nucradshare.com/images/Misc/ACR%20Incidental%20Findings%20Guidelines.pdf.

Get the Right Tests and Ask the Right Questions at Your Physical Exam

Suzanne Steinbaum, MD, DO, attending cardiologist and director of Women and Heart Disease, Lenox Hill Hospital, New York City. Trained as a DO and board-certified as an MD, she combines the holistic approach of osteopathy with conventional medicine. She also is author of *Dr. Suzanne Steinbaum's Heart Book.* SRSheart.com

Annual physicals are a great idea, but not if your doctor's monitoring the wrong things. What are the right things to check? Here's how to get the most from your physical.

When we go to annual physicals, we get poked...we get prodded...we get stuck with needles, but is your doctor testing for all the right things? How do we know?

Remember this annual visit is about you. So go in there with all the questions you have, and make sure those questions get answered before you leave. In fact, talk to your doctor about getting your blood test done before the actual one-on-one visit. So by the time you leave that visit, you have answers about what those blood tests mean and if everything was done. Things that should be checked are risk factors for heart disease—blood pressure should be checked, your height and weight to get a body mass index, and your waist circumference, which can increase your risk for heart disease and prediabetes. Other tests on the blood include hemoglobin A1C, which is a test of sugar...hs-CRP which is an inflammatory marker...and your cholesterol panel. Talk to your doctor about whether or not it's important to do other testing, like a lipid fractionation or some genetic markers that indicate your risk for heart disease.

How many tests are standard and how many tests are "extra" (as in, what won't your insurance pay for)? Be sure to ask your doctor and make sure your doctor clarifies what is absolutely necessary.

One of the tests that's standard is an EKG, but unless you have symptoms, an EKG might not be important, so it's not the most cost-effective test. The other testing that I mentioned, the lipid fractionation, may not be covered by your insurance. If you're at risk for heart disease or you have a family history, call your insurance company and ask your doctor about this test. It might be worth it.

The bottom line on annual physicals is that they save lives. But they're really all about you, so make sure you know which questions you want answered and get those answers from your doctor.

Don't Forget Your Doctor's Words

Charles B. Inlander, a consumer advocate and health-care consultant based in Fogelsville, Pennsylvania, was the founding president of the nonprofit People's Medical Society, a consumer advocacy organization credited with key improvements in the quality of US health care. He is author or coauthor of more than 20 consumer-health books.

A friend of mine recently called me about an hour after his doctor had told him that he had prostate cancer and asked if I could help him decide on the best way to proceed. Of course, I was happy to help. But when I asked exactly what his doctor had said, my friend didn't know! All he remembered hearing were two words—"prostate cancer."

Not remembering what your doctor tells you is extremely common—especially if it's a scary diagnosis or a complicated explanation laden with medical terms. In fact, a classic study conducted by researchers at Allegheny College found that 40% to 80% of the information told to patients by health-care providers is forgotten immediately! The greater the amount of information shared, the greater the percentage that was forgotten. *What helps—you can do any or all of the following, depending on your needs...*

• **Get it in writing and in a picture.** It's long been known that we retain information best when we receive it both verbally and visually. Research backs this up. A study found that when patients were given only verbal medical instructions, just 14% of the information was retained compared with 85% when a visual and text were provided. That means you should always ask your doctor to write down—or give you preprinted information—about your diagnosis. You probably already bring your own pad and pen to take notes at your appointment. But that may not be enough. Ask your doctor to also show you a picture or diagram of what is wrong with you—he/she could use an X-ray, a plastic anatomical model or textbook drawing of the problem area. You can take a photo of the visual with your phone.

Also important: Ask your doctor to give you written instructions about follow-up care and/or how to use prescribed medications, even if you expect to get similar information from your pharmacy. Your doctor may suggest taking the drug less frequently at first or have some other reason for adjusting its typical use.

• **Don't go alone.** We all know that it's smart to bring a family member or friend to important medical appointments so you'll have a second set of ears to remember what the doctor has said. You have a right to have someone with you in the examining room to ask questions or seek clarification. When I recently had surgery, I made sure my wife came with me to every pre- and postoperative appointment. She asked questions I had not thought of and described things that happened during my recovery that I had forgotten. This additional information also helped the doctor in her review of how I was doing.

• **Make a recording.** One of the best ways to not forget what your doctor tells you is to make a brief voice and/or video recording of your medical appointment. Your smartphone likely has an app that enables it to function as a mini tape recorder. If not, you can download one of these apps from your phone's app store. Either hold the phone or put it on a nearby table. Make sure you know how to record beforehand. You can also use your phone's camera to make a video recording (with sound) of your doctor appointment. If you don't have a smartphone, it's worth purchasing a battery-operated handheld digital recorder. You can get one for less than $50. Whatever method you use, just be sure to ask your doctor if it's OK to record the conversa-

Drug Danger Alerts

More problems with PPIs. Long-term use (more than four consecutive weeks) of proton pump inhibitors (PPIs)—drugs such as *esomeprazole* (Nexium) and omeprazole (Prilosec), commonly taken for heartburn and gastroesophageal reflux disease (GERD)—speeds up the aging of blood vessels, which may increase risk for heart disease, kidney failure and dementia.

Why: PPIs reduce the acidity needed to clear waste products from blood vessels, making them more susceptible to blockages.

John Cooke, MD, PhD, chair of cardiovascular sciences, Houston Methodist Research Institute.

Antacids with aspirin may cause bleeding. The side effect is rare—only eight cases have been reported since 2009. But people at risk for stomach or intestinal bleeding should be aware of it. Over-the-counter products such as Alka-Seltzer and Bromo Seltzer contain aspirin. People at bleeding risk include those age 60 or older...with a history of stomach or bleeding problems...who take blood-thinning drugs or medications such as *prednisone*...who take other medicines containing nonsteroidal anti-inflammatory drugs (NSAIDs)...and/or who drink three or more alcoholic drinks per day.

Karen Murry Mahoney, MD, deputy director, division of nonprescription drug products, US Food and Drug Administration, Silver Spring, Maryland.

Antibiotics can cause delirium. More than 50 of the most commonly prescribed antibiotics, including *sulfonamides* (such as Bactrim) and *fluoroquinolones* (such as Cipro), were linked to temporary mental confusion (delirium) in a review of nearly 400 patients (hospitalized and outpatient).

Self-defense: If you're taking an antibiotic and experience symptoms of delirium, such as disorientation, agitation or social withdrawal, a loved one should talk to your doctor about your medication.

Shamik Bhattacharyya, MD, instructor in neurology, Harvard Medical School, Boston.

Antibiotic reaction. The FDA recommends that doctors not prescribe fluoroquinolones, a class of antibiotics that includes Cipro, to people who have sinusitis, bronchitis or uncomplicated urinary tract infections. Side effects from these antibiotics can include pain in the tendons, joints or muscles, a "pins-and-needles sensation," confusion and hallucinations.

WebMD.com

tion. These days, most doctors say it's fine, but you should get their permission to record.

Is It OK to Take a Medication After the Expiration Date?

Amy Tiemeier, PharmD, associate professor of pharmacy practice, St. Louis College of Pharmacy.

In some cases expired drugs are still effective. An FDA review of 122 different drugs found that 88% were still effective a year past their expiration dates. Generally, prescription tablet and capsule medications are good for one year from the date that they are dispensed from the pharmacy...over-the-counter drugs for a year after you open them.

However, these medications may have some potency after that. Powders that are mixed with water to make a liquid solution just before being given to the patient are normally good only for 14 to 21 days. Drugs that require refrigeration are also less likely to remain viable past their expiration dates. You may be able to safely take some drugs that are just past their expiration date, such as *acetaminophen* (Tylenol), but never use any critical medicine, such as insulin, that has expired.

Beware of Whole-Body Cryotherapy

FDA Center for Devices and Radiological Health, Washington, DC.

The benefits of this trendy treatment—in which the entire body is enclosed in a chamber and exposed to freezing nitrogen vapors for several minutes—remain unproved, and the risks are many. Proponents claim that whole-body cryotherapy can ease symptoms of fibromyalgia, rheumatoid arthritis, multiple sclerosis and migraines and that it combats stress and anxiety.

But: People exposed to nitrogen vapors in an enclosed space can suffer from oxygen deprivation and asphyxiation. Other risks include frostbite, eye injuries and worsening of existing medical conditions.

How to Get Faster Test Results

Charles B. Inlander, a consumer advocate and health-care consultant based in Fogelsville, Pennsylvania, was the founding president of the nonprofit People's Medical Society, a consumer advocacy organization credited with key improvements in the quality of US health care. He is author or coauthor of more than 20 consumer-health books.

Sometimes, waiting for your medical test results can cause more anxiety than the actual findings. That's particularly true if you or your doctor suspects that you might have a problem. The longer you have to wait, the more worried you become. But it doesn't have to be that way. *Here are smart steps you can take to get your test results as soon as possible...*

- **Get immediate results.** Immediate results may sound like a very high order, but they are possible. The key is to work closely with your doctor. It probably sounds obvious, but the first step is to let your doctor know that you want to get results as soon as possible—either good or bad news. This increases the chance that your doctor will pass results on quickly to you and that he/she will recommend a lab or center that is known for providing quick results.

Don't assume that you have to wait...and wait. For imaging tests, such as mammograms and other scans, many imaging centers will give you the radiologist-reviewed results on the spot. Ask your doctor to recommend such imaging centers in your area. Or call several centers near you and ask what their policies are on giving patients immediate results. Other centers will let you know if everything is OK but tell you to contact your doctor if there is a problem. In that case, you should immediately call your physician to discuss the results.

My story: When an MRI of my brain found I had a tumor a while back, the results were sent to my physician while I was at the imaging center, and we talked on the phone while I was still there about the next steps.

- **Find out when results will be available.** Of course, not all test results are immediately available. Blood work and other types of tests, such as tissue analysis of a biopsy, can often take several days or even weeks to be analyzed by a pathologist or other medical professional. And quite often your doctor will need to review the results and even discuss them with the pathologist and/or other physicians to make an accurate interpretation of the results. But you can still help move things along by calling your doctor's office as soon as you have completed the test. Let the office know what test you had...where it was done...when it was done...and the best way to reach you as soon as the doctor has the results. Again, let the doctor's office know that you want the results as soon as possible.

Note: If you have a condition, such as cancer, that may require frequent tests and/or biopsies that tend to take a long time for results, be sure to ask your doctor at your follow-up appointments if any future tests are likely or needed and if you should have them sooner rather than later.

- **Go online.** Most major hospitals and large medical practices, along with laboratories and imaging centers that are owned or affiliated with them, now make test results available to the patient online at the same time they become available to the doctor.

Important: The onus is on you to sign up or register for this service. Ask the doctors, hospitals, labs and imaging centers that you use if they offer such online services and how you can enroll.

Helpful: After you have a test but before you get the results, schedule an appointment with your doctor to go over the results.

Note: Some doctors prefer to do this over the phone, which is fine. But be sure to speak directly with the doctor, especially if the results are worrisome.

Doctor's Gender May Matter

Among more than one million patients age 65 and older who were treated for sepsis, pneumonia or other conditions, those with female internists were 4% less likely to die prematurely and 5% less likely to be readmitted to the hospital within 30 days than those with male doctors.

Possible reason: Previous studies have suggested that women internists may be more likely to have better communication with patients and to follow established recommendations for care.

Ashish Jha, MD, MPH, professor of health policy, Harvard T.H. Chan School of Public Health, Boston.

When to Hire Your Own Doctor

Mark V. Pauly, PhD, Bendheim Professor and a professor of health care management and economics and public policy at The Wharton School, University of Pennsylvania, Philadelphia. He received the National Institute of Health Care Management Foundation's Research Award for his investigation of the affordability of health insurance for the uninsured. His research interests include health insurance, health policy and medical economics.

"The doctor can see you immediately." When's the last time you heard that? The shortage of physicians in the US means that you'll probably have to wait about 18 days for an appointment.

By the time you do get in, you can expect a quick visit (13 to 16 minutes, if you're lucky) from a physician who will probably interrupt you within the first 18 seconds that you speak. It's true that some doctors do buck these averages, but the overwhelming majority of patients don't get a lot of hand-holding—let alone a cellphone number for emergencies.

Recent development: Even though the rich and famous have always had personal physicians who go the extra mile, "regular" people are now able to get some of the same attention—at a fraction of the cost that's traditionally been charged by so-called concierge physicians.

What you need to know about the world of concierge medicine today...

FEES ARE DROPPING

Starting in the 1990s, some physicians (mostly primary care doctors) began offering concierge services—also known as "boutique medicine"—to affluent patients. In exchange for an annual fee, they provided same-day appointments... lengthy office visits (about 40 minutes)...e-mail availability...24/7 phone/text access—and even home visits.

But the personal touch didn't come cheap. Some red-carpet practices charged patients $25,000 a year...on top of the usual fees for lab tests, procedures and hospitalization. Patients who ponied up still had to pay for insurance for emergencies and care from specialists.

In the last few years, doctors have begun offering similar services for far less money. Some offer concierge care for as little as a few hundred dollars a year—the national annual average is roughly $1,000 to $2,000. The cost for such services has been reduced due to increasing demand and by changing the scope of services—for example, VIP perks such as limo rides to the office are not offered.

Doctors in these practices accept fewer patients, so they can spend more time with them, and mainly offer basic care, such as physicals and checkups. These services may be covered by insurance, but patients must file their own claims. Other services (such as wellness counseling, which involves discussing issues including nutrition, exercise and stress reduction) may not be covered by standard insurance plans and usually require an extra fee.

A GROWING TREND

Five years ago, there were about 1,000 concierge practices nationwide. There are more than 5,000 now, but they still represent a tiny percentage of medical practices in the US.

Some such practices are run by altruistic primary care physicians who offer lower rates to low-income patients. But most concierge medicine targets patients who have the means to pay for convenience and extra attention.

What do you get for your money? A Tufts University study found that patients in these practices got better service overall (such as faster appointments, less wait time in the office and more personal attention). But there's no evidence yet that these patients are any healthier than those who get their care from traditional practices...or that they have better health outcomes from medical treatments, surgical procedures, etc.

THE REAL BENEFITS

A provision in the Affordable Care Act (ACA) allows a form of concierge services known as "direct primary care" (doctors who largely avoid the insurance system and charge patients a flat monthly or yearly fee, with some charging additional fees for services such as preventive checkups or care for chronic conditions) to meet the required guidelines for ACA-compliant insurance. Patients are still required to have an insurance policy for emergencies and specialists.

There are obvious advantages for doctors. Because they can avoid (or at least limit) their involvement with insurance companies, they can spend less time on record-keeping and filing claims and more time with patients. Many limit the number of patients that they treat to about 800, down from the 2,500 that are common in primary care practices.

Even with the reduced number of patients, the cumulative fees can be lucrative—particularly when they're paid by healthy patients who might not see the doctor more than once or twice a year.

How it can help patients: A concierge practice can make economic sense for some patients, too. Suppose that you have a high-deductible ($1,300 or more per year) insurance plan. If your health care mainly consists of routine checkups and dealing with the occasional (and minor) health problem, you're unlikely to meet the deductible and will be paying for everything out of pocket. You might do better with an annual concierge fee that covers all the services that you're likely to need.*

But you'll still need insurance. The monthly/annual concierge dues are for primary care only—you (or your insurance) will pay extra for visits with specialists, procedures (such as colonoscopy) and many lab tests. These will come on top of the concierge fees. Some direct-care practices have special rates for Medicare patients.

IS IT RIGHT FOR YOU?

Concierge practices give people more face time with their doctors. That's why a concierge practice can make a difference for those with complex medical problems or conditions (such as mental-health issues) that are difficult to address in a rushed medical practice.

On the other hand, a traditional medical practice—and the insurance coverage that's mandated by the ACA—will cover the essentials. Patients still get the necessary exams and tests, including colonoscopies, immunizations, etc. The quality of care is usually at least as good as what can be found anywhere else.

Bottom line: Unless you want to be treated like a VIP and/or have a high deductible, it's probably smarter to find a good doctor in a traditional practice than spend extra money on a concierge practice.

*If you are interested in finding a concierge doctor, consult the American Academy of Private Physicians, AAPP.org, which allows you to search doctors by location.

Watch Out for Your Doctor's Smartphone

Peter J. Papadakos, MD, director of critical care medicine at the University of Rochester Medical Center and professor of anesthesiology, neurology, surgery and neurosurgery at the University of Rochester, both in Rochester, New York. Dr. Papadakos was one of the first experts to identify the potential for distraction from smartphones and to popularize the term "distracted doctoring."

If you're like most people, you love your smartphone, tablet or laptop. Doctors, nurses and other medical personnel are no different. But when they use these devices in the workplace, does that help or hurt your medical care?

It's true that smartphones, tablets and laptops allow doctors to quickly look up the newest drug information and case studies. And it's great to be able to reach your physician in an emergency during off-hours, since doctors will sometimes share their cell-phone numbers and/or e-mail addresses with patients who require extra attention.

But there can also be dangerous downsides for the patient when medical staff has constant access to this type of technology.

A NEW DANGER

Nearly 90% of all doctors currently use smartphones or tablets while at work. *The most significant potential dangers to patients include…*

•**Bacterial contamination.** Even though there are many nonsterile surfaces in a health-care setting, cell phones are of particular concern because they are typically handled so often. When the cell phones of orthopedic surgeons in the operating room were tested, 83% of the phones had infection-causing bacteria on them, according to a study published in *The Journal of Bone & Joint Surgery.*

Self-defense: When admitted to a hospital, ask what the guidelines are for disinfecting electronic devices, particularly any that are brought into and handled in an operating room. Some hospitals now have ultraviolet (UV) sterilizing devices that are 99.9% effective at decontaminating objects in 10 seconds.

If your doctor is holding a cell phone or other personal device, ask him/her if the device was cleaned before attending to you and make sure the doctor washes his hands as well.

Also: When visiting someone in the hospital, don't pull out your cell phone to show photos in an effort to cheer up the patient. Better yet, leave your cell phone at home or in the car.

•**Distractions.** Researchers at Oregon State University and the Oregon Health & Science University tested the impact of distractions on residents performing a simulated gallbladder surgery. When the surgeons were interrupted by a cell-phone ring, the sound of a dropped metal tray clanging or other distraction, 44% made serious errors that could have led to a fatality, including damage to organs and arteries. Only one surgeon made a mistake when there were no interruptions.

Self-defense: To protect yourself from such forms of "distracted doctoring," ask your hospital whether it has a policy on the safe use of electronic devices throughout the hospital, and ask for a copy if it does. If electronic devices are allowed in the operating room, share your concerns with your surgical team.

At the University of Rochester Medical Center, we have a "Code of eConduct" to minimize the distractions of devices such as smartphones and tablets. Guidelines include that devices must be in "silent" mode (no ringing or vibrating) when in a patient's room…work-issued devices should not be used for personal use…and all personal business must be conducted only in break rooms and out of view of patients.

•**Addiction.** Just like everyone else, many doctors and other health-care professionals do not even realize how addicted they are to their smartphones and social media.

In a survey of more than 400 perfusionists (technicians who operate heart-lung bypass machines during heart surgery), more than half admitted that they had used a cell phone during heart bypass procedures to access e-mail, surf the Internet and use social networking sites. While 93% reported that they were not distracted by using their phones, 34% said that they had witnessed other perfusionists being distracted by their phones or texting during procedures.

Are You Addicted to Your Cell Phone?

Researchers at the University of Rochester modified the widely used CAGE survey for alcoholism by replacing the term "drink" with "personal electronic device" to help identify addiction to a smartphone or other devices.

1. Have you ever felt you needed to cut down on your personal electronic device use?
2. Have people annoyed you by criticizing your use of your personal electronic device?
3. Have you felt guilty about your overuse of your personal electronic device?
4. Do you reach for your personal electronic device first thing in the morning?

Two or more "yes" answers suggest an addiction. Recognizing that you have a problem is the first step to cutting down on excessive use of technology.

To make health-care professionals more aware of a possible addiction to technology, my colleagues and I at the University of Rochester modified a widely used screening survey for alcoholism to gauge people's addiction to their phones, texting and/or social media. To take the survey, see the box on the previous page.

•**iPatient.** When doctors are fixated on the computerized record of a patient, what I call an "iPatient," they miss important information such as speech patterns and body language.

Self-defense: Politely ask your doctor to put the device away for a few minutes and listen to you.

Medical Error Is the Third-Leading Cause of Death

Analysis of studies of medical death rate data from 2000 through 2008 by researchers at The Johns Hopkins University School of Medicine, Baltimore, published in *BMJ.*

Medical error is the third-leading cause of death in the US. More than 250,000 people die each year due to medical errors. Only heart disease and cancer cause more deaths annually.

Has Your Doctor Been Sued?

Seth A. Seabury, PhD, an associate professor at the Keck School of Medicine and the Leonard D. Schaeffer Center for Health Policy & Economics at the University of Southern California in Los Angeles. His research has been published in *The New England Journal of Medicine, The Journal of the American Medical Association* and elsewhere.

Some cases of medical malpractice are so egregious—and so shocking—that you have to wonder why some doctors are allowed to continue practicing medicine.

Example: A Missouri woman was permanently disabled after her surgeon mistakenly operated on the wrong side of her brain.

You can guess how you'd vote if you were on the jury. But this and other headline-making lawsuits are exceptional cases. Most malpractice lawsuits involve gray areas...honest mistakes (alleged or proven)...or legitimate disagreements about what should or should not have been done in a particular case.

What does a doctor's history of lawsuits tell patients about his/her ability to practice medicine? To learn more, we spoke with Seth A. Seabury, PhD, a renowned expert on medical malpractice.

How can I find out if my doctor has been sued?

There are public databases, but the availability of this information varies widely from state to state. The Federation of State Medical Boards has a database, DocInfo.org, that includes disciplinary actions taken against physicians by state licensing boards. A doctor could be disciplined for egregious negligence or for unethical or even criminal behavior. You can get similar information, including payments that were made for malpractice lawsuits, from some state medical licensing boards and/or insurance departments or state or county courts.

How often do medical doctors get sued?

A survey of more than 7,000 surgeons found that nearly 25% were recently involved in litigation. If you take into account all of the lawsuits that may occur in a 30- or 40-year career, the risks are much higher.

Research I conducted with colleagues from the University of Southern California and Harvard University suggests that up to 75% of physicians in lower-risk fields—pediatrics, family practice, etc.—will eventually face a malpractice claim. For those in higher-risk specialties, such as neurosurgery, lawsuits are a near certainty.

Isn't it true that bad doctors get sued more than good ones?

It's true that some doctors get sued more than others. A *New England Journal of Medicine* study that appeared earlier this year found that about 1% of doctors who had previously paid two or more malpractice claims accounted for nearly one-third of all paid claims. However, while some of these doctors may indeed provide substandard care, you can't assume that a history of lawsuits/paid claims is a reliable indicator of a doctor's proficiency.

Past research had found that a bad outcome is often what drives malpractice claims. A neurosurgeon who does complicated brain surgery or a cardiac surgeon who mainly treats high-risk patients will have a higher percentage of poor outcomes than doctors who treat the easier cases. As a result, they're more likely to face multiple lawsuits during their careers.

Are these the specialties that face the most lawsuits?

The study mentioned above found that four medical specialties—internal medicine, ob/gyn, surgery and general practice/family medicine—accounted for more than half of all claims.

This is partly due to volume. An internist or family practice physician sees a lot of patients. The more patients a doctor sees, the higher the risk that something will eventually go wrong. Neurosurgeons and cardiac surgeons see fewer patients, but the ones they do see have a higher-than-average risk for complications or death.

If a doctor has a terrible bedside manner, is he more likely to give substandard care—and get sued for it?

I'm not aware of any evidence that a rude doctor is more likely to provide poor care than one who is warm and welcoming. However, one study did find that doctors with a more extensive history of lawsuits also had a history of dealing poorly with patients—ignoring their concerns, not communicating well, etc.

Doctors who show the most empathy—and are willing to admit to, and apologize for, mistakes—might be less vulnerable to lawsuits, but it hasn't been proven. Some states have experimented with so-called "apology laws" to protect doctors who may worry that an apology could be used later against them in court. However, there's no definitive evidence whether or not these laws reduce the number of lawsuits.

So, do most doctors—even good ones—make a lot of mistakes?

Medical errors definitely happen. The Institute of Medicine estimates that tens of thousands of patients die each year due to preventable medical errors. But there is uncertainty as to how well the malpractice system does in discerning actual medical errors from just bad outcomes.

In a number of studies, researchers reviewed the medical records of patients involved in malpractice claims. They often found evidence of medical mistakes (giving a wrong drug dose, for example), but the mistakes were usually minor. Some may have affected how well—or poorly—patients did, but it's safe to assume that many didn't.

According to research, there's actually a weak relationship between medical errors and malpractice claims. A Harvard study found that about 40% of malpractice cases should never have been filed...and that many of the cases showed no evidence of mistakes or proof that patients had been harmed.

Bottom line: Malpractice law entitles patients to compensation if they were injured because their doctor was negligent, which isn't the same as being wrong or unlucky. Practicing medicine is difficult, and sometimes doctors can do everything by the book and a bad outcome can still happen. That isn't to say that malpractice doesn't occur—obviously it does—but sometimes it can be very hard to distinguish between substandard care and outcomes after the fact. That's why you have to sometimes be careful about making a judgment about quality based on the number of malpractice claims a doctor has.

FDA Warns 14 Companies on Bogus Cancer "Cures"

U.S. Food and Drug Administration, news releases.

The U.S. Food and Drug Administration recently posted warning letters to 14 companies that are selling more than 65 fake cancer treatments.

The bogus products include pills, capsules, powders, creams, teas, oils and treatment and diagnostic kits. They're most commonly marketed and sold without FDA approval on websites and social media platforms, the FDA announcement of its action said.

The treatments are frequently advertised as "natural" and often falsely labeled as dietary supplements, the agency added.

"Consumers should not use these or similar unproven products because they may be unsafe and could prevent a person from seeking an appropriate and potentially lifesaving cancer diagnosis or treatment," said Douglas Stearn. He is director of the Office of Enforcement and Import Operations in the FDA's Office of Regulatory Affairs.

"We encourage people to remain vigilant whether online or in a store, and avoid purchasing products marketed to treat cancer without any proof they will work," he said in an FDA news release.

Nicole Kornspan is a consumer safety officer at the FDA. "Anyone who suffers from cancer, or knows someone who does, understands the fear and desperation that can set in. There can be a great temptation to jump at anything that appears to offer a chance for a cure," she said in a second agency news release.

Consumers should be wary of certain phrases often used in the marketing of these treatments: "Treats all forms of cancer," "miraculously kills cancer cells and tumors," "shrinks malignant tumors," "selectively kills cancer cells," "more effective than chemotherapy," "attacks cancer cells, leaving healthy cells intact" and "cures cancer."

The FDA advises patients to always discuss cancer treatment options, including experimental drugs, with a licensed health-care provider.

"There are legal ways for patients to access investigational drugs, for example, taking part in clinical trials," Kornspan said. Information can be found at the U.S. National Cancer Institute's clinical trials website.

Unproven cancer treatments for pets are also common, according to the FDA.

"Increasingly, bogus remedies claiming to cure cancer in cats and dogs are showing up online. People who cannot afford to spend large sums at the animal hospital to treat cancer in their beloved dogs and cats are searching for less expensive remedies," Kornspan said.

The FDA has issued more than 90 warning letters in the past 10 years to companies marketing hundreds of fraudulent products making cancer claims on websites, social media and in stores, the news release noted.

info Visit the U.S. Federal Trade Commission at FTC.gov for more information (search "cancer treatment scams").

Specialists Most Likely to Receive Payments from Drug Companies

Drexel University, news release.

Many American doctors receive payments from drug companies, but few patients know about those financial ties, a recent study finds.

Researchers surveyed 3,500 adult patients and then checked on their doctors in Open Payments, a government website that reports drug and medical device company payments to physicians.

The study found that within the previous year, 65% of patients visited doctors who received payments or gifts from drug or medical device companies, but only 5% of the patients were aware of those doctor-industry links.

Patients who visited certain types of specialists were even more likely to have seen a doctor who had been paid. For example, the rates were 85% among patients who saw an orthopedic surgeon and 77% among patients who saw an obstetrician or gynecologist.

The study was published recently in the *Journal of General Internal Medicine.*

"These findings tell us that if you thought that your doctor was not receiving any money from industry, you're most likely mistaken," said study author Genevieve Pham-Kanter, an assistant professor in Drexel University's Dornsife School of Public Health in Philadelphia.

"Patients should be aware of the incentives that their physicians face that may lead them to not always act in their patients' best interest. And the more informed patients are about their providers and options for care, the better decisions they can make," she said in a news release from Drexel.

Study coauthor Michelle Mello said, "Drug companies have long known that even small gifts to physicians can be influential, and research validates the notion that they tend to induce feelings of reciprocity." Mello is a professor of law and health research and policy at Stanford University in Stanford, California.

The Open Payments data showed that the average amount received in drug and medical device company payments and gifts by doctors was $193. But when the researchers focused only on the doctors visited by patients in the survey, the median payment amount was $510, more than 2.5 times the national average.

"We may be lulled into thinking this isn't a big deal because the average payment amount across all doctors is low," Pham-Kanter said. "But that obscures the fact that most people are seeing doctors who receive the largest payments."

info The American Academy of Family Physicians offers advice on choosing a family doctor at FamilyDoctor.org/choosing-a-family-doctor/.

Struggling with Drug Costs? Ask Your Doctor for Help

University of Michigan, news release.

Many older Americans who have difficulty paying for their medications don't seek help in finding cheaper options, a recent poll indicates.

"We already know that cost can keep patients from taking the drugs they need to maintain health or prevent complications, but these new data suggest that many older adults aren't talking to their doctors or pharmacists about cost and less-expensive alternatives as often as they could," said poll director Preeti Malani, MD. She is a professor of internal medicine at the University of Michigan Medical School.

"This represents an opportunity for patients, clinicians—as well as health systems, insurers and policymakers," Dr. Malani added in a university news release.

The national poll of more than 2,100 adults aged 50 to 80 found that 27% said their prescription drug costs were a financial burden.

About 16% had six or more prescriptions and saw more than one doctor. These patients were the most likely to say they struggled with drug costs, the poll found.

Among the respondents who said their medication costs were a burden, 49% had not talked to their doctors about the issue. But doing so was effective, because 67% of those who talked to their doctor received a recommendation for a less expensive drug, as did 37% of those who talked to their pharmacists.

"Based on these findings, and other evidence, we encourage patients to speak up during their clinic visits, and when they're at the pharmacy, and ask about ways to reduce the cost of their prescriptions," Dr. Malani said.

"But equally, we see a need for health professionals to find ways to more routinely engage with patients about cost—especially through formal medication reviews such as the one that Medicare will cover," she added.

CHAPTER 6

Dental Care Updates

Have Beautiful, Healthy Teeth…At Any Age!

Not that long ago, preteens were just about the only ones whose smiles sparkled with shiny metal, teeth-straightening braces.

Now: The look of braces—and the people who are wearing them—has dramatically changed. Braces are much more discreet than ever before, and about one out of every four patients who seeks this treatment is an adult.

WHY NOW?

There are a variety of reasons why more and more adults are now seeing orthodontists.* Many adults experience crowding of their bottom front teeth as they age. While this shifting of the teeth is perfectly normal, it's usually not aesthetically pleasing. Crowded teeth are also harder for many people to keep clean because rotated and/or overlapping teeth tend to catch more food.

*To find an orthodontist near you, consult the website of the American Association of Orthodontists, MyLifeMySmile.org.

With age, structural changes to the gum and bone also tend to occur, shifting one's normal bite. Orthodontic treatment can often help prevent the wearing down or chipping of teeth that would otherwise result…or, in some cases, guard against gum erosion and problems in the function and comfort of the jaw joint if a person's bite is not properly aligned.

For other people, self-image is the driving force. Many adults have been self-conscious about the appearance of their teeth for years—perhaps even avoiding smiling as a result.

NEW OPTIONS

Fixed braces, "brackets" that are bonded to each tooth and linked with wires, have long been the gold standard. These brackets are ex-

Lee W. Graber, DDS, PhD, an orthodontist in private practice in Vernon Hills and Glenview, Illinois. A past president of both the American Association of Orthodontists and the World Federation of Orthodontists, he has lectured extensively in the US and abroad on adult orthodontic care and is coauthor and editor of *Orthodontics: Current Principles and Techniques*, a graduate textbook.

tremely effective at straightening teeth because precise pressure can be applied by the orthodontist via a connected arch wire. Arch wires may be of varying size, shape and material depending on the stage of treatment. The orthodontist typically makes adjustments once every six to 12 weeks.

Depending on the severity of your condition, treatment for an adult typically lasts one to three years (more complicated problems can require more time). The price for fixed metal braces varies depending on your location, but they generally run about $5,000 to $7,000, according to the American Dental Association.

Note: You may be able to use your Flexible Spending Account to cover orthodontic expenses.

Improved options: Today's standard metal braces are about half the size they were even 15 years ago. So-called "mini braces" are even less conspicuous—about 30% smaller than today's standard braces. Unlike the metal (stainless steel or titanium) that has been widely used, porcelain or ceramic braces are now available and appear tooth-colored or clear.

All of these options are equally effective, but tooth-colored braces placed on the upper teeth may be more expensive, adding about $375 to $500 to the treatment.

Important: For adults who need new crowns, root canals and/or cavity fillings, careful and coordinated planning between the orthodontist, general dentist and other dental specialists, such as periodontists, is often required to achieve an optimal outcome.

In addition, certain medications, such as estrogen hormone replacement therapy...nonsteroidal anti-inflammatory drugs (NSAIDs) and/or long-term aspirin therapy...and osteoporosis medications known as bisphosphonates, such as *alendronate* (Fosamax), can slow down desired tooth movement. With such circumstances, it's crucial for your orthodontist to take a thorough medical history, including the use of any medications, before developing a treatment plan.

TO BE DISCREET

•Clear aligners, such as Invisalign or ClearCorrect, are less visible than traditional braces but more limited in scope. These removable, custom-fit plastic trays are created from 3-D scans of your teeth and can be removed for eating or brushing and flossing.

You'll get a series of trays, which sequentially move teeth to the desired position. To be most effective, patients should wear their aligners at least 22 hours per day.

Patients usually switch their trays every two weeks with treatment lasting from seven to 10 months and up to 24 months for more involved plans. The fees for aligners vary but often are comparable to those for fixed braces.

•Lingual braces attach behind the teeth so no one knows that you're wearing them. Some orthodontists consider lingual braces less efficient and less comfortable than front-of-the-teeth types. Lingual braces are usually more expensive—sometimes costing up to 50% more than traditional metal braces.

OTHER IMPROVEMENTS

In addition to the advancements described earlier, adjunct therapies can potentially be used to improve orthodontic treatment cosmetics, speed and outcome. *For example...*

•SureSmile allows an orthodontist to create a 3-D computer model of your teeth, bite and jaw structures. A truly customized treatment plan is then created using software and virtual simulation tools. The arch wire, which is traditionally manipulated by the orthodontist, is shaped and bent robotically for greater precision based on the orthodontist's prescription.

Use of this technology can reduce treatment time by up to 30%. Some practices may charge an extra $500 to $800, while others include it in your orthodontic costs. Other brace systems that integrate computerized planning and custom fabrication of braces and/or arch wires include Insignia, Incognito Hidden Braces and Harmony.

•AcceleDent is an FDA-cleared device that was introduced in the US in 2012. Resembling a bite guard, the prescription-only device delivers pain-free vibrations, or micropulses, to the teeth, which are thought to accelerate the bone and gum-remodeling processes.

Research findings are mixed, but some studies have found that treatment time may be reduced by 30% to 50%, depending on the type of treatment being provided. AcceleDent should be used for 20 minutes daily to achieve the desired results. Some practices charge an extra $600 to $1,000, while other practices include it in your initial orthodontic cost estimate.

---

5 Little Habits That Can Do Big Damage to Your Teeth

Marvin A. Fier, DDS, FASDA, Diplomate of the American Board of Aesthetic Dentistry. He teaches continuing-education courses to practicing dentists and has a private practice, Cosmetic & Family Dentistry, in Pomona, New York, providing care for residents of the NY Tri-State area and beyond. SmileRockland.com

Are you an ice-chomper or perhaps a nail-biter? These and four other "mouth habits" mean that you should start saving for dental work—you're going to need it.

Brushing and flossing (and dentist visits) won't save your teeth if you engage in mouth-mangling habits. Forget the obvious things such as smoking or chewing on pencils. Habits that seem innocuous actually can cause significant (and expensive) damage…

NAIL-BITING

There's a scientific name for nail biting—onychophagia. It's among the most common nervous habits and is listed in the *Diagnostic and Statistical Manual of Mental Disorder*, fifth edition (DSM-5, the official manual of mental disorders) because some people do it compulsively—in some cases, for hours a day.

Fingernails are harder than you might think, especially if you use nail polish. Constant nibbling can fracture tooth enamel. It damages the cuticle and soft tissue surrounding the nail and exposes your mouth to hand bacteria. It forces your jaw into a protruding position that puts painful pressure on the joint.

My advice: You have to be aware of a habit before you can stop it. An awful-tasting nail polish or cream (such as neem oil, Control-It! or Mavala Stop) will remind you of what you're doing. People are more likely to bite their nails when they're stressed, so it's helpful to substitute healthier (and more soothing) activities—deep breathing, going for walks, etc. Or chew sugarless gum to dispel nervous energy and keep your mouth busy. Also, keep your nails short—they're harder to bite.

HARD BRUSHING

As a dentist, I always encourage people to brush their teeth. Done correctly, it's among the best ways to protect your teeth as well as your gums. But many people think that a soft touch won't get the job done. They apply way too much force or use a brush that's hard enough to clean bathroom grout.

Hard brushing abrades tooth enamel along with gums. It does even more damage to the tooth roots, which are softer than enamel. When I see patients with notches or abrasions in the roots, I know that they're brushing too hard.

Hint: Tooth sensitivity to cold temperatures or sweets can be caused by root damage due to brushing too hard.

My advice: Never buy a hard toothbrush. Those that are labeled "medium" still are too hard. Use only a soft brush. And even with a soft brush, don't bear down when you're brushing—use the lightest touch you can muster. Think "massage," not "scrub."

Helpful: Hold the brush (manual or electric) with your fingertips instead of clenching it in your fist. This makes it almost impossible to apply too much pressure.

CHEWING ICE CUBES

Ice is harder than hard candy. According to the Mohs Scale of Mineral Hardness, it has a hardness of 1.5. That makes it a little harder than talc but not quite as hard as gypsum. No one would think to chew rocks, but that's exactly what you're doing when you munch the ice cubes in your drinks. It can cause microscopic cracks in tooth enamel, which increase the risk for decay and fracturing teeth

My advice: If you can't stop yourself from chomping ice from your drinks, quit putting it in drinks. Stick to chilled beverages without ice. Or use a straw to reduce temptation.

Another option: Use ice chips. They're smaller than cubes and less likely to crack your teeth.

ALL-DAY GRAZING

Snacking isn't bad if your taste runs to nuts, fruits and vegetables. But many people who snack crave sweets. The average American consumes about 20 teaspoons of added sugar a day.

Bacteria in the mouth love sugar. They convert it to acids that damage the teeth as well as the gums.

People who eat a lot of sugary snacks have a much higher risk for cavities and periodontal disease (loss of gum and bone), the leading cause of tooth loss in adults.

My advice: Limit your snacking. Eat larger (nutritionally balanced) meals so that you feel full longer.

When you do snack, keep it healthy. Avoid the usual culprits—sweetened soft drinks... candy bars...hard candies, etc.

Also helpful: If you can't brush after snacks, at least swish your mouth with water. It will remove some of the sugar and bacterial acids.

USING TEETH AS TOOLS

This should be obvious, but many people don't hesitate to use their teeth for all sorts of odd jobs—opening bags, snipping plastic tags off clothes, tearing open clamshell packages and even opening bottles.

I see a lot of patients who have chipped or fractured their teeth because they didn't take the time to look for a pair of scissors or dig through the toolbox for pliers.

My advice: Don't use your teeth as tools. You might think you're saving time by nibbling off a price tag, but the eventual damage and repair will take longer than looking for the right tool—and will cost a lot more.

THE DANGERS OF GRINDING AND CLENCHING YOUR TEETH

Australian researchers made a surprising discovery when they compared human skulls to those of other animals. Using sophisticated engineering software, they found that the human jaw actually generates more biting force than the jaws of great apes. When you use all of your jaw muscles to bite down, you're generating a force as great as 55 pounds.

That's what allows us to chew hard foods. The downside is that it's more than enough to fracture the teeth and even damage the jaw joints. Some of the worst damage I see in my practice comes from bruxism, clenching or grinding the teeth during sleep or times of high stress. It can cause visible wear and flattening of the tooth surfaces.

People who grind their teeth during sleep, known as nocturnal grinders, can protect themselves by wearing a customized mouth guard. Daytime grinders are a bigger challenge because they don't even know they're doing it (and would be unlikely to wear mouth guards while they're awake).

My advice: Start with relaxation exercises. Grinding/clenching almost always increases during times of stress, anger or even deep concentration. People who manage their stress with activities such as yoga, meditation or regular workouts will naturally grind less.

Helpful: The next time you're feeling stressed, pay attention to your shoulders. You'll probably notice that they're tight and hunched upward toward your neck. It's impossible to relax when the shoulders are tensed. Make a conscious effort to relax your shoulders and let them "drop." You'll feel less tension the moment you do this.

Cavities May Have a Genetic Link

Michael Glick, DMD, professor, School of Dental Medicine, University at Buffalo, New York, and editor in chief of *Journal of the American Dental Association*, quoted in *The Wall Street Journal*.

Studies of identical twins have found genetics responsible for up to a 64% higher chance of developing cavities in their "baby" teeth. If you believe that you have a strong likelihood of tooth decay, it is important to brush twice a day, rinse daily with antibacterial mouthwash, see your dentist twice a year and limit consumption of sugar—especially sticky candy and sugary drinks.

Keep on Flossing!

Laurence Grayhills, DMD, MS, MAGD, president, Florida Academy of General Dentistry, and dentist in Wellington, Florida.

Even though recent research showed that there's no real evidence flossing improves dental health, it's important to keep on flossing.

Flossing daily is still recommended as part of a dental hygiene regimen that includes brushing twice a day and visiting your dentist every six months. A recent review found that studies on flossing were poorly designed and that conclusions suggesting that it prevents gum disease and cavities were weak. But weak doesn't mean wrong, so my advice is to keep flossing.

Brushing does not remove food particles between the teeth or under the gums. If these particles are not removed, they can form plaque, a sticky substance that hardens into tartar and causes cavities and gum disease. Flossing every day (with string floss, dental tape or a water flosser) is still necessary to prevent gum disease, the biggest cause of tooth loss.

Don't Let Gum Disease Kill You

Susan Blum, MD, MPH, founder and director, Blum Center for Health, assistant clinical professor, department of preventive medicine, Icahn School of Medicine at Mount Sinai, and integrative medicine specialist, department of medicine, Greenwich Hospital, Connecticut. Dr. Blum is a member of the senior teaching faculty at the Center for Mind-Body Medicine in Washington, DC, and teaches throughout the world in their training programs. She is author of *The Immune System Recovery Plan*.

By now, most of us know that gum disease is linked with heart disease. But if that's not enough to get your attention, how about this—new evidence shows that if you have gum disease, you may be more likely to get serious autoimmune diseases and cancer.

Did that get your attention? If you want to be healthy, act now to keep your mouth and gums in good shape.

Important: It's more than just brushing and flossing.

HOW GUM DISEASE CAN TURN DEADLY

Most of us are aware that the "good" bacteria in our guts, sometimes called the "gut microbiome," play a key role in health. But there's growing evidence that the "mouth microbiome" is extremely important, too. The mouth has billions of "good" bacteria that support digestion and oral health. *But when infection-causing oral bacteria take over, causing gum disease, there's an increased risk for even more serious conditions...*

- **Heart disease and stroke.** Many studies have found a link between gum disease and an increased risk for heart disease and stroke. One reason is that gum infection causes body-wide inflammation that can contribute to these diseases.
- **Type 2 diabetes.** While gum disease hasn't been shown to cause diabetes, people with diabetes tend to have more gum disease—which in turn can raise blood sugar, making diabetes worse.
- **Rheumatoid arthritis.** Researchers at Johns Hopkins University School of Medicine in Baltimore have found that a particular bacterium that causes chronic gum disease can trigger an autoimmune response that is linked to rheumatoid arthritis. The same pathogenic bacteria was found in mouths and diseased joints.
- **Pancreatic cancer.** At NYU Langone Medical Center in New York City, investigators have found that the same bacterium associated with rheumatoid arthritis is also linked with increased risk for pancreatic cancer. Participants in the study who had this bacterium in their mouths were 50% more likely to develop pancreatic cancer than those who did not.

Whether you have a chronic illness or want to avoid one, taking care of your mouth is essential. *Here's how...*

If you're generally healthy and want to prevent gum disease...

You already know the basics—limit sugary foods, don't smoke, do brush after every meal, and floss at least once a day. *More tips...*

- **Floss every night.** It's fine to floss more frequently, such as after every meal, but if you can manage only the once-a-day minimum, make sure you do it at the end of the day.

Here's why: When you sleep, saliva production is at its lowest, enabling bacteria and plaque to get a stronghold on those little bits of food stuck between your teeth.

•**Eat plants.** Vegetarians are less prone to gum disease than meat-eaters, in part because their diets are less inflammatory. Even if you eat meat, make sure you eat a primarily plant-based diet rich in vegetables, fruits, whole grains, legumes, nuts and seeds.

•**Manage stress and get enough sleep.** Stress interferes with saliva production and changes the bacteria in your mouth. Plus, being well-rested and calm helps your immune system stay strong enough to protect against gum disease.

•**Watch out for excessive alcohol.** Moderate drinking isn't a problem, but people who are "alcohol dependent" are much more likely to have lots of gum disease–causing bacteria in their mouths.

•**See your dentist twice a year for cleaning or more often if you're prone to excessive plaque buildup.** (You already knew this, and yet one-third of Americans don't even see their dentists annually.)

If you're starting to show signs of gum disease....

Gingivitis is the earliest, mildest form of gum disease. It's marked by gums that are red, swollen and bleed easily ("pink toothbrush syndrome"). *If this is happening to you, do all of the above and try a little extra dental TLC...*

•**Use a water pick—with added hydrogen peroxide.** (Follow the instructions on your product for where to add it). Using a water pick with water alone will clean between your teeth, but with added hyrogen peroxide, you'll kill "bad" bacteria. (Yes, you'll also kill some "good" bacteria, but it's like pruning a garden—getting rid of the "bad" bacteria will help the "good" ones reestablish themselves.) I recommend doing this daily for two or three months or until gingivitis is resolved, then dropping down to once or twice a week for maintenance.

•**Rinse your mouth with warm saltwater when needed.** Saltwater rinse helps reduce inflammation and kills bacteria. But use this remedy only for flare-ups—daily use can damage teeth.

•**Try oil pulling.** This Ayurvedic practice involves swishing your mouth with a spoonful or so of coconut oil or another plant oil for several minutes and then spitting it out. Although there isn't much scientific proof that it works, my clinical experience is that it is effective at preventing, and even reversing, gingivitis.

•**See your dentist and follow the above recommendations,** but if your dentist recommends it or your gingivitis doesn't get better, make an appointment with a periodontist. Unchecked, gingivitis can proceed to periodontitis, a more serious condition. Advanced periodontitis may require surgery.

If you have dry mouth...

To thrive, the healthful bacteria in your mouth need saliva, which keeps your teeth and gums moist and healthy and helps to wash away "bad" bacteria before they can get established. The good bacteria, it turns out, are more resistant to being washed away by saliva than the bad bacteria.

But many medications—including prescription drugs for high blood pressure (diuretics) and depression and over-the-counter drugs for allergies (antihistamines)—inhibit saliva production. So can some medical conditions such as diabetes. If you take a medication or have a condition that causes dry mouth, drink plenty of water throughout the day. You may also want to look for a chewable probiotic, which will help release saliva even as it helps improve digestive health.

HEALING THE BODY BEGINS IN THE MOUTH

In my work as an integrative medicine specialist, I treat many people with autoimmune diseases, including rheumatoid arthritis, ankylosing spondylitis (a type of arthritis that mainly affects the spine), psoriatic arthritis, lupus and Sjögren's syndrome. My primary approach is to repair the gut, rebuilding the gut "microbiome" with diet and enzymes, probiotics and other supplements. If you have periodontal disease, it can have a negative effect on the gut biome.

In my experience, when my patients improve the microbiomes in their mouths, it helps them manage their diseases. So I always insist that at the outset of my treatment, my patients first see their dentists and then possibly periodontists for evaluation and possible treatment—even if they don't have obvious evidence of gum disease. The truth is, everyone with gum disease should take steps to treat it because it could be triggering system-wide inflammation.

So Long, Splotchy Dark Gums

Alex Farnoosh, DMD, PhD, a cosmetic dentist and periodontist in private practice in Beverly Hills, California, who has published research on the treatment of gingival hyperpigmentation. He also is a clinical professor in the department of periodontology at the University of Southern California in Los Angeles and a diplomate of the American Board of Periodontology. TheTotalSmile.com

Even if their teeth are enviably bright and straight, some women conceal their smiles because they're self-conscious about dark splotches on their gums. Typically there is no medical or periodontal problem—the spots are harmless deposits of the pigment melanin—and sometimes that information alone provides the reassurance people need to let their grins out of hiding.

But when brown or blue-black patches or overall darkness of the gums erode self-confidence, it's understandable to want a solution. Fortunately, there are now easy and effective treatments that allow once-dark gums to be transformed into the "pink of health." However, many people—even dentists—are unaware of that fact.

What's behind those blotches: Genetics plays the primary role in determining who gets gingival hyperpigmentation, the medical term for splotchy or dark gums. Though people of African, Indian, Middle Eastern or Asian descent are particularly prone to produce the extra melanin, darkened gum patches can occur in people of all races, according to Alex Farnoosh, DMD, PhD, a Beverly Hills cosmetic dentist and periodontist (gum specialist). Other contributing factors include smoking and use of oral contraceptives, the antibiotic *minocycline* or certain other medications.

In rare cases, discolored gums can signal an underlying health problem, such as a blood or adrenal gland disorder. That's why it is best to talk with a physician before pursuing cosmetic treatment for dark gum spots, Dr. Farnoosh advised.

Lightening up: Getting rid of gum splotches used to be a risky and painful procedure involving grafting, and results often were unsatisfactory. But today's options, which include laser treatment and/or a nonlaser bleaching technique developed by Dr. Farnoosh, can produce pink gums much more easily—typically in one or two sessions—by breaking down or removing the deposits of melanin. Typically treatment is done under local anesthesia...takes about an hour...involves minimal discomfort...requires no recovery time...and produces immediate results.

Once treated, the dark spots generally do not come back, Dr. Farnoosh said, citing patients he has treated with the nonlaser bleaching method and followed for as long as 20 years. (He noted that there is less long-term data on the permanence of the laser treatment.)

Caveat: Given that smoking contributes to gum discoloration, a patient who continues to smoke after treatment may need a touch-up down the road. The cost starts at about $1,500 depending on the extent of the area treated.

Intrigued? That's understandable...because attractive gums can be part of your loveliest smile. To find a gum specialist in your area, visit the website of the American Academy of Periodontology at Perio.org. But note that not every

Cavity Danger

Beware of silver diamine fluoride (SDF) for cavities, warns Marvin Fier, DDS. Approved by the FDA as a tooth desensitizer for adults age 21 and older, SDF can slow or stop the progression of cavities without drilling, so some dentists are using it off-label for cavities.

But: SDF turns the dentin inside the tooth black, which can show through the tooth.

Marvin Fier, DDS, FASDA, ABAD, is a dentist in private practice in Pomona, New York, and executive vice president of the American Society for Dental Aesthetics.

periodontist knows how to treat dark gums—so you'll want to contact several practitioners to inquire about their experience.

Marijuana May Make Your Gums Go to Pot

Columbia University, news release.

Frequent pot smokers might be dooming themselves to diseased gums, a recent study suggests.

"It is well known that frequent tobacco use can increase the risk of periodontal [gum] disease, but it was surprising to see that recreational cannabis [pot] users may also be at risk," said study lead author Jaffer Shariff. He is a postdoctoral resident in periodontology at Columbia University School of Dental Medicine.

For the study, Shariff's team analyzed data from nearly 2,000 Americans. Of those, 27% reported the use of cannabis (marijuana, hashish or hash oil) one or more times for at least 12 months.

Frequent recreational cannabis users were more likely to have signs of moderate to severe gum disease than less-frequent users, the researchers found.

"The recent spate of new recreational and medical marijuana laws could spell the beginning of a growing oral public health problem," Shariff said in a university news release.

"Even controlling for other factors linked to gum disease, such as cigarette smoking, frequent recreational cannabis smokers are twice as likely as non-frequent users to have signs of periodontal disease," Shariff said.

The association seen in the study doesn't prove a cause-and-effect relationship.

However, in light of the findings, dentists should routinely ask their patients about pot smoking habits, Shariff suggested.

Another gum disease expert agreed that doctors and patients should be aware of the dangers that pot smoking may pose to dental health.

"At a time when the legalization of recreational and medical marijuana is increasing its use in the United States, users should be made aware of the impact that any form of cannabis can have on the health of their gums," said Terrence Griffin, president of the American Academy of Periodontology.

The study was published recently in the *Journal of Periodontology.*

Love Your Toothpaste!

Natalie Hastings, DMD, division chair of clinical general dentistry in the department of preventive and restorative dentistry at the University of California, San Francisco School of Dentistry. Dr. Hastings is a trained prosthodontist and an assistant clinical professor, also serving as the predoctoral director of Fixed Prosthodontics and the Student Dental Implant Program at the university.

Are you a savvy toothpaste shopper? Or do you reach for the same brand that you've always bought...or maybe settle for whatever product is on sale?

With literally dozens of toothpaste varieties on drugstore and supermarket shelves—each one touting different benefits ranging from plaque-fighting to breath-freshening and enamel-protecting—it's tough to know which one is best for you.

You might assume that it's all marketing hype. But the truth is, there are some ingredients that do make a difference—and a few others that you may not need.

Here are answers to the questions that will help you identify the best toothpaste for you...

•**Do I still need fluoride?** You're way past your cavity-prone childhood years, so you really don't need this ingredient, right? Wrong.

Cavities occur at all ages. Your risk depends, in part, on your bacteria levels and diet (sugar provides an ideal breeding ground for bacteria that create decay-promoting acids). Using a fluoride-fortified toothpaste really does help prevent cavities. It strengthens the outer surface of teeth, making the enamel more resistant to tooth decay.

The safety question: In recent years, a growing anti-fluoride movement has asserted that fluoride is a neurotoxin. However, decades of research prove that the amount of fluoride found in toothpaste is not only safe but also

Can Toothpaste Get in the Way?

Some studies say that brushing without toothpaste actually cleans teeth better. Using no toothpaste and looking in the mirror while brushing can make it easier to spot areas of plaque that need extra attention. But use a fluoride rinse after brushing without toothpaste to help strengthen tooth enamel.

Matthew Messina, DDS, spokesperson, American Dental Association, quoted in *Men's Health*.

necessary to guard against cavities. For general oral health, specific brands don't matter too much—just make sure it contains fluoride.

What you may not know: If your dentist spots a cavity in the outer layer of your tooth's enamel, you can permanently reverse it with the use of fluoride toothpaste and mouthwash.

What to do: Follow the standard advice for anyone—brush twice daily with a soft-bristle toothbrush for a full two minutes (use an electric toothbrush with a timer if necessary), then floss—but also swish with a fluoridated mouth rinse, such as ACT Anticavity Fluoride Mouthwash or Crest Pro-Health Advanced Mouthwash. Your dentist may also apply a topical fluoride varnish after a cleaning and provide a prescription for stronger fluoride toothpaste (such as Clinpro 5000 or PreviDent 5000 toothpaste).

• **What will relieve my dry mouth?** Dry mouth is no fun at all. More than 400 medications, including blood pressure drugs and antidepressants, are known to cause dry mouth. (Be sure to tell your doctor if you take medication and have dry mouth—you may be able to switch to a different drug.) Radiation treatments in or near the mouth can also cause it. With dry mouth, you have less saliva, which is needed to help fight cavities by neutralizing acids from food.

What helps: Sip water frequently throughout the day, and try chewing sugar-free gum or sucking on sugar-free mints made with xylitol (a sugar substitute that reduces risk for cavities) between meals to stimulate saliva production.

If you have dry mouth, also consider asking your dentist to prescribe a prescription fluoride toothpaste, such as Clinpro 5000 toothpaste (mentioned earlier). It contains not only more than four times the fluoride of regular toothpaste but also calcium and phosphate to help remineralize and further strengthen your teeth.

Also helpful: Biotène makes a line of xylitol-containing rinses for dry mouth, including Dry Mouth Oral Rinse.

• **What if my teeth are sensitive?** If you've lost some of your enamel due to grinding, clenching, an acidic diet or receding gums, your teeth may be hypersensitive. If that's the case, a desensitizing toothpaste is likely to help—these products contain compounds (such as potassium nitrate) that help block transmission of pain signals from the tooth's outer surface to the nerve.

What helps: Sensodyne Fresh Mint Toothpaste. You'll need to use a desensitizing toothpaste daily for a few weeks before feeling the benefit—stop using it, and the sensitivity will return.

Important new finding: A 2016 study concluded that arginine, an amino acid naturally found in saliva, is superior to other desensitizing agents.

Good product that contains arginine: Colgate Sensitive Pro-Relief Toothpaste.

If you have acid reflux: Don't brush immediately after eating or during an episode of heartburn—food acids may damage tooth enamel over time.

Instead: Dissolve a few teaspoons of baking soda in a bottle of water, then rinse and spit it out after eating to neutralize any acid in your mouth. Wait at least an hour, then brush with a desensitizing toothpaste.

• **What if I prefer a "natural" toothpaste?** Most "natural" toothpastes (such as Kiss My Face and Jason) are free of sodium lauryl sulfate (SLS), a foaming agent that creates that luxurious lather during brushing.

Some people find that SLS irritates their gums, and a small study found that canker sores may be less likely to develop in people who use SLS-free toothpaste. For these individuals, an SLS-free toothpaste is a good option...just make sure it's a product that contains fluoride, such as Tom's of Maine Clean & Gentle with Fluoride Toothpaste, Peppermint.

•To Swish? Or Not to Swish? Not all mouthwashes are created equal. Some, such as Scope, temporarily freshen your breath, but they don't contain the fluoride that is needed to prevent or control tooth decay.

To keep your enamel strong: Stick with a fluoridated rinse such as ACT Anticavity Fluoride Mouthwash. An antibacterial rinse, such as Listerine, can reduce the bacterial count in your mouth to help prevent gingivitis, and it even has a new fluoride-enhanced formulation—just be aware that some versions contain alcohol, which can exacerbate dry mouth. If this is an issue for you, consider an alcohol-free antibacterial mouthwash, such as Listerine Total Care Zero or Crest Pro-Health Advanced (alcohol-free) Mouthwash.

Prevention Is Best When It Comes to Tartar

Laurence Grayhills, DMD, president, Florida Academy of General Dentistry, and dentist in private practice in Wellington, Florida.

Can you remove tartar from your teeth in between dental visits? Do dental tools available online work?

There is no good way to remove tartar at home. The best thing to do is to prevent it from forming in the first place. Your mouth contains bacteria that mix with saliva and food particles to form a sticky goo called plaque. If it's not removed from teeth, plaque can harden into tartar in as little as one day.

At-home dental hygiene tools should not be used to scrape your own teeth. It is too easy for an untrained person to injure his/her gums or teeth. Beware of chemical products that remove tartar, since they can also remove tooth enamel.

Some people (who have a higher amount of calcium and other minerals in saliva, for example) are naturally predisposed to get tartar buildup. They may need dental cleanings more than twice a year. Good hygiene habits—brushing and flossing twice a day and using a plaque-reducing mouth rinse—and avoiding sugary beverages and snacks help keep plaque away.

Beware These Dental Treatments

Fred Quarnstrom, DDS, a dentist with Beacon Hill Dental Associates in Seattle and coauthor of *Open Wider: Your Wallet, Not Your Mouth—Everything You Need to Know When You Visit the Dentist.* OpenWider.org

Dentists sometimes recommend treatments that might not be needed. Large dental chains often require their dentists to meet a quota...today's new dentists graduate from dental school with huge debt...and dental practices must purchase expensive equipment, all of which create pressure to maximize income. *Be cautious if your dentist suggests...*

•Deep cleaning. Also called "scaling," this typically costs $700 or more, often is not well-covered by dental insurance and is appropriate only for patients who have major periodontal problems—that is, problems with their gums or the bones that support their teeth.

Response: If your dentist recommends deep cleaning and you do not have a history of gum problems, ask to see your periodontal chart. If the number five or higher is listed for some of your teeth, you likely have experienced losses to the tissue and bone around those teeth and deep cleaning might be warranted. If not, seek a second opinion.

•Drilling and filling a cavity identified only by laser. "Laser decay finders" have their place in dentistry, but if your dentist can't see decay on your X-ray, there is no reason to treat the cavity, at least for now.

Response: If your dentist says you have a cavity that requires treatment, ask to see this cavity on your X-ray. There should be an obvious dark spot, likely triangular in shape. If you don't see this, get a second opinion.

•Extensive procedures during your first visit. It's a red flag if you have never needed extensive dental work in the past...you go to a new dentist for just a cleaning or what seems to you like a relatively small problem...and your new dentist says you need extensive work.

Response: Get a second opinion.

Dentist Says Time for X-Rays?

Jay W. Friedman, DDS, MPH, a Los Angeles dentist who received the 2012 John W. Knutson Distinguished Service Award in Dental Public Health from the American Public Health Association. He is author of *The Intelligent Consumer's Complete Guide to Dental Health.*

Some dentists recommend patients get dental X-rays every year—even though the vast majority of patients can go two to three years between X-rays. *There are only a small number of legitimate reasons why new X-rays might be prudent after just one year...*

•**Your dentist saw some sign that a problem could be developing on last year's X-rays.** He/she might have made a note on your chart to "watch this" and want to take an X-ray to see if the situation is growing worse and requires action.

•**You have developed new symptoms.**

Dental insurance plans typically will pay for "bitewing" X-rays (showing the upper and lower back teeth in a single view) every year, so some dentists reason that skipping them deprives patients of a service they could have without any out-of-pocket costs. (Other types of dental X-rays might be covered less frequently.) Dental practices have a financial incentive to take annual X-rays, too—doing so significantly increases the income they generate from patients with healthy teeth and gums. Few dentists set out to overtreat or overcharge patients, but many were trained to take new X-rays each year, and in this fee-for-service profession, they have little motivation to question whether that's really necessary.

Unfortunately, patients who do not have dental insurance might have to pay perhaps $60 to $80 for a set of bitewing X-rays and potentially more for other types of X-rays. Taking unnecessary X-rays also subjects patients to unnecessary radiation. The amount of radiation received from typical dental X-rays is small, but the effects of radiation exposure are cumulative.

What to do: If you have had dental X-rays taken within the past two years and your dentist recommends taking another set, ask why they are needed. Turn down these X-rays if the dentist cannot point to a specific reason such as those noted earlier.

Antidepressants Raise Risk for Dental Implant Failure

Latifa Bairam, BDS, a clinical assistant professor of restorative dentistry at University at Buffalo School of Dental Medicine, New York.

A recent study looked at 74 patients who received dental implants. The odds of implant failure were about four times higher among antidepressant users than among those who weren't taking antidepressants.

Takeaway: A patient needs to weigh the risks and benefits of each (and possible alternatives) with his/her psychiatrist and dentist.

Chipped Tooth Concern

Joseph Gambacorta, DDS, assistant dean for clinical affairs, University at Buffalo School of Dental Medicine.

If you've chipped a tooth, it's probably a good idea to see your dentist, even if you're not in pain.

A small chip or crack in a tooth can sometimes get bigger and even trigger an infection in surrounding tissue.

To help determine whether your tooth could be more damaged than it appears, ask yourself the following questions: Is the tooth sensitive to heat or cold? Does the chipped tooth affect your ability to chew or bite? Was the chip caused by an injury? If the answer to any of these questions is yes, then you need to consult your dentist as soon as possible. The interior of the tooth or surrounding tissue could be affected.

Could Prefab Blood Vessels Revolutionize Root Canals?

Oregon Health & Science University, news release.

A new discovery could give root canal patients a reason to smile. Researchers say they've found a way to create new blood vessels that could help these teeth last longer.

Though root canals can save teeth that are infected or decayed, those teeth can become brittle and break over time, the Oregon Health & Science University team said.

Principal investigator Dr. Luiz Bertassoni explained in a university news release that a root canal eliminates a tooth's blood and nerve supply, leaving it without "any biological response or defense mechanism."

He added that "without this functionality, adult teeth may be lost much sooner, which can result in much greater concerns, such as the need for dentures or dental implants."

Bertassoni is an assistant professor of restorative dentistry and biomedical engineering at OHSU.

His team developed a way to engineer new blood vessels in teeth with root canals.

"This result proves that fabrication of artificial blood vessels can be a highly effective strategy for fully regenerating the function of teeth," he said. "We believe that this finding may change the way that root canal treatments are done in the future."

The study was published online in the journal *Scientific Reports.*

More than 15 million root canals a year are performed in the United States. According to the study authors, the current procedure involves removing infected dental tissues and replacing them with synthetic biomaterials covered by a protective crown.

CHAPTER 7

Diabetes Care

4 Hidden Causes of Diabetes

High blood sugar (glucose) is an obvious sign of diabetes. It's worrisome because elevated blood glucose can, over time, lead to serious diabetes-related complications, such as stroke, heart disease and eye damage.

We've long known how diabetes develops: Cells gradually become less responsive ("resistant") to the glucose-regulating hormone insulin...the ability of the pancreas to produce insulin flags...and glucose readings creep upward.

However, it has not been clear, until recently, why people become insulin-resistant in the first place—and what they can do to stop it. Now that's changing.

NEW THINKING

The conventional wisdom is that carbohydrates—particularly foods that are high in "simple" carbs, such as soft drinks, white bread and desserts—are a main driver of insulin resistance and diabetes. *But other factors, some of which are largely hidden, are also important...*

RISK FACTOR #1: **Ectopic fat.** It's clear that being overweight increases risk for diabetes. But we're learning that a specific type of fat that accumulates in the liver and muscles is especially harmful. This ectopic fat impairs the ability of insulin to metabolize glucose and can lead to insulin resistance. Certain people—including some who aren't overweight—have a genetic tendency to develop ectopic fat.

RISK FACTOR #2: **Inflammation.** Persistent, low-grade inflammation—caused by air pollution, obesity, a poor diet, gum disease, etc.—causes cells to produce inflammatory molecules that increase insulin resistance.

George L. King, MD, a professor of medicine at Harvard Medical School. He is also research director, head of the vascular cell biology research section and chief scientific officer of Harvard's Joslin Diabetes Center, the world's largest diabetes research center and clinic, and the author, with Royce Flippin, of *The Diabetes Reset.*

RISK FACTOR #3: **Mitochondrial dysfunction.** Mitochondria, the "batteries" that fuel the body's cells, naturally produce free radicals and other by-products. The harmful molecules are kept in check by endogenous (produced by the body) and dietary antioxidants. A shortage of either type of antioxidant can cause mitochondria to work less efficiently, resulting in less insulin production—and more insulin resistance.

RISK FACTOR #4: **Psychological stress.** A Dutch study found that people who had suffered at least one major stressful event (such as the death of a loved one or serious financial troubles, etc.) within the past five years were 1.2 times more likely to have diabetes.

Why is stress linked to diabetes? Stressed people are more likely to be overweight, eat poor diets and avoid exercise. Also, stress raises levels of cortisol, a hormone that increases insulin resistance and can cause the liver to manufacture excess glucose.

WHAT CAN YOU DO?

Fortunately, the factors described earlier can be managed—and sometimes reversed—with diet, exercise and other changes. *Here's how...*

- **Double the fiber, halve the fat.** The Joslin Diabetes Center recommends an eating plan that's low in fat (15% of total calories) and high in high-fiber veggies, fruits and grains.

- **Forget what you've heard about carbs being bad.** Processed carbs (sugar, high-fructose corn syrup, etc.) are obviously a problem. But healthy complex carbohydrates (such as whole grains, veggies and legumes) are absorbed slowly...do not cause blood sugar spikes...and many are high in inflammation-fighting antioxidants.

Best: An eating plan with a lot of complex carbohydrates—70% of total calories.

We've found that people who follow this diet for eight weeks show significant drops in insulin resistance...have improved blood glucose levels—and lose about 3% of their weight... and have a decrease in abdominal and overall body fat.

- **Be aware of hidden fat.** Excess body fat is one of the main causes of insulin resistance and diabetes—even when the fat isn't readily visible. People with a fatty liver, for example, are five times more likely to develop diabetes. Fat that accumulates in muscle cells might be completely invisible, but it increases inflammation levels and disrupts the action of insulin.

Fat that is visible—on the hips, buttocks and particularly around the waist—is especially troublesome. Most belly fat is visceral fat, which secretes higher levels of inflammatory chemicals than other types of fat. It also increases levels of "hidden" muscle fat. One large study found that obese men (with a BMI of 30 or higher) were seven times more likely to get diabetes than those with a BMI below 25. For obese women, the risk was 12 times higher than that for normal-weight women.

- **Boost natural antioxidants.** Millions of Americans supplement their diets with large doses of vitamin C, vitamin E and other antioxidants. But research has shown that these supplements are unlikely to improve insulin resistance/diabetes—and may be harmful because they can inhibit the action of the body's natural antioxidants.

What helps: Broccoli, blueberries, green tea and other plant foods that are high in phase 2 antioxidants—beneficial plant compounds that activate a protein called Nrf2, which triggers genes that produce antioxidant molecules. People who eat a lot of plant foods have less inflammation, less mitochondrial dysfunction and less insulin resistance.

- **Get off your duff!** Exercise is great for weight loss, but that's not the only reason to do it. People who are sedentary tend to accumulate more fat deposits in muscle cells. These fats inhibit insulin's ability to transport glucose into muscle cells, and insulin-resistant muscle cells are now thought to be a leading cause of diabetes.

It doesn't take hard-core exercise to get the benefits. If you walk three miles a day (about 6,000 steps)—all at once or in five- or 10-minute increments—you'll reduce your diabetes risk by more than 25%.

- **De-stress.** Take up an enjoyable hobby... go for leisurely walks...spend time with loved ones...and try stress-reducing habits, like yoga or meditation. For severe stress (or depression), consider seeing a professional. Any form of stress relief will help manage diabetes—and reduce your risk of getting it.

How to Fight Diabetes with Your Mind

Kyle W. Murdock, PhD, a postdoctoral research fellow in psychology at Rice University and coauthor of the study "Executive functioning and diabetes: The role of anxious arousal and inflammation," published in *Psychoneuroendocrinology.*

The ability to tune out distractions and negative feelings—a cognitive trait psychologists call "inhibition"—can mean less anxiety in your everyday life. And now recent research shows that it may also protect you from developing diabetes—or help you manage diabetes if you have it.

The good news: This is one psychological trait that you can change. That's right—you can fight diabetes with your mind.

STRESS AND ANXIETY

The research isn't the first to show that stress and anxiety can increase the risk of developing type 2 diabetes. But it does show precisely how it can happen...and points to effective mind-body treatments.

The key cognitive trait linked to increased diabetes risk in the recent study is low "inhibition." It's a necessary coping skill—the ability to control your attention and behavior and ignore distracting thoughts and emotions...especially negative emotions.

People with poor inhibition tend to respond impulsively and are easily distracted by anxious thoughts. They also tend to have poor coping skills, including less ability to respond to new challenges with flexible problem-solving. Poor coping, in turn, can increase anxiety, so it can be a vicious cycle.

Researchers at several American universities hypothesized that this inhibition/anxiety connection might affect diabetes risk. So they enlisted 835 midlife men and women (average age 57) who had already taken a battery of psychological tests to also take blood tests that measure inflammation (a key driver of diabetes) and blood sugar.

When individuals are stressed, anxious or depressed, inflammation goes up. The inflammation marker interleukin-6 (IL-6) is also a marker for stress—and it's linked to higher insulin levels, which can set the stage for insulin resistance and, eventually, diabetes. The blood sugar marker was hemoglobin A1c, a measure of blood sugar over the past two or three months.

Results: After adjusting for other variables, people with low inhibition, compared with those with high inhibition, had more anxiety symptoms...higher levels of IL-6...higher levels of hemoglobin A1c...and greater incidence of type 2 diabetes.

People with poor inhibition are also less likely to eat healthy foods, exercise, stick with diets and get enough sleep. So tackling this psychological trait can be a key to unlocking a bounty of health benefits.

STRENGTHENING INHIBITION

Low inhibition is a psychological trait that can have its origins in childhood, so it's not something you can change in a snap. But it can change—and the benefits for your health and your well-being are tremendous. *The first step is to check yourself for common red flags...*

- **Thinking excessively about something stressful.**
- **Restricting yourself to only certain activities because of fear or anxiety.**
- **Acting impulsively.**
- **Engaging in high-risk activities.**

What helps...

- **Mindfulness-based stress reduction therapy (MBSR).** With this therapy, you're taught to keep your attention on the present. Training teaches you to detect and reduce distracting and stressful thoughts. You can try to learn MBSR on your own—there are many books, websites and CDs that teach it. (But seeing a professional will be much better for some people, especially those who tend to need structure imposed from the outside.)
- **Cognitive behavioral therapy (CBT).** This type of talk therapy has been shown to

be an effective treatment for many anxiety disorders—and it's also been shown specifically to strengthen inhibition. The goal of CBT is to learn how to change some negative thought patterns and to modify how you cope with stressful situations. By reducing stress and your body's response to it, you can more easily avoid behaviors (such as impulsive eating) that increase your risk for diabetes.

Anything you can do to reduce your overall stress levels may reduce your risk for diabetes, too. For example, the ancient Chinese mind-body practice of Qigong, which gently exercises the body as it calms the mind, has been shown to reduce stress and reduce blood sugar. The key is to look for a stress fighter that feels right to you!

Do You Have Diabetes? What Your Skin Says...

Yellow-red bumps on your arms and legs may signal problems with blood sugar control. Known as eruptive xanthomas, these bumps can pop up anywhere on the body but are especially common on the buttocks, shoulders, arms and legs. They're caused by very high levels of triglycerides, a type of fat in the bloodstream that is common with insulin resistance, a condition that causes excess blood sugar and can result in prediabetes and diabetes. Once diabetes is treated, triglyceride levels often normalize and skin lesions resolve.

Jeffrey P. Callen, MD, a professor of medicine and chief of the division of dermatology at the University of Louisville School of Medicine in Kentucky.

Diabetes Checklist: Tests and Checkups

American Academy of Periodontology, American Diabetes Association (ADA), American Heart Association (AHA), *Annals of Ibadan Postgraduate Medicine*, *Cell Metabolism*, Joslin Diabetes Center, National Diabetes Education Program, National Diabetes Information Clearing House, National Institute of Diabetes and Digestive and Kidney Diseases (NIDDK), Obesity Action Coalition, MedlinePlus, Oregon Diabetes Resource Bank.

Diabetes—type 1 and type 2—can be well-managed if you keep track of your glucose levels and keep an eye out for complications. This includes having regular checkups with your doctor—and using the checklist below throughout the year. Print it out and keep it where you can use it as a reminder!

SEE YOUR PRIMARY CARE OR DIABETES DOCTOR FOUR TIMES A YEAR

At every visit...

•**Get your blood pressure and weight checked.** If you're overweight or obese, losing just 5% to 10% of your weight can improve glucose control.

•**Get a quick foot exam.** Your doctor can identify—and treat—minor foot problems before they become big ones.

At least twice a year...

•**Get your A1c checked**—at least every other visit. This key number measures your glucose levels over a stretch of three months. Discuss your target with your doctor.

At least once a year...

•**Get your cholesterol and triglyceride levels checked.** Heart disease is the number-one complication of diabetes.

•**Get a complete foot exam.** This exam, more detailed than the quick check at each doctor visit, evaluates circulation, pulses, reflexes, nerves and the skin on your feet.

•**Have two tests to check on the health of your kidneys.** A urine test checks albumin, and a blood test assesses blood creatinine and glomerular filtration rate (GFR).

•**Discuss your sleep habits.** People with diabetes are at increased risk for sleep apnea, which in turn increases heart disease risk.

•**Ask your doctor whether you should have a blood test to check for levels of vitamin B-12 and vitamin D.** Low levels of vitamin D are linked with insulin resistance, and low B-12 can exacerbate nerve problems. Long-term use of the diabetes drug *metformin* may lead to B-12 deficiency.

•**Ask about screening for peripheral artery disease (PAD).** The cardiovascular disease is a particular risk if your glucose levels are unstable.

In the fall…

• **Get a flu shot.** People with diabetes who get the flu are particularly likely to get bronchitis and pneumonia and have a harder time controlling blood glucose.

SEE YOUR OPHTHALMOLOGIST AT LEAST ONCE A YEAR

Make sure you get a "dilated" eye exam. Diabetes increases your risk for retinopathy, cataracts and glaucoma. Find an eye doctor who specializes in diabetes-related eye issues.

SEE YOUR DENTIST TWICE A YEAR

Diabetes increases your risk for gum disease, which makes it harder to control blood glucose.

SEE YOUR DIABETES TEAM AS OFTEN AS YOU NEED TO!

Managing diabetes is a team sport. Your team may include your primary care doctor, a diabetes specialist such as an endocrinologist, a diabetes educator, a registered dietician and other health-care professionals. Make sure you get the help you need to control your blood sugar and stay healthy!

New Way to Reverse Type 2 Diabetes

Newcastle University.

According to a recent study, people who lost about 0.6 g of fat from the pancreas (based on an MRI scan) after weight-loss surgery achieved normal insulin levels within eight weeks.

Bike Away Diabetes

Martin Rasmussen, MSc, research assistant, department of sports science and clinical biomechanics, University of Southern Denmark, Odense.

The more you pedal a bicycle, the less likely you are to develop diabetes, according to a recent study of more than 52,000 adults over age 50. Those who cycled more than two-and-a-half hours a week had a 20% lower risk for diabetes than those who didn't cycle at all.

Tip: Ride a bike whenever possible and/or use a stationary bike.

Diabetes Increases Risk for Deadly Staph Infections

Reimar Thomsen, MD, PhD, an associate professor in clinical epidemiology at Aarhus University Hospital, Aarhus, Denmark.

Up to 30% of patients diagnosed with a Staphylococcus aureus blood infection die within 30 days of diagnosis. People with any form of diabetes are nearly three times more likely than nondiabetics to develop the dangerous infection—and up to seven times more likely if they have type 1 diabetes. Staph can enter the bloodstream through cuts in the skin. Keep cuts clean and covered.

Do Eggs Promote Diabetes? Only in America

Study titled "Egg consumption and risk of type 2 diabetes: A meta-analysis of prospective studies" by researchers at Brigham and Women's Hospital and Harvard Medical School, both in Boston, and Mercy St. Vincent Medical Center, Toledo, Ohio, published in *The American Journal of Clinical Nutrition*.

Katherine Zeratsky, RD, LD, a registered dietician and nutrition educator at the Mayo Clinic, Rochester, Minnesota.

Eggs are funny. If you eat eggs in the US, they increase your risk for diabetes. But if you eat them in Spain or France or Japan, you're fine. No increased diabetes risk. Buen provecho! Bon appetit! Itadakimasu!

So, does living in America somehow make eggs dangerous? Of course that's ridiculous. Here's the real story.

A SCRAMBLED TALE

Eggs, once beloved by all, then shunned because they're high in cholesterol, now are back in nutritionists'—and home cooks'—good graces. After all, dietary cholesterol is no longer a "nutrient of concern" according to the latest Dietary Guidelines.

The only potential spoiler has been diabetes risk. Truth be told, the research has been totally confusing. While a few studies have suggested that dietary cholesterol might increase the risk for diabetes, others show that eating eggs actually improves sensitivity to insulin, which protects against diabetes.

To shed light on the issue, researchers looked at 12 studies from the US, Europe and Japan (nearly 220,000 people).

Taken as a whole, the studies showed no increase in risk for people who ate more eggs compared with those who ate fewer or none.

But when the researchers looked just at the US studies, they found that people who ate three eggs or more a week were 39% more likely to develop diabetes than people who ate fewer eggs or none. Even here, it was dicey—some American studies found no such link.

Some non-US studies even found that eggs were protective. In one Finnish study, for example, men aged 42 to 60 who ate the most eggs on a weekly basis over 19 years were 38% less likely to develop diabetes. A Japanese study also found less diabetes in egg eaters, but only in women.

To put these findings in perspective, we spoke with Katherine Zeratsky, RD, LD, a registered dietician and nutrition educator at the Mayo Clinic in Rochester, Minnesota.

CRACKING THE EGG MYSTERY

First, let's acknowledge that these are primarily observational studies that can't prove cause and effect, explained Zeratsky. *But the studies do hold key clues...*

- **Who's eating lots of eggs?** In the US, people who eat the most eggs tend to also be less physically active, eat more meat and smoke. Egg consumers tend to have a higher body mass index (BMI) than those who don't eat eggs, too. These findings aren't observed outside our borders.

- **What else are they eating?** In the US, people who eat the most eggs tend to also eat more processed meat, such as sausage and bacon.

Since avoiding eggs, especially egg yolks, had long been a health recommendation in the US, it's not surprising that healthier people have been eating fewer eggs—or that people with less healthy lifestyles eat more eggs. That may change now that healthier people are likely to be eating more eggs. We also tend to serve our eggs with bacon, sausage, home fries and lots of toast with butter, not to mention orange juice, which is high in sugar and low in fiber—not the healthiest breakfast pattern.

A HEALTHIER WAY TO EAT EGGS

A single large egg has only 78 calories, a substantial 6 or 7 grams of protein (more than 10% of the Daily Value) and good amounts of iron and zinc, B-12, B-6 and choline, an amino acid key for brain health.

Another egg bonus: They're satiating. In one weight-loss study of people who already had diabetes, those who ate two eggs a day, six days a week, reported feeling less hungry than those who took in the same number of calories but only two eggs a week. Nor was there any difference in blood cholesterol levels between the two groups.

"In the context of an overall healthy diet, eggs are a great, economical source of protein," says Zeratsky. However, she cautions, eggs do contain a moderate amount of saturated fat, which can increase blood cholesterol levels, so moderation is still the best guide. Her recommendation? "Eating up to one egg a day is reasonable." That jives with earlier research that eating an average of one egg a day has no effect on risk for heart disease or stroke. Like a two-egg omelet? That's fine to have three times a week or so. No need to avoid yolks.

Just make the rest of your plate healthy, too. A poached egg or two, with some fruit on the side, is a lovely breakfast, suggests Zeratksy. So is a scramble with red peppers and kale, which add their own nutrients. For lunch, a sliced hard-boiled egg adds protein to any salad—and helps you absorb more vitamins from the greens. When making dinner, try sliding a sunny-side-up egg on top of, say, sautéed chopped Brussels sprouts, for a little extra nutritional punch.

Bottom line: Eggs are once again what they've always been—a versatile, inexpensive, good-tasting, nutritious, low-cal, high-protein staple. For everyone.

Blood Sugar Tip: Eat This, Then That

Study titled "Food Order Has a Significant Impact on Postprandial Glucose and Insulin Levels" by researchers at Weill Cornell Medical College, New York City, published in *Diabetes Care.*

If your blood sugar sometimes runs a little high—and most definitely if you have prediabetes or diabetes—you'll get lots of advice about what to eat but rarely what to eat first in a meal. But the order of what you eat can make a big difference in your blood sugar response.

In a small pilot study of overweight people with type 2 diabetes, on days when they ate carbs at lunch first (ciabatta bread, orange juice), followed 15 minutes later by the foods rich in protein plus some fat (grilled chicken breast, salad with low-fat dressing, steamed broccoli with butter), their blood sugar levels were more than one-third higher 60 minutes later—compared with days on which they reversed the order and ate the protein-rich dish first. Insulin levels were higher, too.

It makes the common practice of munching from the bread basket before your main dish arrives particularly suspect! Instead, whether you're at home or eating out, try starting your meal with something that's high in protein, with some good fats, and perhaps even fiber-rich veggies—for example, veggies and hummus, peanut butter and celery or chilled shrimp with cocktail sauce—before you eat any carb-rich food. What you eat still matters, of course, but eating foods in the right order might help keep your blood sugar levels from spiking after a meal. It also helps if you're a little hungry before you eat.

Cooking Oil vs. Diabetes

While many cooking oils, such as olive and canola oils, have long been associated with heart-health benefits, recent research shows that dietary oils rich in linoleic acid (such as grape seed oil) have special properties that help fight diabetes. Higher blood levels of linoleic acid were linked to lower insulin resistance, a main driver of diabetes. Previous studies showed that as little as one-and-a-half teaspoons of linoleic acid–rich oil daily increased lean body mass and decreased abdominal fat.

Martha Belury, PhD, professor of human nutrition, The Ohio State University, Columbus.

FDA Approves Breakthrough Device for Type 1 Diabetes

Robert A. Gabbay, MD, PhD, chief medical officer at Joslin Diabetes Center and associate professor of medicine at Harvard Medical School, both in Boston.

Medtronic MiniMed 670G monitors blood sugar in people with type 1 diabetes and automatically delivers insulin as needed. Patients still have to count and enter carbs to teach the device how much insulin they need for their intake. Also, the insulin delivery site dressings have to be replaced every three days, so patients must be capable of doing that.

Check Your Neck

Study by researchers at University of Puerto Rico, Medical Sciences Campus, San Juan, published in *Journal of Diabetes Research.*

Neck size is a better measure of disease risk than waist size—which can be influenced by time of day, clothing and other factors. In a study of 1,206 people, those with higher-than-average neck circumference had a higher incidence of prediabetes, hypertension and metabolic syndrome. The average neck size of study participants was 14.2 inches for women and 16.5 inches for men.

Lessons from Diabetes Boot Camp

Michelle Magee, MD, endocrinologist, director, MedStar Diabetes Institute, associate professor of medicine, Georgetown University School of Medicine, both in Washington, DC. Her study, titled "Diabetes Boot Camp Reduces A1c and Health-Care Services Utilization," was presented at the 2016 annual meeting of the American Diabetes Association in New Orleans.

The name makes you think of raw recruits sweating it out on an Army base. "Diabetes Boot Camp" takes the same mental commitment but is a good bit simpler, kinder and easier than that.

The intensive 12-week professionally monitored program for people with hard-to-manage diabetes is also remarkably effective at helping people with type 2 diabetes bring their blood sugar under control, according to a recent study.

Even better: Even if you're not in a boot camp, you can reproduce its essential elements yourself with a little help from your health-care team. To find out more, we spoke with study leader Michelle Magee, MD, director of the MedStar Diabetes Institute and an associate professor of medicine at Georgetown University School of Medicine in Washington, DC. She didn't invent the diabetes boot camp concept, but she is one of the first to study it.

WHEN DIABETES IS OUT OF CONTROL

If you have diabetes, your body responds quickly to what you eat, how active you are and the medications you take. But even if you are checking your finger-stick blood sugars, if you see your doctor only every few months to review your results, it's hard to understand exactly how your daily actions can make a difference.

It is also complicated to live with diabetes if you haven't learned enough to balance all of what you need to know about it. There's a lot to learn about nutrition, not to mention exercise, psychology and medicine. You might have areas of ignorance holding you back.

No wonder millions of Americans have trouble controlling their diabetes. They show up on an urgent basis at their doctor's office. They miss days of work. They get hospitalized or go the the emergency room with episodes of too high or too low blood sugar.

In search of a better way, five primary care practices in and around Washington, DC, enrolled 125 people with hard-to-control diabetes in boot camp. Everyone had had diabetes for at least a year, was taking glucose-lowering medication or insulin, and was asked to regularly monitor their blood sugar.

They all had A1c levels—a measure of average blood sugar over the past two or three months—above 9% and at least one other health concern, such as high blood pressure. (The average A1c level for these patients was even higher—11.4%.) A target A1c for someone with diabetes is usually around 7%, and people with an A1c of 9% or higher are considered to have uncontrolled diabetes.

The great thing is that those out-of-control numbers went down dramatically.

BOOT CAMP CURRICULUM

Here's the program...

In the first week, each participant met twice with a certified diabetes educator (CDE)—a health-care professional who is specially trained to teach people how to manage diabetes. They took a survey to identify knowledge gaps about diabetes—and then were given video clips that addressed the specific diabetes-related information that they didn't know. They were also surveyed on medication adherence and then given tailored support so that they could take their medications as prescribed. Both diet and medications—as well as exercise and other issues—were covered in the two sessions.

That's it for the face-to-face interactions—just two visits. But each participant was also given a "cellular-enabled" blood glucose monitor. As soon as each patient completed a normal finger-stick blood glucose test, the results were displayed in real-time on a "dashboard" visible to their diabetes educator.

Next, participants graduated to "virtual visits," with phone calls, e-mail or text messages instead of face-to-face meetings. Over the course of the next 12 weeks, most patients had eight to 10 interactions with their diabetes educator. "Educators were able to adjust their patients' medications frequently via the virtual visits to help them get to their goal for blood glucose control and to continue to deliver critical 'survival skills' information about lifestyle management," said Dr. Magee.

One of the main benefits was immediate feedback to tie actions taken by the patient to blood glucose results. Say a participant had a big dessert and did a finger-stick test, and the blood glucose dashboard showed a higher-than-desired reading. This would signal a teaching point—the diabetes educator who was monitoring that patient could call or text the patient right away. "Normally, patients wait months in between primary care visits, when their doctors discuss blood sugar levels," says Dr. Magee. "But this almost-immediate response led to a lot of 'eureka moments,' when patients can markedly increase their understanding of how their lifestyle impacts their blood sugar."

BIG BENEFITS

The results were astounding. Within three months, the average A1c levels declined from 11.4% to 8.3%. "Each 1% reduction in A1C is associated with a roughly 15% decline in risk for major cardiovascular events," explains Dr. Magee. *Within six months, when compared with prior use of health-care services by the same participants...*

- **Urgent visits to primary care practices dropped by 92%.**
- **Missed days of work or other activities declined by 77%.**
- **Hospitalization declined by 66%.**

The study is being prepared for publication, so its results are still preliminary—and we don't yet know how well the participants will maintain their A1c levels after the intervention ended. But the results do show just how effective personalized education and counseling combined with timely medication management can be in helping people who are floundering on their own with this complex disease.

BRINGING IT ALL BACK HOME

While this boot camp program is being further developed, almost anyone with diabetes can incorporate its lessons and take steps to help improve their diabetes-care outcomes by working with their own doctor and a certified diabetes educator. *Here's how...*

- **Ask your primary care doctor to refer you to a certified diabetes educator (CDE).** Many large health-care systems and hospitals have them on staff, but you can also find a certified one online at the National Certification Board for Diabetes Education. Most insurance plans pay for this service with a referral from your doctor.
- **Once you meet with your diabetes educator, ask him/her if he can work with you if you use a glucose monitor** that can relay data wirelessly so that you can look at your sugars together more often. These meters are relatively recent, but new ones are coming on the market now. This will allow you to work with your new "coach" more easily.
- **Your provider or educator may recommend that you also try a smartphone diabetes-coaching app program**—these often-free programs provide nutrition info and help you track your carbs and blood sugar—to help you manage your diabetes. "There is emerging evidence that these apps can help with diabetes control, too, and some people do find them helpful," says Dr. Douglas, "but an app is no substitute for working closely with your doctor and your CDE."
- **If you have worked with the CDE on your lifestyle management and your sugars still are not where they should be,** you also need to work with your own doctor so that your diabetes medications can be adjusted to help get you to your targets for blood glucose control.
- **"The more you know, the better you do" may never be more true than it is for people with diabetes.** Get educated.

Working with a diabetes educator isn't new, of course—the profession has been around for decades. But here's what's changing—now that your blood sugar numbers can be transmitted immediately, you, your educator and your doctor can become a much more powerful team. This Diabetes Boot Camp has shown that just a few face-to-face meetings with a handful of "virtual visits" can get you on the right track and keep you on the right track—managing diabetes much better than you have ever been able to do.

Got Diabetes? Don't Let Exercise Mess with Your Blood Sugar

Richard Cotton, MA, ACSM-CEP, exercise physiologist and national director of certification, American College of Sports Medicine, Indianapolis.

If you've been diagnosed with type 2 diabetes, you know that exercise is key for long-term blood sugar control. But it also can affect your blood sugar levels in the short term—and not always in good ways. Exercise too enthusiastically, and you could find your blood sugar level dropping too low—or even spiking.

Here's how people with type 2 diabetes can handle (and even better, avoid) the two most common exercise/blood sugar problems...

PROBLEM #1: BLOOD SUGAR DROPS DURING EXERCISE

When you exercise, your body gets energy first by using blood sugar (glucose) and then by depleting glycogen, the storage form of glucose, from your muscles and liver. (You may also start burning fat for energy.)

The short-term effect is that blood sugar levels fall—and can stay reduced for as long as 24 hours. That's the benefit. But if levels fall too low (hypoglycemia)—below 70 mg/dL if your meter measures whole blood, or below 80 mg/dL if it measures plasma glucose—you may feel symptoms, including shakiness, clammy skin, blurred vision and confusion. A severe drop can be scary or even dangerous.

The good news is that it's rare—and easily prevented. Exercise-induced hypoglycemia is most common in people who take insulin—that is, everyone with type 1 diabetes and some people with type 2. It can also happen if you are taking certain medications that promote insulin secretion, including sulfonylureas and glinides. If low blood sugar during or after exercise happens to you regularly, talk to your doctor about possible solutions such as eating a small snack before (and maybe during) exercise, adjusting your medication dose—or both.

Fortunately, exercise-induced hypoglycemia is quite rare in people who manage their diabetes with lifestyle alone or with a medication such as *metformin*, which instead of promoting insulin secretion makes your body more sensitive to the insulin it already makes. Still, it's possible for a mild drop in blood sugar to happen, especially if you train really hard or for more than an hour. Even a mild blood sugar drop might make you feel tired afterward.

The best advice for everyone with diabetes, especially at the beginning of a new exercise program, is to test your blood sugar three times—before, during and after your workout. Once you get a sense of how your exercise routine is affecting your blood sugar, you can cut back on the testing. Just make sure that you have access to a quick energy source such as an energy bar or fruit juice in case your blood sugar drops.

Tip: To reduce your risk for hypoglycemia, do resistance exercise before aerobic exercise.

PROBLEM #2: BLOOD SUGAR IS TOO HIGH BEFORE OR DURING EXERCISE

Sometimes, blood sugar levels get too high—250 mg/dL or 300 mg/dL or even higher—which can cause you to feel symptoms such as thirst, headache, blurred vision and fatigue. It's called hyperglycemia. It's an indication that you need to adjust your eating pattern, your medications or both so that you can bring blood sugar to more acceptable levels, such as the mid-100s.

Is it safe to exercise if your blood sugar is already somewhat elevated? The answer is yes as long as you're feeling good. Exercise can bring high blood sugar levels down quickly. Indeed, with exercise your muscles can burn up glucose at almost 20 times their normal rate. That's a key reason that regular exercise is so effective in controlling diabetes. Exercising, even a nice brisk walk, is one good way to bring levels down. Make sure you're staying well-hydrated, too, since high blood sugar can lead to frequent urination and thus dehydration.

Exception: Sometimes, if you start exercising when your blood sugar is already running high, rising adrenalin or other exercise-stimulated hormones can stimulate your body to release even more sugar into the blood—temporarily overwhelming the sugar-burning effect of exercise. If that happens, don't sweat it. Just cool down as you would any time you exercise aerobically and then sit quietly to allow your body to rest. After 30 minutes, when you test your blood sugar again, you should find that your blood sugar has gone down to more normal levels. In some cases, it might take an hour.

TAILORING YOUR EXERCISE PROGRAM TO YOUR BLOOD SUGAR PATTERN

The good news is that for most people with diabetes, exercise won't cause any short-term blood sugar problems—and it's one of the best things you can do to control your diabetes.

Check with your doctor before starting a new routine to see if you have any exercise limitations. If you're planning exercise more intense than walking and you have certain risk factors or conditions (such as high blood pressure, high cholesterol, heart disease, kidney problems), your doctor may also recommend that you undergo exercise stress testing, which involves walking fast on a treadmill while your heart is monitored. But most people with diabetes don't need this test.

If you have health issues such as foot problems, eyesight issues, arthritis or other limitations, your doctor can help you tailor an exercise plan that works for you or can refer you to a diabetes educator or an exercise physiologist who can help. It's a good thing that exercise is so safe, because it's so beneficial for people with diabetes.

Water Beats Diet Beverages for Weight Loss

Study of 81 women led by researchers at University of Nottingham, UK, published in *Diabetes, Obesity and Metabolism.*

Overweight women with type 2 diabetes who were placed on a supervised weight-control diet and who drank water five times a week after their main meal at lunch lost an average of 14 pounds in 24 weeks. Those who drank diet beverages lost an average of 11.5 pounds. Body mass index fell by 2.49 in the water drinkers, compared with 2.06 in those using diet drinks. Water drinkers also had greater improvements in fasting insulin, postmeal glucose levels and other measures of diabetes severity.

Psoriasis Increases Risk for Diabetes

Ann Sophie Lønnberg, MD, a psoriasis researcher at Gentofte Hospital, University of Copenhagen, Hellerup, Denmark.

People with the chronic skin condition are 53% more likely to have type 2 diabetes than other people.

Probable connections: Both diseases involve inflammation and have dietary and lifestyle factors in common.

To decrease risk for both: Keep your weight and blood sugar under control. If you have psoriasis, ask your physician to screen you for diabetes.

No Drugs Needed!

Rebecca Shannonhouse, editor, *Bottom Line Health.*

If someone told you that you could reduce your risk for diabetes by 58%—without taking drugs—that would sound pretty good, right?

Not so fast, says the pharmaceutical industry. PhRMA, a trade group that represents the makers of high-priced insulin and other diabetes drugs, has objected to a plan to expand diabetes prevention efforts that have been found to achieve these impressive results.

According to PhRMA, the expansion of the YMCA's nationwide Diabetes Prevention Program is based only on "preliminary" evidence—even though researchers have studied it for more than 20 years and concluded that it's among the best ways to slow the spread of a disease that affects about 25% of older Americans.

The program is based on research showing that people who lost 7% of their body weight—with better diets, more exercise and lifestyle education—reduced their risk for diabetes by 58% versus a 38% reduction in a drug-only group.

What's the program? Each participant attends 25 one-hour YMCA classes—on nutrition, lifestyle changes, etc.—over the course of a year. The goal for each participant is to not only lose weight but also to work up to 150 minutes of exercise a week. Despite drug-industry pushback, it's now being offered at hundreds of Ys nationwide. Cost depends on the Y's location and is usually covered by insurance.

To find a program near you: Go to YMCA.net/diabetes-prevention.

---

5 Diabetes Management Mistakes to Avoid

Gretchen Becker, a Halifax, Vermont–based science and medical writer who was diagnosed with type 2 diabetes in 1996. She is author of *The First Year: Type 2 Diabetes.* GretchenBecker.com

---

One of every four American adults age 65 or older has diabetes—and many don't know it. Even so, every 19 seconds, an American is diagnosed with type 2 diabetes.

My story: After I was diagnosed with type 2 diabetes 20 years ago, I vowed to help people avoid some of the missteps that are commonly made when navigating the trickier aspects of this complex disease. *Mistakes you can avoid...*

***MISTAKE #1:* Assuming that you'll have obvious symptoms.** You may be able to name a few of the classic diabetes symptoms, such as excessive thirst, frequent urination and blurred vision. But maybe you don't have any of these red flags.

Perhaps you do feel a little more tired than usual or have numbness or tingling in your hands or feet that you can't explain. These could be subtle signs that your blood glucose levels are out of whack. The symptoms that I initially dismissed were frequent bathroom breaks, increasing nearsightedness and scratches on my arms that wouldn't heal for more than a month.

Surprisingly, you could even be losing weight. Even though diabetes is commonly associated with being overweight, sometimes people drop a few pounds because they're losing water weight when they are urinating frequently and/or their metabolism is not allowing them to properly absorb calories.

What you should know: If you notice any changes—even if they seem minor—write them down and be sure to discuss them at your next doctor visit.

Important: If your doctor doesn't routinely test your blood glucose levels, ask him/her to do so at least every three years if you're past age 45. If you have any risk factors, such as a family history (in a parent, sibling or child) or being overweight, you may need more frequent testing...and perhaps starting at an earlier age.

Also: Be sure that you're not fighting a cold or some other infection when you're tested—such illnesses can elevate blood glucose levels.

***MISTAKE #2:* Worrying only about sugar.** Lots of people assume that individuals with diabetes simply need to avoid sugar. The truth is, it's much more complicated than that. In fact, virtually everything you eat affects your blood glucose in one way or another.

Carbohydrates (which include starchy foods, such as bread, rice and potatoes, that turn into sugar when they are digested) as well as sugar itself actually have the greatest effect on your blood glucose. Fiber (both soluble fiber, the type that slows down digestion and is found in oat bran, barley, nuts, seeds and beans...and insoluble fiber, the type that adds bulk to your stool and is found in wheat bran and whole grains) also plays a role. It's soluble fiber that can be used to improve your blood glucose levels.

What you should know: Food labels are confusing. Because fiber is a healthy carbohydrate, food labels in the US include it in the total carbohydrate count—for example, a product with 34 g of carbohydrates and 14 g of fiber, has an actual carbohydrate content of 20 g. In other countries, such as those in Europe, the food label would list this same product as having 20 g of carbohydrates and 14 g of fiber. Understanding such quirks in food labeling will help ensure that you're not getting more or less carbs than you think.

MISTAKE #3: **Not keeping close tabs on your numbers.** If you are diagnosed with diabetes, your doctor will no doubt explain that the condition is largely a numbers game—with the prime target being your blood glucose level. Whatever advice your doctor gives you in terms of testing, take it seriously.

Especially in the first year, it's important for most people with diabetes to monitor these levels three to five times throughout the day. Don't try to cut corners. It's true that the test strips you use can be expensive if your insurance limits the number you receive, but the cost of diabetes complications is much greater. If you must economize on test strips, ask your doctor for advice on the best times to test during the day.

Frequent testing will help you understand what causes your blood glucose levels to become elevated. You can then develop strategies to keep them in the normal range—this is the single best way to prevent serious complications, such as kidney failure, diabetic neuropathy and amputation of lower limbs.

In addition to diet, there are other factors that affect blood glucose. Managing stress and increasing physical activity are also important. Aim for 30 minutes of aerobic exercise (such as brisk walking) at least five days a week, but be sure to add some weight lifting a few times a week—it also helps with blood glucose control.

What you should know: Even when your blood glucose levels improve, you can't revert back to old behavior. The improvement simply means that you're doing what you need to do to control your disease and now have the flexibility to make small modifications, such as adding a few more carbs to your diet if you've lost some extra weight. Be sure to keep testing to make sure you don't overdo it. And never stop taking your diabetes medication without consulting your doctor!

MISTAKE #4: **Settling for daily blood glucose testing alone.** Even though your daily blood glucose levels are the main number you need to focus on, other tests are helpful. For example, your doctor should also order (usually quarterly) a hemoglobin A1c test, which measures your average blood glucose for the past two to three months. This will tell you how well your overall diabetes treatment is working. Closely tracking your blood pressure and lipid levels (including cholesterol and triglycerides) is also important.

What you should know: No matter what test you are receiving, always insist on knowing the normal range for the lab. Just asking for the result (without knowing the lab's range) can be very misleading.

MISTAKE #5: **Going it alone.** Other diabetes patients can often provide crucial tips, insights and lifestyle advice that you won't hear from a physician who doesn't live with diabetes on a daily basis.

What you should know: You'll save yourself time and trouble by going online for practical tips. In addition to support groups such as DLife.com and the American Diabetes Association's online community at Diabetes.org, there's an excellent resource that was founded by David Mendosa, a fellow diabetes patient—Mendosa.com/advice.htm. His site is especially useful because he reviews other websites so you can go directly to the ones that offer the best information.

Should Everyone with Diabetes See an Endocrinologist?

Gerald Bernstein, MD, internist and endocrinologist, program coordinator, Friedman Diabetes Program, Lenox Hill Hospital, New York City.

If you've been diagnosed with type 2 diabetes by your primary-care doctor, do you need to see a specialist?

In general, if you have uncomplicated type 2 diabetes, your primary-care doctor can manage your diabetes care. But I do recommend, especially for new-onset diabetes, that you ask your primary-care doctor to refer you to one particular kind of specialist—a certified diabetes educator (CDE).

Among other things, a CDE is specially trained to be able to advise you on lifestyle changes, such as proper nutrition and how much and what kinds of physical activity will help you manage your blood sugar and avoid diabetic complications. Having a CDE assist you with these and other time-consuming elements of treatment relieves some of the burden of care from your doctor, who is not likely to have as much time available during a regular office visit. That's why a CDE needs to be a key part of your health-care team.

Type 1 diabetes is a different story. Anyone who has type 1 diabetes, an autoimmune disorder, should have an endocrinologist on his/her health-care team. An endocrinologist is able to oversee the tightly structured treatment program necessary to manage type 1 diabetes and deal with such things as high-tech insulin pumps, continuous glucose-monitoring devices and so forth.

Some people with type 2 diabetes also should see an endocrinologist. *See one if…*

• **You're having trouble controlling your blood sugar.**

• **You and your primary-care doctor are finding it difficult to find the right mix of medications** to control your blood sugar without worrisome side effects, including low blood sugar.

• **You need to take three or more insulin injections per day or use an insulin pump.**

Even if your type 2 diabetes doesn't include the above challenges, it makes sense to consult an endocrinologist if your doctor recommends it…if your primary-care doctor doesn't have much experience treating diabetes…or if you feel that there are problems communicating with your doctor, such as questions that aren't satisfactorily answered.

Metformin: New Benefits (and Risks) for This Old Diabetes Drug

Kevin M. Pantalone, DO, Endocrine Certification in Neck Ultrasound (ECNU), FACE, a staff endocrinologist at Cleveland Clinic and serves as the director of clinical research for Cleveland Clinic's department of endocrinology, diabetes and metabolism.

If type 2 diabetes is part of your life—whether you have the condition or are at risk of developing it—you've probably heard of a drug called *metformin.* Perhaps your doctor has told you about it, has recently started you on it or has been prescribing it to you for years to keep your blood sugar under control.

It's no newbie. *Metformin* has been available by prescription in the US for more than 20 years and in Europe for more than 40 years. US doctors write nearly 60 million prescriptions a year. It's recommended as the go-to-first prescription for people with diabetes by the American Diabetes Association, the American Association of Clinical Endocrinologists and the American College of Physicians.

Yet, in many ways, metformin remains a mystery. We know broadly but still not exactly, how it works. Even more surprising, new health benefits—and side effects—keep popping up. In fact, we've only recently learned that metformin might protect the heart, fight cancer and even boost longevity. On the other hand, it can, rarely, lead to a potentially fatal side effect, and it can even make a common diabetes complication worse.

It's time to take a closer look at metformin.

MEDIEVAL FLOWER REMEDY, MODERN DRUG

In medieval times, herbalists prescribed *Galega officinalis*—the bloom of the French lilac, also known as goat's rue and Italian fitch—for patients with what we now recognize as diabetes. In the 1950s, medical researchers identified a compound in the lilac, metformin, that appeared to reliably and safely reduce high blood sugar. Metformin became widely available in Europe in the 1970s and was approved by the US Food and Drug Administration in

1995 to treat type 2 diabetes. Some combination prescriptions include metformin with other prescription medications.

HOW IT WORKS

We now know what medieval herbalists didn't—metformin increases the sensitivity of muscle and fat tissue to the hormone insulin. That makes it easier for your body to drive blood glucose (aka blood sugar) into the body's cells where it can be metabolized into energy. It also cuts the amount of sugar that the liver pushes out into the bloodstream. The exact mechanisms aren't known, but the result is lower blood sugar.

WHY IT'S THE BEST FIRST DRUG FOR DIABETES

There are three great things about metformin that set it apart from other diabetes medications. It is very inexpensive. It won't cause your blood sugar to plummet, as some diabetes drugs do. That's a complication that can range from merely bothersome to so dangerous that it lands you in the hospital. Metformin doesn't have that risk.

And it doesn't cause weight gain as many other diabetes drugs do—and may even help some people lose a few pounds. One explanation for this is that the drug enhances the effect of the appetite-suppressing hormone leptin. The weight story is important because many diabetes patients stop taking medications that make them gain weight. Metformin doesn't present that problem.

CANCER PREVENTION...AND LONGEVITY?

It's amazing that this French lilac has been a diabetes remedy for centuries, and metformin has been a drug for more than 50 years, yet every few years there's a new study highlighting a potential new benefit—or entirely new use. *Promising findings...*

- **Cardiovascular protection.** Some observational studies have reported that people with type 2 diabetes who take the drug are less prone to heart disease than those who don't.
- **Cancer treatment.** Metformin's potential to prevent, treat or enhance other treatments for certain cancers has recently emerged. These are based on small, preliminary studies, however. The drug's ability to reduce both blood sugar and insulin levels may play a part in its possible anticancer properties.
- **Longevity.** The latest area of research is the potential for metformin to improve longevity by slowing physiological aging and increasing lifespan. These studies are based on preliminary observations using animal models (roundworms). Much more research in animals—and eventually, humans—will be needed to determine if metformin can have a similar effect in humans...with or without diabetes.

SIDE EFFECTS, OLD AND NEW

The most common complaint with metformin is that it can cause gastrointestinal issues such as abdominal discomfort and diarrhea. Although this may sound minor, it keeps some people from being able to take the drug. An extended-release metformin is available, and in some patients, this version may be better tolerated. *Other side effects include...*

- **A very rare but potentially fatal reaction.** It has been known for many years that if a patient's kidney function is poor when they are taking metformin, there is an increased risk for lactic acidosis, a condition in which too much lactic acid builds up in the blood. This metformin side effect occurs in fewer than 10 out of every 100,000 patients—0.005%—but it's fatal half the time it occurs. That's why your doctor should test you regularly for kidney function if you're taking metformin. Metformin does not cause kidney damage—it is just not safe to take if a patient already has a significant impairment in his or her kidney function.
- **B-12 deficiency.** A recently discovered side effect of metformin, particularly after long-term use, is a deficiency of vitamin B-12. People who are B-12 deficient for a long time may develop cognitive problems and even dementia. Ironically, a B-12 deficiency can also contribute to neuropathy—a burning sensation or lack of sensation in the legs and feet. This common diabetes symptom is usually the effect of high blood sugar causing nerve damage, but B-12 deficiency can cause leg neuropathy or make it worse. It can also cause a form of anemia. If you have type 2 diabetes, have been taking metformin for a long time—and especially if

you are experiencing neuropathy or cognitive issues—ask your doctor to check your B-12 level. The fix can be as simple as a B-12 pill or a monthly B-12 injection.

Generally, metformin is a safe medication. Under the care of a physician, it is safe to take this drug for decades so long as a patient's kidney function remains good and B-12 levels are checked in the appropriate clinical situations, such as in cases of longstanding use, anemia, neuropathy or cognitive issues.

IS METFORMIN RIGHT FOR YOU?

Now that you've got the scoop on this drug—its past, present and future potential—how can you tell if it's right for you? *The following are general guidelines, which may inform you as you tailor your individual treatment plan with your doctor...*

•If you have type 2 diabetes. You may be able to control your blood sugar with lifestyle changes alone, including a healthy diet, weight loss and exercise. However, it is generally recommended that patients start metformin along with lifestyle changes at the time of type 2 diabetes diagnosis. It's an important discussion to have with your doctor.

•If you are at risk for developing type 2 diabetes. People at risk include not only those with prediabetes but also women who developed diabetes during pregnancy (gestational diabetes), because they have a greatly increased risk of developing type 2 diabetes over their lifetimes. It is best to try lifestyle modifications before considering metformin. If that isn't working for you, ask your doctor about metformin.

•If you are a woman with polycystic ovary syndrome (PCOS). This condition increases the risk of developing type 2 diabetes and often leads to infertility. It is marked by high insulin levels, which contribute to a hormonal imbalance. In patients with PCOS, metformin, which tends to reduce insulin resistance, is sometimes prescribed in an attempt to restore ovulation and to improve fertility. If pregnancy is confirmed, metformin is usually continued for at least the first trimester. Always talk with your doctor about your treatment options.

There are, however, practical concerns to be aware of if you don't have diabetes but are taking metformin. Insurers tend to assume that anyone on metformin may have diabetes...even if you're taking it to prevent diabetes. That could affect medical and life insurance coverage. If you are not diabetic but need to take metformin, you may need your doctor to write a letter to your insurer confirming that you do not have diabetes. While there may be many medical reasons to take metformin beyond just type 2 diabetes, a thorough discussion about the role of metformin therapy, and the risks versus benefits, should take place before a patient starts any medication, including metformin.

What Drugs Work Best for Diabetic Nerve Pain?

Caroline Messer, MD, endocrinologist, Lenox Hill Hospital, New York City.

Ajay Misra, MD, chairman, department of neurosciences, Winthrop-University Hospital, Mineola, New York.

Neurology, news release.

Nerve pain and numbness, also known as neuropathy, is a debilitating but common symptom of diabetes.

Now, recent research suggests certain drugs may outperform others in treating diabetic neuropathy.

The new review of the data on the subject was led by Julie Waldfogel, PharmD, of Johns Hopkins Hospital in Baltimore. Her team noted that about half of people with diabetes have some form of nerve damage caused by high levels of blood sugar.

However, not all of them will have symptoms such as pain, numbness and tingling in the legs and feet.

ANTIDEPRESSANTS COME OUT (SOMEWHAT) ON TOP

The Hopkins research group reviewed 106 studies on pain relief for diabetic neuropathy. They found "moderate" evidence that the antidepressants *duloxetine* (Cymbalta) and *venlafaxine* (Effexor) reduce diabetic nerve pain.

However, they only found "weak" evidence that *botulinum toxin* (Botox), the anti-seizure drugs *pregabalin* (Lyrica) and *oxcarbazepine* (Trileptal), and drugs called tricyclic antidepressants and atypical opioids (drugs such as Tramadol) may help reduce pain.

The researchers also noted that *gabapentin* (Neurontin, Gralise) works in a similar manner to pregabalin, and the review found gabapentin no more effective than a placebo.

Long-term use of standard opioids—such as OxyContin, Vicodin or Percocet—is not recommended for chronic pain, including neuropathy, because of a lack of evidence of benefit and the risk of abuse, misuse and overdose, Dr. Waldfogel said.

The anti-seizure drug *valproate* and capsaicin cream were also ineffective, according to the review published online in the journal *Neurology.*

The review was funded by the U.S. Agency for Healthcare Research and Quality.

"Providing pain relief for neuropathy is crucial to managing this complicated disease," Dr. Waldfogel said in a journal news release.

"Unfortunately, more research is still needed, as the current treatments have substantial risk of side effects, and few studies have been done on the long-term effects of these drugs," she added.

EXPERT COMMENTS

Two experts in diabetes care and pain management said the data review is important information for patients.

"This trial was a much needed step in the right direction in an otherwise murky field of medicine," said Caroline Messer, MD, an endocrinologist at Lenox Hill Hospital in New York City.

She noted that "traditional teaching for endocrinologists has always included the use of gabapentin for diabetic neuropathy. Given gabapentin's host of side effects, it will be a relief to remove it from the toolbox."

And Dr. Messer added that "venlafaxine is now an interesting treatment possibility, given that one of its common side effects, weight loss, could prove useful for patients with type 2 diabetes."

Ajay Misra, MD, chair of neurosciences at Winthrop-University Hospital in Mineola, New York, noted that neuropathy can differ for people with type 1 or type 2 diabetes, with neuropathy levels correlating well with blood sugar management in people with type 1 disease, but not as well for those with type 2 diabetes.

As for pain relief, Dr. Misra said "there is clearly no medication which was found to be highly effective" in this recent review, so there is clearly a need for research into better analgesic options for patients.

"We hope our findings are helpful to doctors and people with diabetes who are searching for the most effective way to control pain from neuropathy," researcher Dr. Waldfogel added. "Unfortunately, there was not enough evidence available to determine if these treatments had an impact on quality of life. Future studies are needed to assess this."

info The American Diabetes Association has more on nerve damage from diabetes at Diabetes.org.

Dentists at the Front Line in Diabetes Epidemic

Wijnand Teeuw, DDS, MSc, chief, periodontology clinic, Academic Center for Dentistry Amsterdam, The Netherlands.
Sally Cram, DDS, PC, periodontist, Washington, DC, and spokeswoman, American Dental Association.
Joel Zonszein, MD, director, Clinical Diabetes Center, Montefiore Medical Center, New York City.
BMJ Open Diabetes Research & Care, online.

You'd probably be surprised if your dentist said you might have type 2 diabetes. But recent research reveals that severe gum disease may be a sign the illness is present and undiagnosed.

The study found that nearly one in five people with severe gum disease (periodontitis) had type 2 diabetes and didn't know it. The researchers said these findings suggest that the dentist's office may be a good place for a prediabetes or type 2 diabetes screening.

"Be aware that worsened oral health—in particular, periodontitis—can be a sign of an underlying [condition], such as diabetes," said study author Wijnand Teeuw, DDS. He's the chief of the periodontology clinic at the Academic Center for Dentistry Amsterdam in the Netherlands.

"Early diagnosis and treatment of both periodontitis and diabetes will benefit the patient by preventing further complications," Dr. Teeuw added.

Diabetes is a worldwide epidemic. In 2010, it was estimated that 285 million adults worldwide had diabetes. By 2030, that number is expected to rise to 552 million, according to the study authors. It's suspected that as many as one-third of people who have diabetes are unaware they have the disease.

Untreated, diabetes can lead to a number of serious complications, such as vision problems, serious kidney disease, heart trouble and infections that take a long time to heal, according to the American Diabetes Association.

Periodontitis—an infection that causes inflammation of the gums and destruction of the bones that support the teeth—is often considered a complication of diabetes, Dr. Teeuw said.

Warning signs of gum disease include bleeding gums, receding gums, sensitive teeth, loose teeth, bad breath or a bad taste in the mouth.

STUDY DETAILS

The current study included more than 300 people from a dental clinic in Amsterdam with varying levels of periodontitis or healthy gums. Approximately 125 had mild to moderate periodontitis and almost 80 had severe periodontitis. The rest had healthy gums.

The researchers tested blood sugar levels in all of the study participants using a test called hemoglobin A1c. This test provides an average of blood sugar levels over two to three months.

In people who had never been diagnosed with diabetes, the researchers found that 50% of the group with severe gum troubles had prediabetes, and 18% had type 2 diabetes. In the mild to moderate group, 48% were found to have prediabetes and 10% learned they had type 2 diabetes.

There were even significant numbers of people in the healthy gums group that had prediabetes—37% had prediabetes and 8.5% had type 2 diabetes, the study revealed.

EXPERTS COMMENT

Sally Cram, DDS, a periodontist and a spokeswoman for the American Dental Association, said she sees what the study found in her practice every day.

"I see quite a few patients who don't know they have diabetes, and when they don't respond normally to periodontal therapy, I have to say, 'Go to your doctor and get tested for diabetes,'" she said.

And, on the other side, she explained that people with uncontrolled diabetes often see improvement when their gum disease is under control.

"People with diabetes aren't as able to fight inflammation and infection," Dr. Cram explained.

Diabetes specialist Joel Zonszein, MD, said frequent or slow-to-heal infections are important signs of diabetes.

"People often come in with severe infections in the skin, and I think it's probably the same for infections in the mouth. People have been living for years with high blood sugar, and even if they go to the dentist, they don't get their blood sugar checked," Dr. Zonszein said.

"The relationship between diabetes and gum infections goes two ways. When you improve one, you also improve the other," he added. But it's not clear which comes first, and this study didn't prove a cause-and-effect relationship, only an association, Dr. Zonszein noted.

But the findings do show the importance of collaboration between health-care providers, according to Dr. Zonszein, who is the director of the Clinical Diabetes Center at Montefiore Medical Center in New York City.

Dr. Cram noted that basic prevention goes a long way toward preventing gum disease—99% of dental problems and disease are preventable. "Brush your teeth twice a day and floss once, and see your dentist periodically," she recommended.

The study was published online in *BMJ Open Diabetes Research & Care.*

info Learn more about the connection between diabetes and oral health from the American Diabetes Association at Diabetes.org.

Many People With Type 1 Diabetes Still Make Some Insulin

Uppsala University, news release.

Almost half of people with type 1 diabetes are still producing some insulin more than a decade after being diagnosed with the disease.

The recent findings challenge previous assumptions that people with type 1 diabetes lose the ability to produce any insulin—a hormone that helps usher sugar to cells to be used as fuel—over time.

Researchers at Sweden's Uppsala University, led by post-doctoral researcher Daniel Espes, reached their conclusions after studying more than 100 patients with type 1 diabetes.

The investigators found that people who still produced insulin despite their long-standing type 1 diabetes had higher levels of a protein called interleukin-35. This protein appears to play an important role in the immune system.

Past research had shown that both newly diagnosed people with type 1 diabetes and those who've had the disease for some time had lower average levels of interleukin-35 compared with healthy people.

Type 1 diabetes is an autoimmune disease that causes the body's immune system to mistakenly attack healthy cells in the pancreas that make insulin.

This leaves people without enough insulin to meet the body's daily needs. To survive, people with type 1 diabetes must replace that lost insulin through multiple daily injections or through a tiny tube inserted under the skin every few days and then attached to an insulin pump.

The Uppsala researchers have launched a new study to see if they may be able to boost insulin production in those people with type 1 diabetes who are still making insulin.

Checklist Helps Determine When It's Safe to Drive with Diabetes

Daniel Cox, PhD, AHPP, professor, departments of psychiatry, internal medicine, and ophthalmology, and director, Center for Behavioral Medicine Research and Virginia Driving Safety Laboratories, University of Virginia Health System, Charlottesville, Virginia.

Minisha Sood, MD, endocrinologist, Lenox Hill Hospital, New York City.

Joel Zonszein, MD, director, Clinical Diabetes Center, Montefiore Medical Center, New York City.

Diabetes Care, online.

Having type 1 diabetes can raise your chances of crashing while driving, but recent research offers a checklist that helps determine whether it is safe for you to get behind the wheel.

DRIVING AND DIABETES CAN BE A DANGEROUS MIX

The wrong amounts of insulin and other blood sugar-lowering medications can trigger dangerously low blood sugar levels, which can cause people to pass out or have seizures, the researchers explained.

"People with diabetes need to recognize that they're part of a huge mass of people who have potentially impaired driving, like people with heart disease or narcolepsy. They shouldn't think of themselves as isolated. It's just an issue to deal with," said the author of a recent study on diabetes and driving, Daniel Cox, PhD. He's a professor in psychiatry, internal medicine and ophthalmology at the University of Virginia Health System in Charlottesville.

"By no means are we saying that people with type 1 diabetes shouldn't drive. But, just like pilots go through a pre-flight checklist, drivers with type 1 diabetes need to go through a pre-drive checklist," he suggested.

Dr. Cox explained that some people with diabetes have a higher-than-average risk of driving troubles. This includes people who've already had a serious low blood sugar event (hypoglycemia) while driving, people who mismanage hypoglycemia, people who drive a lot, and people with diabetes who've lost feeling in their feet or legs (diabetic neuropathy), because they can't feel the pedals.

But doctors don't have a standardized assessment to determine who's at high risk for a diabetes-related accident and who's not.

CHECKLIST AND KITS DETER DANGEROUS DRIVING

So, Dr. Cox and his colleagues developed an 11-question test called the Risk Assessment of Diabetic Drivers (RADD). The researchers administered the test to more than 500 drivers with type 1 diabetes from Boston, central Virginia and Minneapolis.

The investigators asked the study participants about their driving "mishaps." A driving mishap —as defined by this study—was a dangerous driving situation that resulted in an accident or a very near miss.

The assessment accurately identified 61% of those who were at high risk for having driving issues, and 75% of those who were at low risk of having driving problems.

The second part of the study included almost 500 drivers with type 1 diabetes from across the country who took the RADD test online. The study found that 372 were identified as high-risk and 118 were considered low-risk.

Half of these people were then given routine care, and the rest were asked to participate in an online intervention.

The intervention aimed to anticipate, prevent, detect and treat hypoglycemia. All of the intervention participants were given a toolkit for their car. It contained a blood sugar meter, a pre-drive checklist, a key chain with a stoplight symbol to remind drivers to stop and treat their low blood sugar if their reading was below 70 milligrams per deciliter (mg/dL), or to be cautious and eat some foods containing carbohydrates before driving if it was between 70 and 90. (Below 70 is considered hypoglycemia.) Over 90 mg/dL is considered a green light, Dr. Cox said.

The kits also contained a fast-acting glucose product, such as glucose tablets or gel.

"Many people with type 1 diabetes didn't know how to properly treat hypoglycemia. They eat something with a lot of fat or protein, and that doesn't make blood glucose rise quickly. If you want a fast rise in blood glucose, glucose tablets will do it," Dr. Cox explained.

He said people with type 1 diabetes should always have fast-acting carbohydrates in their car.

The study found that the intervention tool helped drivers avoid hypoglycemia while driving.

EXPERT COMMENT

Joel Zonszein, MD, said he was glad to see the study bringing attention to the issue. "It reminds us that people with diabetes should be assessed individually, taking into account each individual's medical history as well as the potential related risks associated with driving, as recommended by the American Diabetes Association," he said.

But, he added that "the patients at risk are few, and they are mainly limited to older individuals, and those with advanced complications and type 1 diabetes."

Dr. Zonszein said he'd rather that people and their driving abilities were assessed by their physician or a certified diabetes educator instead of an online program.

Minisha Sood, MD, an endocrinologist from Lenox Hill Hospital in New York City, agreed that it's important to have a doctor or diabetes educator involved in the process.

"The anonymity [of an internet screening] may be a draw for patients who might feel embarrassed or anxious about their potential risk. It would be important for a care provider to have access to the assessment results, however, in order to keep a patient out of harm's way," she said.

Dr. Sood also agreed that anyone with "diabetes should always keep a fast-acting carbohydrate or source of glucose in the car for emergencies."

The study was published online recently in the journal *Diabetes Care*.

Transplant of Insulin-Producing Cells Offers Hope Against Type 1 Diabetes

David Baidal, MD, assistant professor, division of endocrinology, diabetes and metabolism, and clinical cell transplant program, Diabetes Research Institute, University of Miami Miller School of Medicine.
Julia Greenstein, PhD, vice president, discovery research, JDRF.
New England Journal of Medicine.

Scientists report a step forward in the plan to create a truly artificial pancreas, offering new hope to people with type 1 diabetes.

A 43-year-old single mother with dangerously difficult-to-control diabetes had insulin-producing islet cells transplanted into her omentum—a fatty membrane in the belly.

The cells began producing insulin faster than expected, and after one year she is doing well and doesn't need insulin injections, the University of Miami researchers said.

"We're exploring a way to optimize islet cell therapy to a larger population. This study gives us hope for a different transplant approach," said the study's lead author, David Baidal, MD. He's an assistant professor in the university's Diabetes Research Institute.

Others voiced optimism as well. "This study was a good start at evaluating a novel site for transplant," said Julia Greenstein, PhD, vice president of discovery research for JDRF (formerly the Juvenile Diabetes Research Foundation).

TYPE 1 DIABETES AND THE PANCREAS

Type 1 diabetes is an autoimmune disease. That means the body's immune system mistakenly damages healthy cells—in this case, the islet cells found in the pancreas. This leaves people with type 1 diabetes without enough insulin to convert sugars from foods into energy for the body.

As a result, they must take multiple daily insulin injections, or use a pump that delivers insulin via a tube inserted under the skin that must be changed every few days.

ARTIFICIAL "PANCREAS" TO REPLACE LIVER TRANSPLANTS

Currently, islet cells from deceased donors are transplanted into the liver, but that's not an ideal option.

This new research was a proof-of-concept study expected to be the first step on a path toward developing a mini-organ called the BioHub.

In its final stages, the BioHub would mimic a pancreas and act as a home for transplanted islet cells, providing them with oxygen until they could establish their own blood supply.

The hope is that the BioHub also would attempt to tackle the autoimmune attack that causes type 1 diabetes.

But, the first step in developing the BioHub was to find a suitable location in the body. When the liver is used for islet cell transplants, only a limited amount of islet cells can be transplanted. There's also a risk of bleeding when the transplant is done and the possibility of other complications, the researchers said.

"For most people, the liver isn't a problem. It's a great source of blood. It's a good place for insulin to be made. But, there are rare complications that can occur and we want to be able to explant [take the cells out] in case something does happen," said Dr. Greenstein, adding that you can't take the cells out of the liver.

Also, with islet cell transplants in the liver, the underlying autoimmune condition is still there. And, if people didn't take immune-suppressing medication, the new islet cells would likely be destroyed.

TRANSPLANTS RESERVED FOR EXTREME CASES

Because of these and other issues, islet cell transplantation is generally reserved for people whose diabetes is very difficult to control or who no longer have an awareness of potentially dangerous low blood-sugar levels (hypoglycemia unawareness).

The woman in the current study had a 25-year history of type 1 diabetes. She also had severe hypoglycemia unawareness.

"Her quality of life was severely impacted. She had to move in with her parents. And, if she traveled, she had to travel with her father" in case her blood sugar levels dropped dangerously low, Dr. Baidal explained.

The surgery was minimally invasive, and the islet cells were placed on a "scaffold" that eventually dissolved. There were no complications, the researchers said.

"We were happily surprised when her glucose [blood sugar] profile improved quite dramatically," Dr. Baidal said.

INSULIN DISCONTINUED

Normally, after a transplant, doctors wait a while before stopping insulin to give the new islet cells a chance to rest. But the new islet cells worked so well that the injected insulin was causing low blood sugar levels.

"We were able to discontinue insulin sooner than we thought we would. And, the glucose control was very stable," Dr. Baidal said.

Dr. Baidal said the study results need to be replicated in other patients, and the researchers want to see what happens post-treatment over a longer time. The researchers plan to test the omentum as a site in five more patients.

Dr. Greenstein said a big clinical trial isn't necessary because "either the transplant works or it doesn't work," so only a small number of people is needed.

The study's findings were published online in the *New England Journal of Medicine.*

info Learn more about islet cell transplants from the U.S. National Institute of Diabetes, Digestive and Kidney Diseases.

New Diabetes Treatment Teaches Rogue Immune Cells to Behave

Yong Zhao, MD, PhD, associate scientist, Hackensack University Medical Center, Hackensack, New Jersey.
Stem Cells Translational Medicine.

A treatment targeting wayward immune cells in people with type 1 or type 2 diabetes may help even years later, a recent study finds.

For the treatment, researchers take blood from a person with diabetes and separate out the immune system cells (lymphocytes). They briefly expose those cells to stem cells from umbilical cord blood from an unrelated infant. Then they return the lymphocytes to the patient's body.

The researchers have dubbed this treatment "stem cell educator therapy," because when exposed to the stem cells, the errant lymphocytes seem to re-learn how they should behave.

"Stem cell educator therapy is a safe approach" with long-term effectiveness, said the study's lead author, Yong Zhao, MD, PhD. He's an associate scientist at Hackensack University Medical Center in New Jersey.

Researchers have long thought that any cure for type 1 diabetes would have to stop the autoimmune attack, while regenerating or transplanting beta cells.

But Dr. Zhao and his team developed a new approach to the problem—educating the immune cells that had been destroying beta cells so they stop attacking.

In type 2 diabetes, Dr. Zhao said immune cell dysfunction is responsible for chronic inflammation that causes insulin resistance. When someone is insulin resistant, their body's cells can't properly use insulin to usher sugar from foods into cells for use as energy. Instead, the sugar builds up in the blood.

The researchers hoped the stem cell educator would help decrease insulin resistance for people with type 2 diabetes.

In earlier trials, the treatment showed significant promise with up to a year of data. The researchers also showed that the treatment was safe.

STUDY DETAILS

The current study looked at four years of data on nine type 1 diabetes patients in China.

To see how well the treatment works, the researchers measured C-peptide, a protein fragment that's a by-product of insulin production.

Two people with type 1 diabetes who received a stem cell educator treatment shortly after diagnosis (five and eight months later) still had normal C-peptide production and didn't need insulin four years after a single treatment.

Another type 1 patient had had the disease for four years when she got a treatment. She still had improvements in her C-peptide levels, but wasn't considered in remission. The remaining six people with type 1 saw decreases in their C-peptide levels over time. The study authors said this suggests more than one treatment might be needed.

"Because this was a first trial, patients just got one treatment. Now we know it's very safe so patients can receive two or three treatments," Dr. Zhao said.

Researchers also looked at six patients with severe, long-standing (15–24 years) type 2 diabetes. They found that one treatment helped four patients achieve normal C-peptide levels and maintain them over the four-year follow-up.

"For the four type 2 patients, their C-peptide is very stable after one treatment," Dr. Zhao said.

TREATMENT MAY HELP OTHER AUTOIMMUNE DISEASES

In addition to helping people with diabetes, Dr. Zhao said the treatment could help with other autoimmune diseases, too. These might include alopecia areata, which causes significant and sudden hair loss; lupus; Hashimoto's disease; and Sjogren's syndrome, he said.

Dr. Zhao noted that diabetes seems to differ slightly in Chinese populations from Western ones. So, it's not yet clear if this treatment would be as beneficial for people of European descent.

To find out, Dr. Zhao plans to conduct a clinical trial of the new treatment with people with type 1 diabetes at Hackensack Medical Center.

The study was recently published in *Stem Cells Translational Medicine*.

New Nasal Powder Fixes Severe Low Blood Sugar

Elizabeth Seaquist, MD, director, division of diabetes, endocrinology and metabolism, University of Minnesota, Minneapolis.

Cristina Guzman, MD, senior medical advisor, Eli Lilly and Co.

Chad Grothen, global brand development lead, Eli Lilly and Co.

Joel Zonszein, MD, director, Clinical Diabetes Center, Montefiore Medical Center, New York City.

American Diabetes Association meeting, San Diego.

For many people with diabetes, low blood sugar levels are a serious health risk, but researchers report that a new nasal powder quickly reverses the effects of this dangerous condition.

Better yet, it can be administered even when someone is unconscious, the researchers added.

The nasal powder contains the hormone glucagon. This hormone tells the body to release stored sugar, which will generally reverse a low blood sugar episode. Glucagon is currently only available in an injectable form that has to be mixed before it is injected.

"Family members can be terrified to use the injectable form. But 95% of caregivers found nasal glucagon very easy to use," said study leader. Elizabeth Seaquist, MD. She's directs the University of Minnesota's division of diabetes, endocrinology and metabolism.

Dr. Seaquist is also a consultant for Eli Lilly and Co., which plans to make nasal glucagon; the company also makes injectable glucagon kits. The study was funded by Eli Lilly and Locemia, the company that originally developed the nasal glucagon.

WHAT IS HYPOGLYCEMIA?

Low blood sugar, known as hypoglycemia, occurs when blood sugar levels drop too low. This can happen when someone with diabetes takes too much insulin (a hormone that allows the body to use sugar from food for energy). It can also happen if someone doesn't eat enough or exercises harder or longer than planned.

Without enough sugar, the body and brain can't function normally.

Low blood sugar can cause dizziness, hunger, confusion, blurred vision, sweating, slurred speech and irritability, along with other symptoms, according to the U.S. National Institute of Diabetes and Digestive and Kidney Diseases.

To treat low blood sugar, the person needs to have a drink or food containing a fast-acting sugar. Examples include fruit juice, soda with sugar, or sugary candy such as licorice (but not chocolate). Usually, blood sugar levels then quickly return to normal.

Left untreated, a low blood sugar episode will worsen. The continued lack of blood sugar may cause disorientation, seizures, unconsciousness and even death. If symptoms don't subside, or the person is too disoriented to eat or drink, glucagon would usually be given.

The U.S. Centers for Disease Control and Prevention estimates that 300,000 people go to the hospital each year due to severe low blood sugar.

STUDY DETAILS

To evaluate the newly developed nasal glucagon, researchers gave people with type 1 diabetes a nasal device to use when they had a low blood sugar episode.

"Nasal glucagon is a dry powder that exists in a small device. It looks something like a nasal steroid inhaler, but smaller. To use, a family member or caregiver takes it out of the container, puts it in the nose and pushes the bottom of the canister to release the material...It's absorbed through the nose into the bloodstream," Dr. Seaquist explained.

Cristina Guzman, MD, a study author and senior medical advisor for Eli Lilly, added, "Patients don't have to breathe or inhale, which makes it easy to use."

In the study, 69 people had 157 low blood sugar episodes that were treated with nasal glucagon. Their blood sugar levels ranged from 22 to 74 milligrams per deciliter (mg/dL) of blood. A level of 70 mg/dL or under is typically when a low blood sugar episode begins, according to the American Diabetes Association.

In 96% of the episodes, blood sugar levels returned to normal within 30 minutes, the study found. Side effects were similar to injectable glucagon, including nausea and vomiting. The nasal powder also caused some nasal irritation and headache. These side effects tended to last an hour or less, the study found.

Eli Lilly hopes to submit nasal glucagon to the U.S. Food and Drug Administration sometime in 2018, according to Chad Grothen, global brand development lead at Eli Lilly. The company will likely seek approvals in other countries after the United States. Right now, the product doesn't have a name, and Grothen couldn't estimate how much it would cost once it hits the market.

EXPERT COMMENT

Joel Zonszein, MD, director of the Clinical Diabetes Center at Montefiore Medical Center in New York City, expects the new product will be expensive.

But, he said, it will also be welcome.

"The problem with the injectable is that even when [the caregiver] is taught how to do it, they rarely do it, even when the glucagon is available," he explained.

"Nasal glucagon is easier to administer, is absorbed promptly and should be a good formulation," he said.

info Learn more about hypoglycemia from the U.S. National Institute of Diabetes and Digestive and Kidney Diseases at NIDDK.nih.gov.

Inhaled Insulin a Bust

Osama Hamdy, MD, PhD, director, inpatient diabetes program, Joslin Diabetes Center, Boston.

The French drugmaker Sanofi recently canceled its agreement to sell Afrezza in the US due to poor sales. Afrezza was launched in the US in February 2015, but many doctors were put off by the need for spirometry testing before prescribing the drug, and others were concerned about the long-term side effects of inhaled insulin, such as breathing problems in those with chronic obstructive pulmonary disease (COPD) and other lung conditions. The drug was also higher-priced than injectable insulin.

CHAPTER 8

Emotional Rescue

Do This to Beat the Blues

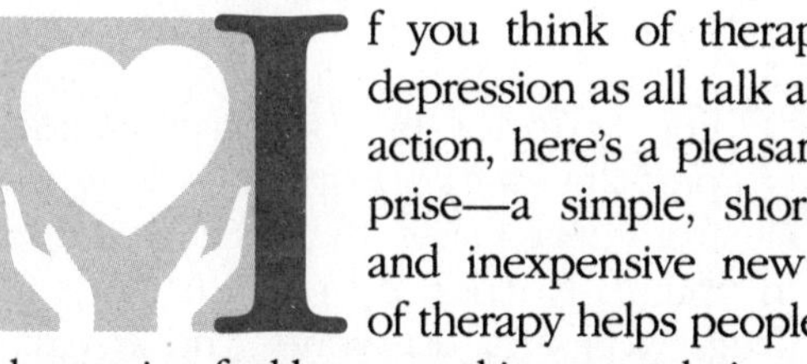

If you think of therapy for depression as all talk and no action, here's a pleasant surprise—a simple, short-term and inexpensive new form of therapy helps people with depression feel better and improve their states of mind by "doing." Doing what? *You'll see...*

TREATING DEPRESSION FROM THE OUTSIDE IN

Behavioral activation (BA), as the approach is called, helps people re-engage with others and with activities that they enjoy—or used to enjoy—rather than focusing on their inner thoughts and feelings.

When people are depressed, they naturally withdraw socially and from activities they used to enjoy—and get pulled in by their negative moods. This sets up a bad cycle.

That's where BA comes in—breaking this negative cycle. It targets inertia, encouraging people to treat their depression through their behavior.

Let's say you enjoy, or used to enjoy, quilting. (In fact, it could be any activity you like, either alone or with others—cooking with friends, hiking, playing piano, being in a book club, drawing, etc.) With BA therapy, you would be encouraged to pursue that pastime in a small, incremental way—perhaps, say, by searching online for local quilting clubs to join. The next step might involve choosing a particular club and making inquiries about when it meets and whether it's open to new members. When internal barriers arise—if you can't mobilize your efforts because you feel so down and tired, for example—you and the therapist would try to

Christopher Martell, PhD, clinic director of the Psychological Services Center at the University of Massachusetts, Amherst, author of two textbooks on behavioral activation (BA) for therapists and coauthor (with Michael Addis, PhD) of the client workbook on BA, *Overcoming Depression One Step at a Time: The New Behavioral Activation Approach to Getting Your Life Back.*

identify what's really standing in your way and what you can do to get around those obstacles.

HOW WELL DOES BA WORK?

BA therapy has developed in its current form only within the past 20 years, so it is not as thoroughly researched as other forms of therapy. *But there's a growing body of supportive evidence...*

• **It works as well as cognitive behavioral therapy (CBT),** according to a recent study published in *The Lancet*. When 440 adults who met a primary diagnosis of depression but who were not yet getting any treatment received at least eight weekly sessions of CBT—a well-established approach that focuses on changing thought patterns and behaviors—or BA, the therapies were found to be equally effective.

• **It works in older people.** A recent study from the Weill Cornell Institute of Geriatric Psychiatry in White Plains, New York, published in *The American Journal of Geriatric Psychiatry,* looked at 48 adults over age 60 with mild-to-moderate depression. After the patients were treated with nine weekly sessions of BA, they were engaged, participating in many more personally rewarding activities—and they experienced a sharp decline in their depressive symptoms.

THE EXERCISE CONNECTION

There's another potential benefit offered by BA. If this therapy could help people with depression become more physically active, the effects could be profound.

Here's why: According to a recent study published in *Psychosomatic Medicine,* 30 minutes of brisk exercise three times a week is not only as effective in treating depression as major antidepressants but also much more effective in preventing the return of depression. Six months after treatment ended, only 8% in the exercise-only group had their depression return, compared with 38% in the drug-only group.

SHOULD YOU TRY IT?

Even though BA isn't successful for everyone, when it works, it can work very quickly. The exact mechanism of action isn't clear, but reengaging in activity can increase positive feelings—and the negative thinking that's associated with depression can change as you change your behavior.

While each patient and each therapist is individual, a typical course of BA consists of weekly 50-minute sessions for up to 24 weeks. It is a nondrug approach but can also work for individuals who are being treated with psychiatric medications, such as antidepressants.

To find a BA therapist, the best place to start is with a therapist trained in CBT (most therapists trained in CBT can do BA). To find a CBT therapist, click on "Find Help," then on "Find a CBT Therapist" at ABCT.org, the site of the Association for Behavioral and Cognitive Therapies. Like other psychotherapies, BA is generally covered by insurance.

And the good news is that the key to this therapy is doing what you enjoy!

The Antidepressant Test

John Logan Black III, MD, professor of psychiatry and codirector of the Personalized Genomics Laboratory in the department of laboratory medicine and pathology at Mayo Clinic in Rochester, Minnesota. *Disclosure:* Dr. Black and Mayo Clinic have financial interests in two companies that perform pharmacogenetic testing and interpret results for physicians.

When a doctor prescribes an antidepressant for a patient who is suffering from depression, there are well over a dozen options to choose from. But none of these drugs works for everyone. And an antidepressant that works well for one person may cause severe or unacceptable side effects (such as headache or nausea) in another person.

Until recently, finding the right antidepressant for each patient has usually involved a considerable amount of trial and error. The process might take weeks and be particularly frustrating for the person suffering from depression.

Now: Doctors are increasingly turning to a more personalized way to tailor the prescription to the patient. With an emerging field known as pharmacogenetics, doctors can test your genes to determine which antidepressant best fits your personal genetic makeup.

HINTS IN YOUR GENES

Other factors (such as one's stress levels and overall physical condition) also come into play, but much of your response to antidepressants —and to many other drugs—is determined by your genes.

How your body deals with medication involves two processes...

- **Pharmacokinetics refers to the way your body metabolizes drugs,** altering them chemically so they can have their desired effect on you and breaking them down to be eliminated. This reaction determines the level of the medication in your body as well as its level of effectiveness for you.

- **Pharmacodynamics is the way drugs interact with specific proteins in your cells**—that is, speeding them up, slowing them down and/or altering the flow of chemical messengers between them. Such changes are the basis of benefits and risks from individual drugs.

In recent years, scientists have identified a number of genes that govern these processes and learned how variations in these genes (or "variants") affect drug response. All proteins in the body are encoded by their genes. While this type of genetic analysis cannot eliminate trial and error altogether, it gives doctors a valuable head start at predicting which antidepressants (and doses) are likely to work well while causing the fewest side effects.

THE SPEED OF METABOLISM

To predict your response to an antidepressant and your odds of experiencing side effects, your doctor can order a blood test or do a swab to collect a sample of cells from the inside of your cheek. A laboratory analysis would look for a family of enzymes, known as cytochrome P450 (CYP) enzymes, that are produced primarily in the liver and play a major role in metabolizing many drugs—including about 20 antidepressants.

Dozens of CYP enzymes, which are encoded by our genes, have been identified, but only a handful are active in metabolizing antidepressants. Most people have two, in particular, which are important in breaking down some of the most widely used antidepressants...

- **Cytochrome P450 2D6 (CYP2D6)** is a key enzyme for antidepressants including *fluoxetine* (Prozac) and *paroxetine* (Paxil).

- **Cytochrome P450 2C19 (CYP2C19)** is the enzyme for antidepressants such as *citalopram* (Celexa) and *escitalopram* (Lexapro).

Depending on which gene variants you've inherited, testing may show how quickly you'll metabolize these and other antidepressants.

Genetic analysis also gives information on how your brain cells are likely to respond to medication. Many antidepressants, including *sertraline* (Zoloft) as well as Prozac, Paxil, Celexa and Lexapro, work primarily by increasing activity of the neurotransmitter serotonin. Genes that influence how brain cells interact with serotonin have been identified.

Also: If your genes suggest that your brain cells are unlikely to be strongly affected by serotonin-only drugs, you may do better with an antidepressant that also works on other neurotransmitters, such as *venlafaxine* (Effexor) or *duloxetine* (Cymbalta).

SHOULD YOU BE TESTED?

Because genetic testing is still relatively new in psychiatry, you may have to mention it to your doctor. *It's worth considering for...*

- **The very young or very old,** who might have trouble communicating how the drug is affecting them.

- **People with very severe depression... or if suicide is a risk**—when it's especially important to get the drug right the first time.

- **People who have been prescribed medication (such as prescription painkillers) in the past** that did not work or produced severe side effects at low doses.

- **People whose close family members have suffered significant side effects from medication, particularly antidepressants.**

Note: People who are already taking an antidepressant may also benefit from testing if they are not achieving a desired response and/or experiencing side effects.

HOW TO GET TESTED

If you opt for genetic analysis, your doctor will order the test. Local and regional laboratories, even large ones, may not do genetic testing, but they can send blood or cheek swab samples to a lab that specializes in this work.

If there is a university medical center in your area, a doctor there who prescribes antidepressants may be able to help you with testing.

Important: Because most physicians are not trained to interpret genetic test results, look for a company whose report translates findings into recommendations for antidepressant prescriptions and doses for your doctor. Such reports are available when the analysis is performed by Assurex Health, Genelex, Genomind and Mayo Clinic.

The cost for this type of genetic testing may range from several hundred to several thousand dollars. Health insurers vary in their willingness to cover this type of testing, so check in advance to find out whether you'll be reimbursed. If your insurer denies coverage, consider asking your doctor to write a letter explaining why the testing is needed and/or filing an appeal.

Antidepressant Is Making Things Worse...

Michael D. Banov, MD, medical director of Northwest Behavioral Medicine, Roswell, Georgia.

Some individuals say that they feel worse when they start taking an antidepressant. *Some possible reasons...*

As the brain and body adapt to higher neurotransmitter levels, side effects such as headache and upset stomach may occur. Worse, some people feel more depressed or anxious than they did before. This may be due to restlessness and agitation provoked by a discharge of serotonin in response to the medication—and may also be behind the increased risk for suicide, which although quite small, is most likely in the first days of treatment.

Other possible reasons: It may be that many people start medication because their depression is worsening, and the drug hasn't started working yet. Or the drug increases mental energy before it improves mood, so people experience negative feelings more strongly.

Most adverse effects go away within a week, but if reactions are severe, the patient should see his or her doctor, who may change the dose or suggest a different drug.

Also, for about 20% of people responding well to an antidepressant, the drug loses its effectiveness after several months or longer. It could be that too much of the drug in the system makes them feel flat and lethargic, and they'll do better on a lower dose. Or the body has learned to metabolize the drug more efficiently, so they need a higher dose or a different drug. Situational factors, such as job stress, could be triggering more distress than the drug can alleviate, and psychotherapy or lifestyle changes may help.

A good professional can advise on why a medication is making a depressed individual feel worse and what to try to make things better.

The 10 Very Best Foods to Prevent Depression

Drew Ramsey, MD, psychiatrist, Columbia University Medical Center, and assistant professor, Columbia University College of Physicians and Surgeons, both in New York City. His latest book is *Eat Complete.* DrewRamseyMD.com

Here's a startling statistic—studies show that people who consume a healthy diet are 40% to 50% less likely to develop depression.

What are the absolutely best nutrients—and most nutrient-packed foods—to protect your brain from depression and other ailments?

What protects mood also protects against dementia and other brain-related conditions. The brain is the biggest asset we have, so we should be selecting foods that specifically nourish the brain.

Here's how to build the healthiest brain possible—starting in your kitchen.

NUTRIENTS BRAINS NEED MOST

These key nutrients are the most important...

•**Long-chain omega-3 fatty acids.** There are two major ones. Docosahexaenoic acid (DHA) creates hormones called "neuroprotectins and resolvins" that combat brain inflammation, which is implicated in the development of depression (as well as dementia). Eicosapentaenoic acid (EPA) protects the cardiovascular system, important for a healthy brain.

•**Zinc.** This mineral plays a major role in the development of new brain cells and can boost the efficacy of antidepressant medications.

•**Folate.** Also known as vitamin B-9, folate is needed for good moods and a healthy brain. It helps produce defensin-1, a molecule that protects the brain and increases the concentration of acetylcholine, a neurotransmitter that's crucial to memory and cognition.

•**Iron.** This essential element is a crucial cofactor in the synthesis of mood-regulating neurotransmitters including dopamine and serotonin.

•**Magnesium.** This mineral is required to keep myelin—the insulation of brain cells—healthy. It also increases brain-derived neurotrophic factor (BDNF), which promotes the growth of new neurons and healthy connections among brain cells. A deficiency in magnesium can lead to depression, anxiety, symptoms of ADHD, insomnia and fatigue.

•**Vitamin B-12.** This vitamin, which often is deficient as we age, helps makes neurotransmitters that are key to mood and memory.

•**Vitamin E.** This potent antioxidant vitamin protects polyunsaturated fatty acids in the brain—including DHA. Vitamin E–rich foods, but not supplements, are linked to the prevention of clinical depression as well as slower progression of Alzheimer's disease. One reason may be that most supplements contain only alpha-tocopherol, while other vitamin E compounds, particularly tocotrienols, play important roles in brain function.

•**Dietary fiber.** A high-fiber diet supports healthy gut bacteria (the gut "microbiome"), which growing evidence suggests is key for mental health.

BOOSTING YOUR MOOD AT THE SUPERMARKET

The best brain foods are mostly plant-based, but seafood, wild game and even some organ meats make the top of the list, too...

•**Leafy greens** such as kale, mustard greens and collard greens.

•**Bell peppers** such as red, green and orange.

•**Cruciferous vegetables** such as cauliflower, broccoli and cabbage.

•**Berries** such as strawberries, raspberries and blueberries.

•**Nuts** such as pecans, walnuts, almonds and cashews.

•**Bivalves** such as oysters, clams and mussels.

•**Crustaceans** such as crab, lobster and shrimp.

•**Fish** such as sardines, salmon and fish roe

•**Organ meats** such as liver, poultry giblets and heart.

•**Game and wild meat** such as bison, elk and duck.

Eating these nutrient-dense foods is likely to help prevent and treat mental illness. When someone with depression is treated, the real goal is to prevent that person from ever getting depressed again.

EVERYDAY BRAIN FOODS

Not into eating beef heart? Having a little trouble stocking up on elk? When it comes to meat, wild game may not be widely available, but grass-fed beef, which is higher in omega-3 fatty acids than conventionally raised beef, is stocked in most supermarkets—and may be independently associated with protection from depression.

Other foods that didn't make it to the top of the Brain Food Scale but that still are very good for the brain include eggs (iron, zinc), beans (fiber, magnesium, iron) and fruits and vegetables of all colors (fiber, antioxidants). Plus, small quantities of dark chocolate, which gives you a little dopamine rush. Dopamine, he explains, is a neurotransmitter that provides a feeling of reward.

Antidepressant Helper

Peter Bongiorno, ND, LAc, naturopathic doctor in New York City and the author of *How Come They're Happy and I'm Not?*

Some psychiatrists are beginning to use natural medicines to help prescription antidepressants work better. Deplin is a prescription form of a natural B vitamin called L-methylfolate. Studies of patients who did not respond well to antidepressants found that those who took 15 mg of Deplin daily responded much better to antidepressant medication.

It appears that folate, which is found in foods like leafy green vegetables, helps to balance levels of the neurotransmitters that regulate mood. Low folate levels can result from poor eating habits, aging, certain drugs, such as antiepileptic medication, and excessive alcohol intake.

The Awesome Power of a Visit to Prevent Depression

Alan Teo, MD, MS, assistant professor of psychiatry at Oregon Health & Science University, and researcher at the VA Portland Health Care System. He is lead author of the study titled "Does Mode of Contact with Different Types of Social Relationships Predict Depression in Older Adults?" published in *Journal of the American Geriatrics Society.*

You know that visiting a friend or relative cheers him or her up, but new research shows that it's far more than a temporary mood lift. When you spend time—even if it's just once a month—it can help prevent that person from becoming depressed. The new research applies to anyone 50 or older, but there are particular insights for those age 70 on up.

While it's no surprise that a real visit packs more emotional punch than a phone call or an e-mail, the new study did uncover unexpected insights. Some ways of contacting people are surprisingly unhelpful...for a certain age group, visits from friends help more than visits from kin...and one particular kind of visit is worse than staying away entirely!

So if you love someone who may be lonely or isolated, read on to learn the best ways to help him or her stay emotionally healthy.

The good news: It doesn't always require a long car ride or trip to the airport.

THE LONELY PATH TO DEPRESSION... AND A WAY OUT

Isolation and loneliness are major contributors to depression. It's true for everyone, but it's especially relevant for older people, who may be dealing with physical limitations, ill health and new living situations and experiencing feelings of loss, anger, frustration—even despair.

Close social support from family and friends has been shown to reduce the risk for depression. But what hasn't been studied much, until now, is how different forms of communication affect depression risk. To find out, researchers at VA Portland Health Care System in Oregon assessed 11,000 US adults aged 50 and older. They were a representative sample, so some had very active social lives—with friends, children and other family members—while others were more isolated. At the beginning of the study, some were depressed but most weren't. Then the researchers looked at depressive symptoms two years later. *Key findings...*

• **Real visits matter.** Individuals who weren't initially depressed who had face-to-face contact with anyone at least once or twice a week had only a 7.3% chance of becoming depressed over the next two years. Those who got together with a friend or relative only once or twice a month fared a little worse—8.1% became depressed. But those who saw friends or family only every few months or even less had an 11.5% chance of becoming depressed within two years.

• **When you're younger, friends help the most.** Between the ages of 50 and 69, frequent in-person contact with friends was the most powerful depression protection. After age 70, in-person contact with the kids was most protective.

• **E-mails, letters and phone calls don't help much.** While there was some indication that frequent e-mails from friends might be somewhat helpful in reducing depressive symptoms, the results were mixed, so no firm conclusions could be reached. Nor did frequent phone calls help prevent depression.

• **Is your loved one already depressed?** Pick up the phone! For subjects who were already depressed at the beginning of the study, frequent phone calls with a friend or relative (two or three times a week) was associated with reduced depressive symptoms. This dovetails with other research that shows that phone-based therapy can be effective, especially for older people with depression.

• **Bad visits are worse than no visits at all.** Driving over, e-mailing or calling just to pick a fight isn't doing anyone a favor. Whether a phone call, letter, e-letter or in-person visit, if the contact involved conflict or was lacking in social support, it increased depressive symptoms, the study found. (The study describes "social support" as feeling understood...having someone to rely on in case of a problem...or having someone to "open up" with to talk about worries.)

THE BEST WAY TO VISIT YOUR LOVED ONE

To make sure your visits are positive experiences, we asked Alan Teo, MD, MS, assistant professor of psychiatry at Oregon Health & Science University and lead author of the study, for his suggestions...

• **Visit regularly and frequently.** It doesn't matter whether the visits are scheduled in advance or spontaneous. It's the regularity and frequency that are most important.

• **Provide social support.** When you visit, be there emotionally as well as physically. Turn off your cell phone, and provide your full attention. Really listen, especially if your friend or loved one is having a hard time. Even if you're not solving any problems, says Dr. Teo, lending an ear shows that you care.

• **Keep it cool.** "People don't always agree, and people do get angry," notes Dr. Teo. That's to be expected. But try not to get too upset when you and your friend or family member disagree. "When that happens, let the other person know this is how you feel and ask to talk it out," he says. When it comes to your loved one's mental health, the quality of the visit really matters.

• **Embrace electronic technology.** Though Dr. Teo stresses the importance of face-to-face contact, he does believe that newer video-streaming technologies—which weren't covered in this study—might help under certain circumstances. "If your older loved one lives too far away to make frequent visits feasible, online video communication, via Skype or Facetime, can be a nice way to bridge the gap between the times when you can visit personally."

Laughing Gas for Depression?

Biological Psychiatry.

Adults with hard-to-treat depression who inhaled nitrous oxide showed improvement within hours. Some had complete relief from depressive symptoms with this experimental treatment.

How to Stop Your Worst Memories from Tormenting You

Ronald A. Ruden, MD, PhD, an internist on the clinical staff at NYU Langone Medical Center and Lenox Hill Hospital. He sees patients at his private practice in New York City. He is author of *Havening Techniques: A Primer* and *When the Past Is Always Present: Emotional Traumatization, Causes and Cures.* Havening.org

What can you do if you suffer from phobias, panic attacks, traumatic memories or other emotional disturbances? Like millions of Americans, you might choose to see a psychiatrist or other therapist. You could engage in some form of talk therapy to gain a fuller understanding of your emotions. You might take an antidepressant or other medication. Both talk therapy and medication (often used together) are helpful, but they may not eliminate the root causes of your distress.

New approach: Havening. It's a technique ("havening" means to put into a safe place) that uses touch to change how electrical signals are transmitted in the brain. After a successful havening session, the traumatic memory is viewed as distant and detached from the emotions, such as fear and anger, that are generated during the event—that is, it no longer causes distress. The havening technique still is considered experimental and is not scientifically proven, but it is inexpensive, safe, rapid and gentle, and there is growing anecdotal experience suggesting that it works.

EMOTIONS LINGER

To understand the theory behind the havening technique, it helps to understand what happens when we experience a traumatic event. Let's say, for example, that you get mugged in an alley—if you're lucky, you'll put it behind you over time. But for some people, the event may be encoded in the brain as a trauma. When you perceive a threat, your brain activates neurons in the amygdala, the region of the brain associated with threat detection and other emotions. If certain criteria are met, cell receptors in the amygdala are potentiated. In other words, they increase in number and remain permanently primed for activation by related stimuli.

Because the encoded receptors are always present, the emotions associated with traumatic memories can be reactivated over and over again. Individuals might experience nightmares, worry every time they walk past an alley or even stop leaving the house altogether. This leads to a worsening of emotional distress.

Experts used to think that traumatic events caused lifelong distress because the memories—and associated emotions—could never be erased. But the brain is essentially an electrochemical system. The theory behind havening is that if you change the brain's circuitry, you can eliminate the response to signals that have been causing emotional pain—even if the memory originally associated with that pain is not gone.

HAVENING TOUCH

The goal of havening therapy is to delink the emotions from the encoded traumatic event. The therapy is designed to generate brain waves that remove the potentiated receptors so that the individual won't experience again those fears or other emotional disturbances associated with the event.

During a typical havening session, a patient is asked to recall the painful memory. This activates the potentiated receptors. He/she then is exposed to "havening touch"—gentle, soothing stroking of the arms, face and hands. At the same time, the patient distracts himself from the memory by counting or singing a song.

How it works: Touching triggers the production of low-frequency delta waves in the brain. Delta waves open calcium channels in the amygdala. The influx of calcium sets off an enzymatic reaction that causes "trauma" receptors to disappear. A patient might still remember the details of the traumatic event, but he will no longer feel disturbed by the memories.

DOES SCIENCE SUPPORT IT?

Only one peer-reviewed, published scientific study has examined the effects of havening. Two others are completed and awaiting publication. The published study, which appeared in *Health Science Journal*, looked at workers in the UK who self-reported that they suffered occupational impairments because of depression and/or anxiety due to a traumatic event. After a havening session, participants showed improvements in tests that measured depression, anxiety and work and social adjustment.

Important caveats: The study was small (27 participants) and didn't include a control group...and the participants weren't randomly selected. In addition, the workers were all health-care professionals, so they might have been more open to—and affected by—psychotherapy than other adults.

WHAT TO DO

In the US, there are only about 40 havening practitioners who have participated in courses and trainer events and have been certified by a Havening Techniques trainer. These practitioners are mainly in New York City and on Long Island and in Chicago and Los Angeles...and there's one in the Louisville, Kentucky, area. Worldwide there are about 140 certified practitioners. The average cost for a havening session is about $200 to $400. But because there are only a small number of havening professionals, some people choose to practice the therapy on their own. In our experience, self-havening often is as effective as practitioner-guided sessions.

What happens in a session...

- **Activate the emotion.** You'll be asked (or you'll ask yourself) to recall the distressing event and all of the details. It might be a street crime...a memory of childhood abuse...even a cruel thing you yourself once did...or another memory that causes you repeated distress. You'll rate the distress that the memory causes on a scale of 0 to 10.

• **Apply havening touch.** The practitioner (or you or a loved one) will offer comforting touch that involves stroking the arms from shoulder to elbow, stroking the forehead and rubbing palms.

• **Distraction.** Simultaneously, with your eyes closed, you will distract yourself by imagining that you're climbing a staircase with 20 steps. Count the steps aloud. With each step, you'll imagine that your distress is diminishing.

After the twentieth step, with eyes still closed, you'll hum two rounds of "Row, Row, Row Your Boat" or another neutral song. You'll open your eyes, look to the right and left, and inhale and exhale deeply. If your distress level is still high, you should repeat the touch/distraction components (using different visualizations and tunes) until the level of distress is zero or remains fixed after two rounds.

The distraction is important because your mind can't process two thoughts at the same time. The idea is that distracting yourself from the memory displaces the recalled event and prevents it from continually activating the amygdala. At the same time, the touch part of the therapy produces the brain waves that de-link the memory from your emotions.

A single session can last for minutes to hours, but a typical session lasts 60 minutes. In my experience, many people will notice permanent improvement after a single session.

Online Therapy Can Relieve Insomnia

Lee M. Ritterband, PhD, director of Center for Behavioral Health and Technology, University of Virginia School of Medicine, Charlottesville.

Online therapy can relieve insomnia, we hear from Lee M. Ritterband, PhD.

Example: After one year, 57% of people using the focused online behavioral-modification program SHUTi were sleeping normally, versus 27% who had received only advice and education. Online programs are based on cognitive behavioral therapy and have proved effective among adults ages 18 to 65. Online programs include SHUTi, $135 for 16 weeks of access, and Sleepio, $300 for one year of access.

It's 3 am and You're Awake...Again!

Michael Breus, PhD, a sleep specialist with a private practice in Los Angeles. Dr. Breus is also author of *The Power of When: Discover Your Chronotype—and the Best Time to Eat Lunch, Ask for a Raise, Have Sex, Write a Novel, Take Your Meds, and More.* TheSleepDoctor.com

In the world of sleep disorders, having difficulty staying asleep is just as troubling as having difficulty falling asleep.

Both sleep problems rob us of the consistent, high-quality rest that helps protect against high blood pressure, obesity, diabetes, stroke and depression.

Plenty of people who have nighttime awakenings turn to a prescription sleep aid, such as *zolpidem* (Ambien). But these pills are only a temporary fix and can cause prolonged drowsiness the next day or, in rare cases, sleepwalking or sleep-eating within hours of taking them.

A better option: Cognitive behavioral therapy for insomnia, known as CBT-I, is now recommended as a first-line treatment for chronic sleep problems.* With CBT-I, you work with a specially trained therapist (typically for six to eight sessions) to identify, challenge and change the patterns of thinking that keep you awake at night. A 2015 study found CBT-I, which is typically covered by health insurance, to be more helpful than *diazepam* (Valium), commonly used as a sleep aid, in treating insomnia.

But if you are not quite ready to commit to a course of CBT-I—or even if you do try it—there are some simple but effective strategies you can use at home to help you stay asleep and get the deep rest you need.

*To find a CBT-I therapist, consult the Society of Behavioral Sleep Medicine, BehavioralSleep.org. You can also try the free CBT-i Coach app, available at iTunes or Google Play.

Best approaches to avoid nighttime awakenings...

•Get more omega-3 fatty acids. While the research is still preliminary, a recent study published in *Sleep Medicine* found that the more omega-3–rich fatty fish adults ate, the better their sleep quality.

My advice: Eat fatty fish...and to ensure adequate levels of omega-3s, consider taking a fish oil supplement (one to two 1,000-mg capsules daily).*

•Avoid "blue light" at night. Exposure to blue light—the kind emitted by smartphones, computers, tablets and LED TVs—disrupts sleep patterns by blocking the release of the sleep hormone melatonin. Even if you do fall asleep fairly easily, blue light exposure may come back to haunt you in the form of a middle-of-the-night wake-up.

If you can't force yourself to power down your electronics within two hours of bedtime, try positioning handheld devices farther away from your eyes than usual.

In addition, consider various apps that filter blue light on your smartphone or tablet. Some operating systems are automatically programmed with this feature—Apple's iOS 9.3 offers Night Shift, for example. Using your device's geolocation and clock, the colors of your display are automatically shifted to the warmer end of the spectrum (which is less disruptive to sleep) around sundown. Free apps for Android devices include Night Shift: Blue Light Filter and Twilight.

•Use special lightbulbs. If you wake up in the middle of the night and make a trip to the bathroom, the glare of the bathroom light tells your brain "It's morning!"

What helps: Use low-blue lightbulbs in your bathroom and bedroom that don't block the release of melatonin. A variety are available from Lighting Science (LSGC.com). Or look online for night-lights designed to emit low levels of blue light.

IF YOU DO WAKE UP

Even if you follow the steps described above, you may still have occasional nighttime awakenings with trouble falling back asleep (meaning you are awake for at least 25 minutes).

Experiment with the following strategies to see what works best for you...

•Resist the urge to check e-mail or do anything else on your phone. Even short exposures to blue light are enough to suppress melatonin. Mentally stimulating activities, such as loud TV, are also best avoided. (However, a TV at low volume with the setting adjusted to dim the screen can be a great distractor for an active mind at night.)

My advice: Choose a relaxing activity like reading, listening to soothing music or knitting. If you read, use a book light or a bedside-table lamp that has one of the special bulbs mentioned earlier.

•Don't look at the clock. If you do, you'll start doing the mental math of how many hours you have left until you need to wake up. This will cause anxiety that will spike your levels of cortisol and adrenaline, sleep-disrupting hormones that make you feel wide awake!

My advice: Turn your clock around, and try counting backward from 300 by threes to distract yourself and promote drowsiness.

Also helpful: Try the "4-7-8 method"—inhale for four seconds...hold your breath for seven...and exhale slowly for eight. Breathe in this manner for up to 15 to 20 minutes or until you fall asleep. Inhaling and holding in air increases oxygen in the body, which means your body doesn't have to expend as much energy. The slow exhale helps you unwind and mimics the slow breathing that takes place during sleep, which will help you fall asleep.

•Turn on some pink noise. The well-known "white noise"—used to mask conversations and potentially startling sounds—is comprised of all frequencies detectable by the human ear. Pink noise, on the other hand, has a lower, softer frequency. Pink noise is generally considered more relaxing and has a steady sound like gentle rain.

Sleep experts believe that our brains respond better to the lower spectrum of pink noise than to the fuller spectrum of white noise. The result is a more peaceful and sleep-conducive feeling.

My advice: Search for a free app that contains pink noise, and listen to it with earphones on

*Consult your doctor if you take medication.

your smartphone, laptop or tablet if you wake up in the middle of the night. Just be sure to glance only briefly at the screen when turning on the device, and turn off the screen light while listening. You can set the pink noise to play for a set amount of time, such as 30 minutes. As an alternative, you can purchase a pink-noise generator online.

Can't Sleep?

Michael Perlis, PhD, director, University of Pennsylvania Behavioral Sleep Medicine Program, Philadelphia.

Get up! In a recent study of more than 400 adults, researchers found that those who try to make up for lost sleep by napping and/or staying in bed longer in the morning reinforce poor sleeping patterns, which can lead to chronic insomnia.

Better: If you intend to wake up at 7:30 am, for example, but find yourself wide awake at 5 am and unable to fall back to sleep, get up and start the day.

It Gets Better

Study of 1,546 people ages 21 to 99 led by researchers at University of California, San Diego, published in *The Journal of Clinical Psychiatry.*

Happiness increases with age. Even though aging is tied to declines in physical health and cognition, older people report more satisfaction, happiness and well-being than younger ones, on average...and less anxiety, stress and depression.

Treatment Less Effective for Executives

Siegfried Kasper, MD, professor and chair of the department of psychiatry and psychotherapy at Medical University of Vienna, Austria.

Treatment for depression is less effective for people with high-status jobs than for people in lower-status positions, reports Siegfried Kasper, MD.

Recent finding: 55.9% of people with the highest-level jobs did not respond to the standard treatment of medication plus psychotherapy...compared with 40.2% of midlevel workers and 44.3% of low-level employees.

Possible reason: People with high-level jobs—and the resulting stress and responsibilities—may find it more difficult to accept or cope with illness.

Fun Way to Stop Cravings

Study of 31 people by researchers at Plymouth University, Devon, UK, and Queensland University of Technology, Brisbane, Australia, published in *Addictive Behaviors.*

Playing Tetris may reduce cravings for food, cigarettes, alcohol, coffee, sleep and sex by up to 21%.

Reason: Playing Tetris affects the parts of the brain involved with visual imagery, keeping the imagination on a single track and distracting it from cravings.

Do You Have a Short Fuse? How to Stop Feeling So Angry...

Bernard Golden, PhD, a psychologist and founder of Anger Management Education, a clinical practice in Chicago. In addition to treating anger issues, he specializes in anxiety, depression and motivation. He is author of *Overcoming Destructive Anger.* AngerManagement Education.com

Here are a few questions worth asking yourself...

Do you often snap at people and later regret it...or continue to stew after a disagreement has passed?

Do friends or loved ones ever call you a hothead?

Does the intensity of your anger sometimes escalate from 0 to 10 in a matter of seconds?

If any of these situations ring true, then you may be experiencing destructive anger.

And it's hurting you!

HEALTHY OR HARMFUL?

Like all emotions, anger can express itself in good or bad ways. Healthy anger motivates us to make important changes in our lives...challenges us to overcome unfairness and social injusticesand is a signal to look inward to identify our core desires, needs and values.

Destructive anger is another story. Whether you quietly simmer with rage or erupt at even slight provocations, destructive anger has been shown to increase one's risk for health problems such as high blood pressure, heart attack, stroke, digestive ailments and depression.

The unfortunate truth: Far too many people assume that they can simply turn off their anger like a spigot. But it doesn't work that way.

THE TOOL THAT WORKS

If you want to reduce your anger, the first step is to realize that out-of-proportion or out-of-control anger stems from a chain of internal experiences and is almost always not just a reaction to whatever has set you off.

For example, you might experience intense anger when someone cuts in front of you in the checkout line, but this triggering event may evoke past anger as well.

To better understand your anger, it helps to complete an anger log, identifying the interplay of your thoughts, feelings and body sensations that occurred before and during your episodes of anger. By doing this, you'll start to see patterns and can interrupt the cycle.

Ideally, you will complete a log entry every time you get angry—but you should wait at least an hour or two so you're calm enough to recognize all of the important elements.

Key aspects to write down...

- **Motivating forces.** People experience anger when they're feeling threatened or when a need—for safety, for respect or to feel important, for example—isn't being met.

Let's say that you shouted an obscenity while arguing with your spouse. Maybe he/she had scolded you for something you did—but did it really warrant that level of verbal retaliation? You might realize that the motivation behind the anger was your (unmet) need for love and connection and respect.

- **Expectations.** We get angry when things run counter to our expectations. In the example above, one expectation might be, "We're a couple, so we should care about each other's feelings." But your conflict is putting that basic expectation into doubt.

- **Triggering event.** Sometimes it's obvious what makes you angry—the car that cuts in front of you...a negative job review...or a curt reply from a store clerk. But sometimes it's less clear—for example, the triggering event could be something that you anticipate will happen. You might, for example, become angry because you anticipate not getting a job for which you interviewed.

- **Body reactions.** Anger evolves in the body. Identifying a pounding heart, sweating palms and other such reactions will help you become more alert to anger in its initial stage.

GIVE IT TIME

You may be surprised by the range of feelings that accompany a "simple" episode of anger.

Example: A client sought my help because of conflicts with her teenage daughter. When she first completed her anger log, she wrote that the motivating factor was "to be respected." Her main expectation was that "she should listen to me."

But the more my client thought about it, the more she realized that the real motivating factor was her desire for closeness and a meaningful relationship with her daughter. She also had the expectation that "our closeness will never change."

Emotional discoveries don't happen all at once. Keeping a log will help you understand the trajectory of your anger—and become much more skillful at altering its course. You'll know you're making progress when there's a decrease in the intensity, duration and/or frequency of anger episodes.

For additional help: Consult The National Anger Management Association, NAMAss.org, for a referral to a therapist.

How to Cure Twitching Eyelids

Twitching eyelids usually are caused by stress or fatigue. Getting rest should stop the twitch. Sometimes twitching results from eyestrain after spending a long time looking at a computer or smartphone screen, so look away at least every 20 minutes.

And: A warm compress can help soothe the area.

Shilpi Agarwal, MD, family physician, Washington, DC, quoted in *Better Homes and Gardens*.

How Compassion Relieves Chronic Pain

Emma Seppälä, PhD, science director, Center for Compassion and Altruism Research and Education, Stanford University School of Medicine, California, and author of *The Happiness Track: How to Apply the Science of Happiness to Accelerate Your Success.*

If you suffer from chronic pain, and perhaps the angry emotions that may result, there's a drug-free treatment that takes only 15 minutes a day and can bring real relief.

It's called compassion meditation. It's not like "regular" meditation. Rather than simply calming your mind, you actively direct your thoughts—toward kindness and altruism. Don't believe this could relieve your pain? Rigorous scientific studies have found that it can—and it may even help you live longer.

THE SCIENCE OF KINDNESS

At the Center for Compassion and Altruism Research and Education at Stanford University School of Medicine, we study the health effects of compassion and altruistic behavior. *Recent research at our center and other institutions has found that compassion meditation helps...*

• **Chronic pain—and anger.** Among people with chronic pain, a nine-week compassion meditation program at Stanford University led to significantly reduced pain severity and greater pain acceptance by the end of the program.

One benefit was that it reduced levels of anger, based on self-evaluations of the patients. Anger has been shown to be an important predictor of chronic pain symptoms, and cultivating compassion has been shown to positively influence how we process emotions, reducing the tendency toward negativity, including anger.

• **Post-traumatic stress disorder (PTSD) symptoms.** In a study at the Veterans Administration's Puget Sound Health Care System in Seattle, researchers found that when veterans with PTSD practiced loving-kindness meditation (a form of compassion meditation) for 12 weeks, they experienced a reduction in PTSD symptoms and depression. The benefits were still evident three months later.

• **Migraines.** A study from the University of Massachusetts Medical School in Worcester found that migraine sufferers who learned loving-kindness meditation in a single session experienced a 33% decrease in pain and a 43% reduction in emotional tension.

• **Longevity.** While there's certainly no conclusive evidence that learning to be compassionate to yourself and to others will help you live longer, there are intriguing clues that it might.

The connection: Telomeres, which are "caps" on the tips of each strand of DNA on your chromosomes.

A study from Massachusetts General Hospital and Harvard Medical School found that people experienced in practicing loving-kindness meditation had longer telomeres, which are associated with greater longevity.

HOW TO PRACTICE COMPASSION MEDITATION

Compassion meditation aims to strengthen feelings of compassion and empathy toward yourself and other people—to generate feelings of kindness toward yourself and others. It's different from the well-known "mindfulness" meditation, which is mostly focused on calming the mind and increasing awareness. In compassion meditation, rather than letting your thoughts come and go without judgment, you focus your attention in specific ways as you silently repeat benevolent phrases or visualize kind wishes.

The goal is to express your intention to move from judgment or dislike to caring, compassion, acceptance and understanding. Compassion meditation involves bringing to mind people you know and love, feeling their love and spreading caring feelings toward strangers or even people you find challenging.

It isn't hard to do.

What to do: Sit quietly, close your eyes, breathe gently and silently repeat a phrase designed to evoke a feeling of goodwill toward yourself, such as *May I be happy, healthy and strong.* Then, extend the good wishes to someone you feel thankful for, then to someone you're indifferent toward, then to someone you find challenging and finally to the world at large.

Practicing loving-kindness or compassion meditation is a way to stretch the "muscles" of kindness, caring and empathy toward everyone and to remember our common humanity. The key is to give your "compassion muscles" a workout by practicing regularly, just as you might any other skill. Doing so will help you cultivate more loving relationships, greater happiness and better health...and could noticeably reduce your chronic pain.

Ready to do it now? You can use my YouTube video, "A Gift of Loving Kindness Meditation," which runs for less than 15 minutes. Close your eyes and follow the prompts. Once you know it by heart, you can do it in your own time and voice.

Grief May Cause Irregular Heartbeat

Study by Danish researchers of 88,612 people newly diagnosed with AF between 1995 and 2014...and 886,120 people without the diagnosis, published in *Open Heart.*

Atrial fibrillation (AFib), which can lead to stroke or other cardiovascular problems, was 41% more common among people mourning the death of a partner than among other people. The effect was even stronger in people younger than age 60—they were more than twice as likely to have AFib after a partner's death. The risk was greatest eight to 14 days after a death and then gradually subsided.

ICU Patients at High Risk for Depression

Dale M. Needham, MD, PhD, professor of medicine at Johns Hopkins University School of Medicine, Baltimore.

One-third of intensive care patients become depressed. That is three to four times the prevalence of depression in the general population. Patients with pre-ICU psychological symptoms and ones who had psychological distress while in the ICU are at greatest risk. Families and caregivers should be alert if patients talk about the ICU being stressful, have flashbacks or delusional memories, act angry or nervous, or exhibit emotional detachment.

Shocking Treatment to Eliminate Bad Habits

The New York Times.

The wristband Pavlok (Pavlok.com, $199) encourages you to break bad habits by delivering a noticeable, but safe, electric shock of varying intensity, loud beeps, vibrations and other means. The device pairs with your phone. You can have the device give you a jolt if you oversleep, or tap the screen to shock yourself if you eat a donut. Online user feedback for Pavlok has been enthusiastic, although there is no scientific evidence supporting the long-term success of this device.

Happy Wife, Happy Life

Study of 1,981 heterosexual couples led by researchers at Michigan State University, East Lansing, published in *Health Psychology.*

A happy spouse is good for your health. People with unhappy partners have more physical problems, engage in less exercise and rate their health worse than people with happy partners.

Possible reason: Happy spouses are more likely to offer social support and to encourage exercise and eating right.

Hold That Pose: Yoga May Ease Tough Depression

Alan Manevitz, MD, clinical psychiatrist, Lenox Hill Hospital, New York City.
Victor Fornari, MD, psychiatrist, Zucker Hillside Hospital, Glen Oaks, New York.
Chris Streeter, associate professor, psychiatry, Boston University Medical Center.
Boston University Medical Center, news release.

The calming poses and meditation of yoga may be just what the doctor ordered when it comes to beating depression, recent research suggests.

Researchers found that weekly sessions of yoga and deep breathing exercises helped ease symptoms of the common condition. They believe the practice may be an alternative or complementary therapy for tough-to-treat cases of depression.

Major depression can be persistent and disabling. Up to 40% of people taking medication for this form of depression will not experience relief, according to the researchers.

The yoga intervention seemed helpful for "people who are not on antidepressants and in those who have been on a stable dose of antidepressants [but] have not achieved a resolution of their symptoms," said study lead author Chris Streeter, MD, in a news release from Boston University Medical Center. Dr. Streeter is a psychiatrist at the hospital and an associate professor of psychiatry and neurology at Boston University.

Prior studies have shown that the ancient practice of yoga may help those with depression.

"The mechanism of action is similar to other exercise techniques that activate the release of 'feel good' brain chemicals," explained Alan Manevitz, MD, a clinical psychiatrist at Lenox Hill Hospital in New York City, who reviewed the new findings.

He added that exercise, especially yoga, may also "reduce immune system chemicals that can worsen depression."

Then there's yoga's meditative quality, as well, Dr. Manevitz said.

"It has been demonstrated that 'mindful' movement—conscious awareness—has a much more beneficial impact on the central nervous system," he said.

STUDY DETAILS

But would this bear out in a rigorous study? To find out, Dr. Streeter's team tracked outcomes for 30 people with major depressive disorder. All were randomly assigned to partake in either a "high-dose" or "low-dose" yoga intervention. The high-dose group had three 90-minute yoga classes each week along with home practice, while the low-dose group engaged in two 90-minute yoga sessions each week in addition to home practice.

The participants practiced Ilyengar yoga, a method that focuses on detail, precision and alignment in posture and breath control.

The study found that both groups had significant reductions in their depression symptoms. Those who took three weekly yoga classes had fewer depressive symptoms than those in the "low-dose" group, but Dr. Streeter's team said even two classes a week was still very effective in improving people's mood.

Dr. Streeter noted that this intervention targets a different neurochemical pathway in the body than mood-altering medications, suggesting that yoga may provide a new, side-effect-free avenue for treatment.

EXPERTS COMMENT

Dr. Manevitz called the study "practical and well-designed." He believes the findings support yoga as a treatment "that can help the millions of people suffering from major depressive disorders around the world."

Victor Fornari, MD, a psychiatrist at Zucker Hillside Hospital in Glen Oaks, New York, agreed that the recent study "supports the use of yoga for the treatment of depression...Yoga, like regular exercise, is good for most people for health maintenance as well as to treat what ails them."

The study was published in the *Journal of Alternative and Complementary Medicine.*

info The National Center for Complementary and Integrative Health has more on yoga at https://nccih.nih.gov/health/yoga/introduction.htm.

This Is No Joke!

Robert Rivest, a Springfield, Massachusetts–based "laughter yoga" teacher, with Rebecca Shannonhouse, editor, *Bottom Line/Health.*

It's been widely reported that meditation provides a veritable treasure trove of health benefits—it can lower blood pressure...improve sleep...and reduce stress, anxiety and depression, along with inflammation.

Now: Researchers are learning that such benefits may also occur with "therapeutic laughter." A study presented at a recent Experimental Biology conference found that people who watched funny videos exhibited the same gamma brain waves that occur during meditation. Gamma waves are associated with feelings of contentment...clearer thinking...and improved focus.

But what if you don't feel like laughing? Go ahead and fake it.

"If you make yourself start laughing, it almost always turns into a real laugh," says Robert Rivest, a Springfield, Massachusetts–based "laughter yoga" teacher who has taught this laughter/stretching/deep-breathing group activity overseas and in many parts of the US. Once you start laughing, you'll likely find that it's hard to stop.

Here's a game to play: The next time you're relaxing with a friend, let loose with "Ha!" When your friend reciprocates, double it: "Ha, ha!" By the time you reach the third "Ha!" chances are you'll both be laughing for real.

Use Your Mind to Treat Your Skin

Skin conditions can be helped by meditation and cognitive behavioral therapy. Stress, anxiety and depression can cause and exacerbate acne, rosacea, psoriasis, itching, eczema, hives and other skin conditions, so treating the mental health issues can help relieve the dermatological issues.

To find help: Go to the website of the Association for Psychocutaneous Medicine of North America (Psychodermatology.us), which includes physicians and psychologists.

American Psychological Association.

Jobs with the Highest Suicide Rates

Data analysis by researchers at Centers for Disease Control and Prevention, Atlanta, published in *Morbidity and Mortality Weekly Report.*

Farmers, fishermen and foresters had a suicide rate of 85 per 100,000 people in 2012 (latest data available). That compares with an overall rate of 16 suicides per 100,000 people in the US. All three high-risk professions involve job isolation, a stressful work environment, less access to mental-health services and, usually, lower income and education. Other higher-than-typical suicide rates were found among construction workers, 53 suicides per 100,000...and in people doing installation, maintenance and repair jobs, 48 suicides per 100,000.

CHAPTER 9

Family Matters

When Your Loved One Is Depressed... and Won't Get Help

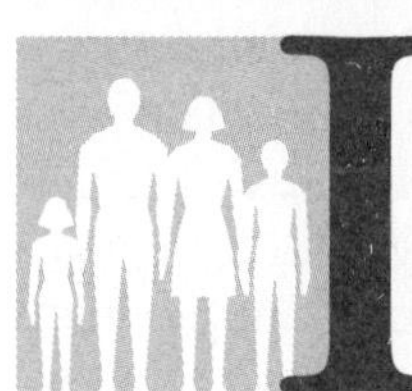

It's gratifying (if a little tiring) to care for a loved one who's recovering from surgery or suffering from a physical illness like the flu. Whether you cook up a pot of chicken soup or help out around the house, your efforts are bound to be appreciated.

But that's rarely the case when a loved one is depressed. Your efforts to help are more likely to be met with silence or withdrawal.

Most people who are depressed don't like to talk about it—assuming they even realize that they are depressed. And it's easy to get frustrated when they won't take the smallest steps to help themselves, especially if they've also stopped pulling their weight with household and family obligations. So what's your best course of action?

YOU CAN HELP

Depression—as well as other mood disorders (such as bipolar disorder)—can literally change the way the mind works. That's why the sufferer may find it nearly impossible to even imagine feeling better. So the nudge to get help often has to come from outside.

It's crucial to do your part because about 80% of those with depression will improve substantially when treated with therapy and/or medication. *What you can do...*

***STEP 1:* Talk about any changes that you've observed.** You're likely aware of many classic signs of depression such as a loss of interest in things that used to be enjoyable... changes in appearance or hygiene...sleeping more or less (or in fragments)...eating more or less than usual...and feelings of hopelessness

Susan J. Noonan, MD, MPH, a physician who has personally suffered from depression and currently counsels patients at McLean Hospital in Belmont, Massachusetts, about depression and recovery. She is also a volunteer consultant at Massachusetts General Hospital in Boston and author of *When Someone You Know Has Depression.* SusanNoonanMD.com

and/or withdrawal from friends and family. But signs of depression can also be less obvious to you (or the person who's suffering).

Examples: Having more bad days at work...and/or drinking more than usual.

If you observe any such changes, you might say something like, "I've noticed that things are different with you lately. You seem to be sleeping a lot more and have not been getting cleaned up in the morning. Do you think it might be depression?"

Your comments might be well received, but don't count on it. Even people who know they are depressed don't like to admit it. Denial is part of the process. You don't have to push the issue right away...but do bring it up again (every four days or so) if the person doesn't start to show more interest in his/her physical and mental well-being.

The gender difference: Women are more likely to see signs of depression in themselves. A man's depression might be marked by less recognizable red flags such as anger, irritability and/or the use of drugs or alcohol. He'll probably be less likely than a woman to seek professional help, so don't hesitate to reach out if you notice behavior or personality changes. Let him know that you're concerned.

STEP 2: **Encourage treatment...but don't push.** The first time you suggest to a loved one that he might want to see a mental health professional, you're likely to get a response such as "I'm fine"...or "Just leave me alone."

At first, just raise the possibility of treatment and give your full—and nonjudgmental—support. You may even offer to help find someone to talk to. When a person is depressed, just picking up the phone to call a doctor or other health-care professional can feel overwhelming. Your loved one's efforts to get help should include a visit to his primary care physician, who can rule out any medical conditions and make a referral to a therapist, if necessary.

Important: People who begin treatment for depression need a lot of encouragement. Treatment can be effective, but it typically takes at least a few months to notice improvement with therapy and/or medication.

STEP 3: **Keep the conversation going.** Most people with depression know (or eventually learn) that they're "off" but need to feel safe before opening up about it.

To encourage the free expression of feelings, I recommend what's known as active listening. When your loved one does open up, remind yourself to be fully present...let him speak without interruption ...and ask "open" questions (such as, "How do you feel about that?") to keep the person talking.

Another good technique is reflection. When talking with your loved one, you identify the emotions that you're hearing the person express. If someone says, "Life is no good," you can "reflect" the emotions by saying something like, "I hear that life feels no good to you right now and everything seems hopeless." With this approach, you acknowledge the person's feelings and show that you're listening closely.

Caution: It's tempting to give assurances by saying something like, "Everything will be fine." To someone who's depressed, this type of response can feel like a brush-off.

STEP 4: **Challenge your loved one's thinking.** Depression causes people to view the world through a negative—and distorted—lens. They may truly believe that "I have no friends." When you hear something like this, offer a more realistic (and fact-based) substitute.

You could say: "What do you mean you have no friends? Didn't you tell me you're getting along with people in your book group?" The idea isn't to argue but to point out the inaccuracy of what's being said.

Also helpful: Encourage your loved one to write two columns on a piece of paper. One column will say "Evidence For"...the other will say "Evidence Against." Seeing evidence that refutes reflexively negative thoughts in writing can help people shift their thinking.

STEP 5: **Recognize that action precedes motivation.** If you don't have depression, you probably do things when you want to do them. But someone who's depressed never feels motivated and might need to commit to an activity—joining a social group, going out to dinner, etc.—despite a lack of enthusiasm.

Example: If a loved one is too depressed to take the long walks you know he used to enjoy, you might say something like, "It's a nice day and I'm going for a short walk. Would you like to come with me?"

Once outside, your loved one may realize how good it feels to get some exercise. Your goal is not to apply pressure...but to encourage an activity until the person feels motivated to do it again.

info For more on supporting a loved one with depression, contact the National Alliance on Mental Illness (NAMI.org). If you're concerned that your loved one could be suicidal, call the National Suicide Prevention Lifeline at 800-273-8255.

What Really Helps a Person Heal

Charles B. Inlander, a consumer advocate and health-care consultant based in Fogelsville, Pennsylvania, was the founding president of the nonprofit People's Medical Society, a consumer advocacy organization credited with key improvements in the quality of US health care. He is author or coauthor of more than 20 consumer-health books.

For a couple of months, I had noticed a few symptoms, such as occasional double vision. At an opera performance, I joked to my wife that some of the duets appeared as quartets. I also started noticing that I had some balance problems. It turns out I had a tumor on the cerebellum portion of my brain. Just a day and a half after it was discovered, I had five hours of brain surgery during which my neurosurgeon was able to remove the entire tumor. The good news is that it was benign.

I am writing this column just five weeks after my surgery. My recovery has been going well. I have a physical therapy regimen that is helping me regain my full balance. The lengthy incisions in my skull are healing nicely. My stamina is returning, although I still am pretty tired by the end of the day. I have no pain.

My doctors are pleased and surprised at how well I am doing (for a 69-year-old man). But I am not at all surprised. I know that the speed of my recovery is due, in large part, to the outpouring of love and support that I have received from family and friends. For many of us, knowing what to do or say to someone who is going through a serious medical issue or lengthy recovery can be difficult. *In the course of my medical saga, here's what I discovered helps a recovering person most—simple steps that anyone can do for a loved one or friend...*

- **Be there.** You might assume that a recovering person wants peace and quiet. Not necessarily! Having people whom you love and trust around you is both helpful and reassuring. In my case, my wife was (and continues to be) incredibly strong. Having her at my side kept me calm. My daughter and son-in-law traveled hundreds of miles to be with me before, during and after my surgery. And one of my former college roommates traveled more than 200 miles to be there when I came out of surgery!

My advice: If at all possible, be available to help a friend or loved one when a serious diagnosis is made. It's very scary to get such news, but having loved ones and friends there for you is more powerful and calming than you may realize. Their presence is also invaluable when it comes to getting questions answered and making a postsurgical or treatment plan. If you're making an in-person visit (contact every couple of weeks is good), just check in to make sure that the patient feels up to it.

- **Stay in touch.** Recovering from major surgery or a serious illness can be very lonely and frustrating. You don't feel well. You have up and down days. Hearing from friends is more healing than just about anything a doctor prescribes.

My advice: Even if you can't physically be with your friend or family member, don't be afraid to be in regular contact with him/her. It's enough to send a short e-mail or card saying that you care. A phone call a few weeks after surgery (when most people assume the hard part is over) can serve as a great pick-me-up. Knowing that people care gives you a reason to work hard to recover.

- **Be positive.** When you make contact, it's OK to say you're sorry that the person is going through a medical ordeal, but quickly shift to a positive, upbeat tone. Don't talk about your own illnesses. Let the person know that you are looking forward to seeing him for lunch, or some other outing, in the near future.

My advice: Have a funny story or wonderful reminiscence to share. Laughter is a great healer—and believe me, it can make the recovering person's day!

Should You Correct Someone Who Has Dementia?

Joanne Koenig Coste, Alzheimer's family therapist in private practice in Framingham, Massachusetts, and author of *Learning to Speak Alzheimer's.*

This question is one of the most frequently asked in caregiver support groups across the country. The dilemma for family members and caregivers in this situation is whether to remind a loved one of his or her present life, correct him or her or try reasoning. None of these options will change the scenario and may cause frustration for you, the caregiver, and agitation for your loved one with dementia.

The ability to reason has most likely diminished or is nonexistent as a result of the dementia. You can not reason with someone who has lost the ability to reason! Short-term memory is slowly being lost, and memories linger of younger days, including times spent with ex-partners or friends and family who have since passed on. Again, reasoning will not help to orient the individual with dementia. When he/she is focused on events far in the past or something imagined, try to redirect him/her...a favorite snack may work well or a change of scenery.

Better Mealtimes for Dementia Patients

Lee Hooper, PhD, senior lecturer in research synthesis & nutrition, University of East Anglia, Norwich, UK.

Family-style meals with caregivers and others can help prevent dehydration and weight loss in dementia patients, a recent study of more than 2,200 people with the disease has found. Patients ate and drank more and were less likely to become agitated when they weren't alone.

Other ways to manage mealtime: Spend more time at the table, play soothing music and talk with the person who has dementia.

Shhh...They'll Never Know They're Eating Vegetables

Missy Chase Lapine, *New York Times* best-selling author, who has written a series of healthy cookbooks, including *The Sneaky Chef.* Her latest, *Sneaky Blends*, features more than 100 all-new healthy recipes. TheSneaky Chef.com

We may try to get the recommended number of servings of fruits and vegetables each day, but most of us fall short. According to the Centers for Disease Control and Prevention, 91% of Americans do not eat enough veggies and 87% aren't getting enough fruit. An easy way to rectify this—and cut calories and fat at the same time—is to add my "sneaky" vegetable and fruit blends to your food (see how to make the blends below). Don't worry—your food still will be delicious, maybe even more so!

These blends can replace one-third to one-half the calories and fat in recipes, so you can lose weight (or stay trim) and continue to eat foods you love. Also, the blends are high in fiber, which helps you feel satisfied longer. A study by Pennsylvania State University researchers found that adults who were given meals made with vegetable purées ate 350 fewer calories a day and reported feeling as full as those who ate the same meals without the vegetables.

Here are recipes for two delicious American favorites made much healthier with my sneaky blends...

Single-Serve Mac and Cheese

This dish may seem decadent, but it has only 302 calories per serving and it is rich in fiber, with six grams per serving.

¾ cup cooked whole-grain rotini pasta
⅓ cup Carrot–Sweet Potato Blend (see recipe below)
1 egg white
⅛ teaspoon mustard powder
½ ounce goat cheese, crumbled
(if you don't like goat cheese, you can double up on the Cheddar and Parmesan)
1 Tablespoon low-fat milk
1 heaping Tablespoon grated sharp Cheddar cheese
½ cup chopped cauliflower florets
Pinch of sea salt and freshly ground black pepper
1 Tablespoon freshly grated Parmesan cheese

Preheat the oven to 400°F. In a large bowl, mix together all of the ingredients except the Parmesan. Pour into an ovenproof bowl, sprinkle the Parmesan over the top, and bake for 20 minutes or until the top is browned and bubbly. Makes one serving.

Not Your Grandma's (Turkey) Meat Loaf

Instead of the refined, nutrient-devoid white bread crumbs in your grandmother's meat loaf, this recipe uses oats and flaxseed, which deliver a hearty dose of fiber, antioxidants and omega-3s. The Black Bean–Blueberry–Baby Kale Blend gives the meat loaf moisture, adds another hit of nutrition and allows you to use half as much meat as needed for most recipes. There are 227 calories and four grams of fiber in a one-and-a-half-inch-thick slice.

½ cup Black Bean–Blueberry–Baby Kale Blend (see recipe below)
¼ teaspoon sea salt
Freshly ground black pepper
¼ teaspoon onion powder
1 large egg
1 teaspoon Worcestershire sauce
2 Tablespoons ground flaxseed
½ cup oats, finely ground
1 Tablespoon tomato paste
½ teaspoon dried oregano
1 pound lean ground turkey breast
Nonstick cooking spray
3 Tablespoons ketchup (optional)

Preheat the oven to 350°F. In a large bowl, combine the first 10 ingredients and mix well with the back of a fork. Mix in the turkey. Transfer to a standard-sized loaf pan that's been misted with cooking spray, and top with the ketchup, if using. Bake for 35 to 45 minutes or until the meat reaches an internal temperature of 160°F. Makes six servings.

THE SNEAKY CHEF VEGETABLE AND FRUIT BLENDS

These blends keep for three days in the refrigerator and three months in the freezer. I like to freeze them in half-cup quantities so that I thaw only what I need.

Carrot–Sweet Potato Blend

This blend has a creamy texture and deliciously sweet flavor. Carrots are high in beta-carotene and other carotenoids—antioxidants that promote eye health and are protective against many cancers. Sweet potatoes also are loaded with beta-carotene, plus fiber, B vitamins and potassium. Unlike white potatoes, which cause a sugar spike and subsequent crash that increases hunger, sweet potatoes stabilize blood sugar levels. Orange vegetables also are protective against heart disease.

In addition to the Mac and Cheese (see above), here are a variety of ways you can use this blend to boost nutrition and replace calories and fat in foods you eat every day...

- **Stir into soups or any red sauces,** such as marinara, to add creaminess (without the cream).
- **Use to replace half the fat and sugar in baked goods** such as muffins and in breakfast favorites such as pancakes and waffles.
- **Mix into salad dressings,** brown gravies and condiments, such as ketchup and mustard.
- **Mix into nut butters and store-bought hummus.**
- **Use in prepared baked beans.**

For this recipe, don't drive yourself crazy dicing the veggies—a rough chop is fine. Just try to make them about the same size so that they cook evenly. Or use frozen diced sweet potatoes, available in many markets. Pick up some frozen carrots, too. Then you can skip the steaming and simply flash-thaw them by pouring hot water over both veggies, and go directly to the blending step. You will need about four cups of frozen chopped sweet potatoes and three cups of frozen chopped carrots.

2 large sweet potatoes or yams, peeled and roughly chopped
6 large carrots, peeled and roughly chopped
Filtered water

Place a steamer basket into a large pot, pour in a few inches of tap water (make sure that the water is below the bottom of the basket) and set it over high heat. Add the sweet potatoes and carrots and steam, covered, for 15 to 20 minutes, until fork-tender. In a blender or food processor, blend the veggies with two to three tablespoons of filtered water until smooth, adding more water as necessary. Makes about four-and-a-half cups.

Black Bean–Blueberry–Baby Kale Blend

This blend combines three nutrition powerhouses. High in fiber and protein, black beans are particularly satisfying and have been shown to reduce the risk for diabetes, heart disease and colon cancer. Blueberries are one of the fruits highest in antioxidants. Kale is high in fiber, calcium, iron, vitamin C and many other antioxidants. It has heart-protective and anticancer properties.

In addition to using this blend in the Turkey Meat Loaf recipe (see above), use it to...

•**Replace half the fat and sugar in chocolaty baked goods,** such as brownies and chocolate cake.

•**Mix into meat dishes,** such as tacos and burgers.

•**Add to a smoothie or a breakfast shake.**

If you prefer dried beans, feel free to sub them in (they will need to be soaked overnight and cooked). And if you don't love kale, swap in fresh baby spinach or your favorite dark leafy green.

4 cups baby kale
2 cups frozen blueberries, ideally wild (I prefer frozen because the berries tend to be cheaper and are available year-round Wild blueberries contain more antioxidants.)
215-ounce cans (BPA-free) black beans, drained and rinsed
Filtered water

Place the kale into a high-powered blender or food processor, and pulse a few times. Rinse the blueberries in cold water to thaw them. Add the berries and the beans to the blender, along with one to two tablespoons of filtered water, and purée until smooth. Makes four cups.

Best Way to Make Up After an Argument

Hal Shorey, PhD, associate professor of clinical psychology, Widener University, Chester, Pennsylvania, quoted in *The Wall Street Journal.*

Address the underlying issue instead of apologizing quickly and trying to move on.

Reason: If you both don't come to a resolution about what started the argument, you will end up getting upset over the same thing later.

Early Antibiotic Use May Raise Allergy Risk

Analysis of studies published between 1966 and 2015 by researchers at Utrecht University, the Netherlands, presented at a recent meeting of the European Respiratory Society.

Babies treated with antibiotics before age two had a 15% to 41% higher risk for eczema and a 14% to 56% increased risk for hay fever later in life. Risk was higher when babies got two courses of antibiotics in early life than when they received one. The study does not prove cause and effect—but it is possible that antibiotics disrupt microorganisms in the gut, leading to reduced immune response.

Don't Swaddle Sleeping Babies

Analysis of data from four studies that included 760 SIDS cases and 1,759 controls by researchers at University of Bristol, UK, published in *Pediatrics.*

Risk for sudden infant death syndrome is about one-third higher in babies who are swaddled than in babies who are not—especially if swaddled infants sleep on their stomachs or sides rather than their backs.

Anesthesia May Affect Children's Brains

Study of 106 children by researchers at University of Cincinnati College of Medicine, published in *Pediatrics.*

Children under age four who received general anesthesia during surgery later scored three to six points lower on listening comprehension tests than similar children of the same age who were never exposed to anesthesia.

Three Questions to Ask Babysitters to Protect Your Children from Abuse

These questions will help you "profile" a sitter's mental state. *What bothered you about the last family you worked for?* A long list, given with a know-it-all and/or angry attitude, is a red flag. *Did you ever make suggestions to the parents?* Listen for negative comments, such as a statement that no one ever listened. *How would you solve a problem such as the kids fighting?* Beware of answers focusing on confrontation or excessive discipline.

Dale Yeager, forensic profiler and criminal behavior analyst and CEO of the security-consulting firm Seraph. DaleYeagerDotCom.Wordpress.com

Stroller and Carriage Accidents Are Common

Study by Center for Injury Research and Policy, Nationwide Children's Hospital, Columbus, Ohio.

Stroller and baby-carriage accidents send about two children a day to hospital emergency rooms. Most occur when kids fall from a stroller or carrier or when it tips over.

Self-defense: Always buckle children into strollers or carriers...keep stroller handles clear of bags...be sure a product is appropriate for the child's age and size...check often for product recalls.

Whole Milk May Be Better for Young Children Than Low-Fat Milk

Study of 2,745 children led by researchers at University of Toronto, published in *American Journal of Clinical Nutrition.*

Healthy children, ages one to six, who drank a cup of whole milk daily had a vitamin D level comparable with that of children who drank nearly three cups of 1% milk. And the whole-milk drinkers had lower body mass.

Possible reason: Vitamin D is better absorbed with fat—and full-fat milk may make a child feel fuller and less inclined to seek out calorie-dense foods that can cause weight gain.

"Uncombable" Hair? Maybe Genes Are to Blame

University of Bonn, news release.

It's not common, but some children have ultra-frizzy hair that can't be combed normally. Now researchers say they've found genes linked to what's known as "uncombable hair syndrome."

"From the [genetic] mutations found, a huge amount can be learned about the mechanisms involved in forming healthy hair, and why disorders sometimes occur," said study coauthor Regina Betz. She is a professor with the Institute for Human Genetics at the University of Bonn in Germany.

"At the same time, we can now secure the clinical diagnosis of 'uncombable hair' with molecular genetic methods," she said in a university news release.

Uncombable hair syndrome is relatively rare. There have only been about 100 documented cases over the past several decades, the researchers said. Some families are especially affected.

"However, we assume that there are many more people affected," Dr. Betz said. "Those who suffer from uncombable hair do not necessarily seek help for this from a doctor or hospital."

Kids with the syndrome have dry, frizzy and often fair hair that can't be combed flat. The family link suggests the syndrome is inherited and connected to genes. So, the researchers found nine children with uncombable hair syndrome and analyzed their genetic makeup. The scientists found mutations in three genes that seem to be linked to the condition.

Is a cure needed? Perhaps not.

According to Dr. Betz, uncombable hair can be a stressful nuisance. "However, those affected have no need to otherwise worry," she said. And, the condition tends to ease as children grow into adulthood.

The study was published in the *American Journal of Human Genetics.*

info For more about hair disorders, visit the University of Maryland Medical Center website at http://www.umm.edu/health/medical/altmed/condition/hair-disorders.

Poison Alerts

***Acetaminophen* is the most common cause of infant poisoning.** The pain reliever found in Tylenol is the medicine most often involved in overdoses in babies less than six months old. Other common poisonings involved gastrointestinal medicines, cough-and-cold products, antibiotics and *ibuprofen.* Nearly half the medication errors—47%—involved incorrect dosage...43% involved giving a medicine too frequently or mistakenly giving the wrong medication.

Review of more than 270,000 calls to poison control centers, led by researchers at Banner-University Medical Center, Phoenix, published in *Pediatrics*.

Essential oils can poison children. Tea-tree oil and other essential oils are derived from plants and used in homeopathic and aromatic products. Reports of poisoning by these oils doubled between 2011 and 2015. Four-fifths of the poisonings involved children—usually ones who tried to swallow the oil but choked on it, so a small amount got into their lungs and caused pneumonia. Less than one-half teaspoon is enough to cause lung damage. Children also have been poisoned by application of too much oil to their skin.

Self-defense: Always store essential oils in a locked cabinet out of children's reach.

Study by specialists at Vanderbilt University Medical Center's Tennessee Poison Center, Nashville.

Moon Myth Debunked

Frontiers in Pediatrics.

Many people swear that they sleep less soundly during full moons. True? Just barely. A 28-month study found that children slept, on average, five minutes less during full moons—not enough to be statistically significant.

Brain Differences Hint at Why Autism Is More Common in Males

Matthew Lorber, MD, acting director, child and adolescent psychiatry, Lenox Hill Hospital, New York City.
Mathew Pletcher, PhD, vice president and head, genomic discovery, Autism Speaks.
JAMA Psychiatry, online

Structural differences in the male brain might explain why autism is more common in men than women, a recent study suggests.

Women were three times more likely to have autism spectrum disorder if their brain anatomy resembled more closely what is typically seen in male brains, the European researchers reported.

"Specifically, these females had much thicker than normal cortical areas, a trait generally seen in male brains," said Matthew Lorber, MD, acting director of child and adolescent psychiatry at Lenox Hill Hospital in New York City, who was not involved in the study.

This could mean there's something about the way the male brain is structured that makes men more apt to develop autism, although the study did not prove that these anatomical differences cause the disorder.

Autism is two to five times more common in men than women, according to background notes in the study. Previous studies have suggested that the biology of men might put them at higher risk for the disorder than women.

STUDY DETAILS

To test that theory, a team led by Christine Ecker, of Goethe University in Frankfurt, Germany, conducted brain scans of 98 right-handed adults with autism. The researchers also scanned the brains of 98 neurologically healthy people for comparison purposes.

The scans focused on the thickness of the cerebral cortex, the gray outer layer of neural tissue in the brain. This thickness typically varies between men and women, and may also be altered in people with autism, the researchers explained.

Children's Lies Show Healthy Mental Growth

Like walking and talking, lying is a developmental milestone. Among verbal two-year-olds, 30% lie to their parents at some point...among three-year-olds, the percentage is 50%...in four-year-olds, 80%. Lying requires children to understand what is in someone else's mind and anticipate the consequences of telling the truth. These are signs of healthy cognitive development, and there is evidence that early liars become more successful in school and in dealing with other children. It's also an opportunity to discuss with the child what a lie is, what truth is and what the implications are for other people.

Study of 58 preschoolers from China led by researchers at University of Toronto, Canada, reported in *The Wall Street Journal.*

Men with autism had brain structures that were similar to those of men without the disorder, the researchers found.

But the brains of women with autism appeared to be more structurally similar to men than to other women, the findings showed.

SIGNIFICANCE OF STUDY

Mathew Pletcher, vice president and head of genomic discovery at Autism Speaks, said, "This work suggests that changes in specific features of the brain may be associated with autism in some females."

Dr. Lorber noted that at this point, no one knows why the thickness of the cortex or other masculine brain structural patterns might be related to autism.

Nonetheless, "these findings give more credibility that biology of the brain plays a major role in the development of autism spectrum disorder," Dr. Lorber said. "It also suggests that when trying to diagnose autism spectrum disorder, it might make sense to examine the cortical regions in the brain."

The study "does not provide direct insights into more effectively treating autism," but future treatments could become available as doctors learn more about how brain structure relates to autism, Dr. Lorber said.

DRAWBACKS OF THE STUDY

Dr. Pletcher warned that too few people were evaluated in the study to draw any firm conclusions.

"Understanding the difference in prevalence in males versus females for autism is an important research topic that could provide critical information on the causes and biology of autism," Dr. Pletcher said.

"Unfortunately, the study does not include enough individuals to be confident that this change in brain structure is meaningful," he added.

"Furthermore, it is not clear that any differences observed in the study have a functional impact on the brain or could play a part in the behavioral and social features of autism," Dr. Pletcher continued.

The recent study was published online in the journal *JAMA Psychiatry.*

info For more about autism, visit the U.S. Department of Health and Human Services at HHS.gov.

Hearing Test May Predict Autism Even Before a Child Is Able to Speak

Study of 77 boys led by researchers from University of Rochester, New York, published in *Autism Research.*

The noninvasive test looks for hearing difficulty in the frequency range of 1-2 kilohertz, which is important for processing speech. The more hearing impairment in that frequency, the greater the severity of autism symptoms in children with autism, on average. The experimental test can be done by specially trained physicians and psychologists in very young children, allowing autism treatment to start as early as age two, when it may be more effective. Currently, autism usually is not diagnosed until a child is at least four years old.

Smartphone Dangers for Children and Teens

Smartphone use linked to dry eyes in children. The more time children spent using smartphones, the more likely they were to develop pediatric dry-eye disease—which can affect vision and school performance. Staring at the screen can reduce blinking, leading to faster evaporation of tears...and the short watching distance to smartphone screens can tire the eyes.

Good news: When children gave up their smartphones for a month, dry-eye symptoms improved significantly.

Study of 916 children by researchers at College of Medicine, Chung-Ang University Hospital, Seoul, South Korea, published in *BMC Ophthalmology.*

Night smartphone use may cause temporary vision loss. Teens (and adults) who lie on one side and use mostly one eye to read a smartphone may think that they've experienced temporary vision loss in that eye. Reason: One eye adapts to the light of the phone's screen, and the other adjusts to the darkness of the room. When you get up, it takes a few minutes for your eyes to equalize and you may be unable to see out of the eye used with the phone for a few moments. The temporary phenomenon is harmless but can be frightening.

Gordon Plant, MD, a neuro-ophthalmologist at Moorfields Eye Hospital, London, UK.

Was Football Safer Back in the Day?

Rodolfo Savica, MD, PhD, assistant professor, neurology, Mayo Clinic, Rochester, Minnesota.

Kenneth Podell, PhD, director, Houston Methodist Concussion Center, Houston.

Mayo Clinic Proceedings, online.

In a finding that suggests football used to be a less dangerous sport, a small study shows that men who played in high school in the 1950s and 1960s may not be at increased risk for dementia or memory problems.

Nor did they show increased rates of Parkinson's disease or amyotrophic lateral sclerosis (ALS), commonly known as Lou Gehrig's disease.

The study used a small group of men, the researchers acknowledged. But, they added, the results are in line with an earlier study that examined men who'd played high school football in the 1940s and 1950s.

"What we can say is, for that era, football did not increase the risks of neurodegenerative disease compared with other sports," said senior researcher Rodolfo Savica, MD, a neurologist at the Mayo Clinic in Rochester, Minnesota.

That might sound surprising, given evidence that former professional football players can face increased risks of degenerative brain diseases. Autopsies have confirmed cases of chronic traumatic encephalopathy (CTE) in numerous former National Football League players. CTE is a progressive brain disease thought to result from repeated head trauma.

But Dr. Savica said that pro and college football is "completely different" from the high school level—in intensity, size and speed of the players, and the number of "hits" they take.

What's more, he added, the recent findings don't prove that high school football carries no long-term risks.

TIMES HAVE CHANGED

Dr. Savica stressed that no one should assume the findings apply to men who played high school football in more recent years.

"That was a different era," he said, referring to the time period his team studied.

High school players have gotten bigger and faster, Dr. Savica said, and there may be more "drive to win at all costs" these days compared with decades ago.

And while there have been advances in protective equipment, he added, that might give some players a "false sense of security" that causes them to be more aggressive, he said.

"You can still get a concussion when you're wearing a helmet," Dr. Savica said.

STUDY DETAILS

The findings, published online in *Mayo Clinic Proceedings*, are based on medical records of 296 men who'd played football at one of two Minnesota high schools, and 190 who'd been involved in swimming, basketball and wrestling. All athletes played from 1956 to 1970.

Over time, the researchers found, seven former football players had been diagnosed with dementia or mild cognitive impairment. That compared with five men who'd played other sports—with no difference in the two groups' overall rates.

Similarly, three men in each group had been diagnosed with Parkinson's disease, while no one had an ALS diagnosis.

EXPERT COMMENT

"It's encouraging that they [the study authors] didn't see any increased risks, but the findings should be considered preliminary," said Kenneth Podell, PhD, director of the Houston Methodist Concussion Center, who was not involved in the research.

And some big questions remain, Dr. Podell said.

One is this: Are there certain people at greater risk of lasting damage from sports-related concussions or repeated knocks to the head?

Dr. Podell also pointed to some things that have changed for the better—particularly in the last decade or so.

Four Traits That Put Teenagers at Risk for Addiction

Sensation-seeking, impulsiveness, anxiety sensitivity and hopelessness increase risk of addiction in teenagers. Sensation seekers are drawn to intense experiences such as those produced by drugs. The other traits are linked to mental-health issues. Impulsiveness is common in people with ADHD—a diagnosis that makes addiction three times more likely. Anxiety sensitivity, being overly aware of physical signs of anxiety and frightened by them, is tied to panic disorder. Hopelessness is tied to depression. Early trials of a new antidrug program suggest that personality testing can identify 90% of the highest-risk children.

Patricia Conrad, PhD, professor of psychiatry, University of Montreal, Canada, quoted in *The New York Times*.

Awareness of concussion and its shorter-term dangers has risen, and management of the condition has changed greatly since the era covered in the recent study, Dr. Podell said.

US states, for example, now have "return to play" laws that typically require players to be immediately removed from the game if a concussion is suspected. And guidelines say that athletes should not return to play until they have a doctor's approval.

Back in the era that Dr. Savica's team studied, blows to the head were typically brushed off as "getting your bell rung."

WHAT PARENTS CAN DO NOW

For now, Dr. Savica suggested that parents remember that sports—including football—can benefit kids. But they should also guard against the risks, he added.

That, he said, includes knowing the symptoms of concussion, and being sure that the trainers and coaches on the sidelines know how to respond to a possible concussion.

According to the U.S. Centers for Disease Control and Prevention, some common concussion symptoms include headache, dizziness, nausea, vision problems, fatigue and confusion.

Football Can Damage Vision

Study of 29 college football players by researchers at Temple University, Philadelphia, published in *JAMA Ophthalmology.*

Repeated low-impact blows to the head may result in double or blurry vision. The muscles that control the eyes become unable to align the eyes properly, so they cannot focus on close-up objects. Players may not notice the condition if it is mild, and it can clear up on its own within weeks after football season ends. However, long-term effects in those who play year-round are unknown.

Teen Energy Drink Danger

Jennifer A. Emond, MSc, PhD, Geisel School of Medicine, Dartmouth College, Hanover, New Hampshire, and lead author of a study of 3,342 adolescents and young adults, published in *Journal of Pediatrics.*

Teens who mix alcohol with energy drinks are much more likely to engage in binge drinking and meet clinically defined criteria for alcohol-use disorder than teens who have tried alcohol but never mixed alcohol with an energy drink. Nearly 10% of teens ages 15 to 17 have consumed an energy drink mixed with alcohol at least once.

Quick Treatment for Concussion Can Speed Recovery

Study of 97 athletes conducted by researchers at University of Florida, Gainesville, published in *Journal of Athletic Training.*

Athletes who did not recognize or report their symptoms immediately after being injured and later were diagnosed with concussions had significantly longer recovery times than similar athletes who were evaluated and treated right away. After suffering a blow to the head, seek medical attention immediately.

You Can Train Your Cat

Sarah Ellis, PhD, feline behavior specialist at International Cat Care, an international charity based in England that provides education and training for veterinarians, breeders, cat boarders, rescue workers and cat owners. She is a visiting fellow in the School of Life Sciences at University of Lincoln in England and coauthor of *The Trainable Cat: A Practical Guide to Making Life Happier for You and Your Cat.* ICatCare.org

Most cat owners would say that their cats have minds of their own and that, unlike dogs, cats cannot be trained. Not true! By following these steps, you can train your cat—even a mature cat—and solve these common cat problems. The training may take a few hours, a day or a few weeks depending on how often you practice and your cat's temperament.

CAT-TRAINING ESSENTIALS

• **Rewards.** The key to successful cat training is a reward that your cat really values. A food treat—animal protein, in particular, because cats are carnivores—likely will be the most motivating reward.

Examples: Tiny pieces of cooked meat or fish, a very small portion of the cat's normal diet or store-bought cat treats such as semimoist or air-dried meat snacks. Always give tiny portions so that your cat doesn't gain weight.

For affectionate cats, stroking can be an effective reward in addition to food. Cats prefer brief strokes, and those that concentrate on the top of the head and under the chin typically produce the most positive response.

• **Comfortable blanket.** You can create a link in the cat's mind between a blanket and relaxation. The blanket can then be used in new places or situations (see below) to elicit relaxation and promote successful training.

Choose a blanket, and place it in front of you on the floor. Reward positive behavior that your cat exhibits toward the blanket, such as sniffing the blanket or a quick step onto it. Because these types of behaviors happen so fast, you can use a verbal marker, such as the word "good," at the precise time the behavior happens, then follow up with the food reward or stroking reward shortly afterward. Eventually, withhold the word "good" and the reward for an extra second each time to build up the amount of time your cat spends on the blanket.

Once your cat is comfortable on the blanket, the next step is to teach the cat to relax there. Any signs of relaxation, such as moving from standing to sitting or lying down, should be rewarded. Keep your voice quiet and calm when saying "good," and intersperse food rewards with chin scratches and gentle stroking of the head.

GETTING YOUR CAT INTO THE CARRIER

Cats typically aren't fond of carriers because they don't like feeling trapped. And many times carriers are associated with negative experiences such as harrowing visits to the vet or a boarding facility. But you can change your cat's response to the carrier to a much more positive one, reducing stress for the cat and for you when you need to use the carrier.

• **Choosing a carrier.** When buying a carrier, make sure that the entry door allows your cat to walk in rather than be lifted in and that the door can be completely removed in the initial training. The lid should be removable, too, so that in the initial training stages the carrier appears less enclosed. (A removable lid also may allow a veterinarian to examine your cat while the animal remains "safe" in the base of the carrier.)

• **Do not hide the carrier.** Most pet owners make the mistake of keeping their carriers tucked away in closets when not in use, but that's a mistake. Your carrier should be left out at all times so that your cat is familiar with it.

• **Familiarize your cat with the carrier well before you have to use it.** Start by removing the lid and the door of the carrier so that you have just the base. If your cat seems very wary of the carrier, begin carrier training by rewarding your cat when he stays in the same room as the base of the carrier. You can take the "relaxation blanket" and slowly move it closer and closer to the carrier, rewarding your cat each time he relaxes on the blanket. Eventually, place the blanket in the carrier. This should be enough to get the cat into the carrier.

Once your cat is comfortable in the base of the carrier—he has slept in it or lays down to groom in it—you can gradually slide the door into place. Start by sliding the door in partway, and reward your cat for staying relaxed. Continue to use the marker word "good" to condition your cat to know a food reward is coming—and continue to reward anytime he does not attempt to leave the carrier. Use the same steps when putting the lid back on.

• **Keep the carrier stable.** Cats find being carried in the air unsettling. Always use two hands to keep the carrier steady, and begin to train your cat to be comfortable in a moving carrier by holding the carrier off the floor for only a few seconds. Progress to walking a few steps at a time, and then farther, always continuing to reward your cat.

THE VET APPOINTMENT

A trip to the vet is terrifying for many cats, so removing as many stressors as possible and preparing your cat ahead of time are key.

•**Choose a cat-friendly clinic.** These veterinary practices treat only cats and/or offer cat-only waiting areas. You can find these practices at CatVets.com/cfp.

•**Take a practice visit to the vet.** Ask the clinic staff if you can visit with your cat during a quiet time to promote a positive association. Simply sit in the waiting room for a short time for the first visit. You even can ask the staff if they will feed your cat some treats, though it may be that your cat will accept treats only from you initially. Once the positive association grows, the cat may then feel comfortable taking treats from the staff.

•**Allow your cat to walk out of the carrier.** At a real visit to the vet, when you are in the examination room, open the door and ignore the cat. Give him time to look around the room from inside the carrier and take the first step out. Many vets make the mistake of pulling cats out of carriers, which is stressful for the cats. Tell your vet ahead of time that you'd like to allow your cat to come out on his own and/or ask whether the examination can take place in the carrier with the lid removed.

•**Practice handling at home.** During a basic veterinary examination, the vet will lift a cat's tail, look in his ears, mouth and eyes, and listen to his heart. To make these routines less stressful, practice them at home with rewards.

For example, while stroking your cat's head, subtly lift his lip. Then reward him. Do the same with widening your cat's eye with your forefinger and looking in his ears. To approximate a stethoscope, familiarize your cat with a spoon. Show it to the cat while giving rewards. Then eventually hold the handle of the spoon in your hand, and press the round part on the cat's chest. Incorporate all these types of touches in your daily routine, and the vet visit will be much less stressful. Also, unless your cat is having gastrointestinal issues or requires an anesthetic, bring treats to the vet to reward your cat during exams.

ACCEPTING MEDICATION

Many times, oral medications prescribed for cats are never actually taken because cats spit them out or refuse to have their mouths opened at all.

•**Before medication is needed, practice with pill pockets or pill putty.** These products, found in pet-supply stores, conceal pills and are tasty to cats. Try a few different brands as treats (with no medicine) to see which brand your cat likes best. Then when you need to give a pill, your cat won't suspect anything and will probably gobble the treat along with the pill without hesitation.

•**Placing a pill in the mouth.** If your cat is not fond of any pill pockets or pill putty or uncovers and rejects pills, you will have to train him to take pills from you. Have the cat sit on the relaxation blanket to help the process. Start by training him to be comfortable with your hand placed over the top of his head, rewarding him along the way. Then progress to placing the forefinger and thumb of your other hand gently on your cat's lower jaw. Give plentiful rewards during this process—and if the cat flinches at all, take time to let him relax again before continuing. The goal is to get the cat to lower his bottom jaw when the jaw is touched. You will need to use a little pressure to open the mouth, but the key is to make sure that the cat is comfortable with this and doesn't find it distressing. As soon as your cat's jaw opens, provide a reward. Once your cat is accustomed to your assisting in opening his mouth—and this can take a number of training sessions!—and you have to give a pill, make the cat open his mouth and then, holding the pill between your thumb and index finger, place it as far back in the cat's mouth as possible.

How to Share a Bed with Your Pet

Pat Miller, a certified dog trainer and owner of Peaceable Paws, LLC, a dog and puppy training center in Fairplay, Maryland. She has more than 35 years of experience in dog training and recently was named one of the 45 people who have changed the dog world by *Dog Fancy* magazine. Miller is author of *The Power of Positive Dog Training*. PeaceablePaws.com

Many of your friends and neighbors are sleeping with someone other than their spouse. According to a recent survey by the American Pet Products Association, the majority of pet cats and nearly half of all pet dogs sleep in their owners' beds.

"Co-sleeping" with pets usually causes few problems. But when pet owners are light sleepers...pets are restless at night...and/or pets act aggressively toward their bed partners, it can lead to a loss of sleep or other issues. Some pet owners who are chronically tired might not even realize that unsettled sleep as a result of having their pets in bed is what's causing their fatigue.

To make these sleep arrangements work well...

•**Give your pet plenty of exercise in the evenings.** A tired pet is less likely to be restless at night. This advice applies to cats as well as dogs—you can teach a cat to play fetch or use treats or toys to encourage him/her to run, jump or climb.

Caution: Do not give cats access to cat toys or treats containing catnip in the evening. Catnip can make it more difficult for cats to settle down.

•**Let your pet have a toy in bed.** Some pets find it comforting to have a favorite toy in bed with them just as some young children find it easier to sleep with a favorite stuffed animal. This should be a soft toy that does not contain any bells or squeakers. The pet-toy-in-bed strategy does not work with all dogs and cats, however—remove the toy from the bedroom if nighttime access to it makes the pet more playful and active.

•**Teach your pet to stay on one particular part of the bed.** Some dogs and many cats disrupt their human bedmates' sleep by getting too close to their faces and/or positioning themselves between human partners. To train a dog or cat to stay on a specific part of the bed, such as near the foot of the bed, lie on the bed at times other than bedtime and invite the pet to join you. When the pet ventures onto the part of the bed where you would like him to sleep, click a clicker, available in pet stores (or say a positive word such as "yes"), and immediately give the pet a treat.

Alternative: If after a few weeks of this training, the pet still is not staying on his part of the bed, cut out a square of cloth large enough for the pet to curl up on. Place this piece of cloth on top of the bed's blankets in the spot where you want the pet to sleep. Use the clicker/treat training technique described above to train the pet to associate positioning himself on this cloth with praise and food.

•**Ignore your pets when they try to get your attention in bed.** Pets who sleep on beds sometimes wake their owners on purpose because they are bored, lonely or hungry. If your pet does this, do not speak to the pet, make eye contact with him or even pick up the animal to move him away—doing any of these things gives the animal the attention he craves, increasing the odds that this problematic behavior will be reinforced and continue.

Instead, ignore the pet when he wakes you intentionally. In fact, pay the pet as little attention as possible whenever you are in bed, at least after the bedroom lights are turned off.

Helpful: If your pet climbs on top of you while you are lying in bed, use the "earthquake technique" to dislodge him rather than picking him up or pushing him—roll from side to side until the animal figures out that this is not a comfortable place to relax.

If your pet gets right in your face while you lie in bed, turn so your face is right at the edge of the bed facing outward so the pet cannot position himself directly in front of you. You also can hide your head under the covers if you prefer.

Ignore a pet's nighttime attention-seeking behavior consistently for a few weeks, and there's a very good chance that he will stop bothering you.

• **Temporarily remove your pet from the bed if he acts aggressively toward an approaching bedmate.** Pets sometimes growl or exhibit other signs of aggression when certain family members (or other pets) approach the bed. A pet might accept the presence of one spouse in the bed but growl at the other, for example.

To overcome this, do not allow the pet into the bed until after this person (or pet) already is in bed. In my experience, dogs and cats that show this sort of aggression generally do so only toward people who are approaching the bed. If these people are already in the bed, the pets usually accept their presence.

Meanwhile, use the clicker/treat training technique described above to teach your pet to get off the bed when told "off." That way, if the pet does get on the bed before this person approaches, your pet can be instructed to temporarily vacate.

Warning: It is much more difficult, though not impossible, to modify the behavior of a pet that acts aggressively toward a person or pet who already is in the bed. The best solution with these pets often is to require them to sleep somewhere other than the bed.

• **Get the pet a baby bassinet if all else fails.** If you want your pet to be close to you at night but letting him sleep in your bed proves too disruptive, purchase a baby bassinet that's about the height of your bed and large enough for the animal, position this next to your bed, then use the clicker/treat training technique to encourage the pet to sleep in the bassinet.

Dog Diarrhea Cure

American Kennel Club. AKC.org

If your dog has diarrhea, try withholding food for 12 to 24 hours and giving the dog small amounts of water frequently. After this time, try feeding the dog white rice or rice water—made by boiling rice in water and straining out the grains...plain canned pumpkin...yogurt, if your dog tolerates milk products. See your veterinarian if diarrhea continues for a week or more...there is any visible blood or a dark tarry color...your dog is very young or elderly...seems feverish or lethargic...or has no appetite.

Xylitol Deadly to Dogs

Carmela Stamper, DVM, FDA Center for Veterinary Medicine, Silver Spring, Maryland, quoted at WebMD.com.

Sugar substitute xylitol can be deadly to dogs. The no-calorie sweetener is widely used in sugar-free candies, chocolate bars, cough syrups, mouthwashes, chewable vitamins, even nut butters such as peanut butter—which some people use to give their dogs medicine. Symptoms include vomiting, lethargy and walking as if unstable or drunk. Read product labels carefully, and contact your veterinarian immediately if your dog shows any symptoms that could indicate xylitol poisoning.

How to Stop a Dog Fight

PetMD.com

Many dog fights are over within seconds. If dogs separate on their own, approach yours calmly, attach your leash and leave the area. If the fight continues, throw water in the dogs' faces—use a hose if possible. If necessary, find something to put between the dogs, such as a board, large branch, blanket or an umbrella that you open quickly to startle them. Check your dog for injuries after the fight.

Caution: To avoid getting injured, never reach for your dog's collar or head while it is fighting.

CHAPTER 10

Heart Health and Stroke Risk

How to Survive a Heart Attack

Every year, about 750,000 Americans have a heart attack. Even though advances in emergency care and cardiology have greatly improved one's odds of survival, roughly one of every six of these individuals dies.

What determines whether a heart attack sufferer lives or dies? Certainly, the person's age and overall health play an important role. But there's another factor that gets far less attention than it should.

Lifesaving strategy: When a person on the scene knows how to recognize that someone is having a heart attack and then respond to the emergency appropriately, it can have a profound effect on whether the victim lives or dies.

Sobering research: When a heart attack occurs, the average sufferer waits two hours or more before calling 911 and going to the hospital. This delay often occurs because victims can't believe that they are really having a heart attack...or they don't want to feel embarrassed at the hospital if it turns out that it's not a heart attack and they've "wasted" everyone's time.

But each minute of delay during a heart attack destroys more heart muscle, putting the victim at greater risk for disability and death.

RECOGNIZE AND RESPOND

My advice for quickly and accurately identifying heart attack symptoms...*

• **Chest discomfort.** Chest pain is widely believed to be the classic heart attack symptom, but severe chest discomfort usually is a more accurate way to describe it. Pain typically is sharp, but the sensation that usually occurs with a heart attack is not sharp but rather a

*There are some exceptions to the heart attack symptoms described in this article. If you have any question, play it safe and call 911.

Gregory S. Thomas, MD, MPH, medical director for the MemorialCare Heart & Vascular Institute at Long Beach Memorial Medical Center in California and clinical professor at the University of California, Irvine.

severe pressure, squeezing or tightness—as if a massive weight had been placed on the chest.

Also: Many women report having no chest discomfort during any part of the heart attack.

How to respond: If a person is having severe chest discomfort, don't assume that it can't be a heart attack because he/she isn't complaining of chest pain. Call 911 immediately. It is important to tell the dispatcher that you believe the person is having a heart attack because saying this increases the likelihood that an ambulance specializing in heart care will be sent.

• **Referred pain.** The nerves that supply the heart also serve many other areas of the body between the jaw and the navel—places that can produce referred pain during a heart attack.

Case history: A woman who had tooth pain while exercising was referred to me. Her exercise stress test showed that her tooth pain was referred pain. In actuality, the pain was due to angina, a sign that her arteries were significantly blocked, putting her at high risk for a heart attack. Other areas of referred pain during heart attack can include one or both arms or shoulders...the upper back or abdomen...the neck and lower part of the face, including the jaw.

• **Other common symptoms.** A heart attack can produce many other symptoms, including sudden shortness of breath...nausea and vomiting...a cold sweat, or feeling cold and clammy... fatigue...and/or light-headedness.

Important: All of these symptoms (except for feeling cold and clammy) tend to be more common in women than in men.

How to respond: If a man has chest discomfort and at least one other symptom...or if a woman has chest, back or jaw pain and at least one other symptom, it's very likely the individual is having a heart attack. Or if a person's discomfort or pain is particularly severe—even without another symptom—a heart attack is also likely. In either instance, call 911.

Another red flag: Sometimes, a victim has a feeling of "impending doom" and asks a loved one or friend to take him to the hospital. If someone says to you, "I think I should go to the hospital," call 911. Never drive a victim to the hospital—lifesaving treatments start when the paramedics show up. The only exception is if you are within a few minutes of emergency care.

KNOW WHO'S AT GREATEST RISK

Knowing one's risk for a heart attack also helps prevent delays in treatment.

While some heart attack victims don't have any of the risk factors described below, people generally are at increased risk due to smoking, age (generally, over age 50 for men and over age 60 for women) and being at least moderately overweight. Diabetes or a chronic inflammatory disease, such as rheumatoid arthritis or lupus, can cause heart disease 10 or 20 years earlier than the norm, increasing risk for heart attack.

Important: Diabetes damages nerves, so a diabetic having a heart attack is less likely to have nerve-generated chest discomfort or referred pain—and more likely to have sudden shortness of breath.

MORE LIFESAVING ACTIONS

In addition to calling 911, do the following to aid a heart attack victim...

• **Position the person correctly.** Contrary to popular opinion, the best position for a conscious heart attack victim is not lying down—this fills the heart with a bit more blood, straining it. The best position is sitting up, which puts the least amount of stress on the heart. An exception is if the person is light-headed, which might indicate low blood pressure. In that case, lay the person down and call 911 immediately.

• **Give aspirin.** Give the person uncoated aspirin—either four 81-mg baby aspirin or one full-strength aspirin (325 mg). The pills should be chewed—this releases clot-busting medicine within 15 minutes into the bloodstream versus up to 30 minutes or more when aspirin is swallowed whole. If someone is already taking a daily blood thinner, aspirin may not be needed. If the person has been prescribed *nitroglycerin,* it should be taken as directed.

• **Reassure.** A heart attack is frightening—and fear floods the body with adrenaline, speeding up and further stressing the heart. Reassure the person that help is on the way and that he will get through this.

If the victim is unconscious: If the individual doesn't appear to be breathing and you cannot feel a pulse or are unable to check for one, start CPR if you know how to do it. If you don't, simply press down on the victim's chest at least two inches deep (where the ribs meet at the base of the breastbone) and pump as fast as you can (100 times per minute). Like CPR, this technique pushes air into the lungs—the best action you can take until paramedics arrive.

A Heart Test We All Need

Rebecca Shannonhouse, editor, *Bottom Line/Health.*

Doctors routinely check for cardiovascular risk factors during annual checkups—things like high blood pressure, elevated cholesterol and diabetes. But unless you have known or suspected heart disease, it's unlikely that you've ever had a cardiorespiratory fitness (CRF) test.

In fact, CRF is the only major heart disease risk factor that isn't evaluated during routine visits. But that may be changing.

What's new: The American Heart Association recently released a report that strongly advises doctors to include a fitness assessment as part of regular exams. Because CRF is potentially a stronger predictor of future heart health than other risk factors, you need to know where you stand.

If you haven't gotten much exercise lately, you have the most to gain. Research has shown that for every one-point increase in aerobic fitness (as measured in METs, a unit used in fitness tests), there's a 10% to 25% improvement in survival.

Your doctor might recommend a cardiopulmonary exercise test, during which you'll be wired to the gills while riding an exercise bike or using a treadmill. It's the best test for CRF, but it can be expensive if your insurance doesn't cover it.

Do-it-yourself option: A one-mile walk test. You map out a course of one mile...walk as fast as you can...check your heart rate when you're done...then enter your heart rate, age, weight and how long it took you to complete the walk into an online calculator, such as ExRx.net/Calculators/Rockport.html. It will give a rating such as "good" or "fair," which you can discuss with your doctor.

To Detect Risk for Heart Attack and Stroke, Get Tested for TMAO

Stanley Hazen, MD, PhD, chair of the department of cellular and molecular medicine at Lerner Research Institute, Cleveland Clinic, and leader of a study published in *European Heart Journal.*

TMAO (*trimethylamine N-oxide*) is produced during the digestion of red meat, eggs and full-fat dairy products. In a recent study of patients who went to the emergency department with chest pain, those with high TMAO levels were six times as likely to have a heart attack or stroke or need surgery to repair a blocked artery within the next month as those with low TMAO levels. A TMAO test costs only about $50 and may be covered by insurance. Patients with high TMAO levels may need more tightly controlled LDL ("bad") cholesterol, closer attention to blood pressure and careful attention to a personalized diet and exercise regimen.

Gallstones and Your Heart

Lu Qi, MD, PhD, professor and director, Tulane University Obesity Research Center, New Orleans.

People who have had gallstones are 23% more likely to develop heart disease than those who have never suffered from gallstones, according to an analysis of more than one million adults over a 30-year period.

Possible explanation: Obesity, high cholesterol and diabetes are common in both conditions.

What to do: Eating a healthful diet that includes fiber-rich foods, such as fruit, vegetables and legumes, may lower risk for gallstones—and heart disease.

Marijuana May Cause Heart Attack and Stroke

Aditi Kalla, MD, a cardiology fellow at Einstein Medical Center in Philadelphia and leader of an analysis of 20 million health records at more than 1,000 US hospitals in 2009 and 2010.

According to recent research, hospital patients ages 18 to 55 who had used marijuana had a 26% increased stroke risk and 10% higher heart failure risk than ones who did not use it. The study did not say how much marijuana patients used or for how long they had been using it. But the analysis—adjusted for common cardiovascular risk factors such as hypertension, diabetes and smoking—found that marijuana appears to be an independent risk factor for cardiac problems.

Loss Can Be Heartbreaking

Simon Graff, MD, researcher, department of public health, Aarhus University, Denmark.

Losing an intimate partner raises risk for atrial fibrillation (AFib)—an irregular heartbeat linked to stroke and heart attack—especially for people under age 60.

Details: In a recent study of nearly one million adults, the newly bereaved were 41% more likely to develop AFib in the first 30 days after a partner's death. Risk was even higher when the death was unexpected.

Why: Severe stress may trigger inflammation and disrupt heart rhythm.

More Cautions on Calcium

Erin D. Michos, MD, MHS, associate director of preventive cardiology, Johns Hopkins Ciccarone Center for the Prevention of Heart Disease, Baltimore.

Recent finding: Calcium supplements raised risk for heart damage and plaque buildup in the coronary arteries by 22% in a 10-year study of more than 2,700 men and women. But those who got their calcium from milk, yogurt, dark leafy greens and other foods were least likely to develop plaque buildup.

Possible reason: The large amount of calcium in a supplement may be stored in soft vascular tissue, not bone.

If you take calcium supplements: Talk to your doctor about the safest dosage. Most people need no more than a 500-mg daily supplement to fill any gap that may exist in their diets.

Is "Healthy Obese" a Myth?

European Congress on Obesity, news release.

The so-called "healthy obese" don't get off scot-free. They still have a higher risk of heart disease than normal-weight people, a recent British study finds.

Folks dubbed healthy obese (see page 27 for more information) don't have metabolic problems typically associated with obesity—such as high cholesterol, poor blood sugar control, diabetes or high blood pressure. But, it's been unclear if they are at increased risk for problems such as heart failure or stroke.

In this study, researchers analyzed 1995-2015 electronic health records of 3.5 million people aged 18 and older in the United Kingdom who were initially free of heart disease.

Compared with normal-weight people with no metabolic problems, healthy obese people had a 50% higher risk of heart disease, a 7% higher risk of stroke, twice the risk of heart failure, and a greater risk of peripheral artery disease (or PAD, which is the narrowing of blood vessels to the arms and legs), the study found.

The researchers also found that the risk of heart disease in obese people rose with the number of metabolic problems. For example, compared with a normal-weight person with no metabolic abnormalities, an obese person with three metabolic abnormalities had almost three times the risk of coronary heart disease and nearly four times the risk for heart failure. Odds of PAD more than doubled, and risk of stroke was 58% higher.

"Metabolically healthy obese individuals are at higher risk of coronary heart disease, cerebrovascular disease and heart failure than normal-weight metabolically healthy individuals," said study author, Rishi Caleyachetty, PhD.

"The priority of health professionals should be to promote and facilitate weight loss among obese persons, regardless of the presence or absence of metabolic abnormalities," said Dr. Caleyachetty, an epidemiologist at the University of Birmingham's College of Medical and Dental Sciences.

The study was presented at the European Congress on Obesity, in Porto, Portugal.

"At the population level, so-called metabolically healthy obesity is not a harmless condition and perhaps it is better not to use this term to describe an obese person, regardless of how many metabolic complications they have," Dr. Caleyachetty said in a meeting news release.

If You're Having a Heart Attack, Don't Drive to the Hospital

Harvard Health Letter. Health. Harvard.edu

If you have heart attack symptoms, don't use a car to get to the hospital. Call 911 for an ambulance because it will have equipment that can restart your heart if it stops—cardiac arrest is rare but is fatal without prompt treatment. And many dispatchers receiving 911 calls about heart attack symptoms send paramedics who are trained to give patients electrocardiograms (ECGs). The ECG results are then sent to the emergency department of the hospital to help speed treatment on arrival.

Dr. Kahn's 7-Step Heart-Health Regimen

Joel K. Kahn, MD, a clinical professor of medicine at Wayne State University School of Medicine in Detroit and founder of the Kahn Center for Cardiac Longevity in Bloomfield Hills, Michigan. He is also an associate professor at Oakland University William Beaumont School of Medicine in Rochester, Michigan, and author of *The Whole Heart Solution*. DrJoelKahn.com

When it comes to keeping your heart healthy, most cardiologists make general recommendations—get regular exercise, eat a balanced diet and don't smoke. But wouldn't it be nice to know exactly what a doctor who specializes in heart disease does to keep his/her own heart healthy?

To find out, we asked Joel K. Kahn, MD, a leading cardiologist, what he does to ensure that his heart stays strong. *Here are his personal heart-health secrets, which he recommends—whether you want to prevent heart disease or already have it...*

SECRET #1: **Drink room-temperature water.** You may not expect an MD who was trained in mainstream Western medicine to practice principles of the ancient Indian wellness philosophy of Ayurveda. But many of these lifestyle habits do carry important health benefits.

For example, according to Ayurvedic medicine, room-temperature water spiked with lemon or lime is good for digestive and cardiovascular health. Because the esophagus is located close to the heart, swigging ice water can cause changes in the heart's normal rhythm in some people.

What I do: If I don't have time to prepare a glass of lemon water, I always drink a big glass of room-temperature water before I get out of bed.

Here's why: We all get dehydrated during the night. Drinking water pumps up the liquid volume of blood, which reduces the risk for blood clots.

I also drink a lot of liquids throughout the day. How much do you need? Divide your weight in half. That's the number of ounces you should drink. A person who weighs, say, 150 pounds, should drink at least 75 ounces (about nine cups) of fluids, including water, every day.

SECRET #2: **Make time for prayer and reflection.** There's a strong link between stress and cardiovascular disease. One landmark study found that heart patients who experienced high levels of stress—along with depression, which is often fueled by stress—were nearly 50% more likely to have a heart attack or die than those with more emotional balance.

What I do: I like meditation and prayer—my routine includes counting my blessings before I get out of bed in the morning and saying a few prayers. I also appreciate the simple miracles of sunrises, hugs and special friends and family.

Other stress reducers: Listening to music and taking long walks.

SECRET #3: **Do fast workouts.** Exercise is crucial to keeping your heart strong, but it's sometimes hard to fit this into a busy schedule. I exercise before breakfast (see below) and eat within 30 minutes after finishing my workout.

What I do: My usual morning workout (six days a week) includes 20 minutes of cardio—on a treadmill, recumbent bike or rowing machine—followed by about 10 minutes of weight lifting.

When I don't have time for a half-hour session, I may do just 12 minutes of high-intensity interval training (HIIT). This typically includes a two-minute warm-up of fast walking on the treadmill, followed by eight minutes of intervals—running all-out for 30 seconds, followed by 30 seconds of walking. I follow this with a two-minute cooldown of slow walking.

HIIT increases cardiorespiratory fitness, builds muscle and reduces inflammation and insulin resistance (which promotes diabetes).

Important: HIIT is strenuous, so check with your doctor before trying it.

SECRET #4: **Have a healthy breakfast.** Millions of Americans skip this important meal. That's a problem because skipping meals has been linked to obesity, high blood pressure, insulin resistance and elevated cholesterol.

Specifically, men who skipped breakfast were found to be 27% more likely to develop coronary heart disease than those who ate a healthy breakfast, according to a study in the journal *Circulation.*

What I do: To save time, I get my breakfast ready the night before. I fill a glass container with oatmeal and almond milk and let it soak in the refrigerator overnight. In the morning, all of the liquid is absorbed, and it's soft and ready to eat. I stir it well and top with a few tablespoons of chopped dried figs, unsweetened coconut flakes or sliced berries.

For variety: I have a "super smoothie" with antioxidant-rich ingredients, such as kale, spinach, frozen blueberries, flax, etc., and organic soy or almond milk.

SECRET #5: **Use heart-healthy supplements.** Dietary supplements aren't the best way to treat cardiovascular disease (although they can help in some cases). Supplements are better for preventing heart problems.

Note: Check with your doctor before taking any of those listed here—they can interact with some medications. *What I take (follow dosage instructions on the label)...*

- **Magnesium glycinate,** which is easily absorbed. People who get enough magnesium (millions of Americans are deficient) are less likely to have a heart attack or stroke than those who don't get adequate amounts of the mineral.
- **Vitamin D.** The evidence isn't yet definitive but suggests that vitamin D may improve heart health.
- **Coenzyme Q10 (CoQ10).** It is a vitamin-like substance that lowers blood pressure and can improve symptoms of heart failure.

SECRET #6: **Eat a plant-based diet.** It's been linked to a reduced risk for diabetes and certain types of cancer as well as heart disease.

What I do: I've been a vegetarian for nearly 40 years. I eat foods with a variety of colors, such as berries and peppers. For me, a huge salad can be a meal! I also enjoy a handful of raw nuts every day.

SECRET #7: **Get enough sleep.** People who sleep at least seven hours a night are 43% less likely to have a fatal heart attack than those who get by on six hours or less.

What I do: I usually get up at 6 am, so I make sure that I'm in bed by 11 pm. I also plan a good night's sleep. For example, I stop drinking caffeinated beverages at least 10 hours before bedtime (this means that I have nothing with caffeine after 1 pm)...and usually stop eating three hours before bed—active digestion makes it harder to fall asleep and increases nighttime awakenings.

Another trick: I have a sleep-promoting bulb in the reading lamp on my nightstand. Typical lightbulbs emit high levels of short-wavelength blue light, which suppresses the brain's production of the sleep-inducing hormone melatonin. You can buy bulbs (such as the Good Night LED or the GE Align PM) that emit small amounts of blue light.

Sex Link to Heart Health Differs for Men and Women

Hui Liu, PhD, associate professor of sociology, Michigan State University, East Lansing.

In a study of more than 2,200 people age 57 and older, men who had sex at least once a week had almost twice the cardiovascular risk of men who were sexually inactive. Women who reported the most satisfying sex had lower risk for high blood pressure and other cardiovascular conditions than other women.

Why: Women may benefit from hormones produced during orgasm, while men might subject themselves to undue stress through exertion or medication for erectile dysfunction.

Takeaway: Sexually active older men should be sure to monitor their cardiovascular health.

Set an Alarm to Stand Up

Bottom Line Personal.

If you're going to be sitting for hours—which is bad for your heart—set an alarm on your phone, watch or computer to chime hourly. When you hear the alarm, get up and walk around for five minutes. According to an Indiana University study, walking just five minutes for every hour you sit is enough to help your heart.

Avoid Strenuous Exercise When You're Upset

Study led by researchers at Population Health Research Institute, McMaster University, Hamilton, Ontario, published in *Circulation*.

People who are angry or upset and work out to help themselves handle the emotions triple their risk of having a heart attack within an hour. Both exercise and emotional stress put a strain on the heart, and the combination creates an even greater strain.

Self-defense: If you find that it helps to work out when you are stressed or upset, be careful not to go beyond your normal routine—the intensity of exercise at times of emotional upset raises cardiovascular risk.

Drink Tea for Your Heart

Moderate tea drinkers (those who drank at least one cup of black or green tea every day) had less calcium buildup in their coronary arteries and a lower rate of cardiovascular events, such as heart attack, than those who drank less tea or the same amount of other beverages, such as coffee, according to a new study of 6,500 adults.

Possible reason: Antioxidants in tea may inhibit the formation of coronary artery calcium, a marker for potential heart disease.

Paul Elliott Miller, MD, instructor of medicine, The Johns Hopkins Hospital, Baltimore.

Diabetes Drug May Help the Heart

Study of 9,340 adults with type 2 diabetes and at high risk for heart disease by researchers at University of North Carolina, Chapel Hill, published in *The New England Journal of Medicine.*

The injectable blood sugar–lowering drug *liraglutide* (Victoza) can reduce heart attack and stroke risk in people with type 2 diabetes. Heart disease is the leading cause of death in people with type 2 diabetes. People who took Victoza, one of a newer class of diabetes drugs known as GLP-1 agonists, had 13% lower risk for heart attack and stroke than those who took a placebo...22% lower risk for death from heart disease...and 15% lower risk for death from any cause.

High Doses of Fish Oil Benefit Heart Attack Patients

Raymond Kwong, MD, MPH, director, cardiac magnetic resonance imaging, Brigham and Women's Hospital, Boston.

Adults who took high doses (4 g per day) of fish oil supplements for six months after a heart attack had better heart function and less scarring of heart muscle than those who didn't take fish oil, according to a new study of 360 heart attack survivors.

Possible reason: Omega-3 fatty acids in fish oil reduce inflammation that harms the heart.

Important: Check with your doctor before taking fish oil—it can interact with blood thinners and certain other medications.

Better Heart Attack Survival

Harlan M. Krumholz, MD, professor of medicine, Yale School of Medicine, New Haven, Connecticut.

Heart attack patients treated at hospitals with better 30-day survival rates live up to one year longer than those treated at poorer performing hospitals, according to a recent study of nearly 120,000 patients.

Possible reason: Many factors are involved in making a hospital high performing, including closer adherence to treatment guidelines and better communication between doctors. Information on hospital mortality and treatment rates can be found at Medicare.gov/hospitalcompare.

Have Your Green Veggies and Coumadin, Too

Timothy S. Harlan, MD, associate professor of medicine at the Tulane University School of Medicine in New Orleans. He is author of *The Dr. Gourmet Diet for Coumadin Users* and *Vegetable Recipes for Coumadin Users.* Dr. Harlan is also executive director of the Goldring Center for Culinary Medicine, the world's first fully operational, full-time teaching kitchen at a medical school. DrGourmet.com

Could a spinach salad ever be considered dangerous? That may sound impossible. But if you're one of the millions of Americans who takes the popular blood thinner *warfarin* (Coumadin, Jantoven, Marevan, etc.) to help prevent stroke, heart attack or pulmonary embolism, chances are your doctor has told you to limit your intake of spinach and other vitamin K–rich foods.

It's true that vitamin K promotes blood clotting, and consuming too many foods that contain abundant amounts of this nutrient could weaken warfarin's effect.

Taken to the extreme, however, this dietary advice often causes warfarin users to become fearful of eating any of the highly nutritious foods that contain vitamin K.

What many people don't realize is that following this guideline too strictly creates almost as much of a problem as getting too much of this crucial nutrient, which has been shown to promote heart and bone health.

The solution: There is a simple way that you can have your warfarin—and your green veggies, too! *Here's how...*

THE STAY-SAFE FORMULA

If you watch TV, you've no doubt seen plenty of ads for the newer generation of blood thinners, such as *apixaban* (Eliquis), *rivaroxaban* (Xarelto) and *dabigatran* (Pradaxa). These medications work similarly to warfarin by blocking production of blood-clotting proteins in the body, but they use a different mechanism that doesn't require vitamin K vigilance.

Even though these newer blood-thinning drugs are being prescribed more and more, warfarin is still the most widely used medication for stroke and heart attack patients.

But the use of warfarin requires a delicate balancing act that weighs the risk for excessive bleeding against the risk for unwanted clotting. To keep tabs on how long it takes a patient's blood to clot, frequent blood testing is used (initially on a daily basis, then gradually decreased until a target level has been reached) to determine the patient's INR, which stands for "international normalized ratio." For most patients, the target for this standardized measurement ranges from about 2.0 to 3.0.

Other risks: In addition to the dietary considerations, warfarin interacts with a number of medications (such as certain antibiotics, other heart medications, cholesterol drugs and antidepressants) as well as supplements (including St. John's wort and ginkgo biloba).

Dr. Harlan's stay-safe formula: There is no definitive research pointing to optimal levels of vitamin K for warfarin users, but I find that most patients thrive on a plan in which their daily intake of this vitamin is about 75 micrograms (mcg) per day—a level that is lower than the recommended daily allowance for adults (90 mcg per day for women...and 120 mcg per day for men). That intake of vitamin K seems to strike the balance between offering an adequate amount of healthful foods rich in the vitamin while allowing warfarin to do its job.

A NEW WAY TO EAT VITAMIN K

It's amazing to see how much the vitamin K content varies depending on the food. Some foods are absolute vitamin K powerhouses—one cup of raw parsley, for example, has a whopping 984 mcg...one cup of cooked spinach contains 888 mcg...and one cup of raw kale, 547 mcg.

Note: Cooking a vegetable will decrease its volume, but won't change the vitamin K content.

To avoid slipping into a vitamin K danger zone, I advise warfarin users to regularly incorporate vegetables with low-to-moderate amounts of vitamin K into their diet (up to 20 mcg per serving).

Good choices (serving sizes are one cup unless otherwise indicated): Arugula (one-half cup), beets, carrots, celery (one stalk), corn, eggplant, sweet red or green peppers, peas (one-half cup), turnips, tomatoes and zucchini.

Other foods that are naturally low in vitamin K include most fruits, cereals, grains, beans, seeds and tubers (such as white potatoes, sweet potatoes and yams).

A good rule of thumb: Stick to side dishes with 20 mcg to 25 mcg of vitamin K per serving and main courses with 35 mcg to 40 mcg per serving. That should keep you at a safe level.

But what if you reach your daily limit and are still craving some sautéed greens or a big kale salad? Don't despair. You can still enjoy these foods...as long as your intake of vitamin K is consistent.

This means that you can exceed 75 mcg of vitamin K per day—but you must consume the same amount of the vitamin every day. So, you can have a spinach salad, but you need to eat that same size salad (or another dish with an equivalent amount of vitamin K) every single day.

Important: Be sure to first tell your doctor if you plan to increase your intake of vitamin K so that you can be closely monitored and, if needed, your dose of warfarin adjusted. The frequency of monitoring depends on the patient's specific circumstances.

To find the vitamin K content of various foods: Go to Dr. Harlan's website, DrGourmet.com/md/warfarincomprehensive.pdf.

THE "SAFE" LIST

Unless you're a nutritionist, you probably don't know the vitamin K content of most foods off the top of your head. To help you stay safe when you're close to reaching your limit of the vitamin, here are some healthful foods that contain virtually no vitamin K in a single serving...

Acorn squash...raw mushrooms...cooked grits...yellow sweet pepper...cooked salmon, halibut or sole...cooked pork...light-meat turkey (no skin)...lemon, lime or orange...almonds... nonfat sour cream...rosemary, garlic powder or ground allspice, ginger or nutmeg.

How to Make Aspirin Therapy Really Work

Mark J. Alberts, MD, a leading stroke specialist and clinical vice-chair in the department of neurology and neurotherapeutics at the University of Texas Southwestern Medical Center in Dallas. He is also a fellow of the American Heart Association and the former director of the stroke program at Northwestern Memorial Hospital in Chicago.

For millions of Americans, popping one or two daily low-dose (81 mg) aspirin pills is an easy way to help prevent heart attacks and strokes.

What most people don't realize: Even though this type of "aspirin therapy" has been used since the 1970s in the US, the majority of patients—as well as many doctors—aren't aware that the drug may not be doing the job for all of those taking it. That's because 15% to 25% of Americans are "aspirin-resistant" and may not fully respond to the drug's cardioprotective properties.

It's troubling because aspirin (typically 81 mg to 162 mg daily) is routinely prescribed for heart patients. Research shows that daily aspirin therapy can reduce the risk for second heart attacks in men and women by about 25% and the risk for second strokes by about 22%.

Recent development: Even though the evidence has long been unclear whether aspirin helps prevent a first heart attack or stroke in both sexes, the American Heart Association has recently recommended that low-dose aspirin therapy be considered in adults age 50 and older who have a 10-year cardiovascular risk of at least 10% but no increased risk for bleeding.* (Uncontrolled high blood pressure and diabetes are among the factors that increase one's 10-year risk.)

Those who are aspirin-resistant, however, face the risks associated with aspirin therapy (mainly gastric bleeding and, in rare cases, hemorrhagic stroke)—without any appreciable gain in long-term health. *Key facts about aspirin therapy...*

A WONDER DRUG...FOR SOME

A daily aspirin prevents blood platelets from clumping and forming clots—the cause of most heart attacks and strokes. But what happens when it doesn't work?

Troubling research: A recent study found that aspirin-resistance in some patients could be linked to a tripling (or more) of major cardiovascular events. This doesn't mean that aspirin isn't an effective treatment. It does work for the majority of patients who take it for its cardioprotective benefits.

But if you don't respond to aspirin...or respond just a little, there may still be a solution.**

THE POSSIBLE CAUSES

Some experts believe that aspirin resistance may not be due to physiological reasons—but instead mainly from improper use.

Example: Many people who take aspirin for cardiovascular health also take other nonsteroidal anti-inflammatory drugs (NSAIDs)—such as *ibuprofen* (Motrin) or *naproxen* (Aleve)—for unrelated conditions. These drugs are believed to antagonize (block) the clot-inhibiting effects of aspirin. *Other possibilities...*

- **Age.** Aspirin resistance is more common in those who are age 75 or older. Age-related declines in stomach acid may limit the absorption of aspirin and make it less effective.

- **Aspirin coatings.** A study in the journal *Circulation* found that the enteric coating on aspirin, used to keep the drug from dissolving in the stomach and ease pain and bleeding for some people with gastritis or ulcers, slowed the

*To calculate your 10-year risk for heart attack or stroke, go to CVRiskCalculator.com.

***Important:* Never start or stop aspirin therapy without consulting your doctor.

effects on platelets. Patients still responded to the treatment, but it took longer (about eight hours) for the drug to be fully absorbed and active.

• **Insufficient dosing.** An analysis of aspirin research by the Antithrombotic Trialists' Collaboration, led by the UK's University of Oxford, concluded that doses lower than 75 mg (commonly used in the UK) might be ineffective. One study found that about 27% of aspirin-resistant patients were taking lower doses than those without resistance. The most effective dose seems to be 75 mg to 150 mg daily, the UK research found.

• **Other causes.** Some patients might have genetic factors that reduce aspirin's effectiveness. Other patients might have high platelet turnover, leaving a smaller percentage of aspirin-affected platelets in the bloodstream. And some might have metabolic pathways that allow platelets to "activate," thus promoting blood clots, even in the presence of aspirin.

WHAT'S THE SOLUTION?

Blood tests can readily detect the effects of aspirin on platelet aggregation, part of the sequence that leads to clotting. The tests are routinely performed on patients who are scheduled for stents or other cardiac procedures. However, they're not commonly used to check for aspirin resistance.

My advice: Anyone who takes aspirin to prevent heart attack or stroke should ask his/her doctor if platelet function testing is needed—and how often. The tests are quick and typically covered by insurance. Your doctor needs to know if you're not responding to aspirin so that he can recommend other approaches (such as those described below) to reduce your clot risks. *What helps…*

• **Use plain aspirin.** As previously explained, research suggests that the rate of aspirin resistance is higher in people who take enteric-coated aspirin. So take plain, uncoated aspirin instead if it doesn't upset your stomach.

• **Consider a higher dose.** In some patients, a dose of 162 mg a day (or even higher) might be more effective, especially if they've had a recent heart attack or stroke. Since higher-dose aspirin can increase GI complications, take more only if your doctor recommends it.

• **Divide the dose.** There's some evidence that taking aspirin in two doses—once in the morning and again in the evening—can reduce resistance. You would take the same daily dose that you did before. Just divide it in two—for example, 81 mg in the morning and 81 mg at night.

• **Space your medicines.** If you are taking aspirin for heart health, try to avoid ibuprofen and similar drugs. If this isn't possible, space the doses—take the nonaspirin NSAID at least two hours before (or two hours after) your daily aspirin.

• **Switch drugs.** Patients who do not respond to aspirin can get similar cardiovascular protection from *clopidogrel* (Plavix), *ticlopidine* (Ticlid) or other blood thinners. Your doctor might recommend aspirin and one of these drugs. Using them together may reduce the resistance to aspirin.

• **Follow directions!** About three-quarters of patients do not. In a study of 136 coronary-artery stent patients, 14% were found to be unresponsive to aspirin therapy one month after discharge. However, all but one patient became responsive after they made a commitment to take aspirin daily, as prescribed.

Should You Take Aspirin? There's an App for That

Article titled "Aspirin for primary prevention of atherosclerotic cardiovascular disease. Advances in diagnosis and treatment" written by Samia Mora, MD, MHS, Harvard Medical School, and JoAnn E. Manson, MD, DrPH, Harvard T.H. Chan School of Public Health, both in Boston, published in *JAMA Internal Medicine*.

Figuring out whether to take a daily low-dose aspirin is tricky. By reducing the tendency of blood to clot, aspirin can help prevent a heart attack or a stroke…but it can also put you at risk for intestinal, even cerebral, bleeding. Do the benefits outweigh the risks—for you?

Even doctors don't always get it right—in some medical practices, nearly two-thirds of patients on aspirin therapy shouldn't be taking it.

Now a new, free smartphone app makes figuring that out easier, faster and safer.

DOC IN A POCKET

Aspirin Guide (currently available for iPhone and iPad only), an app designed by researchers at Brigham and Women's Hospital and Harvard Medical School, is designed for health-care professionals, but it's patient-friendly, too. All you need to know is some basic medical information, such as your systolic blood pressure (the upper number), and your high-density (HDL) and total cholesterol numbers.

The app uses evidence-based algorithms to calculate your 10-year risk for heart attack, stroke and your risk of bleeding based on your answers to certain questions. It then gives two numbers, one for your likelihood of harm and one for your likelihood of benefit.

THE BEST CANDIDATE FOR APP ADVICE

What kind of patient can most benefit from Aspirin Guide? Probably not someone who has already had a heart attack or an ischemic stroke (the kind caused by a blood clot). That's because a low-dose daily aspirin is a well-established therapy, so it's likely that your doctor has already advised you to take it.

But if you are trying to prevent a first heart attack or stroke, the individualized information from the new app is a great starting point for a health-care conversation. What if your benefit is high but your risk of harm is also high? That's a great question to ask your doctor.

New Way to Fight Heart Failure

American Chemical Society.

An experimental gel, injected after a heart attack, may reduce scarring, thinning of the heart muscle and/or heart enlargement—important for preventing heart failure.

Post-Heart Attack Danger Is Real

Johannes Gho, MD, PhD, cardiology resident, University Medical Center Utrecht, the Netherlands.

Nearly 25% of people who had a heart attack developed heart failure within four years, in a recent study of nearly 25,000 heart attack survivors. Risk for post–heart attack heart failure was even higher in those who also had atrial fibrillation (abnormal heartbeat)...diabetes...and/or chronic obstructive pulmonary disease (COPD).

If you've had a heart attack: Make sure your doctor monitors you for symptoms of heart failure, such as edema and shortness of breath.

Better Cardiac Rehab

James A. Blumenthal, PhD, professor of psychiatry and behavioral sciences, Duke University School of Medicine, Durham, North Carolina.

Heart disease patients who attended weekly group stress-management sessions in addition to exercise-based cardiac rehabilitation were half as likely to have complications, such as stroke, heart attack, recurrent angina or even death, as those in a cardiac-rehab group without stress management. Both groups had better cardiac biomarkers than those who didn't participate in cardiac rehab.

Cuts and Blood Thinners: How to Stop the Bleeding

Natalie Evans, MD, vascular medicine specialist, Cleveland Clinic.

If you take a blood thinner you need to take care with minor injuries and bleeding.

For small cuts, simply applying firm pressure for a few minutes should work. You can also try an over-the-counter product, such as styptic powder (Wound Seal or Clubman) or hemostatic gauze, that helps stop bleeding. For bleeding that doesn't stop after 15 minutes of continuous firm pressure (no peeking!), a trip to urgent care or the emergency department may be in order to get a stitch or skin adhesive.

Extra care with knives in the kitchen: Knives should be sharpened regularly so you don't have to push hard to cut—pushing too hard can lead to slipping and injury. When cutting, you should curl the fingers of the hand holding what's being cut under so that only the knuckles are near the knife blade. Cut-resistant safety gloves can further protect the fingers.

Is Surgery Always Necessary for Carotid Artery Blockage?

Deepak L. Bhatt, MD, MPH, executive director of interventional cardiovascular programs, Brigham and Women's Hospital, Boston.

When a carotid artery is 100% blocked and is discovered while testing for another health condition, typically no procedure would be recommended. If the blockage has not already caused a stroke, it is unlikely to do so in the future, and if other arteries are clear, they can continue supplying blood to the brain. Surgery can be risky because there's a chance that a small clot or piece of plaque could break loose and travel to the brain, causing a stroke.

In lieu of surgery, your doctor may recommend medication—aspirin or *clopidogrel* (Plavix), for example—and lifestyle changes. If you begin having symptoms such as dizziness, blurred vision, weakness, and/or numbness, it might make sense to have a procedure to treat it, such as a carotid endarterectomy (surgical removal of plaque) or the insertion of a stent to hold the artery open. All these options should be discussed with your doctor.

Beware of This Stroke Risk

Phyo Myint, MD, chair of old age medicine, University of Aberdeen, Scotland.

Stroke patients with anemia (a lack of healthy red blood cells) were nearly twice as likely to die in the year after their stroke as those without anemia, a study of 30,000 stroke survivors found.

Possible reason: People with anemia may have lower oxygen delivery to the brain.

If you've had a stroke: Make sure you are tested for anemia and receive treatment, such as iron supplements.

Stroke: You Can Do So Much More to Protect Yourself

Ralph L. Sacco, MD, chairman of neurology, the Olemberg Family Chair in Neurological Disorders and the Miller Professor of Neurology, Epidemiology and Public Health, Human Genetics and Neurosurgery at the Miller School of Medicine at the University of Miami, where he is the executive director of the Evelyn McKnight Brain Institute. He is also the chief of the Neurology Service at Jackson Memorial Hospital and the 2014 recipient of the American Heart Association's Cor Vitae Stroke Award.

No one likes to think about having a stroke. But maybe you should.

The grim reality: Stroke strikes about 800,000 Americans each year and is the leading cause of disability.

Now for the remarkable part: About 80% of strokes can be prevented. You may think that you've heard it all when it comes to preventing strokes—it's about controlling your blood pressure, eating a good diet and getting some exercise, right? Actually, that's only part of what you can be doing to protect yourself. *Surprising recent findings on stroke—and the latest advice on how to avoid it...*

•Even "low" high blood pressure is a red flag. High blood pressure—a reading of 140/90 mmHg or higher—is widely known to increase one's odds of having a stroke. But even slight elevations in blood pressure may also be a problem.

An important recent study that looked at data from more than half a million patients found that those with blood pressure readings that were just slightly higher than a normal reading of 120/80 mmHg were more likely to have a stroke.

Any increase in blood pressure is worrisome. In fact, the risk for a stroke or heart attack doubles for each 20-point rise in systolic (the top number) pressure above 115/75 mmHg—and for each 10-point rise in diastolic (the bottom number) pressure.

My advice: Don't wait for your doctor to recommend treatment if your blood pressure is even a few points higher than normal. Tell him/her that you are concerned. Lifestyle changes—such as getting adequate exercise, avoiding excess alcohol and maintaining a healthful diet—often reverse slightly elevated blood pressure. Blood pressure consistently above 140/90 mmHg generally requires medication.

- **Sleep can be dangerous.** People who are sleep deprived—generally defined as getting less than six hours of sleep per night—are at increased risk for stroke.

What most people don't realize is that getting too much sleep is also a problem. When researchers at the University of Cambridge tracked the sleep habits of nearly 10,000 people over a 10-year period, they found that those who slept more than eight hours a night were 46% more likely to have a stroke than those who slept six to eight hours.

It is possible that people who spend less/more time sleeping have other, unrecognized conditions that affect both sleep and stroke risk.

Example: Sleep apnea, a breathing disorder that interferes with sleep, causes an increase in blood pressure that can lead to stroke. Meanwhile, sleeping too much can be a symptom of depression—another stroke risk factor.

My advice: See a doctor if you tend to wake up unrefreshed...are a loud snorer...or often snort or thrash while you sleep. You may have sleep apnea. (For more on this condition, see page 17.) If you sleep too much, also talk to your doctor to see if you are suffering from depression or some other condition that may increase your stroke risk.

What's the sweet spot for nightly shut-eye? When it comes to stroke risk, it's six to eight hours per night.

- **What you drink matters, too.** A Mediterranean-style diet—plenty of whole grains, legumes, nuts, fish, produce and olive oil—is perhaps the best diet going when it comes to minimizing stroke risk. A recent study concluded that about 30% of strokes could be prevented if people simply switched to this diet.

But there's more you can do. Research has found that people who drank six cups of green or black tea a day were 42% less likely to have strokes than people who did not drink tea. With three daily cups, risk dropped by 21%. The antioxidant epigallocatechin gallate or the amino acid L-theanine may be responsible.

- **Emotional stress shouldn't be pooh-poohed.** If you're prone to angry outbursts, don't assume it's no big deal. Emotional stress triggers the release of cortisol, adrenaline and other so-called stress hormones that can increase blood pressure and heart rate, leading to stroke.

In one study, about 30% of stroke patients had heightened negative emotions (such as anger) in the two hours preceding the stroke.

My advice: Don't ignore your mental health—especially anger (it's often a sign of depression, a potent stroke risk factor). If you're suffering from "negative" emotions, exercise regularly, try relaxation strategies (such as meditation) and don't hesitate to get professional help.

- **Be alert for subtle signs of stroke.** The acronym "FAST" helps people identify signs of stroke. "F" stands for facial drooping—does one side of the face droop or is it numb? Is the person's smile uneven? "A" stands for arm weakness—ask the person to raise both arms. Does one arm drift downward? "S" stands for speech difficulty—is speech slurred? Is the person unable to speak or hard to understand? Can he/she repeat a simple sentence such as, "The sky is blue" correctly? "T" stands for time—if a person shows any of these symptoms (even if they go away), call 911 immediately. Note the time so that you know when symptoms first appeared.

But stroke can also cause one symptom that isn't widely known—a loss of touch sensation. This can occur if a stroke causes injury to the parts of the brain that detect touch. If you suddenly can't "feel" your fingers or toes—or have trouble with simple tasks such as buttoning a shirt—you could be having a stroke. You might notice that you can't feel temperatures or that you can't feel it when your feet touch the floor.

It's never normal to lose your sense of touch for an unknown reason—or to have unexpected difficulty seeing, hearing and/or speaking. Get to an emergency room!

Also important: If you think you're having a stroke, don't waste time calling your regular doctor. Call an ambulance, and ask to be taken to the nearest hospital with a primary stroke center. You'll get much better care than you would at a regular hospital emergency room.

A meta-analysis found that there were 21% fewer deaths among patients treated at stroke centers, and the surviving patients had faster recoveries and fewer stroke-related complications.

My advice: If you have any stroke risk factors, including high blood pressure, diabetes or elevated cholesterol, find out now which hospitals in your area have stroke centers. To find one near you, go to Hospitalmaps.heart.org.

The "Silent" Stroke Trigger

Walid Saliba, MD, medical director of the Center for Atrial Fibrillation and director of the Electrophysiology Lab at Cleveland Clinic. His research has been published in many journals, including *Circulation: Arrhythmia and Electrophysiology* and *American Journal of Cardiovascular Drugs.*

When it comes to preventing stroke and heart-related disorders such as heart failure, it's crucial to identify and properly treat "AFib"—short for atrial fibrillation, the most common type of abnormal heart rhythm. Unfortunately, a significant number of the estimated three million Americans who have AFib don't even realize it.

Now: With new diagnostic and treatment approaches, one's chances are greater than ever that this potentially dangerous condition can be spotted and stopped—if you receive the right tests and medical care. *What you need to know...*

WHEN AFIB IS SILENT

If you have AFib, it's possible to experience a range of symptoms including a quivering or fluttering heartbeat...a racing and/or irregular heartbeat...dizziness...extreme fatigue...shortness of breath...and/or chest pain or pressure.

But AFib can also be "silent"—that is, symptoms are so subtle that they go unnoticed by the patient. Silent AFib is sometimes an incidental finding during a physical exam when the doctor detects an irregular heartbeat. It may also be suspected in patients with nonspecific symptoms such as fatigue or shortness of breath—especially in those with a family history of AFib or a condition such as high blood pressure or diabetes that increases risk for AFib. But whether the symptoms are noticeable or not to the patient, the risk for stroke and potentially heart failure remains just as high, so AFib needs to be diagnosed.

To check for AFib: The standard practice has been to perform an electrocardiogram (ECG) for a few minutes in the doctor's office to record the electrical activity driving the heart's contractions. But if AFib episodes are intermittent, the ECG may be normal.

When AFib is suspected based on symptoms such as dizziness and/or palpitations or racing heartbeat, but the ECG is normal, doctors have traditionally recommended monitoring for 24 to 48 hours. This involves wearing a small device that is clipped to a belt, kept in a pocket or hung around your neck and connected to electrodes attached to your chest. But this approach, too, can miss occasional AFib episodes.

What works better: Longer-term monitoring. Research published in *The New England Journal of Medicine* found that AFib was detected in five times more patients when they were monitored for 30 days instead of only 24 hours. Guidelines from the American Heart Association now recommend AFib monitoring for 30 days within six months after a person has suffered a stroke with no known cause.

New option: With a doctor's supervision, mobile ECG devices (about the size of a cell phone) can now be used periodically to record 30-second intervals of your heart rhythm. Ask your doctor for details.

GETTING THE RIGHT TREATMENT

AFib almost always requires treatment. Besides the danger of stroke, the condition tends to worsen if left alone—symptoms become more troublesome, and normal rhythm is harder to restore.

There are numerous options depending on other risk factors, your treatment goals and your own preference. Treatment is chosen based on frequency and severity of symptoms and whether the patient already has heart disease. *Examples...*

•**Prevent stroke.** To keep clots from forming, many patients need blood-thinning medications (anticoagulants). The old standby, *warfarin* (Coumadin), is effective but requires regular blood tests and dietary restrictions.

In recent years, a new generation of easier-to-use anticoagulants has appeared, including *dabigatran* (Pradaxa), *rivaroxaban* (Xarelto) and *apixaban* (Eliquis). These newer drugs have no dietary restrictions and do not require routine blood tests. However, all anticoagulants carry the risk for bleeding, which is harder to stop with the newer drugs.

Some patients at otherwise low risk for stroke may need only low-dose aspirin (such as 81 mg daily).

•**Slow down a rapid heart rate.** This is usually done with a beta-blocker like *atenolol* (Tenormin) or a calcium channel blocker like *amlodipine* (Norvasc) or *diltiazem* (Cardizem).

•**Normalize heart rhythm.** Anti-arrhythmic drugs, such as *amiodarone* (Cordarone), *flecainide* (Tambocor) and *dofetilide* (Tikosyn), are available. However, these are powerful drugs, with potentially serious side effects (such as dizziness and uncontrollable shaking), that can worsen rhythm abnormalities and must be used cautiously.

•**Ablation.** Another option to normalize heart rhythm and reduce stroke risk is known as ablation. With this procedure, the doctor threads a series of catheters up a vein to the heart to destroy the tiny group of cells that generate electrical impulses that cause fibrillation.

The procedure may have to be repeated but may be a good alternative to lifelong drug treatment. Ablation used to be saved for patients who didn't respond to drugs, but it's being offered as first-line therapy nowadays for those who want to avoid lifelong medication.

New procedure: Just last year, the FDA approved a procedure that can sharply reduce AFib stroke risk—left atrial appendage occlusion places a plug in a tiny sac of the atrium where 90% of clots form.

Each of these procedures, which eliminates the need for long-term blood thinning, carries a small risk for serious complications, such as stroke, and is best performed in a hospital that has experience with the surgery and the resources and expertise to provide emergency backup if needed.

•**An anti-AFib lifestyle.** The best way to cut your odds of developing AFib is to modify risk factors. If you have high blood pressure or sleep apnea, get effective treatment. If you're obese, lose weight. Exercise regularly. If you have AFib, these steps will make your treatment work better—and reduce symptoms.

Atrial Fibrillation Can Cause More Than Stroke

Atrial fibrillation is tied to many dangerous conditions, not just stroke, as previously believed.

AFib, a common heart-rhythm disorder, is associated with heart disease, heart failure, kidney disease and sudden cardiac death—as well as death from all causes. The strongest association found was with heart failure, which was five times more likely in people with AFib.

Analysis of 104 studies including more than nine million people, 590,000 of whom had A-fib, by researchers at University of Oxford, UK, and Massachusetts Institute of Technology, Boston, published in *BMJ.*

Alcohol Can Increase AFib Risk

Peter Kistler, MBBS, PhD, is head of clinical electrophysiology research at The Baker IDI Heart and Diabetes Institute at The Alfred hospital, Melbourne, Victoria, Australia.

Risk for irregular heartbeat, also called atrial fibrillation (AFib), is 8% higher for every drink consumed per day. And AFib is a leading cause of stroke and heart failure.

What to do: People with AFib should reduce alcohol consumption to no more than one drink three times a week.

The Best Way to Reverse AFib (It's Not Drugs or Surgery)

Study titled "Long-Term Effect of Goal-Directed Weight Management in an Atrial Fibrillation Cohort" by researchers at University of Adelaide, Australia, et al., published in Journal of the *American College of Cardiology*.

Prashanthan Sanders, MBBS, PhD, director, Centre for Heart Rhythm Disorders, and Knapman-NHF Chair of Cardiology Research, University of Adelaide, and director, Cardiac Electrophysiology and Pacing, Royal Adelaide Hospital, both in Australia.

If you're diagnosed with atrial fibrillation, commonly known as AFib—a chronic condition that creates abnormal heart rhythms, increasing the risk for stroke and heart failure—your doctor may prescribe medications that you need to take for life, and, if that doesn't work, advise a surgical procedure. Not only does each approach have risks, but in many cases you're only controlling the condition, not treating the reasons you have it.

There's a better way.

If you do it the right way, you can virtually reverse this life-threatening condition—while simultaneously dramatically reducing your risk for heart disease and diabetes, finds a recent Australian long-term study. You may wind up needing no medications for this condition at all—and no surgery.

What is this revolutionary new treatment? It's actually pretty old-fashioned—weight loss and managing the associated risk factors such as elevated blood pressure, blood cholesterol and blood sugar. But we're not talking about quick weight-loss schemes here—and losing weight and then regaining a lot of it back can actually backfire, the researchers found.

The good news is that many of the participants in this research lost weight and kept it off for five years. There are lessons here for anyone who needs to lose weight for health.

For someone with AFib, it could be lifesaving.

THE 10% SOLUTION

Obesity is a well-established risk factor for AFib, but the Australian researchers wanted to know the long-term impact of weight loss on heart-rhythm control in obese people with AFib. They were specifically looking at how much weight loss was necessary to see benefits and what the effect of losing and regaining weight (a common occurrence in dieters) would have on AFib.

They studied 355 overweight or obese AFib patients, who were offered weight-loss programs, and followed in a weight-loss registry for five years. To qualify, a 5'10" man would need to weigh more than 188 pounds, although in practice the average weight for someone that height was 235 pounds. Some lost less than 3% of their starting body weight...others lost between 3% and 9%...and some lost at least 10% (an average of 35 pounds). *Results...*

- **The 135 participants who lost at least 10% were six times more likely to be free from arrhythmia** without any need for medication than 220 participants who lost less weight.
- **Losing weight led to normal heart rhythms for many without any need for medication.** That was true for 46% of those who lost at least 10% of their weight...22% of those who lost 3% to 9% of their body weight...and 13% of those who lost less than 3% of their body weight.
- **Two-thirds of the patients who lost at least 10% of their weight were able to maintain the weight loss.**

• **Those who lost more than 10% of their weight had markedly better control of their associated risk factors.**

• **The benefits were drastically reduced in those whose weight fluctuated by more than 5%,** possibly because repeated loss and regain causes physical changes in the heart and can increase the risk for high blood pressure and diabetes. Looking at all the participants, including those still taking medications, researchers found that 85% of the group that lost 10% of their body weight and kept it off were free of AFib—compared with only 44% among those whose weight fluctuated 5% or more.

Researchers don't know exactly how losing weight improves AFib, but obesity causes a number of conditions that are all risk factors for AFib, such as impaired glucose tolerance, high cholesterol, hypertension and sleep apnea. Weight loss in obese patients reduces these risk factors. In fact, the study found that those who lost weight also had reduced blood pressure, better glucose control, lower cholesterol numbers and reduced inflammation. All in all, they were simply much healthier.

Results often happen quickly. With the loss of five or more pounds, patients start feeling much better. Soon they notice they have less AFib and so they become more motivated.

THE BEST WAY TO LOSE WEIGHT

The study also demonstrated that losing weight and keeping it off for years is definitely possible—with the right type of program and support system. The weight-loss program in this study included motivational counseling in a physician-led weight-management program, with regular in-person visits to discuss goals, progress and outcomes—and extra visits if patients requested them. The diet was high protein, low glycemic and calorie-controlled. Most patients just adapted their own eating habits to the guidelines—only 1% to 2% needed meal replacements.

The first lesson was participation—those who followed up more often with the clinic staff were more likely to keep the weight off. *The success of dieters depends on a few key factors...*

• **Individualization.** Look at your own dietary habits, and identify where there is room for improvement. Keep a diary of your food intake and exercise. Specific diets were not the answer. It's more a matter of where you can pare down your diet and how to avoid those foods that are causing trouble. For most people in the Australia diet program, the focus was on eliminating snacking between meals, reducing carbs and sugars, paring meal portions and limiting alcohol.

• **Reasonable goals.** Set achievable, progressive targets to provide a sense of success.

• **Support system.** It's important to have someone to answer to or check in with. While the Australian study relied solely on physicians to help patients identify their problem areas, you can rely on a dietician or nutritionist, says Dr. Sanders. The subjects in the study met with someone once every three months, but those who were having trouble losing weight talked with or e-mailed their doctors weekly.

• **Increased physical activity.** This is important for everyone on a weight-loss program, but anyone with AFib needs to take special precautions. Talk first with your cardiologist and then, if given the green light, set small and achievable goals based on your current level of exercise. For example, if you're walking 10 minutes a day, gradually increase so you're walking 20 minutes on some days and work up to 30 minutes of brisk walking every day. In this study, participants were told to do low-intensity exercise for 20 minutes a day three times a week and then increase that to at least 200 minutes of moderate-intensity activity per week—50 minutes four days a week, for example.

• **Regular medical evaluations—especially for medications.** While waiting for weight loss, make sure you work with your doctor to manage other risk factors that cause AFib, such as high blood pressure, diabetes and sleep apnea. As your weight loss progresses, you may need lower doses—or be able to stop some medications entirely. The treatment for these risk factors needs to be regularly evaluated. Often, with weight loss, patients can be weaned off.

A NEW APPROACH TO AFIB

Currently, if you have AFib, your doctor will discuss medications and possible surgical approaches—and, if you're lucky, mention lifestyle. The recent research suggests that the order should be the opposite—the first line of treatment for someone with AFib is to treat the risk factors, including obesity, that led to it.

For each risk factor that is applicable, work with your doctor to set achievable goals and supervise its management. If, after trying this, you continue to have symptoms, then consider appropriate rhythm-control strategies—such as catheter ablation, in which tiny areas in the heart that are responsible for the abnormal electrical impulses are destroyed.

The good news: Even if you do need treatment, any weight loss you've achieved will likely improve your results. For ablation, for example, patients who lose weight and reduce other risk factors are five times more likely to have their hearts remain in a normal rhythm.

Eggs Slash Stroke Risk

Dominik D. Alexander, PhD, MSPH, principal epidemiologist, EpidStat Institute, Ann Arbor, Michigan.

Eating up to one egg each day cut stroke risk by 12%—without increasing risk for heart disease—a recent study of more than 300,000 adults has found.

Theory: Eggs are rich in antioxidants (shown to reduce inflammation) and protein—both of which help lower blood pressure, an important risk factor for stroke.

Important: The new Dietary Guidelines for Americans eliminates restrictions on dietary cholesterol and notes that eggs are an inexpensive source of important nutrients.

Blood Test for Stroke

Stephen Williams, PhD, assistant professor of neurology, University of Virginia School of Medicine, Charlottesville.

If you've had one ischemic stroke (due to a blocked blood vessel), a common blood test could help your doctor predict whether you'll have another. Stroke patients who had elevated blood levels of C-reactive protein (CRP), an enzyme routinely checked to measure risk of developing heart disease, were more likely to have a second stroke than those with the lowest levels, recent research found. Elevated CRP also indicates higher risk for a first stroke.

Take Control of Your Stroke Risk

Victor C. Urrutia, MD, an associate professor in the department of neurology at The Johns Hopkins University School of Medicine and director of the Comprehensive Stroke Center/Stroke Prevention Clinic at The Johns Hopkins Hospital, both in Baltimore.

If you've ever needed strong proof that you can dramatically influence whether you're struck by a serious medical condition, here's some eye-opening news.

Stunning research finding: When it comes to stroke, the fifth-leading cause of death in the US, 90% of your risk is due to factors that you can control, according to a study published in *The Lancet.*

New development: To incorporate the latest scientifically proven actions that minimize risk for stroke—both ischemic (caused by a blood clot) or hemorrhagic (due to bleeding)—the American Stroke Association has updated its guidelines.

THE STROKE-FIGHTING PLAN

Main steps that reduce one's odds of having a stroke…

***STEP 1:* Test your blood pressure at home.** It's long been known that lowering high blood pressure (hypertension) is the best way to prevent strokes. Unfortunately, not enough is being done to effectively fight hypertension.

Part of the problem is that most people get their blood pressure checked only when they see a doctor. However, blood pressure readings can fluctuate widely throughout the day and from one day to the next—you might have normal pressure in the doctor's office and higher pressure at home...or vice versa.

Important finding: Use of an automated digital upper-arm cuff to measure blood pressure at home helps. A recent study that looked at 450 patients with hypertension found that 72% of those who home-tested achieved good control, compared with 57% of those who did not test at home. Even if you haven't been diagnosed with hypertension, you may want to consider occasional home-testing. Ask your doctor for advice.

Latest thinking: With home-testing, you can see daily changes and identify trends over time that you can discuss with your doctor. It's also a good way to track the effects of medications and/or dose changes. At first, your doctor might advise that you check your blood pressure a few times at different times of the day. After you have steady control, once a day (or even weekly) is usually enough.

STEP 2: **Don't focus so much on LDL "bad" cholesterol.** Until recently, doctors depended on LDL targets when prescribing statins and/or choosing drugs or doses. A desirable reading was generally considered to be below 100 mg/dL...for very high-risk patients with existing cardiovascular disease, a reading below 70 mg/dL was considered optimal.

A better approach: The decision to take a statin—or increase (or decrease) your dose if you're already on one—should be based less on a specific LDL target and more on a patient's 10-year risk of having a stroke or heart attack, according to the new guidelines. Doctors are now advised to use risk calculators (such as CvRiskCalculator.com) before writing prescriptions or changing statin doses. The calculator also takes into account such factors as diabetes and HDL "good" cholesterol levels.

Important: High-sensitivity C-reactive protein (hs-CRP) levels can also help guide treatment.

For people who have not yet had a stroke or heart attack, there is some disagreement about relying solely on such calculators. For now, anyone who has a greater than 7.5% risk of having a stroke in the next 10 years and is between the ages of 40 and 75 will probably need a statin—regardless of his/her LDL level. People with very high LDL (190 mg/dL or higher) will also benefit from taking a statin.

STEP 3: **Don't be afraid to take a blood thinner.** Most strokes are caused by blood clots in blood vessels in the brain. *Warfarin* (Coumadin), the most widely prescribed drug for preventing clots, can reduce stroke risk by about 65% in people with atrial fibrillation, a common heart arrhythmia. But it's a tricky drug to use because it requires frequent blood tests to check/correct the dose...can cause bleeding if it's not carefully monitored...and intake of vitamin K, which affects blood clotting, needs to be carefully controlled. For these reasons, some people refuse to take it.

The updated guidelines include three additional drugs—*apixaban* (Eliquis), rivaroxaban (Xarelto) and *dabigatran* (Pradaxa). They work as well as warfarin, without the need for dietary changes or frequent blood tests. However, they're more expensive than warfarin and have their own limitations (they can't be used by some patients with kidney disease, for example). Bleeding is still a risk with new anticoagulants.

Bottom line: Don't let your concerns about side effects stop you from taking one of these drugs if you need it. Any anticoagulant can potentially cause bleeding, but the stroke-prevention benefit far outweighs the risks.

STEP 4: **Go Mediterranean!** For years, "DASH"—short for "Dietary Approaches to Stop Hypertension"—has been the go-to diet for lowering blood pressure and reducing stroke risk. For the first time, the new guidelines encourage patients to consider a Mediterranean diet, which includes plenty of fish, fresh fruits, vegetables and nuts, along with olive oil and the occasional (optional) glass of wine.

Game-changing research: An influential Spanish study, known as PREDIMED, randomly assigned participants into dietary groups that included people who followed a low-fat diet… and others who followed a modified Mediterranean diet that emphasized an increased intake of walnuts, almonds and hazelnuts.

Results: The Mediterranean group had a lower stroke risk than the low-fat diet group. Based on these findings, the new guidelines advise patients to consider the Mediterranean diet, including a daily one-ounce serving of walnuts, hazelnuts or other unsalted nuts.

STEP 5: **Take migraines seriously.** For reasons that aren't clear, women age 49 and under who suffer migraine-with-aura (a migraine accompanied by visual disturbances such as flashing lights and blind spots) are more than twice as likely to have a stroke (during the headache or at any time) as those without such migraines. For those who also smoke and take oral contraceptives, the risk is 10 times higher.

It's not known whether migraine medication will help prevent stroke in these women.

What does matter: Giving up smoking is critical. Migraineurs-with-aura who smoke and take birth control pills may also want to talk to their doctors about other forms of contraception. In men, migraine-with-aura does not significantly affect stroke risk.

Watch Out for This Stroke Warning

Souvik Sen, MD, MPH, chairman of neurology, University of South Carolina School of Medicine, Columbia.

Recent study: Middle-aged adults who experience an aura (a sensory disturbance, such as flashing lights and/or blind spots) before a migraine are twice as likely to have an ischemic stroke (caused by a blood clot) than migraineurs who don't have auras. Migraines with auras not only affect blood vessels in the brain but may also affect vessels in the heart and neck, loosening existing clots that travel to the brain.

9 Out of 10 Strokes Could Be Prevented, Study Finds

The Lancet, news release.

Stroke is a leading cause of death and disability but the vast majority of strokes are preventable, according to a recent study.

Researchers discovered that 10 controllable risk factors account for 90% of all strokes worldwide. Of these modifiable risk factors, high blood pressure (hypertension) is the most important.

"The study confirms that hypertension is the most important modifiable risk factor in all regions, and the key target in reducing the burden of stroke globally," said study coleader Martin O'Donnell, MB, PhD. He is an associate clinical professor in the Population Health Research Institute at McMaster University in Hamilton, Canada, and the HRB-Clinical Research Facility in Galway, Ireland.

Preventing strokes is a major public health priority and strategies for reducing people's risk should be based on key preventable causes of stroke, the researchers said.

STUDY DETAILS

The study, published in *The Lancet*, involved nearly 27,000 people from every continent.

"This study is of an adequate size and scope to explore stroke risk factors in all major regions of the world, within key populations and within stroke subtypes," Dr. O'Donnell said in a journal news release.

The researchers looked at the proportion of strokes caused by specific risk factors to determine the extent to which eliminating each risk would reduce the impact of stroke. Eliminating high blood pressure was estimated to reduce risk by nearly 48%, the findings showed.

The investigators also calculated potential reductions for eliminating other risk factors:

Physical inactivity: 36%.
Poor diet: 23%.
Obesity: 19%.
Smoking: 12%.

Heart causes: 9%.

Diabetes: 4%.

Alcohol use: 6%.

Stress: 6%.

Lipids (blood fats): 27%.

The combined reduction for all 10 risk factors was 90.7% across all regions, age groups and among both men and women. The study authors noted, however, that the importance of various risk factors vary in different regions. For example, high blood pressure causes about 39% of strokes in North America, Australia and western Europe, but nearly 60% in Southeast Asia.

According to study coleader Salim Yusuf, DPhil, "Our findings will inform the development of global population-level interventions to reduce stroke, and how such programs may be tailored to individual regions, as we did observe some regional differences in the importance of some risk factors by region." Dr. Yusuf is a professor of medicine and executive director of the Population Health Research Institute at McMaster University.

info The American Stroke Association has more about stroke prevention at http://www.strokeassociation.org/.

TV Viewing Raises Risk for Fatal Blood Clots

Study of 86,024 healthy people by researchers at Osaka University Graduate School of Medicine, Japan, published in *Circulation.*

Those who watch TV for two-and-a-half to five hours a day are at 70% higher risk for pulmonary embolism (a blood clot from another part of the body that travels to the lungs) than people who watch TV for less than two-and-a-half hours. Those who watch more than five hours of TV daily have 250% higher risk.

Reason: Prolonged inactivity increases the chance of developing an embolism.

Fidgeting Is Good for You

Study by researchers at University of Missouri, Columbia, published in *American Journal of Physiology: Heart and Circulatory Physiology.*

Sitting for long periods reduces blood flow to the legs and may increase risk for cardiovascular disease. But a small amount of leg fidgeting—such as tapping your foot—increases blood flow to the lower limbs and prevents decline in arterial function.

Take a Statin Drug as Soon as Possible After an Ischemic Stroke

Douglas L. Weeks, PhD, director of research at St. Luke's Rehabilitation Institute and an adjunct professor at Elson S. Floyd College of Medicine and Washington State University's School of Biomedical Sciences, all in Spokane.

Take a statin drug as soon as possible after an ischemic stroke to reduce risk for infection or further strokes.

Recent finding: Infection risk was reduced by 58% in ischemic (blockage) stroke patients who got statins upon hospital admission or early in their stays, compared with similar patients given statins later or not at all.

Take Asprin Immediately After a Ministroke

Peter Rothwell, MD, PhD, professor of clinical neurology and founder and head of Centre for the Prevention of Stroke and Dementia, University of Oxford, UK.

Take aspirin immediately after a ministroke to cut the risk for a fatal or disabling stroke over the next few weeks by up to 80%, reports Peter Rothwell, MD, PhD.

Ministroke symptoms: Muscle weakness, especially on only one side, trouble speaking, numbness/tingling, confusion and/or balance problems. Symptoms may last only a few minutes.

If you suspect a ministroke: Get to the ER, and take a regular-strength, 325-mg aspirin.

New Treatment Improves Movement After a Stroke

Jayme Knutson, PhD, senior staff scientist at MetroHealth Medical Center, Cleveland.

Therapists often use electrical stimulation to elicit contractions in weakened hand muscles. In the new therapy, the patient uses a sensor-equipped glove on the unaffected hand. When he opens his "good" hand, the other one receives corresponding stimulation—strengthening the muscles and possibly changing neural connections. Moderately impaired patients who used the glove showed more than twice the improvement of patients using stimulation on the weaker hand.

Knowing More Than One Language Could Speed Recovery from Stroke

Study of 608 patients led by researchers at National Institute of Mental Health and Neurosciences, Bangalore, India, and University of Edinburgh, UK, published in *Stroke.*

Stroke patients who speak more than one language recover better than similar patients who speak only a single language. Bilingual patients were more likely to recover cognition fully after a stroke than single-language speakers.

Viagra Might Make for a Safer, More Effective Stent

Avneet Singh MD, interventional cardiologist, Long Island Jewish Medical Center, New Hyde Park, New York and North Shore University Hospital, Manhasset, New York.

Carl D. Reimers, MD, associate chairman, cardiovascular medicine, Lenox Hill Hospital, New York City.

American Heart Association, news release.

It's worked wonders for men battling erectile dysfunction, and now early research suggests that Viagra—when added to artery-opening stents—might cut a patient's odds for clots.

Stents are tiny mesh tubes surgically inserted to prop up failing blood vessels. But as South Korean researchers explained, these devices can become less effective over time as the growth of tissue around the metal device narrows the artery again.

But in their recent study in rats, the researchers found that coating stents with Viagra (*sildenafil*) might help prevent this re-closure from happening.

"If similar results are found in clinical trials, sildenafil could be an ideal drug for coating drug-eluting [emitting] stents or to give orally after stent implantation," study lead author Han-Mo Yang, MD, said in a news release from the American Heart Association. Dr. Yang is an associate professor of cardiology at Seoul National University Hospital.

STUDY DETAILS

In laboratory tests, Dr. Yang's team found that Viagra reduced the "bunching" of clot-forming blood platelet cells by 30%.

And when used in rats, the drug also increased the activity of enzymes that prevent artery walls from thickening in response to an injury—suggesting it could also have this effect on people who've had a stent placed, the researchers said.

"Our study is limited by involving only animals," Dr. Yang noted, and experiments conducted in rats sometimes fail to pan out in human clinical trials.

However, "if clinical trials show that sildenafil reduces [artery re-closure] after stent placement, it could be used in the clinical setting right away because the drug is already used in the real world for other purposes," Dr. Yang noted.

EXPERT COMMENT

One heart specialist in the United States believes the approach holds promise.

"The risk of stent closure because of clot and scarring remains the 'Achilles' heel' of this otherwise life-saving procedure," said Avneet Singh, MD.

"This is another example of 'drug repositioning,' where a clinically tested medication is successfully used for an altogether different condition," he said.

Although the research remains preliminary, the use of Viagra in this way "may open the frontiers to making cardiac stenting procedures even safer and more effective," said Dr. Singh, an interventional cardiologist at North Shore University Hospital in Manhasset, New York.

Carl Reimers, MD, helps direct cardiovascular care at Lenox Hill Hospital in New York City. He called the study promising, but pointed out that the drug was tested in the rats' carotid arteries, which lead from the heart to the brain, not the coronary arteries closer to the heart. And because this was conducted in rats only, he said it is "premature to assign clinical significance [to the findings] at this time."

info The U.S. National Heart, Lung, and Blood Institute has more about the risks associated with stents.

Heart Health Might Be a Matter of Geography

Gregory Roth, MD, MPH, assistant professor, cardiology, University of Washington School of Medicine, Seattle.

David Katz, MD, MPH, director, Yale-Griffin Prevention Research Center, Derby, Connecticut, and president, American College of Lifestyle Medicine.

Journal of the American Medical Association.

The county you call home may have a lot to do with your chances of dying from heart disease or stroke, a recent US study reveals.

Although deaths from cardiovascular disease have been dropping overall for the past 35 years in the United States, there are still pockets across the country where these death rates are unusually high, the researchers said. Poverty and lack of access to quality care may doom many Americans to early deaths, the study authors suggested.

"In some counties, the risk of dying from cardiovascular disease is extremely low, while in other counties the risk continues to be very high," said lead researcher Gregory Roth, MD. He is an assistant professor of cardiology at the University of Washington.

In Pitkin County in Colorado, for example, about 35 people out of 100,000 died from heart disease in 2014—the lowest death rate in the United States. In that same year, the highest rate was in Franklin Parish in Louisiana, where 440 people out of 100,000 died from heart disease, the study found.

Two main factors seem to be driving these differences, Dr. Roth said. One is exposure to risks that cause heart disease and stroke, such as high blood pressure, high cholesterol, bad diet, smoking and obesity. The other is a lack of access to good primary care and hospital care, he explained. But the latest research did not look at what specific factors cause these differences, Dr. Roth said. The next step will be to try to understand why these differences exist.

"The really frustrating thing about heart disease disparities like this is we know how to prevent it, and we know the exposures and risks that account for between 70% and 90% of all the heart disease in the country," Dr. Roth said. "This is a highly preventable disease."

STUDY DETAILS: HIGHS AND LOWS ACROSS THE COUNTRY

To estimate death rates from cardiovascular diseases, Dr. Roth and his colleagues culled death records from more than 3,100 US counties.

The overall death rate for cardiovascular disease dropped 50% from 1980 to 2014, from 507 deaths per 100,000 people to 253 deaths per 100,000 people, according to the report.

Across the nation, however, substantial differences between counties was evident. Significant differences also existed for heart failure, atrial fibrillation, disease of the arteries and veins, and other heart-related conditions, he added.

The counties with the highest death rates from cardiovascular disease were located in a swath that extends from southeastern Oklahoma along the Mississippi River Valley to eastern Kentucky, Dr. Roth's team noted.

Outside the South, several clusters where heart disease rates were high included high rates of atrial fibrillation (irregular heartbeat) in the Northwest, aortic aneurysm (a bulge in the body's main artery) in the Midwest, and endocarditis (inflammation of the heart) in the Mountain West and Alaska.

The lowest death rates from heart disease and stroke are in the counties around San Francisco and in central Colorado, northern Nebraska, central Minnesota, northeastern Virginia and southern Florida, the researchers found.

Even in states where people think they are relatively healthy, one can still find places where people are unhealthy, Dr. Roth said. "You can find variation from highway exit to highway exit," he said.

Dr. Roth hopes these data can be used to target areas where death rates are high, and improve health care and lifestyle interventions to reduce deaths from heart disease and stroke.

The report was published in the *Journal of the American Medical Association.*

EXPERT COMMENT

David Katz, MD, is president of the American College of Lifestyle Medicine. He said, "This important paper informs us that while the rising tide of improving cardiovascular medicine in the US may lift all boats, it certainly does not lift them to the same height, or at the same pace."

This study is a reminder of the important role social aspects play in health, he said. These include environment, educational factors, and social and economic status.

Dr. Katz agreed that disparities between counties are likely due to the prevalence of risk factors and to differences in access to quality care.

"Falling rates of death from heart attack and stroke for the US as a whole can mask a lot of important detail about who is and who is not benefiting from such trends. Just such detail is revealed here," he said.

info To see how your county rates, visit the Institute for Health Metrics and Evaluation at the University of Washington.

Head Position May Not Affect Outcome After Stroke

Craig Anderson, MD, PhD, professor, neurology and epidemiology, University of New South Wales, Sydney, Australia, and executive director, The George Institute for Global Health at Peking University Health Science Center, Beijing, China.

Bruce Ovbiagele, MD, MSc, chairman and professor, neurology, Medical University of South Carolina, Charleston.

The New England Journal of Medicine.

New research might turn conventional stroke treatment on its head.

An international study suggests doctors need not ask patients to lie on their backs, eyes trained on the ceiling, for the first 24 hours of their recovery—a popular way to prevent complications. It appears patients do just as well if their heads are elevated, the study found.

"Head positioning does not seem potent enough to produce changes in the brain that make a difference to the chances of survival and recovery from acute stroke in patients," said lead author Craig Anderson, MD, head of a global health institute at Peking University Health Science Center in China.

"They [head positions] also are not the key factor related to the harms associated with impaired swallowing and breathing disturbance after acute stroke," he added.

Doctors have long believed blood flow to the brain is better and swelling is reduced when patients lie on their backs in bed, with the head elevated 30 degrees, Dr. Anderson said. But, he added, "the optimal head position to produce the best outcome from acute stroke, and avoid potential risks, such as aspiration pneumonia, is essentially unknown."

Still, many US and European stroke centers have strict policies for patients with acute ischemic stroke, ones caused by blocked blood flow to the brain.

They require patients to lie on their backs for up to 72 hours and limit trips to the toilet, often prompting complaints, Dr. Anderson said. "In much of the developing world, where most of the stroke burden exists, most patients are positioned lying flat as they do not have modern mechanical or automatic hospital beds that allow the head [to be] elevated," he said.

STUDY DETAILS

To shed more light on the issue, Dr. Anderson's team randomly assigned hospitals in nine countries to treat just over 11,000 patients with acute stroke in one of two ways for the first 24 hours. Those in one group were told to lie on their backs, while the other was allowed to sit up with head elevated at least 30 degrees.

After 90 days, researchers found no significant differences in death rates and disability between the two groups. Nor was there any significant difference in the rate of complications like pneumonia.

The findings could be good news for stroke patients.

Those in the study reported that lying on their backs was less comfortable and led to more back discomfort, Dr. Anderson said. They were also more likely to leave the study, possibly because they were uncomfortable, he said.

EXPERT COMMENT

Bruce Ovbiagele, MD, MSc, chairman of neurology at Medical University of South Carolina, said the findings don't address all of doctors' concerns about bed positioning, because most of the patients studied had suffered milder strokes.

Patients who have more severe strokes are at special risk of developing pneumonia, and it's vital to put them in positions that improve blood flow, he said. The study doesn't offer clear answers about positioning for them, he said, meaning that many physicians won't do anything different.

Lead author Dr. Anderson said stroke patients should feel free to use whatever position they prefer. He added that nurses should position them "in a way that provides best care" and avoids problems with eating, getting to the bathroom and moving around.

Dr. Ovbiagele said, however, that side sleeping is not a good idea for recovering stroke patients because it wouldn't improve blood flow and could make the airway vulnerable.

The study was published in the *The New England Journal of Medicine.*

CHAPTER 11

Infectious Diseases

The Zika Virus: Should You Change Your Travel Plans?

Zika is terrifying. The mosquito-borne illness is continuing to expand throughout Southeast Asia, Central and South America and the Caribbean—where many Americans vacation—and has arrived in Puerto Rico and Florida. It causes serious birth defects, including microcephaly—babies born with "tiny head" syndrome, a condition in which the brain does not develop properly, leading to severe developmental problems, seizures, blindness and more. There's a link to the paralyzing autoimmune disease Guillain-Barré syndrome (GBS), and new research shows that the virus may attack adult brains, too.

There is no vaccine—and no treatment. So, what if you're planning a vacation to a heavily infected area such as Puerto Rico, the Virgin Islands, Barbados, Mexico, Panama or Brazil? Is it time to reconsider?

Surprisingly, for most adults, unless you're pregnant or planning to get pregnant, it's fine to go ahead with your travel plans. Zika is a horrifying illness for women who are pregnant—but for most people, it's either asymptomatic or mild.

Here are the facts...

•**Women who are pregnant should not travel to affected areas, including Puerto Rico and some areas around Miami, Florida.** Women and men who are trying to conceive may also want to avoid these areas, but if you do go, it's time for a pause in your baby-making plans—women should wait at least eight weeks (and men six months) after returning before trying to conceive. The Centers for Disease Control

Phyllis Ellen Kozarsky, MD, a professor of medicine at Emory University School of Medicine, Atlanta, and board-certified in tropical and travel medicine. She has had key roles in the International Society of Travel Medicine and served as project manager for GeoSentinel, a global network of tropical/travel medicine clinics that monitors the trends in travel-related illness and emerging diseases in travelers, immigrants and refugees.

and Prevention (CDC) has expanded its travel alert to dozens of countries. For updates, go to CDC.gov/zika.

•**For all other adults, the travel risk should be minimal.** Eighty percent of the people who get infected with Zika don't ever have symptoms. Even if you do get sick—symptoms may include a fever, rash, joint pain and red eyes. You'll likely just stay home for a few days and then feel better. Most people don't even go to a doctor.

•**What about Guillain-Barré syndrome (GBS)?** There is a link between Zika and GBS, which usually does not result in death but can lead to serious problems, such as muscle weakness or paralysis. With time, we will learn more about post-Zika problems in adults. Many severe illnesses in adults can result in post-infectious syndrome, and we don't know much about this yet. Zika is one of many viruses that can trigger GBS under certain circumstances. In sum, it's a low risk.

•**If you are immunocompromised**—you're taking high-dose steroids...or undergoing chemotherapy, for example—you may want to avoid any travel to a locale where there are serious infectious disease risks, including Zika virus.

•**If you do go to a Zika-affected area, be sure to protect yourself.** Wear insect repellent all the time. The advice used to be to wear repellent when outside from dusk to dawn, but the Aedes mosquito, which carries Zika, can bite indoors or outdoors as well as during the day. Zika isn't the only reason you want to avoid mosquito bites—mosquitoes also can carry other diseases, including dengue fever and chikungunya, which may be more serious than Zika and potentially deadly.

You can use a repellent that contains DEET or, if you want to avoid it, there are CDC-recommended repellents such as those that contain oil of lemon eucalyptus. Be sure to read the directions so that you'll know how to reapply the repellent.

If you do go on vacation or on business to a country that has Zika, you'll want to take precautions when you return. (That's also true if you're welcoming a friend or relative just back from, say, Brazil.) If you get symptoms that might be related to Zika, tell your doctor—and be vigilant about mosquito protection for at least three weeks after you return home. This isn't to protect you, but to protect others, especially pregnant women—by helping to prevent the disease from spreading via mosquitoes in the US.

Zika Warning: Ineffective Repellents

Joseph Conlon, technical adviser for the American Mosquito Control Association, a not-for-profit scientific organization of public health officials, mosquito-control professionals, university researchers, chemical engineers and others. He has 40 years of experience in mosquito control, including 20 as an entomologist for the US Navy. Mosquito.org

---

If you're thinking of going someplace warm this winter, you may be wondering about protecting yourself from the Zika virus.

Beware: Many mosquito-repellent products actually provide little or no protection. These fraudulent products leave consumers just as vulnerable as ever to the Zika virus. Zika can cause fevers, rashes and joint pain...as well as serious birth defects when pregnant women are infected. Zika also has been linked to Guillain-Barré syndrome, which can lead to muscle weakness, temporary paralysis and even death.

Mosquitoes are spreading Zika in South America and Central America as well as in south Florida and Texas. Additional parts of the US could be affected in future years.

Products that have not been scientifically proven to provide significant protection against mosquitoes include ultrasonic mosquito repellers and mosquito-repelling wristbands. Many "natural" or "organic" bug sprays are ineffective as well. The makers of sprays featuring garlic or oil of clove are technically correct when they claim that these ingredients repel mosquitoes... what they don't mention is that their products repel mosquitoes for only very short periods—some last just 20 minutes—and/or work only when used in extremely high concentrations.

What to do: Use a mosquito-control product that has an "EPA Registration Number" printed on its label. Mosquito repellents that have these numbers have been scientifically shown to be both effective and safe when used as directed.

An effective mosquito-repellent almost certainly will feature one of the following active ingredients...

•**DEET.** Choose a product that has a 25% to 35% DEET concentration.

•**Picaridin.** This odorless synthetic product is based on a compound found in black pepper plants. It is as effective as DEET and typically feels lighter and less greasy on the skin. Choose a product that has a 15% to 19% picaridin concentration.

•**Oil of lemon-eucalyptus.** This is the only natural ingredient that has been proven effective against mosquitoes (ticks, too). Choose a product that has an oil of lemon-eucalyptus concentration of around 40%.

The Germ Hot Spots You've Never Thought About

Miryam Z. Wahrman, PhD, professor of biology at William Paterson University in Wayne, New Jersey, where she specializes in microbiology, hand hygiene and the interactions between bacteria and environmental surfaces. Dr. Wahrman also is author of *The Hand Book: Surviving in a Germ-Filled World.*

Whether it's Zika virus, Ebola or MERS (Middle East Respiratory Syndrome), there is a long list of infectious diseases that get our attention when they dominate the news. Even though these are frightening illnesses, this intense level of scrutiny of exotic diseases minimizes the real threat.

The microbes that pose the biggest threat—in terms of annual sickness rates and death—are the potentially fatal ones that we are exposed to every day, such as influenza and hospital-acquired infections known as superbugs.

Why it matters to me: My research on the transmission of infectious disease is fueled, in part, by personal tragedy. Following heart bypass surgery at a highly regarded American hospital, my mother died after contracting a type of virulent hospital-acquired bacterial infection. Hospital-acquired infections kill about 75,000 patients in the US each year. But hospitals aren't the only place where pathogens hang out.

Most people think that they have a good idea where these germs reside. Doorknobs, elevator buttons and handrails in public places are among the best-known hot spots. But hardly anyone thinks about the numerous other places that harbor pesky pathogens.

What you need to know...

HIDDEN GERMS

Effective handwashing removes the germs that can make you sick. But sometimes we fail to recognize hidden sources of microbial contamination, which so often do not get cleaned properly (or at all).

Many of the germs we encounter are not harmful, and a healthy immune system can often handle most of the rest. In fact, some exposure to germs helps strengthen the immune system. However, with the smart hygiene practices described below, you will greatly reduce the odds of putting yourself, your colleagues and your loved ones at risk for a variety of illnesses, ranging from the common cold to the flu and pneumonia. *Germ hot spots that will surprise you...*

•**Neckties.** Some doctors have stopped wearing ties in order to protect their patients. A study at a New York hospital found that nearly half of the ties tested were contaminated with Staph, K. pneumoniae and other disease-causing organisms.

I advise all men (not just doctors) to keep in mind that ties pick up and transmit germs, since they are rarely cleaned, dangle and sweep across surfaces, and are handled frequently. Men who are not working in health-care settings are less likely to pick up drug-resistant superbugs on their ties, but risks still abound, so it's a good idea to clean your ties now and then.

My advice: Buy ties made from microfiber—these textiles tend to resist bacterial contamination more than silk, cotton or polyester. Some ties made of cotton, linen, polyester and/or microfiber can be hand-washed with detergent, air-dried and ironed, but silk and wool usually must be dry-cleaned, which isn't foolproof in killing germs.

Note to women: Handbags have been found to harbor deadly germs, but a sanitizing alcohol wipe can be used to clean straps and the exterior of bags. Vinyl may be easier to clean than cloth or other material.

•**Cell phones.** Have you ever washed your smartphone? It is certainly not recommended to immerse any cell phone in water, but most people don't even wipe off the surface of their phones.

Important finding: A 2011 British study reported that 92% of cell phones had bacteria, with 16% carrying E. coli, bacteria typically found in feces.

My advice: Clean your phone every day by wiping it down with a microfiber cloth (the kind used to clean eyeglasses) that's been moistened with 70% ethyl or isopropyl alcohol (commonly found in drugstores). Or try other products, such as Wireless Wipes, that are made specifically for cell phones.

Another option: An ultraviolet (UV) cellphone sanitizer, such as PhoneSoap Charger or Cellblaster, which uses exposure to UV radiation to kill most bacteria. These products are available online for about $50 to $110.

•**Rings and other jewelry.** Whether you're wearing a plain band or a ring with elaborate settings, bacteria can thrive underneath it—an area that's usually missed by handwashing.

My advice: When possible, remove rings before washing your hands. You should also clean your jewelry, including wristwatches. To avoid water damage, swab the surfaces with 70% ethyl alcohol or use a UV sanitizer device (described earlier).

•**Paper money.** On average, paper currency stays in circulation for about six years. During that time, it comes in contact with wallets, purses, sweaty palms and filthy fingertips. When we tested dollar bills that we collected as change from New York food vendors, we found that about two-thirds were contaminated with different strains of bacteria...and two-thirds of those harbored coliform (fecal) bacteria.

If you use credit cards, you can largely avoid touching money, although sometimes you must hand your credit card to the cashier, which exposes it to someone else's germs. You also have to touch the scanner and stylus, which have been touched by many customers.

My advice: Try to cleanse your hands after handling money, especially before you eat or touch your eyes, nose or mouth. And do not lick your fingers when counting out bills. Coins aren't germ-free, but the metal alloys in the coins tend to inhibit bacterial growth. So it's mainly paper currency that you have to worry about.

•**Airports.** People who travel a lot encounter germs from other travelers. In airplanes, the tray tables, armrests and seat-back pockets can be teeming with pathogens. But there are other hot spots as well.

My advice: At the airport, for example, it's a good idea to put your cell phone, keys and other personal possessions in a Ziploc bag before putting them in a security bin, which has held innumerable shoes, phones...and who knows what.

•**Rental cars.** Even though most rental car agencies vacuum and quickly wipe down surfaces between rentals, studies show the steering wheel may harbor nasty bacteria. Who knows where the previous drivers' hands have been?

My advice: When you rent a car, consider wiping down the steering wheel and door handles with sanitizing alcohol wipes.

Is It OK to Cut Away Mold and Eat the Food?

Stephanie Smith, PhD, food safety specialists, Washington State University, Pullman.

Mold spreads deep beneath the surface rather quickly in soft foods such as breads and strawberries but does not penetrate as deeply in hard foods. You can safely eat firm vegetables and fruits, such as apples and carrots, or hard cheeses if you can cut away at least one inch around the mold and discard it. Any other foods, such as sliced bread, soft fruits and vegetables and meat, that are moldy should be thrown out. Some molds make toxins that can cause severe illness.

Heartburn Meds Linked to Superbug Infections

Sahil Khanna, MBBS, assistant professor, medicine, division of gastroenterology and hepatology, Mayo Clinic, Rochester, Minnesota.

JAMA Internal Medicine, online.

Patients who take certain heartburn medications may be more likely to suffer recurrent bouts of a common "superbug" infection, a recent study suggests.

Proton pump inhibitors, such as Prilosec, Prevacid and Nexium, or so-called H2 blockers, such as Zantac, Pepcid and Tagamet, were linked to a 50% increased risk of developing multiple Clostridium difficile infections, researchers found.

However, the study did not prove these heartburn medications cause recurrent C. difficile infections, just that an association appears to exist.

BACKGROUND ON C. DIFFICILE

C. difficile can cause diarrhea and life-threatening inflammation of the colon. In the United States, about half a million people get sick from C. difficile each year. In recent years, these infections have become more common, more severe and more difficult to treat, according to the Mayo Clinic.

C. difficile most commonly affects older adults in hospitals or in long-term care facilities and typically occurs after use of antibiotics, according to study lead researcher Sahil Khanna, MBBS. He's an assistant professor of medicine at the Mayo Clinic's division of gastroenterology and hepatology in Rochester, Minnesota. Recurrent C. difficile infection is a major problem, with the risk as high as 50% to 60% in people having had three or more infections, he said.

But recent studies have shown increasing rates of infection among younger and healthier individuals without a history of antibiotic use or exposure to health care facilities, Dr. Khanna said.

"Gastric acid suppression medications are commonly prescribed and consumed over-the-counter for gastric reflux disease [GERD], peptic ulcer disease or functional dyspepsia [heartburn], but they are also sometimes prescribed for unnecessary indications, which leads to overuse of these medications," he pointed out.

Dr. Khanna speculated that the suppression of stomach acid might affect the bacteria living in the gut in these people, leaving the door open for C. difficile.

It's also possible that those taking acid suppressors may be in worse health than those not taking them, which in turn might make them more susceptible to infections like C. difficile, Dr. Khanna said.

STUDY DETAILS

To come to their conclusions, Dr. Khanna and his colleagues analyzed 16 studies that included more than 7,700 patients with C. difficile. Among these, 20% developed recurrent infections.

This type of study is called a meta-analysis because it tries to assess previously published studies in the hope of finding a common thread that can apply across all of them. The weakness of such a study is that it mixes findings developed using different approaches and tries to fit them together.

The researchers found that 22% of patients taking acid suppressors experienced recurrent C. difficile infections, compared with 17% among those not taking these drugs.

Dr. Khanna thinks the best way to prevent recurrent C. difficile infections in these patients is to curtail the misuse of acid suppressors.

"Patients with C. difficile should be reevaluated to assess the necessity of using gastric acid suppression medications," Dr. Khanna said.

The report was published online in the journal *JAMA Internal Medicine*.

info For more on C. difficile, visit the U.S. Centers for Disease Control and Prevention at CDC.gov.

A Vaccine for the Common Cold?

Nature Communications.

Animals given vaccines with up to 50 strains of the rhinovirus, the main cause of colds, produced antibodies to fight the illness.

Next step: Human testing.

Smart Flu Testing

William Schaffner, MD, professor of preventive medicine, Vanderbilt University Medical Center, Nashville.

Flu tests are sometimes given to rule out other infections with similar symptoms that may require different treatment. The test is most accurate when given within three days of the onset of symptoms.

However, the antiviral medication *oseltamivir* (Tamiflu) can be given within 48 hours after symptoms begin—even without a flu test. It will help shorten symptoms such as fever, chills, cough and muscle aches. Prompt treatment is especially important for older people and anyone whose immune system is compromised, such as cancer patients or those with chronic kidney or lung conditions. They are more likely to get complications from the flu, such as pneumonia, which can be deadly.

Treated or not, the flu generally goes away within a week or two in healthy people, although some may have a lingering cough or fatigue. Rest, drink plenty of fluids and wash your hands often to keep from spreading the flu to others.

Flu Shot Fights Other Serious Conditions

Eszter Vamos, MD, PhD, research fellow, Imperial College London, UK.

Adults with diabetes who got the seasonal flu vaccine were 24% less likely to die from any cause than those who were unvaccinated, a recent seven-year study of nearly 125,000 adults with diabetes found. They were also less likely to be hospitalized for such conditions as heart failure, stroke or pneumonia.

Why: Flu may lead to other serious conditions, such as heart attack or stroke, in people with chronic conditions, such as diabetes, and the elderly. The CDC recommends flu shots for children and adults, especially those with most chronic health conditions.

Flu Deaths Are Tied to the Super Bowl

People whose home team is in the Super Bowl have a significantly higher rate of death from the flu.

Theory: The game takes place during flu season—and fans of the home team are more likely to attend Super Bowl parties, where the flu virus can spread.

Analysis of mortality data from 1974 to 2009 led by researchers at Tulane University, New Orleans, and College of William and Mary, Williamsburg, Virginia, published in *American Journal of Economics*.

Help for Cracks in the Corner of Your Mouth

Valori Treloar, MD, dermatologist in Newton, Massachusetts. IntegrativeDermatology.com

Painful corner mouth cracks is a fairly common inflammatory condition called angular cheilitis. It can have many causes but often appears in people who breathe through their mouths at night or frequently lick their lips.

An over-the-counter hydrocortisone cream may soothe the irritation, and a dab of petroleum jelly can protect skin from further damage. If these measures don't help after a few days, consult a dermatologist, who can determine if you have a fungal or bacterial infection that requires a prescription ointment.

Drought May Beckon Bigger West Nile Outbreaks

University of California, Santa Cruz, news release.

A parched climate might be the perfect environment for spreading West Nile virus, a recent study suggests.

Mosquitoes become infected with West Nile virus when they feed on infected birds, according to the U.S. Centers for Disease Control and Prevention. Infected mosquitoes can then spread the virus to humans and other animals.

West Nile first appeared in North America in 1999, and since then has caused outbreaks each summer. But there has been significant variation in the severity of those outbreaks, the researchers explained.

That annual variation has ranged from a few hundred severe US cases in some years, to close to 3,000 severe cases in other years, the finding showed. Severe cases include people who suffer brain-damaging meningitis or encephalitis, and sometimes death.

Even at the state level, there have been wildly varying levels of West Nile infection, with case numbers changing 50-fold from year to year, on average, the investigators found.

Researchers examined 15 years of data on West Nile virus infections in people across the United States and found that epidemics were larger during years of drought. There were also significant outbreaks in areas that had not experienced large epidemics of the mosquito-borne virus in the past.

"We found that drought was the dominant weather variable correlated with the size of West Nile virus epidemics," study author Sara Paull, formerly a postdoctoral researcher at the University of California, Santa Cruz, said in a university news release. She is now at the National Center for Atmospheric Research.

It's not clear how drought seems to increase the severity of West Nile virus epidemics. But, the scientists speculated that it might affect transmission of the virus between mosquitoes and birds by stressing birds or changing where they gather.

The researchers said their findings could help direct public health resources to regions most likely to experience future epidemics.

The study was published in the journal *Proceedings of the Royal Society B.*

info The U.S. Centers for Disease Control and Prevention has more on West Nile virus at CDC.gov/westnile/index.html.

Flu Shot Timing

Get your shot in the morning. When adults age 65 and older were vaccinated for influenza, those who got their shots between 9 am and 11 am had a significantly larger concentration of antibodies one month later than those inoculated between 3 pm and 5 pm.

Theory: The body's immune response may be higher in the morning.

Anna C. Phillips, PhD, professor of behavioural medicine, School of Sport, Exercise and Rehabilitation Sciences, University of Birmingham, UK.

How long flu shots last. Flu vaccines protect for six months—enough to get most people through the annual flu season. Vaccination reduces the chance of a doctor's visit for flu by 50% to 70%.

Study of more than 1,700 Americans by researchers at US Naval Health Research Center, San Diego, presented at the 2015 International Conference on Emerging Infectious Diseases, Atlanta.

Viral or Bacterial? This Test Can Tell

Stanford University School of Medicine.

An inexpensive blood test that identifies gene activity that's unique to viral and bacterial infections is now in development.

Possible benefit: A cutback in unnecessary antibiotic use—a current problem since viral and bacterial infections often cause similar symptoms.

How Poison Ivy Spreads

Debra Jaliman, MD, dermatologist in private practice in New York City and author of *Skin Rules.*

It's unlikely that someone who has a poison ivy rash that seems to be spreading could spread it to others.

Poison ivy is an allergic reaction to urushiol, the oily coating on the leaves, stems or roots of the

Surprising Cause of Chronic Constipation

It might be a viral disease, according to Yale researchers. In people infected with the herpes simplex virus, the infection can spread from the genitals and damage nerves in the colon, inhibiting normal digestion.

Cell Host & Microbe.

poison ivy plant. Blisters and a rash develop on the skin in places where a person has come into contact with urushiol. The rash may not appear for several hours or even days after exposure.

The rash itself and fluid from blisters do not spread poison ivy. However, if an individual has urushiol on his clothing or skin and you come into contact with it, you can develop a rash. Avoid this by showering and washing clothing in hot water when coming indoors after being outside near poison ivy.

Better Tick Protection

Thomas Mather, PhD, director, TickEncounter Resource Center, The University of Rhode Island, Kingston. TickEncounter.org

Most ticks are very sensitive to dryness. The first thing you should do once you're in the house after taking a hike or working in the yard is to strip your clothing off and throw it in the dryer—not in the washing machine. Run it on high heat for about 10 minutes to kill deer ticks as well as Lone Star ticks and other species. Gas dryers tend to get hotter than electric dryers, so you might want to add five minutes if you're using an electric dryer.

Ticks are not killed by washing, even in hot water. Clothing just left in the hamper or on the floor may put the next person who touches it at risk. Dry clothes first, then wash. You can also keep ticks off your clothing with insect repellents, such as Insect Shield or Sawyer, that contain long-lasting permethrin.

Rodent Danger

Elizabeth Ervin, MPH, health scientist, Centers for Disease Control and Prevention (CDC), Atlanta.

Any activity that puts you in contact with rodent droppings urine, saliva or nesting materials from mice or rats (such as cleaning and removal) can put you at risk for hantavirus pulmonary syndrome (HPS)—which can be fatal—and other diseases. HPS occurs when people breathe in air that contains the virus, so it's important to avoid actions that raise dust, such as sweeping or vacuuming.

The CDC website has specific instructions for safely cleaning up after rodents (go to CDC.gov/rodents/cleaning/index.html).

Key steps: Air out the area that contains urine, droppings or nesting material. Then, while wearing gloves, spray the area with a disinfectant or a bleach-water mixture (one-and-a-half cups of bleach in one gallon of water). Let soak for five minutes before gently removing the droppings/urine with a paper towel. Wash hands thoroughly after you are done.

Stop Toenail Fungus Spread

Johanna Youner, DPM, podiatric surgeon, New York City. HealthyFeetNY.net

Toenail fungus (onychomycosis) is not highly contagious, but spores can live in warm, moist areas such as shower stalls. Help protect your family by spraying this area with a cleaning product that contains bleach every day. Also, wear flip-flops around public pools or showers. Wear socks to bed to help protect your spouse or yourself, and the family should not share towels, nail clippers or other items with the family member who is infected.

Fungal infection on toenails is difficult to eradicate. Two laser treatments (they may not be covered by insurance) given three months apart plus a topical medication, such as Formula 3, produce the best results for my patients.

I also recommend the SteriShoe, a product that uses ultraviolet light to eliminate fungi and germs from shoes ($150 at SteriShoe.com)...or antimicrobial shoe sprays such as Clean Sweep or Gehwol Foot & Shoe Deodorant (about $30 each).

Better Hip Surgery

William Schairer, MD, orthopedic surgeon, Hospital for Special Surgery, New York City.

If you're considering hip replacement, you may want to put it off for a few months if you've just received a steroid shot in your hip.

Recent study: Infection rates jumped 40% in hip replacement patients who received a steroid injection in the three months prior to surgery...but those who received an injection earlier showed no increased risk. Steroids may weaken the immune system, which could account for the higher infection rate. Although rare, an infection in the hip joint could require additional surgery, intravenous antibiotics and a prolonged recovery.

STDs Hit a Record High in the US

Annual Sexually Transmitted Disease Surveillance 2015 report from the Centers for Disease Control and Prevention, Atlanta.

Between 2014 and 2015 (most recent data available), syphilis cases increased 19%...gonorrhea increased 13%...and chlamydia increased 6%. All the diseases are curable with antibiotics, but many cases go undiagnosed and untreated.

At greatest risk for STDs: People ages 15 to 24 and gay and bisexual men.

Sex Tips to Stay Safe from STDs

Melanie Davis, PhD, a certified sexuality educator and copresident of the Sexuality and Aging Consortium at Widener University in Chester, Pennsylvania, and founder of the website SaferSex4Seniors.org. Through Honest Exchange, LLC, she trains health-care providers, medical students and educators about sexuality and communication.

For older men and women, the fun game is no longer shuffleboard. It's sex. And that's a great thing—except that sexually transmitted diseases (STDs) are on a meteoric rise in this age group. *The latest stats...*

- **Between 2007 and 2011, chlamydia infections among Americans age 65 and over increased by 31%.**
- **Syphilis infections in this age group rose by 52% in the same period.**
- **17% of new cases of HIV infection are in people age 50 and older.**

THE NEW SEXUAL REVOLUTION

One big reason for the rise of STDs—also called "sexually transmitted infections" or STIs—is that more people continue to be sexually active well into their golden years. "The generation of people now hitting this stage of life came of age during the sexual revolution—they're healthier and fitter and expect to keep having sex," explains Melanie Davis, PhD, copresident of the Sexuality and Aging Consortium at Widener University in Chester, Pennsylvania, and founder of the website Safer Sex for Seniors.

Viagra and related erectile dysfunction (ED) drugs play a role, too. One study found that men (average age 61) who used these drugs were twice as likely to have STDs compared with men who didn't. As women become more savvy about managing sexual health after menopause, they also find sex easier to enjoy. It's also liberating for many women to be able to have sex without worrying about getting pregnant.

Being able to enjoy sex later in life, with more comfort and no worries about pregnancy, is all good. But it also opened the door to the new epidemic of STDS.

It has even become an issue in long-term-care facilities. Many STDs are asymptomatic, but most nursing homes and assisted-care facilities don't screen for them. And even if they did, all it would take is one conjugal visit with an infected nonresident for an infection to spread, according to Dr. Davis. Plus, people with chronic conditions may be more susceptible to infection, including STDs.

If you're sexually active, especially if you have recently had multiple sexual partners (or your partner has), being tested for STDs should be a regular part of your preventive medical care. It's so important for the health of seniors that Medicare now covers STD testing as a free preventive service. But as with everything related to health, prevention is always better than treatment. *Here's how to stay safe—and still enjoy yourself...*

HOW TO HAVE MORE FUN IN BED...SAFELY

The single best way to prevent the spread of infection during sex—heterosexual or homosexual—is to use a barrier form of protection such as an external or internal condom or dam, says Dr. Davis.

As bodies change, though, it can take new skills to use barrier protection right. For older men, for example, "the use of an external condom can be tough if he has challenges achieving a firm erection or if his erection waxes and wanes during sex," she explains.

This doesn't mean, however, that it can't be done. Nor does it mean people struggling with this issue must either consign themselves to a having a risky sex life or going back to shuffleboard. *Some tips...*

•**Hold on.** If you change position while wearing a condom during sex, either partner can reach down and keep the condom in place by holding the bottom of it (the part closest to the man's body). One slip and the protective quality of a condom goes down the drain.

•**Try an "innie."** An internal condom (aka a female condom) can be the perfect alternative to a conventional external (aka "male") one. Basically an elongated tube of pliable plastic, this disposable device has soft rings at either end. One ring is inserted into the vagina to hold that end of the condom in place. The other end stays outside the body. "It can look a little weird," says Dr. Davis, "and it takes a little practice, but it has some real advantages. The material it is made of transfers heat well, and that can feel better and more natural for both partners than an external condom," says Dr. Davis. It's fine to use an extra lubricant, but it's often not necessary. "The lubrication inside and outside of the internal condom helps with comfort," she explains. "It's pretty slippery." The female condom is more protective as well. "A conventional condom doesn't cover the base of the penis, which is where the herpes virus likes to hang out," explains Dr. Davis. "Not only does an internal condom solve that problem, it covers the entire labia, essentially providing a barrier against any other organisms as well."

•**Practice safe oral sex, too.** Pretty much any STD you can get on your genitals you also can get in your mouth, according to Dr. Davis. "Use an external condom if you're performing fellatio or an internal condom if you're performing cunnilingus," she advises.

Another option: A "dam," which uses a square of material (similar to a female condom) designed for just this purpose. Says Dr. Davis, "They make flavored condoms and dams for a reason—to be used during oral sex."

•**Lube it or leave it.** With age, vulvar and vaginal tissue gets thinner and dryer so that, even during gentle sex, it can be more easily torn—basically opening the door for a sexually transmitted organism. A woman can increase her pleasure and decrease her risk for infection by using a lubricant. Dr. Davis advises using a silicone-based lube. "It stays viscous longer than water-based lube," she explains. If dryness is a significant problem, talk to your doctor. You may benefit from a topical estrogen cream or another product that moisturizes the tissues. (A condom is still essential for protection, of course.)

•**Tinker with toys.** Safety is only one part of the satisfying senior sex equation. Men and women of a certain age also just want to have fun. "In terms of pleasure," says Dr. Davis, "adult toys are a great idea." For both genders, the older the body the more time and direct stimulation is needed for both arousal and orgasm, she explains. So don't just play it safe—it's fine to just play, too. "Small bullet-style vibrators are great for targeted stimulation of the clitoris," she explains. "Palm-sized vibrators, about the size of a computer mouse, are easy to hold against the vulva, while longer vibrators or dildos (elongated, without vibrations) are good for internal play and keeping the vaginal muscles flexible. For penises, masturbation sleeves, vibrating or not, can be pleasurable—lubricant increases comfort and sensation."

•**Try a little tenderness.** "Consider other types of 'toys' as well," says Dr. Davis. "Brushing a partner's hair is very sensual—with zero STD risk." So is a partner massage. "Massage oil can also enhance sexual experiences," she added.

Sunlight Boosts Immunity

Gerard Ahern, PhD, associate professor in the department of pharmacology and physiology at Georgetown University, Washington, DC.

The blue light found in the rays of the sun makes T cells move faster, so they get to the site of an infection and begin their protective activity more quickly. Thus, short sun exposure can be beneficial.

The Mumps Outbreak Is the Worst in a Decade

William Schaffner, MD, professor of preventive medicine, department of health policy, Vanderbilt University School of Medicine, Nashville.

Cases are especially common on college campuses. If your child is in college, double-check that he/she received both doses of the measles-mumps-rubella (MMR) vaccine in childhood. A third dose may be worthwhile if he is going to an institution with an ongoing mumps outbreak.

Sleep to Boost Immunity

People who sleep less than six hours a night are 400% more likely to get a cold than people who sleep seven hours or more.

Prevention.com

Note: Anyone born before 1957 is likely to have had mumps as a child and doesn't need to be vaccinated.

Regular Dental Cleanings Lower Pneumonia Risk

Michelle E. Doll, MD, MPH, assistant professor and associate hospital epidemiologist in the department of internal medicine, division of infectious diseases, Virginia Commonwealth University School of Medicine, Richmond.

In a study of the records of more than 26,000 people, those who never saw a dentist were 86% more likely to get bacterial pneumonia than those who had dental checkups twice a year. Regular dental cleanings reduce levels of bacteria that cause the lung infection.

Valley Fever Is Misdiagnosed...with Deadly Consequences

John Galgiani, MD, professor of medicine at University of Arizona College of Medicine and director of the university's Valley Fever Center for Excellence, both in Tucson.

The disease, caused by fungi that live in desert soil, is clinically indistinguishable from many other diseases with severe respiratory symptoms. If you live in or have visited the West or Southwest—especially Arizona or central California—and have pneumonia or flu symptoms, ask for a blood test for valley fever.

Patients with an Abscess Recover Better When Antibiotic Is Added to Usual Treatment

Study of more than 1,200 patients at five hospital emergency departments by researchers at David Geffen School of Medicine at UCLA and Olive View–UCLA Medical Center, Sylmar, California, published in *The New England Journal of Medicine.*

Giving patients a seven-day course of *trimethoprim-sulfamethoxazole* (also known as Bactrim) led to a 93% cure rate, compared with an 86% rate for those who had drainage plus a placebo...and it limits the spread of methicillin-resistant Staphylococcus aureus (MRSA). MRSA is the most common cause of skin infections in the US and many other parts of the world.

Swimming Lessons: For Starters, Watch Out for Germs in the Water

Wake Forest Baptist Medical Center, news release.

A dip in a pool, stream or lake on a hot summer day is refreshing, but take some precautions to avoid bacteria and parasites that might lurk in the water.

"One of the worst offenders is the kiddie wading pool," said Dr. Christopher Ohl, a professor of infectious diseases at Wake Forest Baptist Medical Center in Winston-Salem, North Carolina.

"Warm, shallow water and kids in swim diapers—which don't do a good job of containing feces—can create a perfect breeding ground for water-borne infections even though the water is chlorinated," he said. "The best way to prevent young children from getting sick is to keep them from swallowing that water."

Dr. Ohl offered some other tips...

For starters, keep children who have had any type of gastrointestinal illness away from pools or water parks for several days to prevent contamination of the water.

Don't swallow the water when you're in freshwater lakes or streams. It can contain threats such as *leptospirosis,* a bacterium excreted in the urine of mammals that drink from the water. Infection can cause fever with headache or muscle aches, but it's usually treatable, Dr. Ohl said.

Another potential threat is Naegleria, a rare but deadly brain-eating amoeba that is almost impossible to treat. To avoid it, don't jump feet first into a warm, stagnant pond, especially during a very dry summer. Doing so can push water up into the top of the nose where the amoeba can crawl through to get into the brain, Dr. Ohl explained.

Salt water poses a lower risk from bacteria and parasites, but swimmers should stay out of the water if they have a cut or wound that could become infected.

Also, stay away from jellyfish floating on top of the water in the ocean.

"Most people don't realize that the tentacles of some jellyfish, especially Portuguese man-of-war, can be 10 to 15 feet long, so keep a safe distance to keep from being stung," Dr. Ohl said.

info The U.S. Centers for Disease Control and Prevention offers health and safety tips for swimmers at CDC.gov/healthy water/swimming/swimmers/index.html.

CHAPTER 12

Longevity and Optimum Aging

The MIT Anti-Aging Pill

If there were a pill you could take to live longer, wouldn't you? Wouldn't we all?

Well, now there's a dietary supplement on the market that was developed by a famous scientist—from MIT, no less—that supposedly slows aging. It's called Basis. Is it really a fountain of youth?

THE BASICS ABOUT BASIS

You may see some wild claims about the Basis pill in the coming months. *So here's what you need to know to really understand it...*

- **It simulates the benefits of eating less.** When animals are underfed—given an adequate diet but one with about 20% or 30% fewer calories than normal—they live longer. We humans could try to eat less, too, but it's tough to sustain when food is widely available—so anti-aging scientists have homed in on compounds called sirtuins that are stimulated during underfeeding. The theory is that sirtuins—which are proteins that protect mitochondria, tiny energy factories in each of our cells—are responsible for the longevity effect.

- **It's based on science—mostly in animals.** Basis, marketed by a company called Elysium Health, contains two active ingredients that have been shown in animal studies to stimulate the body's production of sirtuins...

  - Nicotinamide riboside (NR)—250 mg. Your body uses NR to make a coenzyme called nicotinamide adenine dinucleotide or NAD+. (Stay with us!) We have less NAD+ in our bodies as we grow older, and it's a hot area of research for scientists who study aging. In one recent mouse study, for example, published in *Cell Metabolism*, boosting NAD+ stimulated energy metabolism, prevented weight gain and improved insulin sensitivity, eye function and

---

Michael Fossel, MD, PhD, a leading expert on the use of telomerase for age-related diseases. He is the founder and president of Telocyte, a company that is investigating telomerase therapy for Alzheimer's disease. He is author of *The Telomerase Revolution: The Enzyme That Holds the Key to Human Aging...and Will Soon Lead to Longer, Healthier Lives.* MichaelFossel.com

bone density. (The study didn't track whether the mice lived longer, however.) NR, also being studied to protect against hearing loss, is found in tiny amounts in many foods, including edamame (young green soy beans) and broccoli.

• Pterostilbene (PT+)—50 mg. Pterostilbene is similar to resveratrol, a compound found in grapes (and wine) that has been studied for its anti-aging and disease-prevention potential, including for Alzheimer's and osteoporosis—but PT+ is more bioavailable and in some ways more powerful. In animal studies, PT+ has had biological effects that may protect against cancer, neurological disease, inflammation, cardiovascular disease and diabetes. It may lower blood pressure and body weight, although some studies suggest that it may also raise cholesterol levels. It's found in tiny amounts in grapes and berries, especially blueberries.

• **Leading scientists developed it.** The scientist behind Elysium Health and Basis is the well-known and well-respected biologist Leonard Guarente, PhD, who has decades of research in aging under his belt. He runs a lab that studies the biology of aging at the Massachusetts Institute of Technology. Elysium Health's scientific board is packed with other big names in science and health, including six Nobel Prize winners.

• **It's probably safe.** As a dietary supplement, Basis isn't regulated by the US Food and Drug Administration, so it didn't need to undergo human safety studies before going on the market. But the safety research to date has been reassuring. According to anti-aging expert Michael Fossel, MD, PhD, who is not involved with Elysium Health or Basis, "I'm not aware of any safety concerns—and there may be none, but you never know."

• **It'll cost you a pretty penny.** Basis is available only online through the company's website. You can buy a single bottle—a one-month supply of the pills, which are taken twice a day—for $60. If you opt for an annual subscription, the monthly cost goes down to $40, or $480 per year.

BUT...WILL BASIS REALLY HELP YOU LIVE LONGER?

We knew you'd ask that question. We suspect you know the answer, too—no one really knows. There's no scientific evidence that Basis works in humans. Elysium Health is studying the short-term effects of the pill in people—on body weight, blood pressure, blood sugar and more—and other human trials are planned on the active ingredients (in Japan, for example), but there are no published results yet. To be fair, it's challenging to study a longevity pill in humans, especially because we live pretty long anyway, so you can't expect actual longevity results for decades. But studies can find out whether Basis reduces risk factors for chronic disease, and we'll know that in the next few years.

Dr. Fossel, for one, isn't convinced that it will actually help us live longer. Yes, we lose NAD+ as we age, he explained, but he doesn't believe that simply pouring more of it into our cells is likely to keep us on this planet longer. "Sirtuins are just part of the longevity puzzle," Dr. Fossel said. He believes a better target to get at the root causes of aging is the telomere—the protective "cap" on our chromosomes that shorten with age.

Here's why: "If I take a young cell, it's operating very nicely, but as it gets older, the pattern of gene expression changes, and that's modulated by the telomere," he said. Telomeres themselves don't cause aging, but they're the most "upstream" target that's currently within our grasp. Unfortunately, scientists still are many years away from safely and effectively being able to fiddle with telomere length and gene expression patterns in humans to extend life. "There is nothing on the market that is a miracle drug at this point," he said.

So go ahead and buy Basis if you want to—and can afford it. It's unlikely that it will hurt you, it may prime your mitochondria to work a little better, and it might reduce your risk for chronic disease. Whether it's a longevity pill is something we won't know—for ages.

If you are being treated for any health condition, let your health-care provider know that you're taking this supplement so you can be monitored for "the usual suspects," such as lipids (including cholesterol), liver function, complete blood count and blood pressure. According to Elysium Health, users report that they sleep better and have more energy and that their hair and nails grow faster—but that's purely anecdotal,

Feeling Old?

You could be at greater risk for health problems, according to recent research involving more than 10,000 adults. People who think of themselves as old (no matter their real age) are more likely to be depressed and in poorer health...have more cognitive decline...and are up to 25% more likely to be hospitalized.

To feel young at any age: Get regular exercise...don't believe negative stereotypes about aging...and stay connected with family and friends.

Yannick Stephan, PhD, associate professor, University of Montpellier, France.

of course. Concluded Dr. Fossel, "I think it probably has about as much efficacy as a good exercise program, a reasonable diet and a safe lifestyle." It is not, of course, a substitute for those things.

To Live Longer, Cook This Way

Helen Vlassara, MD, professor emeritus and former director of the Diabetes and Aging Division at Icahn School of Medicine at Mount Sinai in New York City. She is an endocrinologist and a pioneer in the study of advanced glycation end products and their effects on health and aging. She is coauthor, with Sandra Woodruff, MS, RD, and Gary E. Striker, MD, of *Dr. Vlassara's AGE-Less Diet: How Chemicals in the Foods We Eat Promote Disease, Obesity and Aging, and the Steps We Can Take to Stop It.* TheAgeLessWay.com

When it comes to our health, we often focus on what to eat and what not to eat. But just as important is how we prepare the foods we eat. Certain cooking methods can unleash chemical by-products that have been linked to heart disease, diabetes, Alzheimer's and other chronic diseases.

GLYCOTOXINS

Sugar is a clingy molecule that attaches to amino acids and fats and changes their structures—a process known as glycation. This triggers a complex chemical reaction that culminates in the production of advanced glycation end products (AGEs). They're sometimes called "glycotoxins" because they trigger inflammation and can lead to cell injury and cell death.

Almost all foods contain AGEs. They're naturally produced by the body as well. But their number vastly increases during food preparation, particularly when you cook with dry, high heat.

Small amounts of AGEs aren't a problem—most are excreted through the kidneys. But the foods that many people prefer—particularly those that are high in sugar and fat and are cooked certain ways—are teeming with AGEs. The body can't cope with the excess, so the AGEs pile up over time. *This leads to...*

- **More heart disease.** AGE-modified proteins and fats can accumulate in blood vessel walls and stimulate clots—the cause of most heart attacks. AGEs also form chemical "cross-links" that stiffen blood vessels and cause high blood pressure.
- **Uncontrolled diabetes.** The high blood glucose (blood sugar) that is the hallmark of diabetes provides fuel for AGE formation. AGEs damage pancreatic cells (resulting in less insulin)...make insulin less effective...and increase diabetes complications, including nerve and blood vessel damage.
- **More cognitive decline.** AGEs damage the protective barrier that insulates the brain from the rest of the body. This allows AGEs to damage brain-specific proteins and produce amyloid plaques—the deposits that occur with Alzheimer's disease. In laboratory studies, animals given a high-AGE diet were much more likely to experience harmful brain changes than those given healthier foods.
- **More kidney disease.** AGEs can injure the blood vessels and other parts of the kidneys, causing them to become scarred and shriveled and greatly reducing their ability to excrete AGEs. As kidney function declines, AGE levels rise in the blood, flooding all tissues of the body and setting the stage for even greater damage to the kidneys and all other organs as well. Studies have shown that patients with chronic kidney disease who are treated with a low-AGE diet

have a decrease in circulating AGEs, as well as in levels of markers of inflammation and oxidative stress.

The inflammation from excessive AGEs has been linked to many other conditions, including arthritis, obesity, vision problems and even skin wrinkles.

CUT AGES IN HALF

You can reduce your AGE levels by 50% in as little as one month. *Best steps...*

•**Add moisture, and reduce the heat.** Any form of high-heat cooking—mainly grilling, broiling, frying and roasting—greatly increases AGEs.

Examples: The 500 kilounits (kU) in one serving of raw meat might increase to 5,000 kU after broiling. Moist-heat cooking methods—such as poaching, stewing and braising—are ideal. Consider one serving of chicken. It will contain 600 kU to 1,000 kU when it is stewed or braised, but up to 6,000 kU when it's roasted or grilled.

It is fine to have roasted or grilled food now and then. What's Thanksgiving without roast turkey! But try to limit how often you have these foods.

•**Marinate.** This is a good solution for meat lovers. The acidic ingredients in most marinades—such as lemon juice, wine, tomato juice and vinegar—greatly inhibit AGE formation even when meat is grilled. Depending on the meat's thickness, marinating it for one to two hours will reduce AGEs by up to 50%.

•**Choose lower-AGE foods.** In general, this means eating less meat, cheese and fat and more produce (see list to the right). Beef, poultry and pork have the highest levels of AGEs.

Important: Fatty meats tend to have more AGEs than leaner cuts, but even lean meats will readily produce AGEs when they're prepared with dry heat.

•**Eat minimally processed cheeses.** They aren't cooked, so why are some cheeses so high in AGEs? It is because they're heated during processing and because aging and the removal of liquids during cheese-making increase AGE formation.

My advice: Eat lower-fat cheeses with shorter aging times that undergo the least processing. Cheddar cheese made with 2% milk, for example, has about half the AGEs of cheeses made with whole milk. Avoid Parmesan cheese (2,500 kU) and American cheese (2,600 kU).

•**Get more flavonoids.** These are naturally occurring compounds that appear to activate enzymes that deactivate AGEs, inhibit AGE-related oxidation and trap the molecules that can increase AGE formation.

Good sources: Apples, chili peppers, berries, broccoli, kale and green or black tea. Spices and herbs that have similar effects include turmeric, cinnamon, parsley, rosemary and sage.

•**Go easy on the sweets.** Even though sugar and other sweeteners don't contain a lot of AGEs, levels increase when they're heated—when you're baking, for example, or during the factory production of breakfast cereals. High-sugar foods often contain fats and proteins, which increase the potential for harmful chemical reactions.

Warning: The fructose in many soft drinks and processed foods causes a 10-fold greater rate of glycation than simple glucose. Dark-colored soft drinks (such as colas) are particularly bad because the color comes from caramelized (dry-heated) sugars. Diet colas contain nearly the same amount of AGEs as their sweetened counterparts.

AGE COUNTS

•**Very Low (100 kU/serv or less)—**Bread ...Eggs (poached, scrambled, boiled)...Fruits (fresh)...Grains (boiled, steamed)...Milk...Soy milk...Vegetables (fresh, steamed)...Yogurt.

•**Low (101-500 kU/serv)—**Avocado...Fruits (dried, roasted, grilled)...Legumes (cooked, canned)...Olive oil...Olives...Pasta...Soy veggie burgers...Vegetables (roasted, grilled).

•**Medium (501-1,000 kU/serv)—**Cheese (reduced-fat)...Chicken (poached, steamed, stewed, braised)...Chocolate (dark)...Fish (poached, steamed)...Sunflower and pumpkin seeds (raw)... Tofu (raw)...Tuna or salmon (canned).

•**High (1,001-3,000 kU/serv)—**Beef or pork (stewed, braised)...Butter...Cheese (full-fat and processed varieties)...Fish (grilled, broiled, baked)...French fries...Nuts (raw)...Sweets (donuts, pies, cakes, pastries, etc.).

•**Very High (3,001-5,000 kU/serv)**—Chicken (skinless, broiled, grilled, roasted)... Fish (breaded and fried)...Pork chops (pan-fried)...Single cheeseburger (fast food)...Grilled cheese sandwich...Tofu (broiled, sautéed)...Turkey (roasted).

•**Highest (5,001 kU/serv or more)**—Bacon (fried)...Beef (roasted, grilled, broiled, well-done)...Chicken with skin (broiled, grilled, roasted)...Chicken (fried, fast-food nuggets)... Double cheeseburger (fast food)...Fish sandwich (fast food)...Hot dog...Sausage...Pizza.

"Super Ager" Secrets for Staying Sharp

Bradford Dickerson, MD, a behavioral neurologist, director of the Frontotemporal Disorders Unit at Massachusetts General Hospital and an associate professor of neurology at Harvard Medical School, all in Boston. He is a member of the Mass General Institute for Brain Health, where neuroscientists work with patients who have a high risk for brain disease, as well as with those who are highly motivated to preserve brain function. He is a coeditor of *Dementia: Comprehensive Principles and Practices*.

When it comes to research on memory loss, most studies have shown that it is very common in normal aging to have reduced memory, even in the absence of Alzheimer's disease or other late-life diseases.

But much of this research has been done on people who are in their 80s or older. What happens to memory in those who aren't quite that old? After all, by the time we've reached our 60s or 70s, most of us have memory lapses, whether it's misplaced eyeglasses or a forgotten name.

Important recent discovery: By investigating somewhat younger adults, scientists are now uncovering a new breed of "super agers," who do as well on memory tests as those who are 40 or 50 years younger. This research is contributing to a growing body of evidence that could provide significant clues about new ways to prevent and treat memory loss.

To learn more, we spoke with Bradford Dickerson, MD, a neurologist at Massachusetts General Hospital and a leading expert on brain changes and memory disorders...

How much does memory decline in the typical older adult?

In clinical settings, memory can be tested in a variety of ways. One approach involves giving people a short list of words to memorize. When people in their 20s are presented with a list of 16 words—and given time to really study the list—they'll probably remember 13 or 14 of the words. Most people in their early or mid-70s might remember just eight or nine of the words. This would be considered "normal" memory loss.

To test yourself: Study a list of 16 words for a few minutes and then see how many you can remember 20 minutes later.

But some people do better on these tests? Actually, some do a lot better. Based on research conducted at Northwestern University, it is known that a small percentage of people who are age 80 or older—maybe about 10%—do as well or better on memory tests as people who are in their 50s and 60s.

Our study included adults closer to traditional retirement age. However, we found the same thing—some people simply don't experience the same degree of memory loss as their peers. This has huge implications.

If we can figure out why some people maintain robust memories, we might find ways to prevent or even reverse age-related memory loss—and possibly some forms of dementia, which can cause other cognitive problems such as impaired reasoning and behavior and personality changes.

Do we know how the brains of super agers differ from those of other people?

Even though the brain is roughly the same size in all adults (about the size of a cantaloupe and weighing approximately three pounds), we found in our studies of super agers that the size of specific brain areas correlated with memory—they were larger in those with exceptional memories and smaller in those with normal memories. This means that we now have a "biomarker" that may be used to study age-related memory changes.

Is it possible to strengthen these brain regions and prevent memory loss?

This is the million-dollar question. Some people, due to genetics, may simply be born with "young" brains. We know that exercise (see below) and following a Mediterranean-style diet with fruits and vegetables, fish, legumes and whole grains can stimulate brain growth. Good sleep and reducing stress can also make a difference. Do the brain changes that are associated with these or other activities lead to better memory? At the moment, we're not sure.

How does exercise help?

Aerobic exercise has been shown to reduce circulating cortisol, a stress hormone that can cause brain shrinkage. It also stimulates the release of growth factors (such as brain-derived neurotrophic factor) that prevent brain cells from shrinking and may even help new ones grow.

A recent study showed that sedentary older adults who take up moderate-intensity exercise—for example, a regular walking program for 30 minutes at least four days a week—for six months to a year show growth in the hippocampus (a part of the brain associated with memory) and also do better on memory tests. This reinforces the idea that exercise is protective.

Important: Don't talk on your cell phone while walking or biking, since you may be more likely to fall. Head trauma raises risk for Alzheimer's disease.

What about diet?

Studies suggest that heart-healthy diets (such as the Mediterranean diet) can reduce the risk for Alzheimer's disease and other forms of dementia. We're just not sure whether the diet specifically improves brain functions.

However, in a new study from Mayo Clinic, researchers found (based on MRI scans) that the brains of adults who consumed the most foods typical of a Mediterranean diet for a year—legumes, fish, whole grains and vegetables—had greater thickness in some parts of the cortex, which plays a role in memory, language and other cognitive functions. People who ate large amounts of carbohydrates, sugar and/or red meat had less cortical thickness.

Reading May Help You Live Longer

People who read books for more than three-and-a-half hours per week were 23% less likely to die during a recent study's 12-year follow-up period, compared with those who did not read at all. On average, book readers lived 23 months longer than nonreaders.

Study of 3,635 people by researchers at Yale University, New Haven, Connecticut, published in *Social Science & Medicine.*

And stress reduction?

In studies of older adults, those who participated in an eight-week meditation training program had improved connectivity between the frontal lobes and the hippocampus and other brain structures, which improves memory. It's possible that other relaxing practices, such as yoga, have similar effects. We're hoping to study this more.

How important is sleep?

Very! People who don't sleep well will obviously find it difficult to focus their attention and obtain and retain memories. Also, the brain consolidates memories during sleep (particularly during the deep, slow-wave stages of sleep)—the memories are shifted to brain regions where they become more stable.

It's important to remember, though, that we all require different amounts of sleep. Most adults seem to do best when they get seven to nine hours of sleep a day.

Any other advice?

Socialize. Studies show that adults who regularly connect with friends are less likely to develop dementia. Working past typical retirement age and/or volunteering after retirement also keeps older brains engaged.

More Muscle = Less Disease: The Stay-Strong Formula Proven to Work

Douglas Paddon-Jones, PhD, a professor in the department of nutrition at The University of Texas Medical Branch at Galveston, where he is the director of the physical activity and functional recovery translational research laboratory. His research focuses on mechanisms that promote skeletal muscle protein synthesis and treatments that counteract muscle loss.

Have you ever stopped to think about what it is that makes people look old? Aside from superficial physical characteristics (such as gray hair and saggy jowls), the culprit that doesn't get nearly enough attention is the decade-by-decade loss of muscle mass.

Age-related muscle loss, known as sarcopenia, changes more than just your appearance. It is a slow, insidious process that can rob you of 1% of your muscle mass each year after age 40. It makes it harder to lift things...and more challenging to walk and maintain your balance.

Perhaps the biggest threat is that sarcopenia makes it harder to stay physically active, leaving one at increased risk for at least 35 chronic diseases ranging from heart disease, stroke, diabetes and arthritis to erectile dysfunction, cognitive dysfunction, depression and certain types of cancer.

DIET COMES FIRST

Many people assume that simply hitting the gym will help them preserve their muscles. That's simply not true. To maintain (or increase) muscle mass, you need both exercise and protein. In fact, dietary changes are the smartest place to start because they'll give your body the raw materials that it needs for muscle maintenance. *My advice...*

- **Increase protein.** The recommended dietary allowance calls for 0.8 g of protein per kilogram of body weight each day. (That's about 51 g for a 140-pound woman...or 65 g for a 180-pound man.) But that's not enough for people with sarcopenia. I recommend that adults with sarcopenia (or those at risk) get closer to 80 g to 90 g daily. Men and those who are physically active should check with their doctor about getting even more than this amount.

Caution: People with kidney disease or other medical conditions may need to limit their protein intake. Ask your doctor for advice.

To make it easier: Don't focus on total daily protein. Just make an effort to get 25 g to 30 g of protein with every meal—your body can only utilize about this amount of protein at a time to repair and build muscle tissue. If you need more, enjoy a protein-rich snack between meals.

Good protein sources: A four-ounce serving of lean chicken or pork will provide about 30 g of protein. You'll get about 22 g from three ounces of salmon...11 g from one-half cup of pinto beans...and 12 g from one ounce of soy nuts.

- **Consider a supplement.** I mainly recommend food-based sources of protein, but people who have special needs—those who have trouble chewing, for example, or those who don't have the appetite for adequate meals—can take advantage of protein powders or bars. A scoop of plain whey protein powder (with added honey or fruit for flavor) contains 20 g to 30 g of protein.

Important: Read the label, and avoid products that are high in sugar or fat. Choose one labeled "contains all essential amino acids." Amino acids serve as building blocks for protein used in the body.

- **Always eat breakfast—and make it hearty.** Many people skip it altogether...or make do with a bagel or a bowl of sweet cereal. Get in the habit of starting the day with a few eggs (two will provide about 12 g of protein), along with yogurt (11 g per cup of regular yogurt), almonds (6 g per ounce) or other protein-rich foods.

Another good option: A breakfast burrito made with beef, beans, cheese and eggs.

- **Meat makes it easier.** Animal-based proteins are complete—they contain all of the essential amino acids. People who eat meat don't have to give protein a second thought as long as they meet the per-meal requirement of 25 g to 30 g.

But can you get enough protein if you're a vegetarian or vegan? Absolutely—but you'll have to be aware of the amino acids that are found in different foods, and you'll generally need to consume larger amounts because plant foods contain less protein than meats.

Helpful hint: Eat complementary proteins—food combinations that provide all the essential amino acids needed to build protein in the body. For example, legumes combined with whole grains (such as lentil soup with whole-grain bread) will provide all the amino acids. So will combining dairy with grains or nuts (such as yogurt and granola).

MUSCLE-BUILDING FORMULA

Muscle loss occurs slowly, in part because people tend to reduce activity without realizing it. They start taking elevators instead of stairs... doing less yard work, etc.

Studies have shown that people who are physically active are less likely to develop sarcopenia—or they get it to a lesser degree—than those who are sedentary.

The best way to maintain and increase muscle mass is with protein—and resistance training.*

The American College of Sports Medicine recommends lifting weights two to three days a week—with eight to 15 repetitions of each exercise.

My take: Resistance training doesn't need to be limited to lifting weights. Exercise that uses body weight, such as workouts with resistance bands, yoga, Pilates or even taking the stairs, is helpful.

THE RIGHT WAY TO EXERCISE

Slow walks and easy gym workouts will help maintain muscle, but they won't build it. To boost your strength and gain significant amounts of muscle, you need to do progressive resistance training (PRT). "Progressive" means that you'll strive to lift heavier weights or increase the number of repetitions over time.

Example: When you can easily complete an exercise, it's time to add additional sets. Rather than stopping at 15 repetitions, rest for two or three minutes, then do 15 more.

*Check with your doctor before beginning any exercise program.

Another choice: Increase the weight by 5% to 10% so that you can barely repeat the exercise eight times. Stay at that weight until you can easily do 15 repetitions. Then raise the weight again.

After about four or five months of PRT, people with sarcopenia will often add a few pounds of muscle, research has found. Once you've built muscle with PRT, talk to your doctor about a maintenance plan.

To get a postworkout boost: Have a glass of low-fat chocolate milk after intense exercise. It has about 24 g of carbohydrates and 8 g of protein—the 3:1 ratio that's thought to be ideal for muscle growth. The carbs will quickly provide glycogen (to replenish postexercise energy), and the protein will jump-start muscle growth and repair.

More Seniors Are Using Marijuana

Addiction.

Recreational marijuana use increased by 71% among adults over age 50 between 2006 and 2013.

One concern: The concurrent use of marijuana and prescription drugs could increase physical/mental problems in older adults.

Mouse Study Reveals Antiaging Vitamin

Science.

An "antiaging" vitamin revitalizes stem cells and could reverse age-related declines.

Details: Mice given nicotinamide riboside (a form of vitamin B-3) showed increases in muscle regeneration and longevity.

Makeup Tricks for Women Over 50...and Help for Men, Too

Gail Sagel, CEO of FACES Beautiful cosmetics company, Westport, Connecticut. She is a makeup artist and creator of Brush-On Liquid Mineral Makeup. Sagel is author of *Making Faces Beautiful* and *FACE IT: Five Essential Elements for Living Beautifully—Tips for Beauties Over 50.* FacesBeautiful.com

If you are using the same makeup and skincare regimen that worked for you 10 or 15 years ago, you may be looking older than you need to. As your skin texture and coloring change, your makeup and beauty routine should change, too. *Here, an expert's clever tips for looking fabulous...*

PRIMER AND FOUNDATION

If you have never used primer, now is the time to try it. Primer is a base for foundation that gives a smoother finish and helps your makeup last all day. First apply moisturizer, then primer, then foundation. *Also...*

•**Don't use a heavy foundation**—heavy products settle into creases and pores, emphasizing them. Choose a lightweight, creamy foundation, or try a tinted moisturizer instead of foundation. Avoid powder foundations, which can be drying to the skin and emphasize fine lines.

•**Get the right color.** You may have heard that foundation color should be matched to the color of your neck, but that isn't a useful guideline for most women. Over time, many facial skin tones become progressively darker than the neck because the chin keeps sunlight from reaching the neck. A foundation color that is too pale looks artificial and aging.

Instead, find a foundation color that is midway between the color of your face and your upper chest. Also correct for ruddiness or sallowness by choosing a color that will help to neutralize these undertones.

Example: If your skin has pink or red undertones, choose a color with a very slight yellowish cast. If you are naturally sallow with yellowish undertones, choose a color with just a touch of pink, which will make your overall color more radiant.

•**When you are testing a foundation color,** go outside to see if the color looks natural in bright, natural light.

•**Use a foundation brush rather than your fingers to apply foundation.** A foundation brush distributes makeup more sparingly and more evenly, creating an effect that is both polished and natural. To apply, either put a small amount of foundation on your hand and dip the brush into it...or put a few dots of foundation on your face and then spread with the brush. Try both methods to see which one works best for you.

CONCEALER

Most women apply under-eye concealer before applying foundation. This can cause you to look older. Concealer, which typically is a heavier texture than foundation, will collect in the creases around the eye and call even more attention to wrinkles.

What to do: Apply your other makeup first. Then step back and look at your face closely to see where you need concealer. You may need it in only a few small spots, or you may not need it at all.

Be careful when choosing your concealer color. Don't choose one that is too pale compared with your foundation—lighter colors highlight wrinkles. Use a color that is a similar color or just a touch lighter. A concealer that has a small amount of peach or rose in the color is very helpful in hiding dark circles.

LINER AND EYE SHADOW

Eyes become angular with age. If you are using dark eye shadow to contour the orbital bone above the eye, you may be emphasizing those angles and adding years to your face. *Instead of classic contouring, I recommend the Side V eye shadow technique...*

1. Apply eyeliner along the lash line above and below your eye. Use a kohl pencil or a felt-tip liner—these glide much better than standard pencils, which pull at delicate eyelids. Or use eye shadow as a liner—put a drop of water on a fine brush, and dip the brush into an eye shadow that can be used either wet or dry.

2. Sweep a light-colored shadow along your upper eyelid, from the lash line up to the crease.

3. Using a color darker than the lid shadow but lighter than the liner, brush a sideways "V" on the outside of the lid, with the open part of the "V" facing in toward the nose. Then use a brush to blend the V from the outside corner of the eye inward. The sideways V gives eyes an uplifted appearance.

BROWS

Eyebrows thin out with age. Filling them in is recommended for a youthful, full brow. There are many brow-filling choices—brow balms, brow powders and brow pencils. Eyebrow pencils can make your brows look overdrawn and artificial. Brow balms and brow powders, which are applied with a small-angled brush, typically give the softest, most natural look.

LIPSTICK

The lipstick that you have been wearing may not be the most flattering one for you anymore. Experiment with new lip colors. If you always thought a certain shade was off-limits for your coloring, try it anyway. If you are used to wearing subtle colors, try a bright color...if you typically wear deep colors, see what a nude color looks like on you.

Go to the cosmetics counter, and say to the consultant, "If I were to buy two new lipstick colors, what would make me look more beautiful?" Lipstick is relatively inexpensive—buy those two colors, and see what reaction you get when you wear them.

Using a gentle exfoliator (see below) on the lips when you cleanse is a great way to keep your lip area smooth from wrinkles. To prevent lipstick "bleeding," apply foundation on your lips as well as the rest of your face...then put a small amount of pressed powder on your lips...then apply lipstick. A good long-wearing lip liner can help prevent lipstick bleeding, too.

Here's a trick: Apply lipstick first, then apply lip liner to the edges to define them. This also will make them appear more plump. This technique gives you younger- and fuller-looking lips, and it looks less harsh than outlining your lips first.

FOR MEN, TOO! EXFOLIATION MAKES SKIN LOOK YOUNGER

How men and women clean their facial skin affects how youthful they look. One secret to youthful, radiant skin is cleaning in a way that doesn't dry out your skin but actually forces exfoliation of the topical skin cells. Your body is constantly producing new skin cells and shedding old ones. Unfortunately, skin-cell turnover slows with age, leaving a buildup of dead skin cells that makes skin look dry and dull. Gentle daily exfoliation removes the older skin cells, revealing younger, more supple skin.

Men exfoliate by shaving, but to look their best, they need to exfoliate the rest of their face, as women do.

The simplest way to exfoliate is to clean with a gentle, hydrating, nonsoap, nondetergent facial cleanser using a clean, damp washcloth. A soap-based cleanser leaves buildup on your skin, contributing to the dull look.

At the end of each day, while applying a gentle facial cleanser, use the damp washcloth to gently massage cleanser into your skin. Rinse your face with lukewarm water.

Your skin should look slightly flushed after exfoliating but not bright red and inflamed. Too-rough treatment will damage the skin.

There are many types of exfoliators on the market. Not all of them are suggested for use on facial skin. Avoid using abrasive elements on your face such as loofahs and oatmeal scrubs, apricot scrubs or other cleansers containing abrasive elements. All of these have rough edges that can cause tiny lacerations on the face. But you can use these products on the rest of your body. Keep in mind that even pre-moistened towelettes, which seem mild, are made from paper, which can be harsh to older skin.

Facial cleansers and exfoliators containing fruit acids, such as mango, papaya and citrus extracts, are a very good choice for gentle exfoliation. Vitamin A topical serums and moisturizers stimulate more rapid turnover of skin cells, leading to a more youthful appearance. Start with a mild-strength product. Stronger ones may be too harsh for many skin types, especially older skin.

Parenthood an Elixir for Longevity?

Karin Modig, PhD, assistant professor, epidemiology, Karolinska Institute, Stockholm, Sweden.
Gisele Wolf-Klein, MD, director, geriatric education, Northwell Health, Great Neck, New York.
Journal of Epidemiology & Community Health, online.

It might not feel like it some days, but having children may ultimately help you live a little longer, a recent study suggests.

Parenthood appears to help delay death as you grow older, with parents living longer than those who are childless, Swedish researchers found.

The differences in longevity were not overwhelming, however.

For example, fathers were expected to live two years longer than non-fathers at age 60, while mothers were expected to live one-and-one-half years longer than non-mothers, according to the study.

By age 80, dads were expected to live about eight months longer and moms about seven months longer than non-parents, the findings suggested.

"Parents live longer than non-parents, even in the oldest ages," said lead author Karin Modig, PhD, an assistant professor of epidemiology with the Karolinska Institute in Stockholm.

This survival benefit occurs regardless of whether parents have a son or a daughter, the researchers said, although the study did not prove that having children causes the increase in lifespan.

STUDY DETAILS

Dr. Modig and her colleagues used national Swedish health data to track all men and women born between 1911 and 1925 in that country. The study wound up including nearly 705,000 men and more than 725,000 women.

The researchers compared life expectancy with marital status and parenthood, to see whether having a child influenced how long a person lived.

As expected, the study found that the risk of death rose for everyone as they got older. But the risk remained lower among those who had had at least one child than it was among those who were childless.

"The absolute difference in death risk between parents and non-parents increases with age between age 60 and 100," Dr. Modig said. "These differences persist into, and even grow larger, in old age."

At age 60, the difference in the one-year risk of death was 0.1% among men and 0.2% among women. By the age of 90, these differences had risen to 1.5% among men and to 1.1% among women.

POSSIBLE EXPLANATIONS

The researchers could not say exactly why having a child appears to increase life expectancy.

It's possible that parents have more healthy behaviors than childless people, Dr. Modig said. Childlessness also could be a sign of natural selection, indicating that people who don't have kids are subject to biological or social challenges that affect their life expectancy, she suggested.

A more likely explanation is that parents have adult children around to help care for them as they grow older, Dr. Modig said.

"Children probably provide important support to their aging parents," Dr. Modig said. "Aging individuals without children or other close kin maybe need to get extra support elsewhere."

The link between parenthood and death risk was found for both married and unmarried people, but seemed to be stronger for unmarried men.

Unmarried fathers might be relying more heavily on their children in the absence of a partner, the study authors suggested.

The study was published online in the *Journal of Epidemiology & Community Health.*

HUMANS ARE SOCIAL ANIMALS

Aging parents also probably benefit from more social interaction, thanks to their adult children and grandchildren, said Gisele Wolf-Klein, MD. She is director of geriatric education at Northwell Health in Great Neck, New York.

Social involvement has been shown to be critically important to healthy aging, she noted.

"We humans are social animals, for better or worse. We benefit and thrive from each other's company," Dr. Wolf-Klein said. "My hunch is it does not matter what you do with the kids. If you are exposed to a family, that will maintain you emotionally or physically."

Childless seniors can help extend their life by joining groups, volunteering and essentially building their own family, Dr. Wolf-Klein said. They also can reach out to programs that provide the kind of support one would expect from a son or daughter—for example, programs that help deliver groceries or drive you to doctor appointments.

"If you're childless, that doesn't mean you can't link yourself to a group," Dr. Wolf-Klein said.

info For more about healthy aging, visit the U.S. Centers for Disease Control and Prevention at https://www.cdc.gov/aging/index.html.

The Dangerous Truth About Calcium

Susan Levin, MS, RD, director of nutrition education for the Physicians Committee for Responsible Medicine, a Washington, DC–based nonprofit group dedicated to promoting preventive medicine, better nutrition and higher standards in research.

The calcium supplements that millions of Americans take for bone health may cause serious damage to the heart. That's the conclusion of the latest study examining the long-term risks of these supplements.

The research, published in *Journal of the American Heart Association*, found that people who supplement with calcium are more likely to develop arterial calcification than those who get their calcium from foods. Calcium that accumulates in the arteries can impair circulation and increase the risk for heart disease.

Yet an estimated 43% of Americans continue to supplement with calcium.

WHAT YOUR BONES REALLY NEED

It is a fact that Americans don't get enough calcium. Only 42% meet the estimated average daily requirement of 1,000 milligrams (mg) to 1,200 mg (the exact amount depends on age and gender). It's a serious problem because both women and men need calcium—along with exercise, vitamin D and other nutrients—to prevent bone weakness and osteoporosis, a leading cause of disability and fracture-related deaths.

But supplements aren't the answer for many people. They may slightly increase bone density, but they do little to reduce your risk for bone fractures. In a recent analysis of studies published in *BMJ,* researchers concluded that "evidence that calcium supplements prevent fractures is weak and inconsistent."

The calcium that you get from food is different. It enters the body slowly and in small amounts. That's very different from the calcium rush that you get from supplements. Also, food delivers a "package" that includes calcium along with dozens of other minerals and nutrients, including vitamins, proteins, fiber, amino acids and, in the case of plant foods, phytonutrients. It seems likely that our bodies benefit from nutritional complexity. You don't get this from single-ingredient supplements.

CALCIUM IN THE WRONG PLACES

In the *Journal of the American Heart Association* study, researchers analyzed medical tests that were done on more than 2,700 people who participated in a large heart disease study. They were looking for coronary artery calcium, a heart disease risk factor.

Your calcium score (as measured by a heart CT scan) should be zero. But as people age, levels of calcium-based plaque tend to accumulate in the aorta and other arteries. These levels increase more in people who take calcium supplements.

The study found that people who supplemented with calcium were 22% more likely to have increased coronary calcium scores over a 10-year period than those who didn't supplement. It wasn't the amount of calcium that mattered most—it was the type. People who did not take supplements but who got a lot of calcium from foods (more than 1,400 mg daily) were 27% less likely than those who consumed the least amount of calcium from foods to have calcium scores that indicated an elevated heart risk.

Calcium deposits affect more than just the heart. A high calcium score also has been linked to increased risk for cancer including cancers of the prostate, lung, colon, breast, skin, blood, uterus and ovaries. It also has been linked to lung disease and chronic kidney disease.

Example: A study published in *Journal of the American College of Cardiology: Cardiovascular Imaging* found that people with high coronary calcium scores were 70% more likely to develop kidney disease than those who had low scores.

Caveat: None of the calcium/heart disease studies prove conclusively that supplements increase risks. The only way to know for sure would be to conduct a randomized, double-blind clinical trial in which some participants would take supplements and others wouldn't and then track their health over time. This type of study will probably never be done. The evidence linking calcium supplements and heart disease has become so persuasive that it would be unethical to give supplements to people who don't need them.

WHEN CALCIUM MAKES SENSE

We know that many Americans don't get enough calcium in their diets and that some of these people will never try to get more in their diets. Can supplements take up the slack? Perhaps—but this makes sense only for people who absolutely need to supplement. Are you one of these people? *Here's how to know...*

•Get a workup first. Calcium supplements should be treated as cautiously as prescription drugs. If you're worried about osteoporosis, talk to your doctor. Have your blood-calcium levels tested. If you're deficient, you might be advised to use supplements. Your doctor also should advise you on how to get more calcium in your diet and when to decide if you need supplements.

•Focus on food. Some people—particularly those who have already been diagnosed with osteoporosis or who are at high risk for it—might be advised to supplement despite the possible increase in heart risks. But most people can get more than enough calcium from foods if they make a conscious effort.

Examples: One cup of low-fat yogurt has 415 mg of calcium...one cup of skim milk, 316 mg...one cup of boiled collard greens, 266 mg...one cup of white beans, 161 mg...and one cup of soy milk, 93 mg.

•Consider all of the calcium in your diet. The heart risks from supplemental calcium may be proportional to the dose. You don't want to take any more than you need to. Suppose that you're trying to get 1,200 mg of calcium in total each day. You're already getting some calcium from foods. Keep that in mind before choosing a calcium dose. Why take a high-dose supplement if you need only an extra 200 mg a day?

My advice: Work with a nutritionist to help you find out how much calcium you actually consume in an average day. Or use the Internet—the USDA has a good calcium-content list at NDB.NAL.USDA.gov and click on "Food Search."

If you supplement, keep the doses low—your body can't absorb more than 500 mg at a time. Calcium carbonate has the highest amount of calcium (40% calcium) compared with calcium citrate (21% calcium). But citrate may be better tolerated by those with low stomach acids, which is common among people age 50 and older.

•Get vitamin D and magnesium, too. These help with absorption of calcium. Milk and many breakfast cereals are D-fortified. You also can get vitamin D from sunshine—between five and 30 minutes (depending on your skin type and age) twice a week is probably enough. Or your doctor may advise you to take a vitamin D supplement. There are different types of vitamin D (vitamin D-2, vitamin D-3). It doesn't matter which type you take—research has shown both types to be effective.

Magnesium helps with calcium absorption, too, but you don't need a magnesium supplement. You just need adequate magnesium in your diet. Magnesium is readily available in whole grains, nuts, seeds, beans and leafy greens.

•Don't forget to exercise. Physical activity slows the rate of bone loss in men and women with osteoporosis, and it's among the best ways to strengthen bones before they get weak.

Weight-bearing exercises (such as walking, jogging and weight-lifting) are more efficient for strengthening bones than other types of workouts (such as biking or swimming).

Recommended: 30 to 40 minutes of walking or other weight-bearing exercises most days of the week.

Stand Tall and Live Longer!

Steven Weiniger, DC, managing partner and instructor at BodyZone.com, an organization devoted to improving posture as a way to promote health and longevity. Dr. Weiniger is also author of *Stand Taller–Live Longer: An Anti-Aging Strategy* and developer of the new app PostureZone.

Once you move out of your mother's house, probably no one reminds you to stand up straight. But good posture is not only important for looking your best, it's also essential for good health!

Why: As human beings, our bodies are designed to stand upright, a position that helps us maintain balance. When your shoulders are hunched, you have an increased risk for falls. Plus, hunching causes other parts of your body to compensate to restore balance, which can result in upper and lower back pain, neck pain, headaches and other aches. Additionally, some research has linked bad posture to reduced lung function, poor circulation, digestive issues and much more.

WHY WE HUNCH

Let's face it—hunching is easier than standing up straight. Over the years, your body settles into its most comfortable position, and that becomes your "normal." The problem with this comfortable position is that it contributes to atrophy of the hip, shoulder, upper back and core muscles because they aren't being used to hold your body in alignment. Year by year, this muscle atrophy makes slumping more exaggerated and can lead to the health problems mentioned above.

Modern life also contributes to hunching. According to a 2016 Nielsen report, we spend an average of three hours each day hunched over a smartphone, computer or tablet...and another four hours slouched in front of a TV.

HELP FOR THE HUNCH

To develop good posture and lose the hunch, you need to strengthen the muscles mentioned earlier that help make standing up straight second nature. This simple routine takes no more than about four minutes to complete. If you do the exercises daily, you will start showing results in as little as two weeks.

EXERCISE 1—STABILIZE SHOULDERS DOWN

- **Lie flat on your back on a mat on the floor,** legs extended or knees bent (whatever is most comfortable), with your arms in a "T" position (elbows should be in line with your shoulders). Your face needs to be parallel to the ceiling.
- **Bend your elbows so that your fingers point toward the ceiling and your palms face your feet.**
- **Keeping your elbows on the floor,** pull your shoulders down toward your feet. Then bring your palms toward the floor as far as you comfortably can while keeping your shoulders down. Hold the position for three to five breaths (see the next page for the proper breathing technique).

EXERCISE 2—OPEN CHEST UP

- **Lie flat on your back and bend your elbows** so that your fingers point toward the ceiling and your palms face your feet as in Exercise 1.
- **Bring your hands backward toward the floor as far as you comfortably can.** Your arms will be in a "goalpost" position.

Important: Keep your shoulders down as in Exercise 1. Do not shrug them.

Do this three to five times. Inhale as you point your fingers to the ceiling, and exhale as you bring your hands toward the floor.

EXERCISE 3—FLOOR ANGELS

- **Lie flat on your back as above,** but with your arms flat on the floor in a goalpost position.
- **Keeping your forearms parallel,** and your shoulders on the floor, slide your arms up

and down on the floor. Again, do not shrug your shoulders while performing this exercise.

Do this three to five times. Inhale as you slide your arms up, exhale as you slide your arms down.

Once you master this, make the exercise more challenging by holding and stretching an elastic exercise band between your hands as you move your arms up and down.

EXERCISE 4—PINKIE TOUCH

•**Lie facedown on the floor,** with your forehead resting on the floor. Your arms should be straight at your sides with palms facing down.

•**Keeping shoulders down and elbows straight,** move your hands together beneath your torso so that your pinkie fingers are touching. (You'll have to raise your hips a bit to give your hands room to move.) Hold this position for three to five breaths.

BETTER BREATHING

As you perform these exercises, it's important to breathe from the belly, not the chest.

Why: When you breathe from the chest, your shoulders naturally hunch...but when you breathe from the belly, your shoulders stay in place.

To get the hang of belly breathing: Stretch an elastic exercise band across your lower back, with an end in each hand. Then crisscross the band in front of you, across your waist, about the level of your navel (you will need to exchange the band ends in your hands). Keeping your elbows bent at your sides, make the band snug but not tight. If you are breathing correctly, as you inhale, you will feel your belly pressing against the band, while your chest remains still. Exhale through pursed lips as your belly deflates.

HOW TO MONITOR YOUR POSTURE

To track changes in your posture, ask a friend to take an annual photo of you from the front and side. Or use PostureZone, a free app.

SELF-TEST FOR HUNCHING

Even people who don't think that they hunch their shoulders probably slump to some degree. *Try this simple exercise to find out if you're slumping (you can do this while standing or sitting)...*

•**First,** bring your shoulders forward and in toward your chest, and then bring them up toward your ears. This is an exaggerated hunch.

•**Next, pull your shoulders back and down toward your feet.** This is how your shoulders should be positioned for good posture. If this position feels uncomfortable or painful, you may have a hunching problem.

Feeling Blue?

Optometry and Vision Science.

You may want to get your eyes checked.

Recent finding: Older adults with cataracts were up to 50% more likely to suffer from depressive symptoms.

Your Vision Is Great... Time for an Exam!

Study titled "Value of Routine Eye Examinations in Asymptomatic Patients" by researchers at University of Waterloo, Ontario, Canada, published in *Optometry and Vision Science.*

It's been a few years—OK, let's be honest, more than a few years—since you last had a comprehensive eye exam. But you can see fine with your current prescription. What are the odds that you really need a new exam?

Glad you asked—it's 58%!

That's the finding of a Canadian study of more than 2,500 people who went for a routine comprehensive eye exam. They were all "asymptomatic," meaning that they had no preexisting condition such as an eye disease or diabetes that would require more frequent eye exams.

The last time the 40- to 64-year-olds had been examined was nearly three (2.9) years earlier, on average. For those 65 and older, it was between one and one-and-a-half years earlier. *Findings...*

•**41% needed new spectacle prescriptions.**

•**16% had new "critical" diagnoses,** such as glaucoma or cataracts.

•**31% needed new "management,"** such as a referral to another doctor or a new treatment.

Put it all together and a full 58% of those who went in for a routine eye exam had some benefit from the visit. The older the patient, the more likely the exam turned up something, even if just a prescription change.

HOW OFTEN SHOULD YOU GO FOR AN EYE EXAM?

The American Academy of Ophthalmology recommends that "asymptomatic" men and women get a comprehensive eye exam (which includes checking for glaucoma, age-related macular degeneration and cataracts)...

Age 40 through 54: Every two to four years.

Age 55 through 64: Every one to three years.

Over 65: Every one to two years.

The recent research suggests that it may be prudent to follow the earlier side of those ranges. If your eye doctor recommends more frequent exams based on a specific condition or your health history, follow that advice instead, of course.

We're not talking about just getting your prescription tested by an optician—a full exam can pick up a long list of eye conditions, the earlier the better. The older you are, studies show, the more likely these exams will help not just adjust your prescription but reduce your risk for vision loss. In short, it's an appointment that could save your sight.

Delicious Dry-Eye Remedy

***Pterostilbene* (PS)**, a compound in blueberries, has been found to fight the oxidative damage linked to dry eye.

Details: When PS was added to corneal epithelial cells in the lab, oxidative damage was significantly reduced, curbing the inflammation that leads to dry eye.

Tip: Eat one-half cup of fresh or frozen blueberries daily.

De-Quan Li, MD, PhD, associate professor of ophthalmology, Baylor College of Medicine, Houston.

Stave Off Cataracts

Jeffrey Anshel, OD, optometrist in private practice in Encinitas, California, and author of *Smart Medicine for Your Eyes.*

One of the leading causes of vision loss in older adults, cataracts can only be removed with surgery. But they tend to grow very gradually, and you may be able to slow their progression.

Vitamins C and E and the carotenoids lutein and zeaxanthin have, in some cases, delayed progression of cataracts for 10 years or more. Your doctor can recommend an optimal supplement dosage, but you can reap the benefits of these nutrients by including them in your diet. Citrus fruits, strawberries and broccoli are high in vitamin C. Wheat germ, almonds and sunflower seeds are good sources of vitamin E. Get lutein and zeaxanthin in leafy greens.

Since ultraviolet light raises the risk for cataracts, also be sure to protect your eyes with sunglasses that block both UVA and UVB rays.

Stem Cells for Better Vision

The Association for Research in Vision and Ophthalmology.

Stem cells taken from the skin on a patient's arm and transplanted into the eye slightly improved vision—an important advance for treating macular degeneration, a leading cause of blindness.

My Eye Color Has Changed

Brett Levinson, MD, an ophthalmologist and cornea specialist in private practice in Baltimore. SpecializedEyeCare.com

Eye color (the color of the iris) does not normally change with time. However, as some people grow older, a change in the appearance of the cornea (the clear covering over the front of the eye) can cause the eyes to appear to have a bluish tint.

This condition, called arcus (or arcus senilis or arcus corneae), is harmless and often occurs with age.

Fat deposits in the cornea can cause a visible grayish-blue arc. This appears on the cornea where the white meets the iris. Arcus can start out as a partial arc and eventually become a complete circle, giving the appearance of a blue eye color when someone looks at his/her own eyes in the mirror. But on a comprehensive eye exam by an eye doctor, the iris color will appear the same and the arcus can be seen on the cornea.

Arcus does not affect vision and requires no treatment. In adults over age 60, arcus occurs for no known reason except for aging.

However, when arcus appears in younger people (under age 40), the condition can be a sign of high cholesterol levels that may require treatment.

Also: People who have blue eyes can have a darkening of the iris color due to prostaglandin analog drops, such as *latanoprost* (Xalatan), used to treat glaucoma...or Latisse, a prescription product that lengthens and darkens eyelashes. In rare cases, the prostaglandin that is also an ingredient in Latisse may get into the eye and affect iris pigmentation. These changes can be permanent.

Hearing Loss Is Becoming Less Common

Howard J. Hoffman, director, epidemiology and statistics program, National Institute on Deafness and Other Communication Disorders, Rockville, Maryland, and leader of a study published in *JAMA Otolaryngology-Head & Neck Surgery.*

Hearing loss is becoming less common despite the aging US population and widespread use of headphones and earbuds. Nearly 16% of Americans had hearing loss between 1999 and 2004...compared with 14.1% in 2011–2012.

Pain Relievers Linked to Hearing Loss

Brian M. Lin, MD, a resident in the department of otolaryngology at Massachusetts Eye and Ear/Harvard Medical School, Boston, and leader of a study of pain-reliever use in 55,850 women, published in *American Journal of Epidemiology.*

Pain relievers linked to hearing loss, warns Brian M. Lin, MD. Women who used over-the-counter pain relivers twice a week or more for six years were 16% more likely to report hearing problems than those who took aspirin or no pain reliever. The exact reason for this link is unknown.

The Cochlear Implant Solution

Virginia Ramachandran, AuD, PhD, adjunct assistant professor of communication sciences and disorders, Wayne State University, Detroit.

If hearing loss is a problem for you, a cochlear implant is an excellent option. A cochlear implant is surgically inserted into the inner ear and receives signals from a speech processor that is typically worn on the ear, much like a hearing aid. Electrical impulses generated by the implant directly stimulate the auditory nerve, which sends signals that the brain recognizes as sound. The implant bypasses the damaged inner ear, so many people experience better hearing with an implant than with hearing aids.

With a cochlear implant, the brain must learn to use the signals that are received, which will sound very different than what it is used to. A speech-language pathologist can help you learn to interpret these sounds.

Is There a Ringing in Your Ears?

Murray Grossan, MD, an otolaryngologist at Tower Ear, Nose & Throat in Los Angeles. DrGrossanTinnitus.com

Tinnitus is the perception of ringing, clicking, buzzing or other noise in the ears when no sound is present. It's a fairly common condition that is usually caused by age-related hearing loss, ear damage or certain medications, such as nonsteroidal anti-inflammatory drugs (NSAIDs), including aspirin...loop diuretics...and some antibiotics. Tinnitus that comes and goes may be somatosensory tinnitus, a form of this condition that is caused by external stimulation of nerves in the ear. There is generally no hearing loss or vertigo involved.

Many things can trigger somatosensory tinnitus. Earwax can accumulate in the ear canal and press on the eardrum and auditory nerves. A drop or two of baby oil, eardrops or a warm saline solution applied with a syringe irrigator can soften earwax so that it will come out of the ear. Muscle tension in the face and back of the neck can irritate the auditory nerve. Briefly massaging these muscles when you feel tense may be all that you need to do to avoid tinnitus.

You may also have the jaw joint condition temporomandibular joint (TMJ) disorder, which has been linked to somatosensory tinnitus. While looking in a mirror, put a finger or two in front of each ear at the jawbone, then open and close your mouth. Do you hear the tinnitus sound? If so, the sound you hear may be the cracking of the jaw or another sensation caused by TMJ. Is the spot tender or painful? Is your jaw evenly centered when you open your mouth? If any noise, pain or misalignment causes concern, you may want to consult an otolaryngologist who can provide treatments, such as a mouth guard or exercises to help stretch and strengthen the jaw.

Same-Day Hip Surgery

Matthew S. Austin, MD, an orthopedic surgeon and director of Joint Replacement Services at Thomas Jefferson University Hospital in Philadelphia. He is program director of the Joint Replacement Fellowship at the Rothman Institute and a professor in the department of orthopaedic surgery at Sidney Kimmel Medical College at Thomas Jefferson University.

Until recently, people who needed a hip replacement were operated on in a hospital, spent a few nights there and then went home or to a rehabilitation center to embark on a recovery period of up to three months or more.

Now: An increasing number of people are receiving so-called "same-day" hip surgery—you arrive at a hospital or outpatient center in the morning, have the surgery (typically lasting about an hour or so), spend a few hours recovering from anesthesia and then go home at the end of the day.* Even though this approach may sound appealing, it is not necessarily for everyone.

To learn more about same-day hip surgery, we spoke with Matthew S. Austin, MD, a leading orthopedic surgeon who performs both traditional and same-day hip replacements and researches optimal recovery methods.

First things first—who needs a hip replacement?

It's mainly done in patients with arthritis- or injury-related hip damage that causes persistent pain. Surgery is recommended when people can no longer do the activities they enjoy and/or when they're suffering from chronic pain that isn't relieved by medications or the risks of taking painkillers outweigh the benefits.

How is a hip replacement done?

In a nutshell, the arthritic joint is cut and removed and then replaced with a synthetic "ball-and-socket" that works much like a natural joint...and much better than an arthritic/damaged joint.

Most hip replacements (including same-day surgeries) are done posteriorly. The surgeon enters the back of the hip to access the hip joint.

*If you go to an outpatient center, look for one that's affiliated with a major medical center and/or has accreditation from the Accreditation Association for Ambulatory Healthcare.

The incision is typically about six to 10 inches long, although the same procedure can now be done with smaller incisions.

The operation can also be done anteriorly, with an incision on the front part of the hip...or anterolaterally (on the side). With these two techniques (both of which usually require an incision of about four inches or less), the surgeon moves muscles instead of cutting and reattaching them. A surgeon who's experienced in any of these three surgeries can complete the operation in about an hour.

Is there a preferred technique for same-day surgery?

It makes no difference. The different surgeries have similar success rates—roughly 20 years after surgery, about 85% will still have their implant. Same-day surgery is a different process, not a different surgery.

What do you mean by "process"?

It has to do with the care that's given during the time before and after surgery. The same-day approach involves more of a team effort than conventional surgery...and the process begins well before the actual operation.

Patients have to be medically optimized to reduce the risk for complications and allow them to recover at home instead of in the hospital. A diabetic patient, for example, will be encouraged to stabilize his/her blood sugar before having the surgery. Someone who's obese might be advised to lose weight. Even though these recommendations also apply to people having a conventional hip surgery, they are crucial if a patient wants to go home the same day as the surgery.

The same-day approach also requires an extensive support system. Patients having same-day surgery might meet with team members, such as nurses and physical therapists, to learn such things as how to get around on crutches (usually needed for a couple of weeks)...how to safely climb stairs...how to bathe and use the toilet...and how to manage postsurgical nausea. A discharge planner will ensure that they have adequate support at home—for example, a spouse or a friend who can help them with meals, etc.

In addition, you're encouraged to stay in close contact with doctors, nurses and other support staff. A nurse or doctor should be available 24/7 to answer questions.

Isn't this riskier than staying in the hospital?

Not necessarily. As long as patients are ready for the procedure—in terms of overall health, at-home support, etc.—they'll do about the same as hospitalized patients. The overall complication rate—from blood clots, joint dislocation, poor wound healing or infection—is less than 5% in both same-day and conventional hip replacements.

Who should—or shouldn't—have same-day surgery?

A patient who's 85 years old, lives alone, can barely get around the house and has a variety of health problems would probably be advised not to go home the same day.

On the other hand, a 50-year-old who's in great shape will probably be physiologically able to go home the same day—but you have to consider motivation, as well. It may be easier for some in a hospital, where help is a button-push away.

What about recovery?

The evidence suggests that it's about the same regardless of the type of hip replacement. You can expect to walk a bit soon after surgery, while full recovery might take three months or more. Patients may do physical therapy exercises to strengthen the thighs and hips for six weeks or more.

Do all medical centers offer same-day surgery?

It's not available everywhere, so you'll have to ask your primary care doctor or surgeon or call around. Insurance coverage will probably be similar for inpatient and outpatient procedures.

Important: Whether or not you're considering same-day surgery, choose a board-certified surgeon who does at least 50 hip replacements a year. Studies have found that that's the number at which complication rates start to level off.

Also make sure that the surgeon is experienced in the same type of surgery (anterior, anterolateral or posterior) that you are getting.

To find an experienced surgeon: Check the website of the American Academy of Orthopaedic

Surgeons, AAOS.org...or the American Association of Hip and Knee Surgeons, AAHKS.org.

Make Your Brain Younger

Clinton Wright, MD, scientific director, Evelyn F. McKnight Brain Institute, University of Miami.

Older adults who did regular moderate-to-intense exercise like running or swimming laps had the memory and other cognitive skills of someone a decade younger than those who were sedentary or did light exercise such as gardening, a recent study of 900 older adults found.

Possible reason: Exercise boosts blood flow to the brain and enhances brain cell connections. It also lowers risk for high blood pressure, elevated cholesterol and diabetes—all of which can impair cognitive function.

A Nap After Lunch Makes You Smarter

Junxin Li, PhD, Center for Sleep and Circadian Neurobiology, Perelman School of Medicine, University of Pennsylvania, Philadelphia. Coauthor of the study "Afternoon Napping and Cognition in Chinese Older Adults: Finding from the China Health and Retirement Longitudinal Study Baseline Assessment," published in *Journal of the American Geriatrics Society.*

Afternoon naps are no longer guilty pleasures. Recent research finds that a post-lunch snooze, if it's not too long, is very good for the brain...especially if you're older. Smart napping might even keep your mind younger.

Background: In Spain, China and many other countries, an afternoon nap after lunch is a time-honored cultural tradition, especially for older people. While it's known that short "power naps" of 10 minutes or so can improve alertness and accuracy when performing mental tasks, the jury has been out on the cognitive effects of these longer siesta-type naps.

Study: American researchers studied 3,000 Chinese adults age 65 and older. They were asked to recall their postlunch napping (if any) over the previous month and were then classified as nonnappers, short nappers (less than 30 minutes) moderate nappers (30 to 90 minutes) and long nappers (more than 90 minutes). They were all given cognitive tests that included basic math, memory exercises and copying drawings.

Results: While 60% of the subjects regularly took postlunch naps, not all had cognitive benefits. The sweet spot for optimal performance on brain function tests was a moderate nap of more than 30 but less than 90 minutes. They did better on the cognitive tests than nonnappers, shorter nappers and longer nappers. Second best were the shorter nappers, who had better cognitive test scores than either nonnappers or long nappers.

Surprising finding: Compared with nonnappers/long nappers, the moderate nappers performed on cognitive tests like people who were five years younger.

Bottom line: If you can swing it, take a 30- to 90-minute snooze after lunch—your brain will thank you! The researchers cite other studies to explain what happens. You may wake up feeling a little groggy—it's called "sleep inertia"—but once you fully wake up, your cognitive functioning will be improved for the next 24 hours.

Bonus: Afternoon naps can reduce blood pressure and even are linked to a lower risk for heart attacks and stroke, other studies have found.

The One Sleep Habit That Most Helps Your Health

Study titled "Smoking, Screen-Based Sedentary Behavior, and Diet Associated with Habitual Sleep Duration and Chronotype: Data from the UK Biobank" by Freda Patterson, PhD, assistant professor of biobehavioral health and nutrition at University of Delaware, Newark, and colleagues published in *Annals of Behavioral Medicine.*

If you're trying to live a healthier life and resist the temptation to gobble down that extra piece of chocolate cake tonight and then blow off your workout tomorrow morning...here's a tip from the world of behavioral health science—go to sleep...earlier.

While lifestyle change is never easy, there's growing evidence that becoming less of a night owl and more of a morning lark is a good place to start. Hitting the sack earlier may not only help you get more sleep—a healthy thing in itself—but also make it easier to achieve other healthy lifestyle changes.

You've heard of gateway drugs. But an earlier bedtime may be the opposite...a gateway to healthier behavior.

Yes, you can change. Here's why you should—and how.

BODY CLOCKS, WATCHING TV AND WHAT YOU ATE LAST NIGHT

It's already well known that getting too little sleep, on a chronic basis, is strongly associated with an increased risk for heart disease, stroke, diabetes and other disorders. What the recent research found is that when you hit the hay is linked with three other behaviors that are major risk factors for disease.

The study, published in *Annals of Behavioral Medicine*, which analyzed data from 440,000 British adults, found that those who characterized themselves as "morning people" compared with "evening people" ate 25% more fruit and 13% more vegetables...and spent less time on sedentary activities such as watching TV (about 20 fewer minutes a day) and computer screens (about eight fewer minutes a day). "Morning people" also were 60% less likely to be smokers.

CAN BECOMING A LARK LEAD TO HEALTHIER HABITS?

While the study does not show cause and effect, the study's lead author, Freda Patterson, PhD, assistant professor of health promotion in the department of behavioral health and nutrition at University of Delaware, believes there are good reasons to think that poor sleep habits lead to poor lifestyle habits—not the other way around.

One reason is a body of research about how people use time. People who go to bed later, Dr. Patterson noted, tend to have expanded evening recreation time, which might involve eating less healthy foods late at night and staying on the computer late at night. (Ask yourself—are you more likely to be eating fruits and veggies during the day...or late at night in front of the TV? Are those extra hours at the end of the day likely to be the ones in which you're exercising?)

Physiology plays a role, too. If you've had too little sleep, you may feel sluggish and need an energy boost in the evening...and eating sugary foods may feel like just the ticket. Smokers might get a similar lift from nicotine. Inadequate sleep is also related to stress and anxiety, added Dr. Patterson, which people might "treat" with these bad habits.

A good goal may be to shift your bedtime a half-hour earlier in five- to 10-minute increments, said Dr. Patterson. You'll likely spend less time watching screens and munching, and you may find you have more energy the next day to resist food temptations, eat healthier and be more physically active. "If we can get people to improve sleep, it may percolate to also improve these other risk behaviors," says Dr. Patterson. "Sleep may be the behavior that could facilitate improvements in cardiovascular and metabolic health."

This Blanket May Help You Sleep

Study titled "Positive Effects of a Weighted Blanket on Insomnia" by researchers at University of Gothenburg, Sweden, published in *Journal of Sleep Medicine & Disorders*.

Michael J. Breus, PhD, a sleep specialist in Manhattan Beach, California. His latest book is *The Power of When* TheSleepDoctor.com

Brett Scotch, DO, an osteopathic physician specializing in sleep medicine and otolaryngology and director of Scotch Institute, Wesley Chapel, Florida.

Karen Moore, OTR, an occupational therapist and founder of The Sensory Connection Program in Franconia, New Hampshire.

Move over sleep meds—there's a new solution in town.

WEIGHTED BLANKETS

The comforting heavy covers, filled with small plastic balls that are sewn into compartments for even distribution, have been used for years to treat children with anxiety, ADHD, autism spectrum disorders and other disorders. Parents swear by them, especially to help kids sleep.

Now they're catching on as a simple DIY solution for healthy adults with sleep problems. The theory is that they provide "deep pressure" that helps you feel calmer and more relaxed, making it easier to fall asleep and stay asleep. You might think of it as a kind of swaddling—for grown-ups.

Do they work? Worth a try for better shut-eye? We investigated.

LESSONS FROM INSOMNIAC SWEDES

A recent study from the University of Gothenburg in Sweden looked at the effect of weighted blankets in 33 normal healthy adult men and women with chronic insomnia. Participants wore "actigraph" watches, which recorded the pattern of their movements when they went to bed, and they also kept sleep diaries. In the first week, they slept their usual way. Then for two weeks, they slept under weighted blankets of their choice, which ranged in weight from 13 pounds to 22 pounds—at least 12% of their body weight. During the fourth week, they went back to their normal sleeping conditions.

Results: When they used the weighted blankets, the sleepers spent more time in each phase of sleep, including truly restful deep sleep, and they moved around less during the night. According to their diaries, they found it easier to settle down to sleep, had better quality sleep and felt more refreshed in the morning.

While the Swedish study didn't take anxiety into account, the blankets have a documented calming effect, which may help explain how they enhance sleep, according to sleep expert Michael Breus, PhD. "Most people who have insomnia have some level of anxiety," he said. The sympathetic nervous system, which regulates the "fight or flight" reflex, is often easily aroused in people who have trouble sleeping, he explained. "A weighted blanket puts pressure on the mechanoreceptors—nerve endings under the skin—which sense pressure and signal muscles to relax. That makes us feel safe and supported."

SNUGGLING TIPS

Who's a good candidate to try a weighted blanket? Anyone who is in good health but has trouble falling asleep or staying asleep, according to Dr. Breus.

Who isn't: Anyone with a respiratory disorder (such as severe asthma) or a circulatory disorder, according to Brett Scotch, DO, an osteopathic physician specializing in sleep medicine and otolaryngology in Wesley Chapel, Florida. "The weight on your chest may impede your ability to breathe or decrease circulation to your extremities," he warned. (If you have any serious health condition, consult your doctor before sleeping with a weighted blanket.)

If you do decide to try getting under heavy covers, look for a blanket that weighs about 10% of your body weight or more, has a material that feels good to you and distributes the weight evenly to provide firm, constant tactile stimulation across your body. The blankets are widely available online, from companies such as Sommerfly and Mosaic Weighted Blankets, and cost around $140. "If you're claustrophobic, you may want to start with a lighter one and give it a chance," said Karen Moore, OTR, an occupational therapist and founder of The Sensory Connection Program in Franconia, New Hampshire.

Will it work for you? The Swedish study is relatively small and short-term, so this is not the definitive solution to insomnia. Ultimately, the only way to find out if a weighted blanket will help you get better shut-eye is to try it.

The good news: It's safe and free of side effects. And unlike with prescription sleep medications, there's no "rebound" problem—except, perhaps, to your wallet—if you decide it's not for you. Just stop using it.

Want to Look Four Years Younger?

Smile! In a recent study, 2,000 people were asked to estimate the age of women in photographs. A smile took two to four years off, while people with sad faces looked one year older.

DailyMail.com

CHAPTER 13

Medical Newsmakers

Is Your Body Clock Out of Whack?

The time you go to sleep at night and the time you wake up in the morning can be crucial to your health—and not only because you need enough sleep. It's also because you need to sleep at the right time of the night. For good health, you need to match your bedtime and wake-up times to your personal "clock genes"—genes that control your sleep/wake cycle along with many other biological fluctuations such as blood pressure and blood sugar. *If you don't, circadian disruption can result, putting your health in danger...*

CIRCADIAN DISRUPTION

Your biological rhythms are timed to Earth's 24-hour cycle of light and dark. But your body also runs on internally generated cycles that are a nearly perfect match for the 24-hour rhythm of day and night. Called circadian rhythms, these internal cycles are governed by the suprachiasmatic nucleus (SCN), a "body clock" located in the hypothalamus region of the brain.

Responding to light and dark, the SCN sends signals to every part of your body, regulating when you fall asleep and wake up, when you're hungry, when blood sugar levels rise and fall, when hormones are released—in fact, nearly every biological and behavioral process is regulated by the SCN.

In addition, there are clock genes that produce proteins that regulate rhythms within cells—scientists estimate that 20% of all genes are involved in the body's rhythms. Clock genes help determine whether you tend to go

Phyllis C. Zee, MD, PhD, professor of neurology, neurobiology and physiology in the department of neurology at Northwestern University Feinberg School of Medicine in Chicago and director of the school's Center for Circadian and Sleep Medicine. She is coeditor of *The Handbook of Sleep Medicine* and has authored or coauthored more than 200 scientific papers and reviews on sleep disorders, chronobiology and health, published in leading medical journals.

to bed early and wake up early…or go to bed late and wake up late.

When the external rhythms of light and dark don't match your body's unique circadian rhythms—a condition called circadian disruption—your health suffers. Circadian disruption has been linked to many health problems (see below).

Fortunately, there are ways to prevent or reverse circadian disruption, including the following…

MATCH YOUR RHYTHM TO YOUR SLEEP SCHEDULE

Some people have clock genes that run slightly faster than the 24-hour day-night cycle, making them tired earlier in the evening. Some people have clock genes that run slower, making them tired later in the evening. Which are you?

How to tell: If you usually feel at your best—your most awake and alert—in the morning, you're what I call a "morning type." If you usually feel your best in the evening, you're an "evening type."

To be healthy, you must synchronize these genetic rhythms with your bedtime and wake-up time. In addition to timing, stability of sleep and wake times is important. When there's more than a two-hour difference between the time that is best for you to go to bed and when you actually go to bed, you're desynchronized—and your health is at risk.

What to do: Establish a bedtime and wake-up time that reflect whether you're a morning type (*Example:* A bedtime of 10:30 pm and 6:30 am wake-up time) or an evening type (*Example:* Midnight and 8:00 am). Don't vary those times by more than one-half to one hour. If you work full-time during the week, don't vary those times by more than two hours during the weekend.

GET MORE LIGHT

One study compared people who worked near a window with windowless workers and found that those next to windows had better overall health and slept an average of 46 minutes more per night during the workweek over a one-month period—because daily exposure to light helped prevent desynchronization.

What to do: Try to get natural light during the day. Even 15 or 20 minutes a day can help.

GET LESS LIGHT IN THE EVENING

While bright light in the morning and afternoon is synchronizing, bright light in the evening is desynchronizing—because it blocks the production of melatonin, a hormone that helps regulate the sleep-wake cycle.

Recent research: Exposure to artificial light at night was linked to a 52% increased risk for breast cancer. But reducing artificial light at night—by using a bedtime reading lamp instead of overhead lights, for example—decreased risk by 81%. And a study published in *International Journal of Obesity* found that exposure to artificial light at night was linked to a 97% increased risk for obesity.

What to do: Two to three hours before bedtime, turn off overhead lights to reduce brightness. Use table lamps instead.

At night, avoid the melatonin-suppressing "blue light" of electronic devices, such as computers, tablets and cell phones. LED TV screens give off blue light, too. If you must use blue-light devices at night, wear blue-blocking glasses or goggles, widely available online for less than $10. Or consider downloading an app such as f.lux or Twilight, both of which reduce blue light on your screens at night.

EAT REGULAR MEALS

A regular eating cycle is as important as a regular sleep-wake cycle in keeping you synchronized. Morning types tend to eat a big breakfast and smaller dinner. Evening types tend to favor dinner and skip breakfast.

What to do: Whatever your type, try to eat your three meals at about the same time every day.

Finish dinner at least four hours before bedtime. That habit not only helps you stay synchronized but also helps prevent weight gain—studies show the closer to bedtime you eat, the more likely you are to be overweight.

STRUCTURE YOUR DAY

In addition to regular mealtimes, regular times for socializing, exercising and other daily activities help prevent desynchronization, improving sleep and memory—particularly in people age 55 and older.

What to do: Exercise at the same time, several days a week. Get out of the house, and engage in regular, structured social activities such as going to the library or a place of worship. It's the day-to-day regularity of a structured schedule—doing one or more activities the same time every day, a minimum of three to four days a week—that helps create synchronization.

CONSIDER TAKING MELATONIN

Taking a melatonin supplement in the right dose at the right time can help restore synchronization and may benefit those evening types who can't fall asleep at bedtime.

What to do: Take one-half to one milligram of melatonin five to six hours before your desired bedtime—that's the right amount and timing to maximize melatonin levels at bedtime.

DANGERS OF CIRCADIAN DISRUPTION

Circadian disruption has been linked to many health problems, including...

- **Insomnia**
- **High blood pressure, heart attack and stroke**
- **Obesity and diabetes**
- **Memory problems, dementia and Parkinson's disease**
- **Depression and bipolar disorder**
- **Heartburn, IBS and other digestive diseases**
- **Asthma, emphysema and chronic bronchitis**
- **Poor recovery from surgery**
- **Weakened immune system**
- **Cancer**

Precision Medicine... Just for You

Keith Stewart, MB, ChB, the Carlson and Nelson Endowed Director of the Center for Individualized Medicine and the Vasek and Anna Maria Polak Professor of Cancer Research at the Mayo Clinic in Rochester, Minnesota. A specialist in blood cancers, he is author or coauthor of more than 250 scientific papers.

Modern medicine is more often than not formulaic. Everyone with a certain health problem—for example, heart disease or depression—gets basically the same standard treatment. Typically, this involves one or more medications within a related class of drugs.

New thinking: There's a fresh approach to diagnosis and treatment, variously called personalized medicine, individualized medicine or precision medicine. Rather than treating a disease based on a therapeutic formula, it takes into account a person's unique genetic makeup—his/her DNA, or genome—and customizes treatment to fit the individual.

Personalized medicine is still in its infancy, but some types of individualized diagnoses and treatments are now available...

PHARMACOGENOMICS

DNA testing can help determine whether or not your genes will impact the way a medication affects you. This field of drug-gene interactions is called pharmacogenomics—and it can benefit just about everybody who takes a prescription drug.

Breakthrough research: The Mayo Clinic recently conducted the RIGHT study (the right drug, at the right dose, used at the right time). In this investigation of more than 1,000 patients, 990 of them were discovered to have at least one genetic variant that could impact the way the body processes common medications.

Pharmacogenomics can help your physician determine the likely effectiveness of various drugs and pick the best one for you...choose the right dose for you...and spot possible side effects in advance, including life-threatening reactions that make the drug too risky to take.

At present, pharmacogenomic testing—a simple cheek swab, blood test or saliva test—can help evaluate the individual impact of more than 300 drugs.

Drugs commonly tested include: *Fluorouracil* (Efudex), for colon, skin and other cancers...*clopidogrel* (Plavix) and warfarin (Coumadin), blood thinners used to reduce heart attack and stroke risk...and antidepressants such as *fluoxetine* (Prozac) and *citalopram* (Celexa).

My advice: Before your doctor writes you a new prescription—or if you are having side effects from your current medication—ask about getting genetic testing. The cost of a pharmacogenomic test is becoming more affordable. Some labs are now able to offer the testing for as low as $250. Results are typically available in one to two weeks. Getting such testing done preemptively allows you to have the results at the moment they are needed.

Helpful: You can find a list of the drugs approved by the FDA for genetic testing at Genelex.com/patients/drugs/all.

CANCER

There are many ways that personalized medicine can assist in the treatment of cancer. Tailoring the treatment to the cancer's specific molecular variation is one such approach.

Example: Mayo Clinic research has shown that 65% of patients with various advanced cancers had a genetic target that could potentially be addressed by a matched drug specific to that patient and that cancer.

A cancer gene panel costs $300 to $5,000, depending on whether you are being tested for a specific gene or multiple genes. Insurance may cover all or at least part of this testing. Check with your insurer first.

If you have cancer: Ask your doctor whether having your DNA sequenced would provide information to improve your treatment—especially if your tumor(s) is not responding to treatment.

EARLY DIAGNOSIS

Personalized medicine is also about discovering health issues you may not know you have—so you and your doctor can do something about them to protect yourself.

For example, 25 managers at the Mayo Clinic Center for Individualized Medicine, who were all seemingly healthy, had their genomes sequenced. Five of them—20%—had medically relevant results.

One participant had a genetic predisposition to blood clots, putting that person at almost five times a greater risk for a heart attack or stroke. In another situation, the individual was found to be a carrier of a gene for cystic fibrosis—information that was passed on to the person's adult children so that they could decide whether or not to be tested for the same genetic variant (to determine their own risk and possibly that of any future offspring).

Another person had a genetic condition called malignant hyperthermia, which causes a fast rise in body temperature and severe muscle contractions when anesthesia is administered. Complications can include kidney failure, fluid buildup in the lungs, bleeding and even death. Using certain medications during surgery can prevent these problems.

Helpful: Consider having your genome sequenced to spot any potential, preventable health problems or inheritable conditions you would want your children or grandchildren to know about. Couples who are planning a family and want to understand their genetic risk for inherited diseases also should consider DNA testing. And families with a high risk for cancer may want to be assessed for a predisposition to certain cancers.

A MYSTERY ILLNESS EXPLAINED

In about 30% of cases, precision medicine can detect the cause of an otherwise mysterious disease.

For example, a young man recently treated at the Mayo Clinic had a problem with tremors and had gone from doctor to doctor for years, without getting effective treatment. With genetic testing, a mutation in the gene that controls the movement of potassium into and out of the body's cells was discovered. A potassium-lowering diuretic was prescribed, which significantly reduced the man's tremors.

If you have a mysterious illness or rare disorder—and have visited many doctors without getting a diagnosis and/or successful treatment—ask your doctor whether DNA testing might identify a genetic disorder.

How Your Genes Affect Your Diet

Sharon Moalem, MD, PhD, a physician, scientist and inventor based in New York City. He has served as an associate editor for the Journal of Alzheimer's Disease and has been awarded more than 25 patents for inventions in the fields of biotechnology and health. He is author of *The DNA Restart: Unlock Your Personal Genetic Code to Eat for Your Genes, Lose Weight and Reverse Aging.*

Have you ever wondered why a cup of coffee keeps you up at night, while your spouse downs cup after cup and sleeps like a baby? Or why a glass of wine with supper makes you tipsy, while your friends can keep sipping for hours?

You could chalk it up to random variation, but it's actually not random at all. It's largely determined by your genes. Research has shown that specific genes and gene "variants" (or mutations) can affect how your body metabolizes nutrients and other substances such as caffeine and alcohol.

For certain medical conditions, it's long been established that there is a genetic link to how specific nutrients are metabolized. For example, if you're among those of western European ancestry who have different versions of the HFE gene, it can cause you to absorb two to three times more iron than those without this genetic profile. Hereditary hemochromatosis, commonly known as iron overload disease, can be life-threatening—and is diagnosed, in part, with genetic testing.

But research research in the emerging field of nutrigenetics (the study of how individual genes affect nutrition) shows that there may be important genetic links to many more nutrients and substances than previously thought.

So far, scientists have identified hundreds of genes and gene variants that may affect how your body metabolizes different nutrients and substances.

The question is, can knowing this genetic information help people make smarter nutrition choices? Right now, the jury is still out, but some individuals find that testing helps them identify certain dietary tweaks that may improve their overall health. *Key nutrients and substances with genetic links...*

• **Folate.** Specific versions of the MTHFR gene slow the rate at which the body converts folate into a usable form of the vitamin. People who inherit this gene may be more likely to suffer a heart attack or stroke because of a folate deficiency.

Who might benefit from this test: If you have a personal or family history of heart attack, you may want to discuss this test and/or a blood test for folate deficiency with a nutritionist. If you test positive for the gene and/or a blood test identifies a folate deficiency, ask your doctor about taking a supplement with a methylated (active) form of folate.

• **Caffeine.** The body's ability to metabolize caffeine is controlled mostly by the CYP1A2 gene. People with a particular variant of this gene are "slow metabolizers"—they don't have the same ability to break down caffeine as other people. They might develop high blood pressure from drinking amounts of coffee or tea that wouldn't similarly affect a person without this gene.

Who might benefit from this test: If you have high blood pressure or become jittery when consuming caffeine, you may want to discuss this test with a nutritionist. If you test positive, you would likely benefit from reducing your intake of caffeinated beverages and foods.

• **Alcohol.** Research has found that moderate daily alcohol consumption—up to two alcoholic beverages for men...and up to one for women—can improve cardiovascular health.

But those who have the ALDH2*2 gene might want to disregard this finding. They don't have the same ability to detoxify an alcohol by-product (acetaldehyde), which increases their risk for a deadly esophageal cancer.

Who might benefit from this test: Anyone with Asian ancestry...risk factors for esophageal cancer (such as gastroesophageal reflux disease)...and those who notice their skin becoming red or flushed after drinking alcohol. If you test positive for this gene, avoid alcohol.

GETTING TESTED

A nutritionist or health-care professional (such as a doctor) can order a test kit for nutritional genetic testing online. You provide a saliva sample, and the kit is returned for analysis. The test usually costs a few hundred dollars to check for a set of genes that may have nutritional links. The professional who ordered the test will likely charge you for a follow-up consultation to discuss the results. These fees are unlikely to be covered by insurance.

SELF-TEST FOR ALCOHOL TOLERANCE

If you're interested in learning how your genes might affect the way your body metabolizes alcohol, there's a self-test I have developed based on genetic indicators found in one's earwax. It is not as accurate as genetic testing but will give you some basic information.

Moderate drinking (described in the main article) is considered good for the heart, but some people (such as many of those who become flushed while drinking) should never drink... and everyone's alcohol tolerance is highly individualized. How much alcohol (if any) is right for you?

Take my earwax test. Carefully swab some of your earwax and take a look. People with flaky, dry, gray earwax probably had ancestors from eastern Asia who rarely drank. Those with the wet type of earwax (it's a yellow/brownish color and is somewhat sticky) typically had African or European ancestors who drank alcoholic beverages routinely.

My advice: If you have dry earwax, the safest approach is for you to avoid alcohol altogether—your genetic profile does not prepare you to safely metabolize alcohol. Also, people in this group are likely to have inherited the gene that predisposes them to squamous cell esophageal cancer. For this reason, it's wise to forgo alcohol since it is an important risk factor for this type of cancer. If you have wet earwax, you are unlikely to have the same difficulty metabolizing alcohol.

Have Americans Given Up on Losing Weight?

Jian Zhang, MD, DrPH, associate professor, epidemiology, Georgia Southern University, Statesboro, Georgia.
Mitchell Roslin, MD, chief, obesity surgery, Lenox Hill Hospital, New York City.
Rajpal Chopra, MD, endocrinologist, Northwell Health's Long Island Jewish Forest Hills, Forest Hills, New York.
Journal of the American Medical Association.

More Americans are overweight or obese, but many have given up on trying to lose those excess pounds, a recent study shows.

One in every three people in the United States is now obese, compared with one in five 20 years ago, researchers report.

But people surveyed between 2009 and 2014 were 17% less likely overall to say they'd tried to lose weight during the previous year than those surveyed between 1988 and 1994, the study found.

People who were overweight but not yet obese have experienced the greatest loss of interest in maintaining a healthy weight, said senior researcher Jian Zhang, MD.

"This is not good. We are missing the opportunity to stop overweight from becoming obesity," said Dr. Zhang, who is an associate professor of epidemiology with Georgia Southern University.

STUDY DETAILS

Dr. Zhang and his colleagues analyzed data from the U.S. National Health and Nutrition Examination Survey, a federally funded ongoing survey that keeps track of Americans' health and diet habits.

All racial/ethnic groups across both genders reported decreased interest in weight loss, but women in particular were more likely to say they'd given up on it, the findings showed.

By 2014, black women were 31% less likely to have tried to lose weight compared with two decades prior, and white women were 27% less likely to have made the attempt, the researchers found.

NO MORE DIETING?

People might be giving up on weight loss because it's just too difficult, Dr. Zhang said.

"It's painful," he explained. "It's hard to drop pounds. Many of us tried and failed, tried and failed, and finally failed to try anymore."

Modern medicine also has gotten better at preserving the overall health of overweight people, perhaps causing them to ask why they should bother, Dr. Zhang continued.

"There's increasing evidence that adults with overweight may live as long as and sometimes even longer than normal-weight adults, making many question whether you have to take it seriously," Dr. Zhang said. "In clinical practice, we consider treatment of overweight only when patients have two or more additional risk factors," such as high blood pressure or high cholesterol.

It's also possible that overweight has become the new normal. "Today, we believe that majority are right," Dr. Zhang said. "As more than half of people are overweight, we simply think we are fine, and there's no need to do anything with body weight."

EXPERT COMMENT

Mitchell Roslin, MD, chief of obesity surgery for Lenox Hill Hospital in New York City, added that conflicting diet advice also probably dissuades many from attempting to drop some pounds.

"First they were told don't eat fat, and now we are telling patients to reduce simple carbohydrates," Dr. Roslin said. "While I believe that reducing carbohydrates is key, what the public hears is, 'I might as well eat what I like because all this advice has not worked.'"

According to Rajpal Chopra, MD, these numbers show that doctors, public health officials and the media need to do a better job emphasizing the importance of maintaining a healthy weight. Dr. Chopra is an endocrinologist with Northwell Health's Long Island Jewish Forest Hills, in Forest Hills, New York.

"The path to losing weight is often riddled with lots of ups and downs, and it can be a long and frustrating process. What has to be emphasized is the far-reaching health consequences," Dr. Chopra said.

"Motivation should come from family, friends, physicians and the media in educating about the health risks of being overweight," he added.

HEALTHY LIVING VS. WEIGHT LOSS

Dr. Zhang said that future efforts to improve public health should focus on lifestyle changes that promote healthy eating and exercise for everyone, rather than an emphasis on losing weight.

"It's hard to stop a train; it's hard to drop pounds and keep it off," he said. "We have to tackle overweight and obesity head on. Let's do more to prevent it from happening rather than dropping it off. If fixing a problem is not easy, then we must prevent it from happening, simple as that."

info For more about overweight and obesity, visit the U.S. Centers for Disease Control and Prevention at CDC.gov/obesity.

Cancer Drug Fights Sepsis

Icahn School of Medicine at Mount Sinai.

A minuscule dose of a topoisomerase inhibitor, a cancer drug, attacks the "inflammatory storm" caused by sepsis, a leading cause of death in the US.

Brain Chip Allows Movement in Paralyzed Man

Nature.

After a computerized chip was surgically implanted in his brain, a 24-year-old man who had lost the use of his legs and hands was able to focus his thoughts to move his hand. The finding may pave the way for new advances in "neural engineering."

First Successful Penile Transplant

The New York Times.

The first penile transplant in the US was successful. A 64-year-old man whose penis was amputated when cancer was diagnosed regained urinary function and normal genital appearance less than one month after transplant surgery at Massachusetts General Hospital. Sexual function may return over a period of months as the nerves regenerate.

New Devices Sense Illness

PLOS Biology.

Devices know you're sick before you do. New wearable sensors, similar to an Apple Watch, can detect changes—in heart rate, body temperature, etc.—that could indicate illness before you have symptoms.

Is Potential Human Life Span Unlimited?

McGill University, news release.

Have you ever thought about what it might be like to live into your hundreds?

Now, recent research says there's really no evidence of a limit on how long people can live, though people might need a boost from advances in health care or technology.

A study published recently in the journal *Nature* said that the maximum life span peaks at about 115 years, but a more recent study challenges that conclusion.

"It's hard to guess," said study author Siegfried Hekimi, PhD, from McGill University in Montreal. "Three hundred years ago, many people lived only short lives. If we would have told them that one day most humans might live up to 100, they would have said we were crazy."

The McGill biologists reviewed information on the longest-living people in the United States, the United Kingdom, France and Japan for each year since 1968 and found no evidence for an age limit.

Even if there is a maximum, it has yet to be reached or identified, according to the authors of the recent study, which was also published in *Nature.*

"We just don't know what the age limit might be. In fact, by extending trend lines, we can show that maximum and average life spans could continue to increase far into the foreseeable future," Dr. Hekimi said in a university news release.

He said it's impossible to predict how long people will live in the future, and noted that some scientists believe technology, medical interventions and improvements in living conditions could all increase the upper limit.

info The U.S. National Institute on Aging has more about longevity at www.nia.nih.gov/research/publication/global-health-and-aging/living-longer.

Read On...to Live Longer

Michael Roizen, MD, chief wellness officer at the Cleveland Clinic, with Rebecca Shannonhouse, editor, *Bottom Line Health.*

Most of us spend a good amount of time looking for habits and activities that will help us live longer, healthier lives.

Here's one that might surprise you: Joining a social group, such as a book club.

Book club members live longer, according to research published in *The BMJ.* Yes, really. It's not that readers are necessarily healthier than nonreaders...but getting together to talk about books appears to provide health-promoting effects that are comparable with those of regular exercise.

Surprising finding: When Australian researchers analyzed the habits of more than 400 adults who were transitioning into retirement, they found that those who attended two social groups—such as book clubs and church groups—had a 2% risk of dying over the six-year study period. When participants gave up one group, the risk rose to 5%...and to 12% if they gave up both groups.

Combining friendship with reading and other mental activities is a win-win because it lowers stress, increases serotonin (a feel-good brain chemical) and may even promote the growth of new brain cells.

"Companionship and intellectual stimulation—and thinking quickly during the book club discussions—all of these things are very healthy," explains Michael Roizen, MD, chief wellness officer at the Cleveland Clinic. So why not give it a try? Happy reading!

info To find a book club in your area, check with your local library and/or websites such as Meetup.com or ReadersCircle.org.

Remote Amazon Tribe May Have Healthiest Hearts on Earth

Gregory Thomas, MD, MPH, medical director, MemorialCare Heart & Vascular Institute, Long Beach Memorial, Long Beach, California.

Kim Williams, MD, immediate past president, American College of Cardiology, and chief, cardiology, Rush University Medical Center, Chicago.

Douglas Jacoby, MD, medical director, Penn Medicine Center for Preventive Cardiology and Lipid Management, Philadelphia.

The Lancet, online.

Presentation, American College of Cardiology annual meeting, Washington, DC.

A primitive Amazonian tribe appears to have the best heart health in the world, living a simple existence that inadvertently provides them extraordinary protection against heart disease, researchers report.

The Tsimane people of Bolivia lead an active life of subsistence farming and foraging for food in the Amazon rainforest, said study author Gregory Thomas, MD. He is medical director of the Memorial Care Heart & Vascular Institute at Long Beach Memorial in California.

Thanks to their unique lifestyle, most Tsimane have arteries unclogged by the cholesterol plaques that drastically increase the risk of heart attack and stroke in modern Americans, Dr. Thomas said.

CT scans revealed that hardened arteries are five times less common among the Tsimane than in US adults, Dr. Thomas said.

"We found that based on their lifestyle, 85% of this population can live their whole life without any heart artery atherosclerosis [hardening]," Dr. Thomas said. "They basically have the physiology of a 20-year-old."

The Tsimane also have lower heart rates, blood pressure, cholesterol and blood sugar levels compared with the rest of the world, Dr. Thomas added.

Dr. Thomas and his colleagues have been studying mummies for ancient evidence of heart disease, and have found hardened blood vessels in mummies as old as 3,500 years.

PEOPLE FREE OF HEART DISEASE DISCOVERED

The heart researchers learned of the Tsimane through anthropologists who have been studying the tribe, in a research effort led by Hillard Kaplan, a professor at the University of New Mexico.

"Kaplan and his team felt they had rarely seen any heart disease in this Amazonian tribe," Dr. Thomas said. "They'd only heard of one heart attack that had happened."

Skeptical but intrigued, Dr. Thomas said his team arranged for just over 700 Tsimane to travel by river and jeep from the Amazon rainforest to Trinidad, a city in Bolivia and the nearest city with a CT scanner. It took tribe members one to two days to reach the nearest market town by river, and then another six hours driving to reach Trinidad.

CT scans that look for calcium deposits in arterial plaques confirmed what Kaplan's team had suspected—the Tsimane have the youngest-looking arteries of any population recorded to date.

The scans showed that almost nine in 10 of the Tsimane (85%) had no risk of heart disease because they had no arterial plaques. About

13% of those scanned had low risk, and only 3% had moderate or high risk.

By comparison, only 14% of US residents have a CT scan that suggests no risk of heart disease, while 50% have a moderate or high risk, according to a recent study funded by the U.S. National Institutes of Health.

There appears to be a 24-year lag between when a Tsimane develops any risk of heart disease compared with when an American does, the researchers reported. There's also a 28-year lag between the Tsimane and Americans when heart disease risk becomes moderate or high.

LIFE IS MEDICINE

All this good health can be tracked back to the way the Tsimane live, Dr. Thomas said. They are subsistence farmers; during the day, the men hunt and fish while the women work the farms and tend to children.

Because of this, the men are physically active six to seven hours of their day, and tend to average 17,000 steps a day, Dr. Thomas said. The women are physically active four to six hours a day, and average about 16,000 steps.

The Tsimane also consume a very fresh, extremely low-fat diet, eating only what they can grow or catch, Dr. Thomas said. Nearly three-fourths of what they eat are non-processed carbohydrates, such as rice, plantains, corn, nuts and fruits, and their protein comes from lean wild game and fish.

The tribe's members rarely smoke, Dr. Thomas added. "They mainly use cigarettes to burn these huge flies out of their skin, down there in the rainforest," he said.

"We were really surprised you could prevent heart disease by this amount of exercise and this kind of diet," Dr. Thomas said.

THE CUSHY LIFE CAN HURT YOUR HEART

These results suggest that urbanization could be considered a risk factor for hardening of the arteries, as modern people leave behind lives of struggle for a more cushy existence, he said.

Kim Williams, MD, immediate past president of the American College of Cardiology, agreed, noting that modern medicine has focused less on prevention than on surgeries, procedures and drugs that save and extend the lives of heart attack or stroke victims.

"You can decrease the heart attack death rate, but you're not really decreasing the number of people who have heart attacks," said Dr. Williams, chief of cardiology at Rush University Medical Center in Chicago. "We've been mopping up the floor rather than turning off the faucet."

The findings from the Tsimane also cast some doubt on inflammation as a cause of hardened arteries, which has been a popular theory, Dr. Thomas added.

Thanks to parasites like hookworm, roundworm and giardia, the Tsimane spend most of their lives in a state of infection-induced inflammation, he said. Nevertheless, this inflammation does not appear to have had any effect on their arterial health.

LIVE LIKE AN AMAZONIAN?

People who want to follow the example of the Tsimane would do well to consider US guidelines for physical exercise a starting point rather than a goal, said Douglas Jacoby, MD, medical director of the Penn Medicine Center for Preventive Cardiology and Lipid Management in Philadelphia.

"The guidelines aren't designed to maximally reduce your risk," Dr. Jacoby said. "They are really designed to set up a minimum standard of behavior that we are positive will help reduce heart attacks and strokes."

At the same time, Dr. Jacoby believes the recent study downplays another potential explanation for the remarkable health of the Tsimane—genetics.

"The authors conclude that genetics only play a minor part in the causation of coronary disease. I don't think that's a well-founded statement," Dr. Jacoby said. "There are real genetic risk factors that have an impact on whether a person will have a heart attack or stroke, and living healthy will not fully overcome that risk."

The study was published online in *The Lancet*, to coincide with a presentation on the findings at the American College of Cardiology meeting, in Washington DC.

Marathon Running May Cause Short-Term Kidney Injury

Chirag Parikh, MD, PhD, professor of medicine, and director of applied translational research, Yale University, New Haven, Connecticut.

Cathy Fieseler, MD, primary care sports medicine physician, Christus Trinity Mother Frances Health System, Tyler, Texas.

Peter McCullough, MD, vice chief of medicine, Baylor University Medical Center, Dallas.

American Journal of Kidney Diseases.

Any marathoner will tell you that the grueling 26-mile races can do a number on the hips, knees, ankles and feet.

Now, a small study suggests that these tests of endurance are also tough on the kidneys.

"Marathon runners demonstrate transient or reverse short-term kidney injury," said Chirag Parikh, MD, PhD, professor of medicine at Yale University.

In his study of 22 participants in the 2015 Hartford, Connecticut Marathon, Dr. Parikh found that 82% showed acute kidney injury after the race. In this condition, the kidneys fail to filter waste from the blood.

The good news is that the kidney injury seems to clear up within two days of the race, he said.

"On day 2, they are all fine," Dr. Parikh said.

Runners likely don't even know they've had this transient injury, Dr. Parikh said. "For the short term, I don't think they would notice anything," he said.

Dr. Parikh isn't certain why the strenuous event is linked with kidney injury. But some potential causes include the sustained rise in core body temperature, dehydration or the decreased blood flow to the kidneys that occurs during a marathon, he explained.

When the blood is pumped to the skin and muscles while running, he said, the kidneys may not get as much blood as they normally do.

Nor can Dr. Parikh say whether the effect might be cumulative, getting worse with more marathons run. It may be that the kidney adapts over time instead, he noted.

STUDY DETAILS

To evaluate this type of kidney injury, his team looked at blood and urine samples collected before and after the marathon. These tests included measuring blood creatinine levels and proteins in the urine, along with looking at kidney cells on a microscope. Creatinine is a waste product excreted by the kidneys; measuring it in the blood helps assess kidney health.

In a previous study, published in 2011, Peter McCullough, MD, vice chief of medicine at Baylor University Medical Center in Dallas, and colleagues evaluated 25 men and women marathoners. They found 40% of the runners met the definition of acute kidney injury based on their blood creatinine levels.

In the new study, Dr. Parikh's team also "performed an in-depth evaluation of the urine and found evidence of injury," Dr. McCullough said.

"The larger question looming is whether or not these repeated bouts of injury in endurance athletes lead to chronic kidney disease years later. Can anything be done about the injury at the time including hydration strategy?" Dr. McCullough said. More study is crucial, he added.

Dr. Parikh said additional research is also needed to assess whether certain people may not recover as quickly. For now, those with a family history of kidney disease should let their physician know they run marathons, he suggested.

ADDITIONAL EXPERT ADVICE

Cathy Fieseler, MD, said marathoners who want to reduce their risk of kidney injury should avoid anti-inflammatory drugs before the race. Those drugs include over-the-counter *ibuprofen* (Advil, Motrin IB) and *naproxen* (Aleve), Dr. Fieseler said. *Acetaminophen* (Tylenol) is cleared through the liver.

Dr. Fieseler is a primary care sports medicine doctor at Christus Trinity Mother Frances Health System in Tyler, Texas. She's also medical director of the American Running Association.

The study was published in the *American Journal of Kidney Diseases.*

Less Salt, Fewer Nighttime Bathroom Trips?

European Society of Urology, news release.

Lowering your salt intake could mean fewer trips to the bathroom in the middle of the night, a recent study suggests.

Most people over age 60, and many even younger, wake up to pee one or more times a night. This is called nocturia. This interruption of sleep can lead to problems such as stress, irritability or tiredness, which can affect quality of life.

There are several possible causes of nocturia, including—as this study found—the amount of salt in your diet.

"This is the first study to measure how salt intake affects the frequency of going to the bathroom, so we need to confirm the work with larger studies," said study leader Tomohiro Matsuo, from Nagasaki University in Japan.

"Nighttime urination is a real problem for many people, especially as they get older. This work holds out the possibility that a simply dietary modification might significantly improve the quality of life for many people," he said.

The American Heart Association (AHA) recommends that people consume no more than 2,300 milligrams (2.3 grams) of sodium daily. That's about a teaspoon of salt.

Ideally, the AHA says, people shouldn't have more than 1,500 milligrams (1.5 grams) of sodium per day. Table salt is made up of about 40% sodium, according to the AHA.

STUDY DETAILS

The study included more than 300 Japanese adults. They all had high salt intake and sleeping problems. They were given instructions and help to reduce their salt intake and followed for 12 weeks.

More than 200 people in the study reduced their salt intake. They went from an average of 11 grams per day to 8 grams a day.

With that reduction in salt, the average number of nighttime trips to the bathroom to urinate fell from 2.3 to 1.4 times per night. The number of times people needed to urinate during the day also decreased.

The drop in nighttime bathroom visits also led to an improvement in quality of life, researchers said.

In comparison, the nearly 100 participants whose average salt intake rose—from 9.6 grams per night to 11 grams nightly—had an increase in nighttime trips to the bathroom, from 2.3 to 2.7 times a night, the study revealed.

The study was presented at the European Society of Urology annual meeting, in London. Findings presented at meetings are typically viewed as preliminary until they've been published in a peer-reviewed journal.

EXPERT COMMENT

Marcus Drake, MD, is a professor at the University of Bristol in England and leader of the working group for the ESU Guidelines Office Initiative on Nocturia. "This is an important aspect of how patients potentially can help themselves to reduce the impact of frequent urination. Research generally focuses on reducing the amount of water a patient drinks, and the salt intake is generally not considered," he said.

"Here we have a useful study showing how we need to consider all influences to get the best chance of improving the symptom," Dr. Drake said in an ESU news release.

The National Sleep Foundation has more on nocturia at SleepFoundation.org.

Taking the Stairs May Soon Get Easier

Georgia Institute of Technology, news release.
PLOS ONE, news release.

Does a long staircase leave you weak? Take heart—researchers say they've developed stairs that "recycle" a person's energy, which could be of help to seniors and disabled people.

The stairs use latched springs to store energy when someone goes down them. The energy is then released when a person climbs the stairs again.

According to the researchers from Georgia Institute of Technology and Emory University in Atlanta, the high-tech stairs absorb a person's energy as he or she descends, which cuts forces on the ankle by 26%.

But when the person then ascends the same stairs, that energy is released, making the stairs spring up a bit. The ascent is therefore 37% easier on the knees than it otherwise would be.

"Unlike normal walking where each heel-strike dissipates energy that can be potentially restored, stair ascent is actually very energy efficient; most energy you put in goes into potential energy to lift you up," said Karen Liu, an associate professor in Georgia Tech's School of Interactive Computing.

"But then I realized that going downstairs is quite wasteful," she said in a school news release. "You dissipate energy to stop yourself from falling, and I thought it would be great if we could store the energy wasted during descent and return it to the user during ascent."

Liu said she got the idea for the new technology after watching her 72-year-old mother struggle to climb stairs.

To test the machine, Liu's team analyzed patterns of energy use while nine volunteers went up and down the stairs.

Stairs can be difficult for many elderly and disabled people. Current alternatives such as elevators, stair lifts and escalators are expensive and use a lot of energy, the researchers noted.

Further study is needed, but energy-recycling stairs might become a more practical and affordable option, the study authors suggested. The study was published in the journal *PLOS ONE*.

"Current solutions for people who need help aren't very affordable. Elevators and stair lifts are often impractical to install at home," said Liu. "Low-cost, easily installed assistive stairs could be a way to allow people to retain their ability to use stairs and not move out of their homes."

Info The U.S. Centers for Disease Control and Prevention offers exercise advice for older adults at CDC.gov/physicalactivity/basics/older_adults/index.htm.

Ick! Synthetic Mucus Could Battle Dangerous Bugs

American Society for Biochemistry and Molecular Biology, news release.

Snot, phlegm and other forms of mucus may not be everyone's favorite subject, but scientists say synthetic mucus might help save lives.

Researchers at the Massachusetts Institute of Technology said the lab-made goo could help combat antibiotic-resistant bacteria.

By replicating the natural ability of mucus to control dangerous bacteria, the hope is to find new ways to fight infections.

"I am so excited about mucus because I am convinced it can help us find new strategies for protecting us from infections, in particular those that relate to an overgrowth of harmful microbes," said study author Katharina Ribbeck, an MIT professor of tissue engineering.

A person's body produces about a gallon of mucus every day. Far from being a hindrance, mucus provides a protective coating on more than 2,000 square feet of internal surfaces, including the digestive tract, nose, mouth, eyes, lungs and female reproductive tract.

Mucus also helps maintain a healthy balance between beneficial and potentially harmful germs.

"Over millions of years, the mucus has evolved the ability to keep a number of these problematic pathogenic microbes in check, preventing them from causing damage," Ribbeck said in a society news release. "But the mucus does not kill the microbes. Instead, it tames them."

She said scientists believe, for instance, that a synthetic mucus made with sugar-coated molecules called mucins, which are normally found in saliva, could help prevent tooth decay. The next step is to study the potential role of mucins in other parts of the body.

"My lab and others around the world have begun to engineer mucin-inspired polymers and [synthetic] mucus. We want to use these engineered polymers to control problematic pathogens inside and outside of the body and to stop the growing threat of antibiotic-resistant microbes," Ribbeck said.

info The U.S. Centers for Disease Control and Prevention has more on antibiotic resistance.

Bye-Bye Flu Shot, Hello Patch?

Len Horovitz, MD, pulmonary specialist, Lenox Hill Hospital, New York City.

U.S. National Institute of Biomedical Imaging and Bioengineering, news release.

An experimental flu vaccine patch with dissolving microneedles appears safe and effective, a preliminary study shows.

The patch has 100 solid, water-soluble and painless microneedles that are just long enough to penetrate the skin. Researchers say it could offer a pain-free and more convenient alternative to flu shots.

"This bandage-strip-sized patch of painless and dissolvable needles can transform how we get vaccinated," said Roderic Pettigrew, MD, director of the U.S. National Institute of Biomedical Imaging and Bioengineering, which funded the study.

"A particularly attractive feature is that this vaccination patch could be delivered in the mail and self-administered. In addition, this technology holds promise for delivering other vaccines in the future," he said in an institute news release.

STUDY DETAILS

The study of 100 adults found that the patch triggered a strong immune response and did not cause any serious side effects. At most, some patients developed local skin reactions to the patches, which involved faint redness and mild itching that lasted two to three days.

The flu vaccine is released by the microneedles, which dissolve within a few minutes. The patch is then peeled off and thrown away.

Researchers at Georgia Institute of Technology and Emory University led the study. The results were published online in *The Lancet.*

EXPERTS REPLY

These early results "suggest the emergence of a promising new option for seasonal vaccination," Drs. Katja Hoschler and Maria Zambon wrote in an accompanying editorial. They are with Public Health England's National Infections Service.

The "more exciting features" of the microneedle patch include its low cost, safety, storage convenience and durability, they said.

"Microneedle patches have the potential to become ideal candidates for vaccination programs, not only in poorly resourced settings, but also for individuals who currently prefer not to get vaccinated," the editorialists wrote.

One flu expert agreed.

"The flu microneedle patch is easy to use—it can be self-administered and, like other medication patches, it is well absorbed through the skin," said Len Horovitz, MD, a pulmonary specialist at Lenox Hill Hospital in New York City.

"This development eliminates the need for intramuscular injection [a flu shot] by a health care professional," he added.

Also, "this patch does not need to be refrigerated—it has a long shelf life," Dr. Horovitz noted. "Standard vaccines can loose potency if left out of refrigeration repeatedly, as occurs in most settings."

info The U.S. Centers for Disease Control and Prevention has more on flu vaccination at CDC.gov/flu/protect/vaccine/index.htm.

Scientists Create Part-Human, Part-Pig Embryo for Stem Cell Research

Jun Wu, PhD, staff scientist, Salk Institute, La Jolla, California.
Jason Robert, PhD, director, Lincoln Center for Applied Ethics, Arizona State University, Tempe, Arizona.
Cell, online

It might sound like science fiction, but researchers have successfully used human stem cells to create embryos that are part-human, part-pig.

Scientists said the long-range goal is to better understand and treat an array of human diseases.

The researchers hope to ultimately cultivate human tissue that can be given to patients awaiting transplants.

But that's a long way off, said Jun Wu, PhD, who worked on the research.

"This study is reporting an important first step," said Dr. Wu, a staff scientist at the Salk Institute, in La Jolla, California.

That step, specifically, was to insert human stem cells into pig embryos. Weeks later, some of the embryos showed signs that the human cells were beginning to mature and turn into "tissue precursors."

Such embryos are known as chimeras, and they are controversial.

In 2015, the U.S. National Institutes of Health declared a moratorium on funding chimera research while officials assessed the ethical issues that the work raises. In 2016, the agency proposed changes to that policy—though, it said, certain restrictions would still apply.

WHAT ARE THE ETHICAL CONCERNS?

For one, aspects of the technology make some people uneasy, said Jason Robert, PhD, a bioethicist at Arizona State University.

Before human stem cells are inserted, the animal embryos undergo "gene editing." That capability—altering the genes of an embryo—raises red flags for some, Dr. Robert said.

And then there are the chimeras themselves. Some critics, Dr. Robert said, object on the basis of "human dignity"—arguing that transferring human characteristics to animals could denigrate what it means to be human.

Other concerns are less philosophical. Human stem cells can, in theory, grow into any mature tissue. So, some ask, what if the cells formed human sperm or eggs in the pig, or another animal?

Dr. Robert mentioned another issue some have raised. Could the stem cells get into the brain of a developing animal and endow it with human-like mental abilities or consciousness?

To Dr. Robert, that worry is a "peculiar" one. But he said the bigger point—that human stem cells are powerful, and research needs to proceed cautiously—is well taken.

"This has to be a slow road," Dr. Robert said. And he praised the recent research for its execution.

"These are incredibly careful scientists trying to do good work," Dr. Robert said.

STUDY DETAILS

Dr. Wu and his colleagues detailed the work in an online issue of the journal *Cell*.

First, the researchers experimented with mouse-rat chimeras. They used gene-editing technology to alter mouse embryos—deleting some genes that are critical for the development of a particular organ, such as the heart, pancreas or eyes. The scientists then inserted rat stem cells into the embryos, to see if they would fill the developmental gap.

The resulting chimeric embryos were then implanted into surrogate mouse mothers, where they matured normally, the researchers found. And the rat cells did grow into mature organs.

That offers a "proof-of-principle," Dr. Wu said. Achieving the same feat with human stem cells, and a larger animal, is another story, however.

Dr. Wu said his team chose to work with pig embryos because pig organs are similar in size to humans'. They also used adult human stem cells called induced pluripotent stem cells.

After the pig embryos were injected with stem cells, the researchers implanted them in sows. The investigators allowed the embryos to mature for only four weeks before removing and studying them.

According to Dr. Wu, some embryos showed signs that the human stem cells were beginning to mature and form precursors to tissue.

But, he said, the actual "contribution" of human cells to the organism was low, and that's a hurdle that will have to be overcome.

HOW WILL HUMAN-PIG CELLS BE USED?

Dr. Wu said scientists envision using human-animal chimeras in several ways.

Researchers have long used lab animals to study human diseases and test possible treatments—by, for example, growing human tumor cells in mice.

But actually creating lab animals that have human tissue could prove to be a better way, Dr. Wu said.

Then there's the prospect of using animals as "hosts" to grow human organs for transplant purposes.

"We're nowhere near that yet," Dr. Wu stressed. No one knows, for example, how to direct human stem cells to grow into a specific tissue once they are in an animal embryo.

Even if those scientific challenges are overcome, at least some ethical issues will persist. And they relate to both human and animal welfare.

Some people, Dr. Robert said, will balk at the idea of using animals as "incubators" for human organs, for instance.

Others, he said, "will object to this on the grounds that animal experimentation is wrong."

CHAPTER 14

Men's Health

New Ways to Protect Your Prostate

Drinking a tall glass of water several times each day sounds like one of the best things you can do for your health. But that may not be true for everyone.

Surprising recent finding: In an important study published in April 2016, researchers found that men who drank well water that contained relatively high levels of naturally occurring arsenic had a 10% higher risk of developing prostate cancer. It's a troubling statistic. And arsenic is just one of many other prostate-harming toxins lurking in our environment.

Good news: Scientific evidence now shows that men can build their body's defenses against the effects of these disease-causing toxins.

WORST HABITS FOR MEN

We've all heard it over and over again—eat right and stop smoking. *But men should be especially attentive to the following advice...*

- **Diet.** Two studies published in 2016 showed how crucial food choices are for prostate health.

Study I: Drinking sugary beverages (including not only sodas and sweetened iced tea but also fruit juices) was linked to a three times greater risk for prostate cancer...and eating processed lunch foods (such as pizza and hamburgers) doubled prostate cancer risk.

Study II: Among men who had already been diagnosed with prostate cancer, those who ate lots of saturated fats (found in fatty red meats, cheese and butter) were more likely to have

Geo Espinosa, ND, a naturopathic doctor and expert in prostate cancer and men's health. He is founder and director of the Integrative and Functional Urology Center at New York University's Langone Medical Center in New York City. Dr. Espinosa is author of *THRIVE Don't Only Survive! Dr. Geo's Guide to Living Your Best Life Before & After Prostate Cancer.*

the most aggressive form of the disease...but men who ate diets that emphasized fish and nuts—high in polyunsaturated fats—had less aggressive prostate cancer.

Bottom line on diet: Eat a diet that is rich in fruits, vegetables, nuts, fish, legumes and whole grains...and limit saturated fats, processed foods and sugary beverages.

•**Smoking.** Cigarette smoke is filled with toxins including cadmium, an inhalable metal that has been linked to prostate cancer. A study published in April 2016 showed that the more you smoke—and the longer you smoke—the greater your risk of developing prostate cancer.

Good news: Stopping smoking reduces prostate cancer risk almost immediately.

HERBS AND SUPPLEMENTS

Prostate health is all about detoxifying the body, protecting cells from damage—and reducing the inflammation that can promote the growth of cancers.

Several supplements have one or more of these anticancer effects—get a doctor's advice on which of the following would be most appropriate for you...*

•**Boswellia** reduces levels of *lipoxygenase* (LOX), an inflammatory marker associated with prostate cancer.

Typical dosage: 200 mg to 400 mg a day.

•**Curcumin** helps control *nuclear factor kappa-B* (NF-kB), which is a chemical pathway to inflammation in the body.

Typical dosage: 2,000 mg to 4,000 mg per day, in divided doses (morning, noon and night).

•**Modified citrus pectin (MCP)** may inhibit cancer growth and help remove heavy-metal toxins from the body. Pectins are typically found in the peel and pulp of citrus fruits (such as oranges, lemons and grapefruits). MCP is a form of pectin that is easily absorbed into the body.

Typical dosage: 1,000 mg to 5,000 mg, two or three times a day.

*Consult a physician who is knowledgeable about supplements before using any of those listed here—especially if you take any medication or have a chronic medical condition. To find such a doctor near you, consult The American Association of Naturopathic Physicians, Naturopathic.org.

•**Selenium** is a precursor to *glutathione*, a master antioxidant.

Typical dosage: 200 micrograms (mcg) a day of selenized yeast (other forms of selenium have been linked to increased prostate cancer risk).

MORE WAYS TO DETOXIFY

The strategies below also can enhance your body's natural mechanisms to release toxins...**

•**Sweat it out.** Perspiration is one of the most effective ways for your body to shed toxins.

What to do: Exercise a minimum of three hours per week at an intensity that makes you break a sweat. The type of exercise doesn't matter—sweat is the key ingredient.

Also: If possible, spend 15 minutes a few times a week in a dry-heat sauna.

•**Dry brush.** Another way to detoxify is to dry brush your skin.

What to do: Before you shower, use a dry towel, natural-bristle brush or loofah to gently brush from your hands and feet inward, toward your heart. This promotes the flow of lymphatic fluid, which drains toxins from the body. Brush for a total of three minutes.

•**Try hydrotherapy.** After brushing, shower as usual, but end with a hot water/cold water session of hydrotherapy. This process dilates and constricts blood vessels, promoting better circulation.

What to do: Turn on the hottest water you can tolerate without causing pain or scalding your skin, and let it pour over you for three minutes. Then turn on the cold water—as cold as you can tolerate—for 30 seconds. Repeat this for a total of three hot/cold cycles, ending with cold water.

BEWARE OF CHEMICALS...

Toxins are almost ubiquitous in our modern lives. For example, most plastics contain two problematic chemicals—*bisphenol A* (BPA) and phthalates. These chemicals act like estrogen in the body and may cause or promote the growth of prostate cancer. *While it is impossible to eliminate all contact with plastics, here's how to reduce your exposure...*

**Check first with your doctor if you have conditions that impair circulation, such as diabetes or heart disease, before using a sauna or hydrotherapy.

• **Check your plastic bottles.** All recyclable plastic bottles have a code at the bottom—a number inside a triangle. To reduce your exposure to BPA and phthalates, look for plastics with the number 1, 2, 4 or 5. The worst numbers are 3, 6 and 7—bottles with any of these numbers may contain these and other harmful chemicals.

Also: Most food cans contain BPA. If you opt for canned food, look for "BPA-free" products.

Nuts Reduce Prostate Cancer Deaths

Men with prostate cancer were 34% less likely to die if they ate a one-ounce serving of tree nuts (such as almonds, Brazil nuts, cashews, hazelnuts, macadamias, pecans, pine nuts, pistachios and walnuts) five or more times per week, according to a 26-year study of nearly 50,000 men.

Possible reason: Tree nuts are rich in unsaturated fat and nutrients that may lower inflammation.

However: Nut consumption did not reduce risk of developing prostate cancer.

Ying Bao, MD, ScD, assistant professor of medicine, Harvard Medical School, Boston.

PSA Screening for Baby Boomers

Kirsten Bibbins-Domingo, PhD, MD, MAS, chairperson, US Preventive Services Task Force. She is the Lee Goldman, MD, Endowed Chair in Medicine, professor of medicine, epidemiology and biostatistics, University of California, San Francisco (UCSF). The report is titled, "Prostate Cancer Screening Draft Recommendations," by the US Preventive Services Task Force.

Deciding whether to get screened for prostate cancer just got trickier. For a while, the tide was clearly turning against routine prostate-specific antigen (PSA) screening.

Now it's turning back—a little.

For baby boomers only.

Background: Routine prostate cancer screening—looking for the cancer in a healthy man—is very different from PSA testing in a man who has signs or symptoms of prostate cancer. In 2012, the US Preventive Services Task Force (USPSTF) recommended against routine screening—evidence showed that the harms of screening outweighed its benefits.

Study: The USPSTF has updated its findings by evaluating all high-quality medical research on the topic up through October 2016.

Finding: Recent studies show that the benefits and harms of screening are closely balanced for men between the ages of 55 and 69. That's the core "baby boomer" demographic.

Benefits: For every 1,000 men age 55 to 69 who are screened with a PSA test, one or two will avoid dying from prostate cancer over the next 13 years because of the test. For these men, screening allows early detection so that the cancer can be treated successfully.

Harms: Between 20% and 50% of men age 55 to 69 who are screened and then found to have prostate cancer actually are overdiagnosed—meaning cancer is detected that would never cause any symptoms or endanger their lives.

Here's why: Prostate cancer is usually so slow to grow that these men will end up dying from something else before the prostate cancer has a chance to spread and do damage. For these men, treatment offers no benefit. But it comes with a host of harms, starting with years of additional testing and, if cancer is treated, possible side effects including sexual impotence and urinary incontinence. As the Task Force notes, "Many more men experience harms from prostate cancer screening, diagnosis, and treatment than experience benefit."

Recommendation: The Task Force doesn't go so far as to recommend routine screening for all men age 55 to 69. But it does advise that these men talk with their health-care providers about whether to have the PSA test—weighing their health history and personal preferences. Why preferences? Because in the minds of some men, the small chance of living longer outweighs the larger chance of being harmed by over diagnosis—and for other men, vice versa. Given the complexities of the data, there's no one right

Prostate Cancer Treatment Updates

Watchful waiting compared with more aggressive treatments. Prostate cancer patients with malignancies that haven't spread and who are monitored, but do not receive treatment, have a nearly identical risk for death over the next decade as those who choose surgery and/or radiation, according to a recent study of more than 1,600 men. Surgery and/or radiation (with possible side effects such as incontinence and/or loss of sexual function) lowered the risk of the cancer spreading but did not result in lower risk for death over this 10-year period.

Note: Men with more advanced or aggressive forms of prostate cancer may need prompt treatment.

Jenny Donovan, PhD, professor of social medicine, University of Bristol, UK.

Prostate tumors can differ significantly within the same patient. When a patient has multiple tumors and only the largest one is analyzed using genomic fingerprinting, a smaller but more aggressive tumor may go undetected. Your doctor should consider this when using genomic fingerprinting for prostate cancer treatment.

Hannelore V. Heemers, PhD, associate staff in the department of cancer biology at Lerner Research Institute, Cleveland Clinic. She is lead author of a study published in *European Urology*.

Robotic surgery vs. traditional prostate surgery. Robotic prostate surgery may be no better than traditional surgery done by an experienced doctor.

Recent finding: After three months, people who had either form of surgery had similar levels of complications and urinary and sexual function. And both forms of surgery were equally effective at removing cancerous tissue. The best approach seems to come from finding a urologist the patient respects and whose advice he is comfortable following.

Study of 326 men led by researchers at Royal Brisbane and Women's Hospital, Australia, published in *The Lancet*.

answer. This is a substantial change from the earlier recommendation against all PSA testing in healthy men in this age group.

For men older than 69, the Task Force recommends against routine PSA screening. For these men, the harms of overdiagnosis clearly outweigh the benefits of early detection. (Though again, individual men may feel differently.) The Task Force does not have a recommendation for men younger than age 55.

Surprising finding number one: There is no separate screening advice for men already known to be at high risk for prostate cancer due to race or family history. It's possible that they may benefit more from PSA screening than normal-risk men, but it's just not known. "The Task Force remains concerned about the striking absence of evidence on the potential benefits and harms of screening and treatment for prostate cancer in high-risk men, particularly African American men, and strongly advocates for research in this area. This should be a national priority."

Surprising finding number two: One major reason the Task Force changed its recommendation wasn't improvement in detection—but changes in treatment. The statement makes it clear that active surveillance, when done right, can reduce the harms associated with screening by delaying treatment—and only initiating it if the cancer becomes a more active threat. Active surveillance, which is appropriate for generally healthy men with low-risk disease, involves routine monitoring with PSA tests, office visits and repeat biopsies—rather than immediate surgery, radiation and medications. It's become much more common in recent years.

Bottom line: The updated guidelines emphasize that the choice of screening belongs—as it always has—to each individual man and that the decision should be made in personal consultation with a doctor. With knowledge and proper management, screening does not necessarily lead to unnecessary exploration and treatment.

Prostate Drug for Kidney Stones

Emergency Medicine Foundation.

Patients who were given *tamsulosin* (Flomax) were more likely to pass large stones than those in a control group. The drug could reduce the need for surgery or other kidney stone treatments.

The Bone Danger That Can Kill You

Harris H. McIlwain, MD, founder of McIlwain Medical Group in Tampa and former chair of the Florida Osteoporosis Board. He is board-certified in rheumatology, internal medicine and geriatric medicine. He is the pain expert for Dr. Oz's ShareCare.com website and is a coauthor of *Reversing Osteopenia.*

If you're a man, here's something important you probably don't know—about 25% of men will have an osteoporosis-related bone fracture in their lifetimes, and a man's risk of dying in the year following a hip fracture is twice as high as a woman's.

Women try to protect themselves against osteoporosis because rapid bone loss is a hallmark of menopause. Men eventually will lose as much bone strength as women, but it happens more slowly and later in life—and the consequences of ignoring it can be terrible. *Here's what men need to know to protect their bones...*

MALE BONE LOSS

Bone is always breaking down and building up. This process, known as remodeling, depends on things such as exercise, vitamin D and calcium intake, hormone levels and other factors. Osteoporosis (or osteopenia, an earlier stage of bone loss) occurs when more bone is lost than gained.

Women can lose 20% or more of their total bone mass within just five years of menopause. Men are somewhat protected but only at first. They have more bone mass to begin with... are more likely to have been physically active, which builds bone...and don't have the same midlife estrogen changes that deplete bone. But men may lose bone when testosterone levels are low. Men tend to have their first bone fractures about 10 years later than women.

By the time men have reached their 70s, their osteoporosis risk is the same as women's. In severe cases, the bones can become almost paper thin. This can lead to fragility fractures—bone breaks that are caused by seemingly minor mishaps such as stepping off a curb in an unusual way or merely bumping into a doorframe.

RISK FACTORS

With a few exceptions (see below), men don't need to be tested for osteoporosis until about age 65. Before that age, they should assume that they'll eventually lose bone and start taking steps to prevent it.

The DEXA (dual-energy X-ray absorptiometry) test, which measures bone density at the hip and spine (and sometimes in the wrist), usually costs between $100 and $200 and often is covered by insurance. It assigns a T-score, a measure of your bone density. A negative reading (for example, a score of –1) indicates some bone loss. A score of –2.5 means that you have possible early osteoporosis. Anything lower indicates serious bone loss.

Most at risk: Older men who are underweight are up to 20 times more likely to get osteoporosis than heavier men. Smoking greatly increases bone loss. So does low testosterone, lung disease and a poor diet. Some drugs used to treat prostate cancer and other diseases (including some lung diseases) cause bone loss as a side effect.

Men with any of these risk factors should get tested earlier—say, at about age 50. So should men who have suffered fragility fractures. The fractures usually occur in the hips or spine, although wrist and shoulder fractures also are common. (Broken fingers and toes aren't considered fragility fractures.)

WHAT WILL SAVE YOUR BONES?

Men with early osteoporosis (or a high risk of getting it) can improve their diet, take calcium and vitamin D supplements, and get more exercise. Such men probably won't need medication right away—or ever. *Steps to take...*

•**Plenty of exercise.** Forty minutes a day is ideal. It's the best way for middle-aged men to build bone mass and for older men who already have osteoporosis to slow the rate of bone loss. Research has shown that people who exercise will have fewer hip or spine fractures than those who are sedentary.

Weight-bearing exercises—walking, lifting weights, playing tennis, etc.—are the most effective at slowing bone loss.

My advice: Take frequent walks. Many people enjoy walking more than other forms of exercise, and it's foolproof. It doesn't matter whether you walk slow or fast—simply standing up and working against gravity stimulates bone growth in the hips and spine.

•**More calcium.** You can't build strong bones without calcium. Unfortunately, most Americans don't get enough. The problem is compounded in older adults, who absorb dietary calcium less efficiently. Men and women need a daily calcium intake of 1,000 milligrams (mg) up to age 50 and 1,200 mg thereafter.

Important: The guidelines include the calcium that you get from foods and supplements. There's no reason to take a high-dose calcium supplement if you also get plenty of calcium from dairy, fortified juices or high-calcium foods such as sardines with bones. For most people, a 500-mg calcium supplement is enough—take more if you tend to avoid calcium-rich foods. Your body absorbs calcium more efficiently when it is taken in smaller amounts (500 mg or less) several times a day. Taking 50 mg to 100 mg of magnesium a day also helps with absorption.

•**Add vitamin D.** You can't absorb calcium without enough vitamin D in your system, and older adults' bodies are not very efficient at using sun exposure to create the needed form of vitamin D.

My advice: I recommend taking 1,000 units of vitamin D-2 daily. Check with your doctor to see how often you should get your blood levels tested to make sure that you're getting enough.

•**Go easy on the colas.** Research has shown that people who consume a lot of cola (but not other carbonated beverages) tend to have lower hip-bone densities. It could be that the phosphoric acid in colas reduces calcium absorption or that people who drink a lot of soft drinks tend not to consume calcium-rich foods in general and need to be aware of this. I agree with the National Osteoporosis Foundation recommendation to have no more than five cola soft drinks a week.

If you smoke, do everything you can to quit. Smoking interferes with the hormones that you need for bone strength...decreases blood supply to bones...and slows the production of bone-forming cells. By the age of 80, smokers are about 71% more likely to have bone fractures than nonsmokers.

MEDICATIONS

Men with more advanced disease may need medication. Some of the same drugs used to treat osteoporosis in women also work in men. Bisphosphonates such as Fosamax and Actonel slow the rate of bone loss. The most common side effects include heartburn or an upset stomach. Using bisphosphonates for more than five years has been linked to two rare but serious side effects—thighbone fracture and osteonecrosis (bone death) of the jaw. Prolia, a different type of drug, helps prevent fracture and requires an injection every six months. Discuss this drug with your physician because it too has osteonecrosis of the jaw and thighbone fractures as possible side effects of long-term use. For men with low testosterone, hormone replacement will help increase bone mass and reduce the risk for fractures. Testosterone replacement should be done only under the guidance of a physician because too much testosterone has been linked to stroke and heart attack.

Men Age Faster...But They Don't Have To

Anna C. McCarrey, PhD, lead author of National Institute on Aging study published in *Alzheimer's & Dementia.*
Karen Larson, editor, *Bottom Line Personal.*

Age comes for us all, but it seems to target men first. It's no secret that men die younger than women—nearly five years younger in the US. Now a study by the National Institute on Aging suggests that men tend to experience declines in mental abilities and memory earlier and more rapidly than women, too.

It is possible that behavioral differences between the genders could be playing a role. *If so, the cognitive-decline gender divide points us toward things that men can do...*

- **Eat like a woman.** Surveys suggest that women generally eat more vegetables than men, while men eat more red meat. Perhaps not coincidentally, a study published in *Alzheimer's & Dementia* made a compelling case that consuming a diet featuring plenty of leafy green vegetables, whole grains, nuts, beans and berries—and not much red meat, butter, margarine, cheese, sweets, fried foods and fast food—can significantly slow age-related cognitive decline.

- **Seek out mental challenges.** Women are more likely than men to read books...or take adult-education courses in topics not directly related to their careers. "We know from previous studies that keeping the brain challenged is protective for one's risk for dementia," notes Anna C. McCarrey, PhD, lead author of the National Institute on Aging study.

- **Socialize.** Women tend to have larger social networks than men and are more likely to use social websites. A number of studies have found a link between social engagement and maintaining cognitive function into old age.

Saunas Are Associated with Lower Death Risk

Men in Finland who used a dry sauna two to three times a week over the long term (nearly 21 years) for at least 11 minutes each time had a 22% lower risk of dying from a sudden cardiovascular event than men who used a sauna only once a week. Men who used saunas four to seven times a week had a 63% lower risk of dying from a cardiovascular event.

Possible reason: Sauna use increases the heart rate to a level similar to that when doing low-to-moderate exercise and helps to lower blood pressure.

Study of 2,315 men by researchers at University of Eastern Finland, Kuopio, published in *JAMA Internal Medicine.*

Hey, Men...Ask for Help!

Toni Bernhard, a former law professor and author of *How to Live Well with Chronic Pain and Illness.* ToniBernhard.com

Most people are eager to pitch in when someone needs a helping hand. So why is it so hard to reach out when we're the ones who need a boost?

Let's face it—no one likes to feel needy. Asking for help can make you feel vulnerable or incompetent. You might also worry that you're showing weakness...or wasting someone's time.

Asking for help can be especially tricky for men. Studies have shown that many men who are caring for loved ones don't even talk about the stress...let alone ask for support or assistance.

Here's a little secret: People want to be asked. When we give and receive help, it makes us feel connected. It reduces social isolation... and allows friends and family members to get involved in a positive way.

Toni Bernhard, a former law professor and author of *How to Live Well with Chronic Pain and Illness,* notes that her friends "jump" when given a chance to help.

How to ask...

- **Remember that people really do want to help.** Offers of assistance are virtually always sincere.

- **Start with a list of things you need help with.** It could be a particular errand, walking the dog, etc. Then ask someone to help with just one of those things.

- **Be specific.** Don't just expect someone to magically appear when it's time to rake the leaves—be sure to tell the person exactly what you need...and when.

And don't forget—you feel good when you're able to help someone. Why not give others the same privilege?

Exercise and Testosterone

Hiroshi Kumagai, PhD, researcher, health and sports sciences, University of Tsukuba, Ibaraki, Japan.

Vigorous exercise raised testosterone levels in overweight and obese men who walked or jogged 40 to 60 minutes one to three days per week for 12 weeks.

Possible explanation: Aerobic exercise improves metabolic processes that raise testosterone. Low testosterone can lead to fatigue, decreased sex drive and reduced bone and muscle mass.

Shedding Light on Low Male Libido

Andrea Fagiolini, MD, professor, psychiatry, and chairman, department of mental health and school of specialization in psychiatry, University of Siena, Italy.

Brad Anawalt, MD, endocrinologist and professor, medicine, University of Washington, Seattle.

European College of Neuropsychopharmacology annual meeting, Vienna.

Light therapy, commonly used to treat seasonal depression, may restore a measure of libido to men who struggle with a low sex drive, a small study suggests.

Italian researchers said they found that men exposed to just two weeks of daily doses of bright light saw their testosterone levels increase more than 50%, and their sexual satisfaction levels more than triple.

"We were not surprised to observe our results," said study author Andrea Fagiolini, MD. He is chairman of both the department of mental health and the school of specialization in psychiatry at the University of Siena.

Dr. Fagiolini said that his team's light-box experiment took its cue from nature.

Prior investigations, conducted by his team and other researchers, have found that both sexual interest and testosterone levels naturally go up in tandem during spring and summer.

THE RISE AND FALL OF TESTOSTERONE

Dr. Fagiolini said that, in the northern hemisphere, men typically see their testosterone levels fall off between November and April, before beginning a gradual climb back up during the summer. And while peak testosterone levels aren't reached until October, Dr. Fagiolini said the impact that rising testosterone levels have on sexual activity is evident as early as June.

June ranks as the top month when it comes to maximum rates of conception, he said.

"We thought that light could well have something to do with that," Dr. Fagiolini said.

The research team said up to one-quarter of all men suffer from low sexual desire, with middle-aged men over age 40 particularly vulnerable.

STUDY DETAILS

For the study, half of the male participants spent 30 minutes first thing in the morning sitting about three feet from a special UV-filtered light box that emitted very bright light. The other half of the group, which served as a control group, was exposed to a very low level of light.

The low sex drives seen among the 38 Italian men enrolled in the study were attributed to either hypoactive sexual desire disorder or sexual arousal disorder.

The result: All the men had registered prestudy sexual satisfaction levels at around 2 on a scale of 10. Scores among those in the light-box group hit in excess of 6 by the study's conclusion (two weeks). Light-box treatment was also linked to a notable rise in testosterone levels, up from 2.3 ng/mL to 3.6 ng/mL during the same time frame.

Conversely, those in the control group saw no change in their testosterone levels, while sexual satisfaction rose by less than one point.

Dr. Fagiolini and his colleagues reported their findings at a meeting of the European College of Neuropsychopharmacology, in Vienna, Austria. Research presented at meetings is considered preliminary until published in a peer-reviewed journal.

WHY LIGHT THERAPY MIGHT WORK

Dr. Fagiolini cautioned that, despite the encouraging findings, light-box libido therapy needs more research, involving larger groups of patients.

Still, he offered a few theories as to why bright light might boost sexual desire.

For one, it may have an inhibitory effect on the production of key testosterone-depressing hormones in the brain, Dr. Fagiolini said.

At the same time, light therapy also appears to boost levels of the pituitary gland's luteinizing hormone (LH), which is known to increase testosterone levels. And recent research indicates that light-box therapy increases LH levels by about 70%, he added.

Because LH levels also have an impact on ovulation in women, Dr. Fagiolini suggested that light therapy might help women struggling with fertility issues.

EXPERT COMMENT

Brad Anawalt, MD, an endocrinologist and professor of medicine at the University of Washington in Seattle, offered what he called "two simple plausible explanations" for the study's findings.

Though testosterone levels are usually highest in the morning, inadequate exposure to daytime light might drive morning levels down, he said. "[So] exposure to bright light might raise testosterone concentrations, leading to improved libido," he added.

At the same time, "many men and women with low libido suffer from depression," Dr. Anawalt said. "Bright light that mimics sunshine may help alleviate depression. Improved mood results in improved sex drive," he said.

info Columbia University has more on light therapy at http://www.columbia.edu/~mt12/blt.htm.

Sex Enhancement Supplements for Men May Be Risky

Study of top-selling male sexual-help supplements led by researchers at Wake Forest Baptist Medical Center, Winston-Salem, North Carolina, published in *Journal of Sexual Medicine.*

Sex-enhancement supplements for men may be risky. Some "natural" supplements have been found to contain traces of phosphodiesterase-5-inhibitors (PDE5Is), the medication found in the prescription medicine Viagra, which can be dangerous to men with certain health problems, such as advanced heart disease or severe liver or kidney disease. PDE5Is cannot yet be legally sold over the counter in the US.

Smoking Can Harm Sperm DNA and Affect Fertilization

Analysis of the sperm of 20 smokers and 20 nonsmokers by researchers at São Paulo Federal University, Brazil, published in *BJU International.*

Smoking damages sperm and may make it harder for a man to impregnate a woman.

The DNA in smokers' sperm is more fragmented than the DNA in nonsmokers' sperm—lowering the chance of fertilization.

Diabetes/Infertility Link

Study of 192 men ages 18 to 50 by researchers at Skåne University Hospital and Lund University Hospital, Sweden, published in *Clinical Endocrinology.*

Infertile men have higher risk for diabetes and osteoporosis later in life. Men who have low sperm counts before age 50 are 10 times more likely to have low testosterone levels than men with normal sperm counts...and more likely to have high blood sugar levels and low bone-mineral density in the lumbar spine.

Self-defense: Men under age 50 who have fertility problems should have their hormones checked and should consider lifestyle changes—such as weight loss and increased exercise—and possible testosterone treatment.

A Plug Instead of a Snip for Male Birth Control?

Catherine VandeVoort, PhD, professor, obstetrics and gynecology, University of California, Davis School of Medicine, and scientist, California National Primate Research Center.

Elaine Lissner, founder and trustee, Parsemus Foundation, Berkeley, California.

Landon Trost, MD, urologist and male infertility specialist, Mayo Clinic, Rochester, Minnesota.

Basic and Clinical Andrology, online.

A new gel-based vasectomy has proven effective in a group of monkeys, raising hopes it could one day provide a permanent but easily reversible male contraceptive option in humans.

Vasalgel works by plugging the vas deferens, the two tiny tubes that convey sperm into a male's semen, researchers said.

The gel "doesn't break down. It just sets up a little more, and sticks where you inject it," said lead researcher Catherine VandeVoort, PhD. She's a professor of obstetrics and gynecology with the University of California, Davis School of Medicine.

Traditional vasectomies either sever, crush or tie off the vas deferens, causing tissue damage that can be difficult to reverse, Dr. VandeVoort said.

STUDY DETAILS

The procedure involving the gel starts off much like a traditional vasectomy, with a surgeon opening up the scrotum and exposing the vas deferens, Dr. VandeVoort said. But instead of cutting or crushing the vas, the doctor instead injects a bead of the gel inside the tubes to plug them.

Sixteen male rhesus macaque monkeys injected with the non-hormonal gel have proven incapable of reproduction, according to the study findings.

No females have become pregnant in the males' presence, even though they were housed together for at least one breeding season—about six months.

"We're over two years in a lot of these males we injected with this, and so far they've all remained infertile," said Dr. VandeVoort. "We know that because we check the parentage of every baby that's born at the primate center."

Researchers hope to revise the Vasalgel plug to the point where a simple solution of water and baking soda would flush it out of the vas deferens, easily restoring a man's fertility, said study coauthor Elaine Lissner.

The gel plug has been successfully flushed out of male rabbits in animal testing, but reversibility has not yet been perfected in primates, said Lissner, founder and trustee of the Parsemus Foundation, the nonprofit group funding development of the gel.

The focus of the current study was to see whether Vasalgel would effectively prevent conception, Lissner and Dr. VandeVoort said.

"This tells us whatever challenges we face, the bottom line is it has worked and been safe in animals similar to humans," Lissner said. The Parsemus Foundation, based in Berkeley, California, funded the primate study.

The group is now looking for funding to move to the next step in primates, which will be to test reversibility.

WHAT'S NEXT

Researchers also are preparing for human trials to test whether Vasalgel would work as a contraceptive in men, Lissner said. The Parsemus Foundation hopes to start enrolling men for a clinical trial soon.

However, results obtained in animal studies aren't always replicated in humans, so it's too soon to say Vasalgel will become a viable form of birth control.

The gel first will be tested as a vasectomy alternative in men, before moving into tests of its potential reversibility in humans, Lissner said.

The study results were published online in the journal *Basic and Clinical Andrology.*

EXPERT COMMENT

Landon Trost, MD, a urologist and specialist in male infertility with the Mayo Clinic in Rochester, Minnesota, said there's unlikely to be demand for the gel as a vasectomy alternative unless it's easily reversible.

That's because traditional vasectomy has been honed to the point where it's a very safe and effective procedure that takes four to 10 minutes, Dr. Trost said.

"Vasectomy is about as good as it comes, from a successful outcome standpoint," he said. "Your success rates with the gel, I think, are never going to be able to match up with vasectomy."

Dr. Trost added that the gel might not be as reversible as the theory holds. He's concerned that the gel plug could cause irreparable scarring and damage by its very presence, given that the vas deferens is a very tiny and delicate vessel.

"Even if you can get rid of that plug later, it's not guaranteed you're going to be able to reverse it," Dr. Trost said.

But Lissner and Dr. VandeVoort said results have shown some hope for reversibility.

Some fluid appears able to pass through the gel, potentially reducing pressure that could damage the vas deferens, Lissner said.

In addition, the gel created few complications in the monkeys, the researchers reported.

info For more about vasectomy, visit the U.S. National Institutes of Health at https://medlineplus.gov.

How a Vasectomy Affects Sex...

Sheldon Marks, MD, urologist and microsurgical specialist in private practice in Tucson.

After a vasectomy, partners no longer have to worry about a surprise pregnancy, so in many instances, a couple's sex life improves—sometimes dramatically.

The vasectomy is a 15-minute outpatient surgery that severs the tubes that bring sperm to seminal fluid. The testicles still produce sperm, but it cannot get into the semen. The volume of ejaculation is reduced by less than 10%, which for most men is not noticeable.

Testosterone production is not affected by vasectomy, so sex drive is not impacted. The procedure does not cause nerve damage or impact erections or sensation. It is an extremely safe and effective form of birth control.

Could Good Sex Be Bad for an Older Man's Heart?

Hui Liu, PhD, associate professor, sociology, Michigan State University.

Gregg Fonarow, MD, professor, cardiology, University of California, Los Angeles.

Journal of Health and Social Behavior (online).

Sexually active older men may be more likely to have a heart attack, heart failure or stroke compared with their less lusty peers, recent research suggests.

What's more, older men who say they enjoy frequent sex also appear to face a higher risk for such serious cardiovascular events, the study authors said.

By contrast, an active sex life appears to have no bearing on older women's heart health. And older women who described the sex as enjoyable, pleasurable or satisfying emotionally and/or physically saw some health benefit, the study found.

"The result for men is indeed surprising for us, given our general assumption that sex is always good for health," said study lead author Hui Liu, PhD, an associate professor of sociology at Michigan State University.

Dr. Liu pointed to several potential explanations.

"When men get older, they may have more difficulties reaching an orgasm for medical or emotional reasons," she noted, perhaps leading to overexertion, exhaustion and cardiovascular stress.

Also, medication and supplements to improve sexual function "may have negative effects on their cardiovascular health," Dr. Liu added.

"Moreover, having quite a high frequency of sex may indicate problems of sexual addiction, sexual compulsivity or sexual impulsivity," she said. These may be related to the onset of anxiety and/or depression, which can negatively affect the heart, Dr. Liu said.

STUDY DETAILS

The study researchers evaluated survey responses from more than 2,200 seniors who participated in the U.S. National Social Life, Health and Aging Project. Participants answered sexual behavior questionnaires in 2005–2006 and again five years later. All were 57 to 85 years old at the time of the first survey.

Among the findings: Older men were more likely than older women to say they were sexually active. In the two surveys, about 70% and 50% of men, respectively, said they had had sex in the past year, compared with roughly 40% and 23% of women.

Men were also more likely to say they had more frequent sex. In the two polls, between 20% and 25% of men said they had sex once a week or more in the prior year, compared with 11% of women.

Finally, men were more likely than women to say their sex was "extremely physically pleasurable"—36% versus 23% in the first survey. And 37% of men said their sex was "extremely emotionally satisfying," compared with 25% of women.

Survey responses were then compared with key cardiovascular measures, including blood pressure readings, rapid heart rate, elevated C-reactive protein levels, and incidence of heart attack, heart failure and/or stroke.

Compared with older men who said they weren't sexually active, those who had sex once a week or more were almost twice as likely to experience a heart attack, heart failure or stroke by the second survey.

And men who found sex enjoyable also faced a higher risk for such heart illnesses, the study authors said.

Neither risk was seen among women. Women who said their sex lives were extremely pleasurable or satisfying had a lower risk for high blood pressure than women who didn't, the study found.

EXPERT COMMENT

But at least one cardiologist said he was reluctant to accept the study findings until more research is carried out.

Gregg Fonarow, MD, professor of cardiology at the University of California, Los Angeles, voiced caution about the findings, however.

"Most studies suggest that maintaining an active sexual life seems to be associated with men's cardiovascular and overall health," he said.

Prior studies, Dr. Fonarow added, "have suggested that high frequency of sexual intercourse is associated with lower risk of cardiovascular events and great longevity for men."

Contrary to the recent research, "studies have shown that a reduced frequency of sexual activity was an independent risk factor for cardiovascular events in men," he said. "In addition, studies have documented the risk of cardiovascular events during sexual activity to be very low in absolute terms."

With that in mind, Dr. Fonarow stressed that "the findings of the present study require replication before further consideration."

But he encouraged seniors to broach the subject with their doctors.

"Seniors with or at risk for heart disease should not be shy about talking to their physician about their sex life, implications for heart health, and any concerns," Dr. Fonarow said.

The study findings appear in an online edition of the *Journal of Health and Social Behavior.*

info There's more on heart disease and sex at the American Heart Association, Heart.org.

Odd-Looking Anatomy...

Sheldon Marks, MD, a urologist and microsurgical specialist with a private practice in Tucson, Arizona.

Peyronie's disease is a condition in which scar tissue forms in the penis and causes curvature and sometimes pain during an erection. The condition is usually seen in middle-aged men but can occur at any age.

The exact cause of Peyronie's is not known, but an injury to the penis can cause scar tissue to form. The condition has also been linked to autoimmune disorders, such as scleroderma and lupus. The immune system may attack cells in the penis, which leads to inflammation and scarring.

The curvature is usually upward or to one side. In many cases, the curvature is mild and does not progress, but it can become quite severe and painful.

See a urologist as soon as possible if you suspect that you have this condition. You may need treatment to keep Peyronie's from worsening. Treatment may include oral, topical or injected medication, such as Xiaflex, to soften the scar tissue and reduce pain and curvature.

Other therapies to break up scar tissue include high-intensity focused ultrasound or iontophoresis (a painless, low-level electrical application of medication to the area). Mechanical and vacuum devices used to stretch the penis can also help reduce curvature.

If these measures don't produce results, a urologist may recommend surgery to remove scar tissue and replace it with a skin graft. Some men may require a penile implant.

Guys, a Noisy Bedroom May Not Be Good for Your Fertility

James Nodler, MD, reproductive endocrinology and infertility specialist, Houston Methodist Hospital, Houston.

Jennifer Kawwass, MD, medical director, IVF and third party reproduction, Emory Reproductive Center, Atlanta.

Environmental Pollution.

M*en, take note:* A quiet bedroom might make for strong, healthy sperm.

South Korean researchers found that men who slept where the noise level routinely exceeded that of a suburban neighborhood had worse fertility than men who rested in quieter quarters.

"I think any sort of stressor can contribute to infertility...and I would say bedroom noise can be a chronic stressor in sleep," said James Nodler, MD. He's a reproductive endocrinology and infertility specialist at Houston Methodist Hospital.

"It's basically a protective feature by our bodies—if we're under severe stress, now is not the time to reproduce," added Dr. Nodler, who wasn't involved in the recent research.

About 15% of American couples are unable to conceive after a year of unprotected sex, according to the U.S. National Institutes of Health. Factors contributing to infertility in either sex are wide-ranging—in men, they include problems with sperm concentration, movement or shape.

STUDY DETAILS

In the research, scientists from Seoul National University analyzed health insurance data on more than 206,000 men aged 20 to 59. Noise exposure levels were calculated by combining men's residential location (using postal codes) and information from a national noise information system.

In the eight years covered by the data, about 3,300 of the men had an infertility diagnosis. After adjusting the data for factors such as age, income, smoking and body mass index (BMI), the researchers found men were 14% more likely to be diagnosed with infertility if exposed to night time noise over 55 decibels. That's equivalent to the noise generated by an air conditioner or a suburban street.

Earlier research found a similar association in women, with noise levels linked to an increased risk for premature birth, miscarriage and birth defects, the study authors noted.

Dr. Nodler explained that chronic noise in the bedroom may disrupt the release of a hormone known as GnRH (gonadotropin-releasing hormone) in the brain, which triggers the release of other hormones important to fertility.

"This is biologically plausible to me," Dr. Nodler said. "If you disrupt GnRH, that throws the whole balance of fertility out of whack, both for men and women."

EXPERT COMMENT

Another US fertility expert cautioned that the recent research doesn't establish a cause-and-effect relationship between noisy bedrooms and male infertility.

"It is possible that excessive exposure to high decibels is somehow associated with worsened semen [quality], but the study does not necessarily prove that prolonged noise exposure causes infertility," said Jennifer Kawwass, MD. She's medical director of IVF and third party reproduction at Emory Reproductive Center in Atlanta.

To determine the exact biological reason for the link, Dr. Nodler said future research should measure hormone levels in men with noisier bedrooms compared with men with quieter bedrooms.

Dr. Nodler recommended that men concerned about their fertility keep noise levels down in the bedroom as well as practice good "sleep hygiene" measures. These include avoiding TV or any other screen time while in bed, he said.

"It's an interesting topic to think about, that just reducing bedroom noise [may enhance] fertility," Dr. Nodler added. "It's definitely biologically plausible and—for anyone—having less bedroom noise is better for general health and fertility."

The study, by Kyoung-Bok Min and Jin-Young Min, was published in the journal *Environmental Pollution*.

Info The American Pregnancy Association has more on male infertility at http://americanpregnancy.org/infertility/male-infertility/.

High-Fat Diets May Cause Daytime Sleepiness

Study of questionnaires filled out by 1,800 men by researchers at University of Adelaide School of Medicine and Freemasons Foundation Centre for Men's Health, both in Adelaide, South Australia, Australia, published in *Nutrients*.

Men who ate the highest amount of fat were 78% more likely to have daytime sleepiness and three times more likely to report sleep apnea than men who ate the least fat. The association was strongest in men with high body mass index but was found in all men studied.

CHAPTER 15

Natural Cures

"Best of the Best" Natural Cures

These nondrug approaches cure headache, insomnia, restless legs and more...

Here's a quick fact that may give you pause: Americans use more medication than people living anywhere else in the world. Put another way, Americans make up about 5% of the world's population but consume more than 50% of prescription drugs.

A sad irony: People in parts of the world (including the US) with the highest expenditures on conventional medicine—a treatment category dominated by prescription drugs—actually live shorter, less healthy lives than those in other cultures. How could that be?

Drug reactions and side effects are just part of the problem. The bigger issue is that drugs suppress symptoms but are unlikely to reverse whatever it is that's making you sick.

My advice: Whenever possible, try natural remedies before pharmaceuticals. Natural therapies are more likely to target the "root" causes of illness, increasing the likelihood of a cure. These therapies also have fewer (or no) side effects.

Finding the "best of the best": As a medical doctor who has spent more than 44 years studying the full range of holistic modalities—from supplements to herbs and folk remedies—and treated more than 30,000 patients who have failed to respond to conventional medicine, I have identified the most effective natural therapies for the following common health problems...*

HEADACHES

About 90% of patients who see a doctor for headaches suffer from tension-type headaches.

*Consult your doctor before trying any of these remedies if you take medication or have a chronic medical condition.

C. Norman Shealy, MD, PhD, founding president of the American Holistic Medical Association, editor of the *Journal of Comprehensive Integrative Medicine* and a leading expert in the use of holistic and integrative medicine. He is author of *The Healing Remedies Sourcebook*. NormShealy.com

Despite the name, they're not always related to tension or stress. They are commonly triggered by certain fumes or other sinus irritants.

Nonsteroidal anti-inflammatory drugs (NSAIDs), such as *ibuprofen* (Motrin), are often used for tension headaches, but they can cause side effects, including nausea and diarrhea. *What I prefer...*

•**Coriander seeds.** Coriander, an anti-inflammatory herb, has been used for headache pain for thousands of years. Inhaling the steam will improve sinus drainage and soothe irritated tissues.

What to do: Put about one teaspoon of the seeds in a small bowl...cover with boiling water...drape a towel over your head and the bowl...and carefully inhale the steam for about 15 minutes.

INSOMNIA

Medications for insomnia—such as *zolpidem* (Ambien) and *eszopiclone* (Lunesta)—can cause many troubling side effects such as confusion, lack of coordination and sleepwalking. They also can make you feel like you have a hangover the next morning. *The following natural remedy is very effective for insomnia—without the side effects...*

•**Lavender.** It's a "calming" herb that's among the best natural treatments for sleepless nights. Many people swear by chamomile tea, but I've found that lavender is even more effective.

What to do: Sip a cup of lavender tea at bedtime...or inhale the aroma from a drop of lavender oil placed on a cotton ball under your nose. To use on your skin (for example, on your temples or pulse points on your wrists), add a drop or two of lavender oil to a tablespoon of almond or olive oil to dilute it.

A study at Wesleyan University found that people exposed to the scent of lavender reported more deep sleep and felt better in the morning than those who did not inhale the scent. Lavender can also help you fall asleep more quickly.

RESTLESS LEGS

This neurological disorder causes an irresistible urge to move the legs when you lie down at night—and the drugs that are often prescribed, such as benzodiazepines and muscle relaxants, aren't very effective and can cause drowsiness, confusion and dizziness. *What helps...*

•**Magnesium lotion.** Most Americans don't get enough magnesium, a mineral that reduces overexcitability of the central nervous system. You can take oral supplements, but the absorption is much faster when magnesium is applied to the skin. Apply it to your legs/feet before bedtime.

SHINGLES

This viral infection can cause recurring outbreaks of blisters and rashes—and, in some cases, excruciating pain. Antivirals and other medications can shorten the duration of outbreaks but are unlikely to completely eliminate the discomfort. *The following can be used along with medication to provide more effective relief...*

•**Vitamins A, C and E.** Research has shown that each of these nutrients can reduce pain and the severity of shingles rashes. Combining these vitamins is about four times more effective than taking them individually.

My advice: At the first sign of a shingles outbreak (typically marked by numbness, tingling or itching on the face or abdomen), take 1,000 mg of vitamin C daily...25,000 international units (IU) of beta-carotene (which is converted to vitamin A in the body)**...and 400 IU of vitamin E (the tocopherol form). Keep taking them until your symptoms are gone, typically for several weeks.

TOOTHACHE

Few things are more painful than a toothache—and it always seems to erupt on weekends or late at night, when you can't get to a dentist. *What to try until you can see a dentist...*

•**Cinnamon oil.** Dip a cotton ball in the oil and apply it to the painful area. The oil often curbs pain almost instantly. It's also an antimicrobial that kills oral bacteria and can reduce inflammation and swelling.

**Smokers and heavy drinkers should not take beta-carotene supplements—they may increase cancer and heart disease risk in these people.

If cinnamon oil doesn't help after five to 10 minutes, add crushed garlic. Like cinnamon, it's a natural antibiotic with analgesic properties. If it doesn't hurt too much, you can chew a whole clove, using the tooth (or teeth) that is aching. Or you can crush a clove and apply the pulp to the area that's hurting.

Surprising Castor Oil Cures

Jamison Starbuck, ND, a naturopathic physician in family practice and a guest lecturer at the University of Montana, both in Missoula. She is a past president of the American Association of Naturopathic Physicians and a contributing editor to *The Alternative Advisor: The Complete Guide to Natural Therapies and Alternative Treatments.* DrJamisonStarbuck.com

Mention the words "castor oil" and most people will turn up their noses. That's because castor oil is widely known as a strong laxative. For most adults, just one tablespoon of castor oil, taken in a glass of orange juice (or any other sweet juice) to disguise its oily taste, will fully clear the bowel within six to 12 hours. But because castor oil is such a strong "cathartic" medicine, I don't recommend it for constipation. It can irritate the lining of the intestines and cause cramping and diarrhea that can last for hours in some people, leading to dehydration. It's also a severe irritant to anyone with colitis, diverticulitis or inflammatory bowel disease. If you do want to try castor oil for constipation, be sure to discuss it first with your doctor.

But these dire warnings shouldn't prevent you from trying castor oil for other uses. As a topical medicine, it is very safe and quite effective, and I've recommended it to my patients for more than 30 years. According to research, when castor oil, which is made from the pressing of castor seeds, is applied to the skin, it seems to stimulate lymphocytes, white blood cells that are a part of the body's immune system. Lymphocytes, found in lymph nodes, filter waste and the debris of disease and promote healing. *How castor oil can help...*

• **Gallstones.** The presence of these fat-laden stones in your gallbladder can cause rapidly intensifying pain in the upper-right side of your abdomen, where the gallbladder is located, and even in your right shoulder or in the back between your shoulders if the pain radiates. You can reduce this pain by applying a castor oil pack over the area. This therapy will not cure gallstones but can help ease the pain, along with such therapies as medication and/or shock-wave therapy to break up the stones.

What to do: Get a dish towel–sized piece of cotton cloth (cutting up an old T-shirt works well) and soak it liberally in castor oil. Place the oily cloth directly on your skin in the area of pain...cover it with a dry towel...and put a hot-water bottle or heating pad on top of the towel. Leave the pack in place until the pain subsides—usually for 30 to 60 minutes. You can use this therapy for several days, but consult your doctor if pain becomes severe or lasts for more than a few days.

• **Colic, diverticulitis or colitis.** Castor oil packs can be used by adults with cramping intestines...and are safe for babies with colic (a painful condition believed to be caused by digestive muscle spasms or gas)—just check with the child's pediatrician first. Use a castor oil pack (as described above) over the entire lower abdomen.

• **Eczema, acne and ringworm.** Rub castor oil directly into the skin over a patch of eczema or acne...or a lesion from ringworm (a common fungal infection). Do it twice daily until the skin is healed.

• **Hair loss.** Castor oil helps both patchy and overall hair loss due to stress or illness, such as a parasite infection.

What to do: Rub castor oil into the scalp at night, cover your scalp with a shower cap, and shampoo your hair in the morning. Do this every night for at least a month to see results.

If you decide to use castor oil, go to a health-food store and buy a brand that is sold for human, medicinal use. Castor oil is also used as a machinery lubricant—the seeds for this sort of castor oil are often raised with lots of herbicides and processed with harmful solvents, such as hexane, so you should not use this type of castor oil.

Healing Secrets from Ancient India

Marc Halpern, DC, founder and president of the California College of Ayurveda in Nevada City, the first accredited Ayurvedic doctor program in the US...and cofounder of the National Ayurvedic Medical Association and the National Council on Ayurvedic Education. He is also author of two textbooks on Ayurvedic medicine and *Healing Your Life: Lessons on the Path of Ayurveda.* AyurvedaCollege.com

Can you imagine your doctor telling you that you'll feel better if you wear more orange or blue clothing...watch the sun rise every morning...eat more popcorn...and/or spritz patchouli oil in your home?

Most Americans would assume that their doctor was joking. But for hundreds of millions of people, most of them living in India, such practices from Ayurveda (the "science of life") make perfect sense.

Derived from teachings that originated thousands of years ago in ancient India, Ayurveda asserts that disease can be prevented or even healed by correcting physical, mental and emotional imbalances.

Recent development: Even though Ayurveda has traditionally been supported by its incredibly long history, scientific research is now confirming the effectiveness of some of its key therapies, such as meditation.

WHAT'S YOUR "DOSHA"?

According to Ayurveda, three fundamental forces (known as "doshas") govern the functions of the body and mind—vata (movement, such as blood flow)...pitta (metabolism, such as digestion)...and kapha (structure, such as bones).

Every individual has a unique combination of doshas—your prakruti, or constitution. In most people, a single dosha is predominant and needs to be balanced with an opposite quality.

Example: If your skin is oily (pitta), you need dryness—such as eating more popcorn and toasted breads.

More about the three doshas...

- **Vata (movement).** People with predominant vata tend be thin, with a dull complexion and dry skin, have a variable or picky appetite, get cold easily, speak quickly, sleep lightly and are creative but can lack focus.
- **Pitta (metabolism).** People with predominant pitta tend to be muscular, with a rosy or ruddy complexion and oily skin. They usually have a strong appetite, feel warm, speak precisely, fall asleep easily and are organized and focused but prone to anger.
- **Kapha (structure).** People with predominant kapha tend to be stocky or overweight, with a pale complexion and soft, moist skin, have a slow metabolism, feel neither too cold nor too warm and speak slowly and sleep deeply. They are dependable but can be stubborn.

The key to health: Because imbalanced doshas are seen as the cause of disease, Ayurveda teaches that what you take in through your senses can play a crucial role in restoring your well-being. *Easy ways to balance your dosha...*

SCENTS

One of the fastest natural ways to balance emotions is through the sense of smell, according to aromatherapy research published in *The Journal of Alternative and Complementary Medicine.* That's because olfactory receptors in the sinuses are directly connected to parts of the brain that control emotion.

One of the best approaches to affect smell is with essential oils—the distilled fragrance of a plant. *To bring the emotional tone of your predominant dosha into balance...*

Vata: Use a combination of a few drops of sandalwood and cinnamon.

Pitta: Try a combination of sandalwood and rose.

Kapha: Choose a combination of patchouli and clove.

How to use essential oils: You can opt for an aromatherapy candle or diffuser. Or you can put several drops of each oil into a misting bottle filled with water and spritz the water—in your home, at the office, in your car and/or on your face.

SIGHT

Research from the University of Essex showed that images and colors affect our physical health and state of mind—from the violent and upsetting images of the daily news to calming natural scenes of trees, clouds and rivers. *To maintain health and promote healing, choose colors for your home and office—and the clothes you wear—that help balance your predominant dosha...*

Vata: You need warm, stable colors, such as yellow, orange and green. Avoid or minimize red, white, blue and violet.

Pitta: You need cool colors, such as blue, violet, silver and white. Avoid or minimize red, orange, yellow and purple.

Kapha: You will benefit most from stimulating colors like red, along with other kapha-balancing colors such as orange, yellow and blue. Avoid or minimize brown and black.

SOUND

No matter what your dosha, silence calms the mind and is a powerful tool for healing.

To create more silence in your life: Watch the sun rise or set for 20 minutes...take a 20-minute walk by yourself...and/or spend at least 20 minutes every day not listening to the TV or radio or talking on a cell phone.

HEALTHY EATING

Ayurveda teaches that how we eat is just as important as what we eat.

Habits that aid digestion...

- **Eat in a peaceful, beautiful environment.** Eat quietly, without too much talking. Chew well, until food has a smooth consistency.
- **Have only a small amount of liquid with the meal (no more than one-half cup)**—and no cold or iced liquids, which may slow digestion.
- **Eat until you're 75% full**—never completely full or overfull. Allow at least three hours between meals.

FINDING AN AYURVEDIC PRACTITIONER...

If you would like to consult an Ayurvedic practitioner, consult the National Ayurvedic Medical Association's searchable database at AyurvedaNAMA.org and click on "Find an Ayurveda Professional." (Be sure he/she has graduated from a school accredited by the National Council on Ayurvedic Education.) Cost for an initial consultation ranges from $100 to $150 and is not covered by insurance.

Important: To avoid any possible interactions with medications or other conventional treatments, be sure to tell your primary care doctor about any Ayurvedic therapies, including herbs, that you try.

A Hands-On Approach for Heart Disease, Headache and More

Naresh C. Rao, DO, FAOASM (Fellow of the American Osteopathic Academy of Sports Medicine), clinical assistant professor of family medicine at the New York Institute of Technology College of Osteopathic Medicine, attending faculty in the department of medicine at NYU Langone Medical Center and the department of family medicine at Mount Sinai Beth Israel and partner at Sports Medicine at Chelsea, all in New York City. He is author of *Step Up Your Game.*

When you think of going to a doctor of osteopathic medicine (DO)—if it even occurs to you to see this type of doctor—what often comes to mind is someone who manipulates your joints and muscles to help relieve pain and discomfort. But that's only part of what a DO can do.

Latest development: An increasing body of recent scientific evidence shows that DOs can also effectively treat a host of other ailments, including respiratory problems, headaches and heart disease, with the use of a hands-on therapy known as osteopathic manipulative treatment (OMT).

HANDS-ON THERAPY

Like medical doctors (MDs), DOs attend four years of medical school, complete internships and residencies and are licensed to practice in every area of medicine, from internal medicine to geriatrics.

A key difference: Unlike MDs, DOs receive additional training in the musculoskeletal system—the body's interconnected system of nerves, muscles and bones—learning how to promote wellness and treat illness by using OMT. This method is used to diagnose, treat and prevent illness or injury by moving the patient's muscles and joints with stretches, gentle pressure, isometrics (the tensing and relaxing of muscles) and other hands-on techniques. This approach supplements conventional medical treatments, such as prescription medication and/or surgery when appropriate.

CAN THIS DOCTOR HELP YOU?

In addition to treating muscle or joint pain, such as low-back pain or neck pain, specialized DOs can use OMT—often as an adjunct to conventional care such as medication—to help treat...

•**Respiratory problems.** OMT can help ease respiratory problems, such as pneumonia, chronic obstructive pulmonary disease (COPD) and asthma.

Scientific evidence: In a study published in in the *Journal of the American Osteopathic Association*, 387 people age 50 and older who were hospitalized with pneumonia were divided into groups—one group received a combination of OMT and conventional care (such as antibiotics and fluid replacement), while another received only conventional care. Patients who received OMT had fewer in-hospital deaths...were less likely to require a ventilator...and had hospital stays that were more than a day shorter than the conventional care group. Also, because OMT improves the body's circulation, antibiotics can be more easily delivered.

How osteopathy can be used for respiratory problems: With a technique known as muscle energy, a DO can stretch the muscle in the thorax (between the neck and abdomen), and the patient can perform isometric movements that involve tensing and relaxing muscles to improve lung function.

•**Headaches.** Increasingly, OMT is being used to quell headache and migraine pain.

Scientific evidence: In a study published in *Complementary Therapies in Medicine*, among 105 adults with chronic migraines, those receiving OMT had fewer days with migraines, less pain, better daily function and took less migraine medication.

How osteopathy can be used for headaches: OMT for headaches can include muscle energy and craniosacral manipulation, in which gentle touch is used to relax the cranial bones of the skull. These treatments stimulate the flow of spinal fluid, which is believed to help the central nervous system function better and reduce pain.

•**Cardiovascular disease.** Few people realize that OMT can play an important role in treating cardiovascular disease.

Scientific evidence: In a study published in the *Journal of the American Osteopathic Association*, 53 adults undergoing coronary bypass surgery were divided into three groups—one received daily OMT following surgery, another group got placebo OMT and the last group got only conventional post-op care. Those who received OMT were released from the hospital earlier and were up and about soonest.

How osteopathy can be used for cardiovascular disease: In addition to muscle energy, OMT for cardiovascular disease can include hands-on therapy to improve impaired cardiac lymph flow.

•**Digestive problems.** Digestive diseases, including irritable bowel syndrome (IBS), cause troubling symptoms such as abdominal cramping, flatulence, diarrhea and/or constipation.

Scientific evidence: A review of five studies showed that OMT improved IBS better than conventional care that included fiber supplements, laxatives, antibiotics, antidepressants and psychological treatment. The participants who received OMT had less severity of IBS symptoms, including abdominal pain, and better quality of life. Other research has shown that OMT can improve heartburn and Crohn's disease, an autoimmune disease of the intestines.

How osteopathy can be used: It's believed that OMT helps normalize the flow of blood and lymphatic fluids to restore motility and elasticity of the gastrointestinal tract.

Another common digestive issue occurs in people who suffer from diabetes. Of the approximately 30 million Americans who have diabetes, about 40% of type 1 diabetics and 20% of type 2 diabetics have diabetes-caused nerve damage that leads to gastroparesis—slow emptying of the stomach, which results in symptoms such as heartburn, nausea and bloating. The *Journal of the American Osteopathic Association* includes a report on a diabetes patient who was cured of gastroparesis after six sessions of OMT.

Treatments can include muscle energy, craniosacral manipulation, facilitated positional release and visceral manipulations of the abdomen. Treatments involving the brain-gut axis (the biochemical signaling that takes place between the gastrointestinal tract and the central nervous system) may also be used.

A GROWING TREND

Schools of osteopathic medicine have more than doubled in the US over the past few decades. Nearly one-quarter of all enrolled medical school students are studying to be DOs, and Americans are increasingly relying on them as primary care physicians and specialists.* While insurance companies do not distinguish between care provided by a DO or an MD, coverage of osteopathic manipulative treatment (OMT), like other treatments, depends on the insurance plan. A typical course of treatment from an OMT specialist (for conditions such as those in this article) ranges from six to eight treatments over a two- to four-week period.

*To find a doctor of osteopathic medicine near you, consult the American Osteopathic Association's website, DoctorsThatDo.org.

Can Marijuana Help You? Science Proves It Works for These Conditions

David Bearman, MD, vice president of quality assurance and credentials for the American Academy of Cannabinoid Medicine. He is author of *Drugs Are Not the Devil's Tools: How Discrimination and Greed Created a Dysfunctional Drug Policy and How It Can Be Fixed.* He is in private practice in Goleta, California, specializing in pain management. DavidBearmanMD.com

Almost every state in the US has legalized the medicinal use of marijuana in at least some form. And in early 2017, there was a remarkable development that should lead to greater acceptance of medical marijuana nationally. On January 12, the Health and Medicine division of the National Academies of Sciences, Engineering, and Medicine issued a report on the therapeutic use of cannabis (the term preferred by experts). To write their report, doctors from the Harvard T.H. Chan School of Public Health, Johns Hopkins University, Duke University Medical Center and other leading medical institutions reviewed and summarized the findings of more than 10,000 scientific studies on cannabis.

The studies show that cannabis has "therapeutic effects" on a variety of health conditions, including chronic pain, sleep disorders, anxiety, post-traumatic stress disorder, depression, chemotherapy-induced nausea and vomiting, epilepsy, the muscle spasms of multiple sclerosis, brain injury, Tourette's syndrome and other conditions.

Bottom line: Medical cannabis is a science-supported, effective therapy for symptomatic relief in a wide range of health problems.

Here's what you need to know about the medical benefits of cannabis and—if you decide to try it—how to take advantage of those benefits...

HOW CANNABIS WORKS

Researchers at St. Louis University School of Medicine in Missouri discovered that brain cells (neurons) have receptor sites for cannabinoids, the active compounds in cannabis. (There are more than 100 cannabinoids in cannabis, along with hundreds of other compounds.) In fact, they found that there are more receptors for cannabinoids than there are receptors for any other type of neurotransmitter—the chemicals that relay messages between neurons, activating functions in the brain and the rest of the body.

Scientists also soon found receptors for cannabinoids in the immune system, the peripheral nervous system (outside the brain and spinal cord) and the gut, spleen, liver, heart, kidneys, bones, blood vessels, endocrine glands and reproductive organs.

In subsequent years, they found that the body itself generates cannabinoid-like compounds called endocannabinoids.

Finally, they discovered an entire (and previously undetected) "endocannabinoid system" that regulates many mind-body functions, including memory, mood, aspects of digestion and energy balance. Scientists have concluded that the endocannabinoid system helps regulate a huge number of mental and physical functions.

Medical cannabis works by triggering the endocannabinoid system, which is why its effects are so wide-ranging. What's more, the endocannabinoid system employs a unique type of transmission called retrograde inhibition, which slows excessive activity in the body. With medical cannabis, there can be less pain, fewer muscle spasms, fewer seizures, less exaggerated tremors and less digestive upset.

NEW DISCOVERIES

The National Academies of Sciences report highlights many of the conditions helped by medical cannabis. *Here is a sampling of the most recent research supporting some of the conclusions...*

•**Chronic pain, including diabetic peripheral neuropathy and others.** Many studies have shown that medical cannabis works for chronic pain.

Example: Many people with diabetes suffer from chronic nerve pain in the feet and hands—symptoms include burning, electric shocklike tingling and dismaying numbness. Publishing their results in *Journal of Pain*, researchers from University of California, San Diego, found that medical cannabis could control nerve pain in people with diabetes.

•**Parkinson's disease.** Use of medical cannabis led to improvement in well-being and quality of life for people with Parkinson's disease, according to a study published in *Journal of Psychopharmacology.*

•**Epilepsy.** A study published in *Lancet Neurology* from researchers at major medical schools across the US found that medical cannabis reduced the frequency of seizures in patients with "severe, intractable...treatment-resistant epilepsy."

•**Inflammatory bowel disease (Crohn's).** Israeli researchers at Meir Medical Center, publishing a study in *Clinical Gastroenterology and Hepatology*, found remarkable improvements in 21 Crohn's patients who hadn't responded to conventional medical treatment—five had "complete remission"...10 of the 11 had an average decrease in symptoms of 69%...and three were able to stop taking steroid drugs to control the disease. Many had improved appetite and slept better.

•**Multiple sclerosis.** A study published in *Journal of Neurology, Neurosurgery & Psychiatry* found that cannabis extracts were twice as effective as a placebo in relieving muscle stiffness and pain in people with multiple sclerosis.

USING MEDICAL CANNABIS

In some states where medical cannabis has been legalized, getting a doctor's prescription for use of the medicine might be more or less automatic, just as it is with other sorts of medicines—you might spend a few minutes in the exam room and then be out the door with your prescription. But that is not necessarily a good thing.

You need to know how medical cannabis will work for your problem. You need to know the best dose for symptom control—one that controls your symptoms without a level of mental impairment that is uncomfortable or makes you dysfunctional. Starting with a low dose and slowly increasing the dose is the best approach—an approach that needs monitoring by your doctor and you.

Finding the best strain of cannabis to use for your health problem can be a matter of trial and error. Different cannabinoids have different effects. THC (*tetrahydrocannabinol*) is "psychoactive"—it creates euphoria (and is the reason that so many people use cannabis recreationally). *Cannabidiol* (CBD) is not psychoactive—it partially blocks some of the euphoria caused by THC. You and your doctor need to pick a strain and a dose that work best for you.

There also is the route of administration, which includes both vaping and smoking. Vaping requires the use of a vaporizer, which minimizes respiratory irritability—the plant matter is vaporized into gas rather than burned into smoke. This method is ideal for rapid relief in conditions such as severe, exacerbated chronic pain, migraines, nausea and vomiting, and asthma.

Another option is taking capsules of a cannabis extract such as Dronabinol. This is absorbed more slowly into the bloodstream and can provide three to six hours of therapeutic effect. For example, a dose that delivers five milligrams of THC works for patients who have trouble sleeping because of anxiety—it can provide three to six hours of good sleep if taken one hour before bedtime. There also are topical treatments. For example, topical tincture of cannabis can relieve muscle spasm or arthritic pain in the fingers and wrist.

To find a well-informed doctor, I recommend contacting the American Academy of Cannabinoid Medicine and asking for the name of a doctor near you who is a member of the academy (805-961-9988, info.aacm@gmail.com). Another organization that can help you find a doctor is Leafly (Leafly.com/doctors).

MORE ON SAFETY

As a physician who has worked with thousands of patients using medical marijuana, I can say that it is very safe—and not addictive.

In fact, cannabis creates fewer addictive symptoms than alcohol, nicotine and narcotic painkilling drugs. There is less risk for "dependency" than with any prescription pain or antianxiety medication. Little or no "tolerance" develops (tolerance is when you have to use more and more to achieve the same effect). There are few withdrawal symptoms, if any. All in all, cannabis is about as "addictive" as coffee.

There are possible side effects, however. The main one is coughing, which you can avoid by using a vaporizer or a noninhaled form. Another possible downside is dysphoria (feeling out of touch with reality, dissatisfied with life) or, on the other hand, excessive euphoria, which despite what you might expect can be an unpleasant side effect. Dysphoria or excessive euphoria are most likely when a new user takes a dose of THC that is too high. On the other hand, in patients with cancer or AIDS, a little euphoria to relieve anxiety and depression might be just what the patient needs—again, all of these possibilities can (and should) be worked out in your discussions with your doctor. Don't be afraid of medical cannabis. It has helped a great many people—and can help many more.

Nature's Stress Fighters

Maria Noël Groves, RH, a clinical herbalist and founder of Wintergreen Botanicals Herbal Clinic & Education Center in Allenstown, New Hampshire. She is registered with the American Herbalists Guild and is certified by the Southwest School of Botanical Medicine. She is the author of *Body into Balance: An Herbal Guide to Holistic Self-Care.* WintergreenBotanicals.com

In today's always-on-the-go, connected-to-everyone world, many of us feel constantly stimulated. No wonder up to 90% of all doctor visits are prompted by stress-related complaints, such as fatigue, pain, high blood pressure and cardiovascular disease.

Of course, a doctor visit usually means another prescription. It's not surprising that sedatives, antidepressants and antianxiety drugs are among the best-selling drugs in the US. While these potent pharmaceuticals may temporarily improve mood and other stress-related symptoms, they're not a permanent fix and often come with side effects.

NATURE'S STRESS FIGHTERS

The best way to deal with stress is with some basic—but critical—lifestyle changes, such as getting regular exercise, eating a healthier diet and maintaining a stress-reducing practice, such as meditation.

To augment those healthy habits, you can often use herbal medicines to help your body (and brain) cope with stress-related symptoms.*

For stress-related disorders, so-called adaptogenic herbs work well. Also known as stress modulators, these herbs can create balance when your body's stress-related hormones are too high or too low. The herbs aren't always a substitute for prescription drugs but may help you avoid them.

The following herbs can be taken singly or in combination. If you're combining herbs, be sure to keep their individual properties in mind as they can lessen each other's effects or work in synergy. While you can safely combine most adaptogenic herbs, be aware of what you're

*Before trying herbal therapy, consult your pharmacist or seek a naturopathic doctor or clinical herbalist's assistance, especially if you take prescription medications or have a chronic medical condition.

eating and drinking. Coffee, for example, can negate the calming effects of many herbs.

Options for herbal therapy: You can take the herbs below as a tea, tincture or capsule. Follow the recommended doses listed on the product labels.

BEST STRESS-FIGHTING HERBS

Ashwagandha. This nutty-tasting herb gives a mild energy boost. Paradoxically, it can also improve sleepiness at bedtime.

A study in the *Indian Journal of Psychological Medicine* found that people who took ashwagandha for 60 days had levels of cortisol (one of the main stress hormones) that were nearly 28% lower than those who took a placebo. The herb also gives a mild boost to thyroid function.

Caution: Ashwagandha is in the nightshade family. Try a small amount at first if you react to nightshades such as tomatoes and potatoes. If you have hyperthyroid disease or are on thyroid medication, consult your physician before taking ashwagandha.

Schizandra. It's a "mid-range" adaptogen that both calms and energizes, depending on what your body needs. It can help people with stress-related insomnia. It's also good for boosting vitality, mood and libido, and is one of the best herbs for stimulating digestion and improving liver detoxification.

Caution: Schizandra occasionally aggravates an active ulcer or gastroesophageal reflux disease (GERD).

HERBS FOR ANXIETY

If you mainly suffer from anxiety or stress-related "nerves," try one of the calming adaptogens...

Holy basil. This herb contains eugenol and other aromatic compounds that give it a pleasant odor—and that appear to reduce stress and improve mental clarity.

Studies suggest that holy basil reduces the stress hormone cortisol. In addition, it's often used for reducing anxiety and grief.

You can take this herb as needed or on a long-term basis. I particularly love it as tea and grow it in my garden.

How to try it: Steep one teaspoon to one tablespoon of dried holy basil (or a handful of the fresh herb) in eight ounces of water for 15 minutes. Drink one to three times daily.

Gotu kola. There is some evidence that this herb improves brain circulation and mental functions, while also reducing anxiety. The effects of gotu kola are subtle, making it ideal for long-term emotional balance.

You may not notice significant improvements for two to three months, and you can take it for a year or more. You can also safely combine it with other adaptogens, such as holy basil or ashwagandha, if you feel you need more potent (and faster) effects.

Note: Combination stress formulas are readily available on the market and can often be helpful. Take a look at the ingredients and consider each herb's individual benefits and potential side effects. Pick a formula that makes sense for your needs, and listen to your body.

Using these herbs: Most of the herbal adaptogens listed above will have some effect within one to three days, but with regular use, the effects tend to get more pronounced over the course of several weeks. If you don't notice improvement after two months, try one of the other herbs. Side effects, if any, will usually occur within the first day or two.

While you could take any of these herbs as needed—for example, a cup of holy basil tea on a stressful day—they work better when taken regularly for several months to a year. They're generally not dangerous to take on an ongoing basis, but most people find that they don't need them after a while.

SHOPPING FOR HERBS

You can find good-quality herbs at your local herb shop or natural-food store. Seek organic herbs whenever possible—they are grown without synthetic chemicals and more likely to be good quality. Some of my favorite brands for capsules and tinctures include Gaia Herbs, Herb Pharm, Oregon's Wild Harvest and MegaFood.

Online sources for dried herbs include Zack Woods Herb Farm (ZackWoodsHerbs.com)... and Mountain Rose Herbs (Mountain Rose Herbs.com).

Fast Fixes for Common Conditions

Bill Gottlieb, CHC, a health coach certified by the American Association of Drugless Practitioners. Based in Middletown, California, he is author of 16 health books that have sold more than three million copies and been translated into 10 languages, including *Speed Healing: More Than 2,000 Quick Cures and Fast Fixes to Ease Everything from Arthritis to Wrinkles* (Bottom LineStore.com/shl).

We all want to feel better faster! Here are nine remedies for common health problems that take very little time to implement and that often work in a flash...

1. Arthritis. Nearly half of Americans age 60 and older suffer with the pain of knee arthritis. Ice is the fastest way to relieve that pain—faster than taking a pain pill, says Jason Theodosakis, MD, coauthor of *The Arthritis Cure* and associate clinical professor at University of Arizona College of Medicine in Tucson. But ice often is used incorrectly, undercutting its pain-relieving power. Many people find the feeling of cold uncomfortable, so they either don't ice often enough or at all.

Rapid remedy: Buy a freezable soft gel ice pack and a compression (ACE-type) bandage. Store the gel pack in the freezer. When your knee hurts, place the pack on your knee over a pant leg or a towel, securing it to your knee with the compression bandage. (Never put the ice pack directly on your skin.) Keep the ice pack on for about 15 minutes—just the right amount of time to provide an hour or two of pain relief. Ice packs can bring relief to other parts of the body, too, including the ankle, shoulder and neck.

2. Constipation. In a study published in *World Journal of Gastroenterology*, people with chronic constipation were given a kiwi to eat twice a day for four weeks. For most patients, the number of weekly bowel movements doubled, and laxative use was reduced by 50%. Other research shows that eating kiwi can improve constipation in people with irritable bowel syndrome. Eating the fruit's skin triples the fiber intake and increases the amount of vitamin C when compared with eating just the flesh.

Rapid remedy: Eat one ripe kiwi after breakfast and one after dinner. To determine whether a kiwi is ripe, apply slight pressure to the skin with your thumb. If there's a little give, it's ripe. My health-coaching clients with constipation love this remedy—because it's so much easier than other oft-suggested remedies, such as exercising regularly, trying to eat a variety of high-fiber foods every day or using an herbal or a medicinal laxative.

3. Bug bite relief. I learned this fix from Matthew Schulman, MD, a New York City physician...

Rapid remedy: To stop the discomfort of a bug bite, Dr. Schulman prepares his own topical cream. It consists of two 25-milligram (mg) Benadryl tablets crushed into a powder and mixed into a small amount of over-the-counter 1% hydrocortisone cream (follow the use directions and cautions on the label). "This has an amazing effect that is better than any prescription drug I've tried," he said.

4. Back pain. There are many different causes of back pain. But you can relieve many types by using a simple position that takes weight off your spine while supporting it, says Art Brownstein, MD, director of Princeville Medical Clinic in Hawaii and author of *Healing Back Pain Naturally*.

Rapid remedy: Lie on your back on the floor with your knees bent and your feet resting up on a chair or a bed. Remain in this position for 15 to 20 minutes. Repeat this pose several times a day if needed.

5. Dry eye. Dry eye is one of the most common reasons people visit eye doctors. And one of the most common causes of dry eye is hours of nonstop computer use. There's a quick fix I learned from Robert A. Latkany, MD, founder and director of the Dry Eye Clinic at the New York Eye and Ear Infirmary of Mount Sinai and author of *The Dry Eye Remedy*.

Rapid remedy: Twice an hour, turn away from your computer screen, close your eyes and then move your eyeballs around underneath your closed lids as you count slowly to 10. This bathes and lubricates the eyes.

6. Eczema. The dry, itchy skin of eczema afflicts more than 30 million Americans and is the number-one reason people visit dermatologists. You can stop the itching in one minute with a remedy I learned from Adnan Nasir, MD, professor of dermatology at Duke University and author of *Eczema-Free for Life.*

Rapid remedy: With the heel of your palm, apply firm, deep pressure—equivalent to the weight of a bowling ball—to the site of the itching for one minute. Then apply the same deep pressure to the same part of the body but on the opposite side. For example, if the itch is on your left forearm, first apply pressure there, then apply pressure to your right forearm. "Why this works isn't known," Dr. Nasir told me, "but the anti-itching effect can last from minutes to hours."

7. Osteoporosis. Several studies show that eating prunes can reduce biomarkers of bone loss and build bone density—probably by decreasing bone-damaging oxidation and inflammation. In fact, scientists at Florida State University who conducted the research call prunes "the most effective fruit in preventing and reversing bone loss."

Rapid remedy: A study in *British Journal of Nutrition* shows that eating prunes daily is protective. Aim for five or six a day. Try sprinkling pitted, chopped prunes on oatmeal or ready-to-eat cereal or into pancake batter. Or add them to apple butter, orange marmalade, peanut butter or low-fat cream cheese, and spread on crackers for a delicious snack. Prunes also are great in chicken salad. Or simply eat prunes every day—they make a great dessert.

8. Indigestion. If you've got chronic indigestion or heartburn that medical care hasn't eased (or you don't want to take a dangerous acid-suppressing drug such as a proton pump inhibitor), you might want to try Iberogast. Scientific research shows that this nine-herb remedy from Germany can relieve stomach and abdominal pain, cramps, nausea, bloating and gas.

How it works: Research published in *The American Journal of Gastroenterology* shows that Iberogast relaxes the muscles of the stomach, improves stomach motility (the action of the muscles that move food out of the stomach into the small intestine) and reduces gut inflammation.

Rapid remedy: To ease chronic indigestion or heartburn, take 20 drops, three times a day, right before, with or right after a meal. You can take the drops directly or mix them with one to two ounces of warm water. You can find Iberogast at many online retailers.

Caution: Iberogast should not be taken by anyone with liver disease or by women who are pregnant.

9. Tinnitus. An estimated 35 million Americans suffer from this inner-ear problem that makes sufferers hear sounds such as buzzing, ringing, humming, hissing or clicking. Otolaryngologist Michael D. Seidman, MD, shared with me a rapid remedy for the problem—a combination of zinc and niacin (vitamin B-3).

How it works: The highest concentrations of zinc in the body are in the inner ear, and low levels may affect hearing. Niacin may work by improving circulation to the inner ear.

Rapid remedy: Take 25 mg of zinc once a day and 50 mg of niacin twice a day. (If you're already getting zinc and niacin in a multivitamin/mineral supplement, take enough of the nutrients to reach this level.) This can relieve tinnitus within two weeks or less.

Note: Niacin supplements may cause harmless, temporary but intense facial "flushing" or redness.

Natural Relief for Constipation

Eating three dried figs a day can relieve chronic constipation, according to a recent eight-week clinical trial.

Asian Journal of Clinical Nutrition.

New Treatment For Severe, Chronic Constipation

Jia (Marie) Liu, MD, PhD, China Academy of Chinese Medical Sciences, Beijing, leader of the electroacupuncture study published in *Annals of Internal Medicine.*

Electroacupuncture is acupuncture combined with electrical stimulation. After eight weeks of treatment—three to five sessions a week—31% of people who previously had no more than two bowel movements per week reported having three additional ones each week. The improvement continued during a 12-week follow-up period. Most licensed acupuncturists are trained in electroacupuncture.

Heartburn Remedies You've Never Heard of

Jacob Teitelbaum, MD, board-certified internist and nationally known expert in the fields of chronic fatigue syndrome, fibromyalgia, sleep and pain. Based in Kailua-Kona, Hawaii, he is author of numerous books, including *The Fatigue and Fibromyalgia Solution, Pain-Free 1-2-3* and *Real Cause, Real Cure.* Vitality101.com

If you have heartburn, you may be taking an acid-suppressing drug called a proton pump inhibitor (PPI). About 20 million of us are. PPIs include *esomeprazole* (Nexium), *dexlansoprazole* (Dexilant), *rabeprazole* (Aciphex), *lansoprazole* (Prevacid) and *omeprazole* (Prilosec).

As you may have read or heard, long-term use of PPIs has been linked to serious health problems. *Here, more on the dangers—and what's safer and effective...*

THE DANGERS

Yes, stomach acid may cause heartburn. But stomach acid also is a necessary component of everyday digestion and health. PPIs block the natural production of stomach acid—often with disastrous results. *PPIs have been linked to...*

- **Chronic kidney disease.** Chronic kidney disease (CKD) causes high blood pressure, increasing risk for heart attack and stroke, and can lead to a need for dialysis or a kidney transplant. In people using PPIs long-term, the risk of developing CKD is 50% higher.
- **Bone loss and fractures.** Because PPIs cut the absorption of bone-building calcium and magnesium, they decrease bone density. In one study, using PPIs for less than one year increased the risk for hip fractures by 26% and spinal fractures by 58%.
- **Heart attacks.** Researchers at Stanford University found that people taking PPIs long-term had 16% higher risk for heart attack...and double the risk of dying from heart disease.
- **Cancer.** Long-term use of PPIs can raise the risk for stomach and esophageal cancers, according to Australian researchers in an issue of *Expert Opinion on Drug Safety.*

PPIs also have been linked to dementia, pneumonia, gastrointestinal infection and deficiency of magnesium and/or B-12.

To add insult to injury, a recent study from University of California, San Francisco, published in *JAMA Internal Medicine*, found that up to 70% of PPI prescriptions are "inappropriate." That's because PPIs frequently are prescribed for any digestive complaint, rather than for FDA-approved medical conditions such as gastroesophageal reflux disease, or GERD (the medical term for heartburn), erosive esophagitis (inflammation of the esophagus) and stomach or duodenal ulcers. "Inappropriate" also means that the drugs—which are FDA-approved for only short-term use of a few weeks—often are used long-term.

SAFER REMEDIES

Your body produces stomach acid for a reason—to digest your food. Turning off that stomach acid with PPIs can decrease the pain from heartburn. But it doesn't treat the poor digestion that is causing your heartburn. To put it another way...your real problem isn't excess stomach acid—it's indigestion. Below are my recommendations to banish indigestion—you can try any of these remedies or even all of them at the same time if you wish. Continue to take a PPI drug at first while following these recommendations (see box on page three). You also may want to avoid foods that trigger heartburn, including citrus fruits, tomatoes, garlic, onions and chili.

Important: If problems persist after two months, see your doctor.

- **For quick heartburn relief, try bicarbonate of soda (baking soda).** One-half teaspoon of alkaline bicarbonate of soda (baking soda) in four ounces of water can quickly neutralize stomach acid and relieve the pain. Over-the-counter antacids with alkalinizing minerals (calcium combined with magnesium, such as Rolaids) also work—as little as one-quarter tablet can squelch the pain of heartburn. But there is some evidence that long-term use of calcium is associated with increased risk for heart attacks in women.

•Take digestive enzymes. One of the primary reasons for indigestion in the US is lack of enzymes in food, which have been removed during processing. I recommend the enzyme-containing supplement Complete GEST from Enzymatic Therapy. Take two capsules with every meal to digest food properly.

Caution: Some people find that digestive enzymes irritate the stomach. If this happens, start with GS-Similase—it's the gentler of the two products. If it causes irritation, don't use it. Instead, use the DGL licorice and mastic gum remedies (see below) until your stomach feels better, usually in a month or two—and then start taking digestive enzymes. The enzymes are used long-term to support healthy digestion.

•While eating, sip warm liquid rather than cold. Cold drinks slow and even can stop digestion. Drink warm liquids during meals to aid digestion.

•Avoid coffee, carbonated beverages, alcohol and aspirin. All of them can hurt your stomach. Once your stomach has healed, and indigestion and heartburn are a dim memory, you can use them again in limited amounts. (You'll know you're using too much if indigestion and heartburn return.)

•Take DGL licorice. This herb helps resolve the symptoms of heartburn and underlying indigestion. In fact, research shows it's as effective as the H2 blocker *cimetidine* (Tagamet)—but unlike Tagamet, which has been linked to some of the problems caused by PPIs, DGL licorice is good for you. I recommend Advanced DGL by EuroPharm, which doesn't have the licorice taste. Take one capsule twice a day—after one to two months, it can be used as needed.

Caution: You must use the DGL form of licorice. Other forms can cause high blood pressure.

•Take mastic gum. This gum (resin) from an evergreen tree is a wonderful remedy for heartburn and indigestion. Take mastic gum in supplement form. I recommend one or two 500-mg capsules twice a day for two months, then as needed.

Are You "Addicted" to PPIs?

After reading about the downsides of proton pump inhibitors (PPIs), you may want to stop taking them—immediately. But you may not be able to!

Researchers in Denmark gave *esomeprazole* (Nexium) for two months to 120 people without heartburn. Within two weeks of stopping the drug, 44% of the study participants developed heartburn. In 22%, those symptoms continued for the next four weeks.

Why did healthy people stopping the drug develop heartburn? Because of the phenomenon that the researchers call rebound acid hyper-secretion. It's natural for the stomach to produce stomach acid. If you foil that function and then allow it to resume, it returns with a vengeance, generating huge amounts of stomach acid that cause heartburn.

Best: Use the heartburn remedies from the main article for two months, and then—under your doctor's guidance—start "tapering" your PPI, cutting the dose in half every week (or at the rate your doctor suggests). When you're at the lowest possible dose, switch to Tagamet, which decreases stomach acid without totally turning it off. The Tagamet can be stopped after one month.

Boost Your Mood Naturally

Massachusetts General Hospital's publication *Mind, Mood & Memory.*

Too-low levels of the powerful neurotransmitter serotonin have been linked to depression, anxiety, irritability and mental decline.

Natural ways to raise serotonin levels: Vigorous aerobic exercise...20 minutes a day of peaceful meditation...learning to replace negative thoughts and reactions with more positive ones...exposure to sunlight or to lamps that mimic its effects...consuming probiotic foods such as pickles, sauerkraut, kefir and yogurt with active cultures...adding the spice turmeric to food...eating foods high in omega-3 fatty acids, such as cold-water fish including halibut, herring and salmon as well as flaxseed oil and walnuts.

Natural Ways to Take Care of Your Liver

Rich Snyder, DO, nephrologist, osteopathic physician and clinical professor at Philadelphia College of Osteopathic Medicine. He maintains a part-time nephrology practice at Lehigh Valley Nephrology Associates in Easton, Pennsylvania, and is author of *What You Must Know About Liver Disease: A Practical Guide to Using Conventional and Complementary Treatments.*

Alarming fact—about 30 million Americans have some form of liver disease. That's one-tenth of the population. Yet it's normal for people to go undiagnosed for years or even decades.

Unless liver disease is detected and treated early, it can cause severe inflammation that can lead to scarring (cirrhosis), organ failure and/or cancer—and it even may require a transplant. It is a leading cause of death in the US.

Important: I advise patients who have risk factors for liver disease to get their livers checked—the inexpensive group of blood tests can be done during routine checkups. Risk factors include obesity, metabolic syndrome, hepatitis and a history of alcohol or drug abuse.

If you have liver disease, medications may be required, but herbs and supplements can help reduce inflammation, improve liver function and slow ongoing damage. Always speak with your doctor before taking any natural supplements.

I usually advise patients to start with just one remedy at a time. After six to eight weeks, we reassess to see if there's improvement and if an additional supplement is required. Any of the herbs below can be started first, but milk thistle and turmeric are among the more common options.

MILK THISTLE

Milk thistle has been used for thousands of years for liver health. It's among the most studied herbs for treating hepatitis and other liver diseases.

Milk thistle (a member of the plant family that includes daisies and sunflowers) contains a flavonoid called silymarin. It's an antioxidant that reduces inflammation, blocks the movement of toxins into liver cells and increases the output of enzymes that prevent toxin-related damage.

Research suggests that milk thistle can improve liver function and improve survival in patients with chronic hepatitis and/or cirrhosis. One study found that it reduced the viral load (the amount of viral particles in the blood) in hepatitis C patients who hadn't responded to drug treatments.

Typical dosage: If you have risk factors for liver disease or if you've been diagnosed with liver disease, talk to your doctor about taking 100 mg twice a day, to start—your doctor might recommend a higher dose (between 200 mg and 600 mg) if lab tests aren't improving. Milk thistle is unlikely to cause side effects, although it should be avoided if you're allergic to ragweed or one of its relatives, such as sunflower seeds or chamomile.

TURMERIC

The active ingredient in this spice, curcumin, is an exceptionally potent antioxidant that has been shown to reduce jaundice (the dark urine and/or yellowing of the skin or eyes that often occurs in liver patients).

There's also some evidence that it reduces liver scarring. A study published in *Gut* found that turmeric helped prevent a hepatitis-causing virus from moving from one cell to another.

Typical dosage: Between 500 mg and 1,500 mg of a turmeric supplement daily, divided into two or three doses. (Exact dose will depend on your weight, symptoms and other factors.)

Caution: Turmeric has blood-thinning properties, so it may not be best if you are on a blood thinner such as *warfarin* or if your liver disease is advanced and clotting of the blood is a problem.

N-ACETYLCYSTEINE (NAC)

Doctors who specialize in natural health recommend this supplement for liver patients. It reduces inflammation and increases intracellular levels of glutathione, the "master antioxidant" that is mainly produced and stored in the liver and that is depleted by liver disease.

Doctors give it to improve the viability of transplanted livers. It also is used in patients with liver damage caused by *acetaminophen* overdose (acetaminophen rapidly depletes glutathione).

Typical dosage: 600 mg, twice daily.

GLUTATHIONE

You don't have to take this supplement if you already are using NAC (which is converted to glutathione in the body), but I often advise my patients to take glutathione because it helps rebuild body tissues, including liver cells.

Glutathione is particularly helpful if you regularly use acetaminophen for treating arthritis or another painful condition because acetaminophen, as mentioned before, can deplete glutathione levels. Oral glutathione usually needs to be taken with cysteine, which helps glutathione get into the cells.

Follow dosing directions on the label.

COFFEE

Coffee isn't a cure for liver disease, but there's good evidence that it reduces liver inflammation and may reduce liver-related health risks, including cirrhosis and cancer.

One study found that hepatitis B patients who drank more than four cups of coffee a week were only about half as likely to develop hepatocellular carcinoma (a form of liver cancer) as those who did not drink coffee.

Another study—one that looked at 430,000 people—found that people who drank an extra two cups of coffee a day could potentially reduce their risk for cirrhosis by 44%.

WEIGHT LOSS IS CRUCIAL FOR YOUR LIVER

Non-alcoholic fatty liver disease (NAFLD) is the leading type of liver disease in the US. It affects up to 25% of all adults and is linked to obesity and metabolic syndrome (a constellation of problems that includes high blood pressure, high blood sugar and elevated triglycerides, along with obesity).

A liver is considered "fat" if more than 5% to 10% of its weight comes from fatty tissue. This serious disease can lead to severe inflammation, cirrhosis or liver failure.

You have to lose weight if you've been diagnosed with NAFLD. Studies have shown that it may be possible to eliminate the condition altogether by losing as little as 10% of your total weight.

Also helpful: Alpha lipoic acid. It's a well-researched supplement that can decrease insulin resistance and improve metabolic syndrome. I advise patients with NAFLD to take 200 mg daily, increasing the dose by 100 mg weekly until they reach a maximum dose of 400 mg to 600 mg.

If you have diabetes or are at risk for diabetes, you may need to check your blood glucose levels because alpha lipoic acid has the potential to decrease glucose levels in some individuals.

Beware of Hidden Liver Disease

Jamison Starbuck, ND, a naturopathic physician in family practice and a guest lecturer at the University of Montana, both in Missoula. She is a past president of the American Association of Naturopathic Physicians and a contributing editor to *The Alternative Advisor: The Complete Guide to Natural Therapies and Alternative Treatments.* DrJamisonStarbuck.com

If you think of liver disease, chances are alcoholics and heavy drinkers come to mind. While it's true that these individuals are at increased risk for cirrhosis and certain other liver disorders, there's another condition that can affect this vital organ even in people who drink little (if any) alcohol. Fatty liver is a condition in which fat accumulates in the liver. This disease is very common in people who consume a lot of alcohol, but it's also reaching almost epidemic proportions in the US in nonalcoholics. Among those who aren't drinking heavily, obesity is the main risk factor. Individuals who have high triglycerides, diabetes (or even borderline diabetes) are also at increased risk for fatty liver.

What's most concerning is the insidious way that this condition progresses. As fat continues to accumulate in the liver, the organ becomes inflamed. Months or years of liver inflammation leads to scarring within the liver—and eventually to cirrhosis, possible liver failure (unless the person has a liver transplant) and death. In its early stages, fatty liver causes few symptoms. Your doctor might be able to palpate an enlarged liver, and you may have some indigestion and/or a swollen abdomen. But there is no specific testing for fatty liver, other than a liver biopsy, which involves surgically removing and analyzing a tissue sample from the organ. For this reason, fatty liver disease is usually diagnosed by a doctor based on a physical exam, lifestyle evaluation (red flags include a poor diet and lack of physical activity), excessive body weight and lab tests that show elevated lipids, such as triglycerides, and high blood glucose.

When it comes to treating fatty liver, conventional medical doctors recommend weight loss and perhaps medication for a related condition such as high cholesterol or diabetes. Naturopathic medicine, on the other hand, offers several effective treatment options. *My protocol for fatty liver disease...*

• **Diet.** I agree with medical doctors—If you have fatty liver and are overweight, you must lose weight. But do so slowly. Losing more than three pounds a week is hard on your liver. When planning meals, go low-carb—stay away from pasta, bread and sweets. Limit whole grains to two servings a day. Eat vegetables, fresh fruit, nuts, seeds, legumes and no more than one daily serving each of low-fat dairy, lean meat and fish.

• **Get the right nutrients.** Vitamin C is a powerful antioxidant that can help repair damaged liver cells. And a multivitamin offers other minerals and vitamins necessary for healthy liver function. In addition, I prescribe choline and methionine—these nutrients are essential for the breakdown of fats that can promote fatty liver.

Typical dose: 400 mg each of choline and methionine.

• **Try herbs.** Research shows that artichoke, dandelion and beet can reduce blood fats that promote fatty liver and support the health of liver cells. You can eat these as vegetables...or take them in powdered form in capsules. You can also find general formulas that contain lipotropic botanical compounds, which help protect the liver by breaking down fats in the blood. Follow the manufacturer's recommended dose for each of these supplements.

By taking these steps, under the supervision of your doctor, you may be able to actually reverse fatty liver disease—and in the process improve your digestion...boost your energy levels...and perhaps even increase your life span!

Natural Fixes for Mouth Sores

Jamison Starbuck, ND, a naturopathic physician in family practice and a guest lecturer at the University of Montana, both in Missoula. She is a past president of the American Association of Naturopathic Physicians and a contributing editor to *The Alternative Advisor: The Complete Guide to Natural Therapies and Alternative Treatments.* DrJamisonStarbuck.com.

When he came to see me, Dave complained of painful sores in his mouth and on his lips. When I took a look, I found many circular, yellow-white sores inside his mouth and on his gums and tongue (canker sores) and two large red ulcers on his lower lip (oral herpes). Many people suffer from one or both of these common lesions at some time in their lives, but fortunately, the following remedies can be used individually or simultaneously to help them heal—see what works best for you...*

Canker sores are small, painful, noncontagious lesions that occur inside the mouth. They can be caused by trauma to the mouth (such as biting yourself), dental procedures, digestive problems, food allergies, excess sugar, acidic foods or emotional stress. Canker sores can hurt for seven to 10 days and may take weeks to heal. *To speed the healing process, try...*

• **Licorice root paste.** Licorice root is soothing and reduces local inflammation.

What to do: Make a paste of powdered licorice root (use deglycyrrhizinated licorice, or DGL, if you have high blood pressure—the ingredient that can raise blood pressure has been removed) and water. If you can't find licorice root powder, purchase capsules and open several of them to make the paste. With your finger or a Q-tip, apply the paste to each canker sore several times a day for immediate, though short-lived, pain relief.

• **Chamomile tea.** The tannins in chamomile help with wound healing, including canker sores.

**Caution*: If any mouth sore lasts for more than two weeks, see a doctor to rule out a cancerous lesion. Also, check with your doctor if you take medication or have a chronic health condition, such as diabetes, before using these remedies.

What to do: Steep two chamomile tea bags in 16 ounces of hot water for five minutes. A mouth swish with warm, strong chamomile tea offers pain relief and speeds healing. Swish as often as you like.

Note: Avoid chamomile if you are allergic to plants in the ragweed family.

Also: Avoid coffee, sugar and citrus foods to help heal canker sores.

Oral herpes lesions, commonly referred to as "cold sores" or "fever blisters," most often occur on or near the lips. However, these red, ulcerated sores can spread to other parts of the face, including the eyes, so they should not be touched. Lasting for seven to 10 days, they are caused by the herpes simplex virus and are transmitted by skin-to-skin contact (kissing or touching) or by sharing objects (lip balm, eating utensils, razors, etc.) with a person who has the virus but not necessarily the sores. After the initial outbreak, the virus remains dormant in the body. Future outbreaks can be triggered by stress, illness, sun exposure and allergies. *What helps these sores heal...*

•**Lemon balm.** This herb is a potent antiviral that's highly effective against herpes.

What to do: Use one tablespoon of dried lemon balm in 16 ounces of hot water. Steep, covered, for five minutes. Discard herbs. Apply the tea directly to the lesions with a Q-tip or washcloth four to seven times a day, and drink 16 ounces of lemon balm tea a day for up to a week.

Note: Lemon balm tea can be sedating.

•**Lysine.** This amino acid also helps fight oral herpes. I recommend 3,000 mg of lysine daily while the herpes outbreak is present.

Also: Avoid chocolate and nuts—these foods feed the herpes virus.

Take a Deep Breath to Cure What Ails You

Jane Pernotto Ehrman, MEd, lead behavioral health therapist at the Cleveland Clinic Center for Lifestyle Medicine. Ehrman is also the owner of Images of Wellness, LLC, which teaches stress management to individuals and corporate groups. A variety of her guided meditations can be found on iTunes.

What do stubbing your toe, getting cut off in traffic and worrying about an ill friend have in common?

All these experiences cause us to hold or restrict our breath. When this happens, you are likely not even aware of it, but your breathing becomes shallow...and too little oxygen flows to the body and the brain. You may suffer from poor concentration, memory problems and low energy—or even a panic attack, as shallow breathing triggers the body's fight-or-flight response.

On the other hand, deep, purposeful breathing can have an incredibly positive impact on your well-being. It stimulates the parasympathetic part of your involuntary nervous system, slowing a rapid heartbeat and lowering blood pressure. And now, there's even more proof to back up its benefits.

Recent scientific evidence: Deep breathing, as practiced in meditation, has been linked to a lengthening of people's telomeres (the protective caps on chromosomes that impact aging and longevity), according to research conducted at the University of California, San Francisco.

The benefits don't stop there. Deep breathing has also been shown to help with the following...*

•**Pain.** When we hurt, our muscles often tighten up and we breathe shallowly. In addition to depriving the brain and body of oxygen, this increases inflammation, slowing the healing process and triggering pain-promoting anxiety.

What helps: Combining deep breathing with positive imagery can relax muscles in the affected area, which also decreases inflammation and pain.

*Unless noted otherwise, start with five minutes and work up to 15 to 20 minutes daily.

What to do: Find a quiet spot, and sit or lie in a comfortable position. Picture a place where you feel calm. Close your eyes and begin breathing using a "1:2 inhale-to-exhale ratio." For example, on the inhale, you can count to four and breathe in a feeling of calm, cooling energy...on the exhale, you can count to eight and imagine the painful area getting smaller and smaller and leaving your body.

•**Sleep.** The use of deep breathing with "body scans" (an exercise designed to create awareness of the body) has been shown to improve sleep in older adults—half of whom report sleep troubles.

What to do: While lying comfortably in bed, begin the same 1:2 inhale-to-exhale ratio described above—long, slow exhalations stimulate the brain's vagus nerve, which tells the body: "It's time to relax."

To begin the body scan, concentrate on your feet—wiggle and scrunch your toes, then relax them and notice how comfortable your feet feel simply resting on the bed. Move on to your ankles, perhaps rolling them in circles...then your calves...knees...thighs, etc.

Remember: Keep breathing deeply, and focus on how relaxed and heavy each body part feels, allowing it to become soft and limp like a cooked noodle. You should be asleep before you reach your head! If you're feeling particularly tense, you can tighten each body part before relaxing it.

•**High blood pressure.** For many people, stress can cause the amygdala, the region of the brain that processes danger signals, to activate the release of stress hormones that raise blood pressure.

What to do: Sit tall, with your head held straight, looking forward. Close your eyes or gaze at a single point straight ahead. Breathe in naturally...then exhale more slowly while silently repeating, "I let it go." When your mind wanders, simply refocus on your breath and mantra. By practicing mindful breathing, you will learn to become less reactive to daily stressors.

Extra move: Gratitude breath. As you breathe, focus on a person, place or thing for which you are thankful. Research has linked the positive energy and uplifting mood that results from gratitude with a healthier heart rate.

•**Depression.** This breathing technique activates the parasympathetic nervous system while rewiring the brain for positivity. Consistent practice will heighten your awareness of negative thinking so it will be easier to shift your focus away from sadness and pull yourself out of a downward spiral.

What to do: Breathe in for a count of four... breathe out slowly, counting to eight. Add a mantra that you say silently to yourself. *Possibilities...*

Inhale: In this moment.

Exhale: I am OK.

Inhale: Peace.

Exhale: Calm.

My advice: Whenever you can, do this exercise in a peaceful outdoor setting—nature has a calming, antidepressant effect.

Turmeric May Fight Tuberculosis

Respirology.

Drug-resistant tuberculosis (TB) may respond to turmeric, a popular anti-inflammatory, recent research has found.

Why it helps: The curcumin in turmeric stimulates the immune cells that fight TB.

Eat to Beat Nausea

Jessica Iannotta, MS, RD, CSO, CDN, dietitian and certified specialist in oncology nutrition. She is chief operating officer of Savor Health, a nutrition service that provides individual nutrition solutions for cancer patients and caregivers. She is coauthor of *The Meals to Heal Cookbook.* SavorHealth.com

If you are feeling nauseated for any reason, the last thing you want to do is eat or drink. But that might be the best thing you can do to alleviate that sick feeling in your stomach. An important contributor to nausea is an empty stomach, which leads to irregular contractions of the stomach. Eating small, frequent meals (five or six times a day) helps to reestablish the stomach's rhythm, making you feel better.

Also helpful: For snacks, eat dry foods, such as crackers, toast, pretzels or other high-carbohydrate foods—they are easy on the stomach and absorb excess stomach acid. Drink a half-hour before or after eating, not with meals, because for certain people, the combination of liquid and solid food can aggravate nausea. And drink slowly. Try using plastic silverware because metal can leave a bitter taste in your mouth, especially if you are taking certain medications that can cause severe taste changes (such as antibiotics and chemotherapy drugs).

Be aware of smells that bother you, and try to avoid being around them. And be mindful of your surroundings during meals—make sure to eat in a relaxed, calm setting, which is extremely helpful for efficient digestion.

Here are four delicious recipes that are particularly good for relieving nausea…

Orzo Kale Soup

You can toss cooked shredded chicken into this soothing soup if you like. Reduce or omit the tomatoes if the acid bothers your stomach. (Serves four)

2 Tablespoons olive oil
1 medium-sized onion, chopped
2 medium-sized carrots, peeled and chopped
2 garlic cloves, minced
1 (15-ounce) can diced tomatoes
2 cups vegetable stock
1½ cups cooked white beans, or 1 (15-ounce) can, drained and rinsed
½ cup whole-wheat orzo
4 cups chopped kale
Salt and freshly ground black pepper
¼ cup freshly grated Parmesan cheese (optional)

1. Heat the olive oil in a large pot over medium heat. Add the onion, carrots and garlic, and sauté for one minute.

2. Add the tomatoes, stock and white beans. Bring to a boil, then lower the heat to a simmer. Cover and cook for about 15 minutes.

3. Add the orzo, and simmer the soup for about 10 more minutes or until the orzo becomes tender. Add the kale, and cook for one to two minutes more. Season to taste with salt and pepper.

4. To serve, ladle a generous portion of soup into each bowl.

5. Top with freshly grated Parmesan, if using.

Turkey and Oatmeal Loaf

This simple comfort food is very tasty without being too spicy or heavy for those experiencing nausea. Make meatloaf sandwiches with the leftovers, or you can freeze leftovers for another day. (Serves eight)

¾ cup quick-cooking oats
½ cup milk
1 medium-sized onion, peeled
2 pounds ground turkey breast
½ cup seeded and chopped red bell pepper
2 large eggs, beaten
2 teaspoons Worcestershire sauce
¼ cup ketchup
½ teaspoon salt
Freshly ground black pepper
1 (8-ounce) can tomato sauce

1. Preheat the oven to 350°F.

2. In a small bowl, stir together the oats and milk. Thinly slice one quarter of the onion, and set aside. Finely chop the remaining onion. In a large bowl, combine the turkey, oat mixture, chopped onion, bell pepper, eggs, Worcestershire sauce, ketchup, salt and a few grinds of black pepper. Mix just until well-combined.

3. Transfer the mixture to a nine-by-nine-inch baking dish or a standard loaf pan, and shape into a loaf about five inches wide and two-and-a-half-inches high. Pour the tomato sauce over the meat loaf, and sprinkle with the sliced onion. Bake for about one hour or until an instant-read thermometer inserted into the center registers 160°F.

4. Remove from the oven, and let rest for 10 to 15 minutes before slicing.

Apple Crumble Baked Oatmeal

This oatmeal contains easy-to-digest carbohydrates—and the lightly sweetened warm apple and spice flavors make this an extra flavorful and comforting breakfast. Leftover baked oatmeal can be reheated the following day and served in a bowl with a little milk, yogurt or nut butter. (Serves six)

Unsalted butter or oil, for baking dish
2 cups rolled oats
1 teaspoon baking powder
½ Tablespoon ground cinnamon
¼ teaspoon ground nutmeg
½ teaspoon salt
2 cups milk
¼ cup pure maple syrup
1 large egg
2 Tablespoons unsalted butter or coconut oil, melted
2 teaspoons vanilla extract
3 apples, peeled, cored and cut in half

For the crumble topping...
½ cup roughly chopped walnuts or other nut
1 Tablespoon unsalted butter or coconut oil, melted
Pinch of salt
1 Tablespoon light or dark brown sugar

1. Preheat the oven to 375°F, and grease a nine-by-nine-inch baking dish with unsalted butter or oil.

2. Place the oats, baking powder, cinnamon, nutmeg and salt in a bowl, and stir together. Pour this mixture into the prepared baking dish.

3. In another bowl, combine the milk, maple syrup, egg, melted butter and vanilla. Whisk together completely. Slowly pour this over the oats.

4. Tuck the apple halves into the oats, cut side down.

5. Combine the crumble ingredients in a small bowl, then sprinkle over the top of the oats and apples.

6. Bake for 40 to 45 minutes or until the center is cooked through and the crumble is deep golden and caramelized. Let cool slightly before serving.

Ginger Granita

This recipe creates a slushy drink that is light, refreshing and tasty. It contains ginger, which has been used in China for more than 2,000 years for treating stomach upset, nausea and diarrhea. The gingerroot is rich in gingerols and shogaols, plant substances that relax the intestinal tract. One study found that when cancer patients took one-half to one gram of ginger daily for three days prior to chemotherapy treatment, nausea was reduced significantly, compared with patients who took a placebo.

Depending on how much you crush up the ice (in a food processor or with a spoon), you can drink it with a straw or enjoy it with a spoon. For severe nausea, make a batch and sip throughout the day or about a half-hour before mealtimes. Granita will keep in the freezer for up to five days. (Serves eight, makes four cups)

3 Tablespoons peeled and thickly sliced fresh ginger
3½ cups water, divided
1½ cups sugar
2 teaspoons freshly squeezed lemon juice

1. Chill a baking pan for two hours in the freezer.

2. In a blender or food processor, purée the ginger with one cup of water.

3. Combine the ginger purée, sugar and two-and-half cups of water in a saucepan. Bring to a simmer over high heat, stirring frequently, not allowing the mixture to boil.

4. Strain the mixture through a fine-mesh strainer, reserving the liquid and discarding the pulp.

5. Stir in the lemon juice, and pour into the prechilled baking pan. Place on a level surface in the freezer. Let the mixture freeze overnight until solid.

6. Use a metal spoon to scrape the mixture into a light, granular texture or place broken pieces in a food processor and chop to your desired texture.

Write Your Way to Better Health

James W. Pennebaker, PhD, the Regents Centennial Professor in the department of psychology at The University of Texas at Austin. He is author of numerous books, including *Expressive Writing* and *Opening Up by Writing It Down*.

When it comes to staying healthy (or getting healthy), most people are willing to do whatever it takes—whether it's changing their diet, getting more exercise, using supplements and/or taking medication. But there's another way to improve your health that doesn't get nearly the attention it deserves.

Writing down your feelings not only helps you feel better mentally but also results in beneficial physiological changes, including reduced blood pressure and strengthened immune function. Now researchers are uncovering the best ways to get the greatest health benefits from therapeutic writing.

This may all sound great if you're a would-be novelist or poet. But what if writing has never been your thing...or the rules of grammar leave your head spinning? Don't worry. You can still realize the health benefits of this powerful technique.

To learn more, we spoke with Dr. James W. Pennebaker, a psychologist and pioneer in the field of therapeutic writing.

HOW SECRETS HARM US

Therapeutic writing got started when my colleagues and I became intrigued by a landmark study that found that people who suffered a trauma (such as the death of a loved one, a breakup of an important relationship or a sexual or physical assault)—and kept it a secret—were at higher risk for illness (ranging from colds and flu to ulcers and elevated blood pressure) compared with those who talked about their traumatic experiences.

This finding led us to wonder: If not talking about traumatic events harms health, would asking people to talk—or write—about emotional upsets improve health?

To test this hypothesis, we asked college students to write for 15 minutes a day for four consecutive days on a nonemotional topic or to write about their deepest thoughts and feelings related to a traumatic experience—or a current major conflict or stressor—in their lives. (The latter approach is known as "expressive writing.")

Result: By the last day, most of those who did expressive writing said that the experience was important to them...and four months later, those students had made 43% fewer (onetime) visits to the doctor for sickness than those who wrote about superficial topics.

Since our first study, a growing body of research has revealed specific physiological changes that occur after writing expressively.

The benefits include faster healing following surgery...lower blood pressure...strengthened immune function...reduced physical symptoms as well as better sleep and daytime functioning in cancer patients...and less fatigue in rheumatoid arthritis patients.

GETTING STARTED

To harness the health benefits of expressive writing, plan to write for a minimum of 15 minutes a day for four consecutive days.

Day one: Write your deepest thoughts and feelings about a past trauma or a current emotional upheaval that may be influencing your life now. This could include major life experiences or traumas, such as divorce, a death or a long-lasting conflict in your life.

Simply write about the event itself—how you felt when it was happening and how you feel about it now. Do not worry about grammar, sentence structure or spelling.

Days two, three and four: For the next three days, continue to write about the same trauma, upheaval or major life conflict, digging even deeper into your feelings and thoughts. Write about how this trauma affects all aspects of your life, including your relationships. *Other considerations...*

- **Type or write longhand?** Studies have not found a significant difference in effectiveness. Do whichever you find more comfortable.
- **Plan to throw away your writing.** What you write is for your eyes only. Feel free to destroy or hide it each day when you are done.
- **Don't worry if you initially feel sad.** Give yourself some time after your writing ses-

sion to reflect on what you've written and to relax. Any sadness usually lifts after an hour or so as you move on to other activities. This exercise helps you to get some emotional distance from the trauma. If the sadness doesn't lift, you may want to consider seeing a therapist.

Also: Feel free to experiment. The four-day method, as used in our study, works for many people, but you may prefer writing about your feelings for two days...or six days. You may find it easier to talk into a tape recorder about your deepest emotions rather than writing about them. See what works for you!

Natural Fixes for 4 "Hot Spots"

Jamison Starbuck, ND, a naturopathic physician in family practice and a guest lecturer at the University of Montana, both in Missoula. She is a past president of the American Association of Naturopathic Physicians and a contributing editor to *The Alternative Advisor: The Complete Guide to Natural Therapies and Alternative Treatments.* DrJamisonStarbuck.com

---

Most of us have an "Achilles' heel" or "hot spot" with regard to our health—an area of the body that is more vulnerable to pain or debility, particularly when we are stressed or ill. *Here are several such areas—and my advice on how to keep them as healthy as possible...*

- **Back.** For people who may have had a fall, sports injury or car accident—even if it was years ago—back pain can be a common vulnerability.

What helps: Pay attention to early warning signs—a little tightness in the morning...or a faint grip in the back when you walk. Start stretching (for example, lift your arms overhead and do gentle forward and sideways bending), and rub arnica oil or cream, a very effective anti-inflammatory, on the sore spot. In addition, at the first sign of trouble, consider also using the healing anti-inflammatory herbs boswellia and turmeric for several days (follow dosing instructions on the label).

- **Bowels.** Diarrhea, stomach pain and indigestion can be another Achilles' health heel—especially for anyone with diverticulitis or other digestive issues. At the first hint of gastrointestinal (GI) symptoms, eat light, easy-to-digest foods, including broth, steamed vegetables, fish, roasted chicken, applesauce, soft-boiled eggs and toast. Drinking peppermint, spearmint or chamomile tea between meals can calm your GI tract.* A daily probiotic supplement will also help by keeping the bowel flora balanced.

- **Head.** Headaches are more frequent in people who have had head injuries, meningitis, neck and shoulder injuries or concussion. The brain seems to "remember" a wound, and as stress or inflammation increases in the body, pain flares in the head.

If your health hot spot is your head, consider these steps: First, keep your neck and shoulders limber by doing neck and shoulder stretches when you wake up and at midday. (Consult a physical therapist or massage professional for specific advice.) Second, when you feel tension building in your neck, ice the back of it for five minutes once an hour for several hours—this will reduce inflammation and muscle tension, hopefully warding off a headache. Third, be sure you're drinking enough water. Finally, investigate food allergies, which often go undetected. Start by keeping a journal to see if your headaches seem to be tied to certain foods. You can also consult a naturopathic physician about getting tested for food allergies.

- **Mouth.** Canker sores are a common vulnerability—especially in people with poor immune function. These irritating mouth ulcerations are often triggered by stress...excess sugar consumption...dental procedures...or a high-acid meal.

What I recommend: Licorice root—it is soothing and heals the membrane in the mouth. In some people, it can raise blood pressure, so opt for deglycyrrhizinated licorice (DGL)—the ingredient that can cause blood pressure problems has been removed. It's available in lozenges that are dissolved in the mouth...or in a tincture. For canker sores, swish and swallow a mixture of 60 drops in water four times a day away from meals until the problem clears up.

*Avoid mint teas if you have gastroesophageal reflux disease (GERD), since mint can trigger acid reflux.

---

3 Weeds That Really Work!

Jamison Starbuck, ND, a naturopathic physician in family practice and a guest lecturer at the University of Montana, both in Missoula. She is a past president of the American Association of Naturopathic Physicians and a contributing editor to *The Alternative Advisor: The Complete Guide to Natural Therapies and Alternative Treatments.* DrJamisonStarbuck.com

Every spring, when the dandelions poke their yellow heads out of the soil, I smile with gratitude. This hardy, and often maligned, weed has several under-recognized but well-established health benefits. In fact, it's one of a trio of herbs that I used years ago to clear up a stubborn case of eczema before I had become a naturopathic physician. This "herb tonic" did the job in a matter of weeks and convinced me that natural medicine really does work! My favorite medicinal weeds (available in natural-food and herb stores)...*

- **Dandelion.** This weed, which contains vitamins such as vitamin C, is a member of the daisy family. With roots and leaves that are rich in medicinal properties, dandelion supports liver and gallbladder health...promotes digestion...acts as a diuretic to reduce edema (water retention) in the ankles and hands...and lowers blood pressure.

Note: Check with your doctor before trying dandelion—especially if you take a blood thinner, diabetes medication, a blood pressure drug (such as a diuretic) or other prescription medication.

To consume dandelion, you can eat the leaves in salads or on sandwiches or add to soup as a raw garnish.

Important: Don't cook dandelion leaves in soup or you will lose many of the medicinal benefits—simply add them to the top of your soup for steaming before you serve.

You can also enjoy medicinal dandelion tea. Just put two teaspoons of dried dandelion root in one cup of boiling water. Reduce heat, and simmer for 15 minutes. Drink one cup two times a day, at least 15 minutes before or after eating.

*Before trying any herbal therapy, consult your doctor if you have a chronic medical condition or take prescription medication.

Doing this will aid your digestion and help ease one or more of the conditions described above. For example, edema will typically improve in a few days, while it can take three to four weeks to lower blood pressure. If you like dandelion tea, you can drink it indefinitely. If you opt for dandelion tincture, a typical daily dose is one-quarter teaspoon, in two ounces of water, twice a day, 15 minutes before a meal.

- **Burdock.** Like dandelion, burdock is ubiquitous in the US, popping up around the edges of sidewalks and in abandoned areas. Burdock is also in the daisy family and has what herbalists call "bitter properties"—that is, constituents that help improve digestion. I also use burdock in formulas for skin problems such as psoriasis, eczema and dandruff. Burdock root is mild tasting and can be used in soups and stews as you would carrots. Consult your doctor before using it if you take a blood thinner, diabetes drug or diuretic.

- **Yellow dock.** Because yellow dock is a mild laxative, it relieves constipation in a few days. It's also a good plant source of iron. Like burdock, yellow dock can help with scaly, itchy skin conditions. It is a member of the buckwheat family and tastes very bitter, so it's best taken in tincture (see above) once daily...or mixed in small amounts with other milder plants in a tea.

Caution: Do not use yellow dock if you take *digoxin* (Lanoxin), a diuretic or *warfarin* (Coumadin).

Because these herbs are generally safe for long-term use, I often combine all three in my treatment plans for liver, gallbladder or skin conditions. Many of my patients become fans of these herbs—just as I did—when they experience firsthand the plants' healing powers.

5 Natural Sunburn Soothers

Andrew Rubman, ND, founder and medical director of the Southbury Clinic for Traditional Medicines, Southbury, Connecticut. Naturopath.org

You could have covered up, but you didn't. You could have used more sunscreen, but that didn't happen either. So now you're coming home from a lovely day of swimming, boating, playing golf or otherwise frolicking in the sun—and your skin is feeling hot...and is turning red.

You've got a sunburn...and maybe a windburn, too. Pain is coming. *Here's what to do...*

A NATUROPATH'S FAVORITE SUNBURN HOME REMEDIES

Most of the time when you have a sunburn, you'll feel better faster—and heal faster—by using certain proven-to-work home remedies.

The exception: If you have a blistering burn or one that is covering a large part of your body, or if the burn is accompanied by fever, chills, headache or severe pain, don't treat it at home—see or call your health-care provider. (If you do have blisters, do not break them—it slows healing and increases risk for infection.)

For everyday sunburn and windburn, you can treat your skin with easy-to-find products that you might not have considered. Your first order of business is something most people don't think about—keeping skin moist. With sunburn or wind exposure, the skin's normal ability to retain moisture is disturbed. If the skin starts drying out, it can become inflamed, and then it can become scaly and more vulnerable to infection.

Cooling the skin and keeping it moist can relieve your discomfort and protect the skin from becoming dehydrated. The way to start is not with a lotion, although that's what most people do. Instead, as soon as possible after realizing you have a burn, apply a cool compress to the sunburned or windburned area—a towel or wash cloth soaked in cool water will work for your arms, legs, shoulders or face—and if it's your torso that's sunburned, wear a cotton T shirt that's been soaked in cool water. As the compresses cool, apply fresh ones until the pain is substantially diminished.

Of course, it's not always convenient to walk around garbed in wet clothes and bath linens, so here are some other top remedies. Any and all of these remedies can be combined and used as often as you like, so try different combinations until you find the right one for you. Since they all start working immediately, your skin should start to feel better quickly...

1. Apply witch hazel to the burned area. Using witch hazel, a solution made with an extract from the leaves, twig and bark of the Hamamelis plant, may seem counterintuitive because of its astringent properties. But it is a strong antioxidant with anti-inflammatory effects that are skin soothing and cooling.

2. Coconut oil rubbed into the skin provides a medium-chain fatty acid (lauric acid), which helps keep skin moist. Although the oil is solid at room temperature, it will melt at body temperature and absorb into the skin so you will not leave the house coated in white pasty oil.

3. A soaking bath containing oatmeal powder and a little white vinegar (two or three tablespoons) is soothing, relieves itching and helps the skin regain its normal moisture barrier. The vinegar helps remove inflammatory compounds released by sun-damaged skin and soothes sunburn pain. For the oatmeal powder, try Aveeno, but you can also make your own by grinding uncooked oat cereal in a blender until it becomes a fine powder.

4. Some high-end cosmetics contain squalane, a stablized form of a naturally occurring substance derived from certain plants (and historically from shark liver). Squalane provides good protection against dehydration in damaged skin. Rub squalane on the damaged or dry skin as often as necessary. Squalane doesn't clog pores, it soaks in rather quickly, and it feels very light on the skin. It has no color, odor or taste. The brand Mayumi is inexpensive, made by a reliable company and available in stores and online.

5. Fresh aloe gel is very soothing on damaged skin. If you don't already have an aloe plant, you can purchase one from a home center or nursery for a few dollars. Snip off one of the fronds, squeeze out the gel and apply to your skin. Applying fresh aloe gel feels instantly cooling and soothing. Fresh aloe from a leaf is much better than any store-bought aloe product because the gel's ability to soothe decreases rapidly after it's extracted. Reapply when the soothing effect wears off.

NO MORE SUNBURN

To prevent sunburn the next time you go outside after being burned, especially during peak sun hours, use a sunscreen product with the main active ingredient oxide or titanium dioxide. Because your skin will probably still be somewhat irritated from your previous sunburn, you might be more apt to absorb potentially irritating compounds in other, chemical-based sunscreens. Zinc oxide and titanium dioxide, in contrast, offer a physical barrier, not a chemical one. They may stay white on your skin, but that's the proof that the product is protecting you—and a small price to pay.

CHAPTER 16

Nutrition and Fitness

11 Surprising Ways to Shed Pounds: No Willpower Needed!

If you store boxes of breakfast cereal in the wrong spot in your kitchen, you could end up 20 pounds heavier. If you set serving dishes in the wrong spot at mealtimes, you could consume 20% more calories than you otherwise would have. If you get seated at the wrong table in a restaurant, the odds that you will order a dessert could leap by 73%.

People tend to think that avoiding overeating is mainly a matter of willpower. But willpower alone is never enough. Almost all of us have moments when willpower wavers...and moments when we eat irresponsibly because we are not paying enough attention to eat properly.

The good news is that there are clever, surprising things you can do to avoid overeating without relying on superhuman willpower and vigilance...

FOOD STORAGE TRICKS

- **Segregate snack food.** Each time you open a cupboard that contains empty-calorie snack food, there's a reasonable chance that you will indulge—even if you originally opened the cupboard to retrieve something else.

To avoid this, it's best to just not buy unhealthy snack food. But if that's not in the cards, store all unhealthy snacks, such as potato chips and cookies, in a single cupboard rather than spread them throughout the kitchen as is common. (The typical US kitchen has five cupboards—and snack food is stored in the majority of them.) Do not store anything but snacks in your snack cupboard so that you never accidentally stumble upon temptation.

Healthy snacks such as fruit or whole-grain rice cakes can remain elsewhere in the kitch-

Brian Wansink, PhD, director of the Food and Brand Lab at Cornell University, Ithaca, New York. In 2007, the White House named him the US Department of Agriculture executive director in charge of Dietary Guidelines for 2010. He is author of *Slim By Design: Mindless Eating Solutions for Everyday Life*. SlimByDesign.com

en—there's nothing wrong with stumbling upon these.

Next step: To reduce snacking even further, store unhealthy snacks in a cupboard located in a room that you enter less often than your kitchen, such as the basement or the laundry room.

•Store snacks in single-serving portions. When snack foods leave the kitchen, they rarely come back. Carry a family-sized bag of chips to the living room, for example, and if you're like most people, there's a good chance that you will eat the entire thing...and even if you don't, you likely will eat more than you meant to.

One solution is to buy snacks pre-packaged in single-serving portions—but these tend to cost much more per ounce than larger sizes. Instead, buy economy-sized bags, but immediately repackage these snacks into single-serving-sized plastic bags or other small containers as soon as the snacks enter the house.

•In the refrigerator, store healthy snacks in clear containers...unhealthy ones in opaque ones. Remove fruit from the crisper drawer, and store it in clear plastic bags or storage containers at eye level in your fridge. Meanwhile, wrap unhealthy snacks in tin foil or put them in opaque food containers. The snacks that people are most likely to eat are not the ones they think taste best...they are the ones that they happen to see first.

•Store cereal boxes out of view. It probably comes as no surprise that people are especially likely to eat foods that are "on display" on countertops or exposed shelves in their homes. But what is surprising is that this seems to matter most not with candy but with breakfast cereal.

People who keep candy on display in their homes are, on average, three pounds heavier than people who do not...people who have cookies or crackers on display are about eight pounds heavier...while people who have cereal boxes out where they can be seen are in excess of 20 pounds heavier.

The most likely explanation is that people realize that snacking on candy and cookies is bad for them, so they often manage to stop themselves from grabbing these sugary treats...but breakfast cereal has the aura of healthfulness—even though it usually is quite sugary and fattening—so people who have it out on display are less likely to stop themselves from indulging.

MEALS

•Leave serving dishes and pots on the kitchen counter or stove while you eat. People who fill their plates at least six feet from the table tend to eat around 20% fewer calories at mealtime than people who bring serving dishes or pots to the table. The reason—having additional food within easy reach greatly increases the odds that people will help themselves to seconds or thirds.

Men are particularly likely to do this. They tend to eat faster than their wives and children, so they finish meals first—then take extra helpings even when they are not very hungry because they get bored sitting around doing nothing.

•Eat off slightly undersized plates, and use undersized serving spoons. You might have heard that people eat less when they eat off small plates—small plates make modest amounts of food look more substantial. It turns out that this can be taken too far. If you try to eat dinner off a very small plate, it only increases the odds that you will go back for more. The ideal dinner plate size is around nine inches in diameter—smaller than the typical 10-to-12-inch dinner plate but not so small as to encourage the taking of seconds.

Also: Using serving spoons of modest size reduces consumption, too...as does replacing serving tongs with serving spoons. (Do use tongs to serve salad. Taking large servings of salad makes people less likely to fill up on more fattening foods.) An undersized ice-cream scoop is an especially worthwhile investment—people tend to pay attention to the number of scoops of ice cream they take, not the total amount of ice cream they eat.

But do not try to eat with undersized utensils. It turns out that doesn't make people eat less—it just annoys them.

•Put on slow music, and turn down the lights. These things tend to calm people down—and people who feel calm at mealtimes tend to eat more slowly and eat less.

DINING OUT TRICKS

It's easy to overindulge when you eat out. *These strategies will help...*

- **Ask to be seated at a well-lit table...by a window...at a table that is higher-than-normal table height...or in a bustling part of the dining room.** When people feel on display in restaurants, they tend to order healthier meals, such as fish or salad. When they are seated in booths or dark, private corners, they are more likely to order fattening things such as ribs and desserts.

Example: People seated at the table farthest from a restaurant's front door are 73% more likely to order a dessert than people seated near the entrance.

- **Ask to be seated at least three tables away from the bar.** When people eat dinner at a restaurant's bar—or within two tables of its bar—they order three-and-a-half more alcoholic drinks per party of four. This applies only at dinner, however—people do not drink significantly more when they eat lunch near a restaurant's bar.
- **Adopt trim people's habits at buffets.** Trim people and heavy people tend to exhibit significantly divergent behavior when they dine at buffets—generally without even realizing they are doing so. Thin buffet diners choose tables far from the food (when given a choice of table)...they choose seats that face away from the food...they use smaller plates if multiple plate sizes are available...they use chopsticks (if this is an option)...and they scout out the entire buffet before taking any food. Heavy people tend to do exactly the opposite of each of these things. Act trim, and it will help you be trim!
- **Be aware of your waiter's weight.** If your waiter is overweight, you're more likely to overindulge. In a study of 497 people at 60 full-service restaurants, diners ordered more food—especially dessert—and more alcohol when the waiter had weight to lose than when the waiter was thin. This was true regardless of how much the diners themselves weighed. It's likely that the presence of a heavy person made the diners feel as if they had "permission" to indulge.

You can't control who your waiter is, but just recognizing the effect that a heavy waiter could have on your ordering can help you resist temptation. It's also helpful when eating out to have a "predetermination strategy," such as deciding in advance what you'll order (you usually can view menus online). Or you can have "rules" in place such as only one glass of wine with dinner.

Beware the New Normal for Average Weight

Donald Cutlip, MD, Harvard Medical School, reported by Rebecca Shannonhouse, editor, *Bottom Line Health.*

Most Americans have obviously gotten heavier over the years. What's shocking is how much heavier. A few decades ago, the typical man weighed 181 pounds...now he's 196, according to a recent report from the CDC. For women, the average weight has gone from about 153 to 166.

The dangers of this alarming trend are not new—we all know that being overweight or obese is a risk factor for diabetes, heart disease, stroke and other serious conditions.

So why are so many people still tipping the scales? Part of the problem is how we see ourselves. Now that more than two-thirds of American adults are overweight or obese, "big" has become the new normal. We've simply stopped noticing.

To make matters worse, the main tool for assessing obesity—a weight-to-height ratio known as the body mass index (BMI)—doesn't distinguish patterns of obesity. For example, visceral (abdominal) obesity—often evident from the size of one's belly—is the pattern that's linked to the greatest health risks.

For that reason, a waist-to-hip measurement can also be useful for people who suspect that they may be gaining too much weight, says Donald Cutlip, MD, of Harvard Medical School. All you need is a tape measure.

What to do: Measure your hips...measure your waist just above your belly button...and divide the waist number by the hip number. For women, a good reading is 0.8 or below...men should be 0.9 or under.

Lose the Clutter, Lose the Weight

Reduce clutter to make weight loss easier. People who live with extreme clutter are 76% more likely to struggle with weight issues than those who keep their homes orderly. Clutter causes stress that can lead to overeating and makes it harder to make healthy food choices.

Self-defense: Clear kitchen counters and tables regularly, and throw out anything that makes you feel stressed or guilty, such as expired, never-used spices.

Peter Walsh, professional organizer, Los Angeles, and author of *Lose the Clutter, Lose the Weight*, quoted in RedbookMag.com.

Important: Being underweight—a BMI below 18.5—or suffering unexplained weight loss can be harmful, too.

How to Eat Whole Grains on a Low-Carb Diet

Study titled "Whole grain consumption and risk of cardiovascular disease, cancer, and all cause and cause specific mortality: a systematic review and dose-response meta-analysis of prospective studies" by researchers at Imperial College of London, UK, published in *The BMJ*.

It's easy to feel confused about grains.

On the one hand, you may be reducing your total carbs, which may mean cutting way back on pasta, rice, bread and other grain-based foods.

On the other hand, whole grains such as brown rice, whole wheat, oatmeal, buckwheat, whole-grain cornmeal and quinoa are not only nutritious but linked with protection against heart disease and other chronic ills.

So what's a health-conscious eater to do? What if you're watching your carbs—and your weight?

The good news, based on the latest research, is that you may need just a few servings of whole grains to get big health benefits. That fits nicely into a moderately low-carbohydrate diet.

THE 90-GRAM SOLUTION

To find out how much whole grain is associated with health benefits, an international team of public health researchers reported in *The BMJ* on a statistical meta-analysis of 45 studies from the US, Europe and Asia. *Results...*

- **Key finding.** Eating just three servings of whole grains a day (90 grams) was statistically associated with a 16% reduced risk for cardiovascular disease, an 11% reduced risk for cancer and an 18% reduced risk for early death. (Eating whole grains was also linked with a lower risk for diabetes, respiratory illness and infectious disease, although specific optimal daily servings couldn't be calculated.)
- **People who ate just one or two servings of whole grains a day,** compared with those who ate none at all, were also protected from these chronic illnesses—and early death—in many studies.
- **Eating more than three servings (up to seven a day) was associated with a modest additional increase in benefit**—less heart disease, respiratory illness, cancer and early death in some studies.
- **Not surprisingly, people who ate more refined grains such as white bread received no health benefits.**

WHY IT'S SO EASY TO EAT ENOUGH WHOLE GRAINS

The other key point is that a serving is probably a lot less than you think. The researchers defined it as 30 grams of cooked food, which is about one ounce. The USDA defines a serving, based on one-ounce servings, as one small slice of bread...one-half cup of cooked brown rice...one-half cup of cooked whole-wheat pasta.

So eating just one small bowl of whole-grain cereal at breakfast (30 grams) and one large whole-wheat pita bread at dinner (60 grams) could easily bring you up to three servings for the day. Watch out for "portion distortion," too—a typical bagel, for example, can easily weigh in at four ounces (four servings) or more.

Bottom line: You can get most of the benefits of whole grains in your diet by aiming for three one-ounce (30-gram) servings a day.

Better Lunch Choices

Eric VanEpps, PhD, postdoctoral research fellow, Center for Health Incentives and Behavioral Economics at the Leonard Davis Institute, University of Pennsylvania, Philadelphia.

Cutting calories? Order lunch (or make it) at least one hour before eating.

Recent findings: People who ordered lunch (including a beverage) in advance made more healthful choices and ate about 10% fewer calories than those who ordered just before eating.

Why: When you're not hungry, it's easier to make wise choices—the same reason that experts suggest not grocery shopping on an empty stomach.

To Lose Weight, Cut Carbs...Just Twice a Week

Louis Aronne, MD, professor of medicine, Weill Cornell Medical College, director, Comprehensive Weight Control Center at Weill Cornell Medicine and New York-Presbyterian, both in New York City.

There are many popular ways to lose weight. Lots of people try cutting calories across the board, but then they are hungry a lot of the time. Others dramatically cut carbs, which often helps with hunger, but that is hard to stick with if you love "carb-y" foods. Some people practice intermittent fasting, eating only 500 or 600 calories on certain days, but you might find that overly restrictive, too.

Fortunately, there is another, little-known approach that's just as effective as any of the above—and a whole lot easier for many people to stick with. Like intermittent fasting, it involves restrictive days, and like low-carb dieting, it involves drastically cutting carbohydrates.

But here's the big difference: All you do is go low-carb twice a week, without counting calories at all. The rest of the week you eat as much of a normal healthy diet as you want. It may work by "resetting" the brain so that you're not as hungry—not just on low-carb days but even when you go back to your "normal" way of eating the rest of the week.

Here's how to make it work for you.

THE TWO-DAY LOW-CARB DIET

At the Comprehensive Weight Control Center at Weill Cornell Medical College, we became interested in this new approach when we reviewed a four-month British study of 115 overweight women. *The women were divided into three groups...*

- **Daily dieters cut their calories by 25% to an average of 1,500 a day on a balanced healthy Mediterranean-style diet.**
- **A second group did intermittent fasting on two consecutive days.** It was pretty intense—low-carb and no more than 600 calories a day...and then repeat the next day. The rest of the week, they ate as much as they wanted from a balanced diet.
- **The third group of women also went on an intermittent low-carb diet for two consecutive days, but they didn't have to restrict calories.** It was a big carb reduction—to just 40 grams, slightly less than the amount in one cup of rice. On those days, they were allowed unrestricted protein and healthy fats. The rest of the week they ate as they wanted from a balanced diet.

Results: The two-day-a-week low-carb dieters lost just as much weight as the intermittent fasters...and lost more weight than the everyday dieters. And besides losing more weight (11 versus eight pounds), the two-day-a-weekers also lost more body fat, becoming lighter and leaner.

What was even more intriguing was that just cutting carbs on those two days—and not counting overall calories—was as effective as intermittent fasting. In fact, neither group tended to overeat on days when they weren't, respectively, cutting carbs or fasting.

Could it really be that easy to lose weight—just cut carbs two days a week? Yes, it could—

because carbs do some very particular things to the brain.

THE CARB-BRAIN-APPETITE CONNECTION

When you eat a lot of carbohydrates, especially simple starches and sugars, it can literally damage neurons in the hypothalamus, a part of the brain that helps regulate appetite. The nerve cells in the hypothalamus become surrounded by inflammatory cells, and then they don't function as well as they should.

Quality of fat matters, too. In animal studies, for example, high-saturated-fat diets—the kind of fats that are very prevalent in a typical Western diet—have also been shown to disrupt the appetite-signaling pathways. So the emphasis on healthy, mostly unsaturated fats in the diet may contribute to its effectiveness.

In effect, the brain becomes resistant to input from hormones, including leptin and ghrelin, which play key roles in regulating appetite. The hypothalamus mistakenly sends out signals to eat more. You feel hungrier, you eat more, and you create more damage—and so on.

The secret of the two-day-a-week carb-cutting diet is that the hunger-signaling pathway can be "reset" by giving the damaged neurons a break by cutting carbs, which also tends to cut calories, and by your eating healthy polyunsaturated and monounsaturated fats. When the oxidative load that's hitting those nerves decreases, the whole system can work much better.

That explains why people on this diet don't go crazy with overeating on their "off diet" days. Even after just one day of going very low carbohydrate, the signaling system between the appetite hormones and the hypothalamus works much more efficiently. That effect can last for a few days.

READY TO TRY THE INTERMITTENT LOW-CARB DIET?

In our clinical experience, we have found that there is no need to avoid carbohydrates two days in a row. We tell dieters that they are free to restrict their carbohydrates on any two days of the week.

For a lot of people, just eliminating bread, pasta and sweets (sugars are carbs) gets most of the job done. *But for a little more detail, here's a sample one-day low-carb menu...*

- **Breakfast.** Two or three eggs with spinach and mozzarella cheese, made with one teaspoon of oil.
- **Lunch.** A large vegetable salad with one-third of an avocado, five or more ounces of chicken or grilled shrimp or cheese, and one or two tablespoons of Italian dressing.
- **Snack.** Six to eight ounces of Greek yogurt (0% to 2% fat) with eight walnut halves.
- **Dinner.** Five or more ounces of grilled poultry, fish or red meat, roasted vegetables (such as cauliflower, Brussels sprouts or broccoli) with one or two tablespoons of olive oil, a tossed salad with one tablespoon of oil-and-vinegar and one cup of berries.

True, there's no linguine with clam sauce... no bread-and-jam. But it's only for a few days a week—and on the other five days, you may find that you're not craving carbs as much as you do now. You're almost sure to lose weight.

Cheat Sheet: Know Your Updated Dietary Guidelines

Bob Barnett, editor, *Health Insider* from Bottom Line Health.

United States Department of Agriculture, US Department of Health and Human Services media reports.

The Dietary Guidelines form the backbone of American nutrition regulation, affecting everything from the "plate" food guide to nutrition labels to school lunches. The next revision should occur in 2020.

The most recent update got some things right—and, thanks to intense lobbying by Big Food, they drop the ball on some issues. What does it mean for your health? Here's a quick cheat sheet on what the new official dietary guidelines from the USDA and the US Department of Health and Human Services say—and what they should have said...

- **Sugar.** This is a big change—and a win. For the first time, our national health authorities are urging Americans to limit sugar to no more than 10% of daily calories. Believe it or not, there's never been a specific limit before, but the evidence for the health dangers of a high-sugar diet was just too overwhelming. In a 2,000-calorie diet, 10% is 200 calories—the equivalent of about 12½ teaspoons of sugar. Yet we average 20 teaspoons a day—and some people take in much more.

•**Cholesterol.** It's gone from the guidelines! Based on scientific evidence that's been mounting for decades, dietary cholesterol (as opposed to blood cholesterol) just isn't something we need to worry about anymore. (Eggs, anyone?)

•**Fat.** For the first time, there is no limit on total fat, which is a good thing. However, the advice to limit saturated fat is still in there—even though the evidence that saturated fat leads to heart disease has turned out to be pretty weak.

•**Meat.** An original report associated with the new guidelines called for cutting back on red meat, especially processed meat, but the final official guidelines soft pedal it. That's the work of the meat industry, a very powerful lobbying force. The report does note that teenage boys and men consume too much animal protein (not just red meat but also chicken and other meats) and recommends that they cut back and eat more vegetables. But a strong "eat less meat" message, which the original reported hinted at, never arrived. "I am disappointed that the USDA once again is cutting out recommendations to truly limit red meat intake," University of North Carolina nutrition professor Barry Popkin, PhD, told National Public Radio.

•**Seafood.** This got specific for the first time—aim for at least eight ounces a week, in part to get its heart-healthy nutrients such as omega-3 fatty acids.

•**Sustainability.** The original report called for including sustainability issues in the guidelines—which would mean eating more plant-based food and less animal-based foods. But the USDA administration nixed that idea, too.

Some things didn't change. It is still advised to limit sodium to no more than 2,300 mg a day, rather than the nearly 3,500 that we take in, on average. There's still an emphasis on dairy, especially low-fat and fat-free dairy, both of which are controversial—the recommendations are to eat three servings of low-fat or fat-free dairy each day.

Of course, it is absolutely no surprise to learn that it's a good idea to eat lots of vegetables and to choose whole grains over refined ones, as the new guidelines continue to recommend.

Bottom line: The 2015 dietary guidelines pay lip service to a "dietary pattern" approach to healthier eating, which emphasizes the whole rather than individual nutrients—a very good thing. But by stepping back from embracing a plant-based diet that is better for our health, and the health of the planet, they fall short.

Five Healthy Foods That Can Hurt You

Torey Armul, MS, RD, spokesperson for Academy of Nutrition and Dietetics and a nutritionist in private practice in Lewis Center, Ohio. She is a board-certified specialist in sports dietetics. ToreyJonesArmul.com

What's your favorite superfood? Kale? Quinoa? Avocado? These and other superfoods deserve their superstar status. They're loaded with protein, fiber, healthy fats and other important nutrients. But it is possible to go overboard on even the healthiest of foods—and too much of a good thing can be a bad thing.

See if you face any of these superfood risks...

KALE AND THYROID DISEASE

For the average person, the risk from this superstar green is remote. But some people—particularly those who engage in lengthy, juice-based diets and detoxes—consume extreme amounts of kale. I had a client who drank more than 64 ounces of "liquid kale" a day on a juice cleanse, and it was replacing other vital nutrients in her diet.

Risk: Kale contains thiocyanate, a chemical compound that, in large amounts, interferes with iodine metabolism. Insufficient iodine can cause a drop in thyroid hormones and lead to hypothyroidism. Kale is goitrogenic, meaning that it can affect thyroid hormones if consumed in excess. The body can develop an enlarged thyroid gland (a goiter) in an attempt to compensate for low thyroid levels.

Bottom line: Normal amounts of kale shouldn't cause thyroid problems. Extended juicing, on the other hand, could pose a problem, particularly for those who avoid foods high in iodine. It would be hard to overdo it on cooked kale, but limit juiced kale to less than 10 cups of raw kale per week.

JUICES AND DIABETES

Few things are more refreshing or more all-American than having a glass of juice with breakfast. Millions of people start their day with a glass of orange, grapefruit or other juice.

Risk: A Harvard study found that people who consumed one or more servings of fruit juice daily were up to 21% more likely to develop type 2 diabetes.

Studies also show that people who ingest liquid calories typically don't compensate by eating fewer calories, so they may be more likely to gain weight.

You can blame the lack of fiber. Fruit juices retain the sugary sweet fructose found naturally in whole fruits, but they don't have the fiber found in whole fruits. Fiber is a key component of satiety, or fullness, as well as a factor in weight control and digestive health.

An average-sized orange contains just over 60 calories. The calorie count nearly doubles when you swig an eight-ounce glass of orange juice. And with little fiber, juice is less filling, so you may consume more calories overall.

The same Harvard study found that people who ate at least two servings per week of whole fruit—notably blueberries, grapes and apples—had a 23% reduced risk for type 2 diabetes, compared with those who ate no fruit at all.

Bottom line: You should always try to stick to whole fruits when possible. But if you really love juice, look for one with no added sugar and limit yourself to only an occasional glass of six ounces or less.

QUINOA AND STOMACH UPSET

Quinoa is one of the rare plant foods considered a complete protein, containing all of the essential amino acids. One cup of quinoa has eight grams of protein, twice the amount found in rice or a baked potato. It's also a great source of fiber, with five grams in a one-cup serving, and it is high in folate, manganese, magnesium and B vitamins.

But the outer layer of the quinoa seed contains saponin, a coating that acts as a natural insect repellent. One advantage of saponin is less need for chemical pesticides. The disadvantage of saponin is the potential for stomach upset and even damage to the lining of the small intestine.

Many quinoa brands are prewashed to remove the saponin, but it's a good idea to thoroughly rinse the seeds again prior to cooking.

In addition, try not to overdo it on quinoa. Rapid increases in fiber intake can cause digestive issues and discomfort, such as flatulence, bloating and diarrhea.

Bottom line: If you're not already consuming 21 grams to 38 grams of fiber a day (the recommended amount), increase your quinoa intake slowly. Give your body time to adjust by increasing fiber intake by three to five grams every few days.

Also important: Drink an extra glass or two of water while you're eating more fiber. Fiber absorbs water in the gastrointestinal tract, so you'll need more fluid to keep things moving efficiently.

AVOCADOS AND WEIGHT GAIN

Avocados are loaded with healthy mono- and polyunsaturated fats, which are linked to heart health and cholesterol management. And they're not just for guacamole anymore—avocados add delicious flavor to salads, sandwiches, omelets and tacos. Their creamy texture also provides a healthier alternative to mayo, cheese, sour cream and other high-fat spreads.

Risk: Avocados are shockingly high in calories. One medium-sized avocado delivers 320 calories and 30 grams of fat.

The healthy fats make it worth the calories. One study published in *Journal of the American Heart Association* found that people who ate one avocado a day, in addition to other healthy foods, decreased their LDL (bad) cholesterol by 14 mg/dL.

Bottom line: Enjoy avocados, but limit yourself to one per day and include them in your calorie count.

SALMON AND MERCURY

Dietitians often encourage their clients to eat more fish because it's a nutritional powerhouse. Fish boasts the rare combination of high protein and heart-healthy omega-3 fatty acids.

Risk: Virtually all fish contain some mercury, a neurotoxin that is particularly dangerous for developing brains. This explains why pregnant women and young children are advised to limit their seafood consumption. Adults who consume too much mercury can develop numbness, tremors, headaches and problems with balance or coordination.

Bottom line: Salmon, along with sardines, crab, shrimp and tilapia, is one of the lower-mercury seafoods. (The highest mercury sources include ahi tuna, king mackerel, swordfish and shark.) But mercury poisoning still is possible with excessive salmon intake. Adding salmon to your menu two or three times a week carries little risk and has big health benefits for the whole family. Even pregnant women and children now are encouraged to eat more seafood, with a weekly recommendation of eight to 12 ounces of lower-mercury seafood. However, even adults who are not pregnant should be cautioned against eating salmon much more than that.

Good News About Frying Vegetables...in Olive Oil

Sharon Palmer, RDN, a registered dietitian based in Los Angeles with 16 years of health-care experience. She is author of *The Plant-Powered Diet* and *Plant-Powered for Life: Eat Your Way to Lasting Health with 52 Simple Steps & 125 Delicious Recipes*, and editor of *Environmental Nutrition* and nutrition editor of *Today's Dietician*. SharonPalmer.com

Study titled "Phenols and the antioxidant capacity of Mediterranean vegetables prepared with extra-virgin olive oil using different domestic cooking techniques" by researchers at the University of Granada, published in *Food Chemistry*.

Could frying vegetables in olive oil be the healthiest way to cook them?

That's the suggestion of a recent Spanish study. It found that sautéing vegetables—even frying them—in extra-virgin olive oil resulted in dishes that were richer in certain health-promoting compounds than leaving them raw or boiling them.

But don't start frying all your veggies just yet. There's more to the story.

WHY OLIVE OIL SHOULD TOUCH YOUR VEGGIES WHEN YOU COOK THEM

In the study, researchers at the University of Granada in Spain looked at four vegetables commonly found in the Mediterranean diet—tomato, eggplant, pumpkin and potato. They cubed them and then cooked them different ways—boiled in water, boiled in water plus extra virgin olive oil (EVOO), sautéed in EVOO or fried in EVOO.

Then they measured levels of phenols in the cooked foods as well as in the raw foods.

Results: Frying and sautéing in olive oil yielded the most phenols in the finished dish—significantly increasing both the total amount and the healthful variety of these compounds. Boiling in water, or even water with a little olive oil added in, didn't increase phenols. It was the direct heating of veggies in olive oil that made the difference.

What's so great about phenols? These antioxidant compounds, found in many plant foods (fruits, vegetables, the olives that get turned into olive oil, even champagne) protect the body's cells against oxidation and inflammation that can promote chronic disease. People whose diets are rich in phenols are statistically less likely to develop heart disease, Alzheimer's disease and certain cancers.

To put the recent research in perspective, we spoke with Sharon Palmer, RDN, a registered dietician based in Los Angeles who is author of *The Plant-Powered Diet* and *Plant-Powered for Life*. "Health experts once thought that boring, zero-fat, steamed veggies were the way to go," she said. "But more research is pointing to the advantages of cooking your vegetables in extra-virgin olive oil."

HOW OLIVE OIL MAKES VEGETABLES EVEN HEALTHIER

One way that cooking in olive oil enhanced phenols in the study was that it helped make them easier to absorb. This didn't surprise Palmer. "Other studies have also found that certain antioxidant compounds and nutrients in some vegetables become more bioavailable to your body in the presence of olive oil."

But some of the extra phenols in the cooked dishes came not from a change in the vegetables' phenols, but from additional phenols added from the olive oil itself. You'd get similar benefits from simply including EVOO in your diet—in your salad dressing, for example. You don't need to fry everything! "Olive oil is rich in many phenolic compounds," says Palmer. "A body of science backs up the benefits of eating a Mediterranean diet, which includes a generous dose of extra-virgin olive oil—in a diet filled with minimally processed foods such as grains, vegetables, fruits, legumes, herbs, nuts and seafood." In one major study, called PREDIMED, she notes, each increase of 10 grams a day in EVOO—about two teaspoons—was associated with a 10% reduction in risk for cardiovascular events. Now that's impressive!

What's so special about the golden nectar that is extra-virgin olive oil? Because extra-virgin olive oil is minimally processed, it retains many of those phenolic compounds present in the olive. And it is rich in heart-healthy monounsaturated fats. No wonder EVOO has been linked with many health bonuses, including reducing the risk for cardiovascular disease, improving the management of type 2 diabetes and even breast cancer prevention.

How much is enough? The PREDIMED Study found the most benefits related to consuming 57 grams—about four tablespoons—per day. So that means you can enjoy a little more than a tablespoon per meal drizzled over your foods as your source of additional fat.

THE FORMULA FOR VEGETABLE SUCCESS

So, what's the best way to cook your vegetables with EVOO? "Start with the real deal—extra-virgin olive oil—which works wonderfully in cooking methods as different as sautéing, pan-frying, roasting or grilling," she says. "Don't fall for the myth that more is better. At 120 calories per tablespoon, EVOO is concentrated stuff. If you dump a quarter cup of it over your salad or pasta, you're adding an extra 480 calories to your meal, which most people simply can't afford. If you gain weight, that can quickly erase the potential health benefits from olive oil." The good news is that you don't need much olive oil to pump up both the flavor and healthfulness of your favorite vegetables.

When you're sauteeing vegetables, for example, just heat one or two tablespoons of olive oil in a sauté pan or skillet and then add about four cups of any medley of vegetables. Drizzle a twist of lemon juice and your favorite pinch of spices and herbs, and sauté until just crisp-tender to make about four servings. (For more healthful pan-frying tips, see Bottom Line's article, "What If Fried Foods Were Healthy?" at BottomLineInc.com/health/diet-nutrition/what-if-fried-foods-were-healthy) One or two tablespoons is also a good amount for four servings when you're roasting vegetables or making a salad.

What about boiling vegetables in just a little water or steaming them? That's still nutritious—while it won't enhance their phenols, it actually retains nutrients such as vitamin C best—and you can make it more phenol-rich by simply tossing your steamed (or even microwaved) vegetables with a little EVOO.

Bottom line: It's fine to include some veggies sautéed or even fried in olive oil in your diet, but it's not the only way to get the health benefits of vegetables—or olive oil.

Black Raspberries Love Your Heart

Study titled "Black Raspberry Extract Increased Circulating Endothelial Progenitor Cells and Improved Arterial Stiffness in Patients with Metabolic Syndrome: A Randomized Controlled Trial" by researchers at Korea University Anam Hospital and Gochang Black Raspberry Research Institute, both in Seoul, South Korea, published in *Journal of Medicinal Food.*

Stephen Dunfield, president of BerriHealth, Corvallis, Oregon, which specializes in quality black raspberry products. BerriHealth.com

John La Puma, MD, board-certified specialist in internal medicine and a trained chef. He runs a private nutritional medical practice in Santa Barbara, California, and is cofounder of the popular video series "ChefMD." DrJohnLaPuma.com

---

Let us pause for a moment to savor the sweet and tart black raspberry (Rubus occidentalis). It's got amazing health benefits that you won't get from red raspberries—or blackberries.

This rare native American fruit's fleetingly brief season is just a few mid-summer weeks in many parts of the country. But there are ways you can still enjoy black raspberries year-round—and you'll definitely want to.

Here's why: Black raspberries already have a reputation for anticancer properties. A recent study shows that it's really good for your heart, too.

KEEPING BLOOD VESSELS FLEXIBLE AND HEALTHY

The recent study, from South Korea, looked at men and women with metabolic syndrome, a combination of risk factors such as high blood pressure, belly fat, low HDL levels and insulin resistance that greatly increases the risk for cardiovascular disease and diabetes. Some of them took 750 mg of black raspberry extract daily for 12 weeks while the others took inactive placebo pills.

Result: Those who consumed black raspberry extract had less arterial stiffness, a key contributor to cardiovascular disease risk.

The science behind the benefit: Those who took black raspberry produced more compounds that stimulate the regeneration of the cells lining the blood vessels, helping them function better.

BLACK RASPBERRY POWER

What's so healthy about these berries? For one, they are extraordinarily rich in antioxidants, with 10 times the antioxidant power of most fruits and vegetables—a mere four berries carries the same punch as an entire three-and-a-half ounce serving of, say, spinach.

Foremost among these antioxidants are flavonoid pigments, which give the berries their dark color. These compounds have already been shown to help protect LDL cholesterol from oxidation, a key factor of heart disease. They play a key role in anticancer effects, too—in animal studies, black raspberry extract may slow or reverse the growth of breast, prostate, cervical, colon, oral and esophageal cancers and is now being studied in human clinical trials of colorectal, stomach, oral and prostate cancers as well for the management of inflammatory bowel disease (IBD).

One class of black raspberry flavonoid in particular, anthocyanins, has been shown to improve vision, lower blood pressure, enhance immunity and improve memory. Compared with red raspberries, black raspberries have seven times more anthocyanins per serving.

BLACK RASPBERRY SUPPLEMENTS

If you want to enjoy these health benefits the rest of the year, you can purchase whole freeze-dried black raspberry powder or a liquid extract. One company that makes it and supplies it to researchers in Japan and the US is BerriHealth, based in Corvallis, Oregon. The recommended serving size of its powder is one teaspoon (four grams), which is the equivalent of 20 fresh berries and has 15 calories. You can mix it in water or juice, add it as a topping to yogurt or blend it into smoothies.

How does that amount compare with what was used in the Korean study? It's not possible to make exact comparisons, because that study used a different method to make the extract. But that teaspoon with 20 berries likely represents more than what was used in the study, which was, roughly estimated, the equivalent of seven or eight berries, according to Steve Dunfield, president of BerriHealth.

Cancer research studies have used even larger amounts—as much as 50 grams of freeze-dried black raspberry powder, the equivalent of three cups of fresh black raspberries—about 250 berries.

How much should you take? It depends on why you're taking it. If the purpose is to treat a health condition—especially a serious condition such as cancer—you should work with your doctor to determine what's right for you.

If you just want to enjoy the healthful properties of this berry year round, on the other hand, let food amounts be your guide. After all, that's what the powder is—it's just whole black raspberry, including the seeds, with nothing added. If you put a teaspoon of powder in your smoothie, that's 20 berries. A tablespoon? That's like putting 60 berries in your drink. All that adds are a few extra calories—specifically, 45.

One caveat: Be careful of many black raspberry capsules on the market. Often these capsules do not contain much black raspberry, and many lack authenticity. Best to stick with either freeze-dried powders made from authentic whole black raspberries or well-prepared liquid extracts. According to *Bottom Line* medical contributing editor Andrew Rubman, ND, the Eclectic Institute is another reputable supplier of real black raspberry products, including freeze-dried black raspberry powder in bulk or in capsules.

GET 'EM FRESH...WHILE YOU CAN

Fresh black raspberries are in season primarily in July, so don't hesitate to make tracks to a grocery store or your local farmer's market. They're delicious eaten fresh out of hand, puréed, baked into pie (try two parts black raspberry to one-part blueberry or blackberry), blended into smoothies or preserved in jam. (How to tell the difference between blackberries and black raspberries? Easy—all raspberries have a hollow core.)

Are black raspberries superior to blackberries and red raspberries for the heart? "Neither has been tested against black raspberries for cardiovascular effects," commented food-as-medicine expert John La Puma, MD, who wasn't involved in the study. "But in general, the blacker the berry, the greater the antioxidant effect—and oxidation of LDL cholesterol starts cardiovascular disease."

His advice: "Eat the berry you have, and enjoy it. All of them taste better than prescription medicine!"

Seeds: The Forgotten Superfood

Janet Bond Brill, PhD, RDN, FAND, a registered dietitian nutritionist, a fellow of the Academy of Nutrition and Dietetics and a nationally recognized nutrition, health and fitness expert who specializes in cardiovascular disease prevention. Based in Allentown, Pennsylvania, Dr. Brill is author of *Blood Pressure DOWN, Cholesterol DOWN* and *Prevent a Second Heart Attack.* DrJanet.com

When we think of those ultra-healthy foods known as "superfoods," seeds are one of the least talked about. That's a shame because they are among the most nutrient-rich foods you can consume. But with literally dozens of health-promoting seeds to choose from, does it really matter which ones you add to your diet?

Well, yes. When it comes to research supporting health benefits, two of the heaviest hitters are chia seeds and flaxseeds. Both are spectacularly heart-healthy. But in terms of convenience, chia seeds win hands down. These seeds are more stable than flaxseeds, so you don't have to worry about them going rancid. Chia seeds can also be eaten whole or ground, and you'll still get all the health benefits. Flaxseeds, on the other hand, must be ground before the nutrients are released. Chia seeds also win points because they don't need refrigeration, while flaxseeds must be stored in a preferably dark, airtight container in the fridge or freezer so the nutrients aren't destroyed.

Now, for the nitty-gritty nutritional comparison. *Here's what you'll get from a serving (one ounce) of chia seeds versus one ounce of ground flaxseeds (the calorie count is roughly the same—138 in chia seeds...and 148 in flaxseeds)...*

- **Alpha-linolenic acid (ALA).** Chia seeds and flaxseeds are virtual storehouses of the super-heart-healthy anti-inflammatory omega-3 fat known as ALA. Chia seeds contain 5 g and flaxseeds have 6 g.
- **Fiber.** There's lots of fiber—insoluble and soluble—packed in both of these tiny seeds. Chia seeds edge out flaxseeds—10 g versus 8 g.
- **Protein.** Both seeds contain a respectable amount of vegetable protein (4 g in chia seeds...5 g in flaxseeds). But chia seeds are a "complete" protein because they have all nine of the essential amino acids while flaxseeds do not.
- **Vitamins and minerals.** Both seeds are bursting with vitamins and minerals such as iron, manganese, copper, zinc and niacin, to name just a few. Flaxseeds are higher in folate, magnesium and potassium. But chia seeds, unlike flaxseeds, are a potent source of calcium.
- **Lignans.** When it comes to lignans, a disease-fighting phytochemical, flaxseeds are a much richer source than chia seeds. Lignans may protect against cardiovascular disease and breast and prostate cancers.

Since the nutritional benefits of these two seeds do differ somewhat, how do you choose? To get the best of both worlds nutritionally, I suggest adding both types of seeds to your diet, perhaps alternating days. Both chia seeds and flaxseeds can be sprinkled on yogurt, cereal, oatmeal or salads. Either seed can also be sprinkled on top of one of my favorite snacks—a slice of whole-grain toast topped with peanut butter and banana slices. If you like to bake, replace one-half cup of flour with one-half cup of ground chia seeds or flaxseed meal in muffins, pancake mix or breads. *And for a delicious treat...*

Raspberry chia seed pudding: This festive-looking dessert is perfect for the holidays.

Ingredients for a single serving: One cup of light vanilla soy milk...one-half cup of fresh (or frozen and defrosted) raspberries...one-quarter cup of chia seeds...and mint leaves.

What to do: Mix the raspberries with milk in a blender until smooth. Pour into a mason jar, add chia seeds, cover tightly, give it a good shake and refrigerate overnight. The chia seeds will "gel" to create a pudding-like consistency. (You can add a sweetener of your choice, if desired.) Garnish with mint leaves and enjoy!

Sweet Potato—A Real Superfood

Janet Bond Brill, PhD, RDN, FAND, a registered dietitian nutritionist, a fellow of the Academy of Nutrition and Dietetics and a nationally recognized nutrition, health and fitness expert who specializes in cardiovascular disease prevention. Based in Allentown, Pennsylvania, Dr. Brill is author of *Blood Pressure DOWN, Cholesterol DOWN* and *Prevent a Second Heart Attack.* DrJanet.com

"Don't judge a book by its cover." This well-worn aphorism certainly applies to veggies...especially the sweet potato. This starchy root vegetable is, to be honest, not the most attractive food—with its odd shape, imperfect skin and dusting of dirt. But don't let the appearance stop you from incorporating it into your meals. Chock-full of vital nutrients, including vitamin A, vitamin C, beta-carotene, potassium, folate, fiber, B vitamins and manganese, the sweet potato is one of the healthiest complex carbs around.

Sweet potato or yam? Before we get too far along, let's clear up this confusion about sweet potatoes versus yams.

Here's the truth: Even though they're both tuberous root veggies, a yam is not even botanically related to a sweet potato! Real yams are typically imported from the Caribbean and generally sold only in international food markets in the US. A true yam, which has white interior flesh, is starchier and drier and not nearly as tasty as a sweet potato. It's worth noting, though, that the veggies that are often mislabeled as yams are actually soft sweet potatoes. With their copper-colored skin and orangey flesh, this variety becomes fluffy and moist when cooked. So opt for this one if you want to bake it—and especially if you're looking for that classic roasted sweet potato with the crispy skin and sweet, orange flesh.

Sweet potatoes come in purple, too. Did you know that there's a variety of purple potato that is actually a sweet potato, too? Available commercially in the US for about 10 years now, it is packed with even more antioxidants than its orange cousin. The purple hue is a giveaway that this variety is filled with anthocyanins—the same phytochemicals found in blueberries—which are powerful antioxidant and anti-inflammatory compounds that fight such diseases as heart disease and diabetes. For this reason, it's a good idea to splurge on purple potatoes (they usually cost about twice as much as regular sweet potatoes) whenever possible in lieu of the less nutritious white-fleshed varieties. No matter what type of sweet potato you choose, it's fun to add them to your diet in new ways.

My favorite spud ideas: Cube potatoes, roast them and add to salads or even mac and cheese...bake, scoop out the insides and add to baked goods such muffins or pancake mix. *Or try my sweet potato hummus recipe...*

SWEET POTATO HUMMUS

Change up your basic hummus by making it sweet...or spicy, depending on your taste preference. *Ingredients...*

1 medium sweet potato, washed

1 15-ounce can of garbanzo beans, rinsed, drained

2 Tablespoons of extra-virgin olive oil

1 Tablespoon of tahini (optional)

Sweet spices: 1 teaspoon of cinnamon and 1 teaspoon of pumpkin spice

Spicy spices: ½ teaspoon of cayenne pepper, ½ teaspoon of paprika and 1 teaspoon of cumin

Instructions: Preheat oven to 400°F. With a fork, poke holes in the sweet potato all over (both sides). Place the sweet potato on a baking sheet and bake for 45 to 60 minutes (until you can squeeze it). Once cooked, remove the skin and chop the potato into pieces. Add the chopped sweet potato and the other hummus ingredients into a blender, and mix until it makes a smooth consistency with no visible pieces of sweet potato. Add either sweet or spicy spices. Taste and add more spices, if needed. Then enjoy!

Cooking Tricks for Much Healthier Foods

Lisa R. Young, PhD, RD, a nutritionist in private practice and an adjunct professor in the department of nutrition and food studies at New York University in New York City. She is the author of *The Portion Teller Plan: The No-Diet Reality Guide to Eating, Cheating, and Losing Weight Permanently*.

Loading up your grocery cart with fruits and vegetables is a great start to a healthful diet. But even if you hit the produce section on a regular basis, chances are you're not getting the same level of nutrients in your fruits and vegetables that earlier generations did.

Modern agricultural methods have stripped soil of important nutrients, so produce that is eaten today may be less healthful than it used to be.*

Troubling findings: A study published in the *Journal of the American College of Nutrition* found "reliable declines" in the amount of key vitamins and minerals in 43 fruits and vegetables compared with nutrient levels of those foods in 1950.

Other research has found that the levels of calcium in 12 fresh veggies dropped, on average, by 27%...iron by 37%...and vitamin C by 30% over a 22-year period. Such changes in nutrient values can have a hidden danger by contributing to nutrition deficiencies, which are more common than one might imagine finding in the US.

For these reasons, it's crucial for you to do everything you can to squeeze all of the available nutrition from your foods. Besides stocking up on fruits and veggies, studies have shown that how you store, prepare and cook foods—and even how you combine them—can make a difference. *Six tricks that will help you get the greatest nutrition from your foods...*

• **Make steaming your first choice.** Vegetables are good for you no matter how they're prepared. But to get the most nutrients, steaming is the best choice.

Scientific evidence: Steamed broccoli retained virtually all the tested antioxidants in a study published in the *Journal of the Science of Food and Agriculture*, while microwaved broccoli lost 74% to 97% of these disease-fighting nutrients—possibly because microwaves can generate higher temperatures than other cooking methods.

Boiling is also problematic. The liquid—combined with the high heat and lengthy cooking time—strips out significant levels of important nutrients.

Example: Broccoli that's been boiled loses large amounts of glucosinolate, a compound that's been linked to cancer prevention.

Helpful: The liquid does retain nutrients, so consider using it in a soup.

A caveat: If you simply don't have time to steam your veggies and, as a result, risk not eating them, microwaving can be an acceptable option—if you add only a teaspoon or so of water and cook for the shortest time possible to retain nutrients.

Even though microwaving has been found to remove certain nutrients, it can be one of the best ways to preserve vitamin C and other water-soluble nutrients because the cooking times tend to be shorter. Other methods, such as sautéing and roasting, retain nutrients if you don't cook vegetables at high temperatures or for too long.

*Organic fruits and vegetables may have more nutrients than those that are conventionally grown.

• **Cooked beats fresh.** Fresh, minimally processed foods should usually be your first choice—but not with tomatoes. Cooked tomatoes or canned tomato sauce or paste (best in a BPA-free can or glass jar) provides more lycopene than fresh tomatoes. Lycopene is a well-studied antioxidant that's been linked to reduced risk for prostate and other cancers, along with reduced risk for stroke.

Scientific evidence: A study in *The American Journal of Clinical Nutrition* found that the lycopene in tomato paste has 2.5 times the bioavailability of the lycopene in fresh tomatoes.

Why: The heat used during processing breaks down cell walls and releases more of the compound. Also, the oils that are added to processed tomatoes make it easier for the body to absorb lycopene.

• **Cook first, chop later.** Many people chop their veggies first, then add them to dishes before they go on the stove or into the oven.

Smart idea: Chop most veggies after you've done the cooking.

Here's why: Vitamin C and other nutrients oxidize when they're exposed to air for an extended period of time. An oxidized vitamin loses some of its bioactivity. In addition, chopped or diced vegetables have a greater surface area than whole ones, which allows more nutrients to leach into cooking liquids.

Exception: Onions and garlic should be chopped first (see below).

Scientific evidence: A recent study found that carrots, chopped before cooking, had 25% less falcarinol, a natural anticancer compound, than cooked whole carrots.

• **Try lemon (or lime) to boost iron levels.** Iron deficiency is among the most common nutrition deficiencies in the US, particularly among women of childbearing age. Meats are high in iron, but women with heavy periods might need more.

Low iron can also be a problem for vegetarians/vegans. That's because the non-heme iron in plant foods isn't as readily absorbed as the heme iron in meats.

Helpful: Add a little vitamin C–rich lemon or lime juice to recipes. Research shows that vitamin C can boost the absorption of non-heme iron by four-fold.

Hurrah! High-Fat Cheese Can Be Healthy

High-fat cheese may be as good for you as the low-fat type, when eaten in moderation. In a 12-week study, people who ate three ounces a day of cheese with 25% to 32% fat content had the same blood-chemistry picture—including cholesterol and triglyceride levels—as people who ate three ounces a day of cheese with 13% to 16% fat. And there were no significant differences in body weight change between the groups.

Study of 139 people by researchers at University of Copenhagen, Denmark, published in *The American Journal of Clinical Nutrition*.

• **Add a spoonful of fat.** A garden-fresh salad or a plate of steamed broccoli is undoubtedly healthy. But for an even greater nutrient boost, add a teaspoon of olive oil.

You need fat to absorb vitamin E, beta-carotene, vitamin A and other fat-soluble nutrients/antioxidants. The average meal contains more than enough fat to get the job done, but simpler, fat-free meals won't provide that extra boost.

My advice: Add a little bit of olive oil to dishes...or dress up fat-free dishes with ingredients that contain healthy fats, such as nuts, olives, feta cheese or a hard-boiled egg.

• **Chop garlic, and let it sit.** Many people love the robust flavor of whole garlic cloves that are roasted to buttery smoothness. But you'll get more health benefits from garlic that's been chopped.

Garlic (as well as onions) contains alliin and other sulfur-containing compounds that are locked within cell walls. The cells rupture when these foods are minced or chopped (or well-chewed), which releases enzymes that transform alliin into allicin, a compound with cardiovascular and anticancer benefits.

Good rule of thumb: Chopping and letting garlic or onions sit for about 10 minutes will allow the enzyme to make the healthful conversion. Heating garlic or onions before the completion of the enzymatic reaction will reduce the health benefits.

Small Fish—Big Benefits!

Janet Bond Brill, PhD, RDN, FAND, a registered dietitian nutritionist, a fellow of the Academy of Nutrition and Dietetics and a nationally recognized nutrition, health and fitness expert who specializes in cardiovascular disease prevention. Based in Allentown, Pennsylvania, Dr. Brill is author of *Blood Pressure DOWN, Cholesterol DOWN* and *Prevent a Second Heart Attack.* DrJanet.com

When it comes to fish that people either love or hate, sardines are among the top contenders. Iridescent and tiny, these oily fish within the herring family are oh so flavorful when being enjoyed by their fans! But what if you can't imagine savoring sardines? Well, don't be so quick to swear off this miniature but mighty nutritional powerhouse. Keep reading, and you may just end up with an entirely new appreciation for this budget-friendly, convenient and superbly heart-healthy food.

Fresh sardines are tough to find and are highly perishable, so canned sardines are the go-to option for most people. Because canned sardines generally include the fishes' organs, skin and bones, they are a concentrated source of vitamins and minerals (especially calcium). You may already know that these petite fish are excellent sources of omega-3 fatty acids...are packed with vitamin D...and are rich in protein. But did you realize that one can (3.75 ounces) contains a whopping 1.4 g of heart-healthy omega-3 fat (that's about the same as a serving of sockeye salmon or tuna!) and 23 g of lean protein? Available just about anywhere (even at some gas stations and convenience stores), a can of sardines will cost you a paltry $3.50 or even less on sale. And if that's not enough, consider this: Sardines are very low in heavy metal contaminants such as mercury—they feed on plankton, ranking them very low on the aquatic food chain.

The only bad news is that sardines from certain areas have been overfished and, as a result, appear on the "Avoid" list at SeafoodWatch.org, created by the Monterey Bay Aquarium, a nonprofit educational group that makes science-based recommendations for seafood sustainability. Since 2007, the Pacific sardine population has plunged by 90%—a decline that is believed to have contributed to the deaths of sea lions and brown pelicans across the West Coast. As a result, federal fishery managers have banned nearly all sardine fishing off the West Coast for the second straight year. The good news is that you can still purchase sardines that were canned before the ban—the FDA says sardines from an undamaged, properly stored can are safe to eat for up to five years after packing. You can also find sources of approved sardines from areas not affected by overfishing—they are certified by the Marine Stewardship Council (MSC), MSC.org, an international nonprofit organization established to address the problem of unsustainable fishing and safeguard seafood supplies for the future.

When choosing canned sardines, check the package label. Buy the kind packed in water or extra-virgin olive oil (stay away from those packed in other oils or sugary tomato sauce) and look for the MSC certification. On the convenience scale, sardines rate high because they can be served straight out of the can (or mashed with mustard and onions for a quick and delicious spread on crackers). *You can also try my favorite serving suggestions...*

• **Broiled.** Place your drained can of sardines on a baking tin lined with aluminum foil. Season with a drizzle of extra-virgin olive oil and one-half teaspoon of a fresh herb (such as rosemary), a few capers, a fresh garlic clove (minced) and a spritz of fresh lemon juice. Broil for a few minutes and serve.

• **Sardine-lemon-garlic pasta.** Fry one can of sardines (chopped) with two cloves of fresh

You May Think You Have a Healthy Diet...

Seventy-five percent of Americans say they eat healthfully even though they don't.

That is the percentage that rated their diets good, very good or excellent.

But: More than 80% of Americans don't eat the recommended amount of fruits and vegetables.

Survey by NPR and Truven Health Analytics of 3,000 US adults, reported at NPR.org.

garlic, juice from half a lemon and one-half cup of bread crumbs in extra-virgin olive oil. Add your own tomato sauce to the pasta bowl along with the sardine mixture, parsley and fresh Parmesan. Delizioso!

Just a Few Nuts a Day May Lower Disease Risk

Review of data from 20 prospective studies led by researchers at Imperial College London, UK, and Harvard T.H. Chan School of Public Health, Boston, published in *BMC Medicine.*

In a review of studies, people who ate nuts had a 29% lower risk for coronary heart disease...21% reduced risk for cardiovascular disease...and 15% lower risk for cancer. Nut eaters also had a 52% lower risk for respiratory disease...39% lower risk for diabetes...and 75% reduced risk for infectious disease. Most risk reduction for all diseases occurred in people who ate just one ounce of nuts per day—about two dozen almonds or 15 pecan halves.

Hot Peppers May Protect Against Heart Disease

Benjamin Littenberg, MD, professor of medicine, University of Vermont College of Medicine, Burlington, and coauthor of a study of data on 16,179 Americans, published in *PLOS ONE.*

People who regularly ate hot red chili peppers were 13% less likely to die during a two-decade period—mainly because the group had fewer deaths from heart attack or stroke. The reason for hot peppers' protective effect is not known, but it may be related to the peppers' content of capsaicin, a compound that can improve coronary blood flow.

Avocado Pits Are Edible

Ali Miller, registered dietician, quoted in *Prevention.* Prevention.com

The pits are packed with antioxidants, monounsaturated fats, vitamin E and plant sterols. Grind the pit in a powerful blender, then add two to three teaspoons of the powder to oatmeal or smoothies.

Super-Broth for Super-Health

Sally Fallon Morell, founding president of The Weston A. Price Foundation, which champions nourishing, traditional foods such as bone broths and organ meats and butter and dairy products from grass-fed animals. Based in Brandywine, Maryland, she is author of the best-selling *Nourishing Traditions* and *Nourishing Broth: An Old-Fashioned Remedy for the Modern World.* NourishingTraditions.com

Before the 20th century, almost all soups and stews were made with a stock of bone broth—bones and other animal parts slowly simmered in a cauldron or stockpot, producing a nutrient-rich concoction.

Fast-forward to the 21st century, when food processing has largely replaced home cooking. Today's processed "broth" often is nothing more than a powder or cube dissolved in water and spiked with additives such as MSG that mimic the taste of broth.

The loss of bone broth is a big loss.

What most people don't realize: Traditional bone broth delivers unique, health-giving components that can be hard to find anywhere else in the diet. And a brothless diet may be hurting your health—contributing to arthritis, nagging injuries, indigestion and premature aging.

Good news: Bone broth is simple to make or buy (see below). The optimal "dose" is one cup daily. If you are trying to heal, increase this to two cups.

SUPER-HEALTHY INGREDIENTS

Bone broth, whether it's made from the bones of a chicken, cow, lamb, pig or the like, is extraordinarily rich in the following...

•**Collagen.** The number-one health-giving component of bone broth is melted collagen, or gelatin. Collagen is the most abundant protein in the body, providing strength and structure to tissue. In fact, microscopic cables of collagen literally hold your body together—in joints, tendons, ligaments, muscles, skin and membranes around internal organs.

Your body makes its own collagen, of course. But it becomes harder for your body to make it as you age, leading to arthritis, wrinkled skin and other degenerative conditions.

•**Glucosamine and chondroitin sulfate.** These two nutrients are well-known for helping to ease arthritis pain—and bone broth supplies ample amounts of both.

Glucosamine is created from glucose (sugar) and glutamine (an amino acid, a building block of protein). It's found in cartilage, the part of the joint that provides cushioning and lubrication between bones.

Chondroitin sulfate is a proteoglycan, a type of molecule that helps hydrate cells. It also supplies sulfur, a mineral that nourishes cartilage and balances blood sugar.

•**Glycine.** This amino acid supports the health of blood cells, generates cellular energy, aids in the digestion of fats, speeds wound healing and helps the body rid itself of toxins, such as mercury, lead, cadmium and pesticides. Glycine also regulates dopamine levels, thereby easing anxiety, depression and irritability and improving sleep and memory.

•**Glutamine.** This amino acid nourishes the lining of the gut, aiding the absorption of nutrients. It boosts the strength of the immune system. It helps the body recover from injuries such as burns, wounds and surgery. It also strengthens the liver, helping the body process and expel toxins. And glutamine boosts metabolism and cuts cravings for sugar and carbohydrates, aiding weight loss.

FEEL-BETTER BROTH

Bone broth delivers extra-high levels of all those health-giving compounds, so it's not surprising that it can help prevent and heal many health problems, including...

•**Arthritis and joint pain.** By supplying collagen, glucosamine, chondroitin and other cartilage-nourishing factors, bone broth can repair and rebuild cartilage, preventing osteoarthritis or easing arthritis pain. In fact, bone broth might be the best food for osteoarthritis, which affects more than 30 million Americans.

Compelling research: In a review of seven studies on osteoarthritis and melted collagen (collagen hydrolysate), researchers at University of Illinois College of Medicine in Chicago found that ingesting the compound helped create new cartilage, thus lessening pain and improving everyday functioning.

•**Digestive problems.** In the 19th century, broth and gelatin were widely prescribed—by Florence Nightingale and many others—for convalescents who lacked the strength to digest and assimilate food properly.

Sadly, nutritional therapy for digestive problems went out of fashion after World War II, replaced by pharmaceuticals.

Example: A form of gelatin (gelatin tannate, or Tasectan) is being used as a digestive drug, with studies showing that it can help heal gastroenteritis (stomach and intestinal irritation). The new drug is being hailed as a "gut barrier protector"—but wouldn't it be better to prevent digestive diseases by strengthening your gut with bone broth?

•**Injuries and wounds.** The components in bone broth are crucial for healing broken bones, muscle injuries, burns and wounds—a key benefit for seniors, whose injuries can take longer to heal.

The use of cartilage (a main component of bone broth) for wound healing was championed by John F. Prudden, MD, whose published papers include "The Clinical Acceleration of Healing with a Cartilage Preparation," in the May 3, 1965, issue of *JAMA*. In his research, Dr. Prudden showed that cow cartilage could speed wound healing, produce stronger healing that was less likely to be reinjured and produce smoother, flatter and more natural-looking scars.

More recently, studies have shown that bone broth ingredients—particularly glycine and other amino acids—are uniquely effective at healing wounds, including hard-to-heal diabetic foot ulcers.

•**Infections.** Chicken soup—"Jewish penicillin"—is a classic home remedy for a cold, flu, pneumonia and other infectious diseases. Over the years, researchers studying broth and its components have noted their ability to strengthen immune cells, fight off viruses and calm down the overactive immune system caused by autoimmune diseases such as rheumatoid arthritis, Crohn's disease and psoriasis.

HOW TO MAKE BONE BROTH (OR BUY IT)

Making a very healthful and delicious bone broth may seem daunting—but it's not. Here's a simple way to make a chicken bone broth. You can use the same method for any kind of animal bones. Beef bones (such as rib bones, short ribs and beef shanks) should be browned first in the oven for the best flavor.

How to prepare bone broth: Whenever you eat chicken, save the bones. You can save skin and meat, too—the skin is rich in collagen, and there is some collagen in the meat. Just put all these leftovers in a zipper freezer bag, and store in the freezer until you have enough to fill a standard six-to-seven-quart slow cooker, about six to eight cups. Add a splash of vinegar and one sliced onion. Fill up the slow cooker with filtered water.

Slow-cook on low overnight. (If you don't have a slow cooker, you can make the broth by simmering it all day in a stock pot.)

In the morning, ladle the broth through a strainer and put the broth in the refrigerator. Fill up the slow cooker with water, and cook the bones again overnight, producing a second batch. As with the first batch, ladle the broth through a strainer. You now have about one gallon of chicken broth, which you can refrigerate or freeze.

What to look for: A sign that your broth is rich in collagen is that it gels when chilled. To get a good gel, it is helpful to add chicken feet or a pig's foot to the bone mix.

You can use your broth as a basic ingredient in soups, stews, sauces and gravies. Or just add a little salt, heat it and drink it in a mug.

Try this simple Thai soup: Two cups of chicken broth with one can of coconut milk, the juice of one lime and a pinch of red pepper flakes.

If you want to purchase healthful bone broth, good sources include Bare Bones Broth Company (BareBonesBroth.com), OssoGood (OssoGoodBones.com), Stock Options (StockOptionsOnline.com) and the Brothery (BoneBroth.com). These broths are available by mail order, but you may be able to find them in some gourmet and specialty shops.

Go for Gelato

Lauren Slayton, RD, founder, Foodtrainers, New York City, quoted in *Self* magazine.

Gelato may be better for you than ice cream.

Ice cream has more sugar, fat and calories per ounce than gelato. And because ice cream has a milder flavor and fluffier texture than gelato, it may feel less filling, causing you to eat more of it.

Cool Exercise Treat

Jason Kai Wei Lee, PhD, head, human performance laboratory, DSO National Laboratories, Singapore.

Having a slushy drink before a hot-weather workout may improve performance, recent research has found.

Details: Runners were given about two cups of either a frozen or room-temperature drink 45 minutes before a 10K event in 82°F weather.

Results: Those who drank the slushy ran an average of 15 seconds faster.

Possible reason: The ice increased body heat storage capacity, which allowed runners to improve running time by avoiding overheating. Eating an ice pop may have a similar effect.

Reboot Your Workout

Robert Hopper, PhD, exercise physiologist and author of *Stick with Exercise for a Lifetime,* with Rebecca Shannonhouse, editor, *Bottom Line Health.*

Have your workouts started to feel...well, like work? You might go to the gym, but not as often as you'd like—or need to.

Sooner or later, motivation vanishes from our exercise routines. But the "routine"—which inevitably leads to boredom—is actually part of the problem.

Here's some advice from exercise physiologist Robert Hopper, PhD...

- **Pick an activity that you really enjoy.** Sounds obvious—but how many of us head straight for the treadmill or the same piece of equipment every time we go to the gym? Instead, think of a sport you really love to do. It might be biking, skiing, golf or racquetball. Think of it as your activity, and do it whenever you can.

- **Choose your workouts strategically.** This means opting for activities that support your favorite form of physical activity.

Example: If you're a skier, biking and lower-body weight training will help keep you in shape to hit the slopes.

- **Pay yourself (see also the next article).** A bit too extreme? It actually works for a lot of people.

Helpful: Try one of the motivational smartphone apps—such as Pact Health, which allows you to team up with friends so you can all get paid for working out...or StickK, which donates your contribution to a favorite charity when you meet your fitness goals—or to one you despise when you don't.

How Money Can Get You to Exercise

Study titled "Framing Financial Incentives to Increase Physical Activity Among Overweight and Obese Adults: A Randomized, Controlled Trial" by researchers at Perelman School of Medicine, Wharton School and Leonard Davis Institute of the University of Pennsylvania, Philadelphia, Massachusetts General Hospital, Boston, and Columbia University Medical Center, New York City, published in annals of *Internal Medicine.*

When you're not feeling motivated to drag yourself to the gym or out for a run, a brisk walk or a bike ride, the thought *They'd have to pay me!* might cross your mind.

But would that really work?

In a recent study, employees enrolled in a fitness program were given different financial incentives to achieve a daily walking target of 7,000 steps.

The rewards: Getting a small cash bonus... avoiding a cash fine of the same amount...being entered into a lottery to win big...or no financial incentive at all.

The winner: Avoiding the fine.

Why is avoiding financial pain more motivating than getting financial pleasure? It's called "loss aversion," and it's well-known to behavioral economists—people strongly prefer avoiding a loss over acquiring a gain. We like to win, but we really, really don't like to lose.

Want to "cash in" on these findings? It turns out there is a free app available on both iTunes and Google Play that does just that. With Pact Health, you commit to a health goal and contribute a small amount each week—just a dollar or a few dollars. If you achieve your goal you claim it. If not, you lose it...and the proceeds go to someone else. Yes, it's on the honor system.

In other words, to avoid the financial ouch... get off the couch!

You Can Work Out Like an Olympic Athlete

Timothy Miller, MD, director of the endurance medicine program, which specializes in treating endurance athletes, and associate professor of clinical orthopaedics at The Ohio State University Wexner Medical Center in Columbus. Dr. Miller is also a volunteer team physician for the US Olympic Track and Field Team.

Watching Olympic athletes perform their incredible feats can be awe-inspiring... and humbling. But don't despair.

Even if you're not an Olympic athlete, you can still perform at your highest potential by adding highly effective Olympic training routines to your own workout.

Helpful: You can add all—or just a few—of the exercises below to your current fitness routine to increase your endurance, gain strength and boost bone density...*

FARTLEK WORKOUT

Which Olympic athletes do this? Cyclists and distance runners.

Good for: Anyone who wants to add speed and endurance to a walking, running or cycling routine.

What is it? Short bursts of high-intensity movement—a few seconds to a minute—that take place within a longer aerobic routine. Many people refer to this workout method as Fartlek (which means "speed play" in Swedish), but it is also known as interval training.

How can I do this? Do a 30-minute walk or jog in your neighborhood. Begin with a 10-minute warm-up of a slower-paced run or walk (use a stopwatch to keep track of your time). Once you're warmed up, sprint (or walk fast) between two mailboxes (or telephone poles or any other regularly spaced marker)...then return to your regular pace for the distance of three mailboxes. Sprint or walk fast again, continuing the same interval pattern for 10 minutes. Afterward, return to your regular pace for 10 minutes. Then cool down for a few minutes with a slower run or walk.

For a 30-minute cycling routine, pedal slowly for a 10-minute warm-up. Then do 30-second sprints pedaling as fast as you can followed by one minute of slow pedaling for a total of 10 minutes. Then cycle for 10 minutes at a comfortable pace and end with a cooldown.

*If you have a chronic medical condition or a recent injury, or are at increased risk of falling, consult your doctor before trying these exercises.

ECCENTRIC EXERCISES

Which Olympic athletes do this? Power lifters and gymnasts.

Good for: Anyone who wants to strengthen his/her calves, Achilles tendons and biceps.

What is it? These exercises, which are the most efficient way to build strength, focus on working the muscle when it lengthens. In this phase, you consciously slow the descent of a weight (or gravity). This means that you use resistance twice—once while lifting the weight and once while lowering it.

How can I do this? Biceps curls and heel drops.

Biceps curl: To begin, choose a light hand weight (about three to five pounds)...or use small soup cans. Stand with your feet shoulder-width apart, elbows at your sides and forearms at 90-degree angles from your body, with your palms and weights facing up. Hold your left arm steady. Lift your right arm toward your shoulder for a count of two to three seconds, keeping your elbow at your side.

Lower the weight slowly and with control for a count of three to four seconds, keeping your muscles contracted. This is the eccentric phase of the exercise. Alternate arms for a total of 12 to 15 repetitions on each arm. Perform the whole set two to three times. When you can perform 10 reps easily, increase the weight.

Heel drop: Stand with the balls of your feet on the edge of a stair. Drop your heels as low as you can in a slow, controlled motion, taking about three to four seconds to completely lower them. Then push your heels back up for a count of two to three seconds. Repeat 12 to 15 times. Do two to three sets.

PLYOMETRIC TRAINING

Which Olympic athletes do this? High jumpers, gymnasts, sprinters and basketball players.

Good for: Anyone who wants to build leg strength.

Simple Ways to Improve Balance

See how long you can stand on one foot with your eyes closed, and work on improving your time. Rise up on your toes 10 times with your eyes open and then 10 more times with them closed. Balance yourself on one foot for 10 to 15 seconds, then switch legs. Repeat 10 times, then do it again with your eyes closed. Walk in a straight line, placing the heel of one foot in front of the toes of the other foot.

Caution: When doing these exercises, stand near a wall or some other support.

University of California, *Berkeley Wellness Letter.* BerkeleyWellness.com

What is it? Also known as "jump training," these exercises require your muscles to exert maximum force in short intervals.

How can I do this? Box jumps. Most gyms have jump boxes of varying heights (six inches, 18 inches, etc.), or you can buy one at a sporting-goods store or online. Pick a height you can jump onto so that both feet land squarely on the box.

Stand with feet slightly wider than shoulder-width apart, knees bent. Using your arms to help generate power, jump on the box landing softly on two feet, knees flexed. Keep your hands in front of you for balance. Then jump back down to the starting position. Repeat 10 times for a total of three sets.

A Better Way to Weight Train: You Don't Have to Heave Heavy Weights

Brad Schoenfeld, PhD, a certified strength and conditioning specialist and an assistant professor in exercise science at Lehman College in New York City, where he directs the Human Performance Lab. Dr. Schoenfeld is also the assistant editor in chief of the *National Strength and Conditioning Association's Strength and Conditioning Journal*, and author of *Science and Development of Muscle Hypertrophy*.

To get the biggest bang from your exercise regimen, strength training is a must. It not only builds muscle and bone but also helps manage your weight and control chronic health problems such as diabetes and heart disease.

But not everyone relishes the idea of heaving heavy weights. And the practice can be risky for people with arthritis, osteoporosis and other conditions.

Good news: Researchers have now discovered that people who repeatedly lift light weights get nearly the same benefits as those who do heavy-weight workouts.

Why this matters: Whether you're using hand weights or exercise machines, the lighter-weight approach can make strength training safer and more enjoyable.

Men and women who lift light weights instead of heavy ones are also less likely to experience joint, tendon or ligament injury. Plus, the workouts are easier for older adults...those with arthritis or other health problems...and those who are new to weight lifting.

THE NEW THINKING

According to traditional thinking, you need to lift heavy weights to build your muscles. In practice, this meant identifying your one-repetition maximum—the heaviest weight that you could lift just one time. Then you'd design a workout that required lifting 65% or more of that weight eight to 12 times.

This approach is still favored by many elite athletes because lifting at the edge of your ability targets fast-twitch muscle fibers, the ones that grow quickly and create an admirable physique. But studies now show that slow-twitch fibers, the ones that are stimulated to a greater extent by light lifting, can also develop and grow.

Important finding: In a recent meta-analysis published in the journal *Sports Medicine*, people who lifted lighter weights for six weeks achieved the same muscle growth—although not quite as much strength—as those who lifted heavy weights.

Heavy lifting is still the preferred approach for people who need to develop their strength to the utmost—top athletes, construction workers, movers, etc. But those who simply want to look better and improve their functional capacity—the ability to carry groceries, work in the yard, play recreational sports, etc.—will do just as well with lighter loads.

Bonus: Building muscle mass also helps control blood sugar.

LESS WEIGHT, MORE REPS

Muscle growth occurs only when muscles are exhausted—when you simply can't move the weight one more time. So to get comparable benefits to a traditional heavy-weight workout requiring eight to 12 repetitions, you'll need to do 20 to 25 reps with lighter weights. Your weight workouts will take a little longer, but your muscles will be just as tired when you're done.

A LIGHT-WEIGHT PLAN

Lighter-weight workouts are easier on the joints than those done with heavy weights, and the results are still relatively fast—you'll likely notice an increase in strength/muscle size within a few weeks. *To start...*

• **Choose your weights wisely.** Instead of calculating percentages—a heavy-weight lifter, as described earlier, may aim to lift at least 65% of his/her one-repetition maximum—keep it simple. Forget the percentages, and let repetitions guide your starting weights. For example, do each exercise 20 to 25 times. If you can't complete that many, you're starting too heavy. Conversely, if you can easily do 20 to 25 reps, the weight's too light.*

Important: You're not doing yourself any good if you can easily lift a weight 25 times. You need to strain. On a one-to-10 scale of effort, the last few reps should rate nine-and-a-half or 10.

• **Do multiple sets.** You'll progress more quickly when you do three sets of each exercise—for example, bicep curls. Complete 20 to 25 repetitions...rest for two minutes...do them again...rest...and repeat one more time. If you don't have the time—or the desire—to do three sets, opt for a single-set approach. You'll still notice increases in strength and muscle size, but your gains won't be as great as with a multi-set approach.

• **Work out at least twice a week.** You want to work each muscle group—arms, legs, chest, midsection, etc.—at least twice a week. Three or four times weekly will give even faster results.

Important: Don't work the same muscles two days in a row. Growth occurs during the recovery phase...and injuries are more likely when you stress already-tired muscles.

If you work out every day: Alternate muscle groups—for example, do leg and back exercises on Monday...arm and chest exercises on Tuesday...then more leg and back work on Wednesday, etc.

EXERCISES FOR REAL LIFE

The strength-training exercises below will give you more confidence and power when doing your daily activities—follow the advice above for choosing your weights, repetitions, exercise frequency, etc....

• **Bicep curls.** Exercising this upper-arm muscle will make carrying groceries a bit easier.

What to do: Hold a hand weight in each hand. While keeping your elbows near your sides and your shoulders back, curl the weight toward your shoulder, then lower it back down.

• **One-arm triceps extensions.** This exercise will strengthen your triceps (muscles on the backs of the upper arms), which help balance the biceps—and give your arms a toned appearance. It will help when moving furniture or shoveling snow.

What to do: While sitting, hold a hand weight over your head, with your arm straight up and your elbow close to your head. Bend your elbow and lower the weight just behind your neck, then raise it back up. Repeat with the other arm.

• **Lunges.** This versatile exercise targets the buttocks and thighs, along with the arms, making climbing stairs easier.

What to do: With a weight in each hand, stand with your feet about shoulder-width apart. Take a long step forward with your right foot. As your foot lands, bend the knee until the thigh is nearly parallel to the floor. Pull your right leg back to the starting position, then lunge with the left foot.

*Hand weights are available in neoprene, iron and vinyl at many retail stores and online. I recommend holding various weights in a store to choose the one that feels best.

Sneakers That Strengthen Legs

Study of 38 runners led by researchers at Hong Kong Polytechnic University, Hung Hom, Kowloon, published in *Clinical Biomechanics.*

"Barefoot sneakers" strengthen legs and feet more effectively than regular sneakers. These minimalist shoes have stretchy-fabric uppers, zero heel-to-toe drop and a three-millimeter outer sole—with no midsole cushioning or arch support. Runners who used them for six months had 7% larger leg muscles and 9% larger foot muscles—while those who used regular sneakers had no muscle increase.

Hate to Exercise? Get a Dog

Mathew J. Reeves, PhD, professor of epidemiology and biostatistics, Michigan State University, East Lansing.

Dog owners were 34% more likely to meet the recommended minimum of 150 minutes of moderate exercise a week—and 69% more likely to be physically active—than people who don't own dogs, recent research has found.

Good idea: If you have a dog, work out with your pet. K9FitClub has lots of different classes in cities across the US. Go to K9FitClub.com.

Don't Quit Getting Fit!

J. Carson Smith, PhD, associate professor of kinesiology and director, kinesiology undergraduate honors program, University of Maryland School of Public Health, College Park, and leader of a study of competitive master athletes, published in *Frontiers in Aging Neuroscience.*

Brain benefits of exercise diminish quickly if you stop being active.

When runners stopped exercising, they had much less blood flow in their brains within 10 days.

Bottom line: If you take a break from regular physical activity, don't wait too long to resume it.

What Is "Moderate" Exercise Anyway?

American College of Cardiology.

You've probably heard the U.S. National Institutes of Health's recommendation for most adults to get 30 minutes of moderate exercise on most days to stay fit.

But what exactly is moderate? And how do you know if you're working hard or hardly working?

One of the easiest ways to measure the intensity of your workout is with the "talk test." If you're working in the moderate range, you can talk without too much difficulty. But if you can sing, pick up the exercise pace, according to the American College of Cardiology. And if you're doing vigorous activity, you'll be able to say just a few words before pausing for a breath.

Another way to figure out how hard you're working is to monitor your heart rate.

To do this, first figure out your maximum heart rate. Subtract your age from 220. For a 50-year-old, this would be 170 beats per minute. A person's target heart rate for moderate activity falls between 50% and 70% of their maximum heart rate. So, for that 50-year-old, the sweet spot is between 85 and 119 beats per minute.

Once you calculate your own heart rate range on paper, check to see if you're in this range during exercise by stopping to take your pulse for 30 seconds then multiplying that number by 2.

Walking, playing golf—without using a cart—and general gardening are ways to get moderate exercise. Aerobic dancing, jogging and swimming hard all count as vigorous exercise.

If you're pressed for time (and in good shape), doing more strenuous exercise may be the way to go. Vigorous exercisers only need 15 minutes of activity a day to get the same results as moderate movers.

To learn more about how much exercise is best for good health, visit the U.S. Centers for Disease Control and Prevention at https://www.cdc.gov/physicalactivity/basics/adults/index.htm.

CHAPTER 17

Pain Remedies

The Natural Pain Cures You Need to Try

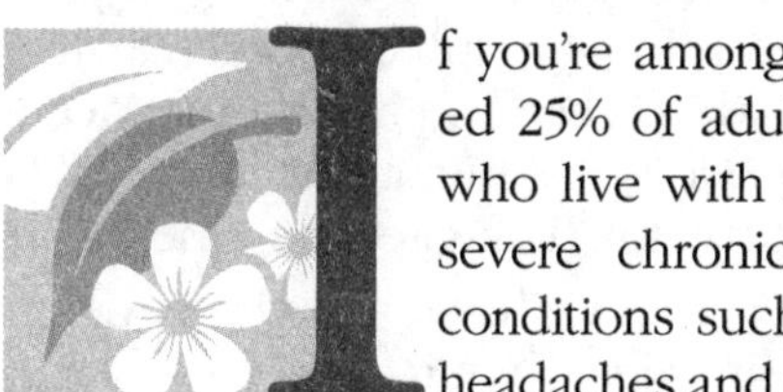

If you're among the estimated 25% of adults in the US who live with moderate-to-severe chronic pain, from conditions such as arthritis, headaches and fibromyalgia, you may be so desperate for relief that you decide to try a powerful opioid—and take your chances with side effects.

It's widely known that people can become dependent on (or addicted to) these drugs—including older standbys such as morphine and codeine...as well as newer heavy hitters such as *hydrocodone* (Vicodin, Norco) and *oxycodone* (OxyContin, Percocet). Yet many doctors are still too quick to prescribe them.

Sadly, these drugs don't stop the root cause of the pain—they simply block the intensity of pain signals that a patient feels. While opioids can be appropriate for acute conditions (including broken bones and postsurgical pain), they rarely are the best choice for chronic pain.

What's more, a recent study published in *JAMA: The Journal of the American Medical Association* found that long-acting opioids, such as OxyContin or *fentanyl* (Duragesic), increase one's risk for death by 65%—due to heart attack and other cardiovascular events.

So what's the best solution for chronic pain? We spoke with Heather Tick, MD, an expert in pain medicine, for answers...

THE PAIN MEDICINE PARADOX

It's an unfortunate paradox that pain medicine can actually worsen pain. In fact, researchers are now finding that patients who are weaned off opioids, using such nondrug therapies as physical therapy and relaxation exercises instead, actually can experience less pain than they did

Heather Tick, MD, who holds the Gunn-Loke Endowed Professorship for Integrative Pain Medicine at the University of Washington in Seattle and is a clinical associate professor in both the departments of family medicine, and anesthesiology and pain medicine. She is author of *Holistic Pain Relief.*

while on opioids, and they have a greater sense of well-being and function better.

Here's what happens: It's relatively easy to develop a tolerance to an opioid, which requires increasingly higher doses for the drug to work. Even when properly prescribed, chronic high doses of these medications can trigger a condition called hyperalgesia, which results in new pain sensitivity either in the primary area of pain or in a new area. For example, a patient who takes an opioid for low-back pain may begin to develop neck pain and headaches.

The good news: Nonopioid therapies that stimulate the parasympathetic nervous system—the branch of the nervous system that helps us feel calm and relaxed—can be highly effective for pain relief.

Chronic pain patients tend to live in the sympathetic nervous system's "fight or flight" mode, which intensifies pain by secreting inflammation-promoting hormones. That's why it's crucial to fire up the parasympathetic system, which tells the body to secrete acetylcholine instead, a neurotransmitter that counteracts inflammation.

There's strong evidence supporting the effectiveness of meditation for fighting pain. It induces the relaxation response—literally altering your body's chemistry. Meditation also lowers stress hormone levels, decreases muscle tension and builds pain tolerance. Other ways to trigger the parasympathetic system's pain-fighting mechanism...*

•**Autogenic training.** Autogenic training (AT) is a relaxation technique based on a set of affirmations (self-directed statements) that are designed to reverse the physical effects of stress. You can buy AT recordings online, in which a person with a soothing voice says the affirmations...or you can repeat them to yourself or make your own recording, using a script like the one below.

What to do: Sit or lie in a comfortable, quiet room. Repeat each of the following statements three times, then dwell on each statement for about 30 seconds afterward. Try to truly feel each sensation in the script. Do this daily.

*Consult your doctor before trying these methods or the supplement described here—especially if you take blood thinners or have a chronic medical condition such as hypertension.

I am completely calm.

My arms feel heavy and warm.

My legs feel heavy and warm.

My heartbeat is calm and regular.

My abdomen is warm and comfortable.

My forehead is pleasantly cool.

My shoulders are heavy and warm.

•**Ujjayi breathing.** Stress causes us to breathe shallowly from the chest instead of deeply from the belly. This leaves stale air trapped in the bottom of the lungs and hinders delivery of healing oxygen to muscles. Any deep-breathing technique can stimulate the parasympathetic system, but Ujjayi (pronounced oo-ja-EE) breathing is particularly effective.

What to do: To get the hang of this technique, inhale deeply through your nose and exhale through your open mouth, gently constricting the muscles at the back of your throat and making a HAAAH sound, as if you were trying to fog up a mirror. Then try to make the same sound on the inhale.

Once you've achieved the correct sound, close your mouth and breathe in and out through your nose, making the HAAAH sound on both the inhale and exhale. Spend equal time (at a pace that's comfortable for you) inhaling and exhaling several times a day. When you first start this technique, try to do it for six minutes at a time. You can work up to 15 to 20 minutes at a time.

Important: If you have a favorite deep-breathing technique of your own, feel free to use that—just be sure that you keep the flow of air constant, and you don't hold your breath for longer than a beat. Otherwise, you will stimulate the sympathetic nervous system, triggering the pain response.

ANOTHER NONDRUG SOLUTION

In addition to the approaches described above, the following supplement can help ease pain by reducing inflammation...

•**Turmeric.** This mildly bitter spice is a powerful analgesic with impressive anti-inflammatory powers. A 2014 study suggested it may be as effective as *ibuprofen* in reducing the pain of knee osteoarthritis.

Capsules are one option to try. But if you like the taste, try making "Golden Milk."

What to do: Combine one-quarter cup of turmeric with one-half cup of water in a pot, and blend to create a thick paste. Heat gently, adding a pinch of ground black pepper and drizzling in water as needed to maintain a thick but stirrable consistency.

Refrigerate the mixture in a glass container, and add one heaping teaspoon to an eight-ounce glass of warm water mixed with a little almond milk every day. You can add some honey to cut the bitterness. Or use warm broth instead of water and a dash of ginger and/or garlic for a tasty soup.

Stop a Migraine Before It Happens

Mark W. Green, MD, a professor of neurology, anesthesiology and rehabilitation medicine at Icahn School of Medicine at Mount Sinai in New York City, where he directs Headache and Pain Medicine and is the vice chair of Neurology for Professional Development and Alumni Relations. He is coauthor of *Managing Your Headaches* and several medical textbooks.

There are more than 37 million Americans who suffer from migraines, but the odds aren't in their favor when it comes to drug treatment.

Sobering statistics: Preventive drugs work for only about half of the people who have these awful headaches—and even when the medication does help, migraine frequency is reduced by only about 50%.

The drugs that stop migraines once they've started—mainly prescription triptans (such as *sumatriptan*, *rizatriptan* and *almotriptan*)...as well as OTC nonsteroidal anti-inflammatory drugs, such as *ibuprofen* (Motrin), and Excedrin Migraine, which contains *acetaminophen*, aspirin and caffeine—are not always effective. They work best when they're taken soon after the pain begins. Some of the drugs also cause side effects, such as fatigue or gastrointestinal bleeding. And taking them too often can lead to more—and more severe—headaches, known as overuse headaches or "rebound" headaches. So preventive drugs may be needed to avoid overuse of these medications.

A COMPLEX PROBLEM

Why are migraines so hard to manage? Experts once believed that migraines were mainly caused by the dilation (widening) of blood vessels in the brain. That's why drugs usually prescribed for other conditions, such as *propranolol*, a blood pressure drug, have been used to reverse these changes.

But we now believe that migraines have more to do with overstimulation of the trigeminal nerve in the face and head—this can cause blood vessels in the brain to expand and become inflamed. Treatments that affect this nerve (see below) are often very effective.

Important: Everyone who suffers from migraines should pay attention to possible triggers that precipitate attacks. Some people react to strong scents. Others are vulnerable to specific foods (such as bacon, ripened cheeses or alcohol)...food additives such as monosodium glutamate (MSG)...emotional stress...bright lights, etc. Avoiding triggers can be an effective way to prevent some attacks.

BEST NONDRUG OPTIONS

Preventing a migraine is always better than trying to treat one that's already taken hold. Unfortunately, not all doctors are aware of the more recent effective migraine-prevention approaches. *Among the best...*

• **Cefaly.** Nearly three years ago, the FDA approved the first device for migraine prevention. Cefaly is known as an external trigeminal nerve stimulation unit. It electrically stimulates branches of the trigeminal nerve, which transmits sensations to the face and head.

How it works: The prescription-only device, which blocks pain signals, includes a battery-powered headband with a reusable, self-adhering electrode. Patients position the headband around the forehead, just above the eyes. It may cause a slight tingling, but no pain. It's used for 20 minutes once a day. Anyone who has an implanted device in the head, a pacemaker or an implanted defibrillator should not use Cefaly.

Scientific evidence: One study found that more than half of migraine patients who used

Cefaly were satisfied and intended to keep using it. The unit costs about $350 and is usually not covered by insurance. The device manufacturer offers a 60-day guarantee, so people can get their money back if it doesn't seem to help.

• **Biofeedback.** Emotional stress is one of the most common migraine triggers. A biofeedback machine allows people to monitor skin temperature, muscle tension, brain waves and other physical stress responses that affect blood flow in the brain. The idea is that once people feel how they react to stress—with tightened forehead muscles, for example—they can modify their reactions with things like deep breathing, muscle relaxation, etc.

Scientific evidence: There's strong research showing that biofeedback can reduce both the frequency and severity of migraines by 45% to 60%—but only for patients who are willing to practice.

Biofeedback can work about as well as many drugs, but it takes most people a few months before they're good at it. It can also be costly because you have to work with an instructor at first. To find a certified biofeedback practitioner, go to the website of the Biofeedback Certification International Alliance, BCIA.org. Insurance often won't cover it.

• **Supplements.** Some people do well when they combine one or more of these supplements with the previous approaches...*

• Riboflavin, a B vitamin, may improve oxygen metabolism in cells. In one study, migraine frequency was reduced by 50% in patients who took riboflavin (400 mg daily).

• Feverfew is an herbal headache remedy. Some research shows that 50 mg to 125 mg daily can help prevent and ease migraines, while other studies suggest that it's no more effective than a placebo. For some people, it might be a helpful addition to more mainstream treatments.

• Magnesium (500 mg daily) can help reduce the frequency of migraines in people with low levels of the mineral.

*Check with your doctor before taking these supplements, since they can interact with certain medications and/or cause side effects such as diarrhea.

BOTOX

Known for smoothing facial wrinkles, these injections were FDA-approved for chronic migraines in 2010. Botox is a good treatment option for patients who have 15 or more days of headaches each month.

We still do not know how Botox works to prevent headaches. It probably deactivates pain receptors in the scalp and blocks the transmission of nerve signals between the scalp and the brain.

How it's done: The drug is injected in multiple locations on the head and neck—and the injections are repeated every three months. It sounds terrible, but the injections are only mildly painful. The procedure takes about 15 minutes, and it's usually covered by insurance if drugs or other treatments haven't worked. Botox treatments are given by headache specialists. Side effects may include swallowing problems, blurred vision and speech difficulties.

Important: I advise patients to commit to at least three treatments. If Botox relieves your pain, you and your doctor can decide how frequently you need additional treatments. If you haven't noticed relief after three treatments, Botox is unlikely to be a good choice for you.

No More Neck Pain

Carol Krucoff, a yoga therapist at Duke Integrative Medicine in Durham, North Carolina, and codirector of Integrative Yoga for Seniors teacher training, which helps yoga instructors safely adapt the practice for older adults. She is also author of *Healing Yoga for Neck & Shoulder Pain* and the forthcoming *Relax into Yoga for Seniors.* HealingMoves.com

About 15% of US adults endure the misery of neck pain at some point each year. When neck pain occurs, the sufferer will do almost anything to get relief—whether it's popping strong painkillers, paying for massages or seeing a chiropractor.

While these and other approaches may be appropriate in some cases, one of the most effective—but underutilized—therapies for neck pain is yoga. Almost all causes of neck pain, including arthritis, can benefit from yoga, which is a great adjunct to medical treatment. It is also helpful to relieve neck pain stemming from poor posture.

Why yoga? Key yoga moves not only stretch tight muscles and strengthen weak ones, but also help create proper body alignment and posture—crucial steps in both preventing and treating neck pain.

To alleviate neck pain and keep it from coming back, practice these steps every day—but be sure to see your doctor first if you're experiencing severe pain...*

HOLD YOUR HEAD RIGHT

The adult head weighs about 10 pounds—roughly the same as a medium-weight bowling ball. So it is important to correctly balance that weight to avoid strain on the neck.

Many daily activities, including sitting at a desk, working at a computer and talking and texting on the phone, cause our shoulders to round...bodies to lean forward...and heads to protrude in front of the shoulders. This posture puts extreme pressure and tension on the neck and shoulders.

What to do: For correct head posture whether sitting or standing, your ears should be directly over your shoulders and your shoulders directly over your hips. Check yourself several times a day to make sure you're doing it. This posture may feel strange to you when you first try it, but learning to keep your head balanced over your shoulder girdle can make you feel better and will eventually seem natural.

CHECK FOR "BODY ARMOR"

When stressed, many people tighten the muscles in the upper back, shoulders and neck. As this physical response becomes habitual, we develop a "body armor" of tight, overused muscles in the neck and shoulders. The pattern becomes so ingrained that we don't even notice that we hold this tension constantly in our bodies.

*Check with your physician before doing any physical activity, including yoga poses, if you have neck pain that is accompanied by numbness, tingling or weakness in your arm or hand...the pain was caused by an injury or accident...you have swollen glands or a lump in your neck...or you have difficulty swallowing or breathing.

To break this cycle, it's important to consciously consider how tension is affecting your neck muscles.

What to do: Set your wristwatch alarm or phone alarm to sound once every waking hour. When you hear the alarm, take a moment to identify any areas of discomfort or tension in your body, including your back, shoulders and neck. Close your eyes, take a deep breath and relax these muscles. With practice and patience, it is often possible to get substantial release of muscle tension.

Also helpful: Repeat a simple mantra, such as "Lips together, teeth apart," throughout the day to avoid clenching the teeth and help relax the jaw, a common site where tension resides. Jaw tightness often radiates downward and exacerbates neck pain.

STRETCH AND STRENGTHEN

Don't worry if you have never done yoga—these are easy poses that will improve your body alignment and gently stretch the shoulders and neck. Practice the following yoga poses throughout the day, while at your desk, a table, while waiting for coffee to brew, etc. The seated mountain pose can be done anytime you're sitting. The other poses can be done once a day. It should take about five minutes to do them all.

- **Seated mountain pose.**

What to do: Sit tall in your chair, with your feet on the floor. Use your hands to gently move the fleshy part of your buttocks aside and allow your "sit bones"—the two rounded knobs at the base of your pelvis—to press down onto the chair seat.

Extend the crown of your head up toward the sky, lengthening your spine. Relax your shoulders down away from your ears, and let your hands rest on your thighs. Be sure your chin is parallel to the ground and neither tilted up nor tucked in.

What helps: Imagine that you have a headlight in the center of your chest at your breastbone—and shine that light forward. Relax your face, and look straight ahead. Linger here for five to 10 slow, easy breaths.

- **Shoulder shrugs.**

What to do: Inhale and lift your shoulders up toward your ears and then exhale as you drop them down. Repeat five to 10 times, moving with the breath—inhale as you lift, then exhale (with a sigh if you like) as you release. Be sure to keep your arms as relaxed as possible.

•Shoulder circles.

What to do: Lift your shoulders straight up as high as they will comfortably go. Then bring them behind you as far as is comfortable. Next, release the shoulders down toward your hips, then bring them forward as far as you comfortably can and finish the circle by bringing them up toward your ears.

Continue circling your shoulders, and avoid holding your breath. Let the movement be easy and get as much motion as possible in your shoulders. Circle five times in this direction, then circle five times in the opposite direction. When you've finished, relax your shoulders and take three to five easy breaths.

•Head turn.

What to do: Inhale and extend the crown of your head toward the sky. Exhale and turn your head as far to the right as comfortably possible, keeping your shoulders still. Allow your eyes to turn also so you can look toward whatever is behind you. Inhale and turn back to center. Exhale and turn to the left. Repeat the set three to six times, moving with the breath.

•Ear to shoulder.

What to do: Sit tall with your hands on your thighs. Inhale and lift the crown of your head toward the sky. Then exhale and drop your right ear down toward your right shoulder, trying not to lift that shoulder toward the ear. Keep your left shoulder down and relax the left side of your neck.

Keep your breath flowing as you take your left hand off your thigh and let your left arm dangle at your side. Stay in this pose for a few breaths while relaxing. Bring your head back to the center and pause. Then repeat on the other side.

Help for Carpal Tunnel

Terry R. Light, MD, professor of orthopaedic surgery and rehabilitation, Loyola University Stritch School of Medicine, Maywood, Illinois.

Carpal tunnel syndrome occurs when tendons within a narrow area of the wrist called the carpal tunnel press on the median nerve, which runs from the forearm to the fingertips, resulting in numbness, pain and sometimes weakness.

Wearing a wrist splint, especially at night, helps decrease tendon swelling and eases symptoms for many people. In some cases, a corticosteroid injection into the carpal tunnel may also provide relief.

A physical or occupational therapist can provide you with hand exercises that can reduce symptoms if done daily. If these techniques do not help relieve pain and stiffness, you may need to consider surgery, which eliminates pressure on the median nerve, providing permanent relief for most people.

When It Comes to Back Pain...Know Your Options

Richard A. Deyo, MD, MPH, Kaiser-Permanente Endowed Professor of Evidence-Based Medicine, department of family medicine at Oregon Health & Science University, Portland. He is author of *Watch Your Back! How the Back Pain Industry Is Costing Us More and Giving Us Less—And What You Can Do to Inform and Empower Yourself in Seeking Treatment.*

Have you ever had an aching lower back? Most likely, your answer is yes—four out of five Americans have experienced low-back pain.

For some, acute low-back pain—lasting one to three months—turns into chronic low-back pain, a long-term problem that can limit activity and interfere with sleep. Back pain is the number-two symptomatic reason for doctor visits, right behind colds.

Problem: The help that most doctors offer is pills—either over-the-counter painkillers, powerful muscle relaxants such as *diazepam* (Valium) or even addictive opioid painkillers such as *oxycodone* (Oxycontin). In fact, guidelines from the American College of Physicians, the main medical society for internists, previously had recommended drugs as the first step in treating low-back pain. But drugs usually are not best!

Surprising development: In February 2017, the American College of Physicians issued new guidelines for treating low-back pain—recommending nondrug treatments as the first choice for acute pain and often for chronic pain, too. *Here's why, plus the nondrug treatments that scientific evidence shows are the most likely to provide real relief...*

MANY DRUGS DON'T WORK WELL

Research shows that many medications commonly prescribed or recommended by doctors for low-back pain don't work to relieve the pain—including *acetaminophen* (Tylenol) and oral steroids. As for opioid medications—they're dangerously addictive, and more than 16,000 Americans die yearly from overdoses.

That said, some medications can help a bit. *Ibuprofen* (Advil, Motrin), *naproxen* (Aleve) or aspirin provide some relief for low-back pain. Muscle relaxants such as *cyclobenzaprine* (Flexeril) also are moderately effective. In my experience, ibuprofen has the fewest side effects. But the truth is, if you have a classic case of low-back pain, you often don't need medication.

MISLEADING IMAGING

Getting an imaging test such as an MRI, a CT scan or an X-ray usually is not a good strategy for diagnosing acute low-back pain. Yes, the imaging may detect an abnormality such as a bulging disk in the spine. But such abnormalities are common and rarely are the cause of low-back pain—and treating them may lead to unnecessary tests and invasive procedures, even surgery, that are not needed.

When imaging is essential: There are several serious problems that can cause back pain and are considered medical emergencies that require imaging. A new episode of back pain could be caused by a tumor. If you have unexplained fever or weight loss and back pain, you may have a rare infection of the bones of the spine or the outermost part of the spinal canal. If you have muscle weakness in the foot or the leg and back pain, you may have a disk problem that requires further treatment.

Bottom line: It is not useful to do imaging in most people who don't have any of the above symptoms or situations. As I tell my patients—if you don't have imaging now and your pain persists, you can always have imaging later. There usually is no rush.

BEST NONDRUG TREATMENTS

The American College of Physicians now recommends the following nondrug treatments as among the best for low-back pain, and I agree...

- **Wait it out.** The little-used but effective strategy for most cases of acute back pain is... don't go to the doctor (and save $150 or more)! That's because low-back pain almost always improves substantially on its own within a month or so. *Instead, try one or more of the following nondrug treatments...*

  - Exercise. There's good scientific evidence that exercise can help relieve chronic low-back pain—and there's little evidence that one type of exercise works better than another.

    Beneficial types of movement include aerobic exercise, such as brisk walking or bicycling...yoga or stretching...and exercises that strengthen your abdominal and spinal muscles, such as Pilates.

    Best: A physical therapist can tailor and guide an exercise program to get you started. For the long term, find an exercise that you enjoy and that you'll stick with.

    For acute back pain, specific back exercises may not be helpful, but it's wise to keep walking and maintain normal activities as much as possible. It's when pain becomes chronic that exercise seems most helpful.

  - Cognitive behavioral therapy (CBT) or mindfulness-based stress reduction (MBSR). I think the most effective regimen for chronic low-back pain often is a combination of exercise and a mind-body approach such as CBT (a psychological therapy that helps you identify dysfunctional patterns of thinking and behavior that increase your pain) or MBSR (which combines the nonjudgmental acceptance of experience with relaxation techniques). By helping you pace yourself in daily life, these techniques ease muscle tension, relieve depression (common in people with chronic pain) and improve sleep.

• Heat. Locally applied heat can soothe acute or chronic back pain. Use a heating pad, a hot-water bottle or an over-the-counter heat wrap such as ThermaCare.

Caution: A temperature that's too hot or an application that's too prolonged could burn your skin.

• Hands-on professionals. Research shows that spinal manipulation (most often performed by chiropractors but sometimes by osteopathic physicians or physical therapists), acupuncture, massage therapy and other hands-on healing techniques can help relieve both acute and chronic back pain.

• Optimism. A recent study I coauthored, published in *Spine,* shows that seniors with low-back pain are more likely to get better if they are confident that their treatment will work. Optimism helps healing!

IF PAIN PERSISTS

If your back pain persists for more than a month without significant improvement, it's wise to see a doctor. (Of course, see a doctor immediately if you have any of the serious symptoms mentioned above.) A physician can create a treatment program that is tailored for you.

If your doctor says that you need medication, you should ask, "What are the relative risks and benefits of this choice? What will happen if I don't take this medication? What are the alternatives?"

And if surgery is recommended, you should probably get a second opinion. The most common surgery for back pain alone is spinal fusion, which is invasive and extensive with a long recovery period.

Even worse: Research shows that the surgery is of questionable effectiveness for many back problems. It also shows that a rigorous rehabilitation program—involving physical therapy and training in pain management—works just as well.

Lean Back to Heal Your Back

David Hanscom, MD, board-certified orthopedic spine surgeon, Seattle Neuroscience Specialists, Swedish Medical Center, Seattle. He is author of *Back in Control: A Spine Surgeon's Roadmap Out of Chronic Pain, Second Edition.* BackInControl.com

Inversion therapy is a form of traction that uses the force of gravity to stretch the spine. Your feet and ankles are securely strapped to a special table or chair, which you then tilt backward until your head is lower than the rest of your body. While inversion therapy hasn't been shown to provide long-term relief for back pain, many people do feel better for a short time while they are doing it and immediately afterward. That brief respite may be enough to allow a long pain-free walk or give you a break from the over-the-counter pain meds that you're taking.

The first thing you should know, though, is that you don't need to literally hang upside down with the soles of your feet pointing toward the ceiling! That's not necessary and isn't even a good idea for most people...at least not when you first try inversion therapy. I'll explain a safer approach below.

First, though, let's look at the potential benefits—and risks.

HOW INVERSION THERAPY CAN HELP

Inversion therapy can work in two very different ways...

• **Mechanical relief.** If pain is being cause by a compressed disc, removing stress on the disc by lying or sitting in an inverted position can reduce the pain.

• **Gravity creates a traction force to muscles and ligaments around the spine,** which temporarily releases muscle spasms. When that tightness disappears, you will feel more relaxed. Relaxation isn't just a nice extra—it's an integral part of treatment. That's especially true if you have back pain that has lasted 12 or more weeks.

Here's why: Living with pain for so long can make you frustrated and anxious, feelings that can become so ingrained that they form new pain pathways. Even after the original source of the pain—say, a pulled muscle—has dissipated, the new pathway still continues to send pain signals. Inversion therapy can relieve your pain so that as you relax, you can begin to "unwind" this nervous system response and break this painful pattern.

While short-term pain relief and relaxation can go a long way, though, they are rarely enough. Treating chronic pain is like fighting a forest fire—it must be attacked from all angles. Staying active is the top recommendation. Getting enough good-quality sleep is key. Nondrug treatments such as yoga, Pilates, tai chi and hypnosis can help.

By itself, then, a few minutes on the inversion table won't help much if you're not also staying active and getting your best sleep. On the positive side, combining inversion therapy with other nonpharmacologic treatments can further reduce pain. For example, hypnosis by itself, or inversion therapy by itself, may each provide only a modest amount of relief, but when you try them both, you may see big improvements in your back pain—without drugs.

WHO SHOULDN'T TRY INVERSION THERAPY

Inversion therapy is not for everybody. When your head is lower than the rest of your body, your heart rate slows but your blood pressure rises—and so does the pressure inside your eyes. If you have heart disease or any cardiovascular problem, including high blood pressure...or glaucoma, retinal detachment or any other eye condition...do not try inversion therapy. Pregnant women and people with hiatal hernia should also avoid it. (If you have any questions about whether it's safe for you, talk to your health-care provider.)

Even if you don't have any of these conditions, you could hurt yourself by being too gung-ho in your approach. If you hang upside down the first time out, you might hurt your ankles or knees. If you stay inverted too long, you might even pull a muscle, which will just make your pain worse.

That's why I recommend a go-slow approach. If you're healthy and you're interested in inversion therapy, speak with your health-care pro-

Better Back-Pain Care

Mindfulness fixes low back pain. Adults with chronic low-back pain showed significant improvement after eight weekly two-hour sessions of mindfulness-based stress reduction (MBSR), a program that combines meditation with simple yoga poses, a recent study found. Participants also practiced MBSR at home.

Details: After six months, 60% of those who did MBSR reported less pain and could more easily perform activities such as walking, climbing stairs and standing for long periods—a better result than those who treated their chronic low-back pain with medication and/or physical therapy. To find an online class in MBSR, go to the Center for Mindfulness, UMASSmed.edu/cfm/stress-reduction.

Daniel Cherkin, PhD, senior investigator, Group Health Research Institute, Seattle.

Exercise prevents back-pain recurrence. Supervised exercise reduced the chance of a repeat episode of back pain by 45% over a one-year period. Shoe orthotics and back belts were almost useless. And the type of exercise did not matter—some programs focused on back muscles, while others combined aerobics with strength and balance training. Patients generally did two to three supervised exercise sessions per week. But the protective effects wore off after a year—probably because many people stopped exercising when they were no longer being closely supervised.

Troubling: About 75% of people who have an episode of debilitating lower-back pain will have another within one year.

Statistical analysis of more than 6,000 studies involving back-pain prevention led by researchers at The George Institute for Global Health, The University of Sydney, Australia, published in *JAMA Internal Medicine.*

vider about first trying it under supervision at a physical therapist's office. You will most likely start gently and slowly by reclining at a slight angle (15 degrees below horizontal is a good start) for just a few minutes. If you feel better, periodically increase the angle and duration of the treatment (be careful not to overdo it). If you find it's really helping you after several sessions at the physical therapist's office, you might want to consider purchasing an inversion table—or an inversion chair, which provides a gentler angle for your body.

Opioids Do Not Help Chronic Low-Back Pain

Analysis of data from 20 trials including 7,295 patients by researchers at University of Sydney, Australia, published in *JAMA Internal Medicine.*

The slight relief they provide is little better than that of NSAIDs, such as aspirin.

Self-defense: Regular exercise and education about its benefits reduce the risk of developing lower-back pain by as much as 45%.

Better Painkiller Safety

Alene Kennedy-Hendricks, PhD, assistant scientist, Johns Hopkins Bloomberg School of Public Health, Baltimore.

Amidst an epidemic of prescription painkiller addiction and overdose deaths, a recent survey found that 60% of patients prescribed opioids don't take all their pills, with many saving leftover pills for later use or even sharing them with others, raising risk for drug abuse.

Better: Dispose of unused or expired medications on National Prescription Drug Take-Back Day (October 22). To find a drop-off location, go to DEAdiversion.usdoj.gov.

Opioid Dependence Can Start in Just a Few Days

Martin Bradley, PharmD, PhD, division of pharmaceutical evaluation and policy, College of Pharmacy, University of Arkansas for Medical Sciences, Little Rock.

Scott Krakower, DO, assistant unit chief, psychiatry, Zucker Hillside Hospital, Glen Oaks, New York.

U.S. Centers for Disease Control and Prevention's *Morbidity and Mortality Weekly Report.*

Doctors who limit the supply of opioids they prescribe to three days or less may help patients avoid the dangers of dependence and addiction, a recent study suggests.

Drug overdose deaths have quadrupled since 1999. More than six out of 10 overdose deaths involve opioid drugs, according to the U.S. Centers for Disease Control and Prevention. Ninety-one people die every day in America from prescription opioids or heroin, the agency says.

Prescriptions for opioids have nearly quadrupled since 1999 even though there's been no overall change in Americans' reported pain levels, according to the CDC.

RESEARCH RESULTS

For the study, researchers looked at a sample of patients drawn from data from health insurers and managed care plans. Specifically, they looked at opioid use among patients not being treated for cancer.

The researchers found that the odds of long-term opioid use increased most sharply in the first days of therapy, particularly after five days of taking the drugs. A single day's supply of a narcotic painkiller can result in 6% of patients being on an opioid a year later. The rate of long-term opioid use increased to about 13% for patients who first took the drugs for eight days or more, according to the report.

"The chances of long-term opioid use—use that lasts one year or more—start increasing with each additional day supplied, starting after the third day, and increase substantially after someone is prescribed five or more days, and especially after someone is prescribed one month of opioid therapy," said senior researcher Martin Bradley, PhD. He is from the division of pharmaceutical evaluation and policy at the University of Arkansas for Medical Sciences.

The odds of chronic opioid use also increase when a second prescription is given or refilled, he noted.

People starting on a long-acting opioid or *tramadol* (Ultram) were more likely to stay on opioids than those given *hydrocodone* (Vicodin) or *oxycodone* (Oxycontin), Dr. Bradley said.

The highest probability of continued opioid use at one and three years was seen among patients who started on a long-acting opioid, followed by patients who started on tramadol, he said.

Tramadol is a narcotic-like painkiller that has been touted as not being addictive. Patients can, however, become dependent on tramadol.

WHAT PATIENTS AND DOCTORS NEED TO DO

Patients need to discuss the use of narcotic painkillers when they are prescribed, Dr. Bradley said.

"Discussions with patients about the long-term use of opioids to manage pain should occur early in the opioid-prescribing process," he said.

"Awareness among prescribers, pharmacists and persons managing pharmacy benefits that authorization of a second opioid prescription doubles the risk for opioid use one year later might deter overprescribing of opioids," Dr. Bradley said.

EXPERT COMMENT

One addiction expert agreed.

"Prescribers should be cautious about what they prescribe, and they should educate patients that if they are going to prescribe opioids, there is a likelihood that patients will have an opioid dependence," said Scott Krakower, DO. He is assistant unit chief of psychiatry at Zucker Hillside Hospital in Glen Oaks, New York.

Given the dangers of opioids, doctors should first think about using non-narcotic pain medications, he suggested.

Dr. Krakower thinks that since the crackdown on opioids, doctors are becoming more cautious when prescribing them. But doctors also need to be cautious about prescribing tramadol, he said.

"No one planned to get hooked on tramadol, but it has some dependent properties," Dr. Krakower noted.

He believes that patients who need a narcotic should be given one. "The problem is that so many patients were prescribed opioids, and the odds of becoming dependent are very high," Dr. Krakower said.

Once someone becomes addicted to opioids, it can take years to kick that dependence, he said.

"If your doctor is going to prescribe an opioid, be educated about what it can potentially do," Dr. Krakower said.

The report was published in the U.S. Centers for Disease Control and Prevention's *Morbidity and Mortality Weekly Report.*

info Visit the U.S. National Institute on Drug Abuse at https://www.drugabuse.gov/drugs-abuse/opioids for more on opioids.

Flirting With Painkillers: Could You Get Hooked?

Michael Weaver, MD, professor of psychiatry and behavioral sciences, and medical director, Center for Neurobehavioral Research on Addiction, The University of Texas Health Science Center at Houston.

If you've heard about the painkiller-addiction epidemic, you're probably scared of these drugs—even wondering if you could become addicted if you ever needed one.

On the one hand, it is very easy to get hooked on painkillers. On the other hand, if you've been prescribed one of these strong opioids, such as *hydrocodone, oxycodone, hydromorphone* or *fentanyl*—which killed the musician Prince in an accidental overdose—and you know exactly how to use it, you don't have to be on a slippery slope to dependency.

What tips the balance? Are you at risk? If you started to get hooked, would you recognize the signs? Would you get help—or even know where to start?

To learn more, we spoke with Michael Weaver, MD, professor and medical director of the Center for Neurobehavioral Research on Addiction at The University of Texas Health Science Center at Houston. He is a clinical expert on opioid-use disorder.

HOW TO KNOW IF YOU'RE AT RISK

Some factors to consider when facing the risk of painkiller addiction....

•**Gender.** Women are more likely to become dependent on prescription painkillers than men are, and not only because they are more likely to have chronic pain—women tend to weigh less than men, so when they are prescribed standard doses, they are in effect taking higher amounts, which can jump-start them on the path to dependence. Also, while men are more likely to abuse illegal "hard" drugs such as heroin or cocaine, women are more likely to fall prey to prescription addictions, especially to opioids.

•**A family history of addiction to any substance.** Said Dr. Weaver, "There is a scientifically based genetic component to addiction." The closer the family member, such as a parent or sibling, the stronger the genetic risk.

•**Symptoms of anxiety and/or depression.** You may knowingly or unknowingly use opioids to numb these symptoms and not just physical pain.

•**A history of abusing another substance**—whether it's nicotine, alcohol, marijuana, stimulants or sedatives. "Substance-use disorders tend to travel in packs," said Dr. Weaver. "If you have one, you are at higher risk to have another."

WARNING SIGNS TO WATCH FOR

Opioid painkillers often are prescribed for chronic pain even though they aren't very effective for chronic pain and should never be the "first line" prescription, according to recent Centers for Disease Control and Prevention guidelines.

Once they are prescribed, often for a hospital procedure, however, some people get used to the drugs' feel-good effects and keep using them...which is to say abusing them. *Here are some signs that that might be happening...*

•**You're using an opioid painkiller for something other than pain**—to improve a bad mood, relieve stress or help you relax or get to sleep.

•**You feel that you have to take a painkiller just to feel normal**—"or what you think normal should feel like," said Dr. Weaver.

•**You find yourself taking higher doses to have the same effect**—that means you're building up a tolerance.

•**Family members or friends express concern about your painkiller use.**

•**You spend a significant amount of time trying to get your hands on one or more painkillers,** using them and recovering from their effects.

•**You find yourself trying to cut down on your use of painkillers—to no avail.**

WHAT TO DO IF YOU THINK YOU MIGHT BE HOOKED

If any of the above describes you, the first and most important tip is, *Don't go it alone.* Talk to your doctor about your concerns and your pattern of use, and ask for guidance on the best way to wean yourself from dependence. "Trying to deal with an addiction on your own is always more difficult," said Dr. Weaver. "It is much easier with help, and there is help available."

"Unlike with some other drugs, quitting opioids cold turkey can be very difficult because it can lead to opioid-withdrawal syndrome, which is very uncomfortable and often leads to relapse," noted Dr. Weaver. Symptoms of opioid withdrawal can feel like a bad case of the flu, without a fever but with nausea, diarrhea, muscle cramps and aches, runny nose and watery eyes. These symptoms often are accompanied by considerable anxiety and "powerful cravings to use opioids since that will make the symptoms go away immediately."

To prevent withdrawal symptoms and improve someone's chances of overcoming an opioid addiction, medication-assisted therapy is often recommended. This involves substituting a different opioid such as *methadone* or *buprenorphine,* which is much less likely to produce euphoria, for the one that's being abused, Dr. Weaver said. "It is better to be slowly tapered off over several days or weeks with a longer-acting, less reinforcing opioid with the help of a qualified physician or treatment program." This is what's often referred to as "detox." Naltrexone, which blocks the effects of other opioids if you do use one, may also be prescribed for long-term maintenance.

Over time, with ongoing counseling or other forms of professional help, people can learn skills to help them quit abusing opioids and avoid relapse for the long haul. There are many effective options available, including individual addiction counseling, group therapy, working with a physician who specializes in addiction medicine or participating in an inpatient or outpatient addiction treatment program.

HOW TO AVOID ADDICTION...AND WHEN ADDICTION IS ACTUALLY OK

Of course, if you are at risk for opioid dependence—if you're almost addicted, as it were—the best thing to do is to nip it in the bud before it becomes a full-blown addiction that needs treatment. "There are lots of nonopioid pain meds available for many different chronic pain conditions, so talk with your doctor about these," said Dr. Weaver. "Think about whether you need a particular dose of opioid at a particular time, or whether you can try to skip it for now, or wait a while by using nonopioid pain management techniques.

"Consider comfort measures such as a heating pad, ice pack, massage or repositioning a painful body part," continued Dr. Weaver. "Other modalities can be useful as alternatives to opioids, such as biofeedback, hypnosis and chiropractic manipulation."

Mind-body approaches can be more effective than opioids for debilitating conditions such as fibromyalgia.

Finally, it should be noted that continuing use of opioid painkillers can sometimes have a place in medicine. The CDC's new guidelines, for example, make it clear that they don't apply to people who are actively battling cancer pain or who are being given opioids for palliative care at the end of life. For these patients, opioid painkillers can be perfectly appropriate.

Beat Knee Pain Without Surgery

Mitchell Yass, DPT, a St. Augustine, Florida–based physical therapist and creator of the Yass Method for treating chronic pain. He is also the author of *The Pain Cure Rx: The Yass Method for Diagnosing and Resolving Chronic Pain* and the PBS special *The Pain Prescription.* MitchellYass.com

Do you wince when you walk, kneel, squat or climb stairs? If so, you are definitely not alone. Nearly 20% of all cases of chronic pain are associated with the knee, and it's severe enough to limit the sufferer's mobility and affect quality of life.

Knee surgery, including knee replacement, is a widely used option, but it's rarely the best choice...and should never be the first choice. Knee pain is often caused by weak and/or imbalanced muscles, which surgery or other invasive treatments do not address.

A much better option: For most people with knee pain, exercise is at least as effective as surgery—with none of the risks, according to research. *What you need to know...*

MUSCLE PAIN

When you see a doctor because of nagging knee pain, you'll probably be advised to have an X-ray or MRI to look for arthritis, torn cartilage or other structural problems that can cause joint pain. But the tests, more often than not, point doctors in the wrong direction.

Eye-opening research: A study of nearly 1,000 patients with arthritis-related knee pain found that 63% had a damaged meniscus (cartilage that cushions and stabilizes the knee). But the same study also found that 60% of patients without pain had the same type of damage.

Most patients—and many doctors—fail to realize that there's a poor correlation between structural problems and knee pain. That's why I often advise clients not to have imaging tests—or consider surgery—until they've first tried my program of targeted exercise. In my experience, about 90% of knee patients have a muscle imbalance or weakness that causes all or most of their symptoms.

Here is a 30- to 60-minute workout that helps specific types of knee pain. Do the exercises on the side that is painful until the pain subsides—once the pain is gone, do the exercises on both sides. Stop if the exercise hurts.

A resistance band, ankle weight or machine in the gym can be used for resistance, which is key for strengthening muscles.* Start at a level where you feel you are working hard but not in pain, and gradually increase resistance.

The exercises can be performed by anyone, including those who have had knee surgery, but check first with your doctor. The quad stretch should be done daily. For each of the other exercises below, do three sets of 10 repetitions (resting 45 to 60 seconds between sets) and repeat the workouts three times a week (with a day between workouts).

WEAK HAMSTRINGS

The thigh muscles (quadriceps) tend to be a lot stronger than the opposing muscles (the hamstrings) on the backs of the legs. Why? It's because virtually all of our daily movements—including walking and climbing stairs—are "forward."

The problem: Weak hamstrings (they are mainly responsible for knee bending) cannot effectively counteract the force of much stronger quadriceps, causing a muscle imbalance.

Result: The quadriceps shorten and pull up on the kneecap, causing excessive pressure and pain. The majority of people with knee pain will improve when they strengthen the hamstrings and stretch the quads.

EXERCISE #1: **Hamstring curls.** While sitting in a chair, tie the ends of a resistance band to a doorknob and slip it around the ankle…or try the seated leg curl machine at the gym.

What to do: Begin with the exercising leg pointing straight out, then bend the knee until it reaches 90 degrees. Return to the starting position.

EXERCISE #2: Hip extensions. This exercise works the gluteus maximus muscles in the buttocks.

*To increase muscle strength, add resistance (with heavier weights or a stronger exercise band) when the exercises become easy.

What to do: While standing, place a resistance band behind one knee. Then attach the ends to a fixed point—such as a doorknob. While standing (you can rest your hand on top of a chair or table for extra support), bring the knee about 10 degrees behind the hip, then return to the starting position.

EXERCISE #3: **Quad stretches.** Tight quadriceps pull the kneecap toward the top of the joint and prevent it from moving smoothly. Tight quads can cause both knee and back pain.

What to do: Stand near a wall (or a dresser, bookcase or other solid support), and use one hand for balance. Reach back with your other hand, and grip the ankle.

Pull the heel upward toward the buttock. The knee should be a few inches behind the hip. Keep pulling until you feel a stretch in the front of the thigh. Hold the stretch for 20 to 30 seconds, and do the stretch twice. Pull gently! If it hurts, you've pulled too far (or too quickly).

QUAD STRAIN

Another common cause of knee pain is quad strain. What are the telltale signs? You might notice a "pulling" sensation at the top of the knee or in the thigh when you walk or climb stairs. A weak quadricep can cause the kneecap to shift out of place. *Try this…*

EXERCISE #1: **Knee extensions.** They strengthen the quadriceps and help the kneecap stay in a "neutral" position.

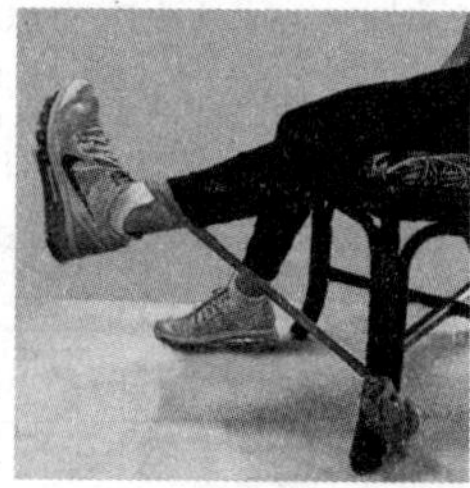

What to do: In a seated position, strap on an ankle weight or tie a resistance band around the front of the ankle and attach the other end to the chair leg. Keep the other foot on the floor. Begin with the knee bent to a 90-degree angle, then straighten it. Return to the starting position.

Important: Make sure that the thigh of the leg being exercised stays on the seat. Raising it will make the exercise less effective.

EXERCISE #2: **Dorsiflexion.** It works the tibialis anterior, a muscle in the front of the shin. Strengthening the muscle can help keep the calf muscle lengthened and allow the knee joint to function properly to prevent knee pain.

What to do: Sit on the floor with one leg extended. Slip an exercise band over the top of the foot and tie the ends to a sturdy table leg. Start with the ankle angled about 30 degrees forward, then pull the foot toward the upper body until it is 10 degrees past perpendicular. Return to the starting position.

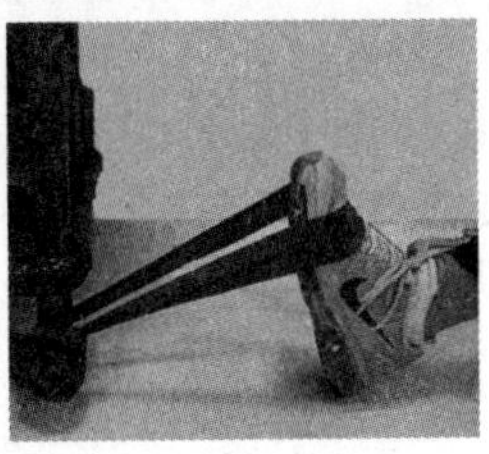

It's Your Butt!

Chris Kolba, PhD, PT, a sports medicine physical therapist and clinical instructor at The Ohio State University Wexner Medical Center in Columbus. He developed The Ohio State Tactical Rehab and Conditioning Program to meet the needs of firefighters, police officers and other tactical operators.

Want to get to the bottom of your persistent back, knee or hip pain? Look behind you, and you'll find the likely cause.

Dormant butt syndrome is the name that I've coined for a serious problem that affects millions of Americans, especially those who spend most of the day sitting. Did you pull a hamstring while playing with your grandkids? Suffer from an aching back after a few hours of TV watching? Weak gluteal (butt) muscles are often the common link. A lack of strength in this area forces other muscles to compensate and do jobs that they're not designed to do alone, resulting in pain in unexpected parts of the body.

THE NEGLECTED CORE

The big muscles in the buttocks do more than give it shape. They absorb shocks and control movements necessary for walking and other activities. When the gluteal muscles are weak, other muscles and joints definitely take the hit.

Dormant butt syndrome strikes people who are generally sedentary—whether they're sitting behind a desk, driving a car or watching their favorite sitcoms. When you're positioned on your derriere for hours on end, the glutes aren't "firing" and there's more tightness in the hip flexor muscles, which can lead to hamstring injuries or back, hip or knee pain. Runners and other athletes who do repetitive motion can also get tight hip flexors.

When I evaluate clients who have lower-body pain, I always check for adequate glute strength. To do this, I ask the patient to lie on his/her stomach and do a leg lift against resistance from my hand to determine how strong his glutes are.

I also put my fingertips lightly on the hamstring and gluteal muscles of the lifted leg to evaluate the "firing pattern" of muscles. Normally, the gluteal muscles will fire (or activate) first, followed by the hamstrings. If the pattern is reversed, I'll know that the gluteal muscles are weaker than they should be.

MORE BANG FOR YOUR BUTT

I advise clients to spend the majority of their waking hours standing, if possible. Since this isn't always practical, at least make an effort to increase your amount of upright time—staying on your feet when watching TV, for example, or standing (and pacing) when talking on the telephone. Six other movements that help—do each one twice a week (except for the hip flexor stretch, which should be done daily)...*

• **Glute Bridge.** It is among the best exercises for targeting the glutes. It gives the abdominal core muscles a bit of a workout, too.

What to do: Lie on your back with your knees bent and your feet flat on the floor. Contract your abdominal muscles slightly. Next, raise your hips up about six inches and hold for a few seconds...then slowly lower yourself back down. Repeat this movement 10 to 12 times.

• **Lunges.** They strengthen the gluteal muscles, along with muscles in the hips and thighs.

What to do: Stand with your feet together and your hands on your hips. Take a step forward with your left leg, while simultaneously bending that leg until the thigh is parallel to the floor. Keep your front foot flat on the floor as you bend your knee (most of the weight should

*Consult your doctor before beginning this regimen—or any other new exercise program, especially if you've had knee, hip or back surgery.

Meditation Beats Morphine

New research: Mindfulness meditation, a technique that focuses on awareness and acceptance of daily thoughts and feelings, activates areas of the brain that reduce pain intensity.

Details: Adults who meditated for 20 minutes a day for four days before being touched with a hot probe reported feeling up to 44% less pain than those who did not meditate—which was twice the benefit provided by opioid drugs such as morphine.

Fadel Zeidan, PhD, assistant professor of neurobiology and anatomy, Wake Forest School of Medicine, Winston-Salem, North Carolina.

go onto your heel), and don't let the front knee extend farther forward than the toes. Return to the starting position, then repeat with the other leg. Work up to 12 to 15 reps on each leg.

Note: If a deep knee bend is painful, don't go down as far.

•**Wall squats.** Squats are popular because they increase both gluteal and thigh strength. This exercise is easier than traditional squats because it requires only body weight and a wall for support.

What to do: Lean back against a wall with your feet shoulder-width apart and out a foot or two. Keep your back and hips against the wall.

Slide down until your thighs are parallel to the floor. Hold the position until your thighs start to say "enough," then rise back up. In the beginning, your thighs might start shaking after just a few seconds. Over time, try to work up to holding the position for 30 to 60 seconds.

If you're out of shape or have weak knees, you can lower yourself about halfway to the parallel position. Don't let your knees collapse inward, and stop if you feel any pain. Work your way toward the full bend as you build strength.

•**Side planks.** For those with dormant butt syndrome, it's important to stretch/strengthen surrounding muscles as well as the glutes themselves. This exercise activates muscles in the midsection, including the hips.

What to do: Lie on your right side, with your legs extended and "stacked" on top of each other. Prop up your upper body by supporting your weight on your forearm, keeping your shoulder aligned with your elbow. Contract the ab muscles and lift your hips and knees off the floor. Hold the position for 10 to 30 seconds, then lower back down. Repeat on the other side. Start with two to three sets, holding the position for 10 seconds, and gradually work up to one minute per set.

•**Single leg balance.** Most people lose some strength, balance and rotational motion (the ability of their joints to rotate) as they get older. This exercise is a good way to improve hip and core stability while challenging balance.

What to do: Stand on one leg, with your arms held slightly away from your body for balance.

Important: For safety, stand next to a counter to catch yourself if you start to topple over. Try to hold the position (without swaying) for 30 to 60 seconds. Then try it on the other leg. It's challenging at first! Once it gets too easy, lift the leg a bit higher and/or try to do it with your eyes closed. This is harder because vision helps the body orient itself.

•**Hip flexor stretch.** Tight hip flexors cause dormant butt syndrome. When these muscles are tight, there's compensatory movement throughout the lower back, which can lead to pain as well as disk damage in the lower back.

What to do: Kneel on your left knee, with your left hand on your hip and your right foot flat on the floor in front of you—the right knee should be bent and the right thigh should be roughly parallel to the floor. Move your left hip forward until it extends beyond the left knee. Don't bend forward during the movement. Hold the position for 20 to 30 seconds, then repeat for three or four reps. Change position and repeat on the other side.

Sprain-Proof Your Ankles

Luke T. Donovan, PhD, ATC, an assistant professor in the department of kinesiology at The University of North Carolina at Charlotte, and past program director of the Post-Professional Athletic Training Program at The University of Toledo. His research interests include chronic ankle instability.

If you haven't sprained an ankle yet, it may be just a matter of time. About 25,000 Americans suffer from these painful injuries every day—that's a total of nine million such injuries each year.

But an ankle sprain is not that serious, right? We've all seen athletes limping off the field, only to return to the game soon after. You've probably done the same thing yourself. You take a wrong step...your foot turns...you hobble for a while...and you forget about it.

What you may not realize: An ankle sprain can cause a lifetime of problems, including persistent ankle weakness, difficulty walking and even arthritis of the ankle. *What you need to know to protect yourself...*

LINGERING DAMAGE

An ankle sprain occurs when a ligament (the band of tissue that connects bone to bone) stretches beyond its normal limits. The more a ligament stretches—or even tears—the more severe the sprain.

Most people who sprain an ankle never see a doctor. They assume that a little rest—along with an over-the-counter pain reliever and perhaps some ice packs—will take care of things. It's true that the immediate symptoms usually clear up quickly...within a matter of days or weeks. But what happens after that?

Studies have shown that more than 30% of people who sprain an ankle go on to develop chronic ankle instability. The joint feels as though it might "give" at any time. As a result, their health may suffer—they tend to exercise less...gain weight...and have more limitations in their daily movements. People who have sprained an ankle are also twice as likely to reinjure it.

To be clear, an ankle sprain does not cause high blood pressure or diabetes, for example, but it often does interfere with the types of activities that help prevent these and other serious chronic conditions. Ankle sprains have also been linked to a 13% to 16% increased risk for arthritic ankles.

SPRAIN-PROOF YOUR ANKLES

The ankles are uniquely prone to injuries due to the mobility and wide range of motion of the ankle joint...and the fact that the ankles support the weight of your entire body.

For these reasons, it's wise for all adults—and especially those who have suffered previous ankle injuries (even if they were years ago)—to do a simple daily regimen of stretching, strengthening and balancing exercises.

Try to do all of the exercises below a few times a day—together, they take only about 10 minutes...

- **Stand on one foot.** This balancing exercise helps prevent ankle sprains by improving ankle muscle reflexes and proprioception, the body's ability to orient itself in space. I tell people to do the exercise when they're standing in line...talking on the phone...or even brushing their teeth.

What to do: Simply stand on one foot near a chair or any other stationary object that you can grab on to if you lose your balance. Stand on one foot for about 30 seconds, then switch sides. Work up to a minute or two on each side.

When it starts to feel easy: Close your eyes while you balance. Taking away the visual feedback forces the muscles and nerves to work harder.

- **Soft-surface stands.** To further improve ankle muscle function and your sense of balance, do one-legged stands (as described above) on a pillow, a foam pad or a balance disc (they're also called balance trainer balls and are available at sporting-goods stores and online).

The unstable surface forces your body to adapt to changes in balance and weight distribution. It makes your muscles more reactive, which can help you adjust to sudden changes in walking surfaces, posture, foot movements, etc.

- **Calf stretches.** The calf muscles connect to the Achilles tendon in the ankle. Stretching and strengthening the calves improves stability and range of motion.

What to do: While facing a wall, stand back about one foot with your palms on the wall for support. Take one step back with your right foot and slightly bend your left leg. You'll feel the stretch in your right calf/ankle. Hold the position for about 10 seconds, then repeat on the other side. Perform the stretch three times on each side and work up to holding it for 30 seconds.

•**Ankle/calf raises.** As mentioned above, stronger calves and Achilles tendons improve ankle stability. This exercise strengthens both.

What to do: While still facing a wall, with your palms on the wall for support, rise up on your toes as far as you can. Hold the stretch for a few seconds, then lower your heels to the floor. Repeat eight to 10 times. It's harder than it sounds! As your muscles get stronger, you can increase the difficulty by taking one foot off the floor when rising/lowering with the other foot.

•**Resistance exercises.** With an elastic resistance band, you can strengthen the ankle by moving it in its complete range of motion.

What to do: While sitting in a chair, wrap an elastic resistance band under the ball of your foot. While holding the band tightly, move the foot/ankle up, down, left and right. Repeat a few times in each direction. Then perform on the other foot.

WHEN TO GET HELP

What if you think that you've actually sprained an ankle? First, see a doctor. You'll need an X-ray to determine whether you have a bone fracture, which typically requires the foot/ankle to be immobilized by a hard cast or boot.

If you have a sprain, don't try to simply "walk it off." The best thing you can do is keep weight off the ankle as much as possible until the pain and swelling are completely gone. An elastic bandage (such as ACE) can help minimize swelling.

During this time, you may also want to immobilize the joint with a brace (such as AirCast) for four to six weeks. Such braces are available online and at most drugstores for about $20 and up.

Also helpful: To reduce pain and swelling, apply a cold pack (or ice wrapped in a towel) to the ankle for 20 minutes, once every hour for up to eight hours a day. Continue with this frequency for at least the first day after the sprain. After that, let pain be your guide—apply cold as long as the pain is severe and cut back as it eases.

To help prevent long-term problems: I advise getting some form of rehabilitation—from a physical therapist or an athletic trainer—after the injury heals.

Ankle Sprain Self-Treatment Works as Well as Supervised Physical Therapy

Study of 503 patients, ages 16 to 79, led by researchers at Queen's University, Kingston, Ontario, Canada, published in *BMJ Open*.

Patients who kept the ankle elevated and applied compression and ice, then gradually increased movement after a sprain did just as well in measurements of quality of life, pain, symptoms and function as patients who received up to seven sessions of physical therapy—including isometric resistance exercises, strength training and stretching. There was no difference between patients in the two groups at one, three or six months after the injury.

The Latest Knee Surgery Is Unproven

Mark D. Miller, MD, professor of orthopaedic surgery and division head for sports medicine at University of Virginia, Charlottesville. He also is a practicing orthopaedic surgeon. UVAHealth.com

If you tear the anterior cruciate ligament (ACL) in one of your knees—a common occurrence—an orthopedic surgeon might recommend repairing it and having your anterolateral ligament repaired as well. A 2013 article in *Journal of Anatomy* speculated that this little-known ligament might play an important role in providing rotational stability to the

Gout Updates

DASH away from gout. The DASH diet (Dietary Approaches to Stop Hypertension)—developed to lower blood pressure—can reduce uric acid levels enough to prevent gout flare-ups. The diet is rich in whole grains, fruits, vegetables and low-fat dairy...and low in salt, red meat, sweets and saturated fats. It sometimes can work as well as antigout medication.

For more information, go to DASHDiet.org.

Stephen P. Juraschek, MD, PhD, research and clinical fellow, The Johns Hopkins University School of Medicine, Baltimore.

New drug for gout. Zurampic (*Lesinurad*), a uric acid reabsorption inhibitor, was recently was approved by the FDA for use in combination with a xanthine oxidase inhibitor, such as *allopurinol* or *febuxostat*, for patients whose serum urate level cannot be controlled with the xanthine oxidase inhibitor alone. After four weeks of treatment, the mean reduction in serum urate with combination therapy in patients receiving 200 mg, 400 mg or 600 mg was 16%, 22% and 30%, respectively. However, Zurampic was approved at a dose of only 200 mg/day—an FDA advisory panel expressed concern about possible side effects at higher doses. Ask your doctor for details.

Study of 208 patients led by researchers at Hospital Universitario Cruces, Barakaldo, Spain, published in *Annals of the Rheumatic Diseases*.

knee, and media reports trumpeting the "discovery" of this new ligament soon followed. In truth, nothing new had been discovered—the anterolateral ligament has been described in medical literature since at least the 19th century. Now some surgeons have begun reconstructing damaged anterolateral ligaments when torn ACLs are reconstructed.

Trouble is, there currently is no evidence that the anterolateral ligament is important or that repairing it is beneficial. This procedure even might turn out to be damaging to the knee—drilling tunnels in leg bones to reattach this repaired ligament could potentially weaken nearby structures.

What to do: If an orthopedic surgeon recommends repairing your anterolateral ligament as part of an ACL reconstruction, seek a second opinion. Research is ongoing, and there is a chance that repairing the anterolateral ligament will be shown to be useful—particularly in people who have had ACL reconstructions fail in the past...or who have extreme amounts of knee instability—but that has not yet been established.

What's more, having your anterolateral ligament reconstructed could turn out to be a mistake even if this ligament is one day shown to be important. That's because whether it is worth performing this procedure is not the only area of contention—there also is not yet any consensus about how to perform it. If you have your anterolateral ligament repaired today, there's a chance the repair will be done in a way that later turns out to be badly flawed.

Compression Braces and Sleeves for Knee Arthritis

Barbara Bergin, MD, orthopedic surgeon, Texas Orthopedics, Sports & Rehabilitation Associates, Austin. She is currently writing a book based on the idea that women should "Sit like a man." DrBarbaraBergin.com

For knee arthritis any kind of sleeve or brace will have a proprioceptive effect, which refers to your brain's ability to sense where your bones, joints and muscles are—even without looking—and take steps to control their function and position.

In other words, the presence of something around the knee—even a piece of duct tape or Kinesio Tape, a type of therapeutic elastic adhesive tape that can be worn for extended periods of time—can actually send more sensory information to the brain, making it more aware of the extremity. Then the brain can send subconscious, corrective impulses down to that extremity—in essence, increasing awareness of the affected part so that your body unconsciously adjusts muscles and joints to accommodate them as you move about.

For example, look at your pinky toe. You might think it is just sitting there limp, resting inside your shoe. But it's not. Your brain is subconsciously putting it there. It's not sticking it up in the air. It's not shoving it down into the sole of your shoe. Now, tell your brain to stick the pinky up in the air. That's not proprioception. That's your conscious brain directing your toe to go there. But let's say you have a blister on your pinky. Now you're not going to walk around all day saying, "Brain! Bend my toe down away from my shoe." Instead, proprioception will eventually take over. The leather on your shoe will act as a messenger to your brain, much as a brace might for your knee, and your wonderful brain will guide that toe away from the abrasive leather.

Proprioception is one reason why a lot of folks with arthritis like the feel of having a sleeve or brace on their knee or anywhere on the body for that matter, such as an ankle sleeve. It's why athletes like to use compression braces and sleeves, tight clothing and Kinesio Tape.

Wearing a compression brace will not directly prevent your knee from twisting in a way that might injure it. But it may help your brain's awareness of your body in space so that you might avoid moves that could cause further injury and pain.

While compression garments and wraps have no potential to cure disorders of bones and joints for those suffering with arthritis or patients with injuries, they just seem to feel better. That's a good enough reason, if you want to try one of these garments or Kinesio Tape—or even an Ace bandage. See if it helps. And yes, you could even try duct tape, a kind of primitive version of Kinesio Tape. It might work quite nicely—although it's going to hurt like hell and give you a waxing when you take it off!

Notes on Knee Pain

Tai chi beats PT for knee pain. Tai chi (a traditional Chinese mind-body practice that combines deep breathing with slow, fluid movement) reduced pain and stiffness as well as physical therapy in adults with knee osteoarthritis who did either regimen twice a week for three months.

Bonus: Those who did tai chi reported significantly greater improvements in depression and overall well-being. To find a class near you, go to AmericanTaiChi.org.

Chenchen Wang, MD, director, Center for Complementary and Integrative Medicine, Tufts Medical Center, Boston.

Vitamin D does not help arthritic knees. The use of vitamin D for this purpose has been controversial.

Recent finding: It does not ease pain or slow the progression of knee osteoarthritis—even in people who are deficient in the vitamin. There currently is no treatment available to stop the loss of cartilage that eventually leads patients to need knee replacements. Symptoms are treated with painkillers, cortisone injections and anti-inflammatory drugs, but these do not slow the disease's progress.

Study of 413 patients with knee osteoarthritis by researchers at University of Tasmania, Hobart, Australia, published in *JAMA*.

You can shower sooner. Knee-replacement patients can shower as soon as two days after surgery if their doctors agree. The usual recommendation is to wait 10 days to two weeks after surgery before showering. But researchers found no difference in bacterial cultures of skin next to incisions in patients who waited and those who were allowed to shower 48 hours after surgery.

Study by researchers at Loyola University Chicago Stritch School of Medicine, published in *Journal of Arthroplasty*.

Arthritis Drug Is Safe Despite Similarity to Vioxx

Steven E. Nissen, MD, MACC, chairman of the department of cardiovascular medicine at the Cleveland Clinic, Ohio, and leader of a study published in *The New England Journal of Medicine.*

Celecoxib (brand name Celebrex) is a COX-2 inhibitor, the same type of drug as Vioxx, which was taken off the market in 2004 when long-term use was found to increase risk of a heart attack. In fact, it is at least as effective as the nonsteroidal anti-inflammatory drugs (NSAIDs) *ibuprofen* and *naproxen* and causes fewer gastrointestinal side effects and kidney-related complications.

To Ease Knee Arthritis Pain, This Depression-Era Treatment Is Newly Popular

Health Insider research.

When it comes to treating the pain of knee arthritis, something old is new again. Prolotherapy, a procedure first developed in the 1930s, is becoming an increasingly prescribed treatment in modern sports rehab clinics and primary care doctors' offices. It involves injections of an innocuous substance such as dextrose, a form of sugar, into the knees.

Why the new popularity? Possibly for the simplest of reasons—the treatment works. We reported in 2013 that it reduces pain and stiffness and improves function, but newer studies have additionally found…

- **It works for people at any weight range**—normal, overweight, obese and morbidly obese.
- **It's effective for people with diabetes,** who hadn't been included in studies before.
- **It may benefit people with severe,** advanced knee arthritis, not just those with mild-to-moderate cases.
- **The benefits last at least two and a half years.**
- **Different kinds of injections work, not just dextrose.** Some researchers recommend a combination for best effect.

Exactly how prolotherapy works isn't understood, but the current hypothesis is that it stimulates short-term inflammation, which promotes a healing response, and recent research suggests that it may help build cartilage—actually modifying the progression of the disease, not just providing symptomatic relief.

Patients usually undergo three to five treatments, sometimes more—side effects are modest, but the procedure itself can be painful. It's not a cure-all, to be sure, but if you have bothersome knee pain from arthritis, it's worth discussing with your doctor.

Total Knee Replacement May Lead to Broken Bones

Sabrina Strickland, MD, a specialist in knee and shoulder surgery at Hospital for Special Surgery and associate professor of orthopedic surgery at Weill Cornell Medical College, both in New York City.

According to a Swedish study, people who have new knees are 19% more likely than others to experience spinal fractures and 4% more likely to break a hip.

Possible reason: Patients become active before they are fully rehabilitated—which increases the risk of falling and breaking a bone.

Self-defense: Ask your physician for balance exercises.

After a Bone Fracture, Check Your Meds

Study titled "Patterns of Prescription Drug Use Before and After Fragility Fracture" by Jeffrey C. Munson, MD, Geisel School of Medicine, Dartmouth College, Lebanon, New Hampshire, and colleagues, published in *JAMA Internal Medicine.*

A broken bone can have devastating consequences for an older person. It can lead to functional decline and loss of independence—even increased risk for death. One of the biggest post-fracture health risks is getting another fracture. But few patients get the right care after a fracture to help them prevent future fractures, a recent study finds—and lots of people keep taking meds that increase fracture risk!

THE DRUG CONNECTION

It's not a secret that many drugs for conditions such as diabetes, depression, high blood pressure, insomnia and even GERD can contribute to increased fracture risk. But breaking a bone should be a loud wake-up call for doctors to reevaluate the meds a patient is taking.

Unfortunately, that isn't happening. A recent study from the Geisel School of Medicine at Dartmouth College looked at 168,000 Medicare recipients who had had bone fractures and found that four months after their fractures, more than 80% of them were still taking at least one medication known to increase risk for fracture. Even more alarming—more patients increased use of fracture-promoting drugs than decreased such use after their breaks!

The list of drugs most associated with fracture risk in the study included...

•**Oral steroids**

•**Proton pump inhibitors** (for peptic ulcers, GERD)

•**Thiazolidinediones** (a class of diabetes drug)

•**Diuretics** (for high blood pressure)

•**Hypnotics** (for insomnia)

•**Selective serotonin reuptake inhibitors** (antidepressants)

•**Antipsychotics**

Some of these drugs increase fracture risk because they increase the risk of falling—for example, hypnotics, antidepressants and even diuretics can make people dizzy. Others, such as proton pump inhibitors, decrease bone density—weakening bones.

Bottom line: If you have had a fracture, be sure to discuss with your doctor whether any of the medications you are taking might either weaken your bones or make falls more likely. You may be able to take a different class of medication to accomplish the same purpose. You may also want to discuss whether you should take medications for osteoporosis, suggest the study authors.

You can also take steps—literally—to strengthen your bones and help keep you steady on your feet. Weight-bearing exercises, such as walking and lifting weights, can help strengthen your bones, while yoga and tai chi help improve balance—and prevent falls.

Ultrasound Does Not Help Fractures Heal

Study of 501 patients led by researchers at McMaster University, Hamilton, Ontario, Canada, published in *BMJ.*

Ultrasound often is used to speed the healing of broken bones. But patients given the popular ultrasound treatment after standard care to repair leg fractures did not heal faster or start bearing weight on their injured legs any faster than people who were treated with a placebo device.

Editor's note: While there is some scientific evidence that certain fractures can show faster healing with the use of ultrasound, there really is no evidence to support its use for routine fracture healing.

Why You Should Roll on a Ball on the Floor

Jill Miller, fitness therapy expert based in Los Angeles, author of *The Roll Model* and creator of the exercise program *Yoga Tune Up.*

Those bright, squishy balls little kids love to play with are for grown-ups, too! In fact, there's a way to "play" with these soft, tactile toys that can help you calm down... stand straighter...and breathe better.

It's inexpensive and easy to do, and it really works. You just have to get down on the floor, lie down with your ball under your abs...and roll around.

Here's how...

A NEW KIND OF ROLL PLAY

Fitness-therapy expert Jill Miller, creator of Yoga Tune Up, author of *The Roll Model* and regular contributor to *Bottom Line,* is so convinced that this exercise is effective that she's created an exercise program called Coregeous—rhymes with "gorgeous." The program uses soft balls to relieve stress and tension, improve posture and breathing, and even to break up deep internal abdominal scars from surgery.

Here's the theory behind it: By lying on a soft ball pushed up against your abdomen, you stimulate the vagus nerve, which is deep inside and runs from your brain stem through your heart and lungs. In medical studies, stimulating the vagus nerve (through an electrical implant) has been shown to help relieve mood disorders such as depression and even help control epileptic seizures.

There's no research—and no such claims—for ball-rolling moves, but Miller has found that they can relieve stress. When you're anxious, she explains, and trying to breathe from deep in your belly—a good way to calm yourself—tense, tight abdominal muscles get in the way. They make it hard to inhale and exhale deeply and fully. But "when you lie face down on the floor with a ball positioned strategically under your abdominals, the pressure will make you aware of tension there that inhibits the full range of motion in your breathing muscles," she explains.

The muscle-and-tension-releasing effects of rolling on a ball also can improve posture. "The pressure of a ball under your belly puts you in touch with any unconscious tension you might be holding in your core," she says. Release that tension, and it's easier to reverse poor posture.

Belly rolling can also create an abdominal massage that mobilizes the fascia, the connective tissues of the body, letting them move the way that they should. Tightness in these tissues can lead to aches and pains in almost everyone, says Miller.

She's also found that these moves can help break up adhesions—including deep, abdominal scar tissue from surgery, such as a C-section, gall bladder surgery or appendectomy. Since such internal scarring "creates compensation within muscles of the core that impact breathing, posture and stress," says Miller, "when you work on your scars, the muscles in your core are freer to get stronger—which in turn improves posture and breathing."

Ready to roll? Here are Miller's beginner tips—plus two moves to start you off.

GET ON THE (RIGHT) BALL

Miller's Coregeous ball (available on her website) is specially designed for the exercises she has developed, but you also can use any very soft and squishy ball, such as a kids' Gertie (which costs about $8 at toy stores and online). "You even can use a small pillow or a rolled-up towel," Miller says. *Her tips...*

Caution: Check with your doctor before doing these moves, especially if you've recently had surgery. It's best to wait until you're cleared for exercise.

- **Take a load off.** If rolling on a hard floor is too uncomfortable, try rolling on a bed or even against a wall. Both will reduce the pressure of your body weight on your stomach.

- **Go slow.** "At first, just the pressure of lying on a ball may be enough to unbind postural and emotional stress," says Miller. "Pay attention to your emotional reactions. Some people who have very negative feelings about their abs or feel ashamed of their bodies can feel vulnerable and even find the position unpleasant in the beginning."

•**Don't bounce back up too quickly.** When you finish with your rolling routine, stay on the floor for a few moments before standing, advises Miller. Jumping upright too quickly can make you dizzy.

Now here are the moves…

BREATH RESET

This helps you ease into the sensation of pressure on your abdominals, brings awareness of your diaphragm and breathing, and provides a gentle belly massage that will soothe your nervous system and help you relax.

•**Place the ball on the floor.** Lie face down on top of it, positioning it in the center of your abdomen. Extend your legs behind you with toes pointed. Bend your arms at the elbow, and let them rest on the floor on either side of your head.

•**Inhale…hold your breath…and then tighten your abs.** Hold for three to five seconds, and then exhale. Repeat five to eight times.

•**Keeping your weight on the ball,** slowly shift your weight from side to side while breathing deeply. Do this for two minutes.

PIN, SPIN, MOBILIZE

This exercise brings more movement to the fascia, which are tight and restricted in their movement in just about everyone. It's also a great exercise if you need to release scar tissue deep in the belly that can restrict breathing and throw off posture.

It will be most effective if you place the ball against your bare skin, so that your skin can grip the ball more tightly and provide traction. Do this only every other day in order to give your tissue time to remodel itself.

•**Position the ball under your abdominals in an area that feels especially tight and restricted.**

•**Use your hands and feet to slowly pivot your entire body in one direction until you feel a pinch.** Stop there, and breathe steadily for 30 to 90 seconds until the pinching feeling dissipates.

•**Then pivot a bit more in the same direction,** just until you feel pinching again. Stop and breathe until the sensation goes away.

•**Repeat the incremental pivoting for as long as the pinching is tolerable.**

Note: You might have heard that the vagus nerve is involved in fainting—the kind that's triggered by things like the sight of blood, for example. Not to worry—this kind of mild exercise is very different from the body's reactions that can cause fainting.

Learn more about how the kind of abdominal massage provided by rolling on a ball might help manage autoimmune conditions, such as asthma, by reading a guest blog by yoga instructor Meredith Hutten Chamorro on the Yoga Tuneup site.

Meanwhile, if you want to keep your body and mind relaxed, be like old man river and just keep rollin'!

Michael Phelps's Sore Muscle Secret: All About Cupping

Jeffrey Zimmerman, OMD, LAc, a doctor of oriental medicine, acupuncturist, martial artist and qigong master who practices in Westport, Connecticut.

The Rio Olympics shined a light on the ancient Chinese medical practice called cupping, with athletes including the best swimmer in history, Michael Phelps, showing up for events with telltale round reddish spots on his arms. What is this practice? Does it hurt? Does it work? Should you try it on yourself?

To explore these questions, we spoke with one of the pioneers of traditional Chinese medicine in the US—Jeffrey Zimmerman, a doctor of oriental medicine, licensed acupuncturist, martial artist and qigong master, who practices in Westport, Connecticut.

Here are his answers to our questions…

What is this cupping that the Olympic athletes are using?

Dr. Zimmerman: It's one of the tools in traditional Chinese medicine.

American and other Olympic athletes saw Chinese swimmers use this in the Beijing Olympics in 2008—and now they're doing it. A special small glass cup is used. Typically, a cotton swab is set on fire inside the cup and then allowed to go out, at which point the cup is quickly placed over the skin. As the heat dissipates, it creates a vacuum, pulling the skin up away from the muscle and lifting the fascia, a web of tissue that supports the muscle. These days, some cups come with a vacuum pump instead, so no fire or heat is used.

What does cupping do?

Dr. Zimmerman: In purely Western terms, it gently pulls up on the muscles, bringing blood flow to an area that may tend to be sore or inflamed—such as certain parts of a swimmer's shoulders and arms. In traditional Chinese medicine terms, it promotes the free flow of chi (vital energy) in the blood in those areas.

What are those big red marks that cupping leaves? Do they hurt?

Dr. Zimmerman: They are caused by the tiny capillaries bursting under the skin. The procedure does not hurt before or afterward, and the red marks go away in a few days.

What are the supposed benefits?

Dr. Zimmerman: By releasing blood flow, cupping reduces swelling, reduces pain and accelerates healing. It's good for swelling and pain caused by intense exercise as well as for sprains. In Chinese medicine terms, these are conditions in which the blood has become stagnant.

Is there evidence that it works?

Dr. Zimmerman: There haven't been many large studies—I hope we can do more research on efficacy. What we have instead is what I call experience-based medicine. A form of cupping has been used not only in China but also in ancient Egypt, and, a fellow acupuncturist told me, in Ireland. It's been used by martial artists for centuries. I don't think Michael Phelps would go around looking like he was attacked by an octopus unless he were getting benefits. While not every traditional medical practice is trustworthy, this is an external technique that can be judged by its efficacy immediately—by reduced swelling, for example.

Could the benefits be merely psychological?

Dr. Zimmerman: I doubt it. You see that it reduces swelling immediately, and it reduces pain quite quickly. If there is any psychological or placebo effect, I think that would just be an additional benefit.

How does dry cupping differ from "wet" cupping?

Dr. Zimmerman: What the Olympic athletes appear to be doing is what is called "dry" cupping, in which the cup is stationary so it is just placed on an area and left there until it is removed. In "wet" cupping, a thin layer of oil, often an essential oil, is placed on the body so that a practitioner can apply the cup, then move it around easily to different spots—without losing the vacuum. For example, if you have back pain, your acupuncturist might place cups on both sides of the spine and move them up and down. As you are sliding them up and down, you can look at the effects. An experienced practitioner will be able to see spots where the skin takes a longer time to become pink, and that's likely where the pain is coming from. Wet cupping takes more time and focus on the part of the practitioner, causing him/her to be more mindful of the process. It's an art. If one particular area needs cupping, then dry cupping is appropriate, but if the blood and qi need to be moved over an area, then wet cupping is the preferred method. The knowledge and skill of the practitioner is the most important part of the treatment.

Don't acupuncturists sometimes draw blood when they cup?

Dr. Zimmerman: Cupping can also be applied to an acupuncture point. I've seen this practiced in China. A patient had a bad case of shingles, which is caused by the herpes Zoster virus, all over his torso. A special needle was used to make a cut on the back of the knee—bladder 40 is the name of the spot—and then it was cupped to draw blood out. The next day, the patient was much improved. But this practice is not generally done in the US, and I don't practice it.

Can cupping be useful for serious medical conditions?

Dr. Zimmerman: Yes, it has been studied for conditions ranging from herpes infection to acne to Bells' palsy to asthma to knee pain, with good results. But if you have a serious medical condition, you need to have Western medicine as well. You need to be examined by all the great technology we have in Western medicine. Then you can also go to someone who is well-educated in traditional Chinese medicine who may use cupping along with other tools, including acupuncture, moxibustion, herbal medicine and nutrition. You don't just go to someone who says, "I'll cup that."

What kind of health practitioner should one go to for cupping?

Dr. Zimmerman: I would start with a licensed acupuncturist. Ask if he/she is experienced with cupping.

Should you avoid cupping if you have certain medical conditions?

Dr. Zimmerman: If you are taking blood-thinning medication, this may be counter-indicated. Go to your doctor first and ask. That's good advice if you are being treated for any condition—ask first if it's safe. It's also important to have a conversation with the health-care practitioner so that you understand why he/she feels that cupping is good for you and your body.

Can people cup themselves or just ask a friend to do it on them?

Dr. Zimmerman: I've heard that there are kits that you can buy online. While it's not particularly dangerous, I'm concerned about people who aren't trained doing this. How would you know if you're making it too tight against the skin? What if you leave it on too long? What if you fall asleep while the cup is on? You don't know what kind of suction you're creating—until you have a big bruise. I'm not aware of any permanent damage that it might cause, but it would take a much longer time for the bruise to heal. When you are being treated by a knowledgeable practitioner, his skill is there with you during the cupping.

Can a health practitioner who isn't well-trained in traditional Chinese medicine do cupping safely?

Dr. Zimmerman: I can imagine chiropractors and physical therapists adapting cupping as a tool. I don't have an objection to that for the treatment of sore muscles and certain injuries. But you want to find someone who has sincerely sought out training on cupping—not someone who took one weekend course. In every profession, there are good and bad practitioners.

Now that so many Americans are learning about cupping from the Olympics, what do you hope they take away about it?

Dr. Zimmerman: I hope people learn to take some of these ancient medical practices more seriously. I would hope that there is more research. For example, after many years, acupuncture has become accepted into mainstream Western medicine for both research and therapy. Traditional Chinese medicine has many tools, including Chinese medical massage, gua sha therapy (in which the skin is scraped to create mild bruising), that have benefits similar to those of cupping. We need to use the technology of Western science to show how these ancient techniques work. I hope that people say to themselves, *If Michael Phelps is using this, maybe I should take a closer look.*

Foot-tastic!

Johanna Youner, DPM, podiatrist and podiatric surgeon. She is founder of Healthy Feet NY, a private practice in New York City. She also is a certified laser specialist for tattoo removal and a member of The American Society for Laser Medicine and Surgery. Healthy FeetNY.net and ParkAvenueLaserTreatment.com

Most of us—75% of Americans—will have foot problems at least sometime in our lives. Think about the stresses that your feet endure. They're subjected to significant impact pressure just from walking—and a lot more from running. They're squeezed into tight shoes and stuffed into hot socks.

But you can treat many foot problems at home—without potent drugs or high-priced medical care.

Natural remedies that work…

ARNICA FOR INJURIES

This homeopathic remedy has become the go-to treatment for athletes—including members of the US Men's National Soccer Team—who need to reduce post-injury swelling, inflammation and bruises.

Arnica pellets (taken internally), ointments, creams and gels contain thymol derivatives, compounds that reduce inflammation. A study published in a rheumatology journal found that homeopathic arnica relieved pain as well as *ibuprofen*—without the side effects that often occur with traditional over-the-counter painkillers.

How to use it: Quickly apply arnica gel, ointment or cream (or put five sublingual arnica pellets under your tongue) after you've banged or twisted your foot or ankle. It works best when it's applied or taken within 10 minutes after an injury. Repeat the treatment three times a day until the pain is gone.

For homeopathic products, I recommend Boiron, a leading manufacturer of these remedies. They're available at pharmacies and supermarkets.

CASTOR OIL FOR ARTHRITIC AND CHRONIC PAIN

Many doctors advise their patients to apply moist heat for arthritic conditions and other chronic pain. Heat dilates blood vessels, stimulates blood flow and increases the supply of oxygen and nutrients…and it accelerates the removal of fluids that cause swelling.

Castor oil is even better because it's an anti-inflammatory and an antioxidant that is readily absorbed by the skin. It contains the unsaturated omega-3 fatty acid ricinoleic acid, which quickly reduces inflammation and pain. Buy hexane-free castor oil (it will say so on the label). Hexane is a petrochemical that may be hazardous.

How to use it: For foot or ankle pain, soak a piece of flannel (flannels are sold online for this purpose) in castor oil…wrap it around the foot…then wrap a warm towel around that…and leave it in place for about one hour. It will reduce the inflammation and swelling. (You also can use a heating pad or hot-water bottle to heat the towel.)

Caution: Castor oil stains! Take a shower after you remove the wrapping…and keep the oil away from your good towels. You can store the flannel in the refrigerator in a plastic bag or container for about one month.

EPSOM SALT FOR CELLULITIS

Cellulitis is a common skin infection that often affects the feet, particularly in patients with athlete's foot, fluid retention in the legs (from poor circulation) and/or diabetes. You might notice redness, swelling or warmth in the early stages.

Epsom salt is an osmotic agent. It pulls material (fluids, pus and even splinters) toward the surface of the skin. When your foot is swollen, an Epsom salt soak will reduce swelling right away—it's almost magical. I use it for many non-emergency foot conditions, including cellulitis, painful warts and infected nails.

How to use it: For a foot bath, add one-half cup of Epsom salt to a basin of warm water.

TEA TREE OIL FOR INFECTIONS AND FUNGUS

Tea tree oil is extracted from the leaves of an Australian tea tree. It has been used for centuries to treat skin infections. Research has shown that it is an effective treatment for athlete's foot as well as nail fungus (onychomycosis).

How to use it: Apply the oil twice a day to new skin infections or toenail infections (don't apply to broken skin). Fungal infections that have gone on for a month or more probably will require a medicated over-the-counter cream such as Tinactin or Lotrimin.

COCONUT OIL TO MOISTURIZE

Feet don't have oil glands. Without this natural lubrication, the skin is naturally dry. Too much dryness can cause itching, peeling or even deep cracks that can be painful and sometimes get infected.

Coconut oil is an excellent moisturizer for the feet—one that also has antibacterial and antifungal properties. It is solid at room temperature and is available in jars at supermarkets and pharmacies.

How to use it: Apply it to your feet several times a day. Because it's readily absorbed, it won't look (or feel) greasy.

MUSTARD, PICKLE JUICE OR VINEGAR FOR FOOT CRAMPS

It sounds like an old wives' tale, but each of these traditional remedies really can help when you have foot or ankle cramps. In a study published on the website of the American College of Sports Medicine, researchers used electricity to induce toe cramps in young athletes who had just completed a workout. The athletes then drank 2.5 ounces of pickle juice or water—or nothing at all. The pickle juice stopped the cramps about 37% faster than water and 45% faster than drinking nothing.

Researchers speculate that a substance in pickle juice—possibly the vinegar—somehow short-circuits muscle-cramp reflexes. Apple cider vinegar has a similar effect, as does prepared yellow mustard (which contains vinegar).

How to use them: Keep any (or all) of them on hand if your feet are prone to cramps. When you feel a cramp coming on, add pickle juice, vinegar and/or mustard to your food.

Important: For most people, dehydration is the main cause of muscle cramps. You must hydrate after exercise. In addition to the vinegar or pickle juice, drink a few glasses of water, juice or a sports beverage.

DRUG-FREE CURES FOR PLANTAR FASCIITIS

Plantar fasciitis affects about 10% of the US population and is one of the most common causes of heel pain. A thick band of tissue (the plantar fascia) runs across the bottom of the foot. It connects the heel bone to the toes and creates the arch. Small tears in the tissue can cause burning/stabbing pain, particularly in the morning.

- **Apply ice.** Hold an ice pack over the painful area for 15 to 20 minutes, three or four times a day.
- **Replace your shoe insoles.** The Powerstep brand of insoles supports and cushions the plantar fascia and helps it heal more quickly. You can buy insoles at pharmacies, sporting-goods stores and online for $15 to $60. In many cases, they work as well as prescription products (which can cost as much as $550).
- **Use a tennis ball or rolling pin** to gently roll along the bottom of your foot (while sitting).
- **Replace worn-out athletic shoes.** They stop cushioning your feet after about 500 miles of use.

A Foot Problem That Gets Misdiagnosed

Mitchell Yass, DPT, a specialist in diagnosing and resolving the cause of pain and creator of the Yass Method for treating chronic pain. He is author of *Overpower Pain: The Strength Training Program That Stops Pain Without Drugs or Surgery* and *The Pain Cure Rx: The Yass Method for Diagnosing and Resolving Chronic Pain* and host of the PBS special *The Pain Prescription.*

If you're age 50 or older, overweight and have recently experienced pain, tingling or numbness in one or both feet, you fit the classic profile of a person with diabetic neuropathy (DN).

This condition occurs when diabetes leads to nerve damage, which most often affects the feet. Sometimes DN hurts, while other times it creates an inability to feel pain, heat or cold. This loss of sensation is serious, because a sore or ulcer can go unnoticed, become infected and sometimes lead to a foot or leg amputation—so your doctor diagnoses you with DN.

Here's the kicker: You may not have DN—or diabetes. Even though people who are overweight are at much greater risk for type 2 diabetes, you may not have the disease.

Still, when doctors see a heavy patient with foot pain, tingling and/or numbness, many are quick to assume that it's DN. Add to that the widespread advertising for *pregabalin* (Lyrica), an antiseizure medication often used to treat the nerve pain of DN, and you can see how many doctors would jump to this treatment. Lyrica can be effective when properly prescribed, but it's a powerful drug with side effects, including dizziness, blurred vision, weight gain, difficulty concentrating and, in rare cases, suicidal thoughts. If you take this drug but don't actually have DN, you put yourself at risk for these side effects...while failing to address the real cause of your foot troubles.

WHAT ELSE COULD IT BE?

If your doctor has diagnosed you with DN, make sure that your blood tests (such as a fasting blood glucose test) confirm that you actually have diabetes. If you are not diabetic but your physician has diagnosed DN, it's time to find a new doctor. But if you don't have DN, then what's causing your foot problems?

UNRAVELING THE CLUES

Based on my experience treating hundreds of patients with foot pain who were misdiagnosed with DN, I recommend special exercises.

To ensure that you're doing the most effective exercises, it's crucial to isolate where you're experiencing pain or numbness in your foot—is it all over...on top...or on the bottom? *What the location may mean...**

If your entire foot is affected—it could be sciatica. This condition, characterized by shooting pain that travels down one or both legs, can occur when the piriformis muscle in the buttocks compresses the sciatic nerve, which runs down the leg before branching off in the foot. The result can be gluteal pain, as well as pain, numbness or a "pins and needles" feeling in the foot. Sciatica often occurs when the gluteus medius muscle above the hip joint is weak, leading the piriformis muscle to compensate.**

Self-test for a weak gluteus medius muscle: Look at yourself in a mirror while standing casually. Does one hip naturally sit higher than the other? A higher hip indicates that the lower back muscle on that side is overworked and shortened, pulling the hip higher. This points to sciatica—not DN—as the cause of your foot discomfort.

To strengthen the muscles of the weaker hip, do these two exercises...

- **Hip abduction.** Lie on your side, with your bottom leg bent at the knee and your top leg (the weaker one) extended in a straight line. Rotate the foot of your extended leg slightly so that your toes point down and your heel is the first to rise. Raise your top leg several inches keeping it parallel with the floor, then lower it, keeping movements controlled.

Perform two to three sets of 10 repetitions, two or three times a week. If doing 10 repetitions is easy, add a weighted ankle cuff (available online). Begin with a one-pound weight and increase weight when the exercise becomes too easy. Do the exercise on your weak leg only.

- **Dorsiflexion.** Slip one end of an elastic resistance band around a sturdy table leg. While wearing sneakers, sit on the floor facing the table. Extend your weak leg, bend your knee and slip the other end of the resistance band over your instep.

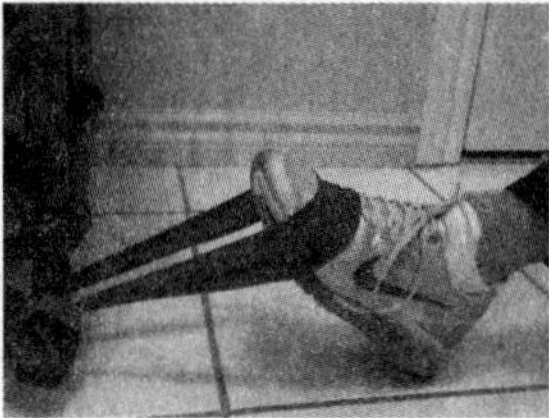

Point and flex, keeping the heel stationary and movements slow and controlled. Perform two to three sets of 10 repetitions, two or three times a week, on your weak leg only.

If just the top of the foot is affected—you may have a pinched peroneal nerve. This happens more frequently in people with strained hip muscles. Symptoms are similar to those of weak gluteal muscles. Unlike sciatica, however, there's no gluteal pain, and the altered foot sensation is on the top of the foot only—not all over. *To strengthen hip muscles, perform the two exercises above, plus this exercise...*

- **Inversion.** Knot a resistance band on one end, and place the knotted end behind a closed door. Sit in a chair, parallel to the door. Loop the other end of the resistance band around your instep. Angle your toes slightly to the outside of the heel, then stretch the band until toes are in line with the heel. Perform two to three sets of 10 repetitions, two or three times a week, on your weak leg only, using slow and controlled motions.

If pain is in the sole of your foot—you may have a collapsed arch.

What can happen: If the gluteus medius or the muscles that support the arch are weak, your arch may flatten. When this occurs, the sole of your mid-foot will be flat on the floor

*If your foot pain, regardless of location, isn't eliminated by these exercises in four weeks, see a neurologist.

**If sciatica causes severe pain or you have trouble controlling your bowels or bladder, see a doctor right away.

when you stand or walk, compressing nerves in the bottom of the foot. This triggers tingling and/or numbness in the sole.

Self-test for a collapsed arch: Wet the sole of your foot, shake off any excess water, then step on a brown paper bag. If the arch side of your footprint is filled in, you may have a collapsed arch.

To alleviate pain, do all three of the exercises above.

Stabbing Pain in the Toes

Johanna Youner, DPM, a podiatric surgeon in New York City. HealthyFeetNY.net

Recently, I had a stabbing pain in my toes while watching TV. It went away but returns now and then. Should I be concerned?

This symptom is probably innocuous. When your legs are dangling, as they might be when you're watching TV, this position can cause pressure on an area of the foot, such as the toe, and trigger pain. This is especially true as we age because the tissues in the foot become slightly worn. Plus, at day's end the foot tissue may be swollen. A neuroma, a benign nerve tumor that occurs from normal wear and tear or from tight shoes, can also cause stabbing pain in the toes.

When you get these pains, a quick self-massage can help, as can using an ice pack (10 minutes on...20 minutes off until the pain eases) or a heating pad. Or try putting your feet up on an ottoman.

To help prevent pain: Practice good foot care. Make sure your shoes fit well and are comfortable. Stay away from pointed, inflexible, thin-soled and high-heeled shoes. A walking shoe is best. These rubber-soled shoes tend to have good arch support and plenty of room for the toes.

However: If stabbing pains occur daily, you should see a board-certified podiatrist. Nerve damage or peripheral neuropathy can cause stabbing pain in the toes, along with tingling or burning sensations. This condition most commonly results from diabetes but can also be caused by certain medications, such as chemotherapy drugs...fibromyalgia...or alcoholism. There's no cure—treatment focuses on good foot care and pain management.

Osteoarthritis can also cause stabbing pain in the toes, often accompanied by stiffness and swelling. A podiatrist can make the diagnosis and recommend treatment.

CHAPTER 18

Women's Health

The Truth About Women and Heart Disease

We've all seen this movie...a man clutches his chest, showing intense pain and collapses on the floor—heart attack. It's usually the first symptom of heart disease in these movie scenes.

You probably think women are different, right? That's been the "new" story in the last several years—that women have very different symptoms from men, often not experiencing the classic chest pains but more often complaining of nausea or back pain or extreme fatigue.

It turns out that almost everything we think we know about women and heart disease symptoms is wrong. That's the finding of a major research study of gender differences in heart disease.

When it comes to heart disease, women are indeed very different from men—even chest pain symptoms are subtly different. Plus, doctors often miss important risk factors in women—or order the wrong diagnostic tests.

A REAL-WORLD LOOK INTO WOMEN'S HEARTS

"Every aspect of the evaluation for heart disease seems to differ between men and women, whether looking at risk factor profile, risk scores, symptoms, the tests that doctors selected and the test results," says Pamela Douglas, MD, Ursula Geller Professor for Research in Cardiovascular Disease at Duke University School of Medicine, and leader of the study team.

While most studies have looked at how to evaluate patients who show up in the ER with a suspected heart attack, we know very little

Pamela Douglas, MD, Ursula Geller Professor for Research in Cardiovascular Disease, Duke University School of Medicine. Dr. Douglas is internationally known for her scientific work in noninvasive imaging, exercise physiology and heart disease in women.

Study titled, "Sex Differences in Demographics, Risk Factors, Presentation, and Noninvasive Testing in Stable Outpatients With Suspected Coronary Artery Disease," by Pamela Douglas, MD, and colleagues, published in *Journal of the American College of Cardiology Imaging.*

about everyday patients who go to their regular doctors with symptoms that may be a sign of heart disease. So Dr. Douglas's team analyzed data from the PROMISE (Prospective Multicenter Imaging Study for Evaluation of Chest Pain) trial, which evaluated about 10,000 patients with suspected coronary artery disease (CAD)—the most common kind—who were seen in outpatient settings. The average age of women was 62 (for men it was 59).

The differences were so big that Dr. Douglas, along with other experts, believes that there should be unique prevention and diagnostic guidelines just for women. Her team's research is supporting that aim and has already uncovered some key differences that all women should know about to protect their hearts—now. *Here's what they found...*

SIMILAR SYMPTOMS

Chest pain was the number-one complaint: Nearly 75% of men and women who went to their primary care doctors to be evaluated for heart disease showed up because they had chest pain. However, there were subtle differences in the types of pain. Women were more likely to experience squeezing or crushing chest pain, while men were more likely to experience aching, dull or burning chest pain.

Both men and women were equally unlikely to complain of less classic symptoms—about 16% of both men and women went to the doctor because they were experiencing shortness of breath, for example. There were some differences in more minor symptoms, but these only brought patients to their doctors less than 4% of the time—women complained of back, neck or jaw pain and palpitations, whereas men complained of fatigue or weakness.

Bottom line: When it comes to heart disease symptoms, both men and women should pay attention to chest pain and, to a lesser extent, shortness of breath. Women don't need to worry so much about unusual symptoms like fatigue or nausea.

RISK FACTORS: A LOST PREVENTION OPPORTUNITY

When women went to the doctor for suspected heart problems, they had a higher prevalence of risk factors for heart disease than men. They were more likely to have hypertension, high cholesterol, vascular disease and a family history of premature CAD, and about as likely to have diabetes. They were also more likely to have nontraditional risk factors that are not measured on risk scales, such as depression and a sedentary lifestyle.

Here's what it means—women, at least until menopause, are somewhat protected against heart disease. It takes more risk factors for them to get to the point that it starts affecting their heart.

While that's a good thing, it also means there is a big missed opportunity for prevention—treating these risk factors before you turn up at your doctor's office with chest pain! Even if these risk factors show up at, say, your annual physical, some doctors may be letting them slide with women.

Another trap: A low score on a heart disease risk calculator such as the Framingham Heart Risk Score. Because these scores don't include factors such as depression or a sedentary lifestyle, they often can underestimate a woman's real heart disease risk. That is, even if your doctor diagnoses you with depression, it wouldn't raise your official heart risk score—even though it does actually increase your risk.

Bottom line: Primary care physicians shouldn't ignore creeping high blood pressure, cholesterol problems, mood conditions or a couch potato lifestyle in their female patients. Doctors should be more aggressive in treating women for risk factors.

A DIFFERENCE IN DIAGNOSTIC TESTING

Compared with men, women were more likely than men to be referred for imaging echocardiography stress tests, which use ultrasound to create an image that shows how well your heart pumps while you exercise. That makes sense since since these tests are known to be more accurate than electrocardiograms in women than men, says Dr. Douglas.

But another difference concerned her. Physicians ordered more stress nuclear tests, in which a radioactive dye is injected, over stress echocardiography tests, for women compared with men. Why the concern? For one, there isn't good evidence that nuclear tests are any better than standard non-nuclear echocardiographs.

Second: Women are more sensitive to the negative health effects of radiation, resulting in a small increase in cancer risk.

Bottom line: If your doctor suggests a nuclear to test your heart health, ask if it's really necessary. (Sometimes there's a good reason, such as comparing new results against previous nuclear test results or because you have breast implants.)

WHAT WE STILL DON'T KNOW ABOUT WOMEN'S HEARTS

To really understand how heart disease differs between the genders, much more work like that of Dr. Douglas's team needs to happen.

One example of what we still don't know: Women are less likely to have a result that indicates a problem (a so-called "positive" test result) from one of these diagnostic tests, compared with men. That sounds like good news, but it's really a paradox. It should mean that women's hearts are healthier than men's. But they're not.

The same percentage of women die from cardiovascular disease as men. This would suggest that, somehow, we are missing something here—we're just not sure what.

Beer May Be Good for Women's Hearts

Study of about 1,500 women over more than 30 years by researchers at Sahlgrenska Academy, University of Gothenburg, Sweden, published in *Scandinavian Journal of Primary Health Care.*

Women who drank one or two beers per week had 30% lower risk for heart attack over three decades than those who drank beer several times per week/daily or never drank beer.

Possible reason: Beer may reduce triglycerides, blood fats that can raise heart attack risk.

Ch-ch-chilly?

Michael Aziz, MD, a board-certified internist and attending physician at Lenox Hill Hospital and founder and director of Midtown Integrative Medicine, both in New York City. Dr. Aziz is also author of *The Perfect 10 Diet*.

You find yourself reaching for a sweater when everyone else is comfortable in short sleeves. Your hands and feet often feel like ice. What's going on? Could something be wrong with you?

It could be perfectly normal. Some people are naturally more prone to feeling chilled—especially women. Ironically, it stems from the way women's bodies keep internal organs warm, which protects the uterus and future generations. In women, insulating body fat is concentrated around their core—leaving toes and fingers in the cold. Plus, when women are exposed to cold, their blood vessels contract more dramatically than men's, which sends more blood to protect inner organs—but leaves their hands and feet colder.

Result: While a woman's core body temperature tends to be slightly warmer than a man's (97.8°F versus 97.4°F), her hands register about three degrees colder—87.2°F versus 90°F. But it isn't just women who are feeling the chill. Men do, too. *Here's why...*

MEDICAL CONDITIONS THAT CAN LEAVE YOU COLD

The following two medical conditions often go undiagnosed. *They affect both genders, although they're more common in women...*

- **Underactive thyroid.** A telltale symptom of hypothyroidism—when the thyroid gland does not produce sufficient thyroid hormone—is feeling constantly cold. Other symptoms can be weight gain, constipation and fatigue. Your doctor can diagnose a low-thyroid condition with a simple blood test. Once your thyroid levels have been normalized, usually by taking daily thyroid hormone medication, your tolerance to cold should improve.

- **Raynaud's disease.** Cold fingers and toes are also symptoms of Raynaud's disease. It's a usually benign condition in which the small blood vessels in the extremities overreact to cold, as well as stress. This causes fingers and toes to feel cold to the touch and, in many cases, to change color—from white to blue or red and back to normal again.

While Raynaud's has no cure, lifestyle modifications can help—such as keeping hands and feet warm by wearing mittens (they keep fingers warmer than gloves) and socks...or keeping hand and foot warmers in your boots or pockets.

More cold culprits...

***COLD CULPRIT #1:* You're too thin.** Muscle generates heat, and fat acts as insulation. But if you're underweight—with a body mass index (BMI) under 18.5—you may lack sufficient body fat or muscle to maintain a normal core body temperature.

My advice: If your low body weight is the result of extreme dieting, a nutritionist can help you adopt healthier dietary strategies. Also, certain medications, including bronchodilators for asthma and the antidepressant *bupropion* (Wellbutrin), can cause weight loss. If you've shed pounds without trying, see your primary care physician to rule out a possible serious medical condition, such as an overactive thyroid, diabetes or cancer.

***COLD CULPRIT #2:* You're on a low-carb diet.** Diets that severely restrict carbohydrates, such as Atkins and Paleo, are popular for their ability to promote quick weight loss. But one of their downsides is that they can make you feel as cold as a caveman. One reason is that carb-restricted diets are very high in protein and fat, which require more energy to be digested, so after a meal your body directs more blood toward your stomach and intestines. Over the long term, a high-protein diet can also inhibit the conversion of thyroid hormone to its active form, which results in feeling cold...or eventually a full-blown underactive thyroid.

My advice: Rather than omit or limit an entire category of food, stick to a balanced 40/40/20 diet—40% of your calories from carbohydrates...40% from (healthy) fats... and 20% from protein. Aim for three meals and one or two snacks per day, depending on your activity level. Your body needs high-quality whole grains, such as brown rice and quinoa, as well as other complex carbohydrates, such as sweet potatoes and squash, for energy and essential vitamins and other nutrients.

A sample day might include a veggie omelet and two slices of rye toast for breakfast...grilled salmon and a mixed greens salad for lunch... chicken with vegetables and brown rice for dinner...and a few chocolate-covered strawberries for dessert.

Also: Don't skip meals. Being hungry causes the body to conserve energy, producing less heat as a result.

***COLD CULPRIT #3:* You don't get enough sleep.** Lack of sleep disturbs the physiological mechanisms of the brain, especially the hypothalamus, which controls body temperature.

My advice: Aim to get seven to eight hours of sleep a night. Don't keep your bedroom too warm—the National Sleep Foundation puts the optimal room temperature for sleep at around 65°F.

If you have trouble falling asleep, give meditation a try. A *JAMA Internal Medicine* study found that meditating five to 20 minutes a day can help you fall asleep more quickly than using basic sleep-hygiene techniques such as establishing a bedtime routine.

***COLD CULPRIT #4:* You're dehydrated.** Your body is 60% water, and if you are dehydrated, it can affect circulation, making you feel colder.

My advice: Be sure to drink plenty of fluids—and drink even more than usual if you are physically active. Water is best, but contrary to common beliefs, tea and coffee can count—your body still holds onto some of these fluids despite their mild diuretic effect.

Best self-check: If your urine is very yellow and concentrated, you are not drinking enough water and other fluids.

***COLD CULPRIT #5:* You're a vegetarian.** Vegetarians are sometimes deficient in iron. Why? Red meat has plenty of iron and it's easily absorbed, while vegetarian sources, such as beans and greens, have less iron and it's in a less available form. Low iron intake can lead to iron-deficiency anemia—and feeling cold is a common symptom. Vegans, who eat only plant-based foods, may also be low in vitamin B-12, found primarily in animal products, including meat, fish, poultry, eggs and dairy. A B-12 deficiency can lead to "pernicious anemia," which can cause you to feel cold as well.

Note: Antacids and proton pump inhibitors, commonly used to treat acid reflux, also can inhibit iron and B-12 absorption. And people who have Crohn's disease and celiac disease are at risk for anemia.

My advice: If you're a vegetarian or vegan, have your doctor run a simple blood test for iron deficiency.

Warning: Only take an iron supplement if it's prescribed, as too much iron can be dangerous.

Vegans also need a supplementary source of B-12, since it's found only in animal foods. But so do many omnivores and lacto-ovo vegetarians.

Here's why: Between 10% and 30% of older adults have gastritis, which interferes with the absorption of B-12 from food—but they can absorb B-12 from supplements and fortified foods. That's why the Institute of Medicine recommends that adults older than age 50 get much of their vitamin B-12 from vitamin supplements or fortified foods.

Tip: If you rely on antacids or proton pump inhibitors, or have a condition such as Crohn's or celiac, get your B-12 levels tested.

IS A DRINK WARMING?

Alcohol, in moderation, dilates blood vessels, making you feel warmer quickly. But here's the rub—the effect is fleeting because your body temperature will drop as heat escapes through those dilated blood vessels.

How a Doctor Beat Her Hashimoto's

Susan Blum, MD, assistant clinical professor in the department of preventive medicine at the Icahn School of Medicine at Mount Sinai in New York City, and an integrative medicine specialist in the medicine department at Greenwich Hospital in Connecticut. The founder and director of the Blum Center for Health in Rye Brook, New York, Dr. Blum is also author of *The Immune System Recovery Plan*. BlumCenterforHealth.com

More than a decade ago, I was diagnosed with Hashimoto's thyroiditis (HT), the most common cause of hypothyroidism, a condition in which the thyroid gland doesn't produce enough thyroid hormones.

Hypothyroidism is more widespread than many people realize, affecting about 14 million Americans. And because thyroid hormones regulate metabolism—key functions such as breathing, heart rate, digestion and body temperature—symptoms are wide ranging. They can include daylong fatigue, weight gain, constipation, low libido, weakness, muscle cramps and aches, cold intolerance, dry skin, poor memory and depression.

HT is typically diagnosed with the same blood tests used to diagnose other causes of hypothyroidism (including those that measure thyroid hormone levels and antithyroid antibodies). With HT, however, an imaging test, such as ultrasound, might also be used to identify the characteristic inflammation of the thyroid gland that occurs with this disease.

My story: When I was diagnosed with HT, my primary care physician said, "No big deal. You'll just take thyroid hormone replacement medication and be fine." I disagreed. As a doctor board-certified in preventive medicine, I wanted to discover the causes of HT, an autoimmune disease in which the immune system mistakes the thyroid for a foreign invader, attacking it and destroying thyroid cells.

For years, I've researched HT for myself and for my patients. *With the help of an increasing body of scientific evidence, I have identified key factors that often trigger and worsen most cases of HT—and the natural therapies that can help...*

MERCURY

When I began to investigate my disease, I discovered that my body had trouble excreting mercury—a toxic metal that can damage tissues and cause autoimmune disease. I've now found that many patients with autoimmune disease have a high mercury level, based on blood and urine tests. One main source of mercury toxicity—eating lots of fish.

My advice: Large fish at the top of the food chain, such as swordfish and tuna, contain the most mercury, but all fish deliver some levels of the toxic metal. That's why I recommend eating fish only twice a week. Opt for varieties that are low in mercury (such as anchovies, sardines, salmon, sole, trout and Arctic char). If you limit your intake of mercury, your body will start to eliminate the excess stored in tissues via urine and stool.

MISSING NUTRIENTS

Two nutrients are key for preventing or healing HT...*

• **Selenium.** This mineral helps create thyroid hormone...helps convert T4 (the less active form of thyroid hormone) to T3 (the active form)...and protects the thyroid gland from oxidative damage. Selenium is so important for thyroid health that several studies suggest that a deficiency of the mineral might trigger HT.

My advice: Each day, take 400 micrograms (mcg) of selenomethionine (the form found in food, which is easier to absorb) for three to six months, then switch to a maintenance dose of 200 mcg.

Important: Selenium is therapeutic when taken in the appropriate dose but toxic in high doses. Never take more than 400 mcg daily. Once selenium levels are restored, you may be able to maintain adequate levels by eating selenium-rich foods (such as Brazil nuts, shrimp and sardines) instead of taking a supplement.

• **Vitamin D.** Researchers have linked low levels of this immune-strengthening nutrient to many autoimmune diseases, including multiple sclerosis, rheumatoid arthritis, lupus, inflammatory bowel disease—and now HT.

Recent research: Greek scientists studied 218 people with HT and found that 85% of them had a vitamin D deficiency.

My advice: Start by getting your vitamin D level checked. If your level is low, take a vitamin D-3 supplement. Most people can safely take up to 4,000 international units (IU) daily, but get your vitamin D level checked every three months. Once you reach an optimal vitamin D level (about 50 ng/mL), cut back to 1,000 IU to 2,000 IU daily.

GLUTEN

This protein, found in wheat, barley and rye, can damage the intestinal lining, triggering increased intestinal permeability (also known as leaky gut), in which gluten and other undigested proteins enter the bloodstream.

Once these undigested proteins are in the bloodstream, the immune system attacks them as if they were foreign invaders. People with gluten sensitivity can end up with leaky gut syndrome...diarrhea, bloating and/or fatigue...an immune system in constant overdrive...and an autoimmune disease such as HT.

Recent research: A study published in the journal *Gastroenterology* showed that people who were sensitive to gluten were seven times more likely to develop HT and other types of autoimmune disease compared with people who did not have gluten sensitivity.

My advice: Eliminate gluten for three weeks—and then eat gluten-containing foods for two or three days. Nine out of 10 of my HT patients feel a lot better after the three-week elimination period, with more energy and mental clarity—and their symptoms return after they reintroduce gluten. This is how you will know whether you are gluten sensitive.

Rice, buckwheat, millet and quinoa are gluten free. Gluten-free breads are often in the frozen section because they are not made with the usual chemical preservatives. For more on gluten-free foods, go to MassGeneral.org/digestive/assets/pdf/gluten_free_diet.pdf.

*Check with your doctor before taking these supplements—they can interact with some medications and affect certain medical conditions.

Mammograms May Predict Heart Disease

Digital mammography was about 70% accurate in predicting the presence of calcium in coronary arteries, an early sign of heart disease, according to a recent study. Researchers report that mammograms were often more accurate in predicting heart disease than standard predictors, such as high blood pressure and elevated cholesterol. If your mammogram shows calcifications in the breast arteries, be sure to follow up with your primary care doctor.

Harvey Hecht, MD, professor of medicine and cardiology, Icahn School of Medicine at Mount Sinai, New York City.

Lower Breast Cancer Risk

Three-step plan lowers breast cancer risk. According to recent research, women can lower their risk for breast cancer by one-third by maintaining a healthy body weight...getting at least 30 minutes of moderate-intensity exercise daily...and avoiding alcohol or limiting it to no more than one drink per day.

Alice Bender, MS, RDN, head of nutrition programs, American Institute for Cancer Research, Washington, DC.

Feed her a high-fiber diet. Women who ate the largest amount of vegetables, fruits, beans and whole grains in the years when their breasts were still developing had a 24% lower risk for breast cancer before menopause, and their lifetime risk was 16% less than those who recalled eating the smallest amount of fiber.

Survey of more than 44,000 US nurses by researchers at Harvard T.H. Chan School of Public Health, Boston, published in *Pediatrics.*

Better Breast Cancer Drug

Paul Goss, MBBCh, PhD, director of breast cancer research, Massachusetts General Hospital Cancer Center, Boston.

Breast cancer survivors who took the estrogen-suppressing drug *letrozole* (Femara) for a decade lowered their recurrence risk by 34%, according to a recent study of nearly 2,000 postmenopausal women.

Bonus: This drug has fewer side effects, such as blood clots and increased risk for stroke, than older hormone suppressants, such as *tamoxifen,* which are typically taken for five years.

Women Who Take Insulin May Be at Increased Risk for Breast Cancer

Gerald Bernstein, MD, coordinator of the diabetes program at Friedman Diabetes Institute at Lenox Hill Hospital, New York City.

According to a small preliminary study, postmenopausal diabetic women who take insulin are about twice as likely to have dense breasts (a risk factor for breast cancer) as women without diabetes. In contrast, those who do not take insulin—they control their diabetes with diet or drugs, such as *metformin*—are at decreased risk. Women who take insulin may benefit from more rigorous breast cancer screening.

Women with Implants Need Extra Mammogram Views

Melissa A. Lazar, MD, assistant professor of surgery, Thomas Jefferson University Hospital, Philadelphia.

Getting implants doesn't increase the risk for cancer, but women with breast implants should continue to have mammograms to screen for breast cancer. (Women of average risk should get them annually, beginning at age 40.)

Note: Women with implants will need extra views at the time of their mammograms to move the implants out of the way, since the X-rays cannot go through silicone or saline implants well enough to view the tissue underneath. The good news is that implants often push the breast tissue closer to the skin and can make it easier to detect a lump. The benefits of getting a mammogram outweigh the risk of damaging the implants. Speak with your doctor about having a mammogram before the surgery and within a year after surgery. The postsurgical mammogram will be your new baseline.

Menopause Help for Breast Cancer Survivors

Andrew M. Kaunitz, MD, University of Florida Research Foundation Professor, associate chair of the department of obstetrics and gynecology, University of Florida College of Medicine, Jacksonville.

Breast cancer treatment often comes with a host of unwelcome side effects. One you may not expect from the treatment that has saved your life is the sometimes sudden and often intense onset of menopausal symptoms, such as hot flashes, night sweats, brain fogginess and vaginal dryness. Some women experience such debilitating symptoms that they skip preventive "adjuvant" cancer therapies just to avoid them. More than half of women in one recent study did just that—a decision with potentially dire consequences down the road.

A better approach: After doing everything possible to prevent a recurrence of breast cancer, explore the many safe ways you can minimize menopausal symptoms.

HOW BREAST CANCER LEADS TO MENOPAUSAL SYMPTOMS

Breast cancer and its treatment doesn't always bring on menopause or make symptoms worse. But it often does. The great majority of women in their 40s receiving chemotherapy for breast cancer, for example, will experience cessation of menstruation, which often is permanent. *Here are the main reasons...*

- **Chemotherapy may have harmful effects on your ovaries.** Chemo drugs attack cancer cells, but they can also damage your ovaries (and your eggs). The result can be a sudden drop in estrogen...and the immediate onset of menopausal symptoms. If you're premenopausal, your periods may stop or become irregular and may not return after treatment.

- **Surgery to remove the ovaries triggers immediate menopause.** Some women with breast cancer are also at a high risk of developing ovarian cancer, particularly those who have the BRCA gene. If your treatment included surgical removal of your ovaries, you'll experience "surgical menopause," which often causes more intense symptoms than natural menopause.

- **Hormonal therapy for some kinds of cancer can make menopause symptoms worse.** Some types of breast cancer are hormone-receptor positive. Receptors—tiny gate-like proteins in the cancer cell—respond to hormones. One treatment for this kind of breast cancer are drugs called selective estrogen receptor modulators (SERMS). These drugs, such as *tamoxifen* and *raloxifene,* can lead to hot flashes, vaginal dryness or other menopausal symptoms. Other hormonal treatments called aromatase inhibitors are used to treat breast cancer in postmenopausal women. They can halt all estrogen production, which worsens menopause symptoms.

WHY HORMONE THERAPY ISN'T RECOMMENDED FOR BREAST CANCER SURVIVORS

Many women ease menopausal symptoms using systemic hormone therapy—a combination of estrogen and progestin (a synthetic progesterone) for women with a uterus...estrogen alone for women without a uterus—that enters the bloodstream. These include pills and skin patches. But that type of relief may be off the table for breast cancer survivors, especially those who are taking drugs to prevent their cancer from returning.

Another type of hormone therapy, vaginal rings, deliver hormones through the vagina. One type of ring, Femring, is not considered suitable for women with a history of breast cancer because it releases hormones into the bloodstream. But another low-dose ring (Estring) may be OK for some breast cancer survivors because it releases lower levels of hormones and isn't considered systemic. More on these below.

In the 1990s, a major study looking at combined estrogen and progestin therapy for menopause symptoms was halted when breast cancer survivors suffered recurrences. Another study going on at the same time didn't show that same increased risk, but researchers called it off anyway to be on the safe side. The US Food and Drug Administration required a "black box" warning on hormone therapy that included an increased risk for breast cancer, prompting women with a history of breast cancer to avoid it. Is it estrogen alone that may affect the safety of hormone therapy for breast cancer survivors, or is it estrogen combined with progestin? The jury remains out.

TREATING MENOPAUSE SYMPTOMS SAFELY

So what should women who have a history of breast cancer do about their bothersome menopause symptoms? Start by talking to your oncologist. Together you can create a treatment plan that works with, not against, your breast cancer treatment or prevention therapy.

For vaginal dryness and painful intercourse...

•**Vaginal moisturizers are available over the counter.** They help to restore moisture to the lining of the vagina. Many are formulated to maintain the vagina's normal pH balance, which can help you avoid infection and irritation.

•**Lubricants ease discomfort during sexual intercourse.** Several types are available—oil-based (which should not be used with latex condoms), silicone-based and water-based. You may need to try a variety of lubricants to find one that you and your partner are happy with. Some women use coconut oil as a lubricant. Keep in mind that while moisturizers are used on a regular basis (regardless of sexual activity), lubricants are used specifically with sexual activity.

•**If these nonhormonal approaches aren't enough, you may want to consider low-dose estrogen therapy**—in the form of vaginal creams, tablets, and, as mentioned above, one brand of vaginal ring (Estring). Because the estrogen is absorbed into vaginal tissues and little makes it into the bloodstream, it's considered a safer option for women who have had breast cancer. Although some oncologists are comfortable with their breast cancer patients using low-dose vaginal estrogen therapy, be aware that the FDA states that even low-dose local vaginal estrogen therapy should not be used in women with a personal history of breast cancer. Talk to your doctor, especially if you take an aromatase inhibitor—because even a small increase in estrogen can be a concern. Women taking tamoxifen to prevent a breast cancer recurrence, on the other hand, may be better candidates for low-dose estrogen therapy. (*Editor's note*: You may also want to ask your doctor about Intrarosa, FDA-approved DHEA suppositories, which create estrogen in vaginal tissues but not in circulation.)

For hot flashes...

•**Avoid spicy foods such as hot peppers.** They have a thermogenic effect, which means they can actually raise your body temperature. Caffeine and alcohol may also trigger hot flashes.

•**Alternative therapies such as deep, paced breathing can lessen the frequency of hot flashes or help you get through them.** Practical solutions such as dressing in layers you can peel off and keeping a fan nearby are also smart.

•**A low dose of an antidepressant**—either a selective serotonin reuptake inhibitor (SSRI) or a selective norepinephrine reuptake inhibitor (SNRI)—may work to treat hot flashes without affecting hormones. *Paroxitene* (Brisdelle) is one low-dose SSRI that is FDA-approved to treat menopause symptoms, including in breast cancer survivors.

Some medications have been shown to be effective nonhormonal treatments for hot flashes, but they are not FDA approved for this purpose. These include *venlafaxine* (an SNRI), the antiseizure medication *gabapentin* (Neurontin), and *clonidine* (Catapres), a blood pressure medication. These may be options to discuss with your doctor.

Keep in mind that these nonhormonal medications are not as effective as hormone therapy for treating hot flashes, and their side effects may be different from hormone therapy.

Bottom line: If you're a breast cancer survivor and have menopause symptoms, you don't have to suffer in silence—or forgo potentially life-saving posttreatment therapies. With the right information and support from your health-care team, you can find the right treatments for you to feel better both physically and emotionally without increasing your risk for a recurrence.

Melatonin Reduces Breast Tumors

Genes & Cancer.

Melatonin, a hormone that regulates sleep, reduced both the size and number of breast tumors in lab research. Researchers speculate that a lack of melatonin, common in sleep-deprived individuals, could increase cancer risks.

Menopause Speeds Aging

Two studies of more than 5,000 women led by researchers at David Geffen School of Medicine and Semel Institute for Neuroscience and Human Behavior, both at University of California, Los Angeles, published in *Proceedings of the National Academy of Sciences* and *Biological Psychiatry,* respectively.

Menopause—and the insomnia that goes with it—speeds aging. Women who start menopause at an earlier age are biologically older than those who begin menopause later in life. Researchers determined that menopause increases cellular aging by an average of 6%. Insomnia, which often accompanies menopause, also leads to faster biological aging, according to another study.

What Your Hot Flashes Say About Your Health

Rebecca C. Thurston, PhD, director, Women's Biobehavioral Health Laboratory, professor of psychiatry, psychology, epidemiology, and clinical and translational science, University of Pittsburgh School of Medicine, Pennsylvania.

When is a hot flash not just a hot flash? When it's a window into future health—of your heart, your bones, your brain and your moods.

"We used to think that hot flashes were just an annoying quality-of-life issue, but now we are learning that they may signal something more about a woman's health," says psychiatry professor Rebecca Thurston, PhD, director of the Women's Biobehavioral Health Laboratory at the University of Pittsburgh in Pennsylvania.

To be sure, just having hot flashes is no cause for concern. After all, in the transition into and through menopause, almost 70% of women experience them. Most of the time, they are merely uncomfortable.

THE VARIETY OF HOT FLASH EXPERIENCES

The trouble is, in the run-up to menopause, when your hot flashes start, when they eventually stop, and how severe they are may be emerging clues to future risks for heart disease, diabetes, osteoporosis, dementia and depression.

Here's how to read those clues—and what to do about it.

As new research emerges, it's becoming clear that many of our assumptions about hot flashes have been way off base. Hot flashes can start many years before menopause and last for many years after your last period is a distant memory...arrive and depart in a year or two... or never happen at all. Now, thanks to a long-term research project called SWAN—it stands for "Study of Women's Health Across the Nation" and has followed about 3,300 women over 15 years—we're getting the real story. While every woman experiences hot flashes differently, *SWAN has identified four distinct trajectories...*

- **Early onset,** with the first hot flash about a decade before the last menstrual period and ending after the last period.
- **Later onset,** with the first hot flash appearing about the time of the final period, persisting several years and later declining.
- **The lucky few,** who have just a few hot flashes around the time of the final menstrual period that don't persist long afterward or never have hot flashes at all.
- **Super flashers,** who have frequent hot flashes from well before menopause and often well into the years afterward.

Women tend to fall fairly equally into these four groups, with the late-onset path being the most common (29%) followed by the lucky few (27%), super flashers (26%) and early onset (18%). SWAN and other studies are also uncovering key associations to health risks. *Here's what hot flashes tell us about....*

THE HEART

A SWAN study has reinforced the connection. Women were asked to track their hot flashes and underwent ultrasound to determine the thickness of the walls of the carotid arteries in their necks—a good measure of atherosclerosis, which increases the risk for heart disease and stroke.

Result: Women who reported more frequent hot flashes (at least every other day) had evidence of atherosclerosis. Also, a different SWAN study found evidence of atherosclerosis in women who had early-onset hot flashes.

Bothersome hot flashes made little or no difference. "We have more often seen effects for frequency than severity," explains Dr. Thurston. But weight increased risk, she adds—if a woman was overweight or obese and had frequent or early-onset hot flashes, the heart risk connection was even stronger.

While the mechanisms aren't well-understood, it may be that women who have less-than-healthy blood vessels (but not yet actual cardiovascular disease) may be particularly susceptible to troublesome hot flashes. So the hot flashes serve as a kind of early warning signal for heart disease risk.

BONES

Hot flashes may also be linked to bone density, osteoporosis and fracture risk. One Korean study found that women who had hot flashes, compared with those who never did, had lower bone density. That was true even after adjusting for other risk factors such as smoking, age, weight and exercise. (Lower bone density increases the risk that you'll develop osteoporosis.)

A separate American study analyzed data from nearly 30,000 women (ages 50 to 79) followed for more than eight years at 40 different medical centers. None were taking hormone therapy. Those with moderate-to-severe hot flashes, compared with those with no hot flashes, were 78% more likely to have a hip fracture.

THE BRAIN

This research is more preliminary, but there may be a hot flash link to brain changes that may increase a woman's risk for dementia. In a small study of 20 healthy midlife women who didn't have cardiovascular disease and weren't taking hormone therapy, hot flashes per se weren't linked with dementia risk, Dr. Thurston and her colleagues have found. But women who had more night sweats—hot flashes during the nighttime—were much more likely to have high levels of "white matter intensities" in their brains. "White matter intensities are a marker of small vessel disease," explains Dr. Thurston, "which is, in turn, a marker for increased risk for dementia." These associations were not accounted for by sleep quality or quantity or hormone levels.

DIABETES

In a long-term Australian study, women who reported having severe, early-onset hot flashes were 55% more likely to develop type 2 diabetes during the 15-year follow-up period than women who had mild hot flashes. A separate SWAN study found that women who had hot flashes or night sweats tended to have more insulin resistance, a precursor to diabetes, than women without them.

DEPRESSION AND ANXIETY

Women who have more hot flashes and night sweats are more likely to suffer from negative mood, such as increased depression and anxiety. These relationships are likely bidirectional—that is, the hot flashes and night sweats cause negative mood, and the negative mood also makes the hot flashes and night sweats less tolerable. In some studies—but not all—disrupted sleep accounts for the associations between night sweats and depressed mood.

WHAT TO DO

The research on hot flashes' links to overall health is still new, so it's too early to draw firm conclusions about cause and effect. In some cases, early, frequent or severe hot flashes might be caused by underlying physiological problems—in other cases, especially with night sweats, bad hot flashes may just make it awfully hard to get a good night's sleep.

But if your hot flashes are frequent or severe, make it a wake-up call to take better care of yourself. "Women who are having a lot of hot flashes or who started having them early should stay on top of their health," says Dr. Thurston. "Watch your diet and remain physically active. Control cholesterol, triglycerides and blood pressure, and see your health-care provider at regular intervals for standard preventive health care." And if you smoke cigarettes, get help so you can quit. Controlling your risk for these factors may help level the playing field, she says.

If you're wondering whether treating your hot flashes will help minimize any or all of the above risks, well, unfortunately, there's no evidence for that.

But one thing is clear: There's no reason to suffer. Hormone therapy, and nonhormonal medications and supplements, have been shown to reduce hot flashes, and mind-body disciplines such as hypnosis and cognitive behavioral therapy can be effective, too.

The best approach: Redouble your efforts to improve your health habits to both curb hot flashes and improve your long-term health. Regular vigorous exercise, along with a largely plant-based diet, may also help reduce hot flashes—and reduce your risk for these chronic diseases. And if treating your night sweats helps you get restorative sleep again, you'll not only feel much better but will be doing your long-term health a world of good.

Hot Flashes After Menopause

Susan Davis, MBBS, PhD, chair of women's health, Monash University, Melbourne, Australia.

Many women experience hot flashes and/or night sweats (episodes of excessive sweating during sleep that can soak clothing and/or sheets) for 10 years or more after menopause.

When researchers at Monash University in Melbourne, Australia, studied 2,020 women ages 40 to 65, they found that 42% of women age 60 and older regularly experienced hot flashes and/or night sweats, and most also reported lack of sexual desire and vaginal dryness.

Women who smoke and those who are overweight were more likely to have long-lasting menopausal symptoms, so talk to your doctor about ways to lose weight if your body mass index (a ratio of weight to height) is more than 25. And if you smoke, you should quit!

Initiation of hormone replacement therapy is generally not recommended for women over age 65, but your doctor may prescribe a vaginal estrogen cream to relieve dryness and discomfort during sex.

A low-dose antidepressant, such as *paroxetine* (Paxil) or *venlafaxine* (Effexor), may also help relieve severe hot flash symptoms.

However, hot flashes and night sweats are not always due to menopause. For this reason, your doctor should check for underlying health conditions, such as high blood pressure, thyroid disease and diabetes.

Night sweats that occur without daytime hot flashes can also be an early symptom of some types of cancer, such as lymphoma or leukemia.

Link to Hearing Loss

Brian M. Lin, MD, resident in otolaryngology, Brigham and Women's Hospital, Boston.

When women ages 48 to 73 used over-the-counter pain relievers such as *ibuprofen* (Motrin) or *acetaminophen* (Tylenol) two or more days a week for more than six years, they were 16% more likely to suffer hearing loss than those who took aspirin or no pain reliever. The exact reason for this link is unknown. Further research is needed to determine whether men could be similarly affected by pain relievers.

Uterine Transplant Breakthrough

Baylor University Medical Center.

A living-donor uterine transplant has succeeded, with no signs of rejection at press time. The patient may be the first to achieve uterine functionality—the ability to sustain a pregnancy.

Menopause Weakens the Lungs

Kai Triebner, MSc, PhD candidate in epidemiology, University of Bergen, Norway, and lead author of article titled "Lung Function Decline Accelerates in Menopausal Women," published online in *American Journal of Respiratory and Critical Care Medicine.*

If the menopausal transition is leaving you fatigued, it may be that your lungs aren't working as well as they used to—because of menopause.

Background: Like so many things, lung function tends to decline with age—in both men and women. Researchers also know that sex hormones, including estrogens in women, play a role. Menopause is associated with more cases of new asthma as well. But the role that menopause, rather than age, plays in declining lung function in women is still being figured out.

Study: European researchers followed 1,438 women for 20 years. None were in menopause at the beginning of the study. By the end, most of them had begun or completed the menopausal transition.

Work Can Make You Sick

Women who worked 60 or more hours per week for decades had about three times the risk for heart disease, cancer, diabetes and asthma and nearly four times the risk for arthritis as women who worked 40 hours a week or less, according to a recent study of nearly 7,500 adults. Men who worked 60 or more hours had twice the risk for arthritis as men who worked less but no increased risk for other health conditions.

Why the gender difference: Women often must balance work with other family duties, leaving little time for self-care.

Allard Dembe, ScD, professor of public health, The Ohio State University, Columbus.

Results: Both forced vital capacity (FVC), a measure of how big lungs are, and forced expiratory volume in one second (FEV1), a measure of how much air can be expelled forcefully in one second, declined significantly in women during and after menopause. One hypothesis to explain the decline is that hormonal changes due to menopause can increase inflammation in the body, which can negatively affect the lungs. Menopause can also increase the risk for osteoporosis, which in turn can shrink the height of the chest vertebrae, limiting the amount of air a woman can breathe in at one time.

Shocking finding: The decline in FVC was comparable to the effect of smoking a pack a day for 10 years, and the decline in FEV1 was comparable to the effect of a pack a day for two years. Not surprisingly, for women who actually smoked, the declines were even more pronounced.

Bottom line: If you have more fatigue during and after the menopausal transition, it may be in part because of a decline in lung function. If you find you're having new breathing problems, such as persistent cough (a possible sign of asthma), see your doctor. To keep your lungs healthy, the most important step is to not smoke, of course, and not to be overweight nor too skinny. And while regular aerobic exercise won't actually make your lungs larger or stronger, it does help your body become more efficient at using oxygen—and that helps combat fatigue. (If you're looking for a specific lung-strengthening exercise–not to mention, a fun one—consider taking up the harmonica.)

Menopause Can Raise Diabetes Risk

Erin LeBlanc, MD, MPH, investigator, Kaiser Permanente Center for Health Research, Portland, Oregon.

Early—or late—menopause can raise diabetes risk. The average age of menopause is 51, but a recent study found that women who had their last period before age 46 were 25%

more likely to develop diabetes. Women who had their last period after age 55 were 12% more likely to develop diabetes.

If you've had an early or late menopause: Ask your doctor whether you should be tested for diabetes.

When Sex Hurts: Intrarosa Is a New Way to Short-Circuit Pain

Andrew L. Rubman, ND, medical director, Southbury Clinic for Traditional Medicines, Southbury, Connecticut. SouthburyClinic.com

If you're a woman approaching menopause or you're already there, you may have discovered a not-so-great fact about the facts of life—during this particular stage of life, sex can hurt.

Here's why: As you transition into and through menopause, you'll have lower levels of estrogen, the hormone that keeps the tissue of the vagina and vulva healthy and lubricated. Vaginal tissue becomes drier and thinner, which can lead to uncomfortable sex, including pain. The medical name for painful sex is dyspareunia.

Women who have it might label it with another name—killjoy.

Vaginal moisturizers, used every few days, as well as lubricants right before sex, can help. But for many women these are not enough to offset thinner, drier vaginal tissue, so there is still some discomfort or pain. In that case, the primary options that women have had from their health-care providers have been prescription vaginal inserts, including rings, or creams that contain estrogen. These are generally safe, since little of this estrogen is absorbed into the bloodstream, and there is no evidence that it increases the risk for uterine or breast cancer. But many women, especially those with a history of breast cancer, are uncomfortable with any circulating estrogen and prefer an approach that doesn't introduce estrogen into the body.

Now they have one. It's a new prescription product that helps you build your own estrogen back in the one place in your body where you need it most for pain-free sex.

WHAT'S A DIETARY SUPPLEMENT DOING IN A VAGINAL SUPPOSITORY?

The US Food and Drug Administration (FDA) has approved Intrarosa, a novel treatment for dyspareunia due to menopause. It comes in the form of a vaginal suppository that's inserted once a day.

The clinical trials submitted to the FDA for approval were conducted by the manufacturer, but many other trials have also found that it's beneficial. In one year-long study, for example, Intrarosa significantly reduced pain—and increased lubrication, orgasms and sexual satisfaction—in postmenopausal women.

What's novel about Intrarosa, and what sets it apart from current treatments for vaginal dryness and dyspareunia, is that its active ingredient is prasterone, which most people know as a dietary supplement called dehydroepiandrosterone (DHEA).

As a vaginal insert, rather than as a dietary supplement, however, DHEA works in a novel way. It's the raw material that vaginal cells use to produce their own estrogen. Don't be confused by the idea that a woman in menopause is able to make her own estrogen. While it's true that the ovaries stop producing estrogen once you've reached menopause, many cells in your body can still produce small amounts of the hormone used within the cells themselves. In this case, the estrogen is actually manufactured, in tiny amounts, by the vaginal tissues.

Even in menopause, the cells that line the vagina and are responsible for its health, including the ability to stay lubricated, remain richly supplied with receptor cells for estrogen (and progesterone). When small amounts of DHEA are applied topically, it stimulates these tissues to convert the DHEA and produce estrogen locally. Voila, natural lubrication, reducing friction—and pain—during sex.

Is this brand new? Not entirely. DHEA creams, both over-the-counter and prescription-only, have been available for many years. Naturopathic physicians regularly prescribe vaginal

DHEA creams, for example. But FDA approval makes this approach available to women from any MD, including their primary care doctors. (*Note*: Intrarosa, manufactured by a Canadian company, doesn't yet have a US distributor but is expected to have one within a few months.) In truth, it's a validation from conventional medicine of an approach that naturopaths have used for years, and that's a good thing.

While Intrarosa is approved for women in menopause, it may be beneficial in perimenopause, when levels of estrogen fluctuate but are still declining. Your health-care provider can let you know with a test called a "maturation index evaluation," done with a Pap smear, what your vaginal estrogen level is. If it is low, you may want to discuss whether Intrarosa is a good idea for you.

IS IT SAFE?

I believe that prasterone is safe, primarily because it does not affect levels of circulating estrogen at all. So there are none of the concerns, for example about increased risk for breast cancer, that come into play with increased levels of circulating estrogen.

Side effects are minor. In clinical trials, about 6% of the women who used it experienced vaginal discharge—primarily from the product itself, since it melts at body temperature. It may affect the results of a Pap smear, and while it's not a safety concern, it's a good idea to remind your doctor before a Pap smear that you're using this product. For a more accurate Pap smear, stop using it three days before your test. There's no need to monitor your hormone levels if you're using Intrarosa.

HOW QUICKLY DOES IT WORK?

Vaginal cells turn over rapidly, so a woman who starts using Intrarosa can expect to experience its feel-good effects fairly rapidly—in three to 10 days. After that, with daily use, there may be no need at all to apply an external lubricant to have the enjoyable, pain-free sex you want. It's even OK to skip using Intrarosa for a day or two if you're having a romantic long weekend and don't want to…be disturbed.

Rethinking Hormone Therapy

Mache Seibel, MD, professor of gynecology and obstetrics, University of Massachusetts Medical School, Worcester, and author of *The Estrogen Window*. Drmache.com

Owen Montgomery, MD, chair, obstetrics and gynecology department, Drexel University College of Medicine, Philadelphia.

Study titled "The mortality toll of estrogen avoidance: an analysis of excess deaths among hysterectomized women aged 50 to 59 years" by researchers at Yale University Medical School, New Haven, Connecticut, published in *American Journal of Public Health*.

Study titled "Vascular Effects of Early versus Late Postmenopausal Treatment with Estradiol" by researchers at University of California, Los Angeles, Stanford University, California, published in *The New England Journal of Medicine*.

"Would you like hormones with your menopause?"

Once upon a time, taking pills that contain estrogen—or later, estrogen plus progestin—was considered the fountain of youth.

Then it became a poison pill.

Now strong new evidence is triggering another look at whether, for certain women, at certain times in their lives, hormone therapy is actually beneficial for long-term health.

"The pendulum had swung from one extreme, where hormone replacement therapy was thought to be beneficial for every woman, to the other, where it was beneficial for no woman," said Owen Montgomery, MD, chair of the obstetrics and gynecology department at Drexel University College of Medicine.

"Now it's shifting again."

When a woman begins hormone therapy, it turns out, is a key factor in determining whether the benefits outweigh the risks—and whether the therapy might even help her live a longer life.

Menopause expert Mache Seibel, MD, a professor of gynecology and obstetrics at the University of Massachusetts, feels so strongly about the difference age makes in the risk/benefit calculation that he named his book *The Estrogen Window*.

A NEW ERA IN MENOPAUSE RESEARCH

The modern era of hormone therapy for menopause started in 2002. Until then, many doctors were prescribing oral estrogen (conjugated equine estrogen), often with progestin (a synthetic form of progesterone), to women going through menopause—not only to treat symptoms such as hot flashes but to reduce risk for chronic diseases that rise with menopause, including heart disease and osteoporosis.

Then the Women's Health Initiative (WHI)—the first relevant randomized placebo-controlled trial, the gold standard of biomedical research—turned those assumptions upside down.

Key finding: Women who took estrogen plus progestin were more likely to get breast cancer and slightly more likely to get heart disease, too. A few years later, a second WHI study in women who had hysterectomies and were taking estrogen only reported an increased risk for stroke as well.

The findings were strong enough that both studies were stopped before they were completed—it was considered unethical to give women hormones when it increased their health risks. The risk wasn't enormous statistically—eight more cases of breast cancer for each 10,000 women, for example. "That's an increase in risk of less than one-tenth of 1%," noted Dr. Seibel. "But in a study that is supposed to be preventive, that was unacceptable."

It should be noted that hormone replacement therapy did decrease fractures—by 23% in the group that received estrogen plus progestin and by 30% to 39% in the estrogen-only group.

Hormone-therapy prescriptions plummeted.

But science marches on. In the original WHI, the women's average age was in the mid 60s—about 15 years after menopause, on average. *A new analysis of the WHI, along with other recent studies, finds a very different story in women who start hormone therapy before age 60...*

- **A 32% reduction in heart disease.**
- **A 39% reduction in all-cause death.**

Women up to age 60 who took estrogen plus progestin also had less colon cancer, although the risk for breast cancer is still slightly elevated at all age groups for women who took estrogen/progestin for at least five years. While that's a particular concern for women with a family history of breast cancer, for most women, the breast cancer risk is dwarfed by the cardiovascular benefits.

"The reality is that heart disease is a much larger threat to most women than breast cancer," said Dr. Montgomery. Statistics back that up—one in every 36 women dies from breast cancer, but one in every three women dies from heart disease. "If the WHI study were repeated with only 50-year-old women taking hormones for 10 years, we would have slightly more cases of breast cancer but, overall, we would have a lot more women alive."

A recent statistical analysis from Yale University School of Medicine makes this fact pretty stark. For women in their 50s who had had hysterectomies, not taking oral hormones that include estrogen may have caused nearly 92,000 women to die before the age of 60 over a 10-year period.

After age 60, the story changes—benefits decline and risks, including cardiovascular risks, increase. In most cases, hormone therapy no longer makes sense. But how can that be? How can the same therapy protect younger women but harm older women?

Recent studies shed light on that, too.

THE HEART PARADOX EXPLAINED

Estrogen protects women against atherosclerosis, narrowing of the arteries. That's one reason why fatal heart attacks are more common in men in their 40s than in women...the women are still producing plenty of estrogen.

But estrogen has another cardiovascular effect—it makes blood slightly more likely to clot, so it's "thicker."

In the WHI studies, some women in their late 60s and 70s began to take estrogen after many years of no estrogen. During that interim period, some of those older women had already developed narrowing of the arteries around their hearts and brains. So when these older women began to take estrogen, they had thickened blood traveling through narrowed arteries. It's no wonder that the incidence of heart attacks, strokes and dementia—which often has a cardiovascular component—increased in this population.

A recent report gives even more credibility to the age effect. When hormone therapy was initiated in women within six years after menopause, it slowed down narrowing of the coronary arteries. But there was no such benefit when hormone therapy was started more than 10 years after menopause.

PUTTING IT ALL TOGETHER: THE NEW MENOPAUSE CALCULUS

The choice to embark on, or forgo, hormone therapy, is a personal decision that requires a careful assessment of each individual's potential risks and benefits. *A few key facts...*

•**Hormone therapy is approved only for the treatment of symptoms of menopause**—such as hot flashes, night sweats and vaginal dryness—even with the new evidence, it's not approved for women without symptoms just for the prevention of heart disease. It hasn't been studied for that purpose.

•**While hormone therapy is approved for prevention of osteoporosis,** there are other therapies that work better, so it is rarely used as a first-line therapy.

•**You don't need to be suffering from unbearable hot flashes to be eligible for treatment.** Painful intercourse caused by changes in vaginal elasticity and lubrication, for example, is a symptom that can be treated with hormone therapy.

•**Unless you've had a hysterectomy,** hormone therapy is always estrogen plus progestin. If you have a uterus, estrogen taken alone increases the risk for endometrial cancer.

•**Early menopause?** In almost all cases, you need hormone therapy. Both Dr. Montgomery and Dr. Seibel agree that the data are clear that women who have gone through menopause before the age of 40 should absolutely be on hormone therapy to replace the hormones that they have lost prematurely. Therapy should last at least until the age of normal physiologic menopause (about age 51). Women who have been through premature menopause are at a much higher risk for cardiovascular disease and dementia if they do not take hormone therapy.

•**Women with certain conditions**—including vaginal bleeding that is not explained, a sensitivity or allergy to estrogen, liver disease, an estrogen-fueled cancer or an increased risk of clotting—should avoid oral hormone therapy.

•**If oral hormone therapy is not appropriate, other forms of estrogen may be**—vaginal creams to treat vaginal dryness, for example, or patches (transdermal estrogen) to treat night sweats. "Women at increased risk of blood clotting may be able to take transdermal estrogen," said Dr. Seibel. "It bypasses the liver and works well on vaginal symptoms, too." Women with estrogen-positive breast cancer, whether survivors or patients under current treatment, can safely use vaginal estrogen, he added.

•**If you don't want to go down the hormone therapy route**—the choice is always yours—there are many nondrug approaches that help relieve symptoms, including supplements, self-hypnosis and more.

BEYOND ONE SIZE FITS ALL

While each woman has a unique set of risks and benefits, the new evidence makes it easier to figure out who may want to consider hormone therapy—and who shouldn't.

Should a 72-year-old woman with no menopause symptoms consider hormones? "No!" replied Dr. Montgomery. "But it's a very different answer when we talk about a 52-year-old woman who is suffering with symptoms that affect her quality of life. For her, it just doesn't make sense to not take a medication for which there are convincing data that it will help keep her alive in the next decade while relieving her symptoms and improving her quality of life."

Even if you do decide to get hormone therapy, a prudent approach is to start with the lowest dose that works—for the shortest duration. The current guidelines call for women who still have their uteruses who get hormone therapy to do so only up to five years and then reevaluate whether it's appropriate to continue for up to another five years. However, said Dr. Seibel, "New data is rapidly supporting that the estrogen window is widening. Stay tuned."

Dr. Montgomery recommended that women who do take hormone therapy revisit the decision every year. "Try drug holidays to see if you are still symptomatic. Menopause symptoms tend to last from one to 10 years, with four years the average—but about 10% of women are still symptomatic in their 70s. It's very individual."

Hormone therapy is not a one-size-fits-all treatment. There is no doubt that there are risks involved, as there are with nearly every drug or supplement, but the benefit-to-harm ratio for you depends on your unique set of circumstances.

Index

D

E

F

G

M

Q

R

S

X

Y

Z